CAMBRIDGE STUDIES IN MUSIC

GENERAL EDITORS: JOHN STEVENS AND PETER LE HURAY

MUSIC AND THEATRE FROM
POLIZIANO TO MONTEVERDI

CAMBRIDGE STUDIES IN MUSIC

GENERAL EDITORS: JOHN STEVENS AND PETER LE HURAY

Volumes in the series include:

Music and the Reformation in England 1549–1660
PETER LE HURAY

Music and Poetry in the Early Tudor Court
JOHN STEVENS

The Music of the English Parish Church
NICHOLAS TEMPERLEY

The Organ Music of J. S. Bach
Volume I: Preludes, Toccatas, Fantasias, Fugues, etc.
Volume II: Works based on Chorales
PETER WILLIAMS

Music and Patronage in Sixteenth-Century Mantua
IAIN FENLON

Patrons and Musicians of the English Renaissance
DAVID PRICE

MUSIC AND THEATRE FROM POLIZIANO TO MONTEVERDI

NINO PIRROTTA AND ELENA POVOLEDO

TRANSLATED BY KAREN EALES

CAMBRIDGE UNIVERSITY PRESS

CAMBRIDGE
LONDON   NEW YORK   NEW ROCHELLE
MELBOURNE   SYDNEY

Published by the Press Syndicate of the University of Cambridge
The Pitt Building, Trumpington Street, Cambridge CB2 1RP
32 East 57th Street, New York, NY 10022, USA
296 Beaconsfield Parade, Middle Park, Melbourne 3206, Australia

First published in Italian as *Li due Orfei* by Eri, Torino, 1969
New edition Copyright © 1975 Giulio Einaudi editore s.p.a., Torino
Now first published in English by the Cambridge University Press 1982
as *Music and Theatre from Poliziano to Monteverdi*
English translation © Cambridge University Press 1982

Printed in Great Britain at the University Press, Cambridge

Library of Congress catalogue card number: 81-3839

British Library Cataloguing in Publication Data
Pirrotta, Nino
Music and Theatre from Poliziano to Monteverdi. – (Cambridge studies in
music)
1. Music in theatres
I. Title   II. Povoledo, Elena   III. Li due Orfei. *English*
780'.945   ML290.2
ISBN 0 521 23259 7

Acknowledgement

Chapter 6 is reprinted from William Austin (ed.): *New looks at Italian
opera – Essays in honor of Donald J. Grout.* Copyright © 1968 by Cornell
University. Used by permission of the publisher, Cornell University Press.

Plates 8, 9, 27, 28 are reproduced by Courtesy of the Trustees of the
British Museum.

Contents

Illustrations

Illustrations

The illustrations were collected and arranged by Elena Povoledo.

Preface

The starting point of the present book was a request we received from Professor Remo Giazotto for a work dealing with the Florentine *Camerata*, to be included in a series he was then editing for ERI, the press of the RAI (Radiotelevisione Italiana). We had some qualms about assigning the *Camerata* a leading role in the creation of opera, but our counterproposal that we should aim at a broader survey of the period leading to the rise of the new genre was readily accepted.

We had already done extensive work in that direction – and indeed one of the chapters in the book had been published as a separate essay. We were eager to go back to materials already explored, to bring them into sharper focus, to look into new sources for new facts, and above all to clarify to ourselves and for our readers the emergence of various trends in the chronological succession of events. We relied heavily on contemporary documents so that the narrative is not encumbered with preconceived views. To be sure, the documents had to be selected and interpreted and a number of essential critical decisions had to be made, not to speak of the translations needed for the present edition, but we hope that a clear distinction has been drawn between proven facts and interpretative suggestions. As one reviewer observed, we have even stressed the fact that we hold different views on a few points.

Li due Orfei, the Italian title of the book, obviously refers to the major works to which we have anchored the two ends of our narrative, Poliziano's *fabula* of 1480 and Striggio and Monteverdi's musical drama of 1607. In the preface to the first edition we remarked that other mythological figures, such as Apollo and Daphne or Cephalus and Aurora, are also prominent both in the theatrical repertory of the late fifteenth century and in the first decades of operatic activity. None of them, however, had been brought on stage as often as Orpheus, or by such outstanding artists; nor could any of them more readily suggest the intimate association of poetry and music which Poliziano achieved with natural ease and the creators of opera had achieved again with spontaneous immediacy, only clouding it in retrospect with theoretical justifications.

Between the two 'Orphic' periods we are mainly dealing with performances of comedies. We even came to think that the archaic note in our title (the use of an obsolete form of the article) recaptured the flavour of many a sixteenth-century title of comedy, only later to realize that we had subconsciously derived it from *Li tre Orfei*, a Venetian comic opera of 1787. Anyway, the increasing demands for scenic realism brought about by the vogue of comedy and soon epitomized in the rules of the so-called Aristotelian unities were highly relevant to our work. Realism excluded music from the most essential sections of the play, reducing its eventual participation to what we would now term incidental music. Realism also had a strong influence on the staging of a play, fostering the creation of the perspective set, which in turn stressed the unity of the place in which, or near which, a unified plot was due to unfold within a reasonably short lapse of time. However, no measure of realism could suppress the fact that the plot, as well as its place and time, belonged to a world removed from the actual life of the spectators. Allegorical or mythological characters, acting in the *intermedi* before and after each act of the play, were called to obliterate everyday reality for a while, and thus help the transition to the presumed reality of fiction. Because of their fantastic nature the *intermedi* promoted the invention of ingenious mechanical devices to produce spectacular events; they also invited music matching the visual marvels with grandiose decorative effects, a varied display of choral and instrumental groups and additional contrasts resulting from the location of such groups in various places within and without the stage.

Early opera has been said to have derived from the *intermedi*, with which it shared the use of mythological plots as a justification for music. It also incorporated some of their grandiose scenic effects and choral displays, most usually in the prologue and at the end of acts, to function as built-in *intermedi*. But the similarities are outnumbered by the differences. In the *intermedi* impressive musical resources were called upon essentially to comment on physical action, on stylized gestures of individuals or groups. In opera, on the other hand almost complete reliance was placed on soloistic singing expressing the inner feelings of the characters. In the patent unrealism of its being 'recited wholly in song' opera was mainly concerned with what we may call a psychological realism aiming to render the dialectics of passion.

This establishes another point of similarity with the mythological plays of the late fifteenth century, which had been essentially spoken but had made recourse to music to enhance the pathos of climactic situations. We have no direct knowledge of such music, due to its being part of an unwritten tradition still predominant at the time even in the most cultivated layers of Italian society. But the comments we read in contemporary sources leave no doubt about the variety and intensity of its emotional effects. That the concern for an affective content apparently declined in the theatrical music of the sixteenth century is only partially related to the advent of comedy and realism and to the later development of the *intermedi*. On the one hand, most of the information we have refers to exceptional theatrical performances, while ordinary performing practices also belonged to a kind of unwritten tradition. On the other, the written and printed tradition of music was dominated during most of the sixteenth century by the deliberate adoption of a polyphonic *maniera*, in which art for art's sake endeavours often obscured the direct expression of feelings.

As in the second edition of 1975, the main substance of the book has been left unchanged in the translation, while additions and revisions have been made in the footnotes, taking into account all that has been published on the subject to date. With so many quotations from old texts there is no way to avoid variant spellings, but readers already familiar with the field will understand this problem. For the musical examples we should mention that two madrigals by Verdelot and one attributed to him, which had been partially reconstructed, are now given complete and with the previously missing authentic Altus part. Thanks are due for this to Professor H. Colin Slim, whose contribution is more specifically acknowledged in the course of the book, and to the Trustees of Oscott College, Sutton Coldfield, England, where the missing partbook has been found. Finally, we gratefully acknowledge Karen Eales' resourcefulness and flexibility in dealing with the many-sided specialization of our texts, as well as the precise, expert advice provided to us by the editorial staff of the Cambridge University Press, more particularly by Rosemary Dooley and Mary Baffoni.

February 1981

NINO PIRROTTA
ELENA POVOLEDO

PART I Studies in the
music of Renaissance theatre

NINO PIRROTTA

to Lea

1 Orpheus, singer of *strambotti*

Ever since Romain Rolland first wrote the essay for which he coined the catchy title 'L'Opéra avant l'Opéra',[1] Angelo Poliziano's *Orfeo* has been assured of a mention in the corresponding introductory paragraph or chapter of every history of opera. Usually, however, the only details given about the work are that the poet composed his dramatic fable for the city of Mantua, where it was performed with some music. The dates given for its performance vary – 1471, 1472, 1474 and 1480 have all been suggested – and when the name of a composer is mentioned at all, it is usually by misapprehension that of an obscure nineteenth-century musician, Pietro Germi, whose Pre-Raphaelite tastes had led him to compose music for Poliziano's text.[2] Nevertheless, Rolland's discussion is still the most thorough treatment of the topic to date, though it concentrates on developing the ideas originally expressed in Alessandro D'Ancona's seminal study *Le origini del teatro italiano*. He studies in some detail the analogies alleged to exist between *Orfeo* and contemporary Florentine religious *rappresentazioni*, the links between these and the later *maggi* (sung May-day plays) of the Tuscan countryside, and the theatrical *ingegni*, stage machines designed and made to work by famous artists such as Brunelleschi and Leonardo da Vinci for use in both sacred and secular performances.[3]

That the text of *Orfeo* is the memorial inscription of a lost musical event is a source of constant frustration to music historians, whose sense of loss is made all the sharper by their awareness of the poetic qualities of the work and its importance as a literary document. I might therefore be induced to think that all I can hope to do is resolve the confusion over the dating of the work, and then move on to another topic. But such is the charm of Poliziano's *operina* (let us not be deceived by the ambiguity of the term *opera* and its diminutives), with its delicate grace and apparent simplicity, that even with

---

[1] This is the title of the first article in Rolland's *Musiciens d'autrefois* (Paris 1908).

[2] Giosue Carducci, in the introduction to his edition of *Le Stanze, l'Orfeo e le Rime* (Florence 1863), p. lxiii, warned people against trying to see *Orfeo* as the first example of true drama. It is possible, he wrote, to call it a tragedy or a pastoral fable, to claim it as the first melodrama or to admire the creation of certain characters and the erudition showing in the fable; 'but, despite all this, *Orfeo* remains basically a [sacred] *rappresentazione* and as such offers no more than a narrative in dialogue form'. Referring to the element of 'melodrama', he hinted at a music master, Signor Germi, who evidently intended to 'adorn the text of *Orfeo* with harmonies, perhaps opening up a new field or a forgotten one by his art'. No one knows what became of this project, but the reference was misinterpreted by Pietro Canal in his 'Della musica in Mantova', *Memorie del R. Istituto Veneto di Scienze Lettere e Arti*. XXI (1879), pp. 655ff. which earned Carducci's obscure contemporary a place in the history of a century not his own. The error was noted by Ferdinando Neri in the introduction to his edition of *L'Orfeo e le Stanze* (Strasbourg 1911), p. 14.

[3] Rolland, *Musiciens d'autrefois*, pp. 21–31.

those flaws bewailed by the poet himself and rather over-stressed by its critics, I have been tempted to do more, and investigate to what extent it does in fact deserve to be considered an *opéra avant l'opéra*. The fame of the work itself and of its author make it all the easier for me to explore what views were held by the generations which preceded the birth of opera about music, theatrical illusion, and how music could be fitted into a dramatic production.

The source of all the speculations about the date of *Orfeo* is a letter which in the oldest manuscripts, in the first edition printed in Bologna in 1494 and in most subsequent editions is attached to the text as a sort of preface. In this, Poliziano, with the coy modesty common to so many authors and so many prefaces, laments the many imperfections of his work, which, he claims, make him wish to see it destroyed rather than preserved and circulated:

Thus I desired that *La fabula d'Orfeo*, which at the request of our Most Reverend Cardinal of Mantua, in the space of two days amid constant tumults, I had composed in the vernacular so as to be better understood by the spectators, should immediately, like Orpheus himself, be torn to pieces: for I know that this creature of mine is of a quality likely to bring shame rather than honour to its father, and to cause him grief rather than joy.[4]

The letter is addressed to one Messer Carlo Canale, one of the retainers of Francesco Gonzaga, cardinal deacon of Santa Maria Nuova ('our Most Reverend Cardinal of Mantua'),[5] and appears to have been written while the cardinal, who died on 21 October 1483, was still alive. From the passage quoted above, it has been inferred that the *Fabula* was written and performed in Mantua – arbitrarily ruling out Rome, where from 1462 onwards the cardinal usually lived, Bologna, to which he had been appointed legate in 1472 though he was not obliged to take up residence there, and all those other places he might have visited either on official business or for pleasure.[6] Even more arbitrarily, scholars have singled out for special attention two particular visits which the cardinal paid to his father's court: those of the summer of 1471 and of August 1472.[7]

Rolland provides us with a clue to this narrowing of the field, though he himself favours 1474 as the most plausible date, when he writes: 'Thus, in 1474, at the height of the Renaissance...Angelo Poliziano, Lorenzo dei Medici's friend, attempted, with resounding success, a stage production of a subject which three centuries of masterpieces were not to stale, and which

---

[4]   Text as in Neri, ed., *L'Orfeo e le Stanze*, p. 33. A description of the *editio princeps* of 1494 was given by Carducci in his introduction to the 1863 edition of *Le Stanze, l'Orfeo e le Rime*, pp. lxxxii–lxxxv. For the early manuscripts of the *Fabula* see Vincenzo Pernicone, 'La tradizione manoscritta dell'Orfeo del Poliziano', in *Studi di varia umanità in onore di Francesco Flora* (Milan 1963), pp. 362–71. The sources are individually described by Ida Maïer, *Les manuscripts d'Ange Politien* (Geneva 1965). See also Cynthia M. Pyle, 'Politian's "Orfeo" and other "favole mitologiche" in the context of Late Quattrocento Northern Italy' (unpublished Ph.D. dissertation, Columbia University 1976).

[5]   Canale remained in Rome after the death of Cardinal Gonzaga and in 1486 became the third husband of Vannozza Cattanei, the notorious favourite of Rodrigo Borgia. See Alessandro Luzio, 'Isabella d'Este e i Borgia', *Archivio storico lombardo*, series V, vol. XLI (1914), pp. 476ff.

[6]   The Bolognese legation was conferred on Franceso Gonzaga by Paul II and reconfirmed by Sixtus IV, who in gratitude also added the abbacy of San Gregorio. Gonzaga occasionally travelled to resting places such as Viterbo or the Bagni della Porretta near Bologna.

[7]   There is little point in considering the earlier visits given the age of Poliziano, who in 1471 was barely seventeen years old.

Gluck was to take up again exactly three centuries later.'[8] By choosing 1474, he is able to draw this exact and satisfying rhetorical parallel with the first Paris performance of Gluck's *Orphée*, but there is a further consideration: it is also the date painted into Andrea Mantegna's frescoes in the so-called Wedding Chamber in the Gonzaga castle of San Giorgio in Mantua. For a long time it was thought possible to recognize a portrait of Poliziano amongst the members of the cardinal's retinue in one of these frescoes, which is still known as 'The meeting between the Marquis Ludovico II and his son Cardinal Francesco', though the identification of Poliziano is now acknowledged to be wrong. The poet was born in 1454 and was said to look young for his age in 1474, while the man depicted in the alleged portrait is much older, though not old enough to justify identifying him as Leon Battista Alberti, who was forty-eight years older than Poliziano.[9] The fresco is therefore useless in establishing when Poliziano was in Mantua, especially as the date of the two main scenes which decorate the Wedding Chamber has ceased to be a matter of prime importance, since the current trend is to reject a precise historical interpretation of them in favour of a more general view that 'it is better to regard them as a free evocation of court life'.[10] They form a collective portrait in which the groupings of the figures and the overall composition were dictated by the artist's tastes and by his expressive and symbolic intentions, though the individual features themselves are true to life.

Even if the Wedding Chamber frescoes cannot be used as evidence for dating *Orfeo*, they are nevertheless valuable, for however different they may be from Poliziano's fable, they do share two of its characteristics. In both there is a sense of theatrical immediacy: though set in a distant time and place, the reality depicted is not remote and detached, confined to a space beyond the surface of a wall or a proscenium arch, but may at any moment come into direct contact with the lives of the spectators. And in both the artists show great skill and inventiveness in overcoming inappropriate or even unfavourable conditions.

Mantegna was faced with the problem of transforming into something much more dignified a rather small room dimly lit by narrow windows cut into the thick walls of a tower. His extraordinary scenic solution has been described somewhat rhapsodically as one in which 'the eye is delighted to see the oppressive walls recede as if by magic, and in their stead appear the supernatural harmony of the most exquisite and delightful scenery'.[11] The spectator is led to feel that he is in a pavilion surrounded on all sides by open arcades. Only two of the walls are actually painted: whenever the room was used to receive important guests, the other two walls were hung with heavy curtains of gilded Cordovan leather, to give the impression that the circle of arches continued behind the temporary hangings. On one of the arcaded walls one's eye is drawn upwards to an open balcony where behind the balustrade a swarm of relatives, retainers, and servants surround the seated figures of the Marquis Ludovico and his wife Barbara of Brandenburg. On the other,

---

[8] Rolland, *Musiciens d'autrefois*, p. 21.

[9] The church of Sant'Andrea was rebuilt according to a plan by Alberti. The start of the project led to the cardinal's visit in 1472.

[10] Luigi Coletti, *La Camera degli Sposi del Mantegna a Mantova* (Milan 1959), p. 11.

[11] Giuseppe Fiocco, *Mantegna* (Milan 1937), p. 57.

one arch frames the scene of the 'Meeting' referred to above, while through the other arches one can see grooms holding horses and dogs ready for the hunt. The figures in the foreground do not block the view of a distant panoramic background quite different from the monotonous flatlands of the Gonzaga domains. The ceiling too is deceptive. It simulates a highly ornate cupola with a round central hole open to the sky, surrounded by a circular balcony from which serving maids, a black slave girl and a peacock can be seen leaning out. The visitor who finds himself in the centre of this varied scene thus becomes a spectator to the lively rhythm of court life, which seems about to spill out of its arcaded frame and involve him too.

The problems involved in *Orfeo* will require a lengthier discussion. It is now almost unanimously accepted that the most probable date for its composition is 1480.[12] It is known that Poliziano was in Mantua in the first six months of that year, whereas there is no evidence that he had ever been outside Florentine territory before then. Cardinal Gonzaga was also in Mantua at that time, having arrived on 20 December 1479 for a short visit which, however, lasted until the following October. In June, the Mantuan court was more than ever involved in 'constant tumults': the betrothal of Chiara Gonzaga (daughter of Federico, who had succeeded his father in 1478) and Gilbert de Montpensier seemed imminent, and did in fact take place shortly afterwards. In addition to this, on 17 June came the news that the Duchess of Ferrara, Eleonora of Aragon-Este and her young daughter Isabella (born in 1474) were about to arrive to take part in the festivities and to celebrate the recently arranged betrothal of Isabella and the young prince Francesco Gonzaga. The two Este princesses reached Mantua on 22 June, and 'preparations were made to hold a great triumph and celebrations', but the same source reveals that 'in those days the lord marquis did not reach an agreement with the ambassadors [sent by Louis XI of France to negotiate the betrothal of Chiara] and nothing came of them' or at least everything was postponed.[13] This explains why those who associate the writing of *Orfeo* with the June celebrations tend also to wonder whether it was actually performed,[14] especially as its author had already left Mantua and by 17 June was back in Florence enthusiastically pursuing his study of philology.[15] As far as I can see, however, one of the stage directions clearly indicates there to have been at least one performance of *Orfeo*. In it, the prescriptive form of the other directions is abandoned in favour of a statement of fact: 'Orpheus on the mountain, singing to the lyre the following Latin verses (which are intended by Messer Baccio Ugolino who acted the part of Orpheus to be in honour of the Cardinal of Mantua), *was interrupted* by a shepherd announcing the death of Eurydice'.[16] Baccio Ugolini, an envoy of the Medici to the cardinal legate

[12]   G. Battista Picotti, 'Sulla data dell'*Orfeo* e delle *Stanze* di Agnolo Poliziano', *Rendiconti della R. Accademia dei Lincei, Classe di scienze morali, storiche e filologiche*, series V, vol. XXIII (1914), pp. 319–57, reprinted in Picotti, *Ricerche umanistiche* (Florence 1955), p. 87ff. Subsequent references are to the later edition.   [13]   Picotti, *Ricerche umanistiche*, pp. 102–5.

[14]   Thus Picotti, *Ricerche umanistiche*, pp. 104 and 105, in contrast to what he had previously written on pp. 90 and 91.

[15]   Ida Maïer, *Ange Politien* (Geneva 1966), pp. 388–90. Though Maïer notes the date of the *subscriptio* added by Poliziano to an incunabulum of Pliny, she maintains that it was still possible for *Orfeo* to have been written between 12 and 15 June.

[16]   The fact that the verb is here in the past tense, whereas all the other directions are written in the present, makes it appear that this was a later addition or modification, in which Poliziano,

of Bologna and to the Gonzaga court, was away from Mantua from Easter (2 April) to June. It is inconceivable that a theatrical performance should have been staged during Lent in those days, so one is forced to push back the possible date to the festive 'tumults' of the carnival, when one occasion in particular appears to lend itself to such a performance: the banquet held by the cardinal for his brothers on the evening of Shrove Tuesday, 15 February 1480.[17] The Latin verses referred to in the stage directions are a Sapphic ode in which no mention is made of Federico Marquis of Mantua or of his marriage alliances. They are entirely in praise of the cardinal, for whom they even predict the triple crown of the papacy.

Though Francesco Gonzaga was made a cardinal before he reached the age of seventeen in Pius II's last creation of cardinals on 18 December 1461, he never became a prominent figure in either politics or the church. To begin with, his father made the mistake of giving him as his secretary Bartolomeo Platina, who twice managed to put him in an embarassing, if not an actually compromising, position with respect to Pope Paul II.[18] As a cardinal, his most intensive political activity was at the time of the 1472 conclave, when with the conclavist Pietro Riario, nephew of the pope-elect and himself the future Cardinal of San Sisto, he campaigned successfully on behalf of Francesco della Rovere (Sixtus IV). The rest of the time Francesco Gonzaga was a reasonably perceptive observer of the political scene, about which he kept his father informed through a regular correspondence. But his main interest was to assert and enjoy his status as a secular prince as well as a prince of the church, living a life of luxury and pleasure, often in the company of Pietro Riario and Rodrigo Borgia. When he arrived as papal legate in Bologna in 1471, the chroniclers made a point of noting that 'he brought with him a most honourable retinue and carried with him a whole silver canteen (*credenza*) whose value was estimated at 20,000 ducats, and a most beautiful tapestry which included one section depicting the battle between Alexander and Pyrrhus [read Porus] in which the figures seemed to be alive'.[19] Though we

while not omitting the tribute to Cardinal Gonzaga, took care to ascribe the sentiment, if not the text itself, to Baccio Ugolini. There was no reason to blame Baccio Ugolini (who frequently visited Cardinal Gonzaga or the Marquis of Mantua on missions for Lorenzo dei Medici) for trying to ingratiate himself with the recipients of his master's messages. But Poliziano must have had uncomfortable memories of his stay in Mantua at a delicate moment in his relationship with Lorenzo – one so delicate that, despairing of regaining favour, he had probably decided to go into the service of Cardinal Gonzaga. Picotti gives a detailed account of the episode in 'Tra il poeta ed il lauro', *Ricerche umanistiche*, pp. 3–86.

[17] I shall return later to Baccio Ugolini. In the two articles already mentioned, Picotti gives detailed information about Ugolini's journeys between Florence and Mantua in the period relevant to the composition of *Orfeo*. Picotti is also the source of information about the banquet offered by the cardinal on 15 February (*Ricerche umanistiche*, p. 101), and he suggests other occasions in that carnival season when a banquet and a theatrical performance might have been held. M. Vitalini, 'A proposito della datazione dell'*Orfeo* del Poliziano'. *Giornale storico della letteratura italiana*, CXLVI (1969), pp. 245–51 also supports the date of 15 February 1480.

[18] Platina was first jailed in 1464–5 for vicious libel against Paul II, in protest against the suppression of the Collegio degli abbreviatori. He spent even longer in jail in 1468–9 when he was involved in the suit against the members of the Accademia pomponiana. However, under Sixtus IV he became Vatican librarian. His association with Cardinal Gonzaga, whose preceptor he might have been for a time, is an indication of the cardinal's humanist interests.

[19] Cherubino Ghirardacci, 'Historia di Bologna'. *Rerum Italicarum Scriptores*, XXXII, part I (Città di Castello 1915), p. 207. On p. 218 it is reported that in 1478 the legate 'ordered the destruction of some houses beside the Palazzo de' Signori [where he lived], and there he built a beautiful garden and surrounded it with high walls'.

know little of his general tastes, he does appear to have had a certain interest in the *studia humanitatis*, a passion for collecting cameos (*camaini*) and bronze figurines,[20] and a love of gardens which he indulged wherever he took up residence, his preference being for ones surrounded by high walls. He wanted the walls of one of these 'secret gardens' decorated with paintings of 'the battle of the Lapiths and centaurs...the story of Theseus...the fable of Meleager', and ordered that Lelio Cosmico should be consulted on their execution and as to whether 'Hercules too should be included'.[21]

This was the man to whom Poliziano, having lost all hope of regaining Lorenzo the Magnificent's favour, seems by about 21 April 1480 to have decided to transfer his allegiance. He might indeed have stayed on in his service as 'chaplain and permanent table-companion'[22] were it not for the fact that the long-awaited message finally arrived, upon which he went back as quickly as he could to Florence, to his lectures at the university there and the writing of his *Sylvae*. This was also the man to whose conviviality and extravagance we owe the creation of *La fabula d'Orfeo*. The connection between conviviality and *Orfeo* need cause no surprise: one has but to read the paragraph entitled 'De conviviis per dominos cardinales faciendis' in an unpublicized plan for curial reform which was probably suggested to Pope Sixtus IV by the untimely death in 1474 of his high-living nephew, Cardinal Pietro Riario. The plan proposed that 'because the banquets given by the afore-mentioned lord cardinals give rise to scandal, we establish and command that henceforth the afore-said banquets should be conducted with sobriety and moderation; that it should suffice to have two kinds of courses, that is one of roast meat and one of stewed...At table, let sacred texts be read...*let there be no music, no profane songs, no acted fables*'.[23]

One of the banquets which had prompted these reforms had been given 'in the house of Mantua' (i.e. in the house of Cardinal Gonzaga) on 16 July 1472, in honour of the ambassadors of the King of France. The Bishop of Novara, Giovanni Arcimboldi, described it to Galeazzo Maria Sforza, relating that 'amongst other worthy things the story of Jason was represented, how he went to capture the golden fleece, and how he slew the dragon and sowed

[20]   In 1472 the cardinal wrote to his father asking that Mantegna (to whom he wished to show the objects) and the musician Malagise, 'to help him not to sleep', should be sent to meet him at the Bagni della Porretta. In the autumn of the same year Mantegna invited the cardinal to dine 'without the walls'. See Paul Kristeller, *Andrea Mantegna* (Berlin 1902), documents 45 and 48.

[21]   Vittorio Rossi, 'Niccolò Lelio Cosmico, poeta padovano del secolo XV', in *Giornale storico della letteratura italiana*, XIII (1889), p. 111. See also notes 18 and 24 of the present chapter.

[22]   The document containing this title is reproduced in Picotti, *Ricerche umanistiche*, pp. 95 and 96. Although the expression normally refers to the close collaborators of a high prelate, it is possible that in Poliziano's case it was purely honorary, a sign of magnanimity used by the cardinal in returning the poet to his legitimate master. For the entire episode, see the references in notes 12 and 16 above.

[23]   'Item cum ex conviviis quae per eosdem Cardd. fiunt scandalum oriatur, statuimus et ordinamus quod de cetero sobrie et modeste praedicta convivia fiant; sufficiantque duo genera ferculorum lissati videlicet et assati. Poterunt etiam in principio mensae aliquibus pasteriis uti et in fine tortibus et fructibus et aliis talibus...Recitetur in mensa aliqua lectio...non soni musici, non cantus saeculares, non histrionum fabulae', from Vatican MS 3884, fol. 122, quoted in Camillo Corvisieri, 'Il trionfo romano di Eleonora d'Aragona nel giugno 1473', *Archivio della Società Romana di Storia Patria*, I (1878), p. 479.

its teeth and ploughed with oxen '.[24] The banquet was offered by 'Monsignor of Santo Sixto', that is by Cardinal Pietro Riario, but took place in Cardinal Gonzaga's palace either because in the summer heat 'the porch overlooking the garden' was preferred ('covered with crimson velvet: with satin curtains all around the walls, all worked with silk and gold filigree, and with other stately decorations'),[25] or because Cardinal Riario, only recently appointed, did not yet have a suitable residence. Soon afterwards he acquired just such a residence, in Piazza Santi Apostoli, and from Eleonora of Aragon's description it would appear to have been most lavish. She was a guest there in June 1473, when she stopped in Rome while on her way to be married to Ercole I d'Este, and she described in detail the fabrics and tapestries of the palace. An awning covering the whole of the piazza was erected for the occasion, and two platforms were put up beneath it, while no fewer than eight hundred lines of Latin verse were composed by two poets, Emilio Boccabella and Porcellio Pandoni, to describe the banquets and stage performances which took place.[26] Although only one detailed account of the banquets of Cardinal Gonzaga exists, again in a letter addressed to the Duke of Milan and dated 2 January 1476, it is unlikely that his were any less splendid than those of Cardinal Riario. The 'royal banquet' of which we have the description was accompanied by 'a show of the conflict between the Virtues and the Vices' which included 'a debate... before the king'.[27] The king of the carnival, played by one of the cardinal's young pages known as Brugnollo, is a late survival from the medieval tradition of the *ludi stultorum* or Feast of Fools.[28]

These convivial performances, which on the whole were very basic and simple, were just one of the various means, which included music, dancing, jugglers' acts and jesters' antics, used to entertain guests in the intervals

---

[24]   Emilio Motta, 'Un pranzo dato in Roma dal cardinale di Mantova agli ambasciatori di Francia', *Bollettino Storico della Svizzera Italiana*, VI (1884), pp. 21 and 22. The title does not actually match the contents of the letter.

[25]   I do not know the location of the cardinal's residence in Rome at that time; it may have been in the 'house or rather palace of Cardinal Mantua', at San Lorenzo in Lucina, or near the church of Santa Prassede, or elsewhere.

[26]   The young princess's letter and the poetic texts which describe the banquet are reproduced by C. Corvisieri in *Archivio della Società Romana di Storia Patria*, X (1887), pp. 629ff, in a text written as the continuation of the article referred to in note 23 above. A useful contribution to this matter has been made by W. Osthoff, *Theatergesang und darstellende Musik* (Tutzing 1968), I, pp. 33–8, and II, pp. 34–44, in which he discusses and reconstructs a song performed towards the end of a verbose allegory attributed to Giovanni Santi and performed in 1474 for Federico da Montefeltro (see A. Saviotti, 'Una rappresentazione allegorica', *Atti e Memorie della R. Accademia Petrarca...in Arezzo*, new series I (1920), pp. 180–236. The song was a quatrain of octosyllabic lines sung by Modesty, Love, two sprites (all sopranos), a *contratenor* and a tenor, and danced by six queens as a *bassadanza* to the tune of 'J'ay pris amour pour ma devise', a rondeau for three voices which was very well known in France and Italy and which can even be read in the inlays of the Urbino *studiolo*. The same music had already been sung, though perhaps with different words, towards the beginning of the performance, during which twelve nymphs also danced to the sound of a virelai (*Gente de Corps*, recalled by Jean Molinet as a *chanson rurale*; see Howard M. Brown, *Music in the French Secular Theater 1400–1550* (Cambridge, Mass. 1963), p. 109). Finally, after another dance, 'all the instruments began to play, and they went on their way'.

[27]   For more precise information see below, p. 287.

[28]   For 'one dressed in royal robes and called the King of Macedonia' at a banquet given by Cardinal Riario in 1473 see P. Ghinzoni, 'Alcune rappresentazioni in Italia nel secolo XV', *Archivio storico lombardo*, series II, vol. X (1893), p. 962. Another text also referred to, on p. 964, mentions the same custom under the name of 'the feast of the King of Beans' (*Re della Fava*).

between courses, the arrival of which, formally and elaborately ushered in, contributed yet another element of theatricality. From this custom derived the various terms by which these entertainments were known: *tramesse, inframesse, tramezzi* and other similar ones, probably partly influenced by the more precise French term *entremets*. The more elaborate performances were probably reserved for the end of the banquet, though even they usually simply consisted of a larger number of characters being called on to sing or recite the praises of the guests of honour. Ten years after Poliziano's *Orfeo*, for example, the performance held in Milan, which is known as *La festa del Paradiso* on account of the *ingegni* designed for it by Leonardo da Vinci, was essentially a parade of gods, Graces and Virtues. Of more interest, however, are certain entertainments performed in 1475 in Bologna, for one of them, a rather free adaptation of a story from Ovid, is possibly the closest known forerunner of Poliziano's fable.[29]

There were three of them, given during the banquets held for the wedding of Count Guido Pepoli and one young Rangoni countess from Modena, and it is likely that the cardinal legate Francesco Gonzaga attended them. The plot of the first is exceedingly simple: 'At the start of the banquet it was pretended that Dodonean Jupiter was arriving in the forest of Dodona to deliver his oracles and to honour the wedding. And first master Tomaso Beccadelli recited the argument of the fable in vernacular verse...and when the argument had been proclaimed and people's attention caught, Jove in the shape of a dove descended from heaven to the same forest...' The argument recited by Beccadelli, poet, notary public and official of the *comune* of Bologna, consists of nineteen lines, though it is difficult to decide whether they form a *sonetto caudato* (i.e. an extended sonnet) or are two octaves plus an extra line. Dodonean Jupiter also recited nineteen lines when he delivered his oracle, though his were slow Latin hexameters in which, besides praising the bride and groom, he also managed to compliment the 'Bentivoglio regnans domus', the Bentivoglio being the ruling house of Bologna. The descent of the dove must have been of particular interest, for it 'spoke' by means of a hollow cane (a *lanza forata*), the voice being that of another poet Francesco Dal Pozzo of Parma, a lecturer in rhetoric and poetry at Bologna from 1468 to 1477 and the probable author of the verses.

'The second fable, included by Ovid in his major [work], was that of Cephalus and Procris. The argument was recited by the aforesaid Tomaso Beccadelli who did not sing it but recited it most elegantly, immediately after the banquet.' So the report continues, raising an interesting question. Had Beccadelli sung the argument of the first *fabula*? In this, the most complex of the three fables, the argument alone consisted of seven octaves; thus when the description gives only six more for the actual performance we are in doubt whether other verses were omitted, and if so how many, or whether a substantial part of the plot was merely mimed. We are told that in the initial scene 'Cephalus, dressed as a hunter...went to the woods for the hunt.' There is no mention of spoken text and though the scene itself is crowded and animated only onomatopoeic sounds are suggested in a reference to horns

[29] The anonymous memoir describing them was published by Filippo Cavicchi, 'Rappresentazioni bolgnesi nel 1475', *Atti e memorie della R. Deputazione di Storia Patria per le provincie di Romagna*, series III, vol. XXVII (1909), pp. 71ff, from which the quoted excerpts are taken.

and hounds. Then 'Aurora, in love with Cephalus and disguised as an old woman, went to Procris and said these words...' which were three octaves of slander against Cephalus, recorded in the description under the heading 'Verba linguae susurrae' ('words of the murmuring tongue'). Procris' answer is a despairing lament in a single octave, after which 'Procris went with the old woman to the forest to see Cephalus who, when he heard her [approaching] pierced her heart with an arrow...' Here at last the text comes to life with something like real dialogue. In one octave Cephalus, realizing his tragic error, curses himself:

> O Cefal traditor, o dispietato
> che con toa mano hai pur sommesso a terra
> costei che amavi più ch'el tuo gran stato!
> Fulmina, Iove! in me tuo arco s[f]erra!
> Non me lassar, o viso mio rosato;
> se lassime convien che teco perra.
> Dime, te prego, o dolce anima mia,
> chi t'ha condutta in questa silva ria?

O Cephalus, traitorous and heartless, with your own hand you have felled to the ground her whom you loved more than your own pride! Thunder, O Jupiter! Discharge your bow against me! And you, my rose, do not leave me. If you do leave, then I shall have to die with you. Tell me, I beg you, O my gentle heart, who brought you here, to this ill-starred forest?

Another octave, some of whose lines are incomplete, is recited by Procris as she lies dying in Cephalus' arms, and ends with the request:

> Per quel amor te prego, per cui moro,
> che Aura non togli, sol per mio ristoro.

By that love for which I die I beg you; stay away from Aura [*sic*]; this shall be my last solace.

And finally 'Cephalus, sitting and clasping her dead body thus in his lap, wept reciting the following song, so that in truth there was no one present who did not weep.' Unfortunately, the writer immediately adds 'this song was stolen, so I have not been able to include it'.

All we are told of the third *fabula* is that 'it was [given] during the evening, after dinner, and consisted of Apollo, the Muses and the three Fates, who all sang in praise of the guests, and the Fates blessed the newlyweds.' This time at least, thanks to the combined efforts of the Muses and the Fates, music won the day.

As we shall see later on, the custom of including dramatic elements in banquet ceremonial survived for some while, so that some of the treatises on cooking or stewardship which date from the following century are useful sources of information on theatrical history. Banquets and dramatic performances were held whenever there were state visits, weddings or other celebrations, but during the carnival they were allowed even without a special reason. 'Festi sese dies offerunt. Personatas licet adducere...' ('Festive days are coming. It is permissible to bring on masked performances...') Thus the prologue of Francesco Ariosto's *Isis*, a Latin 'elegy' acted in Ferrara before Leonello d'Este during the carnival. The performance is noteworthy not only for its early date (1443) but also because of its references to a king of the carnival, to dances, music and songs, and even to 'mountains' which were conjured up for the occasion.[30] Poliziano's *Fabula* belongs to this same tradition of convivial entertainments. Whether it was actually performed during the carnival of 1480 or simply planned for the following June and not performed is immaterial. In either case it must have been conceived to be part of the elaborate pomp and ceremony of a banquet, one of a carefully calculated succession of visual surprises which accompanied the arrival of each course brought in by its stewards, in the midst of a show of precious drapes and tapestry, standards and salvers glistening with silverware or multicoloured heraldic majolica. This in no way affects our judgement of the poetic values of *Orfeo*, but if one bears in mind the implications for its structure of this sort of ceremonial setting, then one is led to a different appreciation of those 'shortcomings' which Poliziano claimed were a result of hasty composition. One has but to compare his fable with the extremely simple standard of the Bolognese spectacles which had preceded it, and indeed of many later ones, rather than seeing it in the light of standards of drama formulated at a much later date, for doubt to be cast on the sincerity of his self-criticism.

Poliziano called his work a *fabula*, and this Latinate term, which he may have chosen for precise philological reasons, is the one best suited to *Orfeo*. Others have preferred *festa*, while manuscript sources also give 'eclogue' and 'comedy'. (A subsequent version of *Orfeo*, in which Poliziano had no hand, was called a *tragoedia*, but I shall return to that later.)[31] The first term, however, was the one most frequently used in Poliziano's own time and even without the addition of the adjective *personata* it implied a dramatic performance. Claims that the term *festa* is to be applied stem from the fact that Poliziano used it in the opening stage directions: 'Mercury announces the *festa*.' To my mind, two considerations militate against the use of the term. In the first place, this is the only time it occurs, and secondly, it is normally applied to sacred *rappresentazioni*. Those who use it here do so in support of the theory that *Orfeo* developed from the performing style of the Florentine religious theatre.[32] I disagree with this thesis. I consider Mercury's two octaves to be the equivalent of the 'arguments' of the Bolognese fables and of many other secular productions. At most, since Mercury is the messenger and therefore the 'angel' of Jupiter, one may see this analogy with the so-called 'annunciations' of sacred plays as a parody similar to that of the king of the

---

[30] Guido Stendardo, 'L'*Iside* di Francesco Ariosto', *Archivum romanicum*, XX (1936), pp. 114ff. The prologue, on p. 117, begins with the exclamation, 'Dive Leonelle noster et Princeps inclyte, spectatoresque optima' ('Our Lord Leonellus, and renowned Prince and best of audiences'), to whom it is then announced, 'Hic mihi Caliopio volenti novam delegavit provinciam, vobis offerrem veridicam fabellam.' ('With Calliope's consent, he assigned to me the new task of bringing you a true little tale.') The reference to the hills is in the joke, still part of the prologue (p. 118): 'Agereque[?] non montes parere, et nasci mures; sed mures parere, *montes* inde nasci...' ('And in the field not mountains [were seen] to travail and bring forth mice, but mice to travail and bring forth mountains...')

[31] Pernicone 'La tradizione manoscritta'. I shall return below to the *Orphei tragoedia*.

[32] 'The angel announces' or 'announces the *festa*' is a common formula in fifteenth-century Florentine *rappresentazioni*. See the three volumes of *Sacre rappresentazioni dei secoli XIV, XV e XVI*, ed. Alessandro D'Ancona (Florence 1872). In the *Rappresentazione di Costantino imperatore*, which is already sixteenth-century, 'a youth with a cither announces' (*ibid.*, pp. 187 and 211).

carnival and like it only permissible in the context of carnival itself. If one accepts that the last two lines of the octave, which do not belong to Mercury, are to be spoken by a Dalmatian shepherd who mispronounces and distorts the words, surely they must have been intended to be humorous:[33]

> Stat'attanto, brigata, bono argurio
> che di ciavolo in terra vien Marcurio.

Tak' keer, goo' folks, it's goo' luck that from haiven to airth there come Marcury.

One might be tempted to regard this first example of rustic realism (which later became more popular) as a precursor of the lively and realistic *frottole* which at a certain point came to replace the angel's 'annunciation' in the Florentine religious *rappresentazioni*, but there is no evidence that such *frottole* were already in use by 1480.[34] (Incidentally, one must take care not to confuse this use of the term *frottola* with its use to describe a genre of poetry to be set to music.) In any case, here it does not replace the 'annunciation', and its sole purpose may have been that Mercury's identity 'might more clearly be understood by the audience'.

The brevity of the 'annunciation' or argument – a mere sixteen lines if one includes the shepherd's – is the first indication of the limited scale of the work. *Orfeo* is an extended and more subtle version of the fables introduced during banquets, official receptions or social dances, and represents a considerable advance on the simple entrances of characters who announce themselves to be such-and-such a person and proceed to praise either the master or the distinguished guest. Nevertheless, despite his greater skill and learning, and his wish to give the *fabula* a richer and more consistent development, it was impossible for Poliziano to overcome the limitations of the genre: *Orfeo* is not planned as an entity in its own right but as a part of the complex social occasion it was intended to embellish. This accounts for the swift transitions and the abrupt and unexpected juxtapositions which critics have variously judged as marking either Poliziano's lack of dramatic talent (a fair enough criticism) or the charm of an immature primitivism. It may be that when, no longer concerned with the practicalities of performance, the author himself came to evaluate his work more critically as a literary text, he saw these flaws as some of the shortcomings of his creation, though given what a delicate craftsman of images he was it is likely that he was more concerned with the occasional imperfect choice of words, dissonant sound or lack of symmetry in his versification.

---

[33] *Schiavone* (literally Slav), as shown by Isidoro Del Lungo, *Florentia* (Florence 1897), pp. 350–6, covered people from both Dalmatia and Illyria. It is impossible to say whether this touch of colour was suggested by some encounter which had taken place during Poliziano's recent visit to Venice, or by the presence in Mantua of a servant, slave or jester from that area. It is present in the older manuscripts but was omitted in the 1494 Bolognese edition.

[34] Lorenzo dei Medici's *Rappresentazione di San Giovanni e Paulo* (c. 1490) still retains the customary annunciation in octaves, but it is given to one of the youths belonging to the Compagnia di San Giovanni who were performing the play. The examples of *frottole* quoted by Alessandro D'Ancona. *Le origini del teatro italiano*, 2nd edn (Turin 1891), I, pp. 379ff. all date from the sixteenth century. According to Vincenzo Borghini, quoted in D'Ancona, *Le origini*, p. 395, it was one of these *frottole* recited without music (the one preceding the *Rappresentazione di Abramo e Agar*) which started the move to abandon the sung delivery of the text in the main plot of the *rappresentazioni*. The term *frottole* derives from the short, seven-syllable lines which closely rhymed.

If one merely reads *Orfeo*, it is not easy to see how much briefer it is than the sacred *rappresentazioni* for, while in *Orfeo* spoken recitation predominates, in contemporary sacred drama monologues and dialogues were still conducted on set patterns of sung recitation which, though extremely simple, nevertheless moved more slowly than spoken words alone.[35] This is a difference which has not been sufficiently stressed, but there is another even more important one to be borne in mind. The subjects of the *rappresentazioni* were always visual and auditory evocations of events in a distant past, which took place on a remote plane of existence quite separate from the lives of the spectators. Contrasting with this, it was quite possible for the world of the mythological or allegorical fables, however unreal or fantastic it might be, to come to interfere temporarily with the present, with reality. The spectators were as close to it as they were to the paintings in Mantegna's Wedding Chamber. It was often actually *brought* to them and involved them;[36] remarks were directly addressed to them and in some cases they themselves were even drawn into the action, as for example in the evening parties in which a dramatic performance of some sort preceded and introduced more general social dancing.

Having thus outlined the tradition to which *Orfeo* belongs, I cannot refrain from pointing out those features which make it a highly individual work. As far as I can see, three of Poliziano's interests combine, not always harmoniously, to make up *Orfeo*. These are his interests in literature, the figurative arts, and music.

[35] See D'Ancona, 'Metro e canto delle rappresentazioni', in *Le origini*, I, pp. 391ff, to which it would not be difficult to add further examples and considerations. The traditional singing formulas must have been well known to the performers and were probably selected to help the identification of certain characters and dramatic situations; they must have derived from the manner of singing which had been called elsewhere *canto passionale* (the narrative way of singing suitable for the Passion or related liturgical times) as opposed to the more festive *canto pasquale* (from the term *Pasqua*, which can be applied in a broader sense not only to Easter but to all the major liturgical feasts). In addition to such formulas of sung recitation, hymns, *laude* or even secular songs, instrumental pieces and dance music were introduced as required by the plot. On the music of sacred plays see also notes 45 and 46 below.

[36] One significant example of scenic elements 'brought' before the spectators is provided by this extract from Giovanni Sabbadino degli Arienti's *Hymeneo*, a description of the entertainment held in Bologna in 1487 to celebrate the marriage between Annibale Bentivoglio and Lucrezia d'Este:

> And suddenly to the sound of trumpets there appeared in the hall a hairy man in sylvan dress...bearing a tree-trunk, with which he parted the people to permit the passage of a wooden tower artfully carried by dancing people. It was not apparent who was carrying it...In this tower was the goddess Juno with two handsome youths...As soon as the tower had been set down, there came a palace, also carried by dancers, which seemed to advance of its own accord, no bearers being visible, and in it was Venus with Cupid with his quiver of arrows and two ladies...Similarly, it was followed by a mountain surrounded by a wood, which incorporated a grotto wherein lived Diana and eight nymphs...Then came a rock, it too carried by dancers, on which was a beautiful girl with eight others dressed in Moorish garb. And when these *edifizi* had been put down, the spectators, of whom there were a large number, were asked to be silent, for the hall was full of the noise of their comments on the arrival of the floats.

The description repeatedly emphasizes the care with which the acts were presented to the dais on which the banqueters were seated. Arienti had the good luck to find a space on the balcony reserved for the six singers. Most of the entertainment consisted of the dialogue between the characters, but it also included dances with a musical accompaniment provided by the six singers or by instruments. See Giovanni Zannoni, 'Una rappresentazione allegorica a Bologna nel 1487', *Rendiconti della R. Accademia dei Lincei*, VII (1891), pp. 414ff.

His choice of the main theme is literary – entirely so, in the sense that it contains no trace of the reflections of Ficino's Orphic mysticism which some have claimed to see in it. I agree rather more with the critic who refers to Poliziano's 'love for harmonic procedures' and like him almost succumb to 'the temptation to place under the sign of Orpheus the whole ideal line of Poliziano's development, and to see his vernacular drama, his *Nutricia, de poetica et poetis*, and the one of his *Sylvae* which contains a sort of profession of faith in the formative virtues of poetry, as being made up of converging themes'.[37] But only the symbol is as yet present in the 'vernacular drama': only later does the 'profession of faith' mature. In *Orfeo*, before the chief protagonist arrives Poliziano portrays a bucolic society conscious of many pleasures, not least that of sung poetry, but he never suggests that this state of affairs is a result of Orpheus' educating influence.

In Mantua, where the myth of Orpheus is depicted in some of the panels in the ceiling of the Wedding Chamber, Poliziano was influenced more by the memory of Virgil, himself from Mantua, and Ovid, than of Horace. It was their tales which he decided to make visible and audible. We shall never know how great a part he himself played in the actual visual presentation of the story; in his text Eurydice is the only figure to be sketched in pictorially, portrayed in the act of picking flowers and, even more vividly, in her agitated and arrested flight. But the various episodes are like a series of bas-relief scenes endowed with speech, not leading into each other but following one another like the symmetric panels of a frieze. This may be an untypical dramatic procedure, but it is hardly a defect from the point of view of the poetry, for it is Poliziano's most authentic form of expression. This 'frieze', with its interwoven memories, allusions and classical quotations, reflects the man whose prime object in life had been the cultivation of the classics. Every image stands out clearly from its background, and all the sounds and stresses are delicately balanced against each other with unrivalled precision.

The classical accounts of the myth of Orpheus are not the only literary sources which inspired the fable. As soon as Mercury has withdrawn, and the Dalmatian shepherd has perhaps been reabsorbed into the anonymity of a group of background figures, the theme of the 'annunciation', which we may perhaps concede to have some parallels with the 'annunciations' of the religious *feste*, gives way to the new theme of the eclogue. This had nothing at all to do with religious drama but was just emerging as a favourite theme of Latin and vernacular humanist poetry.[38] To Poliziano, Mantua could not fail to suggest bucolic Virgilian themes, especially as he may have been hoping to find in Francesco Gonzaga his 'Maecenas atavis editus regibus', a shelter in times of difficulty. Florence too had provided him with plenty of bucolic models in the vernacular, and ones, moreover, rich in dramatic possibilities. He must already have known Bernardo Pulci's translations of Virgil and Girolamo Benivieni's eclogues, for both of these were Florentines,

---

[37] Quoted from Eugenio Garin, 'L'ambiente del Poliziano', in *Il Poliziano e il suo tempo, Atti del IV Convegno Internazionale di Studi sul Rinascimento* (Florence 1957), p. 37. See also Cynthia M. Pyle, 'Il tema di Orfeo, la musica e le favole mitologiche del tardo Quattrocento', in *Ecumenismo della cultura*, vol. II, ed. G. A. Tarugi (Florence 1981).

[38] In manuscript tradition, *Orfeo* appears frequently linked to eclogues. In fact it is even called an eclogue in the Vatican MS Capponi 193.

and he may also have known the eclogues of the two Sienese poets Jacopo Fiorino dei Buoninsegni and Francesco Arsocchi, all of which were soon afterwards collected in the *Bucoliche elegantissimamente composte di varii autori* (Florence 1481; 1482 new style). The search for the lost calf at the start of *Orfeo*, the amorous outpourings of Aristaeus (a youthful shepherd), and the wise counsels he is given by Mopsus (an old shepherd) are all common features of the eclogues. Nor is there anything new in the transition from dialogue to the 'Song of Aristaeus', for it has precedents in eclogues by Leon Battista Alberti, by the Roman Giusto dei Conti, and by Arsocchi. There is no need even to mention (except as an indication of a general trend) the frequent singing to be found in the eclogues of Sannazaro's *Arcadia* and in Boiardo's fifth eclogue, for Poliziano could not have known either work yet.

In *Orfeo*, Poliziano thus has two parallel aims: to bring to life the tale of Orpheus, and to portray a literary myth, the world of the eclogue. A close study of the versification bears out this idea. In line seventeen, Poliziano abandons the metre of the octave in favour of the variety of metres already used by the bucolic authors mentioned above. First comes a passage in *terza rima*, the metre most frequent in the eclogues. Then he shifts to a true *ballata* for the 'Song of Aristaeus' as Alberti does in his eclogues, and finally he reverts to the octave (itself also occasionally used in eclogues) for the resumption of dialogue, which is enlivened by the return of Tirsis, 'servant of Aristaeus', who has recovered the lost calf and describes an encounter with Eurydice (lines 101–8):[39]

> Ma io ho vista una gentil donzella
> che va cogliendo fiori intorno al monte:
> i' non credo che Vener sia più bella,
> più dolce in atto, o più superba in fronte;
> e parla e canta in sì dolce favella
> ch'e' fiumi svolgerebbe in verso el fonte;
> di neve e rose ha il volto e d'or la testa,
> tutta soletta e sotto bianca vesta.

But I have seen a gentle maiden, picking flowers around the mountain. I think Venus could not be more beautiful, sweeter in gesture, prouder in composure. She speaks and sings in such sweet tones that she might turn rivers back towards their source. Her face is snow and roses, her head golden; she walks alone and is all clad in white.

Basically, lines 17 to 137 *are* an eclogue, and as such have nothing – neither theme nor development nor metre – in common with religious drama. Indeed, one of the octaves consists entirely of *versi sdruccioli* (lines with a dactylic ending), which was one characteristic of the bucolic style. And the *frottole* which are also a frequent feature of eclogues (yet another meaning of the term *frottola*, used here to indicate an irregular succession of short lines with frequent adjacent rhymes) can be related to the lively irregular rhythm of the conclusion, in which 'Aristaeus to the fleeing Eurydice speaks thus':[40]

[39] This quotation, and subsequent ones, are taken from the text chosen by Natalino Sapegno in his edition of Poliziano's *Rime* (Rome 1965).

[40] In Boiardo's Eclogue V, it is said that Menalca sings *in frottola*; but the metre of his song is still the *terzina*, though with an extra rhyme in the middle of each verse. Aristeo's invocation to Euridice is the first example of freer versification in the *fabula*; another occurs at the end of the scene set in Hades. The development must have found favour, as it was extended in the later adaptation known as the *Orphei tragoedia*.

Non mi fuggir, donzella,
ch'i' ti son tanto amico,
e che più t'amo che la vita e 'l core.
  Ascolta, o ninfa bella,
ascolta quel ch'io dico;
non fuggir, ninfa, ch'io ti porto amore.
  Non son qui lupo o orso,
ma son tuo amatore:
dunque raffrena il tuo volante corso.
  Poi che 'l pregar non vale
e tu via ti dilegui
el convien ch'io ti segui;
porgimi, Amor, porgimi or le tue ale!

Do not flee me, O maiden, for I am your good friend, and love
  you more than my heart and life.
Hear, O fairest nymph, hear the words I speak; do not flee,
  nymph, for I bring you love.
I am not a wolf or bear, but your own lover; stay then
  your hasty flight.
But if my pleading is to no avail, and you vanish away, I
  must then follow you; lend me, Love, lend me now your wings.

Here no sooner has the nymph appeared than she draws back and flees
without a word; in other eclogues her singing acts as a lure, or else she entices
her lover with blandishments and rejections. Nor is there any reason to
identify the 'mountain' around which she picks flowers before fleeing behind
it as belonging specifically to religious theatre; stage directions for sacred
rappresentazioni do not refer to the mountain often enough to force one to
conclude that it was a permanent and indispensable feature of their staging.
Its use in secular productions, on the other hand, is a response to an urgent
need for scenic properties which could occupy little floor space and would
therefore be able to enter mounted on wheeled platforms (see plates 1, 3 and
4).[41]

It was behind the mountain that Mopsus' calf had got lost; after finding
it, Tirsis 'slides (*sdrucciola*) down the mountain' (Poliziano here puns on
sdrucciola by writing in dactylic lines – *versi sdruccioli*), and it is around the
mountain that Aristaeus pursues the 'hasty flight' of Eurydice, but Orpheus
'appears singing *upon* the mountain'. Poliziano may have intended this to
symbolize that Orpheus' heroic verses, sung in Latin to a lyre accompaniment,
were superior to the more ordinary style of the amorous *ballata* just sung by
Aristaeus 'to the sound of our pipe'.[42] But in a sense the ode sung by Orpheus
(lines 138–89, the longest of Poliziano's known Sapphics, which are mostly
panegyric) should be seen as being part of the eclogue, because it continues
the Virgilian allusions and clarifies their purpose, praising the cardinal as a

[41] See note 36 above.
[42] Ireneo Affò, in his Osservazione IV (reproduced in Carducci, *Le Stanze, l'Orfeo e le Rime*,
pp. 172–4), intending to show that the *Orphei tragoedia* was more authentic than the *Fabula*,
noted a discrepancy between the *fistola*, mentioned by Aristeo in the text of the *ballata*, and the
preceding line 51 in which Mopsus is invited to take from his pocket *la zampogna*. But he mistakenly
derived *zampogna* from *sambuca*, when the correct etymology is from *symphonia*: the term is rightly
used to indicate the instrument which Affò describes as a *fistola*, i.e. the so-called Pan-pipes.
Evidence in favour of the Pan-pipes can be seen in Poliziano's *Stanze per la giostra*, Bk I, octave
116, where Polyphemus' *zampogna* is described as having 100 pipes.

prince who cares for poets and poetry ('qui colit vates citharamque princeps'). The entrance of a shepherd announcing Eurydice's death is conveniently postponed until Poliziano has had time to shower adulatory compliments on his modern Maecenas. Then in one short octave the transition is made from the eclogue, which until then has served to set the atmosphere of the fable, to the treatment of the myth itself.

Orpheus resumes his singing immediately afterwards, this time in octaves in the vernacular (lines 198–229), though these are more a lyrical outpouring than true dialogue. Two of the octaves of Pluto and Minos (lines 230–45), which express their surprise, and further on in the text two other octaves assigned to Proserpina's pleading and Minos' consent (lines 286–301) are definitely dialogue, but the five octaves of Orpheus' prayer can be nothing but song, and therefore should be called not octaves but stanzas or *strambotti*.

The remainder of the underworld scene, with the return journey begun and then fatally interrupted and with the definitive loss of Eurydice, is dealt with in varied and unusual metres. Orpheus' song of victory consists of two Latin distichs ('certain lively verses which are by Ovid, arranged for the occasion'), while the final episode is made up of three short verses which are not really dramatic but certainly show some excitement in their lack of regularity and symmetry:

Eurydice bemoans to Orpheus that she is being forcibly taken from him:

> Oimè, che 'l troppo amore
> n'ha disfatti ambedua.
> Ecco ch'i' ti son tolta a gran furore,
> né sono ormai più tua.
> Ben tendo a te le braccia; ma non vale
> che indreto son tirata. Orfeo mio, vale.

Alas, too much love has undone us both. Now I am taken away from you with great cruelty, and am no longer yours. I stretch out my arms to you, to no avail, for I am pulled back. My Orpheus, farewell.

Orpheus follows Eurydice and speaks thus:

> Oimè, se'mi tu tolta
> Euridice mia bella? O mio furore,
> o duro fato, o ciel nimico, o morte!
> o troppo sventurato el nostro amore!
> Ma pure un'altra volta
> convien ch'io torni alla plutonia corte.

Alas, are you taken from me, fair Eurydice? O rage, O bitter fate, O cruel heavens, O death! O our ill-starred love! But yet, still once more I must return to the kingdom of Pluto.

As Orpheus tries to return towards Pluto, one of the Furies blocks his path and speaks thus:

> Più non venire avanti; anzi el piè ferma,
> e di te stesso ormai teco ti dole.
> Vane son tue parole,
> vano el pianto e 'l dolor; tua legge è ferma.

Advance no further, rather hold your step; and in your sorrow blame only yourself. In vain you spend your words, in vain your tears and sorrow; your fate is sealed.

A later version of *Orfeo* attempted to transform it into what purported to be a five-act *tragoedia*.[43] But whoever was responsible for the attempt had to incorporate new material and new characters and do violence to the original structure, which had consisted basically of three main episodes, which we could describe, imitating the titles later given to the acts of the 'tragedy', as respectively bucolic, heroic and Bacchic. We have already seen each of the first two episodes proceed from a quiet and relaxed beginning to an agitated conclusion. The same is true of the third: Orpheus having returned to the world of the living (though this is not specified by any stage direction) 'bemoans his fate' in four octaves and expresses his intention to renounce all 'feminine association' and to prefer instead 'the springtime of the better sex'. He is evidently overheard by the Bacchantes, who appear out of nowhere. A mere two octaves suffice for their revenge: in the first 'an indignant Bacchante invites her companions to put Orpheus to death', and by the second 'the Bacchante re-enters with the head of Orpheus'. A 'Chorus of Bacchantes' (also entitled 'Sacrifice of the Bacchantes in honour of Bacchus' in one variant) concludes the fable. This is a true carnival song in *ottonari* (octosyllabic lines) with alternating accented and dactylic endings, and even if one is merely reading the text it manages to suggest the unruly and picturesque pantomime (or *moresca*, as it was called) which must have accompanied it.

It seems to me that nothing emerges from this survey of the text of *Orfeo* to support the oft-repeated theory that its dramatic technique is substantially based on that of contemporary religious theatre.[44] Even if one accepts that the phrasing and stage directions of the 'annunciation' (which is itself however quite similar to the 'arguments' of the 1475 nuptial performances in Bologna) are in fact intended as a parody of the annunciation scenes to be found in religious theatre, that is as far as the connection between them goes. The rest of the text hardly bears out the uncompromising statement made by D'Ancona, the most authoritative proponent of that theory, that Poliziano retained the metre of the octave 'in the greater part of his work'. In *Orfeo* one finds a variety of metres never used in contemporary sacred drama, and if the octave does predominate slightly, one must remember that it was the most popular verse form in fifteenth-century secular poetry too. Nor are all octaves alike: in *Orfeo* most of them are used not for narrative or dialogue, but as a vehicle for lyrical expression. More serious are the plot's lack of temporal perspective and the inadequate characterization of the protagonists, but this is a criticism applicable to contemporary theatre in general, whose aim was not to create *ex novo* but rather to re-present a story whose time, setting and characters were already familiar to the audience and had ever been restated in the argument or prologue preceding the action. And whereas in *Orfeo* the visual presentation is rapid and terse, in sacred theatre it is relaxed and unhurried, with a tendency to dwell on minor episodes.

Let us move on now to the musical element, which until now has only been

[43]   I have already mentioned this in notes 40 and 42 above, and shall return to it in the next chapter.

[44]   The most authoritative advocate of these views was D'Ancona, in *Le origini*, II, pp. 2–5. In some ways, the view had already been anticipated by Carducci in his introduction to *Le Stanze, l'Orfeo e le Rime*, in which, however (see the passage quoted in note 2 above), he did not claim that *Orfeo* adopts the same techniques as the *rappresentazioni* but, more accurately, that like them it is a narrative cast in dialogue form.

mentioned in passing. Depending on what one means by 'music', the sacred *rappresentazioni* contained either too much or too little of it. They contained too much if one counts as music the intoned recitation of dialogue; in a sense, however, intoned recitation was music with no musical intent, being only a simplified and formalized vestige of the original custom of singing *laude*, which had itself already developed along different lines.[45] They contained too little of it if one confines oneself to considering those few instances in which the characters are represented in the act of singing, a hymn, a song or a prayer.[46] If in *Orfeo* Poliziano had adopted the technique of intoned recitation typical of sacred drama, the result would have been an interesting forerunner of opera with its alternation of recitative and aria. As it is, he chose instead to follow the tradition of court performances in which spoken recitation alternated with song. Nevertheless, influenced by the bucolic tradition, the nature of its protagonist and the tradition of carnival songs, his fable is exceptionally full of singing.

There can be no doubt that the 'Song of Aristaeus' was actually sung. Its title indicates as much, and even if it did not the lines which precede the song would confirm the supposition, for Aristaeus calls on Mopsus to cooperate with him in making music:

> Ma se punto ti cal delle mie voglie
> deh tra' fuor della tasca la zampogna
> e canterem sotto l'ombrose foglie,
> ch'i' so che la mia ninfa il canto agogna.

But if you care at all for my desires, pray take your panpipes out of your bag, and let us sing among the leafy shadows, for song, I know, is dear to my nymph.

The song is a regular *ballata* of hendecasyllabic lines: four stanzas separated by the regular repetition of a two-line *ripresa*, and apparently accompanied by the sound of Mopsus' panpipes. It is unclear whether Mopsus' part was limited to an instrumental accompaniment or if '*e canterem*' implies that he was being invited to join in the singing in the responsorial style typical of the bucolic tradition. If so, then the reply of the elder, though less Apollonian,

[45]   This derivation becomes clear as the texts of liturgical plays make the transition from *ballata* metre (in the *canto pasquale*) to *sesta* or *ottava rima* (in the *canto passionale*).

[46]   It is not surprising that the problem of music in sacred *rappresentazioni* has never been adequately studied. Until towards the end of the fifteenth century they were normally entirely in song, but the styles and melodic formulas (probably very simple, but varying from one passage to another) belonged to what I would call the music of the unwritten tradition, and can only be guessed at. Information about singing and playing for realistic purposes (that is, as part of the plot) is at times very vague, at times somewhat more precise. (A parallel phenomenon in connection with the performance of comedies is discussed in one of the following chapters.) For example, the following directions taken from *La Regina Ester* (D'Ancona, *Sacre rappresentazioni dei secoli XIV, XV e XVI*) are very general: 'they dance and rejoice' (p. 141), or 'they sing and rejoice and the play is finished' (p. 166). More precise directions have enabled Wolfgang Osthoff to identify in the Panciatichiano MS 27 the music of the *lauda-ballata* 'Chi serve a Dio' sung and danced at the end of the *Rappresentazione di Abramo e Isacco* by Feo Belcari (1499), and the music of a hunters' song 'Jamo alla caccia' in the later *Rappresentazione di Santa Margherita* (W. Osthoff, *Theatergesang*, I, pp. 31 and 43–4; II, pp. 33 and 45–9). The case of the *lauda* 'O vaghe di Jesù. o verginelle', also from the *Santa Margherita*, is unconvincing as Osthoff (*Theatergesang*, II, pp. 38–44) fits to it the music of a late *villota* (a distant derivation of a *ballata* by Sacchetti) taken from a printed source of 1529. It is possible, however, that the *villota* should have picked up musical elements from the tune of the popular song which was also used for the singing of the *lauda*, and indeed, of several *laude*.

shepherd is a *strambotto* of *sdruccioli*, which one assumes was improvised since its last line comments on the return at that moment of the servant who had been sent to search for the lost calf:

The shepherd Mopsus answers:

> E' non è tanto el mormorio piacevole
> delle fresche acque che d'un sasso piombano,
> né quando soffia un ventolino agevole
> fra le cime dei pini e quelle trombano,
> quanto le rime tue son sollazzevole,
> le rime tue che per tutto rimbombano;
> s'ella l'ode verrà come una cucciola.
> Ma ecco Tirsi che del monte sdrucciola.

The gentle murmuring of fresh waters falling from rock to rock, or a pleasant soft wind blowing among pine tops and making them sing, are not as great a solace as your rhymes, your rhymes which echo all around. If she can hear, she'll come here as tame as a puppy. But here is Tirsis sliding down the mountain.

The end of the fable features the Bacchic chorus which combines the evocation of classical myths with contemporary carnival customs which were typically, though not exclusively, Florentine. It is similar to Lorenzo dei Medici's well-known *Triumph of Bacchus and Ariadne* and may perhaps rightly be regarded as its model, though it is richer in suggestions of acting. A large number of polyphonic carnival songs for three or more often four parts has survived but I doubt if there is any point in looking to them for an accurate idea of how the last chorus of Poliziano's fable was performed. Contrary to what is generally thought, the carnival music which survives is not representative of 'the time of Lorenzo the Magnificent'. A small part of it dates from the last years of his life, but most is from the first quarter of the sixteenth century.[47] I believe that at the time when *Orfeo* was conceived both carnival songs and *maggi* had a single vocal part which was supported by one or two instrumental parts, as in Aristaeus' *ballata*.[48] It is more likely that the song of the Bacchantes was performed according to the traditions of dance songs. The choragus probably intoned the first two lines (the *ripresa*) which was immediately repeated by all the Bacchantes, though not polyphonically. She then probably sang all the remaining stanzas, each being separated from the next by choral repetitions of the *ripresa*. The only instruments to have appeared on the stage, if a stage it can rightly be called, would have been percussion instruments such as cymbals and tambourines, which were traditionally associated with Bacchic dancing. If other instruments were used to support the singing they must have been placed elsewhere or hidden.

What I have just been saying ties in with a more general thesis of mine. I have frequently maintained that though polyphony tends to monopolize the attention of music historians to the exclusion of virtually all else, it in fact represents a highly specialized and restricted activity, at any rate in Italy and throughout the fifteenth century.[49] The interest which it arouses is justifiable,

---

[47] See Joseph H. Gallucci, 'Festival Music in Florence ca.1480–ca.1520' (unpublished dissertation, Harvard University 1962).   [48] See note 71 below.

[49] In particular, Pirrotta, 'Ars nova e stil novo', *Rivista italiana di musicologia*, I (1966), pp. 3ff, and 'Music and Cultural Tendencies in 15th-Century Italy', *Journal of the American Musicological Society*, XIX (1966), pp. 127ff.

given its intrinsic value and the fact that its concepts and modes of expression greatly influenced subsequent developments, and, of course, as it was the only form of musical activity associated with a written tradition, its documents comprise all the music we know of the period. But this did not prevent other forms of musical activity from existing alongside it, and these were much more widely influential amongst the common people as well as amongst the wealthy. However, either because they were wholly or partially based on improvisation, or because they were transmitted without the use of written notation, much less evidence about these forms has survived. We cannot afford to overlook this unwritten, and therefore oral, tradition (though in the case of instrumental music one might almost call it a manual one) however elusive it might prove. Indeed, it becomes especially important to consider it carefully when one is studying the different manifestations of humanist culture, for though we are better acquainted with the written tradition, the humanists themselves were almost suspicious of it, associating it as they did with scholasticism.

Poliziano and his contemporaries were quite right in seeing the works of musical theory on which polyphony was based as one of the most typical examples of that convoluted scholastic thought against which they were reacting. They knew little of the music which depended on these theoretical works, and were in any case perhaps less than prepared to understand and appreciate the little they did know. Music to them was something less artificial, more spontaneous. Above all, poetry itself was music – poetry of any sort, which differs from prose in that it is the result of words being combined harmoniously according to proportions of duration, recurring stresses, patterns of rhyme, and a symmetrical disposition of lines, units of metre and stanzas, as well as to that orchestration of sounds and rhythmic elements which 'beautify the harmony of the [overall] structure' ('que...pulcram faciunt armoniam compaginis') to which Dante's theory of versification specifically calls our attention. The frequent recurrence of the rhetorical image of poetry as singing, of the lyre or cither with their strings and plectrum as the instruments of the poet, is an implicit indication that the language of poetry was itself felt to be music. It also shows the close affinity between verbal music and the new musical dimension it can acquire by the addition of a melody and an instrumental accompaniment. We have long been accustomed to consider music and words as at least distinct, if not actually conflicting, elements, which come together as a result of an arbitrary decision usually taken by the composer. The humanist poets on the other hand regarded the musical performance of their verses as a natural extension of the process by which language becomes poetry. This view was still then flourishing, nourished in part perhaps by the antiquity of the rhetorical imagery which encouraged them to believe that they were reverting to the traditions of classical culture, as well as by their awareness that most poetic forms have musical designations.

I will not go so far as to claim that Lorenzo dei Medici and Poliziano were totally indifferent to polyphonic music. (Nothing is known of the musical tastes of Cardinal Francesco Gonzaga.) Lorenzo occasionally corresponded with Dufay through the organist Antonio Squarcialupi, and he certainly kept an eye on the standard of performance of sacred music at Santa Maria del

Fiore and the Baptistry. But even Paolo Cortese, the contemporary writer who seems best disposed towards polyphony (he was a Florentine transplanted to Rome, where the atmosphere of the curia was extremely favourable to an encounter between humanism and polyphony), praises Josquin des Près and mentions with various degrees of approval other contemporary polyphonists, yet still considers the highest level of musical accomplishment the singing *ad lembum* (that is, on the lute), and cites as its most famous exponents Francesco Petrarca (!) and Serafino Aquilano.[50] From Vincenzo Calmeta, only six years younger than Poliziano and a follower of Aquilano, we gather glimpses of a habit common among poets of publicizing verses by singing them personally or by entrusting them to an established singer. Elsewhere, speaking of Antonio Tebaldeo's *Opere d'amore* which appeared in print in 1500, Calmeta observes that by 'hearing today some poet's sonnet, elegy, *strambotto* or epigram *sung* or recited, and then ten or fifteen days later hearing another, and a week later still another, and so on' one formed an impression quite different from the more careful and considered judgement which came from reading the same works collected in one volume.[51] In the case of Tebaldeo's work, he felt the considered opinion to be also the less favourable.

As we have already seen, the most common and best appreciated form of music-making was singing *ad lyram* or *ad citharam*, which when writers allowed themselves to use more familiar expressions was generally translated as 'singing to the viol' (in one case 'vihuola')[52] or 'to the lute' (plates 5 and 6). Lorenzo the Magnificent loved singing, as well as arranging the sequence of steps for dancing *bassedanze*. During one journey in the country, after a certain amount of music-making, he amused himself by 'taking up and trying to refine a certain skilful dancer of local fame'.[53] Of those who surrounded him, Marsilio Ficino, Domenico Benivieni, Antonio Naldi and Baccio Ugolini all sang, as did Poliziano and two of his favourite pupils, Piero dei Medici and Lorenzo Tornabuoni.[54] Florentine singers were generally in demand because

[50] *De cardinalatu libri tres* (Castel Cortese 1510), fol. 74r. For a facsimile reproduction, translation and commentary, see Pirrotta, 'Music and Cultural Tendencies', pp. 151, 155 and 161.

[51] Vincenzo Calmeta, 'La poesia del Tebaldeo' in *Prose e lettere edite e inedite*, ed. Cecil Grayson (Bologna 1959), pp. 15–19. The other passage to which I refer is in 'S'egli è lecito giudicare i vivi' ('If it is permissible to judge the living'; Calmeta did not hesitate to do so): 'A further new way, in addition to printing, has been found, by means of which compositions, especially those in the vernacular ('lingua volgare'), can be brought to light; ... this is the appearance of many citherists, who, while supporting themselves on the efforts of a few poets, publish these works in every princely court, city or land.' (p. 4.)

[52] The spelling is taken from a letter of 1468; see Franca Brambilla Ageno, 'Una nuova lettera di Luigi Pulci a Lorenzo de' Medici', *Giornale storico della letteratura italiana*, CXLI (1964), p. 107. In any case, even without this reference, the close connection between the *vihuela* and the fifteenth-century Italian *viola* is clear.

[53] The *De praticha, seu arte tripudij, vulghare opusculum* by Guglielmo Ebreo of Pesaro, from the MS Magliabechiano XIX, 88, edited by Francesco Zambrini (*Trattato dell'arte del ballo*, Bologna 1873), describes the *bassedanze Venus* and *Zauro* (which should be read *Lauro?*), both preceded by the words 'composed for Lorenzo di Piero di Cosimo de' Medici'. The episode of the provincial dancer is described in a letter written by Poliziano from Acquapendente, in his *Prose volgari inedite e poesie latine e greche*, ed. Isidoro Del Lungo (Florence 1867), p. 47. Del Lungo dates the letter 1476. I must add that both music and dancing followed 'reading a little St Augustine'.

[54] In an earlier piece of work I referred to the sentence about Piero in a letter by Poliziano to Pico: 'Canit etiam, vel notas musicas, vel ad cytharam carmen' (*Epistole inedite di Angelo Poliziano*, ed Lorenzo D'Amore, Naples 1909, pp. 38–40). On 5 June 1490 Poliziano also wrote to Lorenzo, then at Bagno a Morbo: 'Not two evenings ago I heard Piero sing impromptu, for

of their skill and versatility. Part of their art consisted of improvising new verses which they sang to established melodic patterns, and of demonstrating their wit and quickness of mind by rapidly 'swapping' each other's rhymes and poetic themes. Traditional melodies were also used for more ambitious compositions, but quite often the poets themselves composed new melodies for them, or had them composed by others with more musical talent.

My revised understanding of 'the love of harmonic procedures' therefore leads me to see in the character of Poliziano's Orpheus the symbol or personification of this broader definition of poetry as song. The fact that Baccio Ugolini was chosen to play the role is a clear indication that Orpheus was intended to sing, for Poliziano had previously praised him for his skill. There is a further indication that great significance was attached to Orpheus' singing: when, in 1490, the question of a revival of *Orfeo* was raised, one of the greatest problems, despite the existence of plenty of singers in Mantua, was to find one who could satisfactorily play the leading role.[55]

Ugolini was a priest not a professional singer, and as a member of Lorenzo's chancellery had ably and effectively carried out a variety of political and administrative missions. Shortly before his death he was made Bishop of Gaeta, after having acted for Giovanni dei Medici, then Abbot of Montecassino. He was universally well-liked, and was in great demand everywhere because of his jovial nature and skill in singing to the lyre.[56] This was the instrument, whose name lent it an air of classicism despite the fact that it was quite different from the classical lyre (plate 5), which the stage directions tell us he carried when he appeared 'upon the mountain' to sing in Latin the Sapphic ode in praise of Cardinal Gonzaga. It is equally clear that the other Latin text (lines 302–5) was also sung: 'Orpheus returns, after rescuing Eurydice, singing certain lively verses by Ovid, arranged for the occasion.' Between these two Latin texts only one stage direction is as explicit, stating that 'Orpheus singing arrives at the gate of hell.' Strictly speaking, it should refer only to the two octaves which follow it (lines 214–29), but I think it must also apply to the two preceding stanzas (lines 198–213) which are the first expression of Orpheus' grief. In them he turns to his lyre and asks it for a new form of song:

> Dunque piangiamo, o sconsolata lira,
> che più non si convien l'usato canto...

he came to assail me at home with all these improvisers. He pleased me greatly, *et praesertim* in the jokes and retorts, and his ease and pronunciation, so that I seemed to see and hear Your Magnificence in person' (*Prose volgari inedite*, p. 78). He speaks with affection of Lorenzo Tornabuoni in another letter to Pico and adds: 'Dat & Musicis operam'. Paolo Orvieto, 'Angelo Poliziano "compare" della brigata laurenziana', *Lettere italiane*, XXV (1973), pp. 317–18, suggests identifying Poliziano with 'the fellow playing the viol' in the entourage of Lorenzo dei Medici during a trip. [55] D'Ancona, *Le origini*, II, pp. 358ff.

[56] On Baccio Ugolini see Del Lungo, *Florentia*, pp. 307ff. Also Picotti, *Ricerche umanistiche* and *La giovinezza di Leone X* (Milan 1927). On the instrument he played, see Emanuel Winternitz, 'Lira da Braccio', in *Die Musik in Geschichte und Gegenwart* vol. VIII (Kassel 1960), cols. 935ff. which is also notable for the illustrations which deal with the humanists' use of the instrument. Viewed from above, this is easily recognized by a flat box with a round or almond-shaped top into which the pegs which served to tauten the strings were inserted vertically. See plates 5 and 6. An English translation of the same article, in which some of the text has been cut but the illustrations have been reproduced intact, is included in E. Winternitz, *Musical Instruments and their Symbolism in Western Art* (New York 1967).

Weep then with me, unhappy lyre, for no longer can we sing our former song...

Further on a description prefaces the five octaves of Orpheus' prayer: 'Orpheus on his knees speaks thus to Pluto.' The expression 'speaks thus' does not indicate singing, but it does not rule it out either, while the last two lines (lines 291–2) of Proserpina's intercession seem to indicate clearly that Orpheus *has* been singing:

> Dunque tua dura legge a lui si pieghi,
> pel canto, per l'amor, pe' giusti prieghi

Let your stern law then bend for him, for his song, for his love, and for his just prayers.

as do the last two lines (lines 300–1) of the octave in which 'Pluto answers Orpheus and says thus':

> I' son contento che a sì dolce plettro
> s'inchini la potenzia del mio scettro.

I am content that to such a sweet plectrum, even the power of my sceptre should bow.

On the other hand, I doubt whether the four octaves were sung in which Orpheus 'bemoans his fate' once he is back in the land of the living (lines 322–53). A song at this point would have had the power to tame the fury of the Bacchantes,[57] and thus it seems more logical to assume that singing had been reserved for the heroic moment when Orpheus had faced death and fate. But however many verses Baccio Ugolini may have sung as Orpheus, what really matters is that they are octaves, which puts the *strambotto* on a par with the Latin verses as the representatives of the noblest form of sung poetry.

This is not the place to investigate the obscure and controversial origins of the *strambotto*, or to insist on the necessity, already indicated earlier, of distinguishing it from the various other forms of the *ottava rima*. Nor is it the place to advance hypotheses about whether literary *strambotti* were derived from the popular ones, or whether the example of the aristocratic ones filtered down to less educated singers, or if in fact there were even more complex exchanges and reciprocal imitation between the two levels. It is important, however, to point out that from the time of Leonardo Giustinian until the end of the century, the *strambotto* was the form of poetry for music most assiduously cultivated by Italian men of letters as a vehicle for the most passionately lyrical sentiments. It was probably its brevity which made it so popular: while allowing musicians to give their song a more extended and even more florid course, it encouraged in the poets a more precise epigrammatic brevity which not infrequently tended towards preciousness. Certainly a large number of *strambotti* texts were included in contemporary manuscript and printed collections of poems, where they are attributed, not always correctly or consistently, to the best-known poets. The music to which these *strambotti* were sung, however, was not yet written down. Only towards the end of the century does one begin to find examples of *strambotti* in musical as opposed

---

[57] Cynthia M. Pyle, 'Il tema di Orfeo', strongly argues that these octaves must also have been sung. Of course, this would only strengthen my characterization of Poliziano's Orpheus as singer of *strambotti*. Pyle's paper also gives valuable new information on Poliziano's views of Orpheus and music.

to literary manuscripts; and soon some collections appeared which were primarily, if not exclusively, dedicated to settings of *strambotti*.[58]

To what degree these written *strambotti* reflect the unwritten practice is a difficult question to answer with certainty, since one of the terms of comparison is by definition missing. One point which I must make clear is that equating the written tradition with artistic polyphony, as I have done here and elsewhere, does not imply that the music of the unwritten tradition was exclusively monophonic. There are indications that, beginning with the last decades of the fourteenth century, if not before, a way had been found – perhaps not very orthodox from the point of view of official musical teachings – of adding the accompaniment of a second, supporting part to the sung melody.[59] Nor were the two traditions so totally separate that contact between them was impossible: there was nothing to prevent the one less hampered by rules from assimilating for its own ends whatever aspect of the other might be of use. It is probable in fact that some of the 'regular' compositions of Francesco Landini, the blind luminary of fourteenth-century Italian *ars nova*, were incorporated into the other tradition, though possibly in a simplified form and certainly subject to the modifications and variations which were inherent in the procedures of a unwritten tradition.[60]

It is not easy to trace the stages by which it happened, but it seems that singing to the cither, viol, or lute came to imply the addition of a second part, a *tenor*, which accompanied the sung melody. This development had taken place by the time the *strambotto* was at the peak of its popularity, though it applied to the singing of other verse forms as well. A *tenorista* (actually different people at different times) used to travel around with the virtuoso lutenist Pietrobono del Chitarrino of Ferrara, who in his early days had been a singer accustomed to providing his own lute accompaniment and whose career typifies the success of these unwritten musical practices.[61] The *cantus–tenor* relationship remained a fundamental feature of all music which directly or indirectly reflects this unwritten tradition and which musicologists now commonly call *frottola* music, a term derived from its frequent use in the titles of Ottaviano Petrucci's printed collections. It is surprising how readily this type of music later adapted itself to four voices or parts – a feature new to the artistic line of secular polyphony as well.[62] This apparent

[58] See the codices Montecassino, Badia, 871; Perugia, Biblioteca Comunale, 431 (G20); Paris. Bibliothèque Nationale, Réserve Vm.[7] 676; Milan, Biblioteca Trivulziana, 55; Modena, Biblioteca Estense, α.f.9.9. To these one may add some of the more recent compositions appended to the Seville MS, Biblioteca Colombina, 5.1.43, and to its complement in Paris, Bibliothèque Nationale, nouv. acq. frç. 4379.

[59] See Pirrotta 'Musica polifonica per un testo attribuito a Federico II', in *L'Ars nova italiana del Trecento*, II (Certaldo 1968), pp. 97–112, and Pirrotta, 'New Glimpses of an Unwritten Tradition', in *Words and Music: the Scholar's View: Studies in honor of A. Tillmann Merritt*, ed. L. Berman (Cambridge, Mass. 1972), pp. 271–91.

[60] See for example the texts of Landini's *ballate* which figure in the semi-popular repertory of the Treviso MS, Biblioteca Comunale 43, published in Vittorio Cian, 'Ballate e strambotti del secolo XV, tratti da un codice trevisano', *Giornale storico della letteratura italiana*, IV (1884).

[61] For further details see in particular Emile Haraszti, 'Bono, Piero', in *Die Musik in Geschichte und Gegenwart*, vol. II, cols. 117–19, and Pirrotta, 'Music and Cultural Tendencies'. On the *tenorista* (player of the tenor part), see *ibid.*, p. 141 note 53. The style of lute-playing current at the time of Pietrobono still assigned to each player a single melodic line.

[62] It would appear that four-voice writing was accepted for the *strambotto* even more readily than for the *frottola* or *barzelletta*. Nevertheless there are examples of *strambotti* for three voices,

contradiction can however be explained by the fact that the additions to the basic structure of *cantus-tenor* were dictated by chordal or harmonic feeling,[63] whereas in the artistic tradition the tendency was to build in a linear and contrapuntal manner. Furthermore it is quite clear that the fourth part, the *contratenor altus*, was an optional extra omitted in the type of performance which most faithfully adhered to the customs of the unwritten tradition, in which the song was accompanied by the *tenor* and *contratenor bassus* played on a single stringed instrument.[64]

Vincenzo Calmeta, whose volatile and gossipy interest in contemporary events is invaluable to us, informs us of the esteem in which the various types of *frottola* pieces were held. This he does in a tract which takes the form of advice given to 'youths who take delight in works in the vernacular, not for the style of composition, but the better to prevail through them in their amorous endeavours'.[65] Prose composition, for which Boccaccio is the suggested model, is of no interest to us here. But then Calmeta goes on to consider those young lovers 'who, being accustomed to take pleasure in the art of singing, wish by their songs (particularly if they can sing in diminution) to entertain their ladies'. He advises them that 'they must busy themselves with *stanze*, *barzellette*, *frottole* and other pedestrian styles, and not rely upon subtleties and inventions...which when associated with music are not only overshadowed, but obstructed in such a way that they cannot be discerned'.[66] Others, however, might want to aim higher than the 'pedestrian styles'; these

in their manner of singing must imitate Cariteo and Serafino [Benedetto Gareth and Serafino Aquilano]; who in this exercise have been foremost in our day, and have striven to accompany their rhymes with easy and simple music, that the excellence of their witty and sententious words might be better understood; for they have the judgement of a discerning jeweller, who, wanting to display the finest and whitest pearl, will not wrap it in a golden cloth, but in some black silk, that it might show up better.

Such advice, given under the title 'Which of the vernacular poets' styles is to be taken as a model',[67] outlines an aesthetic of music which distinguishes between the pleasure to be drawn from purely musical elements and the subtler and more refined one derived from the interaction of poetic and

not only in the manuscripts mentioned above but also in the *Libro quarto* (1505) of Petrucci's series, which has the unusual title *Strambotti, ode, frottole, sonetti, et modo de cantar versi latini e capituli.*

[63] As a rule the duo formed by *cantus* and *tenor* is a self-sufficient musical structure without the addition of the other parts, and clearly establishes itself as the original nucleus of the piece; deviations from this rule are due to the composer's knowledge that he was to add at least a *contratenor bassus* to the basic structure. The chordal nature of the piece was emphasized by forming the first added part with such notes which would best complete the harmonies outlined by the original duo; the addition of a fourth part, the *contratenor altus*, merely added a richer sound without changing the harmonic substance. To be sure, the basic *cantus–tenor* structure can also be detected in many of the most sophisticated works of fifteenth-century polyphonic art; here, however, the clear definition of vertical harmony gives way to contrapuntal thinking, which is already present in the shaping of the *tenor* line and further developed by the addition of the other parts.

[64] This practice is clearly shown by the title of two collections by Petrucci, *Tenori e contrabassi intabulati col sopran in canto figurato per cantar e sonar col lauto* (*Libro primo* 1509 and *Libro secundo* 1511) and also by Bartolomeo Tromboncino's letter published by Alfred Einstein in *The Italian Madrigal* (Princeton 1949), vol. I, p. 48.   [65] *Prose e lettere...inedite*, pp. 20ff.

[66] *Ibid.*, p. 21.   [67] *Ibid.*, p. 22.

musical values. In the case of the former, music which had the most 'air' or 'spirit' was preferred. This could be dance music, in which, as already seen, even Lorenzo the Magnificent took pleasure; or popular melodies, which might possibly have been used to accompany poetry as deliberately popular in tone and form as that which constitutes a sizeable part of the literary production of Poliziano's circle; or simple melodies with a clearly designed and balanced interplay of lines, which were typical of the *stanze*, *barzellette* and *frottole*; or 'singing in diminution' with its almost instrumental virtuosity; or fully instrumental music played on the lute, organ or the *instrumentum*, better known later as the *clavicembalo* or *gravicembalo* (harpsichord). But where the poetic values were important, music was required to give up some of its prerogatives, and to exert them only to the extent necessary to enhance and intensify the poetry. Therefore, continues Calmeta, 'we must praise the good judgement of those, who in singing put all their effort into expressing the words well... *and have them accompanied by the music in the manner of masters accompanied by their servants,*...not making the thoughts and emotions subservient to the music, but the music to the emotions and thoughts'.[68]

Calmeta's young lover who wishes 'to entertain his lady [with his singing] and to insert amorous words into that music' appears in *Orfeo* in the person of Aristaeus, the wealthy 'youthful shepherd' with a servant. But, perhaps because Aristaeus is also 'a son of Apollo', Poliziano preferred the literary *ballata* form for his song to the more popular *barzelletta*. The fact that by the time of the *Orfeo* the true *ballata* form was archaic may also have influenced his choice: it survived only in Florence, and not even the recrudescence of Petrarchism in the sixteenth century succeeded in reviving it. (Instead it was absorbed into and replaced by the madrigal.)[69] In Aristaeus' song poetic expression tends to be subordinated to musical expression, even to the sensual blandishments of music. And as none of the few contemporary *ballata* settings which survive, essentially those by Arrigo Isaac of texts by Poliziano and Lorenzo dei Medici,[70] are composed on a *ballata* text made up entirely of hendecasyllabic lines like Aristaeus' song, we cannot use them as an indication of what his song was like. His invitation to Eurydice 'to learn to make good use of her beauty' was probably set in two-voice polyphony, with the *tenor* played by Mopsus' pan-pipes, which would have given it a more sensual appeal than the pure and noble notes of Orpheus' lyre.

I have already drawn a parallel between the final chorus of the Bacchantes and Lorenzo's *Triumph of Bacchus and Ariadne*. A plausible reconstruction of the latter has recently been suggested, based on the existing three-voice setting of one of Lorenzo's *laude*,[71] but the overall effect of this reconstruction

---

[68] *Ibid.*

[69] The poems called *ballate* in the *Madrigali del magnifico Signor Luigi Cassola* (Venice 1544 – though most of the texts must be much earlier than the date of publication) no longer retain any traces of the structure of either literary or popular *ballate*, while many of the madrigals set to music by Verdelot, Arcadelt and their contemporaries, though not regular *ballate*, do retain the characteristic return of the initial poetic theme almost in the form of a refrain. On this subject, see Don Harrán, 'Verse Types in the early Madrigal', *Journal of the American Musicological Society*, XXII (1969), p. 27ff.

[70] Most of these appear to have been composed after 1512, in the period of the Medicean restoration.

[71] Walter H. Rubsamen, 'The Music for "Quant'è bella giovinezza" and other Carnival Songs', in *Art, Science and History in the Renaissance*, ed. Charles S. Singleton (Baltimore 1968),

is disappointingly sober and sedate, a result of a rather stolid rhythmic framework and a moderate tempo imposed by a brief passage of more rapid notes. Panic if not Bacchic high spirits are more successfully suggested by the similarly reconstructed music of Poliziano's well-known song *Ben venga maggio* (example I), whose rhythmic abandon and unusual cadences in which the dominant chord omits the third are truly impressive. These features might have been made even more striking and dramatic by spirited recitation and by being accompanied by instruments of the kind which Cortese described as 'offending the discriminating ear by the want of moderation in their notes and by their inordinate noise'[72] rather than on the less aggressive lute.

In their depictions of Apollo, the Muses, Orpheus, or Arion, Renaissance painters and engravers felt free to indulge in extravagant archaeological reconstructions of classical instruments, or of what they imagined were classical instruments. The result was often a fantastic form, highly improbable from a musical or acoustical point of view. Alternatively, they could reproduce instruments in current use, especially since contemporary men of letters often called these by classical names. For the staging of Poliziano's Orpheus, there was no choice but to opt for this second solution, as his instrument had not only to be the visible symbol of his poetic activity but also to accompany his singing. He must therefore have appeared carrying one of the real instruments with which he is most represented: a lute, or a *viola* shaped like the Spanish *vihuela* and like it played by plucking the strings, or the instrument which throughout the sixteenth century and even later was commonly known in Italy as the *lira da braccio* (plates 5 and 6) and which was sometimes plucked, though more often bowed.[73] The odds are in favour of this last, since Baccio Ugolini is always described as 'singing to the lyre', though without specific details about his instrument. He himself once promised to sing the praises of the Marquis Ludovico Gonzaga[74] to the lyre,

pp. 163ff, rightly assigns to the *Trionfo* the music of the *lauda* 'Quanto è grande la bellezza' for three voices in Serafino Razzi, *Libro primo delle laudi spirituali* (Florence 1563), for only two voices in the Florence MS, Biblioteca Nazionale, Rossi-Cassigoli 395, fol. 5v–6 (dated 1522). It had previously been suggested that the *lauda* derived its music from the *Canzone delle Forese*, also by Lorenzo the Magnificent. Even before Rubsamen, Gallucci had reached the same conclusion in 'Festival Music in Florence'. Rubsamen in 'The Music for "Quant'e bella giovinezza"', p. 171, reproduces the inscription which precedes the text of the *Trionfo* in the Florence MS, Biblioteca Nazionale, Magl. VII, 1225, fol. 45: 'Song (*chançona*) composed by Lorenzo the Magnificent who in this carnival had performed the Triumph of Bacchus where they sang the songs written for the lute (*chançone chomposte da leuto*), reproduced below: they were very beautiful.' This seems to me to confirm that only the upper part was sung (probably by soloist and chorus alternately) and that the other parts were played. In Rubsamen's article the *Trionfo* is dated 1489, which by modern reckoning may become 1490.

[72] The reconstruction of the music of *Ben venga maggio* from the *lauda*, *Ecco il Messia* (from Serafino Razzi, *Libro primo delle laudi spirituali*, fol. 15) is also the work of Gallucci in 'Festival Music in Florence'. The printed edition of the *Laudi fatte e composte da piú persone spirituali* (Florence 1 March 1485/6) contains various other *laude* by Feo Belcari, Francesco d'Albizo and Lucrezia dei Medici to be sung to the music of *Ben venga maggio*. *Ecco il Messia* is amongst those by Lucrezia dei Medici, and it must therefore have been written before 1482, the year in which Lorenzo the Magnificent's mother died. *Ben venga maggio* therefore either pre-dates *Orfeo*, or is its contemporary. The quotation about instruments is taken from Paolo Cortese, who uses it to refer to instruments to which he gives the classical names of *barbiti* and *pentades*; see Pirrotta, 'Music and Cultural Tendencies', pp. 149, 153 and 157.   [73] See note 56 above.

[74] From a Latin letter of 1459 which shows how cultured Ugolini was, reproduced in Del Lungo, *Florentia*, p. 309.

Ex. I Angelo Poliziano. *Canzone di Maggio*. Music of the *lauda*. *Ecco il Messia*, on a text by Lucrezia dei Medici. From the Florence manuscript, Biblioteca Nazionale Centrale, Palatino 173, fol. 158r.

'versu ad lyram', so it is likely that he accompanied himself on the *lira da braccio* when singing his Sapphic ode in praise of Cardinal Gonzaga, Ludovico's son. As for the music, the closest parallel I can suggest is a setting by the Veronese Michele Pesenti of Horace's *Integer vitae scelerique purus* (*Carmina* I 22) (example II), which was published by Ottaviano Petrucci in the *Frottole*

Ex. II   Michele Pesenti. Sapphic ode. Words by Horace. From *Frottole libro primo* (O. Petrucci, Venice 1504), fol. 44r (the alto part partially omitted).

libro primo of 1504, almost a quarter of a century after *Orfeo* was written.[75] Despite the fact that the composer, Michele Pesenti, was one of the most lively and inventive of the so-called *frottola* composers, Horace's text is treated with great sobriety, under the influence of a persisting stylistic convention. It is more difficult to find such a parallel for the two elegiac distichs 'by Ovid, arranged for the occasion' which Orpheus sings after Pluto has agreed to the return of Eurydice. Marchetto Cara's music for Propertius' *Quicumque ille fuit*

[75]   Previously printed in Rudolf Schwartz, *Ottaviano Petrucci, Frottole, Buch I und IV* (Leipzig 1935), p. 34 and in *Le Frottole nell'edizione principe di Ottaviano Petrucci*, transcr. Gaetano Cesari, ed. Raffaello Monterosso (Cremona 1954), vol. I, p. 35. It is preceded by another Latin ode also composed by Pesenti on a text attributed to Tebaldeo, which indicates that the musician belonged to the Ferrarese or Mantuan circle. My transcription, like subsequent ones, halves the values of the original notes and places the bar-lines not according to metre but to what seems to me the most likely interpretation of the rhythm. The arrangement of the words beneath the notes, and the suggestion of possible repetitions of the words, follow the same criterion. Furthermore, for music thought to have been played on the lute, lyre or similar instruments, the *contratenor altus* has been omitted (see note 63 above).

31

Ex. III *Strambotto*. Anonymous words and music. From the Paris manuscript, Bibliothèque Nationale, Rés. Vm.⁷ 676, fols. 33v–34r (alto part omitted).

(*Elegies* II 12) was not published until 1517. Not only is the gap between it and *Orfeo* too great for it to provide us with an analogy, but it also has a long interlude (or repetition of the second line) between one distich and the next, which is quite unsuited to the urgency of the situation in *Orfeo*.[76] All we can

[76] It was published in Andrea Antico, ed., *Frottole libro tertio* (Rome 1517?), which also includes a different setting of *Integer vitae* by Bartolomeo Tromboncino. A modern edition of the entire collection has been published, based on the 1518 edition, *Canzoni sonetti strambotti et frottole. Libro tertio (Andrea Antico 1517)*, ed. A. Einstein (Northampton, Mass. 1941).

do therefore is assume a musical setting which followed the principles of plain declamation as applied by Pesenti in his Sapphic ode.

Orpheus' second Latin song celebrates the victory just won by his singing – but by what kind of song? We have already seen that it was a *strambotto*, of which hundreds of examples survive, albeit from a later date. Here I shall restrict myself to three examples, chosen to represent three of the different trends in the varied literature of *strambotti*. The first (example III), whose text and music are both anonymous, is taken from a manuscript in the Bibliothèque Nationale in Paris (Rés. Vm⁷. 676), dated 1502 and originating in one of the courts of Northern Italy, Mantua or Ferrara perhaps, or one of their client courts.[77] The music has an irregular rhythm to which it is difficult to fit the text, which leads me to think it belongs to a type of popular or pseudo-popular *strambotto*, in which moments of plain almost hesitant recitation alternate with passages of pointed rhythmic drive and even with short bursts of vocalization (what Calmeta would have called 'singing in diminution').

My second example comes from the same manuscript, from a small group of settings of texts almost certainly by Serafino Aquilano, who was one of the two poets singled out by Calmeta from amongst his contemporaries as models for those who wished 'to rise above the common throng' and 'succeed in impressing [their poetic expression] not only on amorous hearts but on learned ones too'. The music of *Ite, suspir(i), là dove Amor vi mena* (example IV) is anonymous, as is that of the other texts attributed to Serafino, and does not appear in any other manuscript or printed source. Bearing in mind that Aquilano was in Mantua in 1495, it is possible that this was the music that the poet used to sing, and that he himself composed it.[78] If so, Aquilano fully deserved the praise he received not only for his poetry but also for his music. The *strambotto* has an expressive melodic line with clearly defined contours, and retains something of the rhythmic contrasts observable in my previous example, though here they fit better into the more balanced structure. I could also give an example of the work of Cariteo, Calmeta's other model, for a *strambotto* is included under his name in Petrucci's *Frottole libro nono* (1509, new style). On the whole its style is one of smoother declamation than is the case in the other two *strambotti* already examined, though it too indulges in some simple melismata.[79] But I would rather draw on another contemporary manuscript for a *strambotto* setting which, because it is closer to Poliziano's own circle, might better reflect the style of the songs in *Orfeo*. This is the music for one of the few known *strambotto* texts which are attributed to the singer who played the part of Orpheus, Baccio Ugolini (example V); a sole anonymous version survives in the Biblioteca Trivulziana of Milan, in manuscript 55 which itself consists largely of a collection of *strambotti*.[80] It begins simply and

[77]   Nanie Bridgman. 'Un manuscrit italien au début du XVIᵉ siècle à la Bibliothèque Nationale', *Annales musicologiques*, I (1953), pp. 177ff, gives an accurate description and discusses its content.   [78]   *Ibid.*, pp. 185 and 186.

[79]   A facsimile is to be found as an illustration for W. Rubsamen, 'Frottola', in *Die Musik in Geschichte und Gegenwart*, vol. IV, cols. 1025–26.

[80]   Knud Jeppesen, 'Über einige unbekannte Frottolenhandschriften', *Acta musicologica*, XI (1939), pp. 81ff, was the first to give its content and its concordances. Transcriptions and comments on the compositions it contains are to be found in Remo Giazotto, 'Onde musicali nella corrente poetica di Serafino dall'Aquila', in *Musurgia nova* (Milan 1959), pp. 3–119, which also includes the music of Baccio Ugolini's *strambotto* (pp. 36–7). I have been unable to trace the source which attributes the text to Ugolini. A new edition of the entire MS is included as an appendix in K. Jeppesen, *La frottola* vol. III (Copenhagen 1970), pp. 141–324.

Ex. IV *Strambotto*. Words by Serafino Aquilano. From the Paris manuscript, Bibliothèque Nationale, Rés. Vm.⁷ 676, fols. 74v–75r (alto part omitted).

evenly like the music of Cariteo's *strambotto*, but it is even more restrained, with just a hint of melodic inflexion, and therefore closer to the classical simplicity of the Horatian ode set to music by Michele Pesenti. Remembering the improvising at which Ugolini excelled, as conceded even by the hypercritical Paolo Cortese,[81] one may go so far as to imagine that this might be one of

[81] *De cardinalatu*, Bk III, fol. 164v.

Ex. V *Strambotto*. Words attributed to Baccio Ugolini. From the Milan manuscript, Biblioteca Trivulziana, 55, fols. 15v–16r (alto part omitted).

the melodic formulas which he adapted as necessary to other *strambotto* texts with all the adjustments required each time by the different mood and different accentuation of each text. Such adjustments, we must always bear in mind, were needed even in the singing of a single *strambotto* to fit the same melody to all four distichs.

Whether the music in the Trivulziano codex is really by Baccio Ugolini, and to what extent it reflects the songs he performed on the lyre as Orpheus, are questions to which no definite answers can be given. I can only indicate what Poliziano himself may have expected from the heroic songs of his Orpheus, by quoting some passages from one of his letters, which bear witness to his reactions as a listener to music. The letter in question is addressed to Pico della Mirandola, some ten years after *Orfeo*, and was probably written in Rome.[82] It is a description of music heard during the course of a banquet, offered by Paolo Orsini according to a custom typical of that time. Even more typical is the

[82] It is included in Bk XII of the collection of Poliziano's letters, and can refer, at the earliest, to the voyage to Rome which took place in 1488 for the marriage of Piero dei Medici to Alfonsina Orsini.

fact that as long as he is talking about polyphonic music, Poliziano limits himself to describing the sensual (indeed even visceral) pleasure produced by the voice of one performer, Fabio Orsini, the eleven-year-old son of the host. But his enthusiasm knows no bounds when Fabio goes on to sing in a solo performance:

No sooner were we seated at the table than [Fabio] was ordered to sing, together with some other experts, certain of those songs which are put into writing with those little signs of music [it is difficult to render the sense of contemptuous diffidence conveyed by that 'quaedam...notata Musicis accentiunculis carmina'],[83] and immediately he filled our ears, or rather our hearts ['immo vero in praecordia'], with a voice so sweet that (I do not know about the others) as for myself, I was almost transported out of my senses, and was touched beyond doubt by the unspoken feeling of an altogether divine pleasure. He then performed an heroic song which he had himself recently composed in praise of our own Piero dei Medici...His voice was not entirely that of someone reading, nor entirely that of someone singing; both could be heard, and yet neither separated one from the other; it was, in any case, even or modulated, and changed as required by the passage. Now it was varied, now sustained, now exalted and now restrained, now calm and now vehement, now slowing down and now quickening its pace, but always it was precise, always clear and always pleasant; and his gestures were not indifferent or sluggish, but not posturing or affected either. You might have thought that an adolescent Roscius was acting on the stage.[84]

Calmeta was not alone in insisting prophetically that the music should be 'subservient to the emotions and thoughts' expressed by the words. We find the same idea reasserted by Poliziano and developed to form the basis of a style midway between spoken language and song and which relied for its shades of expression on the performer's flexibility. The basic concepts of monodic reform – the dependence of the music on the text, the recitative or *representative* style, the *sprezzatura* of the performance – had not only been formulated but had even been put into practice more than a century before the birth of opera.

[83] The expression recalls the one used by Poliziano about Piero dei Medici (see note 54 above).

[84] Poliziano's letter is not alone in describing such intensity of 'recitative' or 'representative' delivery. A few decades earlier Antonio di Guido, a surprisingly cultured and poetically talented Florentine strolling player (*cantimpanca*), had amazed learned audiences; his singing was able to render remarkably vivid tales which, merely read, appeared totally insignificant. More recent than Poliziano's letter is Baldassare Castiglione's praise of the singer and composer Bidon for the style of his performance 'so artful, so sensitive, so forcible and excited (*concitata*), with such variety of tunes as to capture and enflame the souls of all his audience' (*Il cortegiano*, I, xxxvii). Angelo Colocci, too, wrote of Serafino Aquilano: 'They recognize the uniqueness of his delivery, but [stress] that he strove to adjust the words to the [sound of the] lute to impress them more forcefully on the souls of the people, as Gracchus had adjusted his lyre in the Senate, now to enflame, now to appease' ('Apologia', in *Le rime di Serafino de' Ciminelli dall'Aquila*, Bologna 1894, p. 27).

2 Classical theatre, *intermedi* and *frottola* music

There is a group of theatrical works, dating from the last twenty years of the fifteenth century and first twenty of the sixteenth, which Italian literary scholars refer to as *drammi mescidati*, hybrid dramas. These works, performed occasionally in conjunction with the more frequently staged Latin comedies in vernacular translations, include mythological plays such as Niccolò da Correggio's *La fabula de Caephalo* and Baldassare Taccone's *Danae*, as well as dramatizations of classically derived stories: both Matteo Maria Boiardo and Galeotto del Carretto based plays on a tale by Lucian, writing respectively *Timone* and *La comedia di Timon greco*, while the latter also wrote *Le nozze di Psiche e Cupidine*, taken from Apuleius, and a self-styled tragedy, *Sofonisba*, for which he drew upon Livy, and which he dedicated to Isabella d'Este Gonzaga, as he had his *Timon greco*. The term *drammi mescidati* also covers a few other plays, based on stories by Boccaccio, such as Bernardo Accolti's *Virginia* and *Filostrato e Panfila* by Antonio Cammelli 'il Pistoia', who dedicated it to Ercole I d'Este, Duke of Ferrara, and sent a copy of it to the duke's daughter the Marchioness of Mantua.[1] These plays were called 'hybrid' because, as the coiner of the term explained, their authors 'sought insofar as possible to impose a certain classical regularity or at least some semblance of classicism on the free ways of popular sacred theatre'.[2] In other words, the authors recognized and imitated some of the more obvious features of classical plays: the prologue, the presentation of the plot, the envoi, and the division into acts, usually five. At the same time, however, they contrived to base their choice of metre, their use of multiple sets and the development of the plot on the traditions of religious theatre, which ignored the requirements of the unities of time and action.

I have already expressed, and need not restate, my reservations about the presumed dependence of Poliziano's *Orfeo* on 'the ways of popular sacred theatre', an idea based on features which are, if anything, typical of the contemporary approach to theatre in general rather than to either sacred or secular theatre in particular. What we now need to do is take a fresh look at the 'classicism' of which the 'hybrid dramas' supposedly fall short. I cannot see how we can reasonably expect to find 'classical regularity' in this period of theatrical activity, since its basic theories and their practical applications

---

[1] The best source for a detailed survey of this particular period and this aspect of Italian cultural history is still the chapter 'Le corti dell'Italia superiore alla fine del secolo', in Vittorio Rossi, *Il Quattrocento*, 3rd edn (Milan 1933), pp. 523ff. More specific information about the authors and performances of the plays is provided by Pyle, 'Politiano's "Orfeo" and other "favole mitologiche" in the context of Late Quattrocento Northern Italy' which includes the text of 'Pasithea' by Gasparo Visconti, possibly never performed and with no directions calling for music.

[2] Rossi, 'Le corti dell'Italia', *Il Quattrocento*, p. 531.

were still being evolved – or even invented – over the next three or four decades. I have come to the conclusion that the whole phase of theatrical activity which began in Ferrara in 1486, when it became fashionable to produce plays by Terence and Plautus, deserves to be described as 'hybrid'; the term would thus cover not only the performances in Ferrara itself but also subsequent ones elsewhere. The Ferrarese dramatists had no real knowledge of authentic classical performing style; all they had to go on were the texts themselves, and these they treated according to the same 'hybrid' criteria which they applied when composing their own works. It was only after actual performances revealed new problems that they were prompted to rethink their ideas on how dramatic works were composed and performed, and to study more closely what classical authors had said about theatre and its various genres.

On 25 January 1486, in Ferrara, and sponsored by Duke Ercole I, 'in the new courtyard of the ducal court the comedy of *I Menechini* was recited, which was most beautiful and pleasing...And it lasted until vespers, that is, four hours; and at the end they lit a tree, or Roman candle, which threw many rockets of fire into the air, all together, very high, with great noise and a most stupendous flame. And thus, with joy, applause and praise, the comedy ended, having been attended by ten thousand people, who watched in silence.' Thus wrote the diarist Bernardino Zambotti,[3] whose words were echoed by another Ferrarese chronicler who also described the 'houses with battlements' on the stage on which 'a farce by Plautus' had been performed, adding only one new detail, that 'then came a flat boat with ten people aboard with oars and sails like a real one, which moved across the courtyard'.[4] *I Menechini* (a translation of *Menaechmi*) was followed in 1487 by another of Plautus' plays, *Amphitrione*. Between these two Niccolò da Correggio's *La fabula de Caephalo* had been staged, but whereas the two Plautine plays were so well-received that they were repeated for many years, the same cannot be said of *Caephalo* and of the majority of the so-called hybrid dramas: even if they were performed once, they were soon forgotten.

The fame of the Ferrarese performances spread rapidly. They were soon copied in every major Italian cultural centre (with the temporary exception of Florence and Naples, due to unfavourable social and political conditions), partly because representatives of other courts had often attended performances at the d'Este court. One such regular spectator from 1486 onwards was Francesco Gonzaga, the Marquis of Mantua, especially after his marriage to Isabella d'Este. Another frequent visitor to Ferrara was his uncle, the apostolic protonotary and bishop-elect Ludovico Gonzaga, who himself later promoted theatrical displays in his residence at Gazzuolo. During the carnival of 1491 the same two Plautine comedies, plus Terence's *Andria*, were given in Ferrara to celebrate the wedding of the fourteen-year-old Alfonso d'Este and the fifteen-year-old Anna Sforza. On that occasion the group of Milanese noblemen who escorted the bride included Giovanni Francesco Sanseverino, Count of Cajazzo, who in 1496 became the promoter of another of the hybrid

[3] B. Zambotti, 'Diario ferrarese dall'anno 1476 sino al 1504', ed. Giuseppe Pardi (Bologna 1934–7) being an appendix in a separate volume to *Rerum Italicarum Scriptores*, vol. XXIV, part VII, pp. 171ff.

[4] *Diario ferrarese di autori incerti*, ed. G. Pardi, in *Rerum Italicarum Scriptores*, vol. XXIV, part VII (Bologna 1927–33), pp. 121ff.

dramas, Taccone's *Danae*, 'a comedy performed in the house of his lordship the Count of Cajazzo for the most illustrious Lord Duke [Ludovico Sforza 'il Moro'] and *for the people of Milan*' (my italics). Even before this performance of *Danae*, Ludovico Sforza, who was married to Beatrice d'Este, had visited Ferrara, in 1493, and had attended performances of comedies including, yet again, *I Menechini*. His father-in-law had returned the visit three months later, taking with him to Milan personnel and props for the performance of three comedies (*Captivi*, *Mercator* and *Penulo*). Charles VIII's invasion of Italy and the ensuing wars temporarily interrupted the Ferrarese performances, but they were resumed with increased fervour in 1499 and 1501, while those staged in 1502 to mark Alfonso d'Este's remarriage to Lucrezia Borgia were particularly impressive.[5]

These performances marked a major development, for they were no longer seen as mere appendages or ornaments to court ceremonies or entertainments, but as entities in their own right and ones which, moreover, were at least nominally open to the public. I have already stressed how this idea was reflected in the title of the Milanese *Danae*, although the idea itself originated in Ferrara. In his brief *Spectacula*, Bartolomeo Prisciano, the astrologer and man of letters who acted as Ercole I's main adviser over the Ferrarese performances, praises his duke's *Celsitude* in no uncertain terms: by this *Celsitude* 'with so many and such well-ordered spectacles you assemble your most faithful and fair people: you delight them: you teach them how to live the life of this world: you encourage them to study and to become learned men to the honour and great benefit of the entire Republic'.[6] Further supporting evidence is provided by those Ferrarese chroniclers who recorded the spectacles of 1486 and 1487. Their descriptions are initially quite extraordinarily detailed (later, as the novelty wears off, so their attention to detail declines), giving exaggerated estimates of the size of the audience, and praising the fact that despite the number of people present they were able 'to watch in silence'. This seems to mark the rebirth of a vague idea of theatre as an institution for the *polis*, and linked to it, the notion of a building whose sole purpose was to house it, whatever the practical problems. Prisciano's tract is essentially a study of ancient Greek and Roman theatres, but for the time being his contemporaries compromised: the only thing their theatres had in common with classical ones was that the sites chosen for the performances were either entirely open or only partially covered by a canopy. On 25 January 1487 a violent thunderstorm disturbed a performance of *Amphitrione* which was taking place, as usual, in the courtyard of the ducal palace, and most of the audience left. The interruption showed that there were problems in reconciling respect for classical models with contemporary custom, which required that except on very special occasions performances should be given primarily during carnival, that is in the depths of winter. An uninterrupted repeat performance of *Amphitrione* was staged on 5 February, but thereafter theatrical performances were given in the main hall of the castle or, if necessary, in an even larger one in the Palazzo della Ragione.[7]

[5]   See the two Ferrarese diaries referred to above, *passim*, and D'Ancona, *Le origini*, II, pp. 13–15 and 127–37.

[6]   Quoted by Giulio Bertoni, *L'Orlando Furioso e la Rinascenza a Ferrara* (Modena 1919), pp. 23ff.

[7]   See the Ferrarese diarists, *passim*.

It is not for me to study the conflicting pressures which influenced the architectural development of theatres, the problems of interpreting data obtained from ancient monuments and classical treatises and of adapting this information to contemporary ideas and conditions. I shall limit myself to observing that initially an attempt was made to give the assembled spectators the illusion of being inside a building designed for a specific purpose – an illusion similar to that created by Mantegna's Wedding Chamber, which I used as the starting point of my discussion in the last chapter. Battista Guarini's verse description of the 1486 apparatus shows that the usual appearance of the castle's internal courtyard had been considerably altered, not only by the stage itself but also by rows of steps for the spectators to sit on and by tapestries which concealed all the entrances:

Et remis puppim et velo sine fluctibus actam
Vidimus in portus nare, Epidamne, tui;
Vidimus effictam celsis cum moenibus urbem,
Structaque per latas tecta superba vias.
Ardua creverunt gradis spectacula multis
Velaruntque omnes stragula picta foros.[8]

We saw a boat moving with oars and sail, yet without waves, in the opening of your harbour, O Epidamnus; we saw the town portrayed with lofty walls, its splendid buildings lining broad streets. Spectator seats rose on many steps, and painted awnings covered all openings.

The chroniclers too describe the tapestries and the steps against the wall opposite the stage, which were intended for the most important spectators: 'our most illustrious Duke, the Marquis of Mantua, Fracasso, son of the Lord Roberto Sanseverino, two ambassadors of the Duke of Milan, and many other knights and foreign gentlemen, as well as local citizens, and doctors and scholars'. Most of the 'ten thousand' spectators stood uncomfortably packed into the space between the steps and the stage, which may explain why the ladies were found safer places 'at the windows of the bedrooms and on the new balcony'.[9]

But the most impressive document connected with this theatrical use of *trompe l'oeil* is not Ferrarese but Mantuan; at least it was sent from Mantua to Ercole I d'Este by one of his courtiers, in 1501. It is a description, in some places quite difficult to interpret, 'of the [theatrical] apparatus ordered by this most illustrious marquis [Francesco Gonzaga, who that year competed with his father-in-law by having four theatrical works performed in as many days of February], most sumptuous and deserving to be put on an equal level with any ancient or modern temporary theatre whatsover'.[10] According to that description, the hall which had been selected was arranged as to appear

[8]   Baptista Guarinus, *Carmina*, Bk IV, quoted by D'Ancona, *Le origini*, II, p. 128 note 2.
[9]   From Zambotti, 'Diario ferrarese', p. 187. Fracasso Sanseverino, listed amongst the spectators attending the performance of *I Menechini*, was the brother of the Count of Cajazzo. His chancellor, Francesco de Nobili, called Cherea, from Lucca, was the man most instrumental in establishing the custom of performing comedies in Venice. In Fracasso's home, on the Giudecca, in 1513, 'was demonstrated a certain shepherds' comedy, by his chancellor Cherea', as Marin Sanudo, *Diarii*, vol. XV (Venice 1889), p. 531, reports.
[10]   Letter by Sigismondo Cantelmo, from Mantua, 13 Feb. 1501, in *Lettere artistiche inedite*, ed. G. Campori (Modena 1886), p. 5. The plays performed were *Philonico* (i.e. probably *Philodico*), *Penulo*, *Ippolito* (probably Seneca's) and Terence's *Adelphi*.

completely surrounded by arches 'with columns harmonizing with and proportioned to the height of the said arches. Their bases and capitals, painted most splendidly and in the finest colours, and decorated with leaves, *represented to the mind a building ancient and eternal, full of beauty* (my italics). The arches on one of the longer sides of the wall were adorned 'with the six panels of the Triumph of Caesar by the inimitable hand of Mantegna';[11] while above the frieze 'there were many tall statues, some silvery, some golden, and of many other metallic colours, some truncated, some whole, which greatly embellished that place. Last came the sky, made of dark blue cloth and spangled with stars with such constellations as they revolved that very night in our hemisphere...' This might seem to be enough, but other details make the description particularly interesting. 'At the corner joining one long and one short side, four tall columns with round bases were to be seen, which supported [the figures of] the four principal winds. Between them was a grotto, artificial yet most natural. Above it was a sky shining with many lights like most brilliant stars, and with a mechanical wheel bearing the signs [of the Zodiac], to the motion of which now the sun, now the moon revolved in their proper houses. Within [the grotto] was the wheel of Fortune with its tenses: *regno, regnavi, regnabo*; and the golden goddess herself was seated in the middle with a sceptre and a dolphin.' We do not know the purpose of the astrological signs and the grotto of Fortune. All we are told about the stage is that at its base were displayed other paintings by Mantegna, depicting the Triumphs of Petrarch, about which nothing more is known, and that 'within the scene were golden drapes and some greenery, as required by the plays'. It would seem then that there was only a vague attempt to sketch in the setting of the play itself, with more attention being paid to creating an illusion of reality centred on the 'most natural grotto' and the suggestion of 'a building ancient and eternal'.

The fact that the Mantuan stage was apparently divided into two segments at right angles to each other, with the grotto of Fortune in the corner between them, suggests that it was a multiple stage, even though this was 1501 and it was a classical tragedy and three classical comedies which were being performed. This is not surprising, for it is not the only time that such a style of staging is indicated. Guarini's verses quoted above, and the descriptions of the chroniclers, suggest that *I Menechini* had been acted on two levels of stage similar to those for which both *Timone* plays have been criticized: a higher level representing the town with its houses with battlements, and a lower level for the harbour where the boat arrived. The same can be said of *Amphitrione*. When this was staged, the 'city' set which had previously been used for Correggio's *Caephalo* was supplemented with a sky which 'had been built high in a corner towards the clock-tower, with lamps burning in the appropriate places behind thin black curtains, and shining like stars; and there were children dressed in white, representing the planets...which sky functioned at the right time as required by the comedy, to the admiration of all well-informed men'.[12] This forerunner of Leonardo da Vinci's *Paradiso*, and

---

[11] There are really nine panels in *Il trionfo di Cesare*, which were moved to England in the seventeenth century. They are painted on paper glued to canvas. Each panel measures 2.74 m × 2.74 m, corresponding to the four *braccia* which Cantelmo gives as the size of the aperture of each arch. The hall adapted to form the theatre must therefore have measured about 24 m × 19 m.   [12] Zambotti, 'Diario ferrarese', p. 179.

of the 1501 Mantuan grotto with the signs of the zodiac, was called for by the final scene of the comedy, in which Jupiter appears and makes prophecies concerning the twins who will be born to Alcmena (lines 1131ff of the Latin text).

The comedies were actually performed in vernacular translations which were of necessity fairly free, partly because of the problems of finding rhymes but especially because modern terms and customs had to be substituted for ancient ones which most of the spectators would have found difficult to understand. By and large, the attitude expressed by Battista Guarini was the one to prevail. He worked on his translations from 1479, and described his basic principles saying 'I try to follow the words of the [original] text, although in some places it seems to me better to take their tenor and work it into a good soprano.'[13] This was none too different from the principles followed in the hybrid dramas. Like them, these were written primarily in two metres: the *ottava*, which was by no means reserved for the exclusive use of sacred plays, and the *terza rima*,[14] a metre fundamentally alien to that sort of representation. And except for formal features such as the prologue, the envoi and the division into acts, they were acted without any real consciousness of classical regularity, if by that we mean the 'classical' unities of time, place and action.

Whether Poliziano actually wanted it to or not – and I would think he did – knowledge of his *Fabula d'Orfeo* must have spread rapidly, if it began so soon to serve as a model for some of the hybrid dramas, two of which are elaborations of it.[15] The first, the *Orphei tragoedia*, on whose subject rivers of

---

[13]   Quoted by Alessandro Luzio and Rodolfo Renier, 'Commedie classiche in Ferrara nel 1499', in *Giornale storico della letteratura italiana*, XI (1888), p. 178. See also Niccolò Cosmico's observations in D'Ancona, *Le origini*, II, pp. 372–3.

[14]   The text used for the 1487 performance was probably the *Amfitrione, commedia di Plauto voltata in terza rima da Pandolfo Collenuccio* (Milan 1864), in which the considerably extended episode of the appearance and prophecy of Jove fits Zambotti's description of the production (see below, p. 49). Pistoia's *Filostrato e Panfila* (performed, it seems, in 1499) is also entirely in *terza rima*, except for the sung *intermedi* which are in a modified *ballata* form. Osthoff, *Theatergesang*, I, pp. 131–43 and II, pp. 55–7, discusses and prints the music by Bartolomeo Tromboncino for the second of these *intermedi*, *Porta ognun del nascimento*, from *Frottole libro nono* by Petrucci (1508–9). Appropriately, the music is sung by four Platonic sirens (not by sea-sirens as Osthoff believes) who, presiding over the movement of the heavens, influence the destinies and fortunes of men. The first *intermedio* is sung by Love, the third by the three Fates, the fourth by Atropos, in accordance with the development of the plot. In my opinion, in the two choral *intermedi* (II and III) the upper part was sung in unison while the other three were played on instruments (cf. Osthoff, *Theatergesang*, I, p. 135).

[15]   I do not believe that one can take seriously Poliziano's reservations about the imperfections of the *Fabula*, or the pretence that the Bologna edition of *Le cose volgare del Politiano* was printed without the knowledge of the author, and that he might have been displeased had he known of it. The printing was supervised by Platone de Benedetti, who in the previous three years had printed or reprinted various Latin works by Poliziano, while the man responsible for the initial idea was Alessandro Sarti, whom Poliziano had praised just a year earlier for his diligence and skill in revising those very editions. The book was dedicated by Sarti to the papal protonotary Anton Galeazzo Bentivoglio who, together with Poliziano, seems to have been Piero dei Medici's favourite candidate for elevation to the cardinalate. It was thus a family affair, and the choice of the *Stanze*, *Orfeo*, the *stanza* of the *Eco*, and of a single very proper *ballata* was well calculated to demonstrate Poliziano's poetic ability without laying him open to charges of futility. As for *Orfeo*, the letter to Carlo Canale has perhaps focussed our attention too much on the possibility of a manuscript original left in Mantua (though in the meantime Canale had found himself a good position in Rome). It is strange that the oldest known manuscript copy, though by no means the first to be made, is the one in the MS Riccardiano 2723, which is Florentine, indeed Medicean,

ink have flowed, is actually nothing more than the *Fabula* itself, enlarged in some places, abbreviated in others, but mainly given the title *tragoedia* and divided into five acts, each with titles and stage directions in Latin.[16] The *Actus primus* corresponds to the eclogue section of the *Fabula* and is entitled *Pastoricus*. The second act has nymphs, *Nymphas habet*, because it offers a glimpse of the fleeing Eurydice as in the fable, and also because of the chorus of Dryads, who announce and lament Eurydice's end. In the *Actus tertius* one of the Dryads takes it upon herself to bring the sad news to Orpheus, and does so in the words which in the fable are given to the shepherd. This act is styled *Heroicus* because of Orpheus' songs which praise persons assumed to be of 'heroic' character and of his firm resolve to attempt to rescue Eurydice. The second and third acts are the ones in which more changes were made; among them the Sapphic ode in honour of Cardinal Gonzaga was replaced by a mere two Latin distichs, taken from Claudian, which praise Hercules – here both the god and the duke. This is the only time that the elaboration is shorter than the original. In addition, a satyr is introduced, to observe and comment on Orpheus' grief. Act IV, in hell, is named *Necromanticus*, and Act V *Bacchanalis*. Both diverge in only minute details from Poliziano's text. The introduction too receives a Latin title and is labelled *Argumentum*, which may also be the name of the abstract character who replaced Mercury and the Slav shepherd and recited their two octaves. The two lines belonging to the latter are modified to emphasize the principal novelty of the new version:

> Or stia ciascuno a tutti gli atti intento,
> che cinque sono, e questo è l'argomento.

Let everyone to each act be now intent, for they are five and this is the argument.

The sole purposes of these changes was to add new elements of visual interest (the Dryads and the satyr) and a new piece of music (the chorus of Dryads), as well as to facilitate the division into five acts, which are in any case extremely short, and of which only the last ends with a chorus.[17] The

though not belonging to the main branch of the family, and is dated 1487. On Sarti's activity in the field of publishing, see Giuliana Hill Cotton, 'Alessandro Sarti e il Poliziano', in *La bibliofilia*, XLIV (1962), pp. 225ff.

[16] From the time of Father Ireneo Affò's discovery of the text of the revised version and of his publication of it under the title of *Orfeo Tragedia di Messer Angelo Poliziano tratta da due vetusti codici e alla sua integrità e perfezione ridotta* (Venice 1776) opinion has been divided as to the accuracy of his attribution of it to Poliziano. (The text, with Affò's preface and appendices, was later reproduced in Carducci's edition of *Le Stanze, l'Orfeo e le Rime*, pp. 113–88, while the text alone appears in F. Neri's edition of *L'Orfeo e le Stanze*, pp. 35–50.) But Margherita Bianca Novaro's linguistic analysis seems to establish quite clearly that the text was not Poliziano's own: see M. B. Novaro, 'L'"Orphei Tragoedia" e la questione della sua attribuzione', in *Scritti vari*, published by the Università degli Studi di Torino, Facoltà di Magistero, II (1951), pp. 209–61, where the entire text is given according to the version in the Codex Estense αM.7.15, which M. B. Novaro believes to be an autograph version by Tebaldeo. Her opinion is confirmed by Vincenzo Pernicone, 'Sul testo delle opere in volgare di A. Poliziano', in *Il Poliziano e il suo tempo, Atti del IV Convegno Internazionale di Studi sul Rinascimento* (Florence 1957), pp. 83–7.

[17] The *Corus Dryadum* which appears in the second act does not bring the act to a close, but is followed by a spoken transitional passage in which one of the nymphs announces the arrival of Orpheus 'with his *citara* in his hand and so happy a face'. The stage-directions at the start of the act specify that the Dryads are to sing: '...interloquuntur item planguntque flebili cantu Dryades' (the chorus was in fact both preceded and succeeded by short spoken passages). Other musical directions are: in Act I 'Cantus Aristei' (Aristaeus has previously asked Mopsus *Fami tenor*

additions, some hundred lines, were certainly not intended to correct any 'imperfections' of the original, for while they do eliminate some of the more abrupt transitions in the action, they create new snags elsewhere. Although Antonio Tebaldeo is generally put forward as being the most probable author of the new version, other poets at the court of Ferrara cannot be ruled out. It may be the work of Niccolò da Correggio, for instance, or even of Matteo Maria Boiardo, if one considers how certain unusual metres which Poliziano barely hinted at are taken up and developed in the reworked version.[18] But whoever it was who wrote it, he must have done so before 1486, that is before the Ferrarese *rappresentazioni* so decisively expanded the size of theatrical spectacle and altered its nature, for there is no trace of such a change in the *Orphei tragoedia*.

The anonymous author of the third version of *Orfeo*, *La favola di Orfeo e Aristeo*, was a man of letters who may have been of Umbrian origin but who almost certainly also worked in Ferrara.[19] He was aware that the *Fabula* was too insubstantial for the new style of theatrical *rappresentazioni*, so he used it as the basis of the second and third acts of his play, and added three more, one before and two after the original ones, deriving his material from the same tales by Ovid and Virgil which had been Poliziano's sources. In the first act Mercury, the inventor of the cither, gives the instrument to Apollo as a gift for Orpheus, the son that the muse Calliope has just borne him. By the end of the act Orpheus is already old enough and well enough known for Diana to give him permission to marry Eurydice, and the act closes with a chorus to Hymen. Act II corresponds to the first two acts of the *Orphei tragoedia* and concludes with a chorus, *Piangiam, Ninfe, il nostro male*, very similar to the chorus of Dryads in the *tragoedia*. This clearly indicates that the author knew the earlier reworking – though perhaps not the original. Act III includes the rest of the plot of *Orfeo*, and ends with a *Canzona de le Bachidi*, which is an almost word-for-word repetition of Poliziano's *Coro delle Baccanti*. The fourth act centres on Aristaeus' grief and the fifth on tales of prodigies: the Maenads are transformed into tree trunks, and a dragon, which has attempted to devour Orpheus' head, is changed into stone. The head itself is carried off by Apollo into the sky, where it becomes a star.

con toa fistula alquanto); in Act III, 'Modulatur lamentaturque cithara Orpheus...', thus referring to the Latin distych at the beginning and to the two *ottave* which express Orpheus' grief: in Act IV 'Verbis flebilibus modulatur Orpheus...' again; in Act V only 'Lamentatur Orpheus...' is all that is said of the hero, but soon afterwards 'interloquuntur agunt et cantant Menades'.

[18]   This is an idea prompted by a consideration of the metres; it may or may not be borne out by a stylistic study of the new parts of the *tragoedia*. At the moment I can only suggest comparing *come succisa rosa/e come colto ziglio* from the Dryads' chorus and *Di corimbi e verdi edere/cinto el capo* with, respectively, vv. 5–6 of the dialogue *Chi te contrista* and v. 58 of the Egloga VII (M. M. Boiardo, *Opere volgari*, ed. Pier Vincenzo Mengaldo (Bari 1962), pp. 108 and 158). As for the metre, we may start from the unusual *ballata* form of the Dryads' chorus (AbaB CddC; ceDDA with the third line from the end divided by an internal rhyme, i.e. *intercisa* according to Boiardo) and with Mnesillo's two *mandriali* (both abCcaB DD) and go on considering the various changes introduced in the infernal scene.

[19]   Guido Mazzoni in *La favola di Orfeo e Aristeo. Festa drammatica del secolo XV* (Florence 1906), p. vii, pointed out that 'the poet was a man of learning and his language enables us to identify him as being from the Umbrian area, south-east of Siena'. Mazzoni also noted, in support of the idea that the *favola* was Ferrarese in origin, that the same codex (MS Riccardiano 1616) contains in the same writing a translation in tercets of Terence's *Formione*, with a prologue which he attributed to Ludovico Ariosto, believing that it was composed for performances in Ferrara between 1508 and 1509.

The *Favola* was richer in material than the *tragoedia*, and its acts were much longer, but these were not the only differences. There was a further major change which must be studied. The *tragoedia* had preserved intact all those parts of Poliziano's *Fabula* which we assume were intended to be sung, and had even added a new choral passage, so that music continued to play a prominent role: the new directions in Latin often indicate that a given passage was to be sung. In *La favola di Orfeo e Aristeo*, however, the only person to whom a song is specifically given is Aristaeus: the *Canzona di Aristeo* in Act II is an exact equivalent of Poliziano's, and indeed has the same metre and an almost identical beginning:

> S'io canto, i fiumi e omni vento tace:
> solo a la Nimpha mia odir non piace.

When I sing, rivers and winds are all stilled; only my nymph does not like my song.

Orpheus too should, and probably did, sing, but neither the metres nor the stage directions give any indication of this. The sections which correspond to Poliziano's *ottave* or *strambotti* are all converted, albeit with extensive and quite obvious borrowing, into *terza rima*, which is the prevalent metre.[20] It seems clear that not only was the plot expanded to five acts, but also that throughout them the predominant style was one of recitation. As if to redress the balance, *La favola di Orfeo e Aristeo*'s author was more consistent than the *tragoedia*'s in placing a choral passage in the metrical form of a *ballata* of octosyllabic lines at the end of every act. In most cases the choral conclusion is entitled *Canzona de le nimphe*, but Act III, as already mentioned, has a *Canzona de le Bachidi*. Act V has neither chorus nor envoi, perhaps because the manuscript is incomplete (in fact a few pages were left blank as if in the hope of adding the missing parts).

Choruses also end the acts of Niccolò da Correggio's *La fabula de Caephalo*, performed on 21 January 1487.[21] Mention is made of them in an octave in the prologue, which is often cited as an early reference to an at least theoretical awareness of the distinctions between dramatic genres:

> Non vi do questa già per comedìa,
> che in tutto non se observa il modo loro;
> non voglio la crediate tragedìa,

---

[20] One can speak of Poliziano's text being entirely recast in *terza rima* in Acts II and III, while even in the other acts the predominant metre is only interrupted by lyric pieces, for which the adapter preferred the octosyllabic *ballata* form aa bcbcca. Only the two pieces most influenced by the original diverge from this pattern, i.e. the *Canzona di Aristeo* (which has the same rhyme scheme but hendecasyllabic lines) and the *Canzona de le Bachidi* which, being Poliziano's own, retains the octosyllabic line and the rhyme scheme abba cdcddb. At the start of Act IV, after the Bacchantes have supplanted the nymphs at the conclusion of Act III, the latter reaffirm their function in a *Corus nimpharum*, which however is in *terza rima*.

[21] For *Caephalo*, see D'Ancona, *Le origini*, II, p. 5–8, and more recently the text in Niccolò da Correggio, *Opere*, ed. A. Tissoni Benvenuti (Bari 1969). The original edition says that the *favola* was 'composed by signor Niccolò da Correggio for the most illustrious Don Hercole, and performed by the latter before his most flourishing people of Ferrara on 21 January 1486'. A. Tissoni Benvenuti, in a note on *Caephalo* in the edition just referred to (pp. 496–99), picks out precise parallels between its versification and that of Poliziano's *Orfeo*, noting especially the recurrence of characteristic irregular metres (for which see above pp. 17–18). To these parallels one can add another: the octave of *versi sdruccioli* (with a dactylic end) (vv. 142–9) and Mopsus' octave in Poliziano's *Fabula* (vv. 85–92). I agree that *Caephalo* is more closely derived from the adaptation in tragedy form than from Poliziano's *Fabula*, that it defines the *terminus ante quem* for the adaptation, and that it casts doubt upon the attribution to Tebaldeo of the adaptation (see above, p. 44 and note 18).

> se ben de Ninfe gli vedrete il coro.
> Fabula o historia quale essa si sia,
> io ve la dono e non per precio d'oro,
> Di quel che segue l'argomento è questo;
> silentio tutti, e intendereti il resto.

I offer this to you not as a comedy, for their manner is not entirely followed; I do not want you to think this is a tragedy, though you will see it has a chorus of nymphs. Fable or story, whatever it may be, I give it to you for no price of gold. I have told you the argument of what follows. Be silent now; you'll understand the rest.

These lines are echoed by the Ferrarese chronicler Bernardino Zambotti, who wrote of *Caephalo*: 'And this *festa* was performed with sounds of various instruments between the acts, because it was done in the manner of a scene or tragedy' ('E tal festa fu facta con soni di diversi instrumenti intermedii a li acti, perché fu facta in modo de sciena o tragedia').[22] Already, and henceforward, the chorus was seen as a distinctive attribute of tragedy, but it was found convenient to apply it also to fables or hybrid drama (although they were often called comedies, as we have seen in the case of *Danae*); and these works thus tended to assume a role somewhere between the genres of comedy and tragedy, which later also became characteristic of sixteenth-century pastorals. In *Caephalo*, as in *La favola di Orfeo e Aristeo*, the nymphs are primarily, though not solely, responsible for retrieving the continuous recitation of the acts by singing and dancing. At the end of Act I they are joined by Aurora, who tells them: 'You sing, I will dance.' At the end of Act II the chorus is replaced by an eclogue sung by two shepherds (in alternation?), and at the end of Act III a satyr and his companions sing and dance 'with strange old-fashioned instruments'.

In Zambotti's words quoted above we find the first occurrence of the classically derived term *intermedi*. There it has the function of an adjective, though later sixteenth-century writers more often used it as a noun. It is not clear if the 'sounds...between the acts' referred to by the chronicler were the choruses themselves of *Caephalo* or *intermedi* introduced into the performance in addition to them, as was often done in sixteenth-century tragedies.[23] What is clear is that from the very start of the Ferrarese performances Plautus' comedies were divided into acts, fourteen years before such a division was officially established by the edition of the Latin texts published by Giovanni Battista Pio in 1500, and that the division was made apparent by interruptions in the main action, but not in the performance, since the intervals were filled by *intermedi*. The Ferrarese chroniclers almost always referred to the latter as 'feste' ('fra li acti forno facte alcune feste'), a further indication that the term was by no means restricted to the sacred *rappresentazioni* (Zambotti even used it to resolve Correggio's hesitations between the terms comedy and tragedy). Other terms in frequent use at the end of the fifteenth century were *intramesse*, *tramesse*, *tramezzi* and *introdutti*, all reminiscent of the convivial

---

[22] Zambotti, 'Diario ferrarese', p. 178. Choruses, or their equivalent, actually end the five acts; after the last chorus, however 'enters Calliope to sing the last stanza' – again an octave.

[23] But on rereading the text of *Caephalo* I am convinced that the *suoni intermedi* were those required to accompany the songs. On the *intermedi* see Nino Pirrotta, 'Intermedium', in *Die Musik in Geschichte und Gegenwart*, vol VI (Kassel 1957), col. 1310ff. and Elena Povoledo, 'Intermezzo: Dalle origini al secolo XVIII...Italia', in *Enciclopedia dello spettacolo*, vol. VI (Rome 1959), pp. 572ff.

entremets introduced in the banqueting hall. One might say, as in a mythological tale, that the *feste* – whether comedies or *drammi mescidati* – outgrew and devoured the *entremets* from which they had originated; but the latter lived on within them as *intermedi*, and before long took their revenge. Most of the descriptions of *intermedi* come from letters which usually make only passing reference to the main performance, while going on at great length about its accessories. The addressees of these letters presumably already knew the main text from previous performances or from reading it in manuscript or early prints; yet one cannot dismiss the suspicion that before long the spectators began to be more interested in the accessories (i.e. the *intermedi*) than in the plays they accompanied. By the middle of the sixteenth century repeated and explicit contemporary statements confirm this suspicion. By contrast, the published texts of comedies, tragedies, eclogues and the like seldom contain any indication of *intermedi*; in the few instances where such indications do exist, they are there to act as a record of how the play had been presented on a particular occasion rather than as an indication of how future performances should be conducted. Most of the time there is no mention of them, not because the performance could do without them, but because they varied according to the tastes, means and skill of those who embarked on a theatrical performance. As early as the Ferrarese spectacles of 1499 we have an example of a comedy, Terence's *Eunuco*, which was repeated but with different *intermedi* only four days after its previous performance.[24]

An anonymous *Farsa recitata agli excelsi Signori di Firenze*, in an undated Florentine print which must belong to the period of the Medicean exile, provides a rare example of prescriptive rather than descriptive directions. Once again, the exception proves the rule, since the directions added at the end of the five *tempi* suggest the simplest and most democratic solution: 'here, play or sing'.[25] This was the type of *intermedio* which was later called *non apparente* ('invisible'), because while the sound of instruments or voices, or a combination of the two, could be heard, the stage itself, though open, remained empty. From the earliest days of *intermedi* attempts were made to conceal the source of the music. In *Danae* (Milan 1496) mention is made more than once of instruments 'hidden behind those devices of the stage', or of 'fifes, bagpipes and other hidden instruments'. In *Danae* (which despite being called a 'comedy' and being divided into five acts is among the *drammi mescidati* which are closest to the type of the earlier allegorical or mythological actions) the preference for hidden instruments was probably dictated by the fact that music was quite often also performed in the course of the acts themselves. The division between them had therefore to be marked more obviously by

[24] Luzio and Renier, 'Commedie classiche in Ferrara nel 1499', pp. 188 and 189.

[25] D'Ancona, *Le origini*, II, pp. 37ff. The title continues: 'and first, in place of a Prologue, Proem and Argument, a man with a lyre says'; what is said 'on the lyre' is not, as D'Ancona notes, merely a long tirade on the variety of human desires, but also a long series of *ottave*, which once more raises the problem of sung recitation of long poems either in *ottave* or in other metres. These long poems include the *cantari* and the epic poems, and the style of recitation was particularly popular in Florence, where it flourished as much amongst the strolling players (*cantimpanche*) of San Martino as amongst the heralds or *canterini* employed by the Signoria. I shall return below to the final *ottava* of this tirade, in the chapter called 'Temporal perspective and music'. The work must have been divided into phases (*tempi*) rather than acts because they knew that the *Farsa* did not respect the unity of time, and also perhaps because anything which smacked too much of classicism was suspect in post-Savonarolan Florence.

clearing the stage during the intervals and filling the gap with music coming from hidden sources. There were also, however, some *intermedi apparenti* (i.e. 'visible' *intermedi*): at the end of Act II, after a piece for fifes and bagpipes, a *capitolo* of love was recited 'by one who carried a labyrinth of love (?), as an *intermedio*' ('*per intermediare*'); at the end of the following act another *capitolo* was also recited 'of one man who went sowing', an obvious allusion to the act which had just ended with the legendary shower of gold: '... for a time gold was seen raining from the sky and Jupiter disappeared visibly (?), and here so many instruments were played that they were beyond counting or one's imagination.'[26]

In other cases it is difficult to determine why 'invisible' *intermedi* were preferred. They were by and large the simplest solution, but it is not always possible to conclude that this was the real reason behind the choice. In the first Ferrarese performances the two types alternated, but later on 'visible' *intermedi* prevailed. In Urbino in 1513, the first performance of *La calandria* by Bernardo Bibbiena had 'visible' *intramesse*; but another comedy performed with the same stage setting (possibly one of the first examples of perspective scenery) had 'strange music...all hidden and [located] in different places'.[27] Similarly, in the performance of *I suppositi* by Ludovico Ariosto, given in Rome in 1519 in the presence of Leo X, 'there was an *intermedio* for every act with music of fifes, bagpipes, two *cornetti*, viols and lutes, and the small organ whose sound is so varied, which was given to the Pope by the late-lamented most illustrious Monsignor [Cardinal Luigi d'Aragona, who had died at the beginning of that year]; and together with them there was a flute and a voice which received much praise; there was also a concert of voices *in music*, which did not appear, in my opinion, as successful as the other music. The last *intermedio* was the *moresca*, which represented the story of the Gorgon and was very beautiful.'[28] Our informant again shows the humanist preference for solo singing voices and for musical instruments, combined with scant sympathy for compositions in more rigorous polyphony such as the concert of voices 'in music'.

By 'visible' *intermedi* they obviously meant those in which something was seen to happen rather than just to be heard – in connection with which one must also bear in mind that the boundary between stage and audience was still far from clearly marked. The oldest accounts refer to final *intermedi*, to which, to be sure, the name of *intermedi* should not properly apply, though this is what they were called; after *Amphitrione*, on 2 February 1487, 'all the

[26] D'Ancona, *Le origini*, II, pp. 13ff. For the complete text see *La Danae commedia di B. Taccone*, nuptial publication by A. Spinelli (Bologna 1888). Taccone was also the author of a pastoral eclogue and of *Atteone*, an old-style *rappresentazione* whose text consists of five *ottave* and a few *terzine* (cf. Rossi, *Il Quattrocento*, p. 538). More than once *Danae* involved the opening of 'a beautiful sky...wherein was Jove with the other gods, with innumerable lights for stars'. Mercury, Jove's ambassador, made flying descents, obviously using stage machinery. As one of many possible examples of music played in the course of the main play one can cite the fifth act, in which 'certain nymphs who were going hunting, seeing in the sky an unusual star, with a song (*con una musica*) asked Jove to explain the phenomenon'. The influence on *Danae* of *Amphitrione*, which the Count of Cajazzo had seen performed in Ferrara in 1491, seems obvious.

[27] Augusto Vernarecci, 'Di alcune rappresentazioni drammatiche alla Corte di Urbino nel 1513', in *Archivio storico per le Marche e l'Umbria*, III (1886), pp. 181ff.

[28] Letter by the Este ambassador Alfonso Paolucci quoted by D'Ancona, *Le origini*, II, pp. 89 and 90, and by Giuseppe Campori, *Notizie inedite di Raffaello da Urbino* (Modena 1863).

labours of Hercules appeared on the stage (*per suxo il tribunale*), that is Antaeus, the Pillars of Hercules, the Bull, the Amazons, the Centaur, the Wild-boar, the Hydra, Cachus with the cattle being led backwards by the tail, and many others'.[29] This final procession of *Amphitrione*, which was in reality an expansion of the scene of Jupiter's apparition and prophecy, was not repeated in the frequent performances of the comedy in the following years; but the final scene continued to impress the public 'with a sky which opened in a circle on the ceiling of the hall'.[30] The apparition of Jupiter had been made into a fully-fledged final *intermedio* with music, which was briefly mentioned together 'with other *feste* between all the acts, exceedingly beautiful'. In 1491 a humorous scene served as final *intermedio* for *I Menechini*: 'The end of the comedy was that Menechino had all his possessions auctioned off, saying that he would give them away for 1700 ounces of gold with his wife thrown into the bargain; and here the trumpeter urged everyone who had an ill-natured wife and did not like her to do the same.'[31] A possible explanation for the habit of such final *intermedi* is suggested in connection with a Ferrarese performance of *L'asinaria* in 1500, in a letter that mentions how 'one of those *tramezzi* was presented at the close and after the end of the comedy, that it might serve as restraint to hold back the crowd, lest they rise with such great turmoil and disorderly noise as they so often do'.[32] Whatever the reason, with a final *intermedio* as well as one preceding or associated with the prologue it became quite common for there to be six *intermedi* rather than the four which would have sufficed to mark the division into five acts.

Evidence of how important the *intermedi* had become even before the beginning of the sixteenth century is contained in a series of letters by one Giano Pencaro. He regularly kept Isabella d'Este informed about what was going on in Ferrara, and in 1499 wrote to her describing in minute detail the sixteen *intermedi* which accompanied the four spectacles (*Eunuco, Trinummo, Penulo* and a repeat of *Eunuco*) performed during the carnival that year.[33] At the request of the Duke, Ercole I, the entire theatrical series had a prelude; that is, 'first there was a parade along the stage of all those who were to perform in all the comedies, and they were one hundred and thirty-three, all dressed in new costumes, specially made...After these appeared those of the *tramezzi*, who were one hundred and forty-four, similarly dressed with all new costumes, some as peasants, some as pages, nymphs, fools and spongers.' The rest of the first letter, from which the above passage is taken, deals with the four *intermedi* of the first evening; but of the comedy itself, the informant states, 'there is nothing more to be said, for anyone can read it in the works of its author'. The same happens in the subsequent letters, although the writer, who must have been well acquainted with the tastes of the Marchioness of Mantua, never neglects to add precise

[29]   *Diario ferrarese di autori incerti*, p. 133.
[30]   Zambotti, 'Diario ferrarese', p. 221.
[31]   Letter from the Milanese ambassadors who attended the 1491 performance, quoted in D'Ancona, *Le origini*, II, pp. 130 and 131, note.
[32]   Quoted by Luzio and Renier, 'Commedie classiche in Ferrara nel 1499', p. 180, note 3.
[33]   *Ibid.*, pp. 182ff. The Marchioness of Mantua's informant was also the author of the letter referred to in the previous note. The codex Estense X.*.34, which also contains a translation of *I Menechini*, attributes two sonnets to him, while Pistoia wrote a sonnet beginning *Pincaro, io ho veduto un tuo capitolo.*

details of the most beautiful dresses worn by the ladies attending the performance.

The nature of the *intermedi* described by Pencaro varies, but in all of them dancing is the single most important element.

In the first *tramezo* [of the first performance of *Eunuco*] there appeared a group of ten peasants, who, in six exercises, reaped the harvest of their well-cultivated land; inasmuch as, having first entered leaping on to the stage in the fashion of a *moresca*, they began with their tools to hoe the ground; and, always, every act, movement and measure kept to the tempo and the proportion of the playing, so that several men all seemed to be moved by a single spirit, according to the tempo of the musician. Having thus entered and cultivated the ground, they sowed it with golden seeds, still keeping the measure and tempo I have mentioned above, so that every footstep, every motion of their hands, or turn of their heads was always in time to the sound. When the grain they had sown had grown, they proceeded to mow it in the same mode and measure, so that one swing of a sickle, one gathering of hay, one tying of a bundle, were all [one] tempo and [one] measure. Thereafter with the above said tempi they threshed it, shovelled it with shovels, and, having stored it in their bags, they prepared as a final entertainment a fine banquet, with singing, acting and dancing; and then, amidst merriment and music, they gave place to the second act. In the second *tramezo* there came twelve people led by a clown, all dressed in fine clothes of silk, with hose of nine stripes, golden bells and shining ornaments; and these, after a *chiaranzana* was played, danced a vigorous and most beautiful *moresca* (*una moresca gagliarda et bellissima*). In the third *tramezo* six nymphs entered led by a musician, all joyous and free; and after them a few sorrowful youths, who sang with sweet harmony plaintive songs, bewailing their cruel fate of being slaves to such ladies who cared nothing for their plight; they were in chains in the manner of slaves.

In the fourth *tramezo*, too long to describe in full, preparations for a banquet in the open air were interrupted by a bear, 'who performed its role so well that it seemed real to many'. Someone gets killed, but finally the bear is taken and chained, and the banquet is resumed 'with all the appearances of joy'. As *intermedi* to the other comedies there were maidens who flirted with old and rich lovers, but in fact preferred the young smartly dressed ones; *moresche* performed by dancers carrying lighted torches, and other displays of lights with tapers arranged in various patterns; hunting scenes. One 'beautiful lady, [who was] amorously dancing and parading before the audience with great charm and composure', was threatened with arrows by 'eight elegant youths', but saved by Love 'from those who had wanted to take her by might and main'. 'From one corner [of the stage] jumped out a fool with his antics, and soon after a drummer playing a *dordoglione* (i.e., a *tourdion*), both being after a Fortune'; and later on 'ten stalwart youths with rich and elegant clothes, following the measure of the music, approached the said Fortune; but she always seemed [to be falling] into the hands of this one, or that one, but she always escaped them all'. Finally, 'the little fool, made bold by desperation... seized her by the hair on her forehead and dragged her into a house. The youths departed despairing with sorrow and anger.'

On other occasions the action of the *intermedi* is quite sedate. In the fourth one of *Penulo* 'six musicians entered, leading the same number of ladies, who walked graciously always heeding the music, words and gestures; and so they went around without quarrel, still making harmony, and then made their exit'. Similarly, in the second *intermedio* for the repeat performance of *Eunuco*, 'following the [usual] drummer and fool, six men came out, held in chains by six women dressed in old-fashioned garb; with sweet and gentle melody they sang their amorous passion'. But in most cases the action is brisk and varied, its rhythm often being marked by the sound of a small drum on the stage. The term *moresca* was so often repeated that it soon became an almost perfect synonym of *intermedio*. This is the term which Isabella d'Este chose to use when she wrote to her absent husband describing the comedies performed in Ferrara in 1502 for the arrival of Lucrezia Borgia. According to her, *Epidico* 'was not too beautiful in language and poetry; but the *moresche* performed between acts made a good show with great gallantry'; the *Bachide* 'was so long and tedious, and with no dances in between...only two *moresche* were inserted'.[34] The use of the term *moresca* is more easily understood when it refers to an appearance of 'soldiers dressed in the ancient fashion', or 'yeomen armed with helmet, gorge, breastplate, corselet and greaves', whose dances simulated a variety of combats with different weapons. In other cases the plot is incredibly twisted, as in the second *moresca* of the *Bachide*, which features

ten men who simulated a nakedness, with a veil across their bodies and heads of tinsel hair, and held horns of plenty in their hands, having inside four lighted resinous lamps which blazed up as the horns were moved. Before these a young maid had entered and crossed the stage to the other end, in great fear and without a sound. A dragon then came in, threatening to devour her; but a foot soldier stood by her as protection, and, fighting with the dragon, captured it; and as he was leading it about in chains, the maid followed, arm in arm with a youth, and the naked ones went dancing around, setting the resin ablaze.[35]

It is a very complex pantomine, the mythological or allegorical meaning of which the Marchioness of Mantua was either unable or unwilling to interpret, feeling as she did tired and bored, and above all ill-disposed toward her new sister-in-law.[36]

In some ways, what the *intermedi* were about was of only limited importance: subjects could be repeated, since what really mattered was the novelty of the way in which they were presented. This is very much what Giano Pencaro tells the Marchioness of Mantua when he writes 'although frequently a drummer and a fool are said to appear on stage, it is not always the same, [being] neither the same gestures nor the same music, but different invention, costumes and music'.[37] We have already begun to establish quite how varied this inventiveness was; virtually any form of entertainment was acceptable. There was no objection to including clowns and jugglers not only

[34] Quoted by D'Ancona, *Le origini*, I, p. 385.
[35] *Ibid.*
[36] It is interesting to compare his account with the still more confused one by a certain Niccolò Cagnolo, who belonged to the retinue of the French ambassador. His memoir on the 1502 festivities was included in the edition of Zambotti's 'Diario ferrarese' (p. 326). He wrote: 'There appeared another band of *morescanti*, of ten men dressed in white with blue hats in the Turkish style, and carrying a reed, or a bladder shaped like a rather elongated gourd. With them came a man who was naked, except for his hose, whom they were beating. They pulled him off his horse and took down his hose and beat him. This was followed by the presentation of a large winged dragon who with much beating of wings advanced to attack a young girl. And then entered an armed man who fought the dragon, and having wounded it in the neck with a spear he immediately tied a chain about its neck, and led it about the proscenium miming a *moresca*.'
[37] Luzio and Renier, 'Commedie classiche in Ferrara nel 1499', pp. 188 and 189.

in comic *moresche* (of peasants beating one another, or cooks drumming on their pans) and in vaguely exotic ones, but also in ones based on myths or on political or moral allegories. Pencaro provides a fine example of the widespread interest in costumes when he describes some 'old lovers, neatly combed, with braces after the fashion of Borso [and, therefore, old-fashioned], long robes with fringes, and open breeches with draping shirts, as well as some little greenery in their huge berets with dangling pendants' – almost an anticipation of the character of the 'magnificent' Pantalone. He has less to say about the music; to his comments quoted above we can add references to 'the playing of a vigorous (*gagliardo*) and lively *brando*', the 'singing of certain sweet words as a lament', and to a piece 'played in the Swiss style' (*sonata alla sguizera*) by the customary drummer, in an *intermedio* which later on included 'two kettle-drums playing in the Hungarian style' (*sonando alla ongaresca*). It is not much, and possibly the most important piece of information to be gathered from his letters is that music was sometimes temporarily absent. Fortune, whom I have already mentioned, 'in eight lines *recited* (*pronuncioe*) who she was and her powers'; Love, having freed the virtuous lady, also *recited* (again *pronuncioe*) the reasons for his intervention, 'because, Love said, I will not allow in my kingdom anything but intelligence and faithfulness'. At the end of an *intermedio* in which 'hunters, always keeping the order and measure, went gracefully after their prey,...a hunter was discovered, who, *speaking* in German, acted as if he was drunk, and, searching in the thickets with horns and darts, flushed out a monkey which was hidden there'.[38]

Isabella d'Este might have told us more about the music in the 1502 performances, for although she could not compete with her detested sister-in-law in either elegance or graceful dancing, she could at least assert her own superiority when 'with a lute in her hands she sang various *canzonette* with [beautiful] tunes and utmost sweetness'.[39] But because she was so bad-tempered and unenthusiastic, she confined herself almost exclusively to describing the music performed by the musicians of her own court: 'In the third act [of *L'asinaria*] came the band of Tromboncino, Paula, Pozino and their companions, by means of which the Mantuans made a better show than the Ferrarese,' In *Casina* 'first entered the music of Tromboncino, singing a *barcelletta* in praise of the newlyweds'; and 'in the third act came the consort of six viols, amongst which was Signor Don Alfonso...'.[40] The third *intermedio* of *Epidico* was dismissed by the Marchioness of Mantua as 'extremely dull music'; but from another source we learn that it was a *moresca*, presented 'on a cart drawn by a horse in the shape of a unicorn, led by a young maid, upon which were some men tied to a mast and four singers with a lute...They were then untied by the said damsel, and climbing down did a *moresca* and sang four most beautiful songs.'[41] Other *intermedi*

[38]   *Ibid.*, passim.
[39]   Account by Cagnolo in Zambotti, 'Diario ferrarese', p. 327.
[40]   A. Luzio, 'Isabella d'Este e i Borgia' in *Archivio storico lombardo*, series V, vol. XLI (1914), p. 545, note 1. The complete text of these two letters is now given in Iain Fenlon, *Music and Patronage in Sixteenth-Century Mantua* (Cambridge, 1980), docs. 2 and 3, pp. 171–2.
[41]   Account by Cagnolo in Zambotti, 'Diario ferrarese', p. 325. As previously in 1499, on the first day of the festivities, 3 February 1502, 'five comedies were presented, with all their characters masked and dressed for the performances...One of them, named Plautus, only told the plots of these comedies. Then the company of only one of them, *Epidico*, moved to a large hall with a high ceiling. The hall was decorated and arranged as a scene [i.e. as a theatre], with

not mentioned by Isabella are of no less interest. The first of *L'asinaria* had 'fourteen satyrs, one of whom carried the silvery head of an ass, having inside a pipe, and another a Turkish drum and a whistle; and they made their entrance one by one, playing their instruments. And then, having gone out for a while, they re-entered with pipes of muted reeds in their mouths, and all playing danced in the Moorish fashion' (*balavano a la morescha*). In another *intermedio* (perhaps an 'invisible' one) there was 'a harmony of whistles of great elegance'. In an *intermedio* of *Casina* 'a Wild Man (*homo salvatico*) blowing a horn entered, as did a beautiful maiden, whom he pursued with other wild men, all dancing a *moresca* very properly. And suddenly there appeared the god of Love, who chased the said wild men and struck them, accompanied by certain musicians who surrounded the said damsel singing sweetly.' From the same source we have a more detailed description than that given by Isabella of the consort of viols in which Prince Alfonso had also taken part: 'there came out an enormous sphere, which opened into two [halves] in the middle of the proscenium, and inside was a most beautiful music of lyres and a sweet harmony of voices'.[42] The cart of *Epidico* and the sphere of *Casina* are among the first instances of music and musicians being brought on stage by a vehicle of some sort.

Would that it were possible to emulate those peasants in so many *intermedi* who, having sown their seed, gather in 'with the same manner and measure' a bountiful harvest and rejoice in its abundance. Alas, our harvest is one of empty husks. All these quotations merely serve to emphasize how little we know: the varied, almost continuous music by which the *intermedi* counter-balanced the predominantly spoken main action has become little more than a string of empty words which fail to convey how the music really sounded. We can see how commonly instruments were used to mark the rhythm, beginning with the almost omnipresent tambourine, whose entrance on stage accompanied by a fool seems to have been part of a ritual repeated in many *intermedi*. But the rhythms with which the drummer accompanied the jests and pirouettes of the fool must have depended in each case on the personality of the clown and the characteristics of his repertory. Quite often the tambourine, and in one case 'two kettle-drums playing in the Hungarian style', seem to have been able to sustain long stretches of mimed or danced action on their own. This obviously also applied to non-theatrical dancing too, for it is said that on the same occasion 'milady the bride (Lucrezia Borgia) danced many dances to the sound of her tambourines, in the Roman and

its upper and lower seats arranged in a circle and on one side the proscenium with several rooms, all crenellated and decorated with turrets, which housed the mimers and actors who were performing the comedy, and in the middle was the orchestra, where the most illustrious men and the ambassadors sat'(*ibid.*, pp. 324–5). The passage is worth noticing not only because it described this general prologue which was recited in a different location, but also because of its use of the terms 'company' and 'orchestra', because it mentions the circular (or semicircular) form of the tiers of seats, and the central orchestra as the place of honour. It is worth wondering whether the *intermedio* which Isabella d'Este judged to be 'very poor' might not have been performed by actors employed and sent by Cesare Borgia; D'Ancona, *Le origini*, II, pp. 72 and 73 mentions pantomimes performed in the Vatican before Lucrezia left 'in which Cesare too took part disguised as the symbolic Unicorn'. Cesare Borgia did not attend the Ferrara festivities, but was represented: amongst his representatives were 'Nicolò the musician with one companion' (Zambotti, 'Diario ferrarese', p. 336).

[42] *Ibid.*, pp. 329–31. Cagnolo also records that there were four *rappresentazioni* when the bride arrived at the gates of the city.

Spanish fashions'[43] However it is also possible, though not explicitly stated, that while the tambourine or the kettle-drums remained the only 'visible' instruments on stage, other kinds of instruments might have been involved 'invisibly' from off-stage. Sometimes the instrument on stage was not a tambourine but another instrument, unspecified in the case of the 'six nymphs led by a musician', better identified in the case of 'a piper playing in a peasant style and eight villains behind him'. The horns given to one 'wild man' or to hunters and huntresses seem to be part of a realism more onomatopoeic than musical, which is peculiar to hunting scenes. Their bearers 'with noise and sound of horns flushed out of certain bushes bears, lions, panthers and one ape'; yet it is also said that other unnamed, and therefore probably 'invisible' instruments gave 'order and measure' to this action. Sometimes the rhythms were those of established dances, such as the *chiaranzana*, the 'lively and vigorous *brando*' or a *moresca gagliarda e bellissima* which may have been a galliard. At times there is a brusque transition from one rhythm to another: 'and having suddenly changed the sound, there began a vigorous *brando*'. On other occasions the transition is gradual: after ten dancers with flaming torches had come out, 'the measure which had hitherto been very broad, was narrowed'; or else, 'the measure began to be narrowed, and these [ten characters dressed in white, with tunics in Hungarian garb, richly embroidered with gold, and with head-dresses quite beautiful to see] began to strike one another...And as the measure was further narrowed, they multiplied their blows, which was increasingly beautiful to the eye and pleasing to the ear...and thus, furiously striking each other, they made their exit...never missing one measure, while the sound did the same.'[44] In two instances, both of which I have already mentioned, *moresche* of satyrs were accompanied by 'strange and old-fashioned instruments' (*La fabula de Caephalo* 1487) and by 'pipes of muted reeds' and whistles (*L'asinaria* 1502). Also mentioned in connection with the latter is the 'silvery head of an ass',[45] which recalls the lyre in the shape of a horse skull similarly decorated with silver inlay, which Leonardo da Vinci once brought with him from Florence to Milan; the instrument used in the *intermedio*, however, is a *fistula* (which might mean either a single pipe or a multiple flute, the so-called Pan-pipe) hidden in the skull of the animal.[46] In both cases we are dealing with the early manifestations of a fancied musical archaeology, of which contemporary figurative art also offers many examples.

This was true pantomime, in the sense that most of the action was undoubtedly mimed without words and that even the music was suspended when gesture, either symbolic or realistic, became particularly important. On the other hand, the fact that action was usually stylized and subordinated to the regular rhythm of the music justifies the use of the term *moresca* in its strictest and most precise sense of a representational dance whose performers

[43] *Ibid.*, p. 324.

[44] My main source is Pencaro's description in Luzio and Renier, 'Commedie classiche in Ferrara nel 1499', *passim*.

[45] *Diario ferrarese di autori incerti*, p. 285, and N. Cagnolo's 'Memoria' in Zambotti, 'Diario ferrarese', p. 329.

[46] For Leonardo da Vinci's musical knowledge and skills, see the article by Emanuel Winternitz in *Die Musik in Geschichte und Gegenwart*, vol. XIII (1966), col. 1664ff. On the strange results of various attempts at musical archaeology, see Winternitz, *Musical Instruments and their Symbolism in Western Art*.

impersonate exotic, bizarre or comic characters. (It was originally a dance of Moorish slaves but later, as we have seen, came to include satyrs, ancient warriors, peasants, cooks, or modern soldiers of fortune of various nationalities, such as Swiss guards, Greek *stratiotes* or German *landsknechts*.) It is worth noting that the *bassadanza* is never once mentioned in connection with these mimed scenes, despite the fact that it was the major social dance of the day, so that Pencaro mentions one only on the occasion when he speaks of dances performed at a reception rather than at dramatic performances. It may have been used in some of the *intermedi*, for example when the 'fair lady dancing amorously' or the ladies and gentlemen who spoke of love while 'promenading with grace' appeared. But the only named dances which occur in connection with the real *moresche* are either ones like the *chiaranzana* which never entered the repertory of social dances, or ones which did so at a later date and in a modified form more suited to courtly decorum. One such dance was the *dordoglione* or more correctly the *tordiglione*, the French *tourdion*.

The term most frequently used is *brando*, almost always accompanied by the adjectives *gagliardo* (vigorous) and *allegro* (lively). It must have been characterized by that 'nimbleness of foot and doubled stamping', which Castiglione considered to be suitable for professional dancers, though not for his courtier. Castiglione, however, follows his prohibition with a compromise, or rather a series of interesting compromises, conceding that 'in private quarters [the courtier] might be permitted...to dance *moresche* and *brandi*; but not so in public, except when in disguise...for the wearing of a costume carries with it a certain freedom and licence...and a certain carefree manner [*sprezzatura*] concerning unimportant matters'.[47] The *brando*, so far as I know, is mentioned only once as a non-theatrical dance, in a letter by Girolamo Muzio (1525) describing the carnival at Valperga in Piedmont: 'The dance which they call *brando* was danced, in which all the men dance with all the women, and, leaving the one they have first, they kiss the next one they take hold of, and so they continue until they take back their own, and in so doing they kiss her.' This suggests that the dance was rustic in origin and that it may perhaps have no relationship with the French *branle*, with which it is generally identified. Finally the *piva*, mentioned in one *intermedio* as the instrument accompanying the entrance and dancing of peasant men and women, is also the name of a dance in a rhythm twice as fast as that of the *bassadanza*; it is declared to be a typical country folk-dance in the dance treatise of Domenico da Piacenza, also known as Domenico da Ferrara.[48]

---

[47] Baldassare Castiglione, *Il cortegiano*, II, xi. There are many indications that men of gentle birth took part in both comedies and *intermedi*: Tebaldeo and Ariosto played main parts; Cesare Borgia, according to the source referred to in note 41 above, took part in *intermedi*; not only Cagnolo's account but Marin Sanudo's *Diarii* (vol. IV) confirm that Alfonso d'Este participated in the 1502 *intermedi*, and indeed from what Isabella d'Este said it would appear likely that both he and his brother Giulio took part in other *intermedi* as well. (See also note 40.)

[48] 'I am called *piva* [literally 'bagpipe'], and of the dance measures I am the humblest, for I am used by peasants, and I stand out so much because of my speed that I last only half the measure of the *bassadanza*' – a description by Domenico da Piacenza in the Paris manuscript, Bibliothèque Nationale, fonds ital. 972, and printed in Dante Bianchi, 'Un trattato inedito di Domenico da Piacenza', in *La bibliofilia*, LXV (1963), p. 119. It is echoed (and misunderstood) by Thoinot Arbeau (i.e. Jehan Tabourot) in *Orchésographie* (Langres 1589), p. xix: 'I am called the *cornemuse*, and of the measures I am the humblest, for I am used by the peasants, and am so lacking in speed that I hold the centre of the measure of the *basse dance*' ('et la prestese me fait tellement défaut que je tiens le milieu de la mesure de la basse dance'). Even more interesting

It is already apparent that the meaning of some *intermedi* was at times rather unclear even to fairly educated people. In one instance, in the interests of comprehensibility, Fortune begins by declaring her nature and attributes in eight lines of verse. I am convinced that the same purpose was served by a certain type of piece which appeared with some frequency in the *frottola* collections of Ottaviano Petrucci from his *Libro sesto* onwards; in these pieces a group of people, evidently a masquerade, begins by declaring the trade or social status which they all have in common. In the *Libro sesto* (1506) there are four such pieces, all with anonymous music: two are sung by pilgrims (*romei*), one by beggars, and one by peddlers of millet bread. The *Libro ottavo* (1508) includes a piece (*Nui siamo segatori* – We are carpenters) by Antonio Stringari of Padua and one by Bartolomeo Tromboncino (sung by peddlers of chestnuts, *Ai maroni, ai bei maroni*). In the *Libro nono* (1508) there are two by Filippo di Lurano (or da Luprano) (about Amazons, *Noi l'amazone siamo*, and pilgrims, *De paesi oltramontani*), plus an anonymous one (about old men, *Giunti siamo alla vecchiezza*). One in dialect (by vendors of beans, *Fabbe e fasoi*) appears in the *Libro undecimo*, attributed to an unidentifiable A.T. Furthermore, three by Ansano Senese (about convicts, *Noi siamo galeotti*; Turks, *Chi volessi turchi siamo*; and quarter-masters, *Logiamenti noi cerchiamo*) are found in *Canzoni sonetti strambotti et frottole libro primo* (Siena 1515). The following, from Petrucci's *Libro sesto*, may serve as an example of their texts:

> Forestieri a la ventura
> giunti siam a Roma sancta;
> ciascheduno nui si canta
> a più modi cum misura.
>
> Nui cantiamo per b molle,
> per b quadro et per natura;
> cosa alcuna a nui non tolle
> il cantar che sempre dura,
> cum ingegno e gran mesura,
> giorno e note, hor alto hor basso,
> ch'ogni cor afflicto e lasso
> levarem d'ogn'altra cura.
>
> Forestieri, etc.

Foreigners in search of fortune, we have come to holy Rome; each one of us can sing various modes with good measure. We can sing with a b flat, or b-mi, or else natural; no restraint can ever keep us from our unceasing singing, day and night, high and low, with fine talent and great measure. From all hearts tired or afflicted shall all care by this be lifted. Foreigners, etc.

All this forms the *ripresa* and first stanza, which are followed by four more stanzas. The music (example VI) is evidently intended to be sung in all four

---

is Antonio Cornazano's description: 'This [the *piva*], although at the time of our ancestors it was the chief music (*sono*) for the dance, nowadays, because men know better things, it is scorned and despised by people of rank and by good dancers. Nevertheless if this too happens to be danced, it is proper for the lady to perform only natural steps and to help the man with his turns, according to whatever hops and jumps he may choose to perform, either straight or backwards, bent inwards or outwards ('dritti e riversi, e dentro e fuori'). She needs to be alert and skilled in such a dance as this, because its measure [the measure of the *piva*] runs faster than any other'; see Curzio Mazzi, 'Il "Libro dell'arte del danzare" di Antonio Cornazano', in *La bibliofilia*, XVII (1916), p. 11.

Ex. VI Pilgrims masquerade. Anonymous words and music. From *Frottole libro sesto* (O. Petrucci, Venice 1506), fols. 43v–44r.

parts and gives great emphasis to the text by strictly syllabic delivery, and a strong sense of vertical harmony despite some slight shifts in rhythm, which occur first between the two higher and the two lower voices, then between the soprano and the other three parts. The initial self-introduction resembles in all respects that of most Florentine *canti carnascialeschi*, as does the music. A short passage in ternary rhythm in the *volta* provides a transition to the final phrases, which are a recapitulation of the *ripresa*.

The introduction is effected in a different way in a hunting scene, whose music was never printed, yet must have travelled to a number of places since it is found in various manuscript sources (and in Florence was even used with a rather unusual *lauda* as text).[49] Here too one can only assume that the music was intended for use in the theatre, an hypothesis supported by the fact that the text is polymetric, as parts of comedy texts were just starting to be:

A la chaza, a la chaza,
su, su, su, su, ognun se spaza.
A questa nostra chaza
veniti volentieri;
con brachi e con levrieri
chi vol venir si spaza.
Non aspectar el zorno,
sona el corno, o capo de caza;
spaza, spaza, spaza!
 Te' qui, Balzan, te' qui, Liom,
te' qui, Fasam, te' qui, Falcom,
te' qui, Tristam, te' qui, Pizom,
te' qui, Alam, te' qui, Carbom!
Chiama li brachi del monte, babiom!
 Te' qui, Pizolo,
te' qui, Spagnolo,
habi bon ochio
al capriolo!
A te, Augustino, a te!
a te, Spagnolo, a te!
Vidila, vidila, vidila,
a spalla, a spalla, pilgiala,
che li cani non la stracia.

To the hunt, to the hunt! up, up, up, up, everyone hurry! Come with us to the hunt eagerly, with pointers and with hounds; who wants to come must hurry. Do not wait for day-break, blow your horn, master of the hunt! Hurry, hurry, hurry!

Here now, Balzan, here now, Lion, here now Fasan, here now, Falcon, here now Tristan, here now Pizon, here now, Alan, here now, Carbon! Call the hounds from the mountain, you fool!

Come here now, Pizolo; come here now, Spagnolo! Keep a sharp eye for the deer. To you, Augustino, to you! To you, Spagnolo, to you! Look at that, look at that, look at that! Take it now on your shoulders, that the dogs may not tear it.

---

[49] The text is taken from the Seville MS, Biblioteca Colombina, 5.1.34, fols. 32–4, for which see Dragan Plamenac, 'A Reconstruction of the French Chansonnier in the Biblioteca Colombina Seville', in *The Musical Quarterly*, XXXVII (1951) and XXXVIII (1952), especially, XXXVIII, pp. 98 and 99. The music was published (from another source – see note 50) by Fausto Torrefranca, *Il segreto del Quattrocento* (Milan 1939), pp. 412–15. The *lauda*, which is atypical in that it is non-strophic and polymetric, is no. CCLXIV in *Laudi spirituali di Feo Belcari, di Lorenzo de' Medici...e di altri* (Florence 1863). The incipit *Jamo a Maria* is closer to the variant incipit of the secular text *Jamo a la caza* given in the Florence MS, Biblioteca Nazionale, Panciatichi 27, fols. 44–5. Osthoff, *Theatergesang*, II, pp. 52–65, analyses this version of the Florence MS; he obviously considers it closer to the hunters' song called for in the Florentine *Rappresentazione di Santa Margherita* (see note 46 of the previous chapter). I do not see why he transcribes it as 'Erster Teil' and has it followed by its other version, the one found in MSS from Northern Italy, whose text and dialect are somewhat different. The stage directions for the first 'day' of the Florentine *Rappresentazione di Santa Uliva* also called for the singing of *Su alla caccia* as one of the many musical insertions of a realistic nature used in the play. These, together with the pieces of music needed for very elaborate allegorical *intermedi*, are all features setting the date of this *rappresentazione* well beyond the end of the fifteenth century.

Ex. VII   Hunting scene. Anonymous words and music. From the Paris manuscript, Bibliothèque Nationale, Rés. Vm.⁷ 676, fols. 63v–65r.

The music (example VII) shows the same variety of rhythms: it begins with a rather broad measure and gets increasingly fast, until it finally broadens again for the last line. Here too syllabic recitation and chordal setting predominate, though the four voices tend to divide themselves into groups which answer one another more often than in the masquerade. Similar to

61

this is a fishing scene attributed to an otherwise unknown 'Iannes plice' (presumably a Frenchman, if the form of his first name is anything to go by), though here the distribution of the music amongst individuals and groups of voices is rather more varied, which would have made it more difficult to perform on stage. The only manuscript in which it appears is dated 1502 and

also includes the hunting scene described above, and a masquerade of *landsknechts* (*Sergonta bergonta*), as well as various other pieces from Mantua and Ferrara.[50]

[50] This is the Paris codex, Bibliothèque Nationale, Musique, Rés. Vm.⁷ 676, described by Nanie Bridgman, 'Un manuscript italien du début du XVIᵉ siècle à la Bibliothèque Nationale', in *Annales musicologiques*, I (1953), pp. 177–267. The manuscript is now available in a facsimile edition, *Manuscript italian de frottole 1502*, ed. François Lesure (Geneva 1979). It includes some compositions on occasional texts, amongst which are *O triumphale diamante*, in praise of Ercole

63

d'Este, and *Apresso il santo uccel(lo)* by G. L. (Giorgio Luppato?), both *strambotti*, while the sole incipit, *Turcho Turcho et Isabella*, is given of another. Zambotti, describing Isabella d'Este's arrival in Mantua, in 1490, says 'she was received with great joy and merrymaking, being acclaimed with shouts of *Hisabella* and *Diamante*'. He also recalls a joust attended by Ercole d'Este, 'in Turkish costume' ('Diario ferrarese', p. 215), but it is more likely that the nickname 'Turk' was used to refer to Francesco Gonzaga, as it had previously been to other members of his family.

Other pieces exist which might have been used in theatrical performances without having been composed for that specific purpose. Amongst these I would include Michele Pesenti's *Dal lecto me levava* and Josquin d'Ascanio's *Il grillo è buon cantore*, in Petrucci's *Libro secondo* and *Libro tertio* respectively.[51] There is another *frottola* in Petrucci's *Libro tertio* which is more likely to have been composed with the intention of using it in an *intermedio*, for in its text, as in an *intermedio* to which I have frequently referred, the character addressing the audience is the goddess Fortune:

> Son Fortuna onnipotente,
> son regina all'universo;
> se a me piace, fia submerso
> chi non crede al mio talento.
>   Son Fortuna, etc.

> Però creder el bisogna:
> esser ben sempre a cavallo
> e lassare l'altrui rogna
> per exempio longo è fallo.
> Se tu prendi questo ballo
> sarai grato a nostra gente.
>   Son Fortuna, etc.

I am all-powerful Fortune, I am queen of the universe; if it pleases me I overpower whoever doesn't fear my might. I am Fortune, etc.

This must everyone remember: to have always the upper hand, and ignore the other's mishap is by long experience wrong. Come, if you enter this dance, you shall please our people all. I am Fortune, etc.

A mere ten lines serve to introduce not a group of characters but one individual. It might therefore have been not a collective masquerade but a *trionfo*, recalling Mantegna's paintings of the Triumphs of Petrarch which adorned the Mantuan stage in 1501, as well as the non-Petrarchan Triumph of Fortune which on the same occasion was placed almost as a pivot between two sections of the stage. The music is by Filippo da Lurano, one of the most gifted and versatile of the so-called *frottola* composers. His outstanding ability is clear from the very start of the piece (example VIII),[52] in the imperious virtuosity of the vocal part, the imitative interplay of the lower parts (probably played by viols or *cornetti*) and above all in the precise and energetic rhythmic and harmonic drive.

I do not claim to be able to establish a firm connection between any of the musical pieces which I have given as examples and specific theatrical performances. Indeed, if we set the *frottola* of Fortune against the plot of the entire Ferrarese *moresca* of 1499 which featured the same goddess, we can

---

[51]   Both published in *Le frottole nell'edizione principe di Ottaviano Petrucci*, vol. I (the only one published), Bks I, II and III (Cremona 1954), ed. Gaetano Cesari and Raffaello Monterosso, with a preface by Benvenuto Disertori, respectively on pp. 22–3 and 140. On Josquin and Ascanio see E. E. Lowinsky, 'Ascanio Sforza's life: a key to Josquin's biography and an aid to the chronology of his works', in *Josquin des Prez: Proceedings of the International Josquin Festival Conference*, ed. E. E. Lowinsky (New York 1976), pp. 31–75.

[52]   *Le frottole nell'edizione principe*, pp. 95 and 96. It had already been published by Rudolf Schwartz, 'Nochmals "die Frottole im 15. Jahrhundert"', in *Jahrbuch der Musikbibliothek Peters*, XXXI (1924), Notenbeilage, pp. 1–2.

Ex. VIII Filippo da Lurano. *Frottola*. From *Frottole libro tertio* (O. Petrucci, Venice 1505) fols. 4v–5r.

see quite clearly that each of my musical examples could only have formed a small part of a complete *intermedio*. Even so, there are very few pieces in the entire corpus of *frottola* literature in either manuscript or print which in themselves suggest that they were intended for even such a limited theatrical function. In fact, though there may be more, I can actually think of only two,

both by a certain Rossino da Mantova. Petrucci included the first, which opens with a vocal imitation of the sound of bagpipes (*Lirum, bililirum, lirum*) in his *Frottole libro secondo* (1505). It is a piece which could have been adapted to many peasant scenes, as its title or caption indicates: 'A sound of bagpipes in *fachinesco*', that is in the Bergamasque dialect spoken by many manual labourers. The second (example IX) is in the *Frottole libro tertio* (also 1505)

and though not in actual dialect it does have all the flavour of a rustic serenade:

> Perché fai, donna, el gaton,
> s'io t'amo, anci t'adoro?

Why do you play the coy kitten, woman, if I love you, nay I adore you?

The style of the four parts would appear to indicate that both pieces[53] were intended to be sung by a soloist with an instrumental accompaniment (wind instruments in the 'bagpipe' piece). But their words and structure also suggest that the instrumentalists might have provided intermittent vocal support for the main voice part, in the first piece imitating the sound of bagpipes, in the second echoing the caterwauling of the main actor of the serenade as he gives vent to his anguish:

> ...Gnao, gnao, vo gridando, Gnao, gnao! è 'l mio desio
> gnao, per tutto il dolor mio; per haver conclusïon?
> e col gnao vo suspirando,   Perché fai, donna, etc.
> ma al morir col gnao m'invio.

Miaow, miaow, I go wailing, miaow, for my harrowing pain; but for all my miaows and sighs to my death miaowing I go. Miaow, miaow! shall my desire ever be fulfilled? Why do you play, woman, etc.

[53] To be found in *Le frottole nell'edizione principe*, I, respectively on pp. 69–70 and 100–2.

Ex. IX   Rossino Mantovano, *Frottola*. From *Frottole libro tertio* (O. Petrucci, Venice 1505) fols. 9v–11r.

The idea that both pieces were intended to be used in theatrical performances is strongly supported by the hints of mimicry conveyed by the onomatopoeia and emphasized by skilful scoring. However there are plenty of other serenades in the *frottola* repertory which, while less overtly clownish, nevertheless tend to exaggerate the sorrows of love to the point of caricature: Marchetto Cara's *Udite voi, finestre*, in Petrucci's *Libro primo*, the anonymous

Ite, caldi suspir mei in the *Libro secondo*, and from the *Libro tertio*, another anonymous piece, *Se non dormi, donna, ascolta*, and Filippo da Lurano's *Aldi, donna, non dormire*. Similarly, there are many other pieces which may either have been written specifically for an *intermedio* (though this is impossible to establish, as only *scenari* of *intermedi*, not texts, have survived) or may have been chosen from the current repertory because they fitted the plot of an *intermedio*. Besides the customary praises of the god of Love, the surviving

frottola repertory includes words and settings which deal with all the vicissitudes of love, with its entreaties, spurnings, laments and scornings, which are described in the *intermedi*. One description actually specifies that 'a *strambotto* and a *barzelletta*' were sung. Furthermore, Petrucci's printed collections, which provide the broadest idea of the contemporary repertory of court music, feature a number of settings intended to be used with any text of a given metrical structure. The *Frottole libro primo* contains a *Modus*

Ex. X Marchetto Cara. *Aer de capitoli*. From *Frottole libro nono* (O. Petrucci, Venice 1509) fol. 2v (alto part omitted).

Na_sce la spe_me mia da un dol _ ce ri _ so,

o _ gni mio ben da un hu _ mil sguardo pen _ de,

La mia fe_li_ci_tà sta in un bel vi_so.

dicendi capitula (Manner of reciting *capitoli*) by Michele Pesenti, while the full title of the *Libro quarto, Strambotti, ode, frottole, sonetti et modo de cantar versi latini e capituli*, itself gives a clear indication of the contents of the work, which include an *Aer de versi latini* (Air for Latin verses) by the Brescian Antonio Caprioli, an *Aer de capituli* (Air for *capitoli*) by Filippo di Lurano, and an anonymous *Modo de cantar sonetti* (Manner of singing sonnets). Other anonymous *modi* for sonnets are to be found in the *Libro quinto* and *Libro sexto*, while authors of 'airs' for *capitoli* are named in the *Libro octavo* (I. B. Zesso), *nono* (Marchetto Cara) and *undecimo* (Joannes Lulinus Venetus). Of these three types of composition, the *capitolo* is the one most frequently mentioned in descriptions of *intermedi*. Even when such descriptions tell of 'spoken' (*detti*) *capitoli*, it is possible that they were recited to music, as the texts were such that for the sake of clarity they had to be recited syllabically, and a short, direct and well-balanced melody like Marchetto Cara's *Aer de capitoli* (example X) would have suited them well.

The only musicians whose names are more precisely linked to particular *intermedi* are Gian Pietro della Viola, a Florentine who moved to Northern Italy, and Bartolomeo Tromboncino. None of della Viola's musical works survive, with the possible exception of a piece I shall discuss later.[54] He wrote a *Festa de Lauro*, performed in Mantua for the Feast of the Ascension in 1486: D'Ancona thinks that this is yet another name for a *rappresentazione* which was sometimes called *di Phebo e di Phetonte* (i.e. Python), sometimes *di Phebo et Cupido*, and sometimes *di Daphne*. It must have been a short scene quite similar to the one in *La fabula d'Orfeo*, with Apollo playing the cither and perhaps singing an amorous lament in *terza rima* or a *strambotto* in memory of Daphne, transformed into a laurel. The vocal pieces were probably set to music and performed by the author himself, one of the many Florentine singers who, like Ugolini, and Bellincioni in Milan, were appreciated and sought-after in the courts of Northern Italy.[55] It is interesting to note that even then there was a division of labour, which later became customary, between those who composed the vocal music for theatrical works and the dance experts who composed or selected the music for the choreographic work within the same production. The author himself informs us that the final *moresca* of his *La rappresentazione di Daphne* was commissioned from Lorenzo Lavagnolo, the most sought-after dancer in the courts of Ferrara, Mantua and Urbino.[56] Tradition attributes the music of the 1487 *intermedi* for Correggio's *La fabula de Caephalo* to Gian Pietro della Viola. I have been unable to establish whether or not he did write it, but insofar as there might be an element of truth in the tradition, I would imagine it to refer to the choruses at the end of the acts, since the *intermedi* themselves, if any were performed, would have taken the form of either dances or instrumental pieces.

More is known about Bartolomeo Tromboncino than about Gian Pietro della Viola, though not as much as one would like. He and Marchetto Cara are the two most famous composers of *frottola* music, with Tromboncino writing rather more than his colleague. He was the son of one Bernardino Piffero, who was already in the service of the Gonzaga court in 1477;[57] obviously Tromboncino (on one occasion 'Trombetino') was not a real name but a nickname based on the instrument he played. The diminutive form would seem to indicate that his fame began when he was still very young; he too was in service at the Mantuan court as early as 1489, and remained associated with it until at least 1512, though with short interruptions. He then moved to Venice, where he was still alive and composing in 1535. Because our information about him and the *intermedi* is fragmentary and erratic, we do not know when he began to compose and perform music for *intermedi*, though it is said that he went to Casale in 1489 to take part in the performance of Galeotto del Carretto's *Beatrice*, a comedy (?) whose text is lost.[58] It is more certain that he participated in the Ferrarese *intermedi* of 1502, since all the reports agree on this. It is likely that the only one of the many works attributed to him which has a clearly theatrical text dates from the same year. His *Crudel, fuggi se sai* (example XI) is one of three *frottole* (or *barzellette*) in Galeotto del Carretto's mythological play *Le nozze di Psiche e Cupidine* which was also performed in Casale in 1502 before Guglielmo IX Paleologo. Its text is a series

[54]   See note 47 to the next chapter.

[55]   D'Ancona, *Le origini*, II, pp. 350–2, note.   [56]   *Ibid.*, p. 351, note.

[57]   Professor William Prizer of the University of California, Santa Barbara, kindly tells me he has evidence that Tromboncino was the son of another Bernardino Piffero.

[58]   A. Luzio and R. Renier, 'Niccolò da Correggio', in *Giornale storico della letteratura italiana*, XXI (1893), p. 247.

Ex. XI   Bartolomeo Tromboncino. Pan's song from *Le nozze di Psiche e Cupidine* by Galeotto del Carretto. From *Frottole libro tertio* (G. Mazzocchi, Rome 1518) fol. 42v (alto part omitted).

of short stanzas of four lines each, but it was not part of an *intermedio* since it is sung to Syrinx by Pan, who holds a *fistula* in his hand – a further reflection of Poliziano's Aristaeus and Eurydice.[59] Here, as in the *Canzona di Aristeo*, a

[59]   Previously published by A. Einstein in his edition of *Canzoni sonetti strambotti et frottole. Libro tertio*, pp. 56 and 57, and now by Osthoff, *Theatergesang*, II, pp. 58–9. The statement that

wind accompaniment is required to simulate the sound of Pan-pipes. It is ironic that while there is no doubt that the text was intended for theatrical use, the authorship of its music is disputed: there are two separate printed editions of the music, one of which attributes it to Tromboncino, while the other identifies it as being by his colleague at the Mantuan court, Marchetto Cara.[60]

Tromboncino must have had certain qualities which made him a particularly good stage performer, but when chamber singing is being discussed, as in Castiglione's *Il cortegiano*, he is not even mentioned: all the praise is for 'the singing of our Marchetto Cara', who 'by his quiet manner full of gentle sweetness softens and penetrates all souls, impressing them delicately with pleasing passions'.[61] Both composed *frottole* about the shifts and changes brought about by Fortune: Marchetto wrote *Non è tempo d'aspectare*, in Petrucci's *Libro primo*, and *Ogni ben fa la fortuna*, in his *Libro tertio*, while Tromboncino produced *Chi se fida de fortuna*, also in the *Libro tertio*. All these could well have served as comments on the events and vicissitudes of a comedy. But there is no way of knowing whether Cara actually set out to compose music for the stage: maybe he did, maybe he did not – or, as the start of yet another of his *frottole* and the famous Gonzaga motto have it, *Forsi che si, forsi che no*.

this is the only text amongst those attributed to Tromboncino which was definitely composed for the theatre must be modified in view of the additions, pointed out by Osthoff, of the music for the second *intermedio* of *Filostrato e Panfila* (cf. note 14 above) and the *ballata, Queste lacrime mie*, from Castiglione's eclogue *Tirsi*. For the music of the latter, see Osthoff, *Theatergesang*, II, pp. 60–3. And there is a lot of music in the course of the acts of *Le nozze di Psiche*. In this there should have been five acts, but it is unclear where the text divides, at any rate in the undated edition I have seen, as only the beginnings of Acts III and V are actually marked. The most surprising music is that to be performed by the two sisters of Psyche, as it clearly has no realistic function.

[60]   This is the arrangement for keyboard instruments contained in the collection of *Frottole intabulate da sonar organi, libro primo*, also by Andrea Antico, which is dated Rome, 17 January 1517. There is also an anonymous version of the same piece in the Venice MS, Biblioteca S. Marco, Ital. Cl. IV, 1795–98, note 59.

[61]   B. Castiglione, *Il cortegiano*, I, xxxvii. On Cara see William Prizer, *Marchetto Cara and the North Italian Frottola*, Ph. D. dissertation, University of North Carolina 1974, as well as his book on the same subject published Boston, Mass. 1979.

3 Realistic use of music in comedy

The *intermedi* which more and more frequently came to be inserted during the last decades of the fifteenth century between the acts of a comedy or of a so-called 'hybrid' drama served to emphasize to the spectators a feature which at the time appeared to be typical of the new classical style of theatrical performance: the division into acts, preferably five in number. It is equally possible, however, to argue that, regardless of whether the division into acts could be proved to be authentically classical,[1] the organizers of spectacles in a classical style were more easily persuaded to accept it because the *intermedi* were practical and effective in providing a temporary diversion, after which the spectator's attention could be refocussed on the main action with renewed interest. One must remember that these performances, like their classical prototypes, used or needed to run from beginning to end without interruption, although the main action itself could be broken up. They could last for up to four hours, and frequently even longer than that,[2] during which time not only was it virtually impossible for the spectators to leave, but a large number of them were forced to stand throughout and yet were expected to listen quietly. The division into acts and the *intermedi* were thus classical at least in the sense that they were a solution to a basic human need for variety if attention is to be held over a long period. Besides this, by creating a diversion, they satisfied another basic psychological need: they gave rhythm and order to the audience's perception of events.

For the *intermedi* to accomplish their formal function successfully, it was necessary that their style should distinguish them from the acts between which they were inserted. The dominant feature of these acts was spoken recitation, eminently realistic and essentially prosaic, in spite of occasional experiments in different verse forms aimed at mirroring the verse forms of the classical models.[3] For contrast, music and rhythmic gesture dominated

---

[1]   Both Horace and Donatus indicated a division into acts, and specified that they should be five in number, but it is doubtful whether Plautus and Terence observed these rules in their comedies.

[2]   See the previous chapter, p. 46.

[3]   The first translations of classical comedies (for example, Pandolfo Collenuccio's *Amphitryon* for use in the 1487 performances, already referred to in note 14 of the previous chapter) were normally in *terza rima*. Iacopo Nardi's comedies were in *terzine* and *ottave*, the latter being used primarily by the more dignified characters. Later, the prevalent verse form was hendecasyllabic blank verse, used on occasion by writers of prose comedies too. The most typical example of the conflict between the desire to find metres comparable to the ones used in the classical models and the impulse towards the greater realism of prose is to be found in the work of Ariosto. He may originally have written in irregular verse with frequent rhymes (see note 6 below), then adopted prose, but later revised even those comedies which had been written and performed, rewriting them in *endecasillabi sciolti sdruccioli* (blank hendecasyllabic verses with dactylic endings) which sought to reproduce the rhythm of the iambic trimeter. A similar attempt was

the *intermedi*, and the use of words, especially of spoken words without music, was reduced to a minimum. Nevertheless, despite this fundamental distinction, a few musical elements did find their way into the main spectacle and into the principal plot of the acts, where, however, they were subject to the dictates of realism, a basic principle recently learnt from the classical models.

In the case of comedies, by far the most frequently performed spectacles, the idea of the theatre as a mirror or an imitation of life and human customs was translated into the reproduction on stage of urban middle-class or working-class daily life, initially, however nominally, of classical times,[4] but very soon, and most explicitly, also of modern. One of the first symptoms of this realism, and of the attempt to break free of classical themes in order to link the plot more closely to contemporary experience was the increased attention paid to the short story, as the only literary form then existing in which observation of character and custom played any part. This was already the case with Bernardo Accolti's *Virginia*, performed in Siena in 1494, and in 1499 with *Filostrato e Panfila* by Antonio Cammelli known as 'il Pistoia' – though the latter play claimed to be a tragedy, not a comedy. Both were based on well-known short stories by Boccaccio, an indication that from the very beginning the dramatists were less concerned with inventing new characters and plots than with the means of giving them the immediacy of real life. At the same time, attention was also focussed on realistically representing the location of the plot. The most immediate consequence of this was the adoption of the perspective set, and consequently of the notion of unity of place. This is already clearly indicated in the description of the 1508 Ferrarese performance, under the patronage of Cardinal Ippolito d'Este, of Ludovico Ariosto's first comedy, *La cassaria*.

The best part of all these plays and *feste* has been the scenes against which they were performed, which were made by one Maestro Peregrino, a painter employed by the Lord [Pellegrino da Udine, then serving the new Duke of Ferrara, Alfonso d'Este, the cardinal's brother]; there is a road and a perspective of a town with houses, churches, belfries and gardens. A person cannot tire of looking at it for the divers things there depicted, all cleverly contrived and well-planned...[5]

On that occasion the urban scene so realistically represented was taken to be Taranto.[6] The following year, 1509, even greater attention was paid to realism in Ariosto's *I suppositi*, 'a delightful modern comedy' whose argument 'was recited by the author and is most beautiful, and *well-suited to our ways and*

later made by Luigi Alamanni in his *Flora* (1549), which was in sixteen-syllable verse with dactylic endings.

   [4]   Attempts at modernization began with the very first translations of Plautus's comedies. On this matter, see the texts by Battista Guarini and Niccolò Cosmico mentioned in note 13 of the previous chapter.

   [5]   From a frequently reproduced letter by Bernardino Prosperi to Isabella d'Este, published by G. Campori, *Notizie per la vita di Ludovico Ariosto* (Florence 1896), p. 51.

   [6]   *Ibid.* In the prose version handed down in print, *La cassaria* is set in Metellino; in the poetic version, it is set in Sibari. An indication that the 1508 set represented Taranto, and another, also in Prosperi's letter, that the play 'was translated in the form of a *barzeleta* or *frotola*' have raised the possibility of a first version in poetry. See Ireneo Sanesi, *La commedia* (Milan 1954), I. pp. 222–5. If one accepts this theory, which has met with much opposition, then the expression '*barzeleta* or *frotola*' would be taken to indicate versification either in hendecasyllabic lines with frequent internal rhymes, or else in seven- or eight-syllable couplets rhyming ab, bc, cd etc., i.e. with the second line of one couplet providing the rhyme for the first line of the next.

customs, since the action took place in Ferrara' (see plate 21).[7] Nine years later the prologue to Niccolò Machiavelli's *La mandragola* announced:[8] 'Behold the setting, as it is shown before you: this is your Florence; another time it will be Rome or Pisa.' And it goes on to point out 'that entrance which is on my right...that road which is tucked away on that side...that temple which is placed opposite it' and so forth, further emphasizing the evidence of what the audience could in fact see. The frequent use of prose, which ultimately prevailed over the experiments with verse, was also a response to the dictates of realism. Anyway, either in prose or in verse, even the less talented Florentine dramatists made such vivid and idiomatic use of language, that their plays are a rich mine for anyone who cares for colourful specimens of linguistic and folkloristic usage. Non-Florentine authors tended instead to exploit a range of dialects and of specific jargons as an effective way not only of enlivening the comic dialogue but also of characterizing types, classes and social groups. Finally, from the wish to stay close to real life derived the need to place limits on the duration of the action, and this need too was embodied in one of the famous Aristotelian rules of unity, the unity of time, which we will have cause to examine later.

In this general context, the inclusion of music in the main action also took on a realistic function: the characters could be made to sing, play or dance on stage in those ways and in those circumstances in which singing, playing and dancing would be plausible and acceptable in ordinary life. The classic example, and indeed the earliest which I can cite, is that of the 'roguish youth' who at night 'comes by all alone, clad in a beggar's short coat and playing the lute' in Act IV scene 9 of *La mandragola*, and is snatched up, taken into Messer Nicia's house and introduced into Lucrezia's bedchamber. Of course, what is being carried out is a lover's plot which had been worked out in advance and outlined by Ligurio, in scene 3 of the same act, in a single rapid line: 'As soon as you appear at the street corner, we shall be there, take your lute, grab you, turn you round, carry you inside, put you to bed; and the rest will be up to you.' The roguish youth, who is the lovesick Callimaco in disguise, advances singing two lines which, whether invented by Machiavelli or taken from the current repertory,[9] must have been the start of a cheeky Tuscan *strambotto* or *rispetto*, and were well-suited to the nature of the disguise:

> Venir ti possa el diavolo allo letto,
> dapoi che io non ci posso venir io.

> May the Devil steal into your bed,
> Since I myself can't join you there.

Similarly, the action of Pietro Aretino's *Il marescalco*, composed for Mantua between 1526 and 1527, opens with a little song which is full of the interruptions and repetitions typical of popular songs:

---

[7]   From another letter by Prosperi to Isabella d'Este, in Campori, *Notizie*, p. 58.

[8]   On dating the first performance of *La mandragola* 1518, see the next chapter.

[9]   Alessandro D'Ancona, *La poesia popolare italiana* (Livorno 1906), p. 101, noted that the first line is used in the *incatenatura*, i.e. a *quodlibet*, a poem made up of quotations of either incipits or refrains of well-known songs, known as the *Serenata* by Bronzino (the painter Agnolo Allori). As this could simply be an echo of the comedy, more important is the similarity with popular texts from Istria and the Marches.

Il mio padron to' moglie...
il mio padron to' moglie in questa terra
in questa terra.
La torrà, non la torrà,
ei l'avrà, e' non l'avrà
in questa sera, in questa sera.

My master takes a bride,
my master takes a bride in the neighbourhood,
in the neighbourhood. Will he take her or not?
Will he have her or not
this very night, this very night?

Gianicco is singing, and with his song he immediately characterizes the
setting as the Po valley (the set was assumed to represent Mantua), and
announces the theme of the trick being played on the protagonist, the marshal
himself. Gianicco is the marshal's young servant, whom the prologue has just
identified as a 'sly little thief' and a 'greedy glutton'. Part of his impudence
and sauciness is expressed in the songs he frequently sings: these are three,
one after the other, in Act II scene 3, all of them taken from the contemporary
popular or vernacular repertory. The first is the beginning (part of the *ripresa*)
of a long *barzelletta* telling the dialogue between a courtesan and her admirer,
in itself a farcical, if not a comic, scene:[10]

– Deh, averzi, Marcolina. –
– Va con Dio, scarpe pontie! –
– Deh, averzi, Marcolina. –

– Marcolina, open your door! –
– Go with God, you booted boor! –
– Marcolina, open your door! –

Another is on the common theme of a girl who wants a husband:[11]

Cara mare, maridemi,
che non posso più durar.
Caro pare, maridemi,
ch'io la sento...

Mother dear, do get me married, for I can stand it no longer. Father dear, do get me
married, you don't know how it feels.

The third too is on a not uncommon theme:[12]

La vedovella quando dorme sola
lamentarsi di me non ha ragione,
non ha ragione,
non ragione.

The little widow, when she sleeps alone, can't blame it on me, can't blame it on me.

---

[10]   Vittorio Rossi, 'Balli e canzoni del secolo XVI', appendix III to the edition of Andrea Calmo,
Le lettere (Turin 1888), pp. 441 and 442, gives the complete text according to an early
sixteenth-century printed edition.
[11]   D'Ancona, *La poesia popolare*, p. 108 note 2 gives several examples on the same subject.
[12]   *Ibid.*, p. 106. These are frequent but less precise examples. The quotation in the *argomento*
of *I tre tiranni* by Agostino Ricchi is worth noting. For further details, see below, p. 87.

In Act III scene 10 of *L'ipocrito* (1542), also by Aretino, one of the servants sings a verse which was certainly a *frottola* refrain:[13]

> Tempo fu che bene andò:
> vissi lieto senza pene.
> Bene andò che l'andò bene,
> or va mal quanto la può.

Time was when all went well; happy I was, I had no worry. The time when all went well has well and truly gone; now all goes as badly as can be.

Another servant answers him with a snatch of a song decidedly more popular in tone, which is however known through polyphonic elaborations handed down in *frottola* literature: '*E quando...quando andrastu al monte*' ('And when, O when, will you go to the mountain').[14]

By contrast, the portrayal of the 'Pedant, alone, who enters singing' at the end of Act III of Aretino's *Il marescalco*, is pure caricature. His song is a curious distich in Latin, a parody partly of didactic and mnemonic methods and partly of a way of approaching music which had been common amongst humanists a few decades previously:

> Scribere clericulis paro doctrinale novellis
> rectis as es a a, tibi dat declinatio prima.

I am getting ready to write instructions for virtuous new young students: 'as es a a' makes the first declension.

But whereas in Aretino's comedy both singer and song are of secondary importance, they figure much more conspicuously in Francesco Belo's *Il pedante*, performed in Rome in 1528, in a serenade which the protagonist organizes in honour of his beloved, and which is skilfully exploited so as to allow the trick played against him to be developed. Prudenzio, the pedant, has assembled as many singers as he has been able to recruit. These include a Venetian lutenist, presumptuous enough to boast (Act IV scene 1) 'For the gospel of San Zacharia I...don't envy any man alive his ability to produce a *romanzesca*, a *pavana*', i.e. a song in the Paduan dialect. But when it comes to it, the most moving thing he can contribute is a *frottola* rather reminiscent of the one by Rossino da Mantova in *Frottole libro tertio* of 1504 (1505 new style):[15]

> Mi s'è tanto inamorao
> in sta donna mia vicina,
> che me dà gran disciplina.
> che me vedo desperao.
> Gnao, gnao, gnao, gnao,
> mi s'è tanto inamorao.

Me, I am so much in love with a girl living next door. But she keeps being so hard on me, that I feel quite forlorn. Miaow, miaow, miaow, me, I am so much in love.

[13] Compare this with *E la va come la va* by Bartolomeo Tromboncino, transcribed by A. Einstein in *Canzoni sonetti strambotti et frottole. Libro tertio*, pp. 47–50.

[14] This song too is recalled in the *argomento* of Ricchi's *I tre tiranni*. For other quotations see E. Lovarini, *Studi sul Ruzzante e la letteratura pavana*, ed. G. F. Folena (Padua 1965), p. 216.

[15] See above, pp. 77ff. The text of *Il pedante* is included in I. Sanesi, ed., *Commedie del Cinquecento* (Bari 1912; reprint Bari 1975), I, pp. 83ff.

The second recruit is more recalcitrant. This is the boy Luzio, the pedant's pupil, who had been beaten by his master at the start of the comedy. Now he is called upon to sing a series of Latin couplets haphazardly thrown together with classical overtones. Even more uncooperative, Malfatto the servant has obstinately refused to take part, but at the last moment interrupts irrepressibly from a window of the pedant's house with a couplet from a *strambotto* or a Neapolitan *villanesca*:

> O fatte alla finestra dello muro
> e mostrame lo pertuso dello...

O come to the window in the wall. Show me the hole of the...

In *Gli ingannati*, the anonymous first comedy of the Sienese Accademia degli Intronati (1531), there is also a pedant in the cast, but he utters his howlers without singing. The housemaid Pasquella, however, does sing, to ward off the advances of an ardent Giglio, 'a Spaniard' (this also gives scope for several gibes aimed at his compatriots). The first song seems to be the *ripresa* of some sort of *ballata* which may have been popular in Siena as it also appears in a short story by the Sienese Pietro Fortini:[16]

> Che fa lo mio amor ch'egli non viene?
> l'amor d'un'altra donna me lo tiene.

> What is my love doing? Why does he never come?
> Loving another, he's kept away from me.

The comedy gives only one line of the other song: 'Non ti posso servir, signor mio caro' ('I cannot serve you, my dear sir'). It is difficult to say where it comes from, but it immediately provokes an angry reply from the Spaniard: 'This music is badly chosen. It is not suitable for my presence here.' In *L'amore costante* (1536) Alessandro Piccolomini, another member of the Intronati, did not hesitate to bring in the *abbattimento* (duelling on stage) more than once (Act IV scene 11; Act V scene 1) as well as singing (Act II scene 7). But, above all, one is struck by the joyous finale which incorporates dances: 'Here there is a *moresca in pietosa* with a kiss' (Act V scene 11); 'Here there is a *moresca gagliarda*' (Act V scene 12); 'Here there is an *intrecciato*' (Act V scene 13). The instrumental accompaniment of pipes or bagpipes and drums is hinted at in the words of two of the characters: 'More dancing, more dancing. Play! tifr, tru lu ru u u u! Rejoice! rejoice!' (the 'German') and 'Play, play drums, sirs' (once again the 'Spaniard').

Of course, one must immediately point out that these examples, and all the others one could add, represent the exception rather than the rule.[17] In most of the comedies published during the sixteenth century, the *intermedi* which

---

[16] D'Ancona, *La poesia popolare*, p. 110, note 1. For the text of the comedy, see '*Gli ingannati*' degli Accademici Intronati di Siena. An Italian Comedy of the Sixteenth Century (Edinburgh and London 1943) and Sanesi, *op. cit.*, I, pp. 311ff.

[17] One cannot fail to reach this conclusion when, after consulting numerous editions of comedies, one finds one has collected much the same examples as are to be found in the works of D'Ancona, Rossi, and Lovarini. The later the play, the fewer were the realistic insertions; Ciacco's songs in Act II scene 1 of *Il ragazzo* by Ludovico Dolce (see Sanesi, *Commedie del Cinquecento*, II, pp. 205ff) and the two *strambotti* in Act III of *Il roffiano*, by the same man, which were sung by a servant who attributed the first to 'one of Petrarch's clerks, and set to music on the lute by Tromboncino', and the second to Bembo, were thus exceptions.

had been performed or were to be performed between the acts are rarely mentioned; but even rarer are the indications of musical pieces forming part of the acts themselves. On one hand one is led to conclude that the growing concern with formal observances tended to preserve the contrast between the main plot and its formal framework, restricting the use of music to the latter, i.e. to the *intermedi*. The examples we have looked at do in fact come from works by authors who tended to forsake the beaten track, such as Machiavelli, who not only knew the Latin models but had glanced at works by Aristophanes;[18] by Belo and the extremely unconventional Aretino, both of whom must certainly have recalled the vivacious but unorthodox performing styles of the Sienese comedians who had been summoned to Rome by Pope Leo X;[19] or by Sienese authors, members of the Accademia degli Intronati and certainly well aware of the precedents established by their coarser precursors and contemporaries. On the other hand, one cannot rule out the possibility that the absence of references to music, whether intended to achieve a formal or a realistic purpose, was determined by purely practical considerations: although the *intermedi* were a necessary part of each performance of a comedy, they were not specified because only the performers themselves, aware of their own capabilities, could make the final choice. Similarly, it is possible that the dramatists were not opposed to the inclusion of musical elements as realistic ornaments to their texts, but again simply left the responsibility to the performers. This possibility is borne out by the tendency of sixteenth-century Italian theatre to develop on two distinct levels: as a literary activity, which is naturally the aspect most often reflected in the printed works, and as a practical activity, mainly motivated by the desire to please and entertain. This does not mean that the learned writers of printed comedies did not also intend their work to be performed, or that they were not concerned with favourable audience reactions. But the fact that they were men of letters, in addition to making them aware, though not always observant, of those precepts being hammered out in the course of theorizing and polemic criticism, also led them to concentrate on those elements which they deemed to be most essential: on the invention of a plot (though rarely a truly original one), on its development through a series of scenes, and on the dialogue. They were aware that they had no control over many other elements of the performance, such as scenery, costumes, lighting, style and pace of the delivery, *intermedi*, and, one might well add, realistic musical insertions.

Viewed in this light, it becomes clear that even then the literary text of a comedy was nothing more than an outline to be fully realized in the performance, prefiguring the way in which *scenari* were soon to be used in the *commedia dell'arte*. We learn more about music from what was done by those comic actors who, whilst not yet truly professional, were becoming increasingly specialized in actual staging, than from the texts of literary comedy. The single act of the anonymous Sienese *Comedia di Pidinzuolo* (1517)[20] included hymns (which were probably bawled in a tone which was

---

[18] According to Giuliano de Ricci, Machiavelli 'composed...in imitation of Aristophanes' 'Clouds' and other comedies, a discussion in the shape of a comedy to be performed in acts, and he called it *Le maschere*'. Quoted in Sanesi, *La commedia*, I, p. 253.

[19] D'Ancona, *Le origini*, II, pp. 81 and 84.

[20] In *Commedie del Cinquecento*, ed. Aldo Borlenghi (Milan 1959), II, pp. 905ff.

a caricature, just as the figure of the celebrant Ser Adagio was also a caricature) and dances in the piazza to celebrate the elevation to the cardinalate of Giovanni Piccolomini. The protagonist also first sang a *strambotto* with a partner, and then added a serenade to be sung for his 'Dolovica'. The choice of music for the latter was left to the performers; the stage-directions only say 'They perform the serenade and the singers sing...' The *ballo alla martorella* (i.e. in the peasant style) and Pidinzuolo's *strambotto* on the *cetarino* (lyre), are amongst the early, but not the earliest, of many brought on stage in the varied theatrical productions by those Sienese amateurs, mainly artisans, who in 1531 formed an academy, or rather a group, which they called the Congrega dei Rozzi.[21] The Congrega's historian has recorded various examples of *strambotti* sung either by one man alone or else in alternation by two singers vying to out-do each other. In one example, in *Il solfinello* by Pier Antonio della Stricca Legacci (Siena 1521), they alternate in singing the quatrains and tercets of a sonnet, one actor delivering his lines 'straight', the other singing a distorted parody.[22] In *Il vitio muliebre* by Mariano Maniscalco da Siena (Siena 1519) two girls, Virginia and Camilla, sing *strambotti* to relieve 'the assault on their hearts', and when one asks the other 'who will judge our words', the reply reflects the culture of the author, varied enough but picked up by ear:

> Imolo (!) e Pan con diritta ragione
> come altra volta eletti a questo offitio.

Imolus [possibly Tymolus] and Pan, whom a good choice has called to perform such a task as they had before.

The *ballo* too recurs frequently: *alla martorella* with instruments, or *ballo tondo* (round dance) accompanied by song, and even occasionally the *abbattimento*, i.e. duelling to the sound of music, and the *moresca*. In Giovanni Roncaglia's *Scanniccio* (Siena, undated), the scene of one 'shepherd' playing and another dancing 'a dance in the Ethiopian style' (another expression for a *moresca*) is seen through the description and comments of the rustic protagonist:[23]

> Io so' stato a veder più di due ore
>   se costoro han la febbre tedesca.
> Deh, mira come [e'] van saltellando;
> oh, ch'io non veddi mai la maggior tresca!
>   E' va co' piedi e con le man naspando;
> or cade, or no, e fa mille attaregli;
> attienti, eccolo giù va giocolando;
>   oh, mira, mira, quanti campanegli!
> Alle guagnel, che questo è un bel gioco!
> quanto a me, mai n'ho visti de' sì begli!
>   Io vo' stare a veder un altro poco
> s'i' potessi imparare. Oh, i' l'are' caro
> più che aver l'amicizia di un cuoco!

---

[21] Curzio Mazzi, *La congrega dei Rozzi di Siena* (Florence 1882), I, pp. 84ff.

[22] *Ibid.*, pp. 153–4. In *Gli errori d'Amore* by the Mantuan Marco Guazzi (Venice 1525) the division into acts is not explicit, but amongst the interlocutors are listed Berto and Bertun, *vilani intermedi*, who in one of their appearances on stage sing *strambotti*, singing alternately for the first couplets and in unison for the last.

[23] Mazzi, *La congrega dei Rozzi di Siena*, I, p. 207. Also on the Rozzi see Roberto Alonge, *Il teatro dei Rozzi di Siena* (Florence 1967).

I've been peering at them more than two hours, wondering if they don't have some kind of fever. Look at how they're hopping; sure, I never saw so lively a jig! Now he's raising his feet, waving his hands; he falls, he jumps, he makes a thousand twists. Watch him come down – he's having great fun. Goodness, how many pirouettes! My God, I think this game is such a feat the like of which I've never seen! I shall watch more of it here; O, I wish I could learn! I would hold it so dear, dearer than making friends with a cook!

These were the musical numbers used by the Sienese comedians who, albeit in groups recruited just for the occasion, were more than once summoned to Rome to enliven the carnivals of Leo X, and who later also acted in Naples, if not in 1536, at least in 1540.[24] Songs and dances were also used to enliven other non-literary comedies such as *Gli errori d'Amore* by the Mantuan Marco Guazzi (Venice 1525) or *I tre tiranni* by Agostino Ricchi. The latter, a neo-classical morality rather than a real comedy, had the privilege of being 'performed in Bologna before our Lord [the pope] and Caesar, on the day of the commemoration of the crowning of His Majesty', i.e. in February 1530. It is interesting to note that at such a time the play presented amongst other things a lover playing a real madrigal on his lute: *Non vedrà mai queste mie luci asciutte / in alcun tempo il cielo* ('Never shall the heavens see my eyes henceforeward dry').[25] And finally it is particularly worth noting the abundance of musical talent displayed by Ruzzante and his associates, whose theatrical activity in Padua, Venice and Ferrara was one of the greatest incentives (perhaps with Andrea Calmo as intermediary) to the formation of the first groups of professional comedians. Ruzzante's *La pastorale* and *La vaccaria* both closed with dances; *L'anconitana* is full of references to the protagonist's abilities as a singer and dancer. The exuberant actor-cum-author had already given proof of both these talents in *Moscheta*.[26] Besides Ruzzante, 'who was a good singer', at least two of his principal partners, Menato (Aurelio Alvarotto) and Vezzo (Girolamo Zanetti), also sang, and others who took both male and female parts may have done so as well. Indeed, even outside the context of the comedies 'Ruzzante and five comrades and two women' could entertain with 'beautiful songs and madrigals in the Paduan dialect'.[27] It should therefore come as no surprise that one Francesco 'of the lyre' was amongst 'the comrades recorded below' who on 25 February

---

[24]   See below, pp. 106–8 on the Neapolitan plays.

[25]   The first known printed edition of madrigals is the *Libro primo de la serena*, also published in Rome in 1530 (all that remains of it is the 'alto' part in the Biblioteca Colombina in Seville). Besides Chrisaulo's madrigal, the *lauda* of a pilgrim setting off, in Act IV, for Santiago of Galicia (and already back in Act V) could also have been sung. The comedy, already mentioned in connection with the songs referred to in its *argomento*, was published in 1533, 'with Apostolic and Venetian licence', and was dedicated by its Ferrarese author to Cardinal Ippolito dei Medici. For a modern edition see Sanesi, *Commedie del Cinquecento*, I, pp. 163ff.

[26]   See the copious information given by Lovarini in various papers now collected into the volume entitled *Studi sul Ruzzante e la letteratura pavana*. Most of the time Ruzzante must have invented if not the tunes at least the words of his songs, as I have failed to trace any musical pieces corresponding to those songs which feature in his comedies.

[27]   From the description of a banquet held in Ferrara in January 1529, in Cristoforo da Messiburgo, *Banchetti, compositioni di vivande e apparecchio generale* (Ferrara 1549), c. 7r (reprinted in facsimile, ed. F. Bandini, Venice 1960). See also *ibid.*, c. 4, the description of a banquet in June of the same year, when 'there were five who sang certain songs as used in Padua, in a rustic dialect which it was a wonder to hear'.

1545, in Padua, formed one of the first real companies of comic actors,[28] or that the Neapolitan Guglielmo Perillo, Angelo Michele from Bologna, and Marcantonio Veneto, drawing up the contract in 1567 in Genoa for the formation of a 'societatem insimul recitandi comedias', should take on the task of 'sonandi, cantandi, balandi' ('playing, singing, dancing') (plate 24).[29] Apart from the numerous collections of *scenari*, hardly any documents survive on the improvised acting style of the *comici dell'arte*, which left each actor free to draw at will upon his own repertory of characteristic lines, *tirate*, *lazzi* and even acrobatics, pirouettes, songs and dances. But the *scenari* merely outlined the points needing to be agreed in advance between the performers, their entrances and exits, and the essential elements that each was to contribute to the development of the plot. It follows logically that they include only a few general references to music, and that the lists of properties necessary for the performances hardly ever include instruments, since each actor would obviously have used his own.[30]

That music was widely used does emerge from the pictorial documents providing evidence about *commedia dell'arte* (plate 25), such as rare book illustrations, the engravings of the 'recueil dit de Fossard', the frescoes decorating the Trausnitz castle, the Franco-Flemish paintings which record the first visits of the Italian comic actors to the French court and, a little later, the engravings of *I capricci* and *I balli di Sfessania* by Jacques Callot, which depict mainly Neapolitan masks and characters. But there exist few actual examples of musical pieces which can with confidence be linked with the theatre, and those which do exist are largely of too late a date to be considered here. Only an *Aria della comedia* and one *della comedia nova* in *Il secondo libro d'intavolatura, di balli d'arpicordo* by a Venetian, one Marco Facoli (Venice 1588), belong to the sixteenth century, and they have survived in an instrumental version, without a text which would have helped us to establish the nature of their theatrical function.[31] Otherwise, we have to rely on a kind of evidence resembling that provided by pictorial sources, which one might call 'musical iconography', if one wished to emphasize just such an analogy. In late fifteenth- and sixteenth-century musical literature several pieces, while not themselves performed in comedies, are in some way reflections of ones which were; it is possible from them to come up with a fairly faithful image of the originals, provided we take due account of the nature of the pieces acting as mirrors.

This is easier in the case of evidently popular strophes or refrains which may have been either sung unaccompanied by a character intent on his tasks or chores, or quoted almost as a proverb in the middle of a dialogue to add force to an argument. Students of literary folklore have collected large

[28] Ester Cocco, 'Una compagnia comica nella prima metà del secolo XVI', in *Giornale storico della letteratura italiana*, 65 (1915), p. 55.

[29] Quoted in Sanesi, *La commedia*, II, p. 2.

[30] For an extensive bibliography see under the appropriate entry in the *Enciclopedia dello spettacolo*, III, especially section II (Italy) which also provides, in col. 1202, a list of collections of *scenari*. In these, lists of 'robe per l'opera' (properties to be used in the play) are not uncommon. Note the generic use of the term 'opera'.

[31] Transcription in modern notation edited by Willi Apel and published under the same title in Rome (?) 1963. In addition, see the article referred to below in note 43.

numbers of quotations, and even gone as far as to record how pervasively and obsessively some of the songs may have resounded at the height of their popularity.[32] The main sources are not so much comedies, as short stories, narrative poems and *incatenature* ('chains'), verse compositions in which some witty soul took pleasure in aligning all the fragments he could recall, linking them together either according to far-fetched associations of ideas or for pure convenience of rhyme. Occasionally, it has been possible to reconstruct the complete text of some songs, or at least one of the many versions of them, thanks to the printing of popular booklets, through which the words were made available at the time to people who had already learned them in incomplete form, picking them up along with the tune.[33] There are also musical *incatenature* (the so-called *quodlibets*) analogous to the literary ones and yet belonging on a sensibly higher cultural level, since the task of combining simultaneously various already extant tunes required considerably skill in counterpoint. As a result, the fragments are generally brief (as indeed are those of the literary *incatenature*) and it is difficult to determine where, after the characteristic start, the changes may begin which were needed to achieve an harmonious blend with the themes proposed by the other voices. Much research has already been done into the music too, and detailed comparisons have been made;[34] nevertheless, three new examples can be added here, which are more than mere beginnings, and come from a collection which is clearly of the fifteenth century.[35] *Nencioza mia* (example XII) must have been a Tuscan song; it was used as the tenor part in a piece for four voices by Johannes Martini of Armentières, who was a singer in Milan in 1474 and then in Ferrara from 1475 until circa 1490, and was also Isabella d'Este's music teacher.[36] The other two songs, tenors of anonymous pieces in the same

[32] Besides the works already referred to by D'Ancona, Rossi and Lovarini, see the various articles by Severino Ferrari, and Francesco Novati's 'Contributo alla storia della lirica musicale italiana popolare e popolareggiante', in *Miscellanea Rodolfo Renier* (Turin 1912), pp. 899–980.

[33] In the absence of a more comprehensive bibliography, see Arnaldo Segarizzi, *Le stampe popolari della Biblioteca Marciana* (Bergamo 1907); Carlo Angeleri, *Bibliografia della stampe popolari...nella Biblioteca Nazionale di Firenze* (Florence 1953); Caterina Santoro, *Stampe popolari a carattere profano della Biblioteca Trivulziana* (Milan 1964). Most of the extant editions tend to be relatively recent and thus, while they provide evidence of the continued popularity of a song, do not help establish its chronology.

[34] I refer primarily to the article by Knud Jeppesen, 'Venetian Folk-Songs of the Renaissance' in *Papers Read at the International Congress of Musicology*, ed. A. Mendel et al. (New York 1944), pp. 62ff, and to Torrefranca's *Il segreto del Quattrocento*. Since this chapter first appeared, Jeppesen has published a fuller and more systematic study than the one referred to above, called 'Frottola und Volkslied', in Jeppesen, *La frottola*, III, pp. 9–140. References to this in subsequent notes will give only the author's name and the number he assigned to each tune.

[35] This is the Seville MS, Biblioteca Colombina 5.I.43 from which Jeppesen, 'Venetian Folk-Songs', draws the tune of *Villana che sai tu far*. Dragan Plamenac noticed the three tenor parts, though he mentioned them only briefly in part I (p. 527) of his valuable study 'A Reconstruction of the French Chansonnier in the Biblioteca Colombina Seville' in *The Musical Quarterly*, XXXVII (1951), pp. 501ff; XXXVIII (1952), pp. 85ff and pp. 245ff. The manuscript, of Italian origin though much of its content is French, has also been published in a facsimile edition, ed. Plamenac, *Seville 5.I.43 and Paris N.A.Fr 4379 (pt. I)* (Brooklyn, New York 1962). See also Jeppesen, 293–5.

[36] Seville 5.I.43, fol. 130v–131r. The incipit *Lenchioza mia* is easily corrected on the basis of the concordance in Petrucci's *Canti C* (Venice 1503; 1504 new style). The tune largely corresponds with the one used by another foreigner, Johannes Japart, which can be found in *Harmonice Musices Odhecaton A*, ed. Helen Hewitt (Cambridge, Mass. 1942), pp. 233–4. On Martini see the article by Ludwig Finscher in *Die Musik in Geschichte und Gegenwart*, vol. VIII (though the liturgical codex which led Finscher to assume a stay in Modena is in fact to be related to the Este court in Ferrara).

Ex. XII *Nencioza mia, Nencioza balarina.* Tenor of the piece with the same title. From the Seville manuscript, Biblioteca Colombina, 5.I.43, fol. 130v.

manuscript, seem to originate from the Po valley.[37] The melody of *O zano, bello zano* (example XIII) is repeated seven times, though the words change: that of *Cavalcha Sinisbaldo* (example XIV) is fitted to two lines of twelve syllables followed by a refrain, and should then be repeated with four more rather unedifying couplets, all followed by the same refrain. It is interesting to note how all three examples suddenly switch to a compound triple metre, as a rhythmic variation of the main melody in the first two, as a characteristic of the new refrain in the third.

Fragments, of varying lengths, of popular songs are also to be found in a small group of pieces which, although themselves not true *frottole*, belong to the *frottola* period. They appear in early sixteenth-century musical editions beginning with the publication of Petrucci's *Frottole libro septimo* (Venice 1507). The words of this anonymous piece show how they were presented:

> Forzato dal dolore
> che l'alma mi tormenta,
> a ciò che lei mi senta,
> che intenda il mio martire,
> dispost'ò tutto dire
> una canzon novella
> tra l'altre la più bella:
> *La vedovella quando dorme sola*
> *lamentarsi di me non ha ragione,*
> *lamentarsi di me non ha ragione.*

I am compelled by grief which gnaws my soul, to let her know the pains I am enduring. To make her hear me, I want all to be told in a new song, the most beautiful of all: *The little widow, when she sleeps alone, cannot blame it on me, cannot blame it on me.*

Unfortunately the only surviving partbook of the undated printed edition

---

[37] *Ibid.,* fols. 131v–132r and 133v–134r, both *unica. Ibid.,* fols. 134v–135r is a composition on the tenor *Che fa la rama(n)zina che fala che la non vem,* the tune of which is familiar through other sources. It would appear that the whole group of compositions was intended to be played on instruments.

Ex. XIII *O zano, bello zano.* Tenor from the homonymous piece. From the Seville manuscript, Biblioteca Colombina, 5.I.43, fol. 131v.

```
O        za _ no   bel _ lo   za _ no,   ca _ za   fo _ ra   le   ca _    pre,
U _ na   ro _ sa   l'al _ tra   ne _ gra,   l'al _ tra   me _ za   bian _ cha.
la      fil _ gio _ la   de   lo   re   fa   fa _ re   u _ na        tor _ ta
```

```
D'un   a _ gne _ lo,   d'un   por _ ce _ lo,   d'u _ na   ca _ pra   mo _ za.
Chi   se   tro _ va   se _ cha   ca _ na   si   po _ rà   trin _ ca _ re.
```

```
O        za _ no,   bel _ lo   za _ no,   ca _ za   fo _ ra   le   ca _   pre,
U _ na   ro _ sa,   l'al _ tra   ne _ gra,   l'al _ tra   me _ za   bian _ cha.
```

Ex. XIV *Cavalcha Sinisbaldo.* Tenor from the homonymous piece. From the Seville manuscript, Biblioteca Colombina, 5.I.43, fol. 133v (part of the text omitted).

```
Ca _ val _ cha   Si _ ni _ sbal _ do   tu _ ta   la   noc _ te        E
```

```
tan _ to   ca _ val _ chò   che   a   le   por _ te   zun _ se.   Pan   e   pa _
```

```
_ na _ da,   man   a   la   bra _ ga,   Pe _ re,   me _ le,   nu _ se,   ca _
```

```
_ sta _ gne,   Fig   e   la _ sa _ gn'e   Do'   su _ si _ ne   fre _ sche.
```

Trovo bella fantina, basar la volse
Fantina fo cortese, bochim li porse

El cavalier vilan in terra la pose
Fantina tenerella i ochi stravolse

containing the piece is the one of the alto, whose melody is certainly not the tune of the couplet quoted in Aretino's *Il marescalco*.[38] However we are luckier with another text which is mentioned, but not sung, in Aretino's *L'ipocrito* (Act III scene 10);[39] the music is provided by a piece by the almost unknown Eneas Dupré in the *Frottole libro septimo* (example XV):

[38] See above, p. 79. The publication, undated but not prior to 1530, is *Il libro primo de la Fortuna*. What little survives of the music was transcribed by Torrefranca, *Il segreto del Quattrocento*, p. 571. See also Jeppesen, 148.
[39] On the appearances in literature of this refrain and the previous one, see Lovarini, *Studi sul Ruzzante*, pp. 216 and 170.

Ex. XV Eneas Dupré. *Canzone* with refrain. From *Frottole libro septimo* (O. Petrucci, Venice 1507), fol. 33v.

Chi à mar _ _ tel _ _ lo, Dio gli'l to _ _ _ glia,

Ch'io ne son al tut _ _ to fo _ re.

Ho mu _ ta _ to sti _ le e vo _ _ _ glia,

Chi à martello Dio gl'il toglia,
ch'io ne son al tutto fore.
Ho mutato stile e voglia,
ho raccolto mecho il core.
Cantian donque con amore,
con serena e lieta fronte:
E quando, quando andarastu al monte,
bel pegoraro,
fradel mio caro, oimè.

He who grieves may God help him; as for me I am free of pain. I have so changed my mind and ways as to keep my heart with me. Let us sing, then, lovingly, looking most happy and serene: When, O when will you go to the mountain, you handsome shepherd, dear brother, Ah me.

The most remarkable find is a piece by the Bolognese Alessandro Demophon, *Vidi hor cogliendo rose*;[40] in it the same lay-out with the final quotation of a

⁴⁰ Published, from *Frottole libro septimo*, in Luigi Torchi, *L'arte musicale in Italia*, I (Milan 1897); in an arrangement for voice and lute from *Tenori e contrabassi intabulati...libro secundo* (Fossombrone 1511), in Benvenuto Disertori, *Le frottole pel canto e liuto* etc. (Milan 1964), pp. 493–5. I am not convinced that the soprano line, given by Jeppesen, 83, is the tune of the popular

song is repeated for five verses. This gives us a complete ten-line *rispetto*, which is quoted in a list of *balli* in the so-called *Egloga rusticale* (1508), which was a brief entertainment by Cesare Nappi, also from Bologna, somewhat similar to the popular Sienese performances.[41] The complete text appears below:

> Deh, levate la stringa dallo pecto
> e lassami mirar quelle viole,
> e lassa star el paradiso aperto
> dove se leva la luna col sole.
> El sol se leva e la luna se posa,
> dagli la buona sera a quella rosa.
> Dagli la buona sera e 'l buon dormire,
> e chi usa falsità possa morire;
> possa morire e far la mala morte,
> star in pregion e far la mala sorte.

Loose that piece of ribbon lacing your bosom, and let me admire those violets of yours, and leave the sight of paradise open, where the moon rises as well as the sun. The sun rises there and there sets the moon; let's wish good-night to that beautiful rose. Let's wish good-night to her, may she sleep well, and may those who slander die. May they all die without being at peace, stay long in prison and be forever ill-fated.

If these refrains were dances, as Nappi's list, which includes several of them, seems to suggest, then it would be logical to infer that the *strofe* of pieces of this sort included in the collection of *frottole* must have imitated the *strofette* of the *ballo tondo* which were sung or spoken by whoever was leading the dance. These *strofette* regularly reintroduced the danced refrain. This hypothesis is confirmed by the existence of a third group of settings of very brief texts dialectal in flavour – generally set in chordal polyphony and with their tune usually given in the tenor – which are nothing more than the usual refrains.[42] *E quando andarè tu al monte* features here once more in a setting of I. B. Zesso from *Frottole libro septimo* (example XVI) together with *D'un bel mattin d'amore*, also by Zesso (*Frottole libro septimo*), *E d'un bel mattin d'amore* by the Brescian Antonio Caprioli (*Frottole libro nono*), and *A pe' de la montagna* by Rossino da Mantova (*Frottole libro octavo*). Their brevity, and the lack of additional texts for further repetitions, lead me to think that they might have been used in comedies as choral refrains for the *ballo tondo*: the *additamenta* or 'calls', i.e. the *strofette* of the leader of the dance, would have been recited,

song. There are three compositions of this type by Antonio Caprioli: *Sotto un verde alto cupresso* (quoting the refrain *E d'un bel mattin d'amore*), *Una legiadra nimpha* (quoting *Cavalcha*) and *Chi propitio à la sua stella* (quoting *La vilanela*). The first is from Petrucci's *Libro octavo*, the other two from his *Libro nono*. See Jeppesen, 91 and 98. (The reservations I expressed about 83 apply here too.) Other compositions are in *Frottole libro secondo* (Rome 1516?), part of the series published by Andrea Antico; amongst them *Per fuggir d'amor le ponte* by Marchetto Cara (quoting *Deh tiente alora, tiente alora ruzenenta*) already in *Tenori e contrabassi intabulati . . . libro secondo* (and therefore to be found in Disertori, *Le frottole per canto e liuto*). It is not included in Jeppesen's list, though he cites other sources (87–90, 92 and 94).

[41] On the rustic rather than arcadian nature of the eclogues, see the summary by Sanesi, *La commedia*, I, pp. 407–8. For the list of dances, refer to the article by Frati in the next note.

[42] The list also includes *el Pegoraro*; *el Turlurú*; *Tiente alora*; *Me livava un bel mattino*; *Torela mo, villan* and *Fortuna d'un gran tempo*: see Luigi Frati, 'Un'egloga rusticale del 1508', in *Giornale storico della letteratura italiana*, 20 (1897), pp. 186ff. The *strambotto* had already been noted by Novati, *Contributo alla storia della lirica popolare*, pp. 926 and 927.

Ex. XVI Ioan Battista Zesso, Choral refrain. From *Frottole libro septimo* (O. Petrucci, Venice 1507), fol. 55v.

not sung, more or less as was the case, until a few decades ago, in the now obsolete country-dance. The result must have been a curious mixture of realism (the dance) and convention (the polyphonic elaboration of the refrain).

It is not purely by chance that musical literature enables us to trace some of the melodies used in comedy. From the very start of the sixteenth century strong similarities developed between music, or at any rate certain types of music, and theatre.[43] I have concentrated until this point primarily on plays which imitated those of Terence and Plautus, but one must not neglect those minor theatrical genres (eclogues, farces, *frottole*, *gliommeri* or *mariazi*), which usually formed a subcultural background to more consciously literary drama, but at least once, in the hands of Ruzzante, acquired a major importance. They mostly dealt with pastoral topics, but fluctuated between idealized expressions of arcadian nymphs and shepherds and more realistic portrayals in which the characters were rustic villagers whose passions were at times not devoid of spontaneous refinement, but more often crude and elemental. This uncertain fluctuation between the idyllic and the rustic style of pastoral is clearly exemplified in the popular drama which flourished in Siena. It is also likely to have characterized many of the Venetian performances of which there survive only scattered and brief records, such as the *Egloga pastoral* performed in 1508 by Francesco Cherea, or the *Comedia, et...demonstration vestiti a la vilota* staged in 1512 by 'a company of gentlemen Gardeners'. This was performed in Murano following a decree by the Senate in 1509, 'quod Comoediae, recitationes, et representationes comoediales seu tragoediales, eglogae, omnino banniantur'. Nevertheless, also in 1512, for a Contarini marriage, there was 'the beautiful demonstration of a tragedy and a pastoral eclogue' staged by Francesco Cherea, and in the following year he organized a 'certain demonstration of a comedy of shepherds'.[44] This list could be extended to include the 'rustic comedy staged by one Paduan named Ruzzante, who speaks most excellently as a rustic' (13 February 1520). This was *La pastorale* by Angelo Beolco, to whom the nickname 'Ruzzante' was given after the part he had performed in that performance.[45] However, more important for our purpose are corresponding trends of musical taste. The nymph who opened *La pastorale* with her song had been prefigured at least thirteen years before by the solitary huntress whose wandering in the woods had led to the singing of the above-quoted *rispetto* in Demophon's composition and by the 'graceful nymph' in a similar piece by Caprioli (*Una legiadra nimpha* in Petrucci's *Libro nono*). These, and other pieces, are idyllic, Giorgionesque scenes: in another of Caprioli's pieces (from Petrucci's *Libro octavo*) the female figure is encamped 'beneath a tall green cypress'. Yet the songs that they sing clearly belong to the genre of *chanson rustique*,[46] so much so that one of them, that of the *pegoraro* or shepherd, is extended and dramatized into a dialogue of rustic seduction set to music by one Ioan Pietro Mantuan (example XVII).[47]

---

[43]   I had already mentioned this several years ago in 'Commedia dell'arte e melodramma', in *Manifestazioni culturali dell'Accademia Nazionale di Santa Cecilia* (1954), later reprinted as 'Commedia dell'Arte and Opera', in *The Musical Quarterly*, LXI (1955), pp. 305ff.

[44]   D'Ancona, *Le origini*, II, pp. 111ff.

[45]   *Ibid.*, pp. 120 and 121, and Lovarini, *Studi sul Ruzzante*, pp. 81ff.

[46]   I am deliberately using this term to emphasize a relationship parallel with that of French *chansons rustiques* and *chansons musicales* discussed by Brown, *Music in the French Secular Theater*, pp. 113ff.

[47]   From *Tenori e contrabassi intabulati...libro secundo*, and therefore in Disertori, *Le frottole per canto e liuto*, pp. 548–51, which includes a more complete text than is given with the music. Jeppesen does not refer to it. It is tempting to identify its author as Gian Pietro della Viola, a Florentine attached to the court of Mantua, who was the author of the text and of the music (?) of a *Festa de Lauro* performed in Mantua in 1486; see D'Ancona, *Le origini*, II, pp. 351 and 352, note.

Ex. XVII Ioan Pietro Mantuan. Rustic idyll. From *Tenori e contrabassi intabulati col sopran in canto figurato per cantar e sonar col lauto libro secundo. Francisci Bossinensis Opus* (O. Petrucci, Fossombrone 1511), fols. 41r–42r.

Ex. XVIII *De voltate in qua.* Refrain of the anonymous piece *Poi che 'l cielo e la Fortuna.* From *Frottole libro septimo* (O. Petrucci, Venice 1507) fols. 24v–25r.

Ruzzante scholars have not found it easy to trace literary texts precisely corresponding to (and not merely resembling) the many songs and dances which were performed, or simply referred to, in his comedies. As for the music, there are only three songs amongst the many listed by Nale in the *Betía* whose tunes I can firmly identify. *D'un bel mattin d'amore* is a brief refrain of which more than one version is known. *De voltate in qua e do, bella Rosina* (example XVIII) recurs as a refrain placed in the upper part at the end of each verse of *Poi che'l ciel e la Fortuna*, from the *Libro septimo* of Petrucci's series.[48] Torrefranca published a facsimile and a transcription of a setting for four voices of *E levòmi d'una bella mattina* (example XIX) which is referred to by Nale and by the character Ruzzante in *L'anconitana*. It is classified as a *villota* in the index of the Venetian manuscript in which it appears,[49] though in fact it too is a choral refrain with the popular melody placed in the tenor. It does not therefore belong in the category of the *villota* '*in contrappunto arioso*' which flourished primarily in the decade between 1520 and 1530, although earlier examples do exist (Torrefranca thought these much older and credited them with a decisive role in the evolution of the sixteenth-century madrigal). Information about 'beautiful *canzoni* and madrigals *alla pavana*' which were sung in Ferrara in 1529 by Ruzzante and his colleagues probably relates to this sort of polyphony; however, it is also conceivable that the pieces *in contrappunto arioso*[50] were here called madrigals and those having a mainly

[48] Jeppesen, 65–70, lists these and other compositions in which either the complete melody or fragments of it appear in whatever form.

[49] *Il segreto del Quattrocento*, pp. 356 and 357 (facsimile), 451 and 452 (transcription), from the Venetian MS, Biblioteca Marciana, It. Cl. IV, 1795–8. One anomaly of the melody in the tenor line as it appears in the composition, is that it begins in the key of F (B flat is understood according to the rules of solmization) and ends in the key of C, extending over a ninth. It is likely that the whole of the repeat was sung in the original tune a fourth higher than it appears in the composition; this would have restored the tonal consistency of the whole and turned its range into a sixth, more common in this sort of song. See also Jeppesen, 50–2.

[50] Torrefranca's theory is well known. He maintained that the contrapuntal *villota* (to which he attributed considerable antiquity) was, to play with words, the matrix of the madrigal. As has frequently been pointed out, most of the examples on which he based his theory either do not display the characteristics on which he based his argument, or else came from manuscripts and printed editions not earlier than 1520. And yet the *contrappunto arioso* (a happy choice of words) did have a precursor, in the work of a musician from Verona or Vicenza, one Michele Pesenti. From the first book of Petrucci's *Frottole* (1504) he appeared not only as the harmonizer of a popular *filastrocca*, but also as the originator of the contrapuntal *villota* in which all the lines make some use of bits of popular melodic material. This is not the place to go into the connection

Ex. XIX   Choral refrain on *E levòmi d'una bella matina*. From the Venice manuscript, Biblioteca San Marco, Ital., Cl.IV, 1795–98.

chordal texture and the popular melody in the tenor were called *canzoni*. Such an hypothesis is supported by the fact that the 'Canzone di Ruzzante', *Zoia zentil che per segreta via*, set *in musica* (that is, 'revised according to the rules of musical art') by Adrian Willaert, is of this second type.[51] It is precisely because Ruzzante was an authentic singer as well as a writer of comedies that no trace remains of the many other songs which he composed: he himself made up the verses in a popular style and adapted tunes, according to the traditional rules and customs of unwritten music.

between the *contrappunto arioso* and the contemporary French *chanson*. But it is interesting to note that alongside the tendency towards the more erudite madrigal motivated by its Petrarchan suggestions, there was also a contrary tendency towards a pastoral and popular form, perhaps influenced by the derivation of *mandriale* from *mandria*, suggested by Antonio da Tempo, whose fourteenth-century treatise was printed in 1507. These two tendencies are interestingly paralleled in the theatre, where side by side with imitation of the classics one finds Alessandro Vellutello's theory that 'Comedy had been invented by the shepherds...for in that language [Greek] *comi* means "country"'' (in the 'Avviso ai lettori' which precedes *I tre tiranni* by Agostino Ricchi).

   [51]   Transcribed by Fernando Liuzzi and revised by R. Cumar and P. L. Petrobelli in Lovarini, *Studi sul Ruzzante*, figs. xxvi–xxxii, from *Canzoni villanesche alla napolitana di Messer Adriano a quattro voci con la canzon di Ruzante* (Venice 1548). See also A. Willaert, *Volkstümliche Italienische Lieder*, ed. E. Hertzmann (Wolfenbüttel, n.d.) ('Das Chorwerk', vol. 8), pp. 8–10.

Another lead to be followed is that of the frequent participation by musicians in theatrical activities, and of comic authors or actors in musical ones. At the very beginning of the sixteenth century a Latin comedy staged in Venice, the *Stephanium*, gave Sabellico the chance to claim, in a *Carmen*, the superiority of contemporary Venetian life over classical, and to declare: 'saltamus aptius: sonamus dulcius lyra: monaulo: barbito psalterio' ('our dancing is superior: our playing of the lyre, the pipe, the lute and the psaltery is sweeter'). The author, and actor, of the *Stephanium* was a friar from Abruzzo, Giovanni Armonio, later employed as an organist in Saint Mark's, from 16 September 1516 until November 1552.[52] Farces by one Antonio Ricco were also performed in Venice in the first years of the century. Antonio Ricco was a Neapolitan who had some connection with the Gonzaga family, and I would like to think he is the D. Antonio Rigum by whom at least one piece of music is known.[53] Far better known as a dramatist, short-story writer, and musician is Girolamo Parabosco of Piacenza, who was in Venice from 1540 as a pupil of Adrian Willaert and in 1551 became organist of the first organ in Saint Mark's. His *Madrigali a cinque* appeared, printed by Gardane,

[52]   Emanuele A. Cicogna, *Delle iscrizioni veneziane*, V. (Venice 1842), pp. 551 and 552, refers to Latin verses composed by him and set to music in honour of Anne of Hungary, and sung in 1502 by Pietro de Fossis. Even Bembo sought his company.

[53]   *Donna, ascolta*, in *Frottole libro primo* (Venice 1504). He was chapel-master at Ferrara. On Ricco, see Sanesi, *La commedia*, I, pp. 206 and 207. His links with the Gonzagas are shown by the dedications to his verses in 1518 and 1520.

in 1546, the year in which his first comedies, *La notte* and *Il viluppo* were also published. Over a period of a few years these were followed by another six, one of them in verse, and by a tragedy, *Progne*. Another dramatist, Andrea Calmo (1510–71), though not himself a professional actor, was amongst those who paved the way for the development of acting as a profession. Calmo's earliest biographer wrote of him that 'he entered into the famous companies of comic actors then flourishing in Italy. There, acting the part of Pantalone and of the singer, he advanced so rapidly that he gained the highest reputation of all.' The wording is anachronistic, in that the author assumes a multiplicity of companies and a clear differentiation of roles which in fact only appeared in the next generation, but Calmo was certainly interested in music: there is evidence of this interest in his *cheribizzi*, curious letters in dialect, some of which are addressed to musicians and singers. In one, obviously autobiographical in tone, he boasts of having 'reinstated the idiom of the ancients and restored the singing of *strambotti* (*strambotizar*) in music'.[54] By the 'idiom of the ancients' he meant that dialect which he elsewhere referred to as the 'vulgar antiqua lengua Veneta', the 'ancient Venetian vernacular'. A similar claim could be made for the merchant, actor and dramatist Antonio Molino, known as Burchiella. The narratives which frame Gianfrancesco Straparola's short stories in his collection *Le piacevoli notti* (a series of carnival reunions held on Murano in about 1536, in which Pietro Bembo and Bernardo Cappello would seem to have been involved), mention Burchiella's abilities as a player of a variety of instruments: the *viola* or lyre, the *lirone* and the lute. He and Fra Giovanni Armonio together sponsored a musical Academy, which may be the same as the one mentioned by Anton Francesco Doni, which gathered together the cream of the Venetian musicians as well as a fair number of amateurs. Significantly, we are told that in order 'better to establish this Academy, he [Molino] engaged in demonstrating how good he was at acting comedies. And he was the first to change them, reciting them in several languages...copying the so-called "Greek" and the Bergamask'.[55]

One might think that it was in the *intermedi* that the connection between the musical and comic arts was primarily developed, but in my opinion what we know of Calmo and Molino indicates that this was not the case. It seems that Calmo specialized in portraying typical traits of angry and complaining old age, its obstinacy, its suspicious avarice and its constant use of Venetian dialect as opposed to the frequent use of Tuscan by the couples of young lovers and of Bergamask dialect by most of the servants in comedies. These traits later became essential features of the mask of Pantalone. Given the report on Calmo's supposed abilities as a singer and his claim that he had 'restored the singing of *strambotti* in music', it seems more than likely that Pantalone-

[54] Calmo, *Le lettere*, p. 29. The biographical information is by Alessandro Zilioli, from p. xxx of Rossi's introduction. Calmo was certainly a friend of Parabosco (*ibid.*, p. xi) and besides addressing one of his humorous dialect letters to him also wrote others to Giammaria del Cornetto, Anton Francesco Doni, Ippolito Tromboncino and Adrian Willaert.

[55] From the dedication of Molino's *I fatti, e le prodezze di Manoli Blessi, Strathioto* (Venice 1561), a mock-heroic poem in *lingua greghesca* (i.e. the mixture of Greek and Venetian used by the *stratioti* in the service of Venice). The dedication was written by Ludovico Dolce, which indicates that even if Molino was not noble, he was of considerable rank. Using the Bergamo dialect, Molino tells the fourth story from the fifth night of Straparola's *Piacevoli notti*. In 1568, when he published one volume of his own madrigals for four voices, Molino referred to his 'great age'.

Calmo, or whatever he was called on stage, was, in the throes of love, apt to come out with little comic nonsense songs, of the sort which a 1570 collection of pieces called *justiniane*.[56] One of these, *Anchonononor che col partire*, was a parody of a famous madrigal by Cipriano de Rore. In it, not only were the words distorted, but they were embroidered with the insistent repetition of a nasal syllable which seems to have been one of the character's phonetic habits or vices:[57]

> Anchonononor che col partire
> me senenenento sgagiolire,
> scampar vorave ogn'hora ogni momenenenenento.
> Tant'è 'l furor che sento
> che coro intorno intorno
> e cusí mille schite schito al zorno,
> e qualche volta ogn'hora
> buto per vu, crudel cara signonononora.

Althoug-hough in departing I am feeling mi-mi-miserable, I'd treasure every hour, every mo-moment. Such is the frenzy I am in that I am running all around, and stop to shit a thousand times a day; and often every hour you make me sick, cruel dear my-my-my lady.

In another *justiniana*, *Chi nde darà la bose*, the *strambotizar* lays claims to a spurious technical knowledge of music:

> Chi nde darà la bose al solfizar
> per dirve a vu, brigenti, una canzon?
> Amor, ti priego, fande scomenzar
> musicalmente qualche dolce ton,
> ma del be quadro non send'impazemo
> perch'el bemole è quel che sempre usemo.
>
> Ut re mi fa sol la, la sol fa mi,
> e po la sesquialtera in driana,
> golizanando, fradei, ti e mi e ti
> per favorir questa stella diana
> che nde fa consumar la nott'e 'l di.
> Fande, te prieg', Amor, zusta rason
> e traghe nella panza un vereton.

Who will lend a good voice to our solfa, that we may sing for you a pleasant song. I pray you, Love, help us to begin in a sweet tone and most melodiously; but of sharpening a B don't give a thought, for we can do no more than sing B flat.

Doh ray me fah soh lah, lah soh fah me, as well as sesquialtera in a triplet. Let's go on, brothers, singing trills and runs, to honour she who is our morning star, because of whom we are burnt out day and night. I pray you, Love, to do us justice by throwing in her belly a huge dart.

---

[56]   *Il primo libro delle justiniane a tre voci di diversi eccellentissimi musici* (Vincenzo Bell'haver, Francesco Bonardo, Donato Baldissera, Andrea Gabrieli, Claudio Merulo and Gasparo Vinciguerra). The collection, like many others, is varied in content, and the example chosen by Einstein, *The Italian Madrigal*, III, note 60, is not very representative. It contains a beggars' masquerade, and some of the *justiniane* are also masquerades of three old men, while others are individual expressions of love, and therefore suited to the character of Pantalone (they belong to the type of the *strambotto*). A couple are *zorziane*, i.e. songs of a youthful, vain and empty-headed character, and are also suited to appearing in comedies.

[57]   Alfonso d'Avalos' original text was made famous by the music for four voices by Cipriano de Rore, published as early as 1547.

103

Ex. XX   Andrea Gabrieli. Start of a five-voice *greghesca*. From *Di Manoli Blessi il primo libro delle greghesche con la musicha disopra, composta da diversi autori* (A. Gardano, Venice 1564).

Molino's case was similar. None of his comedies survive, so we do not know how often they featured the part of the swaggering *stratioto*, a local version of the *landsknecht* or the Spanish captain who appear in non-Venetian comedies. (The *stratioti* were Albanian mercenaries in the service of the Venetian republic.) But we have his mock-heroic poem *in lingua greghesca* (in the jargon of the 'Greeks'), *I fatti, e le prodezze di Manoli Blessi, Strathioto*, which was published in Venice in 1561. In turn, the hero of this poem appears as the supposed author of the texts in the collection *Di Manoli Blessi il primo libro delle greghesche con la musicha disopra, composta da diversi autori* (Venice 1564). Also by Manoli Blessi, which can only have been a pseudonym for Molino,[58]

---

[58]   Einstein, *The Italian Madrigal*, p. 528, notes that Manoli is an anagram of Molino (more or less), and prints its joking dedication. But the best confirmation is the dedication of the 1571 edition of *Greghesche e iustiniane di Andrea Gabrieli a tre voci*.

is the dedication 'To the most excellent musicians Messer Paulo Vergerio, M. Claudio da Currezo [Claudio Merulo], M. Francesco Bunardi', all of whom are represented in the collection, along with many others, including Willaert and Rore. The most heavily represented of them is Andrea Gabrieli:[59] the beginning of one of his pieces gives some idea of the musical style of this collection (see example XX).

Let it be clear that neither these pieces, nor any of the 1570 *justiniane*, nor any of the 1571 *Greghesche et iustiniane di Andrea Gabrieli a tre voci*, may, except in two or three cases, have been those sung by Calmo or Molino in their respective stage roles.[60] These are simply reflections of the originals either in

<hr />

[59] With seven pieces, while the others have one or two each, and only Annibale Padovano has three.

[60] The three-voice compositions would better lend themselves to such use, but Gabrieli claimed they were his, and there is no reason to doubt him.

the form of a masquerade or of an idealized musical evocation of picturesque figures and songs which had been so vivid and successful on stage that they had exerted a strong appeal on the imaginations of the most famous musicians in Venice.

Elsewhere, in Naples, something similar happened. There the viceroy Don Pedro di Toledo, though he ruled the city with an iron fist in the name of Charles V, nevertheless favoured a resumption of those literary and artistic activities which the wars and troubles of the first three decades of the sixteenth century had either scattered or stifled. It is interesting that Ferrante Sanseverino,[61] Prince of Salerno and nephew of the Count of Cajazzo and of Fracasso Sanseverino, was particularly influential in the 'attempt to promote in Naples a taste for the theatre and to develop it to the level it had reached in other Italian cities', for in their own day his uncles had promoted some of the first performances in the classical style to be given in Milan and Venice.[62] This makes it all the more interesting to see how he revived the idea of the civic function of the theatre, albeit only in the interests of popularity:

He was the first man in Naples to introduce the acting of comedies with most stately apparatus, which greatly increased the love of the *popolo* [i.e. the middle class] for him, for he took the trouble to stand, on the days when Comedies were performed, at the doors [of his palace] to permit the citizens to enter to view and hear them in comfort...[63]

The first theatrical enterprise of any importance by the prince was 'the beautiful comedy' which he sponsored in 1536 in honour of the emperor's visit to Naples.[64] He supported two further performances in 1540, *Calando* and *Beco*, for the marriage of Maria di Cardona, Marchioness of La Padula, with Francesco d'Este. The plays were performed by actors brought from Siena, whom he may also have employed in 1536.[65] We have already stressed the joyous propensity for music which was a characteristic of the Sienese theatre, so it will come as no surprise that the names of a good many musicians feature in the list of those who acted in the first comedy known to have been performed in Naples by local artists. The comedy was *Gli ingannati*, a Sienese comedy already referred to above. In the Neapolitan version of 1545, the parts of the two servants were played by the Neapolitan Luigi Dentice, the author of a celebrated music treatise, and by the Sienese Scipione delle Palle, famous for having later taught Giulio Caccini. Fabrizio Dentice, Luigi's son(?) and a composer of madrigals, played Pasquella, the

[61] Following the treaty of October 1505, his father regained his possessions and married Maria of Aragon. The prince 'by nature most generous...kept in his highly prosperous court men of letters, musicians, artists and men of arms'. Proud of his eminence amongst the nobles of the kingdom, he clashed with Viceroy di Toledo, left Naples in 1552 and was declared a rebel.
[62] See the previous chapter.
[63] Gio. Antonio Summonte, *Historia della città e regno di Napoli* (Naples 1675), IV, p. 235.
[64] Charles V reached Naples in November 1535 and remained there for the whole of the following carnival season. On 6 January the marriage was celebrated of Margaret of Austria 'daughter of the emperor, despite her tender age, with the Duke of Florence Alessandro dei Medici...On the morning of February 2, the day of Candlemas, the emperor ate at the home of the Prince of Salerno, where that evening came the noblest ladies and all the gentlewomen of Naples, and a splendid comedy was performed...The rest of the carnival passed in constant masquerades, entertainments, banquets, music, comedies, farces and other recreations' (from Gregorio Rosso, *Istoria delle cose di Napoli*, Naples 1770, pp. 66–70).
[65] Benedetto Croce, *I teatri di Napoli* (Bari 1926), pp. 21ff, assumed that they were Bibbiena's *La calandria* and Francesco Belo's *Beco*.

crafty and meddling elderly servant, the abbot Giovan Leonardo Salernitano (Giovan Leonardo dell'Arpa?) played one of the old men, and Giulio Cesare Brancaccio the lover Flaminio.[66] The historian Antonino Castaldo, who also took part in the performance and therefore had a particular interest in describing it, added that 'Zoppino, a famous and judicious musician of the time, was in charge of the choice of music, and also of the consort of instruments; wherefore was the Music truly heavenly, especially as Dentice with his falsetto and Brancaccio with his bass performed miracles'. The same source also records that 'the following year, 1546, another Comedy was acted, a work of Mariconda [who had also been involved in the 1545 production] known as "la Filenia", performed by almost all the same actors with excellent Music, which was a great success'. On this occasion Vincenzo da Venafro was in charge of the music, aided once again by 'the most divine signor Luigi Dentice'.[67]

Although the version of *Gli ingannati* printed in 1537 had already been full of hints for music, I think it obvious that many more pieces must have been inserted into the Neapolitan version in order to satisfy the talents of so many musicians. The 1537 text had left ample scope for such additions: a servant describes Gherardo in his dotage saying: '...now that he has been driven to such an amorous frenzy, he depilates and combs himself, walks about [the house of] his lady, goes at night to dancing parties armed with a curved knife, sing-songs all day long with a disgraceful, rattling voice to [the sound of] a bad lute even more out of tune than himself. And finally he has even become addicted to composing *fistole, sognetti, capogirli, strenfiotti, materiali* [i.e. epistles, sonnets, *capitoli, strambotti* and madrigals] and other jests by the thousand' (Act I scene 5).[68] There is no indication in the text that the parts of the servants or of Flaminio involved singing at all, and yet in Naples two of the most famous singers of the century were employed: Scipione delle Palle and the bass Brancaccio, the latter so well-known that he was even praised in a madrigal by Giovanbattista Guarini.[69] Nor can the songs for which there are directions in the text have been the same as those used in the original performances, or there would have been no need for a 'choice of Music'. Furthermore, although *Gli ingannati* is set in Modena, and was set there even

[66] *Dell'istoria di Notar Antonino Castaldo libri quattro* (Naples 1769), pp. 71–2. Luigi Dentice was the author of *Due dialoghi della musica* (Naples 1552). Fabrizio must still have been very young in 1545. G. Cesare Brancaccio, after an adventurous life, was still admired about 1580 as an amateur singer (*gentiluomo cantore*) at the court of Ferrara. I shall return to Scipione delle Palle, Caccini's master, in the chapter entitled 'The wondrous show, alas, of the *intermedi*!'. Giovan Leonardo dell'Arpa, if indeed it was him, was known primarily as a writer of *villanelle* in the Neapolitan style, and was still being praised as a lutenist by Count Fontanelli in 1594. A. Newcomb, 'The musica segreta of Ferrara in the 1580s', Ph.D. dissertation, Princeton University 1970, biographical appendix.

[67] The comedy is included in the collection *Commedie del Cinquecento*, ed. A. Borlenghi, vol. assumed that in 1546 the plays were performed by 'certain actors from Modena'. But the reference in the prologue of *Philenia*, which led Croce to alter its supposed date and to assume that a Modenese company had arrived in 1546, is in fact a reference to the performances of *Gli ingannati*, supposedly set in Modena.

[68] The comedy is included in the collection *Commedie del Cinquecento*, ed. A. Borlenghi, vol. I. The quotation is to be found on pp. 186 and 187.

[69] Entitled *Il basso del Brancazio*. Brancaccio is also mentioned in Vincenzo Giustiniani's *Discorso sopra la musica* (c. 1628). See Ercole Bottrigari, *Il desiderio*, and Vincenzo Giustiniani, *Discorso sopra la musica*, both transl. and ed. Carol MacClintock, American Institute of Musicology, 1962.

in the Neapolitan production,[70] I have a suspicion that, at least musically, the 1545 'Modena' was heavily Neapolitan. I have no idea whether the ironic anti-Spanish jibes which appear in the text published in Venice were left out or at least toned down, but I think it more likely that Pasquella (Fabrizio Dentice) taunted her Spaniard by singing derisive *napoletane*, and that the other characters might also have sung *villanelle alla napoletana*, especially Brancaccio and Giovan Leonardo Salernitano, if we are correct in assuming the latter to be the same person as dell'Arpa.[71]

Amongst the many signs of the revival of cultural activity in Naples, one occurrence is of some interest. This was the publication in 1537 of a small collection entitled *Canzoni villanesche alla napolitana...libro primo*.[72] It was never followed, it seems, by a *Libro secondo*; nevertheless it was the source of an abundant crop of *napoletane*, mainly published in Venice, to which not just Neapolitans but musicians from all over Italy and from beyond the Alps soon contributed. The anonymous and undedicated *Canzoni villanesche* of 1537 contain no indication as to who was responsible for having them printed, but their very anonymity implies that they were, or were intended to be taken for, popular pieces, a manifestation of 'that natural [musical] instinct with which', according to a contemporary description of the beauties of Naples and its traditions, 'it seems that heaven has endowed every Neapolitan spirit, so that, as everyone supplements nature with art, divers harmonies, both vocal and instrumental, of an exquisite sweetness are heard both day and night in a variety of places'.[73] Many subsequent *napoletane* were published under the author's name, though they might still have incorporated popular melodies of their day. Such an idea seems to me to be supported by a request to the senate of Milan, put forward in 1559 by the Neapolitan Massimo Troiano. He asked to be granted privilege to publish some songs 'in the dialect and musical harmony of Naples' which he had 'written down bringing them to fit the rules of music'.[74] The songs were probably those pieces which were later reprinted in Venice in 1568 by Girolamo Scotto.[75]

Also dating from 1568 is an account – not a *scenario* – of *La cortigiana innamorata*, a comedy performed with improvised dialogue at the court of Monaco and based on a plot conceived by Troiano. Orlando di Lasso, who

---

[70]   See note 67.

[71]   Croce, in *I teatri di Napoli*, p. 26, mentioned Giovan Leonardo dell'Arpa, along with Scipione delle Palle, the Spaniard Cornelius who sang in the viceregal chapel, and one Phomia (madonna Eufemia) as being amongst the performers in the *intermedi* of Alessandro Piccolomini's *Alessandro*, put on in 1558 at the wish of the Marquis of Vasto.

[72]   This is the first known example of an Italian musical edition printed with movable type 'Printed in Naples by Joanne de Colonia on the 23 October 1537'. Donna G. Cardamone, 'The Debut of the "Canzone villanesca alla napolitana"', *Studi musicali*, IV, 1975, pp. 65–130.

[73]   Benedetto di Falco, *Descrittione dei luoghi antichi di Napoli e del suo amenissimo distretto* (Naples n.d. – but c. 1535). For further testimony see Donna G. Cardamone, 'The "Canzone villanesca alla napolitana" and related Italian Vocal Part-Music'. Ph. D. dissertation, Harvard University, 1972, pp. 354–7.

[74]   'Maximus Troianus neapolitanus musicus, in aula Ill. Ducis Suessae in provincia Mediolanensis Gubernatoris multum acceptus, cum quasdam cantiones neapolitano idiomate et concentu scriptas in artem musicam redegisset et edere vellet, ne suis laboribus et sumptibus frauderetur, petit a nostro Senatu Mediolanensi facultatem, et privilegium sibi concedi' etc, from Mariangela Donà, *La stampa musicale a Milano fino all'anno 1700* (Florence 1961), p. 127.

[75]   *Di Massimo Troiano di Corduba da Napoli il primo et secondo libro delle canzoni alla napolitana* (Venice 1568). The absence of a dedication indicates that it was a reprint.

during his youthful stay in Italy had spent some time in Naples in 1549–50 and taken part in the activities of the Accademia dei Sereni,[76] played the part of the 'magnificent Messer Pantalone di Bisognosi...with a long jacket of crimson satin, Venetian-style scarlet hose and a black gown down to the floor, a mask the sight of which forced everyone to laugh, and carrying a lute, playing and singing':

> Chi passa per questa strada e non sospira,
> beato se...

Blessed is he who can walk this street without a sigh...

Troiano played three parts: 'the prologue as a rustic fool, the lover, Polidoro, and the despairing Spaniard'. His account is couched in dialogue form, and informs us that the prologue was 'a country bumpkin, from Cava dei Tirreni [near Naples] so clumsily dressed that he seemed the ambassador of the country of laughter'.[77] The other parts were taken by a variety of people, amongst whom was a young musician named Ercole Terzo, who played the part of the courtesan's servant, probably an old woman.[78] Alfred Einstein inaccurately defined *La cortigiana innamorata* as 'a sort of madrigalistic comedy': it was rather a comedy performed by amateurs in the style of the *comici dell'arte*,[79] and like the latter's plays was divided into three instead of five acts, though its *intermedi* were more suited to a court than to the halls used by the professional comic actors. The only song specifically mentioned in the plot was Pantalone's song, sung and played by Orlando di Lasso,[80] and there was music at the end of the play because 'Camilla [the courtesan] was wedded to Zanne [Pantalone's servant], and in honour of this marriage they performed a *ballo* in the Italian style.' Yet I cannot imagine that, either as a rustic from Cava or as a lover, Troiano refrained from singing *napoletane*, ironic in tone, like the one blandishing an old bawd in the 1537 *Canzoni villanesche* (see example XXI). As a despairing Spaniard he might have sung

---

[76]   Horst Leuchtmann, *Orlando di Lasso* (Wiesbaden 1976), pp. 45–6, 86–7 and 92–3.

[77]   From *Discorsi delli triomfi...nell'anno 1568 a' 22 di febraro* (Munich 1568) in which Troiano maintained that the comedy was put on at only a day's notice. The quotation is taken from Enzo Petraccone, *La commedia dell'arte* (Naples 1927), pp. 297ff.

[78]   K. M. Lea, *Italian Popular Comedy* (New York 1962), p. 27, pointed out that Battista Scolari of Trent, who played Zanne, was a goldsmith. The part of Camilla was taken by the Marquis Malaspina. Ercole Terzo is mentioned in the 1568 account-books of the court of Munich as 'Lucio geigers sonn' and from 1659 onwards as 'Hercules', often qualified as 'trombonist'; his full name, 'Hercole Tertzio' is listed amongst the names of the trombonists in 1577. Simon Gatto, whose name does not figure amongst those of the actors but who received payment for the comedy, was also an instrumentalist.

[79]   The *intermedi* were: after the prologue 'a sweet madrigal à 5'; after the first act 'a piece for five *viole da gamba* and an equal number of voices'; after the second act 'a piece for four voices, with two lutes, a keyboard instrument (*uno strumento da penna*), a fife and a bass *viola da gamba*'. For a more precise view on the nature of *commedia madrigalesca* see below pp. 115ff.

[80]   The song had already been identified (Jeppesen, 405–6). A more elaborate version is to be found in F. Azzaiolo, *Il primo libro de villotte alla padoana con alcune napolitane a quatro voci* (Venice 1557), and it is also quoted in A. Striggio's 'Serenata' (part I, à 5) in his *Primo libro de madrigali à sei voci* (Venice 1560), itself not a first edition. Several versions for lute, sometimes in the rhythm of galliards, pavans, *passamezzi* or *saltarelli* show that it was internationally famous: see H. M. Brown, *Instrumental Music before 1600. A Bibliography* (Cambridge, Mass. 1967), *passim*. For the early seventeenth century, see J. M. Ward, 'Apropos the British Broadside Ballad and its Music', in *Journal of the American Musicological Society*, XX (1967), p. 34. Jeppesen, 405, gives the *cantus* of Azzaiolo's version, whereas I feel that the tenor line is in fact closer to the popular melody.

Ex. XXI *O vecchia, tu che guardi.* From *Canzoni villanesche alla napolitana novamente stampate. Libro primo* (Joanne de Colonia, Naples 1537). The bass part is missing in the only known copy.

the 'Aria alla spagnola a quattro voci' *O passos esparzidos* (adapted for soloist with the accompaniment of a stringed instrument), a piece listed on the frontispiece itself of the fourth book of his *Rime, & canzoni alla napolitana a tre voci* (Venice 1569). Its text, a translation of Petrarch's sonnet *O passi sparsi*, may have resulted in a very apt caricature when it was sung in honour of a courtesan besieged by many lovers but finally married to the servant Zanne.

Literary echoes, and even Petrarchisms, are not uncommon in the texts of the *villanelle alla napoletana*: in the 1537 collection one which begins in pure Tuscan style *Dove nascesti, o viso angelicato?* stands alongside the colourful dialect of *Voccuccia de no pierzeco apreturo, / musillo de na fico lattarola*. However, I do not believe that these echoes of literary preciosity were intended to be parodies, just as I have opposed for several years the interpretation that the famous parallel fifths so frequent in the *napoletane* were intended to mock the rules of counterpoint and the refined polyphony of the madrigal.[81] As far as the texts are concerned – and I am speaking here specifically of the truly dialectal ones, not those used later when the *napoletana* had become a genre imitated by non-Neapolitans – there was nothing rustic about the *villanesco*. It was popular poetry of the city; and Naples in its long history as a capital had seen and heard plenty of illustrious troubadours. And as for the music, I see those fifths not as an irreverent mockery of Messer Adriano or of his pupil Zarlino, but as an attempt at reproducing by a madrigalian type of polyphony the harmonic procedures and the techniques of instrumental accompaniment of popular singers, so closely interrelated as to form a

[81] In the article 'Tragédie et comédie dans la Camerata Fiorentina', in *Musique et poésie au XVIe siècle* (Paris 1954), p. 202. On its first flowering see D. G. Cardamone, 'The "Canzone villanesca alla napolitana"', as well as the same author's 'The Debut of the "Canzone villanesca alla napolitana"' in *Studi musicali*, IV, pp. 65–130. See also *Studi musicali*, IX (1980), pp. 191–217.

Ex. XXII   Giovanni Tommaso di Maio. *Napoletana*. From *Canzon vilanesche di Giovan Thomaso di Maio Musico napoletano Libro primo A tre voci* (A. Gardane, Venice 1546).

characteristic musical language of their own. The fifths were already an important part of the *napoletana* reproduced above. But, lest anyone be tempted to think that they were simply a result of my handling of the tenor part, missing in that first anonymous example, here is another example, on a capriciously picturesque text. It is entirely authentic, and undoubtedly by a Neapolitan composer (example XXII).

Even in their original form of solo songs with instrumental accompaniments, the *napolitane* were certainly no more than an evocative reflection of popular songs, themselves accompanied on the *cetola* or the *colascione*, just as all the polyphonic elaborations which we have studied have been reflections. This taste for picturesque musical evocation becomes even more marked in the *moresche* (a familiar term put to new use to designate comic snatches of dialogue in the jargon of the Moorish slaves), published several times, generally anonymously, though one *moresca* was attributed to Orlando di Lasso,[82] in a 1562 edition. A *moresca* was also included in the *Libro terzo* (Venice 1567) of Massimo Troiano's *napoletane*, together with a *Battaglia de la gatta e la cornacchia* and an *Amascherata alla turchesca*. In the same year there appeared in print *Il cicalamento delle donne al bucato et la Caccia* by Alessandro Striggio (Venice 1567) to which the 1569 reprint also added a *Gioco di primiera*. As Alfred Einstein rightly stated, *Il cicalamento* was 'a musical *divertimento*, not a precursor of musical drama'.[83] It contains elements of dialogue, but the musician followed their thread only to the extent that was needed to create the impression in the mind of the listeners of voices one on top of the other, of a turmoil of exclamations, of an overall picture of brawls and reconciliations. In view of the general thesis of this chapter, it is interesting to note that every so often snatches of songs are interpolated into the various chatterings of the housewives. One of these insertions enables us to reconstruct the tune of a song which had been used several decades earlier in a comedy:[84] *Che fa lo mio amore che non viene?* (example XXIII).

Amongst the scenes evoked, which include those of the quarrelling washerwomen, a game of cards, and a hunt, there is also an evocation of the theatre in one of its most characteristic and picturesque aspects: the dialogue between Zanni and Pantalone is dealt with in an eight-voice (!) version by Orlando di Lasso, published in Paris in 1581, and in a version by Johannes Eccard, presumed to be a pupil of Lasso, which appeared in his *Newe Lieder*, published in Königsberg in 1589.[85] More than ever, since the pieces were being aimed at foreign audiences, the words spoken in the dialogue were in themselves unimportant, a mere pretext for the impressionistic effect of a variety of voices superimposed and intertwined, Zanni's squeaking falsetto against the menacing or exasperated tones of Pantalone's grumbling bass. To round up the impressionistic evocation, Eccard added a third sound floating in mid-air between the other two, a snatch of a tune given to the quinto part, repeated many times at different pitches, *E la bella Franceschina, ninina, bufina, la filibustachina*.[86] The stage is thus set for Orazio Vecchi's *L'Amfiparnaso*

[82]   Einstein, *The Italian Madrigal*, I, p. 373, casts doubt upon this attribution.

[83]   *Ibid.*, II, p. 766. On the following page Einstein goes so far as to call a *romanesca* the popular song quoted below.

[84]   Already recalled in connection with the Intronati di Siena's anonymous comedy *Gli ingannati*, and a short story by the Sienese Pietro Fortini (cf. note 16 above). It is worth remembering that Virginia Vagnoli, Striggio's wife, was Sienese.

[85]   See J. Eccard, *Newe geistliche und weltliche Lieder...Königsberg 1589*, ed. R. Eitner ('Publikationen älterer...Musikwerke' vol. XXI, Leipzig 1897), pp. 95–7. It is to be noticed that Eccard, by repeating the tune at different pitch levels, gives it each time in a different mode.

[86]   Jeppesen, 333–4, gives two versions which differ from Eccard's. The second is the instrumental dance in the Venice MS, Biblioteca Marciana, Ital. IV.1227. Jeppesen also refers the reader to his own edition of *Balli antichi veneziani per cembalo* (Copenhagen 1962), no. 2. The Marciana manuscript was also known to F. Torrefranca, who frequently referred to the song in *Il segreto del Quattrocento*. In a lecture held on 7 May 1953 at the Accademia Nazionale di

Ex. XXIII   Alessandro Striggio. Fragment from *Il cicalamento delle donne al bucato* (G. Scotto, Venice 1567). Only the cantus and bass are given.

Santa Cecilia in Rome, he also reported that Annibale Caro had heard it as far afield as Belgium; indeed, A. Caro, *Lettere familiari*, ed. A. Greco (Florence 1957), I, p. 311, refers to 'concerts of bells' in a letter from Brussels dated 29 October 1544, and immediately adds 'Your Excellency [Pierluigi Farnese] must not laugh at me for noting this music, for in this country the bells even play *la bella Franceschina*.' Also of interest in the letter is the description of a masquerade of Amazons in which Ottavio Farnese took part: the celebrations were to mark the arrival in Brussels of the daughter of Charles V who was to marry the Duke of Orléans, to seal the peace of Crespy.

comedia harmonica (Venice 1597, but performed prior to publication). Set, that is, figuratively speaking, for as the prologue says:

> ...la città dove si rappresenta
> quest'opra, è 'l gran Theatro
> del mondo, perch'ognun desia d'udirla:
> Ma voi sappiat' intanto,
> che questo di cui parlo
> spettacolo, si mira con la mente,
> dov'entra per l'orecchie, e non per gl'occhi...

...the stage of this play is not a city, it is the greatest Theatre, the World, for everyone would like to attend. Meanwhile you should take notice that the spectacle I am talking about is only seen in your minds, which are reached through your ears, not through your eyes...

For a moment Vecchi takes seriously his task as a dramatist, and in the discourse 'To the Readers' holds forth on the comedy which 'as a mirror of human life aims no less at being useful than pleasing, and not merely at moving to laughter, as perhaps some people may think this musical comedy of mine is going to do'. Nevertheless, he immediately goes on to admit that 'the plot is briefer than it should be, for as plain speech is more rapid than singing combined with words, so it was not good to go into certain details of the fable'. Even this was more of an excuse than a reason, for the need to keep the text brief did not prevent Vecchi from repeating phrases purely for the musical effect. Much nearer the mark is the passage in which he adds:

But whoever should desire more in this plot, let him relate everything he finds missing to the premises which have been implied though not actually expressed, for in this way he will create a complete fable in his own mind...Thus I shall treat in full some parts of this Harmonic Comedy of mine, those which are necessary, others I shall treat more briefly, and merely hint at others.

In other words, what he intended to do was not to develop a comedy in an orderly fashion, but to evoke in the minds of his spectators the vision of a comedy being performed. In the brief passages of dialogue, too, there is sometimes some hint of an attempt to identify each character with a different grouping of voices, but the attempt is soon abandoned, since what primarily interested the composer was the musical development of his ideas. Most coherently developed as individual pieces are the lyrical outpourings of the serious characters, which are expressed as fully fledged madrigals for five voices, though climactic passages of dialogue are at times also expressed in a similar madrigalian style, as is the case of the dialogue in which Frulla reveals to the despairing Isabella that Lucio is not dead (example XXIV).

We have already been acquainted with parodies of Cipriano de Rore's madrigal *Ancor che col partire*; here it becomes

> Anchor ch'al parturire   l'acqua vita m'ha pist'e pur ai torne.
> al se stenta a murire,   E così mille mele al far del zorne
> patir vurrei ꞁ'hor senza tormiente.   padir agn'hor vurrei,
> Tant'è 'l piaser Vincenze   tanto son dolci i Storni ai denti miei.

> Although all births are as trying as death I should like my departure to be without pain...

Ex. XXIV Orazio Vecchi. Fragment of Frulla's narrative. From *L'Amfiparnaso comedia harmonica* (A. Gardano, Venice 1597). Act II scene 5.

It is sung by Doctor Graziano, invited by Pantalone ('Cantè su un pochetin / un Madregaletin') after the latter has granted him the hand of Isabella. The woodcut which precedes the four-voice madrigal (see plate 23) shows the doctor playing the lute beneath the window of his beloved, while Pantalone and Francatrippa stand to one side. This provides yet further pictorial evidence of realistic insertions in comedies. But although it would not have been impossible for the music to be arranged for voice and lute, it was not intended to be performed like that, for that would have dulled the point of the joke. The composer in fact preserved intact the upper part of Rore's piece, and beneath it developed a different and highly personal madrigalian counterpoint.

The same author's *Il convito musicale* is no more a banquet than *L'amfiparnaso* is a real comedy. Instead of food, his 'banquet' offers the musical *entremets* which we have already learnt to recognize as the forerunners of theatrical *intermedi*. The comedy, *L'Amfiparnaso*, was the author's excuse for a series of genre vignettes, some picturesque, some caricatures, some sentimental, all bearing witness to the author's flexible inventiveness. While Vecchi was careful to refrain from using the same pretext twice, as starting point for his inventions, one of his admirers and imitators, Banchieri, was less discreet. At least three times he attempted to reunite the two Parnassus – more than three times if one bears in mind that some of his so-called 'madrigal comedies' were each issued several times, on each occasion with alterations, additions and omissions. An eager polygraph, as well as a musical composer, performer and theoretician, Banchieri also wrote, under the pseudonym of Camillo Scaligeri della Fratta, a whole series of comedies, in a mixture of languages and dialects, with associated *intermedi*, at times 'visible', at times 'invisible'. He therefore knew all that he needed to about comedy, but in his musical comedies he worked even more schematically than Orazio Vecchi, and actually his plots, characters and situations are merely slight variations on those of *L'Amfiparnaso*. At most, the roles of the two old men are at times reversed: instead of allowing his daughter to marry Doctor Graziano, Pantalone himself becomes the luckless hopeful suitor. However, most important of all, especially for the *intermedi*, of which there were none in *L'Amfiparnaso*, but which here played an important part, is the fact that the comedy is each time set somewhere new; this allows the author to vary the local colour and to have the masquerades refer to different characteristic trades. If you like, *La pazzia senile* (1598), *Il metamorfosi musicale* (1600) and *La saviezza giovanile* (1608) were three different performances of the same *scenario*, altered on each occasion to include a different dialogue, different retorts and different musical *lazzi*. But these pseudo-comedies do provide confirmation of which occasions were held to be most suited to the use of music in comedies. Music was used realistically in the course of the action, with songs, serenades and dances as required by, or at any rate compatible with, its development. In addition it served a formal purpose in the *intermedi*, though these were also linked, after a fashion, to the main action when they consisted of trade masquerades or of characters typical of the urban life of the place where the plot was supposed to unfold. Both *L'Amfiparnaso* and Banchieri's comedies also hint, albeit vaguely, at the possibility that musical pieces might have been inserted in love dialogues or soliloquies contributing to give them some kind of formal organization; if such pieces really were used in comedy, in the same way as verse *chiusette* appear to have been used at the end of emotional speeches in the *commedia dell'arte*, then they must surely have made easier the acceptance, later on, of the convention of set pieces, be they called *ariette* or *scherzi*, interrupting the flow of the operatic recitative.

One final point is made by Banchieri: he did not follow the model of *L'Amfiparnaso* and use the normal madrigal group of five voices. Not only did he persist in each of his comedies in writing for only three voices, he even went so far as to rewrite his model in the same texture. This he did in the *Studio dilettevole fiorito dall' Amfiparnaso* (Milan 1600), which he listed amongst his own works as the *Libro terzo delle canzonette a 3 voci*. Only the *Libro primo* of the series is made up of simple *canzonette* (amongst them a *napolitana*, a *villotta* and a *villanella*, a masquerade and a *balletto*). *La pazzia senile* in its various editions is always listed as the *Libro secondo*, *Il metamorfosi musicale* appears as the *Libro quarto*, and *La saviezza giovanile* as the *Quinto libro degli terzetti*. It is obvious that Banchieri was aware of a tradition which linked comedy music to the tuneful and graceful genre of the *villotta–villanesca–villanella–canzonetta*.

4 Temporal perspective and music

I do not know whether any special meaning has ever been attached to the vignettes on the title pages of the two earliest editions of *La comedia di Callimaco: & di Lucrezia* (i.e. of Niccolò Machiavelli's *La mandragola*).[1] They both represent a character playing a Renaissance lyre with a bow, like the one played by Orpheus in Poliziano's 'fable'. The first of these editions was certainly printed in Florence, but bears no typographical notes; nevertheless Roberto Ridolfi, who is convinced that the comedy was first performed during the carnival of 1518, assigns it to that same year. In it, the lyre-player is a centaur, undoubtedly wise Chiron.[2] In the second edition, printed in Venice in 1522 by Alessandro Bindoni, the lyre-player is Homer, blind and left-handed.[3] This second edition is based on the previous one, and may have followed the lead of the earlier illustration for no other specific reason. But the possibility exists that the image on the title page of the first edition reflects the way in which the comedy had initially been presented to an audience.

An introduction by a character singing on a lyre occurs in other Florentine plays of the time. The most telling example is in a *Farsa recitata agli Excelsi Signori di Firenze*, printed without a date but certainly pre-1512, where it is said that 'instead of a Prologue, Proem and Argument one [man] with a lyre recites'. (What he recites is a long series of octaves described by D'Ancona as 'a rambling sermon on the vanity of human desires'.)[4] In two other comedies the luxury of a song 'on the lyre' did not imply giving up either prologue or argument. Iacopo Nardi's *La comedia di amicitia*, almost certainly given in 1512,[5] ends with a comment: 'The stanzas noted below were sung

[1] On this title see Roberto Ridolfi, 'Composizione, rappresentazione e prima edizione della Mandragola', in *La bibliofilia*, LXIV (1962), pp. 285–300, as well as his introduction to Niccolò Machiavelli, *La mandragola per la prima volta restituita alla sua integrità* (Florence 1965), pp. 17–18. Both works were published with additions and some alterations in R. Ridolfi, *Studi sulle commedie del Machiavelli* (Pisa 1968).

[2] Reproduced in both the works referred to above.

[3] Reproduced in Machiavelli, *La mandragola*, edn cit., p. 21 and in Ridolfi, *Studi sulle commedie del Machiavelli*, p. 53. But my colleague H. C. Slim has drawn my attention to the fact that we are dealing with a drawing which recurred in various roughly contemporary prints, though not always produced from the same matrix; see, for example, the two figures reproduced in *La bibliofilia*, X (1908–9), p. 429. I may be wrong in believing the player to be Homer, though there is no doubt that the image is reversed, since he is holding his bow in his left hand. What is significant though, is that the one element in common with the vignette of the first edition is that a lyre is being played, especially, as Ridolfi showed in *Studi*, p. 56, as 'the Venetian edition does not merely depend on the first edition for its text, but is a real...typographical copy of it...page by page, line by line'.

[4] D'Ancona, *Le origini*, II, pp. 37ff.

[5] No place-name or date are given, but it was certainly printed in Florence, and is preceded by a Latin dedication to Lorenzo di Filippo Strozzi. I suggest it was performed in 1512, despite the reservations expressed by Sanesi, *La commedia*, I, p. 470, because of an invocation in the

on the lyre in the presence of the Signoria when the above comedy was recited.' It is unlikely, however, that the stanzas – four octaves paying homage to the 'high, holy and noble See' – were recited at the end of the play, where they appear in the edition, for by then the audience would have been impatient to leave the place of the performance. Like the octaves of the *Farsa*, they must have formed part of the preliminaries of the entertainment. We can assume the same of *I due felici rivali*, also by Nardi, performed on 17 February 1513. By then, the political situation was markedly different, so that 'the comedy was performed in the presence of the Most Revered Lords Giuliano and Lorenzo dei Medici'.[6] Accordingly, eloquent homage was paid to the newly ascendant Medicean constellation.

The stanzas which were then 'sung on the lyre [by one actor] impersonating the poet Orpheus returning from the Elysian fields' begin as follows:

> Dal loco della eterna primavera,
> che nel suo sen le felici alme accoglie,
> gode tra l'altre una honorata schiera,
> libera hormai dalle terrestri spoglie,
> di sé contenta, e di sue opera altera,
> a l'ombra delle verdi e sacre foglie;
> qual m'ha commesso che io demonstri, e vuole,
> la mente sua con mie roze parole.

From the site of eternal spring I come. There, where all the blessed spirits are assembled, an honoured host rejoices among the others. Free at last of their terrestrial bodies, they take pride in themselves and in their works under the shadow of the sacred green leaves [of the laurel]; they have sent me and asked me to speak their mind with simple words.

Instead of Orpheus, any other poet might have been called upon 'to speak their mind': Homer, Ovid, or Virgil. Though not a poet, even the wise centaur Chiron might have been called upon to perform this task. Whoever was selected was to add joy to a day 'on which the feats of the ancients' were once more 'displayed and celebrated'. The words I use here are the same as those used in the *canzone* which precedes the beginning of Machiavelli's *Clizia*.

Machiavelli took over the idea and used it in the carnival of 1525 to introduce *Clizia* to his friends and an eager audience crowding the garden of Jacopo di Filippo Falconetti, called 'il Fornaciaio'. However, the task of mediating between the audience and the fictitious world of play (an almost

prologue which already heralds the imminent restoration of the Medici: 'Ma sia chi a me insegni/in questa nostra etate/Augusto o Mecenate/il qual conforti e sproni' ('But let there be someone who points out to me in this modern age some Augustus or Maecenas to encourage and spur on'). The octaves sung to the *lira* reply auguring a future in which 'the sky having assumed a happier aspect,/the Golden Age shall be renewed on earth,' (see the following note). By comparing the prologue of *L'amicitia* with that of the *Commedia di Justitia* by Eufrosino Bonini (Fortunato Pintor, 'Una commedia politica per la restaurazione medicea del 1512', in *Dai tempi antichi ai tempi moderni*, Milan 1904, for the Scherillo–Negri marriage, pp. 404–5), it would appear that Bonini clearly remembered *L'amicitia*.

6   Alessandro Ferraioli, *I due felici rivali. Commedia inedita di Jacopo Nardi* (Rome 1901) (for the Pizzarini–Sterbini marriage), p. 71. Vasari mentions Nardi as the inventor of the six *Trionfi* performed for the same carnival of 1513 by the Broncone company, whose leader was Lorenzo dei Medici. The last of the *Trionfi* was of the Golden Age. The comedy is to be found in the Vatican MS Barberini XLV, 5, dedicatory copy offered to G. Battista della Palla. In the dedication it is described as 'Laurentii Medicis auspicis acta'.

spiritualistic conjuring job) was no longer given to a single character but to a group made up of one nymph and three shepherds, 'blessed spirits' belonging to another 'honoured host', that of the Arcadians:

Quanto sia lieto il giorno
nel qual le cose antiche
son hor da voi dimostre et celebrate,
si vede perch'intorno
tutte le genti amiche
si sono in questa parte ragunate.
Noi che la nostra etate
nei boschi e nelle selve consumiamo,
venuti anchor nui siamo
– io ninfa – e noi pastori –
e giam cantand'insieme i nostri amori.

Chiari giorni e quieti,
felice e bel paese
dove del nostro canto il suon s'udia!
Pertanto, allegri e lieti,
a queste vostre imprese
farem col cantar nostro compagnia
con sì dolce armonia
qual mai sentita più non fu da voi:
e partiremci poi
– io ninfa – e noi pastori –
e torneremci ai nostri antichi amori.

How joyful is this day, on which the feats of the ancients are now by you displayed and celebrated, can be seen from the friends who have assembled here from all around. We too, who spend our lives in the groves and the woods, we too have come to join – I, a nymph, and shepherds we – singing together the story of our loves.

Bright and quiet were the days, happy and beautiful the land in which the sound of our song used to be heard! Happy and cheerful, therefore, we shall unite our singing to your present endeavour, with a harmony so sweet you have never heard the like of it before. And then we shall depart – I, a nymph, and shepherds we – and shall return to our timeless loves.

'You have never heard the like of it before' was no empty boast. The music of the *canzone* has been identified and partially published by Alfred Einstein from *Il primo libro de madrigali di Verdelotto*.[7] The music in this collection was still a novelty when engraved by Andrea Antico and published in Venice eight years after the first performance of *Clizia*. In 1525 there was even more cause for the five 'madrigals' – one before the prologue and one after each of the first four acts – to be regarded as a novelty.[8] Not only was the madrigal genre

[7]   *The Italian Madrigal*, I, pp. 250–1, and by Osthoff, *Theatergesang*, II, p. 65.
[8]   The use of madrigals as *intermedi* was a novelty compared with the *intermedi* performed in 1518 with Lorenzo di Filippo Strozzi's first comedy (it is now accepted that this was the *Commedia senza nome* formerly attributed to Machiavelli). The earlier ones too were described as new in the account given in an incomplete biography of the author which precedes L. Strozzi, *Le vite degli uomini illustri della casa Strozzi*, ed. P. Stromboli (Florence 1892), p. xiii: '...having provided divers instruments from various places, he divided them in this fashion: that before the Comedy the full-bodied sounds (*i suoni grossi*) should begin, such as trumpets, cornemuses, fifes, that they might stir up the souls of the audience; he had the second act introduced by three

itself then new, but it was probably also the first time it was used in the performance of a comedy: I know no example of such a use prior to that of *Clizia*.

For this reason I cannot bring myself to agree with a highly respected Machiavelli scholar who, having set out to publish his handsome edition of *La mandragola* 'restored for the first time to its integrity', felt obliged for the sake of that integrity to confine to an appendix the '*canzoni* written for the performance in Faenza',[9] with which I shall soon deal in more detail. From the strictly philological point of view (the eternal nostalgia for an Urtext!) he was quite justified in doing this, for the *canzoni* are not present in the manuscript text dated 1519 on which his edition is based, neither do they feature in any of the early printed editions nor in the more recent ones up to 1782–3.[10] But if we are interested in *La mandragola* in all its theatrical aspects, then it is hard to dismiss what he calls 'a superstructure, incidentally added, and for one performance alone, for the sake of the beautiful Barbera, who was to have sung them [the *canzoni*]'.[11] After all, *intermedi* of some kind were always necessary, indeed as necesary as a stage setting,[12] for the

richly-attired Moors with three lutes, who in the silence sweetly delighted each listener; in the third, soprano voices sang to four *violoni*, rising according to the requirements of the comedy. To the clamouring tumult of the fourth act he set the shrillest quilled instruments; and the last music was of four trombones which artfully and sweetly modulated their voices. Such kinds of music have since been imitated several times, but previously they had not been used, nor even considered.' The biographer, Filippo Zeffi, was tutor to the two sons of Filippo Strozzi the younger. It was to the younger of his two pupils that he addressed his unfinished *Ragionamento*, recalling their participation in the performance and how they were praised: he was obviously an eye-witness. The novelty to which he refers may have lain in the fact that at least some of Strozzi's five *intermedi* were 'visible' (the one preceding Act II certainly was, and the next one too, probably). Their being linked to the main plot may also have been new: the singing 'according to the requirements of the Comedy' in Act III, the instruments set to 'the clamouring tumult of the fourth act', the 'sweet' sound of the trombones (which we will find often associated with the darkness of night) in Act V. Zeffi (*ibid.*, pp. xiii–xiv) reports that Lorenzo 'took great delight in the music, and in the singing played his role with such great charm that at times he appeared lascivious, especially when bestowing his love to the sound of the lute'. He had been taught by the composer of polyphonic music, Baccio degli Organi (F. D'Accone, 'Alessandro Coppini and Bartolomeo degli Organi', in *Analecta musicologica*, 4, pp. 38ff), but, though younger than Poliziano, he belonged to a generation still fond of expressive singing to the lute.

[9]   This is the edition referred to in note 1; the *canzoni* are to be found on pp. 195–9 and were written for a performance intended to be presented in Faenza, but which in the event never took place.

[10]   The edition is based on the text found by Ridolfi in the Laurentian MS Rediano 129 (see the table of contents appended to E. Pasquini, 'Una bucolica anonima del primo Cinquecento' in *Giornale storico della letteratura italiana*, 144 (1967), pp. 224–31) which does not seem to depend on the printed editions. The *canzoni* appeared for the first time in 1782–3 in Cambiagi's edition; Ridolfi believes that they were taken from the papers of Guicciardini, which were at that time broken up by his heirs.

[11]   Ridolfi, introduction to Machiavelli, *La mandragola*, edn cit., p. 47; on the following page he adds: 'I am quite sure that had the author lived long enough to still be able to present and publish the comedy, he would have abandoned that ephemeral structure.' The fact remains, however, that music too was composed for at least one of the new texts.

[12]   On the apparatus for *La mandragola*, see, in the periodical directed by Ridolfi, the long and interesting, albeit unconvincing, article by Alessandro Parronchi, 'La prima rappresentazione della "Mandragola". Il modello dell' apparato. L'allegoria', in *La bibliofilia*, LXIV (1962), pp. 37–86. Parronchi's thesis on the first performance is that *La mandragola* was the first of three comedies to be performed, in September 1518, to celebrate the arrival in Florence of Lorenzo dei Medici the Younger with his recently married French bride, Madeleine de la Tour d'Auvergne. The second would have been the 'comedy without a name' previously attributed to Machiavelli and now to Filippo Strozzi and named, by some, *Falargo* on the basis of some rather devious reasoning.

performance of a comedy, and we are lucky to have a complete series of *intermedi* created by the author himself for *La mandragola*, though not for its first performance. Indeed we are doubly lucky in that, together with the *intermedi* of *Clizia*, they represent the starting point of a new concept of *intermedi*.

Nothing is known of the *intermedi* which had been used in previous performances of *La mandragola*, nor of those in the first performance itself; we do not even know the date of that first performance, though it seems reasonable to assume that Ridolfi's hypothesis is correct that it took place during the carnival of 1518.[13] Chiron may have introduced it with a series of octaves sung on a lyre; thereafter the more flexible practice suggested by the directions printed in *La farsa recitata agli Excelsi Signori di Firenze*, 'here let someone play or sing', may have prevailed once more. The same kind of directions are also found in the anonymous *Commedia di Adulazione*, in which one character, Ligurio, has the same name as one in *La mandragola*.[14] The novelty introduced with *Clizia* and intended to apply also to the planned performance of *La mandragola* in Faenza, was above all a musical one; the 'sweet harmony' of madrigalian polyphony performed by a group of singers replaced the introduction by a single player accompanying himself on a lyre. A further novel aspect was also at least partly musical. This was the unification of the musical pieces between the acts, achieved by having them all performed by the same group.

The example set by Machiavelli's comedies was soon taken up by other authors. A cycle of madrigals resembling those in *Clizia* and *La mandragola* can be recognized amongst the pieces contained in *Il terzo libro de i madrigali novissimi d'Archadelt a quattro voci*, published by Girolamo Scotto in Venice in 1539. I have not been able to identify the comedy to which they belonged, but though the edition claimed to be brand new, I am inclined to think that the cycle had been written eight or ten years earlier.[15] Judging from the text of what must have been the '*canzone* before the comedy', the whole cycle must have been sung by a group of ancient poets, so that 'this girl here in a gown' would have been Sappho:

> Dai dolci campi Elisi, ove tra' fiori
> viviam, sempre ridendo in festa e canti,
> vegniam sol per udir le gioie e pianti

The third was *La Pisana*, also by Strozzi. The key to his reasoning is the sentence in the Prologue: 'This is your Florence; another time it will be Rome or Pisa.' But, besides what Elena Povoledo has to say on p. 322, note 20, it is tautological. Even if *La mandragola* was selected for performance on this occasion, it is highly unlikely that the bitter and personal prologue, on which Parronchi's reasoning rests, would have been retained, as it contains no mention of the glory of the Medici and no prophesies of good fortune for the bride and groom. Remove the prologue, and the argument itself collapses, and with it the allegorical interpretation. Parronchi quotes extensively from the passage of Zeffi's *Ragionamento* quoted above, in note 8, but he fails to note that Zeffi mentions a single comedy by Lorenzo Strozzi performed in the Medici palace (his first, and therefore the so-called *Commedia senza nome*). This rules out the attribution of *La Pisana* to Strozzi, and so another element in Parronchi's ingenious argument is destroyed.

[13]   'Composizione, rappresentazione e prima edizione della "Mandragola"', in *La bibliofilia*, LXIV (1962), pp. 285–300, and later included in the volume *Studi sulle commedie*, pp. 11–35.

[14]   Fortunato Pintor, 'Un'antica commedia fiorentina', in *Miscellanea di studi critici...in onore di Guido Mazzoni*, ed. A. Della Torre and P. L. Rambaldi (Florence 1907), I, pp. 433ff.

[15]   See below, p. 151.

de' liet'afflitt'amanti;
e, come fummo già, così cantori
siam oggi; e questa in gonna
fu sì leggiadra donna,
ch'ancor molti di qua par ch'inamori.
Hor voi, cortes'e benigni auditori,
s'Amor vi face ogn'hor contenti e lieti,
ch'a noi dat' audienza intenti e cheti.

From the sweet Elysian fields, where we live amidst flowers, always rejoicing in feasts and songs, we have come only to listen to the joys and sorrows of these happy–sad lovers. As we were once, so are we singers today; and this girl here in a gown was so enchanting a lady that still she seems to charm many in this world. But now, courteous and kind listeners, if Love has always made you happy and contented, listen to us quietly and attentively.

The other madrigals of the cycle (here listed in the order in which they are most likely to have appeared in the performance of the comedy) are those which begin *Foll'è chi crede la prudenz'e gli anni / ponghin il freno all'amorose voglie* ('A fool is he who thinks prudence and age may ever restrain one's amorous desires', a Machiavellian sort of text, possibly to be sung after Act I), *Ecco che pur doppo sí lungh'affanni / doppo tante fatich', angosc'e pianti, / i desiosi amanti / verran'al fin de gli amorosi inganni* ('Behold, after long grieving, after so much distress, anguish and tears, our desirous lovers shall reach the goal of their amorous schemes', maybe to be sung after Act IV), and *Quanto fra voi mortali / poss'un accorto e virtuoso ingegno, / si vede ne' passati vostri mali* ('How much an ingenious and sharp mind can achieve amongst you mortals is seen in your past tribulations'; evidently the last element in the series. The madrigals after Acts II and III would thus appear to be missing).[16] In Donato Giannotti's *Il vecchio amoroso*, written between 1533 and 1536, a group of hermits make up the masquerade which introduces and comments on the play:

Dal più solingo loco
del vostro almo paese,
ov'al Rettor del ciel devoti siamo,
per celebrare il gioco
a cui sono oggi intese
le menti vostre, qui venuti siamo;
e come noi prendiamo
de' leti aspetti vostri
uno immenso diletto,
così non sia interdetto
il simil fare a voi de' canti nostri.

[16]   They are respectively madrigals 17, 8, 6 and 14 in Jacques Arcadelt, *Opera omnia*, ed. Albert Seay, vol. IV, American Institute of Musicology (1968). Also Osthoff, *Theatergesang*, I, pp. 270–4, recognizes three of the four madrigals by Arcadelt as belonging to a series of *intermedi* (he does not include *Foll'è chi crede*, despite the obvious reference to a senile love). However, I do not agree that *Ecco che pur* should hold the final place in the series; this placing is refuted by the 'verran'al fin' ('shall come at the end') in the fourth verse, which announces the future *dénouement* in the course of the last act. The part of the 'song after the last act' is more suited to *Quanto fra voi mortali* (of which Osthoff gives the complete text) with the eulogy of the 'shrewd and virtuous mind' which has succeeded in guiding the love affair 'to port, to the desired goal'. It is however necessary to adjust the third verse so that it fits in with the initial apostrophe, reading it as 'can be seen in *your* past ills'.

From the remotest corner of this noble land of yours, where we live, devoted to the Ruler of heaven, we have come to solemnize the game on which your minds are all so intent today; and as we get the utmost pleasure from watching your happy faces, so we hope you may get pleasure from our songs.

Their first 'chorus' precedes the prologue, which is not in verse; each of the other 'choruses' precedes one of the acts, beginning from Act I.[17] Thus, even without a final *intermedio*, the total of six was reached, which was to become the norm for the kind of *intermedi* which I like to term 'courtly'.

L'ammalata, by Giovanni Maria Cecchi (in verse, date uncertain) also had six *intermedi*, beginning with one before the prologue: 'First *Intermedio*. Let Truth appear, who recites, and must be accompanied by the following, who sing: Time, Adventure, Innocence, and Aesculapius, the god of Medicine...' The lines recited by Truth are in fact followed by a

> Madrigale. – Càntino
>
> Venite lieti, e del nostro valore
> gustate quante sian l'opere, e quali...

> Madrigal. – Let them sing
> Come gladly, and rejoice in the number and greatness of our deeds of valour...

The subsequent *intermedi*, from the 'second' to the 'sixth', precede the five acts, and all begin with Truth reciting and being answered by the singing of the other four allegorical characters.[18] The same playwright's *Maiana* goes so far as to derive its title not from the plot nor from the comic characters but from the protagonist of the *intermedi*, 'the goddess Maia, mother of Mercury, who recites. With her [enter] the six Pleiades, her sisters and the daughters of Atlas, who sing.'[19] In the printed edition only the first madrigal is given, in which a new political trend begins to appear:

> Vivi eterna e felice,
> bella e gioconda Flora,
> sott'il manto di Cosmo e Leonora...

May you have an eternal and happy life, beautiful and merry Flora [i.e. Florence], under the protection of Cosmo and Leonora...

Anton Francesco Grazzini had in mind new themes for the *intermedi* to accompany the performance of his *La gelosia* (1550), but 'for lack of time, and because they were difficult and expensive, they could not be enacted... so that their place was taken by those [*intermedi*] which are printed with the comedy'.[20] In other words, the performance had to fall back on the customary

[17] D. Giannotti, *Opere politiche e letterarie* (Florence 1850), vol. II, pp. 195, 199, 211, 231, 249, 265.

[18] G. M. Cecchi, *Commedie*, published by G. Milanesi (Florence 1856), vol. I, pp. 91–2, 107–8, 122–3, 142–3, 161. The chronology of Cecchi's works is extremely unclear.

[19] *Ibid.*, I, pp. 301–2.

[20] A. F. Grazzini, *Teatro*, ed. Giovanni Grazzini (Bari 1953), pp. 15–16, 31, 45, 66, 85–6, 106–7. The *intermedi* are different in the 1551 and 1568 editions; those of the latter, the original ones which could not be performed, have the following titles: (1) Diana's priestesses; (2) Satyrs who go to plunder; (3) Witches; (4) Elfin spirits; (5) Satyrs who have seized nymphs, and nymphs abducted by force; (6) Dreams. Although they appear unconnected, they too are linked to the time of the comedy. The author in fact explained that he had made them all nocturnal as the main action of the comedy is nocturnal. These are perhaps more recent than another series of

set of six 'madrigals', no longer a novelty, whose singers introduced themselves as 'the ancient ministers and priests of the great temple of Love'. The only new feature was the placing of the 'First Madrigal' after the prologue, the final words of which announced it: '...I see the chorus already entering; you listen to their music, while I retire inside.' As a result, the 'Sixth and Last Madrigal' was sung after Act V. However, the *intermedi*, sung by a group of 'slaves of Love', of Giovan Battista Gelli's *L'errore* ('recited on the occasion of a dinner offered by Roberto di Filippo Pandolfini to the Compagnia dei Fantastichi, in the year 1555'),[21] and Andrea Lori's *intermedi* for the Florentine performance of Luigi Alamanni's *Flora* in 1556,[22] furnish us with evidence that the older custom of singing the madrigals before the acts had not died out.

I have already mentioned the task of mediating between the audience and the fictional world on stage, originally performed by a single character and later assigned to a group. This role, however, was barely hinted at in the texts of a few *intermedi* and was never explicitly formulated, so that it was easily supplanted. For example, an attempt was made to use the *intermedi* to provide a frame, somewhat similar to the sort commonly found in collections of short stories, for the comedy's re-presentation of past events. (The events of *La mandragola* were supposed to have taken place in 1504, and those of *Clizia* in 1506.) This is yet another sign of the influence exerted on the theatre by stories, especially Boccaccio's *Decameron*. But in the stories the framework was realistic, whilst the stories themselves, though realistic in nature, were removed from reality by the words of the narrator which projected them into the minds of the listeners or readers; in the comedies the realism of the main characters and of the comic plot was contrasted with an unreal framework, despite the latter being made almost tangible by the miracle of being acted on stage. The unreality of the framework seems to have been intended to ease the transition from the present, to which both spectators and spectacle were bound, to the fictitious time in which the action on stage was supposed to take place.

The nature of music itself and the need to justify its introduction between the acts as an element of variety and diversion may have played a part in this inversion. It is certainly more logical to have Orpheus, the poet-cum-singer of antiquity, the shepherds and nymphs of Arcadia, or any kind of allegorical, mythological or fantastic creature sing than it is to have realistic characters do so. Nevertheless, we do find that Trissino had seen nothing against having a chorus of sailors in his *I simillimi* (published in 1548) sing between the acts as well as take part with the other characters in the acts and dialogue. Of

five madrigals for *intermedi* which are to be found amongst Grazzini's poems, with no indication of the comedy with which they were to be performed. The series opens with the words ''Le stesse Ninfe siam che voi pur dianzi | vedeste un'altra volta, | che per farvi passar con gioia molta | questo bel giorno, vi venghiamo innanzi; | dove alla vostra festa, compagnia | farem, cantando con dolce armonia | e con soavi accenti, | purché voi stiate ad ascoltare intenti'. ('We are the same nymphs which you before | saw on a different occasion, | and to enable you to pass with great delight | this fine day, we come before you; | here we shall accompany your entertainment | singing with gentle harmony | and soft accents | provided you stay to listen attentively.')

[21] G. B. Gelli, *Opere*, ed. I. Sanesi (Turin 1952), pp. 503, 513, 533 and 541.

[22] L. Alamanni, *Versi e prose*, ed. Pietro Raffaelli (Florence 1589), vol. II, pp. 321–2, 336–7, 351–2, 365–6 and 388. The printed editions of *La suocera* by Benedetto Varchi also contain five madrigals, though there are no indications as to who sang them.

course, Trissino felt himself justified because in doing this he was following the example of a classical author, Aristophanes. He was critical of the *intermedi* because 'they are something quite different from what happens in the comedy' and often perversely become 'another comedy... which makes it impossible to appraise the wisdom of the [main] comedy'.[23] Nevertheless, he seems not to have been concerned with the propriety of having a group of normal people suddenly burst into song, with a miraculous concordance of opinion and musical expression. All doubts in his mind were dispelled by the magic power of the word 'chorus' and of its classical precedents. We must conclude then that one of the reasons for having an unrealistic frame was to justify singing, but that this was neither the sole reason nor even the main one. In my opinion, more important was the fact that by its unreality and its music the frame helped to create what we might call the illusion of a temporal perspective.

The Renaissance theatre had begun to observe the so-called Aristotelian unities long before their rules, rooted in the authority of 'the philosopher', were formulated by the theorists. In retrospect, it is obvious that the adoption of a set which was both fixed and designed according to the rules of perspective would foster the development of the unity of place. Not only did such a set preclude any change in location, but by its design it clearly defined and reduced distances, and made it necessary to abandon the previously accepted convention of the multiple set.[24] Similarly it made it impossible, for example, to represent a long journey between two distant places by the convention of taking a few steps from one corner of the stage to another, each corner representing one of those places. It is almost equally obvious that the unity of action was influenced by the fact that the stage became much narrower whilst at the same time serving as the focal point for all the activities of the main characters: thus the stage directions of *La mandragola* require that the set include the houses of Messer Nicia and Lucrezia, that of Callimaco and the church of Fra Timoteo. As for the unity of time, its original significance is now obscured by our familiarity with later theatrical conventions and with the sixteenth-century prescriptions, themselves formulated some time after the first spontaneous applications of the idea.

Machiavelli's contemporaries may have become aware of the need for the unity of time through the first performances of classical tragedies, in which the chorus was either continuously present on stage or constantly returning to it; and no sooner had the chorus finished commenting on what had just happened than it was already spotting the arrival of the main characters for a new episode.[25] This established an uninterrupted sequence of events, which

[23]   Gian Giorgio Trissino, *La quinta e la sesta divisione della poetica* (Venice 1562), c. 32v–33.
[24]   A trace survives in the fact that the set generally includes the 'houses' of the main characters.
[25]   This is so, for example, in the case of Seneca's *Hippolytus*, performed in Ferrara during the 1509 carnival. On 8 February Bernardino Prosperi described it thus to Isabella d'Este: 'The tragedy of Phaedra and Hippolytus... was performed with excellent voices and gestures, nor did it take place without the tears of many for the cruelty therein contained. As a chorus there appeared all four times ten people garbed in double dresses, the first reaching the knee, the other the floor. In the first [chorus] one of them sang a tercet and another played the *lira*. In the second chorus these ten were divided into three parts and in song recited certain verses, and in the third and fourth chorus, divided into two parts, they again sang, but in different tones, more melancholy than sweet. No other *intermedi* were performed, but it was orderly and sumptuous

naturally gave rise to the idea that the plot should be completed within a reasonable length of time. The most obvious solution was to adopt as the norm the time between sunrise and sunset – the time, that is, between the awakening of all the characters, including the members of the chorus, from their nocturnal rest, and the moment when, after an eventful day crowded with strong emotions, they would succumb to fatigue and the need to sleep. Eventually it came to be felt that very unusual circumstances in the plot might conceivably upset normal habits and that the succession of fictional events might proceed throughout the whole night or even into part of the next day. But even the narrower span of fifteen or sixteen hours of daytime was at least three times the acceptable length of a performance which, as we have seen, permitted no interruption. It was therefore necessary that the four or five hours of a performance should give the impression of spanning sixteen, or twenty-four, or even more, hours of fictional time. This could only be achieved by means of an artificial effect of temporal perspective, a compression of time akin to the artificial compression of space achieved by either linear or theatrical perspective.

Not every playwright clearly perceived the problems which were soon to give rise to the rule of unity of time,[26] but a keen sense of reality gave the Florentines a more ready understanding of them. Even the anonymous author of *La farsa* (which has been mentioned a number of times), while failing to observe any of the rules of unity, nevertheless felt obliged to warn the audience (in the long rambling sermon sung on the lyre in place of a prologue) that his work was not 'a properly ordered comedy...neatly divided into five acts...with its whole plot contained within one single day'. Rather it unfolded 'in the manner of an imaginary story and [was] divided into *tempi*, one more than five'.[27] In other words, the author recognized that in *La farsa* he had indulged in temporal shifts between the episodes, and that whereas these shifts were perfectly acceptable when demanded of the imagination in a narrative, in general they were to be avoided in theatrical performances.[28] Another dramatist, Iacopo Nardi, ended Act IV of *I due felici rivali* by sending to sleep two old men, Menedemo and Cremete, and leaving the servant Strobilo alone on stage to address the audience. Strobilo winks at them, with one of those gestures of mutual connivance which was later to become typical of servants in the *commedia dell'arte*:[29]

Let's go home. But you must not leave, O spectators, for we want to get to the end of this comedy, and it is not our fault that it has to pause, but the old men are in need of some sleep. This I tell you lest somebody should later say that the crux of

and as well-conducted as any performance I have seen in my days.' Quoted in A. Luzio and R. Renier, 'La coltura e le relazioni letterarie di Isabella d'Este', in *Giornale storico della letteratura italiana* 33 (1899), p. 54, note 3.

[26] I have already, on p. 84 and in the appropriate note, referred to the case of *I tre tiranni* by Agostino Ricchi, which dates from 1530. Ricchi declared in his prologue that he had desired 'thus to detach himself somewhat from the style and customs of the ancients', and that he had wished 'that the present set/(as required by the story)/should serve for many days and nights, up to one year'. [27] D'Ancona, *Le origini*, II, p. 39.

[28] One comes to the same conclusion even if one chooses to interpret the expression 'imagined story' (*storia imaginata*) in the sense of a pictorial representation of several scenes, each one illustrating an episode of the tale, and omitting the intermediate events.

[29] A. Ferraioli, *I due felici rivali. Commedia inedita*, p. 58.

the plot should or could not have been postponed to the next day, thus wrongly blaming our author.

Thus Machiavelli was not exceptional in having Fra Timoteo, at the end of Act IV of *La mandragola*, recite the following monologue:

They are all snugly at home, and I shall go to the cloister. And you, spectators, do not criticize what we do,[10] for nobody is going to sleep tonight, so that the acts will not be interrupted by time [off]. I shall recite my office; Ligurio and Siro will dine, for they have not eaten all day long, and the doctor will be trotting back and forth from the bedroom to the living room, to make sure the pot keeps on the boil. As for Callimaco and Madonna Lucrezia, they will not sleep, for I know for sure that we would not sleep, were I in his place and you [the ladies in the audience] in hers.[11]

On the next page, or possibly on the same one (after all, we are in the habit of reading *La mandragola*), Act V begins with another soliloquy by the same friar:

All night long I could not close my eyes, I was so anxious to know how Callimaco and the others had fared. And to while away the time I attended to various chores: I recited matins, read the life of one of the Holy Fathers, went to the church to rekindle a lamp that had gone out, changed the veil on a miraculous statue of Our Lady...

Similarly, Act V of *Clizia* opens with a soliloquy by Doria:

I have never laughed so much, nor do I think I shall ever do so again...Sofronia, Sostrata, Cleandro, Eustachio, they are all laughing too. We have spent the whole night measuring the passing of time and saying 'Now Nicomaco is entering the bedroom, now he is undressing, now he has gone to bed beside his bride, now he is engaging her in battle, and now he is being more valiantly counter-attacked.

(The 'bride', of course, is actually a young man.) To us, such passages as these are but colourful touches sparkling with the author's *vis comica*. We are not in the least concerned about the hours which have lapsed between the end of Act IV and the beginning of Act V, used as we are to mentally filling the gap with the shutting and reopening of the curtains and an intermission spent smoking in the corridors. But for an author and an audience used to an uninterrupted progression of the spectacle, they provided necessary reassurance that the life of the characters had not been interrupted for a single moment and that their consciousness had been alert all the time. 'The acts will not be interrupted', but the length of the vigil between them is reduced and compressed by the insertion of *intermedi*. These were either 'invisible' (*intermedi non apparenti*), introduced by such directions as 'here let somebody play or sing', or, more refined and less generic, were marked by the arrival of nymphs and shepherds whose return provided the frame for a choral comment, such as the '*Canzone* after Act IV' in *La mandragola*:

[10]   This is the meaning of 'non ci appuntate'.
[11]   The passage had already attracted the attention of R. Ridolfi, *Studi*, p. 21 (as well as the first version of it in *La bibliofilia*, LXIV (1962), pp. 285–300), who considers it as a semi-serious reference to unity of time (*ibid.*, p. 173).

Ex. XXV Philippe Verdelot. Song before the prologue of Niccolò Machiavelli's *Clizia*. From *Il primo libro de madrigali di Verdelotto* (O. Scotto, Venice 1537).

Oh dolce notte, oh sante
ore notturne e quete
ch'i disïosi amanti accompagnate;
in voi s'adunan tante
letizie, onde voi siete
sole cagion di far l'alme beate.
Voi giusti premi date
all'amorose schiere,
delle lunghe fatiche;
voi fate, o felici ore,
ogni gelato petto arder d'amore.

O sweet night, O sacred hours of nocturnal quiet, bringing together all the desirous lovers; in your span so many joys are compounded that you are the only source of bliss to their souls. On hosts of lovers you bestow just rewards for long labours; O happy hours, you kindle the iciest heart with flames of love.

Let us therefore restore due credit to the 'canzoni after the acts' of *La mandragola*, for they served a precise function and, of all the various types

of *intermedi* in use at the time, they were the one which most consistently sought to maintain some relationship with the plot of the comedy. Like them, the *canzoni* of *Clizia* were also undoubtedly written for the beautiful Barbera Salutati, then an intimate friend of 'il Fornaciaio' in whose gardens the comedy was first staged.[32] In the *canzone* which introduces the comedy (example XXV) Verdelot's music has a gesture in the soprano part, immediately echoed by the three lower voices, that would seem to reflect the gracious bow she and her companion singers must have performed at the end of each strophe, while singing 'I, a nymph, and shepherds we'. The same vocal distribution, for a soprano and three male voices, is found in the music for the *canzoni* to be sung after Acts I and IV (examples XXVI and XXVII) unknown to Einstein. These appear in a manuscript now in the Newberry Library of Chicago, and are certainly by Verdelot, though they are unascribed in the manuscript.[33] As far as I know, the other three songs are missing.[34]

---

[32] The precise status of the young Barbera Salutati, who later married and out-lived one of the Raffacani family, is unclear.

According to Domenico Puligo's life written by Vasari in the second edition of *Le vite*, the artist 'also painted a portrait of the Florentine Barbara, who was at the time a very beautiful courtesan, loved by many for her beauty as well as for her good manners; more particularly, she was an excellent musician and sang divinely'. (On her portrait see H. Colin Slim, 'A Motet for Machiavelli's Mistress and a Chanson for a Courtesan', in *Essays Presented to Myron P. Gilmore*, ed. S. Bertelli and G. Ramakus (Florence 1978), vol. II, pp. 457–72).

She also wrote poetry, and may have been kept by Jacopo di Filippo Falconetti, a rich plebeian known as 'il Fornaciaio', in whose villa outside the walls at San Frediano *Clizia* was performed on 13 January 1525, before a large crowd. Machiavelli had fallen in love with Barbera and made wry fun of himself, even going so far as to devise for Nicomaco, the elderly character in the comedy who is disappointed in love, a name which incorporated the beginnings of his Christian name and surname. Perhaps Palamede's rejoinder (*Clizia*, Act I scene 1) is part of the same joke: '...I have always understood there to be three types of man to be avoided: singers, old men, and lovers'. Or is it aimed at one of Barbera's singers?

[33] It is a handsome contemporary MS, of which the Newberry Library owns all the partbooks but the Altus; it contains a collection of motets and madrigals for four, five and six voices, all anonymous, but largely identifiable from other sources. Verdelot is amply represented. A detailed study and an edition of its contents were published in H. Colin Slim, *A Gift of Madrigals and Motets* (Chicago, Illinois 1972); the two madrigals are included in vol. II, pp. 344–9.

According to Slim, it would appear that the manuscript, illuminated by G. Boccardi, was compiled for an unidentified purchaser in Florence between 1525 and 1529, and eventually sent as a gift to Henry VIII of England, in whose honour a motet was added to the previously arranged series – a politically motivated gesture which could have come only from the Florentine Signoria intent on defending the threatened independence of the city. Iain Fenlon, 'La diffusion de la chanson continentale dans les manuscrits anglais', paper given at the Vingtième Colloque International d'Etudes Humanistes in Tours 1977, states that the manuscript must have been intended for Henry VIII from the outset, and suggests 1526 as its date.

Both Professor Slim and I have made attempts at reconstructing the missing Altus part. We can now compare our results with the original, for the missing partbook has recently been found at Oscott College; see H. C. Slim, 'A Royal Treasure at Sutton Coldfield', in *Early Music*, 6 (1978), pp. 57–74, as well as his *Ten Altus Parts at Oscott College Sutton Coldfield* (n.p., n.d.). Accordingly, examples XXVI and XXVII (of which I gave only partial transcriptions in 1969 and 1975) as well as example XXIX are now given with the original altus part.

Osthoff, even though he did not know the madrigals in the Newberry Library manuscript, wrote a whole chapter on 'Verdelots Musik zu Machiavelli-Komödien und das Madrigal' (*Theatergesang*, I, pp. 213–49) with corresponding transcriptions (II, pp. 65–73). I think it unlikely that the isolated five-voice madrigal *Sí soave è l'inganno* by A. Marri (*ibid.*, II, pp. 79–84) can be linked to performances of one of Machiavelli's comedies.

[34] *Clizia* has six songs: one before the comedy and one at the end of each act, including the last.

Ex. XXVI Philippe Verdelot. Song after the first act of Niccolò Machiavelli's *Clizia* (and after the first act of *La mandragola*). From the manuscript. Chicago. The Newberry Library, Case MS-VM 1578. M91. Altus part reproduced by permission of the Trustees of Oscott College, Sutton Coldfield. MS Case B no. 4.

135

Having perhaps introduced a new kind of *intermedio* with *Clizia*, it was only natural that Machiavelli should wish to do the same for a new performance of *La mandragola*. Plans for such a performance, to be held in Faenza where Francesco Guicciardini was then living as the main representative of the papal government in Romagna, must have originated in the summer of 1525 when

Machiavelli visited Faenza. During his visit they must have discussed his comedies, previously unknown to Guicciardini, and the plan became a recurrent theme in the correspondence the friends exchanged between August 1525 and February 1526. First mention of the *intermedi* appears in an undated letter by Machiavelli, thought by Ridolfi to have been written on 20 October:[35] 'While you are putting pressure there, we are not sleeping here,

[35] R. Ridolfi, *Vita di Niccolò Machiavelli*, 2nd edn (Rome 1954), p. 465, note 6.

137

Ex. XXVII   Philippe Verdelot. Song after the fourth act of Niccolò Machiavelli's *Clizia* (and after the third act of *La mandragola*). From the manuscript Chicago. The Newberry Library, Case MS-VM 1578. M91. Altus part reproduced by permission of the Trustees of Oscott College, Sutton Coldfield. MS Case B no. 4.

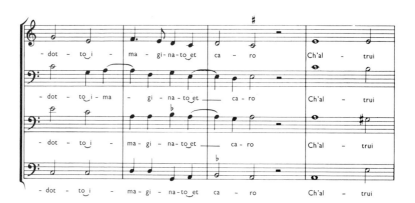

for Lodovico Alamanni and myself recently had dinner one night with Barbera and spoke of the comedy, so that she happened to suggest coming herself with her singers to be the chorus between the acts; and I undertook to write the *canzonette*, suiting them to the acts.' The performance never took place, though as late as 3 January 1526 Machiavelli was still hoping that it would be given, and sent the texts of the *canzonette* to Guicciardini, enclosed in a

letter.[36] But he had only partly fulfilled his pledge to write them anew, 'suiting them to the acts'. Two of them, namely those to be sung after Acts I and III, were the ones he had already used after Acts I and IV of *Clizia*.[37] However,

[36] *Ibid.*, note 9.

[37] Fortunately, these are the two contained in the Newberry Library manuscript (examples XXVI and XXVII), which also contains *Quanto sia lieto il giorno* from *Clizia* and *Quanta dolcezza, Amore* from *La mandragola*, and a *ballata*, written by Machiavelli for Barbera, *Amor, io sento l'alma*. In any case, the question as to whether the music for the *intermedi* of *La mandragola* was ever written has been answered. H. C. Slim, *A Gift of Madrigals*, I, pp. 92–100, discusses in minute detail the circumstances of the theatrical collaboration between Machiavelli and Verdelot; *ibid.*,

they fitted well into their new context, and, after all, he had kept the promise as far as the places where it mattered most: in the 'canzone before the comedy', in the one after Act II which refers to Messer Nicia, and the one after Act IV which hints at the secret pleasures of Lucrezia and Callimaco and prevents a gap from breaking the continuity of time.[38]

Machiavelli must have attached additional importance to the canzone before the comedy because his friend Guicciardini had told him that the original prologue, so full of personal bitterness, was to be replaced by another, more easily comprehensible to actors and audience.[39] Machiavelli got his own back by giving an equally bitter twist to the beginning of the new canzone:

> Perché la vita è brieve
> e molte son le pene
> che vivendo e stentando ognun sostiene,
>
> dietro alle nostre voglie
> andiam passando e consumando gli anni;
> ché chi il piacer si toglie
> per viver con angosce e con affanni,
> non conosce gli inganni
> del mondo; o da quai mali
> e da che strani casi
> oppressi quasi – sian tutti i mortali.

Since life is short and many the pains which in living and toiling we sustain, let us spend our years in pursuit of all our desires; for whoever forsakes pleasure to live in grief and anguish does not know the deceptions of the world, or the evils or all the strange events by which most mortals are oppressed.

In the eyes of the audience, the nymphs and shepherds of La mandragola would not have seemed too different from those of Clizia who come from remote Arcadia.[40] To the poet himself, however, they seem to have represented spectres for some personal Arcadia, a lonely contemplative and welcome refuge from the drudgery of life, which is why it comes as a shock to find that they go on to bestow courtly praise on Guicciardini in their third strophe,

II, pp. 333–5 and 341–9, he gives transcriptions of the four madrigals. Two further pieces by Verdelot which he thinks may have been intended for use in the theatre are (ibid., I, pp. 100–4) a chorus from Tullia by Ludovico Martelli (Quante lagrime, oimè, quanti sospiri, in Il terzo libro di Madrigali di Verdelotto, Venice 1537) and one of Orpheus' octaves, vv. 322–9, from Poliziano's Fabula (Qual sarà mai sí miserabil canto, in Madrigali a cinque. Libro primo, Venice 1535?). But it is inconceivable that Poliziano's text was still being performed forty years after its appearance; and Martelli's tragedy remained unfinished because the author died. In any case, the attribution of the two madrigals is open to discussion. Osthoff, Theatergesang, I, pp. 179–80, discusses another madrigal, Fuggite l'amorose cure acerbe (itself also of doubtful attribution) as a possible song for a tragedy (though not a chorus); but Slim, A Gift of Madrigals, I, p. 101, identifies the text as being an Epitaphio by Bernardo Accolti.

[38] Unlike Clizia, La mandragola has no final intermedio after the conclusion of the comedy.

[39] Prologues, like intermedi, were often replaced, but literary critics are not as instinctively suspicious of them as they are of what was intended to be linked to music.

[40] Arcadia is the 'happy and beautiful land' whence come the nymph and three shepherds in Clizia (see the text of the song before the comedy, on p. 122). It is strange that characters who belong to a mythical prehistoric past should have been called on to introduce an evocation of a relatively recent past (Clizia is set in the Florence of 1506). The timeless Arcadia of the first 'chorus' of La mandragola is more logical: no indication is given of the provenance of the characters, but the second stanza explains that they are 'graceful youths and nymphs', represented musically by two male and two female voices.

Ex. XXVIII   Philippe Verdelot. Song after the fourth act of Niccolò Machiavelli's *La mandragola*.
From *Il terzo libro de madrigali di Verdelotto* (O. Scotto, Venice 1537).

and even add a hint of a bow in the direction of Clement VII. The music unfortunately is missing, as is that of the *canzone* after Act II which referred to Messer Nicia's frenzy to have children. But the music of the songs transferred from *Clizia* survives, and furthermore *Il terzo libro de madrigali di Verdelotto* (Ottaviano Scotto, Venice 1537) contains the music of the *canzone* after Act IV, the one we might well call a hymn to Night (example XXVIII).

144

Machiavelli always called them *canzoni*; Verdelot, or his Venetian printers, used instead the term *madrigali*, which had recently become fashionable in the language of music printing.[41] Actually the new, or rather rediscovered, term[42] is the one better suited to the short poems to be sung after the acts, for they have the free form, without a predetermined metrical scheme, most typical of the sixteenth-century madrigal. The term is less suitable when applied to the two songs before the comedies, which are both strophic. We have already seen that in the song of *Clizia* the composer simply had the music of the first strophe repeated for the second. He may have done the same for the two strophes of the song in *La mandragola* which, however, are preceded by an initial section not unlike the *ripresa* of a *ballata* (though it is not one, as the subsequent structure in no way resembles a *ballata*). Composers of madrigals generally avoided strophic repetitions of music because the genre required the new poetical content of each strophe to be matched by new music. Nevertheless, the definition of the madrigal as 'the singing of shepherds', and the related theory according to which the term derived from *mandria* (herd),[43] clearly applies to the two *canzoni*, for in both of them the singers assert their Arcadian, idyllic and pastoral origins. The contradiction shows that nobody at that time was as eager as we are to define with complete clarity and precision the meaning of the term 'madrigal'. The rules of the genre had not yet crystallized and become as exclusive as we are inclined to believe them: indeed even later they never became too rigid,[44] the emphasis probably being on an entirely vocal polyphony and a particularly refined musical style.[45]

Chordal texture, a prevailing feature in many of the earlier madrigals, is also predominant in the music for Machiavelli's comedies, where it was doubly important because words spoken on stage needed to be especially clearly enunciated. However, the composer always felt free to depart from and revert to it as best suited the progress of his music. Such intentional freedom is evident in Verdelot's setting of *Quanto sia lieto il giorno* (example XXV) which opens with a dialogue between two pairs of voices and is on the whole more contrapuntally active than any of the other *canzoni* for the two comedies. It also presents a real instance of a 'madrigalism', not so much in the passage already mentioned, which opposes the voice of the nymph to the voices of the male singers as in the waves of vocalization suddenly starting on the words *e giam cantand'insieme i nostri amori* ('singing together the story of our loves'). The nymph and shepherds repeat in both strophes the gesture which is matched to the words 'I, a nymph, and shepherds we', but the madrigalism illustrating the idea of singing loses its original point when it comes to be

---

[41]   See above, note 8.

[42]   The name 'madrigal' covers a wide range of metrical forms, on which see the most informative study by Don Harrán, 'Verse Types on the early Madrigal', in *Journal of the American Musicological Society*, XXII (1969), pp. 27ff.

[43]   Invented by Antonio da Tempo for the fourteenth-century madrigal.

[44]   On the various elements concurring to give origin to the madrigal, partly influenced by differing interpretations of the meaning of the term, see the previous chapter, p. 99 and note 50.

[45]   Nevertheless, even this fact is not without exceptions. I shall confine myself, as it is immediately connected to the music I am discussing, to the case of the Venetian edition of a selection of twenty-two madrigals by Verdelot with a lute tablature for the lower parts and only the upper part written out for voice. (Both the 1536 edition and a later 1540 reprint attribute the arrangement to Willaert.) It includes the first song from *Clizia*, and as the nymph's part alone was sung, her 'io ninfa' is left without the shepherd's reply. See Osthoff's transcription, *Theatergesang*, II, pp. 69–73.

repeated matched to new words, *e torneremci ai nostri antichi amori* ('and shall return to our timeless loves'). *Chi non fa prov', Amore* (example XXVI) is also remarkable for the contrapuntal fluidity of its beginning and the *cantabile* smoothness of all the voices. *Sí suave è l'inganno* had an ambiguous, ironical role where it was originally placed, after Act IV of *Clizia*, where it filled a nocturnal pause with its praise of the intrigue bringing victory of Love, at the same time as a much desired amorous conquest was actually turning into a cruel discomfiture for Messer Nicomaco (see Daria's soliloquy quoted above). The composer disregarded the ambiguity: his predominantly chordal madrigal (example XXVII) is full of nocturnal secrecy in its low murmured beginning, and more resonant and full when proclaiming Love's praise. *O dolce notte* (example XXVIII), also mainly chordal, opens on a tender touch of chromaticism which compensates for the higher range and less nocturnal colour of its vocal orchestration. It then proceeds to unfold with even greater directness than *Sí suave*, in a crescendo which links the soft tones full of mystery of the initial invocation–evocation to the half cadence which paves the way for the threefold statement of the final line.

Verdelot, alias Philippe Deslouges, is a composer whose life is shrouded in obscurity. He may have been still young when he arrived in Florence shortly after 1520;[46] certainly he quickly became so well integrated into his new surroundings that he whole-heartedly embraced the cause of Florentine republicanism in the events which led to the siege of 1530.[47] His complete mastery of Italian, evidenced in his madrigals by the flexible variety with which the lines of text are recited individually and moulded into an overall

[46]   More precisely, before 1 July 1523, when he was appointed chapel-master in the Baptistery of St John. He held the post until 10 August 1525, but remained in Florence beyond then. He may have been in Rome at the beginning of the next decade, and after about 1533 he may have been in Venice. His hypothetical return to Florence after 1540 is even more shrouded in obscurity. On him, see Anne-Marie Bragard's monograph. *Etude bio-bibliographique sur Philippe Verdelot, musicien français de la Renaissance* (Brussels 1964) and her own up-dating of the information, *sub voce*, in *Die Musik in Geschichte und Gegenwart*, vol. XIII, cols. 1421–6. I am sceptical about Bragard's hypothesis that Verdelot died around 1552; the sentence 'Verdelot, the Frenchman, was in his day exceptional', in the *Catalogo dei musici* by Ortensio Lando, seems to me to indicate a more distant past. The most recent and accurate discussion of the available information, by H. C. Slim, *A Gift of Madrigals*, I, pp. 41–65, casts doubt upon Bragard's suggestion that Verdelot spent some time in Rome after his Florentine sojourn and that he returned to Florence after 1540. Slim believes that Verdelot may have died in Florence during the 1529 siege (see the next note), or in Venice in the course of the next decade. It is generally accepted that Verdelot reached Florence via Venice (or even, I think, Padua), but Slim's idea that Verdelot was born circa 1470 seems to me improbable: it is based on dubious interpretations of a poem by Jean Molinet and a no longer extant painting attributed to Sebastiano del Piombo. A date somewhere around 1485 strikes me as more plausible.

[47]   Verdelot appears perfectly at home on the Florentine stage in one of the dialogues of *I marmi* by Anton Francesco Doni (see the edition by Ezio Chiorboli, Bari 1928, vol. I, pp. 202ff), in which he holds his own against the lively Zinzera and tells two short stories. From one passage (*ibid.*, p. 208) it transpires that as a good Frenchman he disliked Spaniards. Anton Francesco Grazzini has a *madrigalone* addressed to 'Nannina Zinzera Cortigiana' (*Rime burlesche*, Florence 1882, p. 244). H. C. Slim, *A Gift of Madrigals*, I, p. 55, still on the basis of *I marmi*, points out that Zinzera used to appear as a singer during the meetings of the Orti Oricellari, which Machiavelli too attended. Verdelot's active participation in the cause of republican Florence during the siege of 1529–30 was first indicated by E. E. Lowinsky, 'A Newly Discovered Sixteenth-Century Motet Manuscript at the Biblioteca Vallicelliana in Rome', in *Journal of the American Musicological Society*, II (1950), pp. 173–232. It is re-examined, together with A. M. Bragard's occasionally different views, by Slim, *A Gift of Madrigals*, I, pp. 55–62, since the Newberry Library manuscript also contains some of the motets in which Verdelot expresses support for the Florentine cause.

oratorical line, is most impressive, given that he was a foreigner used to the sharper accents of his native French. Still present in his madrigals of 1525 are the natural accentuation of the text and many features of rhythm and phrasing, which had typified the '*modi dicendi*' for *capitoli*, *strambotti*, sonnets, and even Latin poems. In the decades immediately before and after the turn of the century these features had been typical of the more classical, recitative trends of musical humanism, not of its popular aspects. Now they had become additionally effective in that, adopting the free metres of the madrigal, they had freed themselves from the habit of melodic repetitions reflecting repetitions of similar metrical elements in the texts.[48] Similarly, the obsessive drive toward very definite tonal goals which had been prevalent among the composers of *frottole* was softened by a new harmonic feeling; composers benefited from the tonal experience acquired in the practice of counterpoint and applied it to an essentially chordal musical texture, combining variety with a coherent and controlled sense of tonal direction.

I have mentioned above other madrigal texts which were meant to be sung as *intermedi* in comedies by Florentine writers, but have been unable to trace any of their musical settings. Other such texts must however have existed, possibly in large numbers, for use in later repetitions of the same comedies or in performances of other plays whose editions do not mention *intermedi*, as can be inferred from the presence in madrigalian literature of pieces certainly intended for such a use. One such piece, again by Verdelot, is the madrigal *Mandati qui d'Amor noi siam venuti*, included in the collection of his *Madrigali a sei voci*, printed in Venice in 1546 by Antonio Gardane.[49] Verdelot may also have been the author of a short, gently refined anonymous madrigal set to the following text:[50]

> Quanta dolcezza, Amore,
> arrechi seco il tuo dolce veneno,
> se non è gentil core
> no'l può sentir, non che ritrarlo appieno;
>
> ché un sol sguardo sereno
> seco ha tanto di bene
> che ristora tante onte e mille pene.

How much sweetness, Love, your sweet venom can bring none but a gentle heart can feel, let alone fully express; for a single kind glance has in it so much goodness that it repays much contempt and suffering.

---

[48] Even now, only a small part of Verdelot's work has been published, and there is no overall critical study of it. It is interesting to note the judgement of one of his contemporaries, Cosimo Bartoli, who wrote: '...you already know that here in Florence Verdelot was my dearest friend by whom I would be so bold as to say...that there were, and indeed still are, an infinite number of musical compositions which even today cause the most discerning composers to marvel. For according to the character of the words being set, these compositions can be light or weighty, gentle or compassionate, fast or slow, benign or wrathful, or have fugues. And I have heard it said by many who understand these matters, that not since Josquin has there been a man who better understood the right manner of composing' (from the *Ragionamenti accademici*, Venice 1567, c. 36). This judgement too emphasizes the general expressive tone rather than the detailed (and often strained) interpretation of individual poetic concepts which is a feature of later madrigal writing.

[49] The Pleiades in the one *intermedio* of Giovanni Maria Cecchi's *Maiana* (see above, p. 126) also sang à 6, and though they were Pleiades it is impossible that all six voices were female. The music of Verdelot's madrigal is published in Osthoff, *Theatergesang*, II, pp. 180–6.

[50] As in the case of the two 'choruses' by Machiavelli, the attribution is based on the fact that the Newberry–Oscott Library manuscript in which it is to be found contains, anonymously, numerous works by Verdelot, as well as on the delicacy and precision of the piece. The madrigal has now been published by H. C. Slim, *A Gift of Madrigals*, II, pp. 336–7. For the altus part in example XXIX, see above, note 33.

Ex. XXIX Philippe Verdelot (?). Madrigal for four treble voices, probably for an *intermedio* to a comedy. From the manuscript Chicago, The Newberry Library, Case MS-VM 1578. M91. Second treble part reproduced by permission of the Trustees of Oscott College, Sutton Coldfield. MS Case B no. 4.

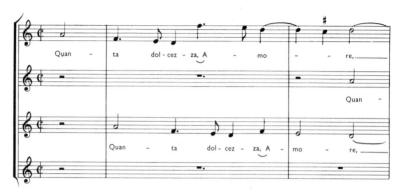

We have here (example XXIX) another praise of Love, sung this time by four high-pitched voices (of nymphs? of cupids?). Again we find the voices divided into pairs, as in *Quanto sia lieto il giorno* and *Chi non fa prov', Amore*, but here the more uniform colour and range of the voices led the composer to extend their dialogue, give the initial theme a sharper contour and reduce to a

minimum the use of chordal texture. We also find that the musical phrase which corresponds to the first two lines of the text is repeated almost identically for the next two, which have the same rhyme and metre. Such a procedure, also to be found in *Quanto sia lieto il giorno* and *Sí suave è l'inganno*, stresses the metrical structure of the texts, which consists of two symmetrical *piedi* and an undivided *sirima*, and is actually a late application of a procedure which had been customary in the setting of stanzas of *canzoni* since the early decades of the century.[51] The composer, however, did not regard it as a binding rule and actually availed himself of this procedure only when it gave clarity to his musical and poetic expression: *O dolce notte* does without it altogether, though its text has a similar metrical structure.

'Following in his [Verdelot's] steps, Archadel proceeded to assert himself very well during his stays in Florence', wrote Cosimo Bartoli.[52] His statement dispels all doubts about Arcadelt's sojourn in Florence, but leaves unspecified the dates and the length of it. As mentioned above, the *Terzo libro de i madrigali novissimi d'Archadelt*, which included four madrigals probably derived from a comedy, was published in Venice in February 1539, but despite being advertised as '*novissimi*', all the madrigals in this *Terzo libro* were probably older than those of the previous two books, also published in Venice.[53] It is likely then that the four *intermedi* belonged to a Florentine comedy, especially as they all resemble Machiavelli's *canzone*, and the text of one of them (*Foll'è chi crede la prudenz'o gli anni*) suggests a situation similar to one in *Clizia*.[54] In *Il vero secondo libro di madrigali d'Archadelt* (A. Gardane, Venice 1539) however, one madrigal, *Deh fuggite, o mortali*, whose text is given below, appears to have come from a tragedy:[55]

> Deh fuggite, o mortali,
> metter il piè su l'amoroso varco,
> cagion di tutti i mali,
> ché stral non tien poi scoccato l'arco.
> O periglioso incarco,
> che tragge l'huom alla sua morte interna!
> Ma chi la mente volta
> al ciel, dove ogni pena è ascosa e tolta,
> sgombr'e scem' ogni doglia sempiterna,
> poi gode gloria eterna.

Refrain, O mortals, from setting your foot in the path of Love, prime cause of all evils, for no dart from his bow shall ever be halted. O dangerous calamity, driving man to his inward death! But he who turns his mind to heaven, where every suffering is solaced and appeased, he shall avoid or discard distress for ever, then enjoy eternal glory.

[51] Other traces are to be found in *Chi non fa prov'*, *Amore* in the similarity of the passage corresponding to *indarno spera* and *mai fede vera*. The parallels between musical phrases and rhymes derive from *frottola* technique, which in turn must have inherited them from an earlier technique of improvisation.

[52] In the *Ragionamenti accademici* it immediately follows the passage on Verdelot quoted above (note 48). Einstein, *The Italian Madrigal*, I, pp. 159ff recalls a piece lamenting the departure from Florence of an unnamed person, and another setting of words attributed (not uncontestedly) to Lorenzino dei Medici.

[53] The enormous success of Arcadelt's first two books of madrigals, which were published by Antonio Gardane in February 1539, must have moved the latter's rival, Ottaviano Scotto, to cobble together a third book out of pieces by Arcadelt not included in the previous two collections. Biographical detail on Arcadelt too is uncertain or full of lacunae, especially on the period preceding 1539, when it is known that he was in Rome, a singer in the Capella Giulia. On 30 December 1539 (or 1540) he joined the papal chapel where he remained employed until 1552. Prior to 1539 he was certainly in Florence and later in Venice, but it is impossible to pinpoint either the dates or the circumstances of his presence in those places.

[54] It is also remarkable how closely the language and poetic images resemble Machiavelli's *canzoni*.

[55] Included in *Opera omnia*, ed. A. Seay, vol. III, pp. 8–9.

Studies in the music of Renaissance theatre

Ex. XXX   Jacques Arcadelt. Beginning of a madrigal probably composed for an *intermedio* to a comedy. From *Il terzo libro de i madrigali novissimi di Archadelt* (A. Gardane, Venice 1541).

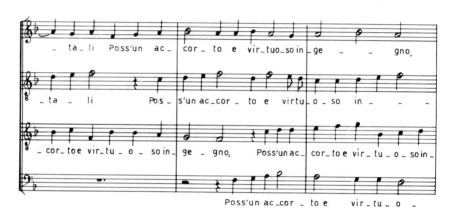

Chordal declamation also prevails in such settings by Arcadelt, but at least one of them indicates that no prejudice existed against the theatrical use of the kind of fugal beginning soon to become typical of the madrigal in its more mature phase (example XXX). Repetition, suggested either by metre or by rhyme, is also avoided. Indeed only the text given above has a structure with *piedi* and *sirima*.

Short as such pieces were – they usually lasted no more than a couple of minutes, plus a few seconds to allow for the arrival and departure of the singers – they were relied on to reduce drastically the temporal dimension, and thus to produce the perspective effect necessary to the rule of unity, or continuity, of time. Outside Florence *moresche* or jester plays, survivals from the old *feste*,[56] were still being used as *intermedi*, and, as Trissino complained, were really comedies within the comedy – at least four within the major one. But in Florence, while the *intermedi* still retained some links with the past (we have seen them develop out of the announcements made by 'one singing on the lyre', who was none other than the herald of the Signoria), they had acquired a classical dignity through being equated with tragic choruses. As early as 1525 Machiavelli had done this, purely instinctively and without

[56] See chapter 2.

theorizing.[57] True, sixteenth-century theorists from Bernardino Daniello onwards,[58] were all too eager to exorcise and canonize the most unruly and least classical kinds of *intermedi* by applying to them the magic name of 'chorus'; but the Florentine *intermedi* were real choruses, engaged in the task, once performed by the classical choruses, of commenting on the events within the play and adding an almost hieratic sense of celebration to the performance.[59] What was new was the fact that their members were unreal beings – shadows from a world outside this one and outside real time – who could more plausibly express themselves in song. As a result, it became easier for the *intermedi* to substitute the rhythmic pulse of musical time, ruled by art, for the realistic pulse of time within the play, and thus reduce the gaps between the acts.

It is in the first of the great courtly spectacles of sixteenth-century Florence that we find the clearest and most coherent example of this effect of temporal perspective achieved by means of *intermedi*, which supports the idea that it was primarily, though perhaps not exclusively, a Florentine achievement.[60] The spectacle took place in 1539, on the occasion of the wedding of Cosimo dei Medici and Eleonora of Toledo, and its *intermedi* represented then the *ne plus ultra* of theatrical refinement and magnificence.

Both external and domestic political pressures required that the celebration of the wedding of the new Duke of Tuscany be surrounded by the greatest possible splendour. The choice of a viceregal bride (for want of an imperial one)[61] emphasized the duke's alignment with the policies of Charles V, an inevitable course, to be accepted as gracefully as possible in order that it might be as profitable as possible. And as a major internal threat had recently been eliminated with the defeat at Montemurlo of the anti-Medici exiles, the full

---

[57]   See, above, the excerpt from the letter assumed to have been written on 20 October 1525, in which Machiavelli refers to Barbera's offer 'to come and act as the chorus between the acts'. A. F. Grazzini, in *La gelosia*, and, closer to Machiavelli, Donato Giannotti in *Il vecchio amoroso*, refer respectively to the 'chorus' (in the sense of a group of people) and to the 'choruses' (the songs). The anonymous author of *Il cocchio* must have been slightly later; he already complains that 'excessive and splendid *intermedi* are put on, out of all proportion to the main plot, treating it in this respect as a tragedy', i.e. having the *intermedi* act as choruses in the main play. He also bewails the fact 'that the spectators ask for nothing besides the *intermedi*, and the poor comedy, which is the main event and the basis of the whole performance, is left to pass in boredom'. And finally, still according to the same anonymous writer, the ancients did not have *intermedi* at all, 'except to allow the actors to pause and change their dress, to eat something and, as is said colloquially, *far otta* (to take time); and whenever they chose to have a song it was sung from within'. It is difficult to decide on the exact temporal implications of *far otta*.

[58]   B. Daniello, *La poetica* (Venice 1536), p. 39.

[59]   For Machiavelli it was 'the day | on which the things of old | are now by you displayed and celebrated', while for Giannotti it was a question of 'celebrating that game | upon which today | your minds are intent...' But its origins are much earlier, as is shown by the solemnity with which the feast known as the Paliliae was celebrated in Rome on 13 and 14 February 1514 (though in honour of Giuliano and Lorenzo dei Medici). It also included a performance of *Poenulus*.

[60]   I cannot rule out the possibility that non-Florentine examples might exist, but all the examples I have come across have been Florentine.

[61]   Cosimo seems first to have thought of Margaret of Austria, the illegitimate daughter of Charles V and the widow of Alessandro dei Medici, but instead she married Ottavio Farnese. His choice then fell on one of the daughters of Don Pedro di Toledo, viceroy of Naples and one of the emperor's most important representatives in Italy. Even in this choice, insofar as it was his choice, Cosimo had good luck, and succeeded in obtaining not the elder but the younger of the viceroy's daughters; he had been struck by her dignity and beauty three years previously in Naples, at the wedding of Alessandro dei Medici and Margaret of Austria.

loyalty of the duke's subjects was expressed in a parade of allegorical characters representing the major towns of Tuscany – Florence, Volterra, Arezzo, Cortona and Pistoia – and the river Tiber, who all marched in an elaborate procession during the banquet of 6 July and sang madrigals in praise of the newly wedded couple.[62] They had been preceded by a chorus of the nine Muses, each holding a musical instrument, who had also sung a nine-voice madrigal by Francesco Corteccia.[63] Each character in the group had been introduced by Apollo, clad in purple and gold, with a long series of descriptive and eulogistic octaves, sung once more to a bowed lyre.[64]

The banquet was held in the Medici palace in the Via Larga (now known as the Riccardi palace). The second courtyard had been covered for the occasion with 'a sky of tautly-stretched blue *rovescio* cloth', and decked on three sides with rich tapestries. There were no tapestries on the northern side so that people could admire the stage already set for the comedy to be performed after another banquet three days later. The comedy performed on 9 July 1539, *Il commodo* by Antonio Landi, now remembered solely because of the solemn occasion of its performance, takes place in Pisa. The official narrative of the nuptials by Pierfrancesco Giambullari does not include a description of the stage setting, but we can easily supply one from the prologue of *Il vecchio amoroso* by Donato Giannotti, written only a few years earlier:

The setting represents that section of Pisa where the church of St Nicholas is located; this building in front of you is the church itself. The street on its right side is Via Santa Maria, leading to the Duomo. The other street, whose beginning is also there, is a street leading to the city walls. The street running parallel to the facade of the church is Via dell'Ulivo...And we are acting this comedy for you in the square in front of the church. The street in front of me is the Lungarno. And you, spectators, are watching this feast from within the Arno river. Rest assured, however; you will not get wet.[65]

In the 1539 play, too, the fore of the stage represented one of Pisa's Lungarni, at the foot of which 'was seen a very wide canal, all painted within and without to resemble the river Arno. From the seaward side of this, three naked sirens suddenly appeared..., three sea nymphs..., three sea monsters...' The quotation is from the description of the *intermedio* which followed Act II – the third in the series, for one had been performed before the prologue. In it, 'all these characters travelled upstream, indicating that they were looking for the Most Illustrious Lady Duchess, who had left Naples, and sang sweetly...'. The

[62] Pierfrancesco Giambullari, in his *Apparato et feste nelle nozze del Illustrissimo Signor Duca di Firenze...con le sue stanze, madriali, comedia, et intermedii, in quelle recitati* (Giunti, Florence 1539) gives a detailed description complete with all the texts. It is revealing that the description takes the form of a long letter written by Giambullari to the Florentine ambassador at the imperial court. The quotations in subsequent notes are from Antonio Landi, *Il commodo* 'comedia... nuovamente ristampata' (Florence 1566).

[63] Each Muse was provided with a musical instrument as a means of identification, though there is no evidence that it was then used in the performance of the music. Thalia was given a trombone, Euterpe a *dolzaina*, Erato a *violone*, Melpomene a fife, Clio a flute, Terpsichore a lute, Polymnia a *storta*, and Urania a *cornetta*.

[64] Apollo sang no less than forty *stanze*, accompanying himself on a *lira ad arco*; these alternated with *madriali* sung polyphonically by the Muses and the various cities and rivers of Tuscany. Apollo's words are recorded, though not the music, in the edition mentioned in note 62.

[65] *Opere politiche e letterarie*, II, p. 197. The set for *Il commodo* was described by Vasari (see Elena Povoledo's essay, pp. 342ff).

next *intermedio* paid homage to the duke, shown as a solar figure: a Virgilian Silenus sang the following *canzonetta*, accompanying himself on a *violone da gamba* hidden in a tortoise-shell,[66] though his song was in fact a *madriale*, with a structure as typically fourteenth-century as its name.[67]

> O begli Anni de l'Oro, o secol divo!
> alhor non rastro, o falce; alhor non era
> visco, né laccio; et no 'l rio ferro e'l tosco;
>
> ma sen gia puro latte il fresco rivo;
> mel sudavan le querce; ivano a schiera
> Nymfe insieme et Pastori, al chiaro e'l fosco.
>
> O begli anni del Or, vedrovvi io mai?
> Tornagli, o nuovo Sol, tornagli homai.

O blessed golden years, age divine! then neither sickle nor rake, neither bird-lime nor net, neither cruel sword nor venom existed yet. Fresh rivers ran pure milk; oaks oozed honey; nymphs and shepherds together rambled day and night without fear. O blessed golden years, shall I ever see you? Bring them back, at last, to us, O rising Sun.

The *intermedi* thus paid due homage to the ducal couple, for whom, though pure milk did not always run in the Arno, the future had in store reasonably happy years. But their main theme was the continuity of time, and their function was to create the feeling of this continuity, compressed by the use of temporal perspective into the shorter span of the theatrical fiction. The *intermedio* before the prologue started to do this by having Dawn appear in the sky on the right hand of the stage, i.e. from the east, as the stage was set on the northern side of the courtyard. 'Following Dawn, the Sun was seen to rise slowly in the sky of the stage; and with its gentle motion it made known the hour of the fictional day, act after act, and similarly it later set and disappeared at the end of Act V, shortly before the appearance of Night.' At the end of Act I, 'twelve shepherds crossed the stage, each couple differently dressed and adorned', and singing a madrigal they implored the sun god to moderate 'the summer heat's...great fire and fierce ardour' in the day which had just started. No sooner had the sirens, sea nymphs and marine monsters of the *intermedio* after Act II sung to honour the bride, than they swiftly hastened to take refuge in the shade, and in the fourth *intermedio* 'that Silenus, whom Virgil described in his Sixth Eclogue, was found at noon by

---

[66] Landi, *Il commodo*, p. 56: '...when asked to sing, he placed between his goat-like legs a tortoise, in which was an excellent *violone*; and with a bow shaped like a dry snake, he began sweetly to play and sing the following *canzonetta*...' The tortoise-shell was obviously derived from the legend of Mercury's invention of the lyre, but it was not the first instrument to appear in camouflage in the *intermedi* to *Il commodo*. In the *intermedio* after Act I, in several of the pairs of shepherds 'one carried what appeared externally to be a length of fresh and leafy cane, though inside it was really a *storta*'. In the case of the other pairs the disguise varied, and in the last pair 'one of them played that instrument with seven pipes borne by the God of the countryside, which artfully contained a *stortina*...' Even in the *intermedio* after Act II the nymphs and marine monsters had 'transformed' instruments. See also note 71.

[67] The man who devised the *intermedi* and their costumes and wrote the words was Giovanbattista Strozzi the elder, son of Lorenzo di Filippo (mentioned several times in this chapter for his comedies). The choice of a Petrarchan rhyme-scheme for Silenus' song was probably deliberate. Even the terms *madriale* or *matriale* for *madrigale* go back to fourteenth-century Florentine usage.

Mnasillus and Chromis and fairest Egle as he rested asleep in a grotto...which showed that in the comedy it was already the hour of noon'. At the end of Act IV, 'in order to show that evening was approaching, eight hunting nymphs walked across the stage...singing, indicating that they were back from their hunting'. Finally, at the end of the comedy, Night came on stage, 'clad in black silken gauze, with a blue head-dress spangled with stars and with the Moon on her forehead'. She too sang, inviting all to go to rest, but

so sweet was her song, that lest the audience fall asleep there suddenly entered on stage XX followers of Bacchus, ten of whom were females and the others satyrs...of all these, eight played, eight sang and danced in the centre of the stage, and two on each side acted as if they were drunk...The eight singers and dancers were four satyrs and four females...The words they sang again and again were BACCHUS BACCHUS EUOE, with roaring laughs and various merry actions and jests like the drunken people they were supposed to be.

Thus, for the sake of a joyous finale (at which point food and iced wine were to be distributed to the audience too), the cycle was expanded to include a seventh *intermedio*, though they avoided numbering it as such.

There is further evidence in the dialogue of the comedy of the author's concern with the passage of time. He even brings in subjective factors which may affect one's perception of time, so that a brief moment may seem never to end, while what appears to be but a brief pause may be made to represent a longer time-span. At the beginning of Act II, Leandro, who had gone home at the end of Act I, returns saying 'I thought I would wait for the middleman's answer, to find out what hopes I have; but I was home less than one hour, and it seemed to me to be more than a hundred...' At the start of Act III the servant Currado twice mentions the fact that it is past lunchtime. Paradoxically, however, while they were stressing the observance of the classical or pseudo-classical rule of the unity of time, they had abandoned the unity of the frame, i.e. the custom of bringing back the same group at the end of each act to comment on the progress of the story. By doing this, they were destroying the last trace of similarity between the *intermedi* and tragic choruses, despite the fact that the continued presence of the latter in stage performances of tragedy had been the most effective element in enforcing all the rules of unity. Now each *intermedio* had new characters and a new subject, unrelated to each other or to the main plot except insofar as they acted as a clock. Even the unity of place was beginning to break down. The shepherds after Act I and the hunting nymphs after Act IV crossed the stage representing Pisa, and the Bacchants of the finale danced and behaved drunkenly on the same stage, but for Dawn and Night who appeared in the sky, for the sea creatures travelling up the Arno, and for Silenus asleep in a grotto the stage had to expand either upwards or downwards.

Lesser local composers, and one from the Roman milieu, Costanzo Festa,[68]

[68] Alongside the publication of Giambullari's description, the music for the nuptial entertainments appeared in Venice, in August 1539, printed by Antonio Gardane under the title of *Musiche fatte nelle nozze dello Illustrissimo Duca di Firenze il signor Cosimo de' Medici et della Illustrissima consorte sua mad. Leonora da Tolleto*. Festa composed the two madrigals to be sung by Florence and Arezzo; Ser Mattia Rampollini two madrigals also à 4 for Pisa and Pistoia; Gio. Pietro Masaconi the madrigal à 5 for Volterra; Baccio Moschini that à 4 for Cortona and the one à 5 for the Tiber. Corteccia was asked to provide not only all the music for the *intermedi*

contributed to the music for the 1539 nuptials. But Francesco Corteccia (1502–71)[69] did by far the largest share, and also wrote the music for all the *intermedi* of Landi's comedy. The most striking feature of this music is the richness and variety of its sound, of its changing groups and textures, which is all the more impressive if contrasted to the sparse sobriety of the four-voice madrigal choruses in the *intermedi* which we have just examined. The only comparable pieces are the *intermedio* of hunting nymphs and the Bacchic final chorus, both four-part pieces too, though both require that each part be doubled by two singers.[70] Furthermore, the final chorus adds to its eight singing dancers an equal number of instrumentalists with a drum, a whistle, two *cornetti*, two *storte*, one *ribechino* and a harp, all variously camouflaged.[71]

but also the motet for eight voices *Ingredere* ('sung above the arch of the Porta al Prato by twenty-four voices on one side, and on the other by four trombones and four *cornetti*...'), and the nine-voice madrigal for the Muses. All the music for the 1539 wedding festivities has recently been transcribed and published by Andrew C. Minor and Bonner Mitchell, *A Renaissance Entertainment. Festivities for the Marriage of Cosimo I, Duke of Florence, in 1539* (University of Missouri Press, Columbia, Mo. 1968), which also includes the English translation of Giambullari's description and the text of the comedy, and an extensive historical introduction. See also Osthoff, *Theatergesang*, I, pp. 334–41, and II, pp. 90–109, and H. W. Kaufmann, 'Music for a Noble Florentine Wedding' in *Words and Music* (referred to above, p. 28 note 59) pp. 161–88; Alois M. Nagler, *Theatre Festivals of the Medici* (New Haven 1964); *Il luogo teatrale a Firenze, spettacolo e musica nella Firenze medicea, documenti e restituzioni.* I (Milan 1975).

[69] Corteccia's date of birth has recently been corrected, and the matter enriched by new information, by Mario Fabbri, 'La vita e l'ignota opera-prima di Francesco Corteccia...' in *Chigiana*, XXII (1965), pp. 185ff. Born in Florence in 1502 (and not in Arezzo in 1504) of a Florentine family, he sang as a chorister from 1515 to 1522 in San Giovanni Battista, where he studied with Bernardo Pisano, and served there as a chaplain from 1527. In 1531 he became first chaplain, then organist, in the basilica of San Lorenzo; he was made a 'supernumerary' canon in January 1549–50 and a 'full' canon in 1563. In 1540 (i.e. shortly after the nuptial celebrations) he was named chapel-master of the baptistery of San Giovanni and of the Medici court, his appointment being back-dated to the beginning of the year. In addition to the music for the 1539 comedy, Corteccia wrote the music for Francesco d'Ambra's *Il furto*, performed by the Accademia Fiorentina in 1544. This music took the form of five *intermedi* madrigals not recorded in any of the printed editions of the comedy but included in a reprint of the *Libro primo de madriali a quattro voci...con l'aggiunta d'alcuni madriali novamente fatti per la comedia del Furto*. With these one seems to be back in the mainstream of Florentine *intermedio* tradition, with the comedy being presented by a chorus of 'gypsies' who also comment on its developments (see the first two *intermedi* in Federico Ghisi, *Feste musicali della Firenze medicea*, Florence 1939, pp. 65–73). Various other *madriali* by Corteccia may have been composed to serve as *intermedi* to comedies, or even as tragic choruses; amongst this latter category I would include *A che ne stringi, o scellerata fame | dell'oro, l'appetito de' mortali!* for a male chorus (*Libro primo de madriali a quattro*). I shall return later to Corteccia's involvement in the 1565 *intermedi*. About Florentine *intermedi* in general see Alois M. Nagler, *Theatre Festivals of the Medici* as well as *Il luogo teatrale a Firenze*, and the second part of *Il potere e lo spazio. La scena del principe* (Florence 1980).

[70] For the first see Landi, *Il commodo*, p. 72, where reference is made to 'eight huntress nymphs' who sang, while the madrigal is for four voices; for the second see the description quoted below.

[71] *Ibid.*, pp. 93–4:

Immediately twenty Bacchants appeared on stage, of whom ten were women, and the others satyrs. And of all these, eight played, eight sang [i.e. voices and instruments were doubled] and danced in the middle of the stage and two on either side behaved as if drunk...And these were the players' instruments. A wineskin which hid a drum and a spigot instead of a drumstick with which to beat it, together with a dried-up human shin-bone containing a flageolet. A stag's head containing a rebec. A goat's horn, containing a *cornetta*. A crane's shin-bone and foot, containing a *storta*. A barrel-hoop with reeds, containing a harp. A swan's plumage with head and neck, containing a straight *cornetta*. A root and branches of elder, containing a *storta*. These eight who danced and sang were four satyrs and four women...

Ex. XXXI Francesco Corteccia. Music for *Il commodo* by A. Landi. Beginning of the song 'sung and danced by 4 Bacchants and 4 satyrs, with divers instruments all together, which...was the end of the comedy'. From *Musiche fatte nelle nozze dello Illustrissimo Duca di Firenze* (A. Gardane, Venice 1539).

The texture is simple and wholly chordal in the Bacchic chorus (example XXXI), which was to be danced in a lively ternary rhythm marked by the drum, the only percussion instrument in the whole series of *intermedi*. But the chorus of nymphs (example XXXII), written in the more modern *misura breve*, though meant to express cheerfulness, begins in counterpoint with curiously broken and twisted rhythms and only later relaxes in a fuller chordal chorus.[72] More persistent and more diversified is the counterpoint in the six-voice *canzonetta* which served as an *intermedio* after Act I and was performed by twelve shepherds, six of whom played and six danced. In spite of the contrapuntal writing (typically of Corteccia's music, the imitations were rhythmic more often than melodic) its low texture – two basses, three tenors and one contratenor – must have produced a thick chorality, possibly inspired by the

For a more detailed description of the instruments involved here as in other Florentine *intermedi*, and for a systematic attempt to reconstruct their scoring, see Howard M. Brown, *Sixteenth-Century Instrumentation: The Music of the Florentine Intermedi*, American Institute of Musicology 1973.

[72] Ghisi, *Feste musicali*, pp. 58–62, gives the music of the nymphs' chorus, which also appears in Minor and Mitchell, *A Renaissance Entertainment*, pp. 319–23. *Ibid.*, pp. 351–2, is the final Bacchic chorus, of which both Osthoff and Kaufmann give further transcriptions.

Ex. XXXII Francesco Corteccia. Music for *Il commodo* by A. Landi. Beginning of the song 'sung at the end of the fourth act by eight huntress nymphs'. From F. Corteccia, *Libro secondo de madriali a quattro voci* (A. Gardane, Venice 1547).

rural sound of pastoral reed instruments. The piece was actually performed twice. Initially it was played entirely instrumentally, with four *storte*, one *stortina* and one straight *cornetto*,[73] all camouflaged as canes, branches and animal horns so that the sound might appear to be produced by a cornemuse and a set of panpipes which were the only visible objects having the appearance of ancient instruments.[74] There then followed a sung repetition, accompanied by the same instruments. With the song of Silenus after Act III we come back to a four-part texture, but Giambullari's description and the edition of the music both indicate that only the upper part was sung, by a singer who simultaneously played all four parts on a *violone*. This instrument is related to the bowed lyre, though lower in range,[75] and to emphasize its classical origins it was disguised as a tortoise-shell, in memory of the myth of

[73] As elsewhere (cf. note 71) Giambullari speaks of a '*cornetta*', obviously referring to an instrument of the family of the wooden or ivory *cornetto* with a metal mouthpiece and six holes. *Storte* and *stortine* are instruments belonging to the crumhorn family, with a double reed and a cylindrical body curved at the end like a walking-stick handle.

[74] See the passage about the *intermedio* after Act I, quoted in note 66.

[75] It was not played held between the knees, but standing up, the instrument resting on the floor.

Ex. XXXIII   Francesco Corteccia. Music for *Il commodo* by A. Landi. Song 'sung by Dawn, and played on a harpsichord, small organs and various instruments at the start of the comedy'. From F. Corteccia, *Libro secondo de madriali a quattro voci* (A. Gardane, Venice 1547).

_ scel _ li: U _ sci _ te, u _ sci_t',o pa _ sto _ rel_ li, u _

_ sci_te, Nim _ phe bion_de, Fuor del bel ni _ d'a _ dor _ no; O _

_ gnun si sve_gli, o _gnun si sveglie muo _ _ va al mio ri _ torno, o _

_ gnun si sve_ gli, .o _ gnun si svegliet muo _ _ va al mio ri_

_ tor_no, al mio ri _ tor _ _ _ _ no.

the lyre's invention by Mercury. If such a piece was to be performed at all it would have had to be simple in style and plainly recited.[76] The songs of Dawn and Night must have been accompanied by an instrumental sound nearly as dense as that of the six-voice *canzonetta*. The first of them, also in the *misura breve*, had however a higher range (example XXXIII) and the solo voice which sang the upper part stood out alone against a variegated combination of sounds which we would find rather difficult to reproduce today, as they came from 'one *grave cembalo* with two stops, and under it [?] organ, flute, harps and bird calls, and one *violone*'. This strange mixture combined symbolic and naturalistic motifs with the requirements of musical practice, and was made even more intriguing by the fact that all the instruments were invisible,[77] as were those accompanying the song of Night, pitched high against the soft, dark and hypnotic sound of four trombones (example XXXIV).[78]

Much more technically demanding must have been the task of writing the music for the eight-voice motet *Ingredere*, which greeted the arrival in Florence of Eleonora of Toledo, or the nine-voice chorus of the Muses which opened the banquet of 6 July 1539. But Corteccia's main artistic achievement, and one in which he was aided by the advice of Giovanbattista Strozzi, was the sharply diversified characterization of the *intermedi* of the comedy, though this variety was largely lost when he had the seven pieces reprinted in 1547 as simple '*madriali*'.[79] In his desire for variety he had three of the *intermedi* sung chorally (at least two of them with two singers per part) and three performed by a solo voice with an instrumental accompaniment. The latter style has often and not unreasonably been seen as a precursor of the later monodic style of the turn of the century, but it was also an extension of the earlier humanist style of singing accompanied by a stringed instrument, or of the *frottola* singing accompanied by several instruments, for which the voice accompanied by tenor and bass parts 'intabulated' for the lute was also a possible alternative. Actually, Corteccia's style was no longer truly *frottola*-like;

---

[76]   See the music in Minor and Mitchell, *A Renaissance Entertainment*, pp. 299–303. It was previously published in Arnold Schering, *Geschichte der Musik in Beispielen* (Leipzig 1931).

[77]   The harpsichord, organ and *violone* must have served to fill the chords (with the *violone* strengthening the bass) whilst preserving a discreet, almost ethereal sonority. Their task was made easier by the fact that they remained off-stage. At that time harps and harpsichords were often used to characterize heavenly scenes (see Robert L. Weaver, 'Sixteenth-Century Instrumentation', in *The Musical Quarterly*, XLVII, 1961, pp. 262ff). Flutes and birdsongs were of course intended to evoke the sounds of nature awakening at dawn. I doubt whether the 'sounds of birds' were actual musical instruments or just a sort of whistle or other gadget suitable for imitating the songs of specific birds. The music has been published in its madrigal version by Minor and Mitchell, *A Renaissance Entertainment*, pp. 225–8, and by Osthoff, *Theatergesang*, II, pp. 90–3. H. M. Brown, *Sixteenth-Century Instrumentation*, p. 89, suggests the use of a 'claviorganum with a harp stop on the harpsichord and flute and nightingale stops on the organ, and bass viola da gamba'; I do not see, however, that the reduction of a number of instruments to mere stops on the two parts of the claviorganum can be inferred from Giambullari's description.

[78]   Minor and Mitchell, *A Renaissance Entertainment*, pp. 343–8, and Osthoff, *Theatergesang*, II, pp. 101–7. On trombones, see also the article by Weaver referred to in the note above. The slide-trombones in use during the Renaissance had a softer, gentler and deeper tone than modern ones, and created an atmosphere of mystery and deep night (cf. the description above, in note 8). This led to their being associated with infernal beings; but they reflected merely their subterranean nature, not the horror of their environment.

[79]   I.e. with all the parts provided with their texts, as indeed already in the 1539 edition, but with no indication which might suggest their performance 'by singing and playing' let alone the desired instrumental effects.

Ex. XXXIV Francesco Corteccia. Music for *Il commodo* by A. Landi. Song 'sung at the end of the fifth act by Night, and played by four trombones'. From F. Corteccia, *Libro primo de madriali a cinque & a sei voci* (A. Gardane, Venice 1547).

it still retained in 1539 a typical feature of the most sophisticated *frottole*, an essentially harmonic texture dissimulated by a counterpoint consisting more of rhythmic animation than of real thematic work; but whereas the harmonies in *frottole* gave the impression of a clear tonal direction, Corteccia deliberately diversified his for the sake of different, and more artistic, developments. Even in the choral pieces he gave the upper parts an almost unchallenged predominance and a recitative accentuation derived from the declamatory style of humanist music as it had been practised in the first decades of the sixteenth century, though his concern for variety led him to include sudden contractions of rhythm and sharp contrasts which make his music sound twisted and jerky. The general impression conveyed is that of a stylistic venture still rooted in an earlier tradition but striving hard to give it some element of novelty. Of the 1539 *intermedi*, the piece which most succeeded in doing this, in my opinion, occurs in the *intermedio* which followed Act II, a six-voice piece (example XXXV) which displays great contrapuntal fluency, and it is all the more interesting, if my interpretation

Ex. XXXV Francesco Corteccia. Music for *Il commodo* by A. Landi. Song 'sung at the end of the second act by three sirens, and played on three transverse flutes by three marine monsters, and on three lutes by three marine nymphs all together'. From F. Corteccia, *Libro primo de madriali a cinque & a sei voci* (A. Gardane, Venice 1547).

is correct, for having been performed in a *concertato* style, with the three upper parts sung by the three sirens and the three lower ones played by the sea nymphs and marine monsters, who may also have doubled the upper parts with their instruments.[80] Here too the instruments were disguised. We are told

<hr />

[80] It seems to me that both Giambullari's description and the one contained in the *Tavola* of the musical edition of 1539 imply very clearly that only the three sirens sang. The latter description says that the piece was 'sung at the end of the second act by three sirens, and played by three sea-monsters with three *traverse* and by three sea nymphs with three lutes all together'. Thus the three upper parts were sung by the sirens, the three lower ones were played by the sea-monsters on flutes, and the whole piece was accompanied by chords played by the lutes. The 'traverse' were played as modern flutes are, held across the body. They had no keys, only holes which were held open or closed by the fingers. The description of how they were disguised in

that each nymph 'had a lute hidden within a shell, and by playing it sweetly harmonized with the singing of the sirens', while the marine monsters 'each played a transverse flute transformed in its appearance: for the first looked like a fish's long backbone, with head and tail attached but no ribs; the second looked like the shell of a sea-snail, and the third like a marsh reed'. The hidden lutes had the practical function of providing basic harmonic support for the singing, but characterization must have been mainly achieved by the liquid sound of the transverse flutes, which the audience must have imagined came from the snail-shell, as if from a marine trumpet.

Nine years after the nuptials of Cosimo I, another comedy, not performed in Florence but in several respects Florentine, also opened with Dawn

the 1539 *intermedio* implies that they were rather larger than their modern equivalent, and thus had a lower range which corresponded to the lower parts of the composition. The music is in Minor and Mitchell, *A Renaissance Entertainment*, pp. 277–88, as well as in Osthoff, *Theatergesang*, II, pp. 94–100.

appearing on a chariot drawn by two cocks, and ended with the arrival of Night on a chariot drawn by two owls. Dawn sang the following madrigal, accompanied 'by two spinets and four German flutes (*flauti d'Alemagna*)':[81]

> Io son nuntia del sol, che la prim'ora
> imperlo, ed egli indora:
> spenga il cielo ogni stella,
> rend'al mondo i color che 'l vespro invola;
> ch'omai, gelata e sola,
> all'opre usate appella
> ciascun la casta Aurora
> e 'nvita a sospirar chi Amore adora.

I am the herald of the Sun. I tinge the early hour the colour of pearls; he gilds it. Let the sky extinguish every star and restore to this world the colours which vespers stole; for now chaste Aurora, chilled and lonely, summons all back to their work and invites him who adores Love to sigh.

Night answered with another solo.[82] But between the first *intermedio* and the last, which was actually the eighth, no emphasis was placed on the progress of time as had been done in *Il commodo*; the feeling for the continuity of time seems to have been frozen into the rigid rule of unity, with a time-span inflexibly defined by the beginning and ending of the solar day. The comedy, *La calandria*, by Cardinal Bibbiena, a Medicean if not a Florentine author, was performed in Lyons on 27 September 1548 to honour the solemn entrance into that town of the French king, Henry II, and of his queen, Catherine dei Medici. 'The Florentines had it recited at the request of Her Most Christian Queen.' The artists in charge of decorating the 'great hall of St John and of preparing the stage sets' were Florentines, and the actors had been brought from Italy for the occasion.[83] The Florentine nature of the spectacle was all the more remarkable as it was mainly sponsored by an illustrious representative of the culture of Northern Italy, Cardinal Ippolito II d'Este.

The Lyons performance of *La calandria* had eight *intermedi*, achieved by doubling the *intermedio* before the prologue and the one after Act V. One could say that Dawn and Night framed the customary frame, or else that the frame had been enlarged and structured as a number of concentric elements. The figure of 'one singing on a lyre' was recreated in Apollo, who in the second and seventh *intermedi* (also placed before the prologue and after Act V) came on stage to sing a series of octaves, to pay homage to the most important

[81] Described by Angelo Solerti, 'La rappresentazione della "Calandria" a Lione nel 1548', in *Raccolta di studi critici dedicata ad Alessandro D'Ancona* (Florence 1901), pp. 693ff, taken from *La magnifica et triumphale entrata del Christianiss. Re di Francia Henrico secondo...colla particulare descritione della comedia che fece recitare la natione fiorentina* (Lyons 1549). The two spinets and the flutes are a simplified reflection of the instruments which had accompanied the Florentine 'Dawn' of 1539.

[82] 'To close...came Night on a chariot drawn by two owls and she too sang a strophe' (Solerti, 'La rappresentazione', p. 696). The instruments which accompanied the song are not mentioned.

[83] The *Particulare descritione della comedia* deals at length with the hangings and the set, the work of master Nannoccio, a Florentine, who was aided by one master Zanobi, sculptor. Thanks to them the 'hall of San Gianni' was transformed. Brantôme, quoted by Solerti, 'La rappresentazione', p. 694, expressed himself thus: '...this beautiful hall, which still exists, he [the Cardinal d'Este] had it arranged just as one sees it now: for previously it was huge, ugly, and with no sort of beauty or grace'.

spectators and to introduce the play. 'Having descended on this very day from my immortal sojourn as one summoned by the call of his desire', he announced in the second of his six octaves in the *intermedio*, his rôle of presenter:

> Et per farvi l'honor che mai non soglio
> ad altri far che cosa sia mortale,
> quant'oprat'ho già mai mostrar vi voglio
> da poi che per l'Olimpo apersi l'ale;
> *e 'n un momento innanzi a voi raccoglio*
> *quel che gran tempo a ripensar non vale:*
> le tre passate età, con quella ch'ora
> (benché dispiaccia a voi) qua giù dimora.

And to honour you as I never honoured any mortal, I wish to show you what I have accomplished since first I spread my wings throughout Olympus. *Before you I shall assemble in one brief moment what a lengthy time will not suffice to recall*: the three past ages, and with them this present one (though it displeases you).

Both this introduction and the effect of temporal perspective no longer apply to the comedy, but to the *intermedi* alone. Apollo is accompanied by four characters whom he introduces one by one. They represent figures, with their symbols, who will return in sequence in the four real *intermedi* between the acts. In reverse order of time, they were the present age 'as cruel as iron, for it reigns over all possible ugliness', the Age of Bronze 'in which lived those to whom you gave the name of Heroes: Jason, Hercules, Theseus...', the Age of Silver, devoted to agriculture, and the Golden Age, 'when there was no pain, fear, toil, heat or ice'. After Act I there entered the Age of Iron, accompanied by Cruelty, Avarice and Envy. She recited one *canzone* stanza (i.e. a madrigal) and then, during a parade of all the allegorical characters, 'the lines which the Age of Iron had recited were sung to music by four voices inside the stage, while the same music was played by four *violoni da gamba* and four German flutes. And when the music was over the Age of Iron paid homage to the king and...made her exit with her companions.' In the following *intermedi* the Age of Bronze was accompanied by Fortitude, Fame and Revenge; the Age of Silver by Ceres, Pales and Agriculture; and the Golden Age by Peace, Justice and Religion. After Act V Apollo returned with the Golden Age, sang four stanzas and left: the Golden Age sang a further seven, then climbed down from the stage and approached the queen, to present her with a weighty gold lily, a gift from the Florentine Nation. We are told that all the musical pieces 'were composed and the instruments consorted (*concertati*) by Messer Pietro Mannucci, who is the organist of the Florentine Nation here at [the church of] Notre Dame'.

Neither Apollo nor the four Ages said anything relating to the events in the comedy. Two years later Anton Francesco Grazzini ('il Lasca') devised for his comedy, *La gelosia*, *intermedi* which were remarkable for their variety and inventiveness, though unfortunately they were never performed. And like the earlier *intermedi* at Lyons, their only link with the comedy and with each other was the fact that they dealt with nocturnal themes.[84] 'Il Lasca', who was reluctantly obliged to fall back on the usual frame consisting of choral

---

[84]   See above, note 20.

commentaries (sung by some 'slaves of Love'), had little right to complain of the abuse to which he referred in his well-known humorous madrigal 'Comedy complaining about the *intermedi*':

> Misera, da costor che già trovati
> fur per servirmi e per mio ornamento
> lacerar tutta e consumarmi sento.
>   Questi empi e scelerati a poco a poco
> preso han lena e vigore,
> e tanto hanno or favore
> ch'ognun di me si prende scherno e gioco,
> *e sol dalla brigata*
> *s'aspetta e brama e guata*
> *la meraviglia, ohimè! degli intermedi;*
> e se tu non provvedi,
> mi fia tosto da lor tolto la vita;
> misericordia, Febo! aita, aita!

Woe is me, for I am rent and ruined by those very creations once devised to serve me and be my ornament. Little by little the wicked felons have gained strength and vigour; they are now so much in favour that I am scorned and abused by everyone: *nothing else is sought, desired and admired by the audience save the wondrous show, alas, of the intermedi*! If you take no action, they will soon take my life; have mercy upon me, Phoebus! help me! help!

5 'The wondrous show, alas, of the *intermedi*!'

An autograph 'Register of [my] works'[1] by Anton Francesco Grazzini still survives, in which the prolific writer, whose comment on the *intermedi* forms the title of this chapter, follows his entry of 'Sonnets, about five hundred' with a reference to 'Madrigals, about four hundred, including those written as *intermedi* for comedies by myself or others', all nine hundred items being grouped under the general heading of 'Petrarchan Rhymes'.[2] Grazzini, also known as 'il Lasca', wrote six or seven comedies, but only one of these, *La gelosia*, was printed with its *intermedi*.[3] I have come across no other comedies which were printed including verses written by il Lasca for use in *intermedi*. This confirms the hypothesis that though most printed comedies make no mention of *intermedi*, this by no means necessarily signifies that the plays were produced without them. Again, the many comedies by Ludovico Dolce were all printed without *intermedi*, yet at the end of Act I of his *Il capitano*[4] the servant Truffa concludes his comments on the events of the act by saying:

> Ma, che genti son quelle che compaiono
> in Scena? s'addimandano intermedij
> che 'l mondo usa di por ne le Comedie.

But who are those people who are now appearing on the stage? They are called *intermedi*, such as we are now used to having in comedies.

Our automatic reaction is to assume that a curtain closed and an interval filled in the gap between acts, but this was not so in sixteenth-century theatre. Indeed, it is this lack of information which has meant that we think of *intermedi* as being all of a type which in fact represents the exception rather than the rule, though admittedly an exception of great historical and artistic importance. In this category of 'exceptional' *intermedi* belong those which were intended to celebrate some particularly important event in the life of a court and to impress all the guests with their inventiveness and extravagance. In order that members of both allied and rival courts should hear of these spectacles and be suitably impressed, a detailed description was usually printed immediately afterwards, reporting on the stage sets, the decorations, the attributes and symbolic meanings of each of the characters, the quality and colour of the materials used, the wonders of the stage machinery and even, on occasion, including a list of the instruments used to perform the musical pieces.

---

[1] See the conclusion of the previous chapter.

[2] Reproduced in A. F. Grazzini, *Le rime burlesche* (Florence 1882), p. cxxi, facsimile on the facing plate. See also Robert J. Rodini, *Antonfrancesco Grazzini: Poet, Dramatist and Novelliere, 1503–1584* (Madison, Wisconsin 1970), appendix 1.   [3] See above, pp. 126–7.

[4] *Il capitano* '...performed in Mantua before His Excellency the Duke' (Venice 1545).

I have already suggested that these special *intermedi* should be described as 'aulic' or courtly.[5] They were performed at many courts, but the Florentines were particularly anxious to publicize theirs; the Florentine court had only recently asserted its political power and the Medici may have been eager for their banking and trading past to be forgotten. Both the Florentine spectacles of 1539 and those given in Lyons in 1548 belong in this category, though for convenience I have dealt with them elsewhere. That they were in fact exceptional is clear: even in Florence more than a quarter of a century elapsed before entertainments similar to those of 1539 again took place, though within this period 'ordinary' performances of comedies continued. These may have been more frequent than we realize, and were generally sponsored by the Accademia Fiorentina under the patronage of Cosimo I,[6] but none of the productions was as solemn or as lavish as that of *Il commodo* had been. It was Cosimo's restless and pleasure-seeking eldest son, Francesco, recently put in charge of routine state administration, who was responsible for a new burst of intense theatrical activity; on St Stephen's day (26 December) 1565 Francesco d'Ambra's *La cofanaria* was performed with *intermedi* by Giovanbattista Cini 'for the nuptials of the Most Illustrious Prince Don Francesco dei Medici and of the Most Serene Queen Giovanna of Austria', sister of the Emperor Maximilian II. The masquerades of the carnival of 1566[7] formed what was tantamount to a continuation of the wedding festivities, with the Accademia Fiorentina staging a performance of Leonardo Salviati's *Il granchio* with *intermedi* by Bernardo de Nerli, a member of the Accademia.

We shall consider the *intermedi* for *Il granchio* before those of *La cofanaria*, for despite being later than these, they were more similar in style to the performances we have already examined. Indeed, they were either modelled directly on the 1548 Lyons *intermedi* for *La calandria* or shared with them a common source as their model. In spite of the fact that both Duke Cosimo and Prince Francesco had 'lent their money and support to this public spectacle',[8] the Accademia did not want things to be overdone, so there were only six, not eight, *intermedi*. The 'declaration', added by their author to the

[5]   'Intermedium', in *Die Musik in Geschichte und Gegenwart*, VI, col. 1314.

[6]   Of this sort were the comedies of 1544, 1547, 1550 and 1560, mentioned by Ghisi, *Feste musicali*, pp. xxii–xxv. On the first of these, see note 69 of the previous chapter (but to Ghisi's publication of the first two madrigals Osthoff has now added the remaining three, in *Theatergesang*, II, pp. 110–21); for the 1550 comedy, the only one published with the text of the *intermedi*, see note 20 of the same chapter.

[7]   These were: the *Canto dei Sogni* 'sent out by the most Illustrious and most Excellent Prince of Florence, and of Siena. The second day of February, 1565' (Florence 1566); the *Mascherata della geneologia degl'iddei de' Gentili* 'sent out by the most Illustrious and most Excellent Duke of Florence and Siena. The day of 21 of February M.D.LXV' (Florence 1566); and the *Dieci mascherate delle bufole* 'sent out in Florence the day of carnival the year 1565' (Florence 1566). All the dates on the title-pages are according to the Florentine style, *ab Incarnatione*, i.e. with the year beginning on 25 March. Even the printed edition of *Il granchio* (Florence 1566) was dedicated by Tommaso del Nero to Francesco dei Medici (see next note). The masquerades too deserve a chapter of their own; on them see for example Ghisi, *Feste musicali della Firenze medicea*; Jean Seznec, *The Survival of the Pagan Gods* (Princeton 1953); Nagler, *Theatre Festivals of the Medici*; G. G. Bertelà and A. M. Petrioli Tofani, *Feste e apparati medicei da Cosimo I a Cosimo II* (Florence 1969).

[8]   In his dedication of *Il granchio* to Francesco dei Medici. Tommaso del Nero described the Florentine Accademia as a 'garden...planted, looked after, and enriched by the generosity of His Excellency the Duke your father'; but further on he indicates, in the phrase quoted, that Francesco too had contributed towards the cost of the comedy.

printed edition of the comedy,[9] insisted on their resemblance to 'the chorus
of the ancient fables of the Greeks' and maintained that, 'as the *intermedi*
correspond to the *canzoni* sung by the chorus, and as these were [placed]
neither before, nor after the fable, but only sung in the middle of it, it seems
reasonable that the *intermedi*...should take place only between one act and
the other...For these reasons there are but four [real] *intermedi* in the present
comedy; and they are [those representing] the four ages of human life, namely
Childhood, Youth, Virility and Senility.' According to Bernardo de Nerli, 'the
two madrigals of the Muses, one of which is [placed] before the comedy and
the other after it, are not *intermedi*'; they are 'added to the four *intermedi*...to
avoid a departure from custom, as well as to please the theatre...accustomed
to seeing something before and after the comedy'. Nerli dwells (possibly with
a hint of criticism of the recently performed *intermedi* of *La cofanaria*) on two
qualities of his true *intermedi* (the central ones): 'first, that they are clear and
easily understood', and secondly, that in a comedy 'dealing with private,
domestic actions', he has avoided bringing on stage for the *intermedi* 'most
illustrious characters of marvellous appearance, such as kings, gods and the
like'. This does not apply as well to his two 'madrigals of the Muses', both
because the Muses were neither 'private' nor 'domestic' characters, and
because their appearance on the stage depended on the audience knowing
their previous lengthy story which involved an even more illustrious character,
Apollo, and, to some extent, even Jove.

Whatever Nerli may have felt, one thing is evident: there is a clear
distinction between the general framework and the *intermedi* within it, with
the latter again given the task of marking the passage of time. The link
between the framework and the plot is casual and contrived. On Apollo's
advice the Muses have 'abandoned their beautiful Parnassus, now inhabited
by a cruel, barbarous nation' (an allusion to the Turkish occupation of
Greece), and have come to Florence on a cloud. Apollo has suggested 'that
they enter the city and go immediately to the Accademia, [a place] full of
virtuous men, among their truest followers; when they arrive, they should
wait there till the next morning', when he will show them Fiesole, 'which
is in no way inferior to Parnassus'. In fact, the Muses, 'covered by a
cloud...arrive at the Accademia...at the very moment when all the people
are getting ready to start acting the comedy without delay, with the curtains
covering the stage [already] lowered'. The Muses sing their madrigal and leave
the stage; 'and when the comedy is over, and morning come, the Muses
return...and, moving toward the hills of Fiesole, their new Parnassus, they
praise the country and its Princes'. The looseness of the external frame has
a parallel in the vague analogy by which the central *intermedi* allude to the
passage of time. The comedy 'lasts a little less than one revolution of the sun
[in the sky], beginning about noon [one day] and ending before noon the next;
but, as within such a period one can observe, and there exist, only four
separate "hours", Morning, Noon, Evening and Night...and as each of those
ages [the four ages of man] corresponds to one of the said hours...each age
is brought on stage as an *intermedio* at the appropriate hour...which it

---

[9] The full title is *Intermedii della commedia del Granchio, Dichiarazione di essi, e discorso dell'autore*.
It forms a separate section, signature I, not present in all copies, although the frontispieces of
all of them mention 'gli intermedii di Bernardo de Nerli. Accademico Fiorentino'.

represents'. For the sake of this correspondence Nerli was obliged to have the *intermedio* of Youth performed after Act I and to postpone the *intermedio* of Childhood until after Act IV. Despite the fact that his 'Discourse' is so lengthy, he fails to include in it any information about the music, its composers and how it was performed, an omission for which it is hard to forgive him.

Much has recently been written about the performance of *La cofanaria*, and much had previously been written,[10] starting with a pompous preface to the first edition of the comedy[11] by one Alessandro Ceccherelli: 'It is commonly held amongst those who know best...that of all the spectacles that are performed, the most worthwhile and worth listening to and seeing is comedy...Especially as for some time it has become usual to make them [more] attractive and ornate, by performing wonderfully inventive and skilfully contrived *intermedi* between their acts.' This almost seems to be leading up to a justification of *intermedi* in terms of their educational and moral values, but Ceccherelli stops short of that, merely stating that thanks to them 'nowadays a comedy, representing various actions simultaneously, brings no less wonder to its audience than did the tragedies with their choruses in ancient times'. Although the *intermedi* of *La cofanaria* do include choral parts, they share none of the functions of tragic choruses, but it is true to say that they enable different stories to be represented simultaneously. Giovanbattista Cini's six *intermedi* have a plot of their own which is carried through from one *intermedio* to the next, so that while they act as *intermedi* to the acts of the comedy, these can also be seen as functioning as *intermedi* to them. There is supposed to be some connection between the two plots: 'All the *intermedi* were...derived from the story of Psyche and Amor...and we have proceeded to select those parts [of the story] that seemed most essential, fitting them to the comedy with as much skill as possible, to make it appear that what the gods were doing in the fable of the *intermedi* the humans, too, would later do in the comedy, compelled as it were, by a superior power.'[12]

As far as I know, this is the first instance in which the plots of the *intermedi* and the comedy are integrated. The result is an action which develops on two levels, alternating between the divine and the human, the latter influenced

[10] My main source has been the *Descrizione degl'intermedii rappresentati colla commedia nelle nozze* etc. (Florence 1566), appended with its own frontispiece and pagination to the printed edition of *La cofanaria* (Florence 1566) 'by the sons of Lorenzo Torrentino and Carlo Pettinari, partners'. In the dedication to the bridal pair the author of the description is declared to be il Lasca, i.e. Anton Francesco Grazzini, and he mentions that the *intermedi* had previously been 'brought out in haste and therefore carelessly...based on a simple description made by their author before their being performed'. U. Angeli, *Notizie per la storia del teatro a Firenze* (Modena 1891), pp. 13–14, knew a *Descritione dell'apparato della commedia. Et intermedii d'essa...ristampata, con nuova aggiunta* in 1566, and another with the same title but *Quarta impressione*, also of 1566; they differ little between themselves or il Lasca's version, except insofar as the latter does not describe the apparatus. Studies include the anonymous nuptial booklet *Apparato per le nozze di Francesco de' Medici con Giovanna d'Austria* (Leghorn 1870); Ubaldo Angeli's 1891 study referred to above; O. G. T. Sonneck's work referred to in note 15; Ghisi, *Feste musicali della Firenze medicea*, also already referred to; and now a more recent publication by Howard Mayer Brown (see note 32). Pier Ginori Conti, *L'Apparato per le nozze di Francesco de' Medici e di Giovanna d'Austria* (Florence 1936), although full of detailed information which shows the enormous care which went into the preparations, says nothing about either the comedy or the *intermedi* and their music. Finally, see Osthoff, *Theatergesang*, I, pp. 342–6, and II, pp. 122–31.
[11] Already referred to in the previous note.
[12] Grazzini, *Descrizione degl'intermedii*, p. 3.

by the former, though its characters do not realize it. This at least, was the intention; but in fact Psyche's story is outlined in such a sketchy and discontinuous way that it could hardly be followed without a precise knowledge of the myth as well as Apuleius' story – a knowledge which Cini, Ceccherelli and Grazzini (for he, too, was involved) must have worked hard to revive in the minds of as many spectators as possible. Nor is it made clear how its development exerts an influence on the events which involve the characters of *La cofanaria*. In the first *intermedio*,

shortly after the curtains, which concealed the perspective [i.e. the stage] from the eye of the spectators had fallen,[13] the arc of the sky was seen to open up, showing a second most artistic sky;[14] from this a cloud was seen emerging little by little, on which a gilded, jewelled chariot had been fixed with singular mastery; it was understood to be Venus' chariot because it was seen pulled by two very white swans, while that most beautiful goddess, naked and all garlanded with myrtle and roses, sat majestically in it as its mistress and driver...She had the three Graces in her company, also identified by being completely naked and with the fairest of hair...and the four-winged Horae as well...They could all be seen...sitting on the said cloud; which, descending little by little, appeared to leave behind it in the sky Jupiter, Juno, Saturn, Mars and Mercury and the other gods, from whom a sweetest harmony descended, more divine than human, as well as...the most delightful and precious scents. Meanwhile Amor was seen entering from a corner of the stage, winged and yet seeming to walk about on foot...and accompanied by his four main passions...that is, by Hope...Fear...Joy...and Sorrow...Approaching the chariot, which in the meantime had reached the floor, they stood there while the Horae and Graces slowly stepped down from the cloud; and these, surrounding Venus who had risen to her feet...helped her to sing the first two stanzas of the *ballatetta* given below; and all the while the Horae were showering garlands, made of various flowers by the thousand, on the audience around them; and when they had finished and all resumed their places, the cloud, the chariot and the swans were seen to climb back slowly into the sky; and when they reached it, suddenly it closed leaving no trace...Meanwhile Amor, walking about the stage with his companions who accompanied him in harmony, continued to sing the final stanza of the *ballata*; he also threw many darts, intimating by this that the lovers, who thereafter continued to recite, had been moved by their wounds to give birth to the following comedy...

Although I have pruned a lot of detail about costumes and properties, the description still preserves as its main feature an almost hieratic slowness of motion: the cloud bringing Venus' chariot descended little by little; slowly the Horae and Graces stepped down from it; little by little the cloud raised them back to the concave sky by which they were swallowed, though this time suddenly. The movement was slow partly because the machinery was cumbersome, but its main purpose was to give the audience all the time they needed to absorb the variety of visual, aural and olfactory stimuli, to appreciate the ingenuity of the artifice involved, to perceive all the details, to relish the piquancy of the female nudes. All in all, the spectacle was a sort of *tableau vivant* rather than a pantomime,[15] with movement kept to a

[13]   *Ibid.*; the ceremonial which introduced the performance of a comedy included the falling of the curtain, often preceded by the sound of trumpets, and followed by a brief interval before the start of the first *intermedio* or the prologue.

[14]   *Ibid.*; on the concave panoramic background of sky see Elena Povoledo's essay, p. 350.

[15]   Oscar G. T. Sonneck, 'A Description of Alessandro Striggio and Francesco Corteccia's *intermedi* "Psyche and Amor" 1565', in *Miscellaneous Studies in the History of Music* (New York

minimum, lest it upset the overall effect. A fairly specific allusion to pictorial art occurs in the reference to the Graces, 'identified by their being all naked and with the fairest of hair'.[16] Even more precise is the reference in the fourth *intermedio* of a comedy performed the following year, in which Calumny was shown 'between two women who were whispering in her ears, as once portrayed by Apelles, the ancient painter';[17] it should not be too difficult to trace more such visual correspondences by examining contemporary painting in Florence.[18]

For all the lavishness and slowness of the presentation, the only development in the first *intermedio* of *La cofanaria* is contained in a short passage of dialogue between Venus and Amor:

VENERE

> A me, che fatta son negletta, e sola,
> non più gl'altar, né i voti;
> ma, di Psiche devoti,
> a lei sola si danno, ella gl'invola.

> Dunque, se mai di me ti calse, ò cale,
> figlio, l'armi tue prendi,
> e questa folle accendi
> di vilissimo Amor d'huomo mortale.

AMORE

> Ecco, Madre, andiàn noi: chi l'Arco dammi?
> chi le saette? ond'io
> con l'alto valor mio
> tutti i cor vinca, leghi, apra & infiammi?

VENUS

> To me, neglected, nay deserted, are dedicated neither altars nor vows; to Psyche alone they go; to her alone are offered; she steals them all.

> Therefore, if ever you cared for me, or care, my son, take up your weapons and fire this fool's heart with basest love of mortal man.

AMOR

> Behold, Mother, we are departing: who shall give me my bow? Who my darts? that by them with my great powers I might win, tie, open and enflame all hearts.

Both characters express themselves in a way fully in keeping with the solemn and stylized scene, for Venus' song is a madrigal for eight voices, and Amor's answer one for five. The Horae and Graces 'helped her [Venus] to sing the first two stanzas'; Amor sang his 'with his companions who accompanied him in harmony'.[19] In addition, Venus' descent had been accompanied by 'a

1921), p. 271 (reprinted from the *Musical Antiquary* of October 1911), defined them as pantomimes, rightly reacting against the widespread concern to see the *intermedi* as forerunners of opera. I have no intention of contradicting his statement; I merely wish to define it more closely.

[16] Grazzini, *Descrizione degl'intermedii*, p. 4. It is difficult to establish precisely which portrayal of the Graces the authors had in mind.

[17] Certainly they were not recalling the ancient painting; if anything, they would have thought of Botticelli's, now in the Galleria degli Uffizi.

[18] One must bear in mind that Vasari was responsible for the visual element of the *intermedi*.

[19] Grazzini, *Descrizione degl'intermedii*, p. 5.

sweetest harmony...more divine than human', appearing to descend from the images of the gods placed in the farthermost sky – obviously the sound of hidden instruments, which was possibly repeated while the goddess rose again and disappeared.[20]

The musical settings for *La cofanaria* – those of the first, second and fifth *intermedi* by Alessandro Striggio, those of the third, fourth and sixth by Francesco Corteccia – were scheduled for publication.[21] Probably this never happened; nor have the pieces been found in manuscript sources, with a single lucky exception which I shall discuss later. In addition to vocal sections, they must have included a considerable amount of instrumental music. In the second *intermedio* 'from one of the four roads [of the set]...a small cupid was seen to enter, who seemed graciously to hold in his arms a swan, within which a *violone* not too large in size had been hidden with great mastery;[22] this cupid, while pretending to play with a cane of marshy reed (under which a bow was hidden) held in one hand, played most sweetly'. Music, entering immediately after, had no need to disguise her instrument, 'the beautiful, large *lirone* on which she was playing'.[23] Following her, and following other characters (Zephyrus, Play and Laughter, also represented as small cupids), 'there came four more cupids...playing four very beautiful lutes'. Thus there were three different kinds of 'visible' instrumental music played on stage: solo music for *violone* and for *lirone*, and ensemble music for the lutes.[24] Then all these characters, plus four more singing cupids, joined together to sing and play a madrigal about Amor, 'now prey to himself and to Psyche'.[25] In the

[20] *Ibid.*, p. 6. incorrectly numbered p. 8. The musical information in the body of the description needs to be considered in conjunction with the more precise details added at the end (p. 16) 'to satisfy curious Musicians'. First of all they tell us that 'because, besides being wondrously beautiful, the hall was also singularly large and high, and perhaps the largest known at this time, it was necessary to make the consorts of music very full in tone'. In the first intermedio 'four double harpsichords...four *viole d'arco*...two trombones...two tenor flutes...a mute *cornetto*...a transverse flute...two lutes...with excellent voluntaries (*ricerche*)...gave enough time for the descent of the chariot, and for the Hours and Graces to reach their appointed places'. The music of Venus' two short stanzas 'was à 8; sung on stage by voices only, and accompanied from within, though with singular difficulty and artifice, by two harpsichords, four *violoni*, a medium-sized lute, a mute *cornetto*, a trombone and two recorders'. The stanza assigned to Amore 'was à 5, also sung on the stage by voices alone and accompanied within by two harpsichords, by a large lute, by a double-bass viol added to the parts ('Da un sotto basso di viola aggiunto sopra le parti'), by an added treble viol and a flute similarly added, by four transverse flutes and a trombone'. I take this last passage to mean that the five voices were doubled by the transverse flutes and the trombone, and that the bass and soprano parts were further strengthened by the 'added' instruments. The harpsichords and the lute would have fulfilled the same role as later played by the continuo. It is interesting to note the 'beautiful voluntaries' (*ricerche*) mentioned in connection with the instrumental piece; they indicate a contrapuntal style (cf. *ricercare*).

[21] *Ibid.*, p. 16, it says 'as will be seen when the music is printed' (*stampandosi le musiche*).

[22] *Ibid.*, p. 7. It is generally assumed that the *violone* must have been played rested on the ground (and it is not uncommon to consider it a forerunner of the double-bass). Here we have an indication that there existed scaled-down *violoni* held in the player's arms. (Besides, the French name for a violin is even now *violon*.) On p. 17 the same instrument is called a *viola d'arco*.

[23] *Ibid.*, p. 7. What I have said above about the *violone* applies equally to the *lirone*. Music's *lirone* must have been larger than the usual *lira* but still of a size to be held in her arms, as she 'approached playing'.

[24] *Ibid.*, p. 8. As elsewhere in il Lasca's description, the impression here conveyed is that the lutes each played a single melodic line; cf. the next note.

[25] 'These, having made themselves almost into a chorus, sang and played the following madrigal', *ibid.*, p. 8. The second *intermedio* presents several problems of musical practice: there were nine characters (including the first cupid and Music) on stage, but the music to be performed

third *intermedio* 'there were seen to rise little by little [from the ground] first seven, then seven more Deceptions', unleashed because Amor was caught in the tangle of his love for Psyche. 'Some of them held snares in their hands, some fish-hooks, and others hooks and grapples, under each of which were hidden musical *storte*.' First they played a madrigal for six voices on them, and then both played and sang it.[26] The rising of the characters of the fourth *intermedio* (Discord, Anger, Cruelty, etc.) out of smoking holes may have been either silent or accompanied by noise; but then 'two Anthropophagi or Laestrigones…by playing two trombones disguised as ordinary trumpets, seemed to incite all those present to fight'.[27] Also present on stage were the Furores, 'armed with drums, iron whips and various weapons, under which various instruments were hidden';[28] after all the others had played and sung a madrigal, the Furores performed a new and curious *moresca* as if they were fighting.[29] Finally, in the sixth *intermedio*, Mount Helicon was seen to rise on stage, from which all the good characters of the fable descended with Hymenaeus; two *canzonette* were sung and played, the second accompanying 'a novel and most joyous dance'. The instruments, played by Pan and nine satyrs, were 'pastoral…under which other musical instruments were hidden'.[30]

Psyche, the focal point of the whole story, did not appear until the fifth *intermedio*, when, 'clothed in desperation' (*sic*), she is 'dispatched by Venus to the infernal Proserpina'. She is escorted by Jealousy, Envy, Worry or

was for four voices. I think that the lower parts of the piece were sung by Zephyrus, Laughter and Play, and the soprano part by the four cupids without lutes. On pp. 17–18 it says: 'The second [*intermedio*] was à 4, sung on stage by four voices and played by four lutes, a *viola d'arco*, and a *lirone*. And within by three harpsichords, a large lute, a soprano viol, a contralto flute, a large tenor flute, a bass trombone and a mute *cornetto* which played an additional soprano fifth part'. In the 'visible' group, each lute would have reinforced one voice. The function of the *viola d'arco* (or small *violone*) and of the *lirone* is unclear. In the 'invisible' group inside, the voices were reinforced by an interesting combination of instruments: in descending order of pitch, viol, transverse flute, large flute and trombone. The mute *cornetto* evidently had a new part, and the other instruments provided as it were a continuo.

[26] *Ibid.*, pp. 8–9. 'Love being intent on work other than inflaming human hearts, it seemed at the end of the second act almost as if the floor of the stage were rising to form seven little hillocks, whence were seen to emerge, little by little…' etc. And on p. 18 'The third *intermedio*, à 6, was sung and played entirely on stage, i.e. by five *storte*, a mute *cornetto* and eight voices reinforcing the sopranos and basses'. Osthoff, *Theatergesang*, I, p. 346, emphasizes this doubling of the highest and lowest parts as being indicative of those tendencies which were eventually to lead to accompanied monody. See also note 20 above.

[27] Grazzini, *Descrizione degl'intermedii*, p. 10. As has already become clear from the other details of the orchestration of the *intermedi*, it is impossible to ascribe to each instrument a fixed and unchanging ethos. The trombones which we saw connected with nocturnal and subterranean images appear quite differently characterized in the first and second *intermedi*. Here in the fourth *intermedio*, although there is some slight hint of an infernal element, they are associated with warlike noises.

[28] *Ibid.*

[29] *Ibid.*, p. 18. 'The music of the fourth was also à 6 [and] sung and played in similar fashion, all on stage doubling the voices in all the parts, and adding to them two trombones, a *dolzaina*, two ordinary *cornetti*, a large *cornetto* and two drums.' There is no mention of how the *moresca* was accompanied.

[30] *Ibid.*, p. 14. On pp. 18–19: 'The last, à 4, was most gay and full in tone, quadrupling all the voices. And adding to them two mute *cornetti*, two trombones, a *dolzaina*, a *stortina*, a *lirone*, a *lira*, a rebec and two lutes. They all played and sang in the first *canzonetta*. In the second [which is in *ballata* metre] as long as the stanzas were recited in the course of the dance, only eight voices sang, and the *lira* and the *lirone* played, but its refrain, as though to reawaken the souls of the audience, was heard to be played and sung with renewed gaiety by all'.

Ex. XXXVI Alessandro Striggio. Start of Psyche's lament, from the 5th *intermedio* of *La cofanaria* by F. d'Ambra. Reconstruction by H. M. Brown from the lute tablature in Vincenzo Galilei, *Fronimo* (G. Scotto, Venice 1568).

Concern, and Scorn (all female characters), who harass her and then fight four snakes who emerge from the ground; then, 'while striking them [the snakes] in many ways with thorny rods they held in their hands (in which four bows were hidden)...suddenly a sad, yet very soft and sweet harmony was heard, while Psyche sang the following madrigal; this because four *violoni* had been arranged with great skill inside the snakes; and then she sang with such grace that it was seen to draw tears from many eyes'.[31] The whole *intermedio* centres on Psyche's lament:

> Fuggi, spene mia, fuggi,
> e fuggi per non far più mai ritorno.
> Sola tu, che distruggi
> ogni mia pace, à far vienne soggiorno,
> Invidia, Gelosia, Pensiero e Scorno,
> meco nel cieco Inferno
> ove l'aspro martir mio viva eterno.

You forsake me, my hope, you forsake me never to return. But you alone who destroy my peace, you come to stay with me – you Envy, Jealousy, Concern and Scorn – in gloomy hell, where my cruel torment shall last forever.

The action did not stop there; for after Psyche's lament 'a huge gulf opened in the floor, causing all the ladies in the audience no small scare, and from it smoke and flames in great quantity emerged unceasingly. Then, suddenly, infernal Cerberus was seen with his three heads, and his frightful bark was heard; Psyche was seen to throw him one of two flat cakes she was holding and after a while Charon, accompanied by various monsters, appeared in his

[31] *Ibid.*, p. 13–14.

boat, in which Psyche took her place, in the tiresome and unpleasant company of her four tormentors.'

Fortunately an American musicologist has successfully made a skilful reconstruction of the music of Psyche's pathetic madrigal (example XXXVI), which was accompanied by four trombones and one *lirone* in addition to the four *violoni* playing on stage.[32] It becomes increasingly evident, however, that all that occurred before and after this must have taken place without music. The old identification of the *intermedi* with 'madrigals' or choruses is giving way to a new situation, in which music, no matter how rich and varied in its vocal and instrumental combinations, or even impassioned and moving as in Psyche's lament, represents only one of many elements contributing to the 'wondrous show of the *intermedi*'. It is clearly subordinate to the lavishness of the plastic and pictorial figurations, the opening of skies, the *dei ex machina* and *ex nube*, or the structures emerging from the ground during each *intermedio*, which were superimposed on the settings designed for the action of the comedy and completely altered their appearance.[33] Cerberus' frightful bark, or 'the uproar of Chaos' of a later *intermedio* (producing 'a thunder similar to the report of a musket')[34] are as important a part of the spectacle as the *lirone* played by Music herself.

In the Florentine *intermedi* of 1567/8, performed to celebrate the christening of Francesco's first child, a daughter, and in those of 1569, given 'to honour the Most Illustrious presence of his Most Serene Highness, the Most Excellent Archduke of Austria' (a 'presence' anticipating the imperial decision to promote the Florentine duchy into a grand-duchy), variety and surprise were once more regarded as more important than giving the *intermedi* some kind of a plot or even some element of continuity. Admittedly, the overall tone of

[32]   *Ibid.*, p. 18: 'In the fifth à 5 a single soprano voice was accompanied on stage by four *violoni* and from within by a *lirone* and four trombones'. I must here express my gratitude to Professor Howard M. Brown of the University of Chicago who generously allowed me to use his study 'Psyche's Lament: Some Music for the Medici Wedding in 1565', which was in the process of being published at the time I was writing this chapter and which has since appeared in *Words and Music: The Scholar's View*, pp. 1–16 (the music on pp. 17–27). I felt I should leave to him both the task of pointing out the source (the second edition, Venice 1584, of Vincenzo Galilei's *Fronimo*) and the criteria of the reconstruction, as well as the credit for so doing; I therefore confined myself to quoting but a brief incipit of this extremely important example of recitative music *ante litteram*. (I have doubts about the lengthy coloratura passages, in my opinion not suited to a lament, suggested by the transcriber). Another piece of music for the *intermedi* of *La cofanaria* (the madrigal for eight voices, also by Striggio, with which Venus turns to Love in the first *intermedio*) has been published by Osthoff, *Theatergesang*, II, pp. 122–31, from a 1584 printed collection either incompletely described, or not described at all, in the main bibliographical catalogues.

[33]   In *La cofanaria* there was one single, permanent set for the comedy. The scene did not change for the *intermedi*, but descending clouds, floats, hillocks and whirlpools, flames and smoke and a succession of fantastic apparitions all served to obliterate its normal appearance, which was probably further altered by lighting changes. See Elena Povoledo's essay in connection with this matter.

[34]   This was the first *intermedio* of *Le due Persilie* by Giovanni Fedini, a Florentine painter. The play was commissioned by the Counts of San Secondo and performed on 16 February 1582/3 'in the presence of the Great Princesses of Tuscany'. In the first *intermedio*, Demogorgon, the father of the gods, and Eternity sing in dialogue, and 'the song being over, there followed the uproar of Chaos, which came from beneath the stage…and having offended [the ears of] the audience with thunder like the report of a musket…Demogorgon drew from it Strife, the god Pan, the three Fates, and thus Demogorgon began to sing, followed by the others'. A little further on we are informed that 'The music of the first *intermedio* was by Messer Iacopo Peri alias Zazzerino', Peri at the time was twenty-one years of age.

the 1567/8 *intermedi* was rather more moralizing than that of earlier ones: perhaps the more rigorous moral climate established by the Council of Trent had made someone feel that the 1565 *intermedi* had been rather too pagan. Yet the description by Alessandro Ceccherelli[35] reveals no single moral idea unifying the admonishments, full of references to classical characters and authors, which were showered on the innocent Leonora (while they would have been more appropriate if addressed to Francesco or Cosimo) and only occasionally is there any link between the events of *I Fabii*, the comedy by Lotto del Mazza, and those of the *intermedi*.[36] Despite Nerli's plea in the previous year, the latter were far from being models of 'clarity and easy comprehensibility': indeed more than once the allegories and classical allusions were quite beyond Ceccherelli's understanding.[37] Luckily for us, his information about music is more precise, having been received directly from 'the Excellent Messer Alessandro Striggio di Pieroni from Mantua, who had composed and concerted it with all kinds of instruments that are apt to be employed in such things'.

In the first *intermedio* three Furies, two Danaids, one Lapith (representing Gluttony) and a host of 'men most famed for their vices' (of whom only Ixion, Tantalus, Tityus, Sisyphus, Salmonaeus and Phlegias are mentioned by name) came out from the mouth of hell (described as having 'long sharp fangs' and an open throat, from which fire and flame emerged). Before scattering 'through all the streets of the stage, step by step they formed a [half-]moon and...sang and twice played a madrigal for six male voices, sung by six [voices] and played by five *dolzaine* and one trombone'.[38] The six voices were probably one bass and five tenors, anticipating the practice of seventeenth-century opera of giving old women (or such unsympathetic female characters as the Furies or Discord) a tenor voice. In the second *intermedio* Pleasure (in female attire and singing soprano) engaged in a dialogue with Hercules (a bass, anticipating another later operatic convention); and 'from within [that is, either in the wings, or behind the backdrop] three *gravicembali*, three lutes, four trombones, four bowed viols, two flutes and one transverse flute were played'.[39]

PIACERE

> Perché, giovine, a te perigli, oltraggio
> cerchi, che bello sei oltra misura?

[35] *Descrizione di tutte le feste, e le mascherate fatte in Firenze per il carnovale, questo anno, 1567. E insieme l'ordine del battesimo della primogenita dell'Illust. et Eccell. S. Principe di Firenze, e Siena, con gl'intermedij della commedia, et dell'apparato fatto per detto battesimo...* (Florence 1567).

[36] See below notes 42 and 43.

[37] Examples of this are the confused descriptions of the fifth and sixth *intermedi*.

[38] There were twelve characters on stage, and singers and instruments are also given as coming to a total of twelve. Six of the characters must therefore have had musical instruments which had been disguised to resemble attributes appropriate to their owners. The *dolzaina*, a double-reeded wind instrument, is always associated with male voices in the *intermedi*. See Brown, *Sixteenth-Century Instrumentation*, p. 102.

[39] Although the description does not say so, it seems to me reasonable to assume that, as it was a dialogue or else an argument, the instruments listed did not all play at once, but formed different groups to accompany one or other of the characters. For example, the three harpsichords, four trombones and four viols might have accompanied Hercules, and the three lutes, two flutes and a transverse flute Pleasure. But it is also possible that some instruments (for example the harpsichords) might have been used for both.

ERCOLE

Che mi giova beltà senza 'l bel raggio
di vertù 'n questa vita, o m'assicura?

PIACERE

Io che beato altrui rendo e felice.

ERCOLE

Donna, chi siete voi?

PIACERE

Quella che dura
mai sempre, d'ogni ben viva radice.

ERCOLE

Ditemi il nome vostro, e per qual via
seguir vi deggio dunque, alma Beatrice.

PIACERE

Per questa piana, amor, che dolce invia
al contento, e tralascia ogni fatica.

ERCOLE

Dunque l'Hidra, il Leone, e l'aspra ria
schiera domar non deggio, empia nemica
a l'huomo in questa vita? o qual mercede
dar mi potete a par di questa, amica?

PIACERE

Il Piacer, ch'ogni ben nel mondo eccede.

ERCOLE

Non impedir, malvagia, il mio viaggio,
ch'io per seguirti mai non torco il piede,
seguendo sol virtude e 'l suo dir saggio.

Pleasure: Why do you want to face perils, and be injured, young man who are so exceedingly handsome? *Hercules*: What's beauty's worth in life without the shining light of virtue? whom should I trust? *Pleas.*: Trust me, for I can bring happiness and bliss. *Herc.*: Who are you, lady? *Pleas.*: One who lasts forever, living root of all joy. *Herc.*: Tell me your name, tell me on which road should I follow you, kind dispenser of bliss. *Pleas.*: My love, on the easy one, which smoothly leads to joy and shuns all toil. *Herc.*: Then should I never conquer Hydra, the Lion, and the fierce, cruel host which besets man in this life? and what reward, my friend, could you ever grant me as precious as that? *Pleas.*: Pleasure, exceeding all other good things in life. *Herc.*: No longer impede my path, O temptress; for I shall never change my course for you, but only follow virtue's just advice.

All the fabulous monsters of Hercules' labours were on stage during this dialogue; and once the hero had rejected Pleasure's blandishments, they 'sang a Madrigal à 10, ten voices all on the stage with no added instruments'. In the third *intermedio* four shepherds and four nymphs made their entrance, 'and when these had entered, suddenly a vaulted vine-trellis was seen to appear in the middle of the stage...[40] and when the shepherds, who had four

[40]   Note in this and in the fourth *intermedio* the appearance of scenographic elements adding to those already on stage. Unlike the whirlpools and hillocks already considered in connection with the *intermedi* of *La cofanaria*, the sudden appearance of the pergola and of King Midas' royal seat have no real dramatic justification in the *intermedio*; they are merely a sign that all principles

violoni, had seated themselves under it while the nymphs stood, two at the farthest end [of the trellis], two at the nearest', they all performed a madrigal for eight parts, the nymphs singing four soprano parts most sweetly, and the shepherds playing their four *bassi di violone*.[41] So far so good, but we have no indication of how the music, whether vocal or instrumental went in the final part of the *intermedio*, when 'four satyrs having arrived, and the terror-striken shepherds fled, the nymphs were seized and abducted by them [the satyrs]'.[42] Anyway this is the full text sung by the nymphs:

> In questi verdi prati
> e ballando, e cantando, chiare e snelle
> a i più soavi e grati
> canti de i dolci uccelli, a questi amati
> presso, lete sem noi; haggia le belle
> gemme, e l'oro chi 'l vuole,
> poi che noi sen felici, o quanto, e sole.
>   Poni a te, Dafne, hor questa,
> a te quest'altra, o biondo Aminta, o nostro
> Tirsi, ghirlanda in testa,
> di ben mille viole e fior contesta.
> Ma quel nemico là, quel fero mostro
> che sguarda? ecco le belve!
> fuggian, misere, oh, oh, fuggian le selve.

On these green meadows we sing and dance, swift and gay, to the sweet and pleasant songs of lovely birds: near to these, whom we so love, we are happy. Let whoever wants them have fine jewels and gold: happy we are, how happy, in solitude.

Now, Daphnis, place this garland on your head; and you this one, fair Aminta, and you, dear Tirsis, all woven with thousands of violets and flowers. But lo, the enemy there, the cruel monster, what's he after? Here come the wild beasts! Let's flee, alas, alas, let's leave the woods!

In the fourth *intermedio*, Ceccherelli tells us, 'Calumny was represented... as once portrayed by Apelles, the ancient painter', adding that the music of the *intermedio* 'was for five parts, sung by five singers and played by a *storta* as the bass, plus two trombones and two *cornetti muti*'. I cannot help thinking that this selection, more particularly the *storta* and the two *cornetti muti*, may in itself have been meant as a madrigalism *sui generis*, an allusion to the *distortion* of truth and to the *whispering* of two women (Ignorance and Fear) in the ears of King Midas.[43] Again, some of the female characters must have

---

of verisimilitude have been abandoned. Ceccherelli also gives some technical details which explain how these appearances and subsequent disappearances were effected.

[41] The piece was to be 'sung and played', but the instruments obviously played different parts from the vocal ones.

[42] 'By which *intermedio* it is pointed out that when a man thinks himself to be happy and prosperous, and nearly blessed, and when he is enjoying pleasures and delights, some strange accident results which deprives him of all contentedness, just as one saw happen in connection with the comedy' (Ceccherelli, *Descrizione*, c. 21 r–v).

[43] The fact that the instruments were probably 'invisible' and that only a few of the spectators would have been able to identify with any degree of certainty their tones and hence the allusion, does not rule out this interpretation. In general, we are inclined to interpret the so-called 'madrigalisms' as means of expression, and as such we judge them to have been arid and intellectualistic; I consider it more likely that they were really suggestions coming from the text,

sung in a tenor voice.[44] The most surprising thing is that the wicked characters take part in singing a text which somehow sides with the slandered victim and with Truth, who is also present, 'a most beautiful lady, all naked but for some veils surrounding parts of her figure'. Anyone who recalls Botticelli's *Calumny of Apelles*, with characters immobilized in flight, may find it hard to visualize the characters in the *intermedio*, who, 'having all entered and formed a [half-]moon on the stage' were so grouped that 'the king sat in the middle...on a royal chair, which had suddenly emerged from under the stage floor;[45] and thus all together they sang and played the following *canzone*':

D'ogni altra furia e peste
sicur' è l'Innocenza,
non già, non già da queste
fiamme, che 'l buono, e' 'l rio n'hanno temenza,
e guai a chi pel crine
tengon legato e stretto:
Calumnia, Livor, Fraude, Onta e Sospetto.
   Ma Penitenza pur ne stringe alfine;
alle più delle genti
queste si trovan chiuse
regali orecchie, à noi così patenti.
E ben tal'hor deluse
sem dalla Veritade
ch'assedia nostre strade.

Safe as she is from all other plagues and furies, Innocence is not safe from these burning flames, feared by good and bad alike. Woe to him, who, caught by his hair, is pressed by Calumny, Shame, Fraud, Envy and Suspicion.

But punishment will reach us in the end. Those kingly ears, deaf to most people, are opened wide to us; and yet we are often defeated by Truth, who obstructs our ways.

According to Ceccherelli, the fifth *intermedio* 'answers the first, in which the Vices had dispersed, so that they have [by now] infested the whole world'.[46] Love, Fear, Hope, Envy, Honour, Joy, Glory, Reward and Virtue enter one after another, 'raising their eyes to the sky, from which a cloud descended and covered the whole stage, in the middle of which [cloud] the nine Muses and three graces[47] were seen, descending with the cloud little by little.'

and leading the musicians' imagination in one direction rather than another – a catalyst of artistic expression, yet quite distinct from it, and therefore not requiring recognition by the audience.

[44] It is unlikely that five of the characters on stage played instruments, even disguised ones, as their characters provided no excuse for carrying them. All ten, or perhaps only five of them, merely sang, while the instruments were played off-stage. But even if one assumes that five characters sang, only two were male, while the use of the *storta* and two trombones indicates that there must have been three low male voices.

[45] This is another of those elements to appear before the audience without there being any natural justification for its rising from the floor – the only explanation being the intervention of magical or supernatural powers.

[46] Ceccherelli's description shows that he understood little of the meaning of this *intermedio*. His confused account misled U. Angeli and F. Ghisi, who named as vices Love, Fear, Glory and Honour, omitted other characters, and incorrectly distributed the dialogue between the two groups.

[47] The descent of the 'cloud which covered the whole scene' (Ceccherelli, *Descrizione*, c. 25 v) had already been seen in *La cofanaria* in 1565 and in the 1566 initial *intermedio/non-intermedio*

Elsewhere, with reference to the music, we are told that 'twelve [characters] descended from the sky, and sang a madrigal for five parts, with which four viols, one *cornetto muto*, two trombones, one lyre and one lute were also played. Those on the earth answered with a madrigal in four parts, sung by four voices and played by two trombones and three flutes, which made nine...Then all of them, that is, twenty-one, sang another *canzone* à 6, with all these voices and instruments; finally twelve departed, but nine remained, who sang the canzone *Vatten'o bella schiera.*' For all its glorious display of voices and instruments,[48] the *intermedio* ends on a distressing note: Muses and Graces must forsake Virtue because the Vices have taken Joy, Reward and Glory away from her! The only compensation lay in the fact that the cloud, reascending into the sky, revealed that during the *intermedio* 'the second perspective had been revolved, showing the square of San Giovanni, which made an even richer and more beautiful sight'.[49]

Act V was performed in this new setting, and then the sky once more opened to reveal the gods, who had assembled to celebrate with a banquet the birth of Venus.[50] They were only puppets, made 'with painted pasteboard, one by one, making a beautiful show'; but then when 'the sky had been closed, all the gods came [down] on stage, and there were twenty-nine of them, for the stage could have contained no more'. They sang and then repeated 'a *canzone* for six parts, played by two *cornetti*, four trombones, six lutes, bass and

of *Il granchio*, so that the description, after recounting that on it were to be seen the Muses and the Graces 'their instruments in their hands', immediately goes on to say 'and as they have often been seen I shall not trouble to describe them' (an indication that not only the machines but also parts of the decorations, costumes and properties were being re-used). Instead, Ceccherelli described how the twelve characters were arranged on the cloud. Bastiano de Rossi, who in 1586 described another descent by cloud of celestial characters in the first *intermedio* of *L'amico fido*, was wrong when he wrote: 'Which marvels of clouds...have never before been seen. For in that [cloud] made by this artist [Bernardo Buontalenti] at the wedding of Her Serene Highness Giovanna of Austria, and in the one made by Baldassare Lanci in honour of the Archduke Charles, they were seen to rise up again empty [in the 1586 performance the cloud was made to disappear] and one could see the hook.' But already in 1565 the cloud had borne Venus and her suite aloft again, and in 1567/8 the cloud bearing the personified Clouds did not descend at all, but was wafted eastwards by the breath of the Winds. In 1567/8, and later in 1569, the cloud was used to hide the stage while the set was changed.

   [48]   In the group of nine Muses and three Graces, five sang and the rest played; in the 'earthly' group, possibly made up of Love, the Vices, and Love's suite, four sang and five played. Since none of the instruments was of a sort to lend itself to a sort of continuo playing, there is in each case a numerical disparity between the vocal and instrumental parts, which is repeated when the groups sing together (nine voices, twelve instruments). It may be that some of the instruments had a part independent of that of the voices. Note too the use of trombones in both groups: this is unlike their usual characterization.

   [49]   This is one of the first known cases of a change of scene in a comedy. Nevertheless, it was not the author of the comedy who so disregarded the rule of unity: it was the set designer. When the situation recurred in 1569, G. B. Cini, the author of *La vedova*, inserted between Acts II and III of the printed edition the following note, in which he noted the change of scene which occurred at this point but refused to accept literary responsibility: 'At the end of this second act, while the *intermedio* was being performed before the eyes of all, the whole perspective was seen to turn and change with marvellous artistry: which [perspective] having until then represented one section of the city, with the revolving I have described brought into view some of the most magnificent villas and most attractive gardens of delightful Arcetri, to which [change] not without skill the previous and subsequent parts of the comedy were ably adapted; nevertheless it has been felt necessary to permit it to appear in the form in which it is here to be read', i.e. with no change of locale.

   [50]   Ceccherelli also gave a confused description of this *intermedio*. The description is in no way improved by an appeal to the authority of Plato.

soprano viols, two flutes and one *traversa*, and sung by all the others [that is, by twelve]; these, voices and instruments, were all mingled according to the decisions made by the expert judgement of the said Messer Alessandro [Striggio]; and the said pieces of music were marvellous and exquisite'.[51]

Last in this series of spectacles came *La vedova* by Giovanbattista Cini. It was performed in 1569, with *intermedi* invented and described by Cini himself.[52] One feature of the comedy was its medley of dialects – Venetian, Bergamask, Neapolitan, Sicilian and Tuscan.[53] In the *intermedi* the author's vague classical aspirations, or rather his attempts to 'improve on the classics', were intermingled with various suggestions made by those in charge of the scenery and by the musical adviser, who was again Striggio. Only two pairs of the *intermedi* are in any way related: the first and second, and the third and fourth; otherwise the desire prevailed to achieve the utmost variety and spectacular effects. The curtain had just fallen, and the audience was still admiring the set which depicted 'the city of Florence' and 'the corner of the Antellesi, from which the façade of the Ducal Palace and the three giants at

[51]   The effects of a fascination with numbers begin to show: in the fifth *intermedio* there were twenty-one performers on stage, in the sixth twenty-nine. Note that the vocal parts of the piece à 6 were performed by twelve voices, i.e. all the parts were uniformly doubled. The accompanying instruments were less uniformly doubled: the two *cornetti*, four trombones and six lutes may have been assigned one to each part, but this distribution leaves a less homogeneous residuum of five instruments, namely two viols, two flutes and a transverse flute.

[52]   I know of two descriptions of performances of *La vedova*: the *Raccolto delle feste fatte in Fiorenza...Nella venuta del Serenissimo Arciduca Carlo d'Austria* (Florence 1569) and the *Descrittione dell'intermedii fatti nel felicissimo palazo del Gran Duca Cosimo etc.*, 'Appresso Bartholomeo Sermartelli' (Florence, undated, though the address to the reader is dated 9 May 1569). In the former publication the comedy is first mentioned on p. 10, and on p. 11 it says: 'I shall narrate to you the apparatus and the contents of these *intermedi* in a few words, leaving the rest to emerge in the description of them brought out (so they say) by the author'. Clearly this is a reference to the *Descrittione*.

[53]   The description requests applause for 'the Fable with its mixture of tongues'. Amongst the characters of the play, Burchiello the servant speaks the dialect of Bergamo, while Messer Marino and Donna Benetta (two aged Venetians), Signor Cola Francesco (a young Neapolitan), and Fiaccavento (a Sicilian soldier) all speak their native dialects. The rest of the cast speaks Florentine, as the scene is set in Florence. The Neapolitan has literary and musical pretensions: in Act III scene 5 he gives us a taste of his talents as a poet and singer with 'a little song of mine, half according to our tradition and half according to the one Petrarch used...':

> Dica cui dire vole
> e laudi pure maritate o zitelle,
> ch'a me piaceno sole
> gl'uocchi e le trezze delle bedolelle.

> Let whoever wishes to, speak, and let him praise both wed and unwed women, for I like the eyes and plaits of the little widows.

He then informs us that the song is 'in imitation of that beautiful one by Gian Leonardo dell'Arpa which runs:

> Villanella crudel, mi fai morire
> con ss'uocchi e con ssa bocca saporita;
> tu mi dài morte, ahimè, tu mi dài vita.'

> Cruel country lass, you make me die with your eyes and your tasty mouth; you give me death, alas, you given me life.

This last song really was by G. Leonardo dell'Arpa, from the *Secondo libro delle canzoni alla napolitana a tre voci* (G. Scotto, Venice 1571) – see Benedetto Croce's edition of *La vedova* (Naples 1953), p. 139. In Act IV scene 3 it is night, and the Neapolitan sings to give himself dignity 'S'io avissi tantillo, tantillo di speranza' ('If I had a little, just a little hope'); he is immediately answered by Fiaccavento's 'S'eu avissi tanticchiu, tanticchiu de bastuni' ('If I had a few, just a few cudgels'). This song too was by G. Leonardo dell'Arpa in G. Leonardo Primavera, *Il primo*

its base' could be seen[54] (plate 30), when from one side of the stage Fame came in triumph, 'riding a most beautiful oval gilded chariot...driven by Time Present, all clad in red satin meaning Vitality, and by Time Past, clad in azure satin meaning Divinity'. While on the subject of the allegorical significance of the costumes we might also add that Fame herself was 'clad in azure satin hemmed with gold, had nice gilded sandals, puffs of white voile on her shoulders, golden wings, and her head...covered by a rich diadem of gold, gracefully ending in a row of stars; for she is the one who raises man to the stars'. With all this taking place immediately in front of the Ducal Palace, nobody could miss who was going to be raised to the stars. With Fame came 'many people', unidentified in the description although they represented 'the famous ones', and nine Florentine youths and nine girls came from the opposite side to meet them. Their prayers to Fame, and her answers 'filled the place with the sweet harmony of the following pleasant dialogue'. The texts are given next, from which we gather that the exchange in the crowded square was both opened and closed by Fame; nothing is said, however, as to whether she sang alone or was joined by her entourage,[55] while the song of her Florentine suppliants seems to have been a madrigal à 6, sung by three singers to each part. For this, as for the subsequent *intermedi*, no mention is made of accompanying instruments; if any were used, they must have been 'invisible'.

There was dialogue too in the second *intermedio*; 'Eritone (a sorceress, made famous by the rhymes of poets) came on stage and while singing traced some magic rings on the ground, from which emerged suddenly large numbers of all kinds of spirits...When they had sung, she forced them back amongst the dead, and in a most wondrous manner they were made to return to the place from which they had come.'[56] In this early scene of magic *avant l'opéra* the

libro de canzoni napoletane a tre voci...con alcune napolitane di Io. Leonardo de L'Arpa (G. Scotto, Venice 1570), also mentioned in Croce, *La vedova*, p. 270. In Act IV scene 8 Cola Francesco also sings:

> Chisso mussillo d'oro
> mi da guai, & martoro,
> ma chiss'uocchi lucenti
> al cor me danno foco, & fiamme ardenti.

> This little golden face punishes me most cruelly, but these bright eyes enflame my heart with fire.

[54] I.e. the façade of the Palazzo Vecchio, viewed from the Uffizi then under construction. As the performance took place inside the palace, the view of the outside while one was within was a curiosity which prefigured Bernini's idea of presenting the audience of an opera in Palazzo Barberini with an *intermedio* depicting the audience leaving that same palazzo after the performance.

[55] The *Raccolto delle feste* merely says that lads and lasses 'beseeching Fame, and she replying to their requests, filled with gentle harmony in such pleasant dialogue the whole place'. The *Descrittione dell'intermedii* on the other hand gives the texts of the *intermedi*, which show that Fame sang first and answered last, but we have already seen, in the 1565 *intermedi*, that it was possible for an abstract or divine character to speak through a chorus.

[56] It would seem quite clear that the musical dialogue was here between the soloist and the chorus. As Eritone appears alone on stage without musical instruments, those accompanying her must have been 'invisible'. But though this was what I believed, and wrote in that belief, I must now admit that I have been proved wrong by the Brussels manuscript, Bibl. du Conservatoire 27.731 (quoted by Ghisi, *Feste musicali*, pp. xxxi–xxxiv) which I ignored because of its fragmentary state. (It is the *cantus* part of a large collection of madrigals, and also includes the *cantus secundus* for only a few pieces.) Both the sorceress' invocation (fol. 86v), and the song

sorceress must have sung solo (accompanied by hidden instruments) an incantation whose main purpose was to add to the visions of Time Past and Present of the previous *intermedio* a prophecy about Time Future:

> Ombre, fuor dallo scuro
> abisso, a ripigliar l'antica veste
> venite, e non vi tenga fossa, ò muro;
> dite se le moleste
> cure haran fine.[57] Hor preste
> uscite; io vel comando, Eriton maga,
> che del tornarvi in terra son sì vaga.

Shades, arise from the darkness of the abyss to resume your old shapes; let neither grave nor wall restrain you. Say if the harrowing worries come to an end. Come quickly, I, the sorceress Eritone, command you, who am eager to return you to earth.

As expected, the answer given by the souls she has evoked (of poets, painters, sculptors, musicians and alchemists) is reassuring:

> ...il gran travaglio
> tosto si cangia, e torna dolce, eterno
> gioire...

...the great distress [?] is quickly dispelled, and sweet rejoicing returns for ever...

The third *intermedio*, of Winds and Clouds, was entirely choral: real clouds appeared on the stage and completely covered it, 'showing such tangles as one is wont to see when they [the clouds] are thick in the sky and collide', as well as personifications of clouds 'in the shape of women with wet locks of fair hair, clad in the colours that are usually seen in them, such as silver, red, yellow, green...and all sitting on one [cloud], which moved from west to east'. One of the two chroniclers who reported on the event gives us a clue about the *intermedio*, writing: 'We saw represented most pleasantly something that had first been done by the witty Aristophanes in his most amusing comedy *Nephelai* – the invention of a chorus of Clouds. But here he was surpassed and outdone, inasmuch as after their song the Winds rose up...blew them [the Clouds] away and cleared the sky, while singing most sweetly; which was a real delight to watch and listen to.'[58] The ancients were

in which she dismisses the souls she has questioned and reassures the spectators (fol. 87: 'Now, human mind, live free of pain, for the evil which now besets you shall be short-lived and mild') are madrigals for four voices, and the sorceress cannot have sung them to an instrumental accompaniment as the *cantus* of the former lacks some words and it is unlikely that she would have sung any other part. She must therefore have mimed, while behind the stage a chorus sang her part. See James Haar, 'Madrigals from three generations: the MS Brussels, Bibl. du Conservatoire Royal, 27.731', *Rivista italiana di musicologia*, X (1975) pp. 242–64; and Iain Fenlon and James Haar, 'Fonti e cronologia dei madrigali di Costanzo Festa', *Rivista italiana di musicologia*, XIII (1979), pp. 212–42: esp. 215ff. The madrigal sung by the souls (fols. 87v–88 of the MS 27.731) is for six voices. Neither the *Descrittione* nor the *Raccolto* gives any information about how many people performed the music or the quality of their accompaniment.

   [57] I cannot identify the troublesome cares to which Eritone refers and from which the chorus of spirits promises relief.

   [58] *Raccolto delle feste*, pp. 12–13. Cini (assuming the *Descrittione* to be by him) says nothing about it, though he makes it clear that the 'sixteen winged Winds, with a great flapping of veils' emerged from underground and 'pretended to push by their breath the Clouds towards the east, raising to their lips a long silver conch and they sang...' Wind instruments would have been hidden within the silver shells. The Clouds' madrigal was for four voices (the *cantus* is on fol. 84v of the Brussels manuscript referred to in note 56); the Wind's madrigal was for eight voices (*cantus primus* and *secundus* on fols. 85v–86 of the same manuscript).

once more 'improved upon' in the fourth *intermedio* in a 'transformation of peasants into frogs, upon a prayer of Latona (as told by Ovid)'. Again the *intermedio* develops as a dialogue. A gay chorus of peasants (in lavish costumes) is interrupted by the arrival of Latona, 'who, dying of thirst and carrying her [two] small children in her arms, went to the water there to quench her thirst'. Here, at least on paper, the dialogue begins to move more briskly.

CONTADINI

> Non toccar l'acqua, o folle.

LATONA

> Perché, se l'è comun non vuoi ch'io brami
> questa?

CONTADINI

> I nodosi rami
> tu aspetti, et esser molle
> di pianto.

LATONA

> Questo no; poi che satolle
> non fien le brame mie, quetate i figli.

CONTADINI

> Che ci torbi, o scompigli?

LATONA

> O sommo Giove, i tuoi
> dolci figli non vedi in che dispregio
> questi malvagi hor hanno? e giusto vuoi
> soffrir l'empio collegio
> di così ingrati? o fa, Padre, che puoi
> ciò che tu vuoi, che mai
> non gustin chiaro il rio; ma torbo in guai.

Peasants: Do not touch the water, you fool. *Latona*: Why, if it belongs to all, should I not want it? *Peas*: You ask for knotty cudgels and shedding tears. *Latona*: O no! but then, if you do not let me quench my thirst, help my children, at least. *Peas.*: Why are you causing so much trouble and confusion? *Latona*: Jupiter supreme, do you not see in what contempt your sweet children are held by those rogues? can you bear the impious gang of miscreants such as those? O Father, who have power to do all that you want, may they never enjoy the stream clear; let it be muddy and bitter.

Like the rest of the text, the wording of the prayer is hardly particularly clear. And yet it must have found favour with Jupiter; for suddenly 'with masterly art, the whole crowd was seen transformed into frogs, so realistic that even the real frogs could look no more true to life. They were seen to leap into the pool and resuming their *canzone* they were seen to swim about in the water with a thousand most natural gestures, and to sing with gurgling noises.' The sight gave tremendous pleasure to the whole audience, but especially to the '*literati*, for they saw, put into action and even surpassed because of the transformation, that [novelty] which had been introduced by the Greek poet Aristophanes in the comedy of *The Frogs*, so called from the ones that formed its chorus.'

The fifth *intermedio* saw 'a most beautiful chorus and a large gathering of nymphs...dressed in the most gallant garb that has ever been seen. These, numbering thirty-six, followed Diana in good order through the land, some singing, some playing; and then those who were playing stood aside, the others, sweetly matching their song to the instruments, danced most gracefully around Diana, who (as figured by the poets) was a full head taller than all the rest.' In the final *intermedio* 'Heaven suddenly opened, and so bright was it because of the lights reflecting on the gold that one's sight was blinded by a shimmering light which the eye could not bear...Within this heaven, divided into different tiers,...a great number of gods...sang a beautiful *canzone* in the form of a dialogue of sweetest harmony, with Jupiter and the upper Gods beginning first, the lower ones answering them, and...all finally repeating the last line.'[59]

The *intermedi* for *La vedova* were in fact less freely invented than they first appear, for though not restricted by the plot of the comedy, they are bound by the requirements of the stage setting and the music. In the third *intermedio*, the Clouds piled up on stage served to hide the stage while the set revolved quickly on pivots and revealed a different painted surface, changing the set from an urban to a rural view, so that as the Clouds were swept away by sixteen blowing Winds, there appeared 'several of the most magnificent villas and finest gardens of most delightful Arcetri'. The next two *intermedi* were affected by the need for a subject 'which suited the new set' even more than by Aristophanes' model (although the Clouds in the third *intermedio* may have led to the frogs in the fourth, and the advantage of having at hand a dancing Diana of unusual stature to the topic of the fifth). Finally, the machinery invented by Vasari in 1565 was re-employed in the last *intermedio* for the benefit of the imperial guest, to produce the opening of the hollow sky and the appearance through it of a second one in the remoter distance. As for the music, it must have influenced the style of the *intermedi* more than the actual choice of subject for them. *Intermedi* which included dialogue had first appeared in 1565, and by 1569 that was the predominant style. According to the descriptions, only the thirty-six nymphs who followed Diana in the fifth *intermedio* sang, played and danced without engaging in any dialogue at all, whether dramatic or purely musical. Dialogues, on the contrary, are clearly specified in the others, although it is not clear, as I have already mentioned, whether a soloist and chorus, two choral groups, or even two choruses and a soloist may have constituted the first *intermedio*. The second *intermedio* developed as a soloist–chorus–soloist sequence;[60] in the third the dialogue was carried on by Clouds and Winds, two choral groups; in the fourth and most diversified one, the initial chorus of peasants and the final one of frogs symmetrically framed the recitative dialogue and the aria prayer of Latona quoted above. In the last *intermedio* the dialogue alternated between the two choral groups of the superior, spatially more remote gods and the inferior, nearer ones, the two combining forces to repeat the final lines.[61] We are reminded of similar spatial effects that Striggio had sought to

---

[59] This is the first time lighting effects are mentioned. In this *intermedio* the gods of the upper sky sang, or rather were the first to propose the song; since they were puppets, their song in fact came from off-stage.

[60] One must now bear in mind those arguments which militate against such a solution, as put forward in note 56. Nevertheless, the dialogue between two differently constituted groups still holds good.   [61] See note 59.

achieve a year earlier on the occasion of the nuptials of Duke William of Bavaria with Renée of Lorraine, when he wrote a motet for forty voices (distributed between four choruses of 6, 8, 10 and 16 voices respectively), accompanied by eight trombones, eight bowed viols, eight large flutes, one harpsichord (*instrumento da penna*) and one large lute.[62]

Alessandro Striggio, sole author of the music of the 1567 and 1569 *intermedi*, as well as of the music for many of the masquerades performed in those years, is an artist who deserves more attention than he has so far received. Such attention as has been paid to him has centred not on the artistic merits of his work but on the whimsical aspects of his *Cicalamento delle donne al bucato* (*The chattering of women at the laundry*), which had, after all, appeared in 1567, before the *intermedi* for *La vedova*, in the same print with *Dido's Lament* by Rore.[63] A very gifted performer, as well as a composer, he was 'not only excellent but supreme in playing the viol and in making four parts heard on it at once, with such grace and musical knowledge (con tanta leggiadria e con tanta musica) that all listeners marvel; and in addition his compositions are held to be as rich in music and as good (*musicali e buone*) as any others that we hear nowadays'.[64] Cosimo Bartoli, who wrote these lines, must have found 'rich in music and good' the pieces in Striggio's *Primo libro de madrigali a cinque voci* and in his *Primo libro* for six voices, both first issued circa 1560 and reprinted many times, the former until as late as 1585 and the latter until 1592.[65] The wording of this praise, if we scrutinize it more closely, shows that Bartoli admired the combination of a solid technical mastery (the *ars musicae*) with a felicity and charm of invention, evidently not too often found together. In terms of his techniques of harmony and counterpoint, Striggio may not have broken new ground. However, his search for new combinations of voices and instruments, his qualitative and quantitative decisions about the sound mixtures most suited to different performing conditions and most likely to

[62]   See Max Schneider, *Die Anfänge des Basso continuo und seiner Bezifferung* (Leipzig 1918), p. 67 and facsimile. The information on the circumstances of the performance and the instruments involved is taken from Massimo Troiano, *Dialoghi ne' quali si narrano le cose più notabili fatte nelle nozze* etc. (Venice 1569). The *instrumento da penna* was the harpsichord, which Striggio evidently favoured as a *concertante* instrument. On the significance of these first examples of continuo, see the next chapter, pp. 246–47. There are now indications that the motet may have originally been a *musica a quaranta voci* on a secular text performed in Florence in 1561, then presented to Guglielmo Gonzaga. See Fenlon, *Music and Patronage in Sixteenth-Century Mantua*, pp. 86–7 and doc. 24. Fenlon further suggests that the music might survive as the 40-voice motet *Ecce beatam lucem*.

[63]   Alessandro Striggio...deserves to be considered as a great Florentine musician in an entirely special way...Generally he is classed – in the strength of a series of *intermezzi* composed for a few ceremonies at the Medicean court – amongst the precursors of Florentine monody. But he was something more: he was the most varied and extraordinary Italian musician of the second half of the sixteenth century. Had he lived longer...Galilei, N. Vicentino, Bottrigari, Caccini and Peri would have been much less important, and Monteverdi would have had a great and worthy precursor.

Thus wrote Alfred Einstein, 'Firenze prima della monodia', in *Rassegna musicale*, VII (1934), p. 263. Striggio's *La caccia* has recently been published, in a critical edition by F. Mompellio (Rome 1972).

[64]   Information taken from Cosimo Bartoli, *Ragionamenti accademici* (1567).

[65]   I do not know on what basis Ray J. Tadlock, 'Striggio, Alessandro', in *Die Musik in Geschichte und Gegenwart*, vol. XII, col. 1607, dates the *Primo libro* for five voices as 1558, but two 1560 reprints are known, and then those of 1564, 1566 (again two), 1569 and 1585. The *Primo libro* for six voices appeared in 1560 and was reprinted in 1565, 1566 (twice), 1569, 1578, 1579, 1585 and 1592.

achieve the expressive effects he desired, his exploitation of the different placing of vocal and instrumental groups (or even of the single elements in a group, the judicious 'alternation' of voices and instruments praised by Ceccherelli apropos of the 1567 *intermedi*), and finally his persistent and varied use of musical dialogue, as shown in the descriptions of *intermedi*, all prove him to have been truly innovative. On a reduced scale, within the limits of a madrigalistic group, these qualities are evident in the few madrigals by Striggio available in modern editions;[66] the sample I can give here (example XXXVII) is exquisite in the skilful part leading, and, particularly in its first section, in the poignant recitative quality of the single voices as well as of the whole ensemble; the voices diverge in the next section, once more creating the effect of a musical dialogue. Striggio has also been considered a pioneer in the use of *basso continuo*, and rightly so, for in the *intermedi* he anticipated the use of 'perfect' instruments (that is, capable of producing full chords), such as harpsichords, lutes, and possibly the *lirone*, to connect separate, or even contrasting, elements of a composition. This means that he anticipated the use of continuo in a *concertato* style and indeed the style itself. He might also have anticipated the use of continuo in support of a single singing voice, as later used by Caccini and Peri, had he not been inclined, because of his skill as a *viola* player, to accompany the voice on his own instrument, on which he expertly played several contrapuntal lines. This might also explain his tendency to be rather conservative in his use of harmony and counterpoint.[67]

Striggio is less important as an anticipator of the monodic style, even though in his *intermedi* he made frequent use of solo voices, supported by either 'visible' or 'invisible' instruments. As we have seen, this custom had very early origins, and had never been abandoned in sixteenth-century musical practice, although most of the extant music, either printed or manuscript, is presented in ways which point to a polyphonic performance by a group of

[66] They are still limited almost exclusively to the five (excellently chosen, but too few) included in Luigi Torchi, *L'arte musicale in Italia*, I.

[67] As well as in the work referred to in note 65, Tadlock also speaks of conservatism in the article entitled 'Alessandro Striggio, Madrigalist', in *Journal of the American Musicological Society*, XI (1958), p. 39:

> The use of dissonance is quite conservative...His madrigals reflect the growing feeling for tonality of the time, with an accompanying use of actual modulation. He shows the influence of the harmonic innovations of his contemporaries but makes no experiments himself, remaining entirely conservative in his use of chromaticism. He actually makes no use of real or direct chromaticism, though he makes an increased use of accidentals.

Tadlock reflects the widespread but misleading assumption that dissonances and chromaticisms monopolized expressiveness. Besides, the just but too exclusive interest taken in some harmonic experiments must not blind us to the fact that their acceptance as a part of musical language was only gradual and that their absence is not therefore necessarily a sign of conservatism. Striggio's harmonies were strongly chordal as is shown by his propensity for using chords almost exclusively in root position and specifying, by means of accidentals, the major or minor harmonies, in places where the performer might have hesitated between the two. Our idea of modulation, dependent as it is on our concept of tonality, did not yet exist as such in the sixteenth century, so it is difficult to distinguish a modulation achieved by means of accidentals from 'a real or direct chromaticism'. Striggio's artistry lies largely in the wealth of contrapuntal invention which he manages to develop even within the bounds of quite precisely defined harmonies. The result is an *arioso* counterpoint, illuminated by the modulation (which, implying precise tonal directives, is in itself *arioso*). For his use of expressive dissonance see the beginning of the penultimate bar of the first section of the first madrigal used as an example.

Ex. XXXVII   Alessandro Striggio. Madrigal (first part and start of the second part). From *I lieti amanti*, *Primo libro de madrigali a cinque voci, di diversi eccellentissimi musici* (G. Vincenzi and R. Amadino, Venice 1586).

unaccompanied singers.[68] Among Striggio's madrigals à 5 or à 6 it is likely that those prevalently homophonic in texture were conceived for solo performance, accompanied by an instrument on which all the lower parts could be played, more particularly the viol, which he played so well.[69] This, after all, would have been but a continuation of the practice as it is documented by the tablature for voice and lute, attributed to Willaert, of a number of Verdelot's madrigals. As to solo singing on stage, we know of at least one antecedent, namely that of the first, third and last *intermedio* of 1539. And although it is a pity that no manuscript or print has preserved the solo pieces composed by Striggio for the Florentine *intermedi* of the 1565–9 period, we would probably not think too highly of them if they had survived; their texts were so shallow and elaborate that all he could do was to encase them skilfully in an agreeable but essentially decorative wrapping of sounds. It might prove more interesting to know how Striggio solved the problem of quick repartee as in the dialogues between Hercules and Pleasure, or Latona and the peasants. Only occasionally – in Psyche's lament, and perhaps in Latona's prayer – when the text or the dramatic situation was striking enough to allow him to develop it in a style distinct from the usual illustrative or decorative *intermedio* music, did Striggio succeed in expressing 'the sadness of those lines with such an intensity of emotion' by means of a style whose

[68] The editions of the 1539 and 1589 *intermedi*, exactly half a century apart, are typical examples of this tendency. In them, even those pieces performed by soloists with an instrumental accompaniment have the text of all the parts.

[69] Either on the *lirone* or on the *arciviolata lira*. It is difficult for us to distinguish between the two, but they both had more strings than most other instruments, and an only slightly curved bridge which made it easier to play four or even five strings simultaneously.

chief features were simplicity, naturalness and restraint, precise declamation and a sober but pointed use of chromaticism.[70]

Even the use of accompanied monody to express emotions was nothing new, for it derives, in a line whose continuity we are beginning to perceive, from the humanistic ideals of the late fifteenth century and early sixteenth century.[71] Nor was Striggio its only representative in Florence. It might be interesting to examine the music by Stefano Rossetti, a restless composer, who was the master of the chapel of the Florentine Duomo in 1564, and who in 1566, when he was already in the service of the then very young Cardinal Ferdinando dei Medici,[72] dedicated his *Musica nova...A cinque voci* (printed in Rome by the Dorico brothers) to the Most Serene Princess of Florence and Siena, Giovanna of Austria. It might pay to look, in his *Primo libro de madrigali a quattro voci. Insieme alquanti madrigali ariosi & con alcuni versi di Virgilio* (A. Gardano, Venice 1560), at the settings of sonnets by Petrarch that are specifically marked as *madrigali ariosi*[73] and at Coridone's lament *O crudelis Alexis* from Virgil's Second Eclogue (lines 6ff); or else to see how a *Lamento d'Olimpia*, giving the title to another edition of Rossetti's compositions (published in Venice by G. Scotto in 1567), follows the pattern of Ariosto's stanzas, and alternates the narrative with the impassioned outbursts of the heroine herself.

In the carnival of 1567 Rossetti shared with Striggio the task of writing the music for the masquerades, helped in one by Caccini's teacher, the Sienese Scipione del Palla (or delle Palle).[74] This last piece of information, which oddly enough had escaped my own attention as well as that of other scholars,[75] clarifies where and when Caccini may have studied with Palla and adds to

---

[70] Vincenzo Galilei, *Fronimo* (Venice 1584), p. 48. The 'so sorrowful verses' are those of Psyche's lament in the fifth 1565 *intermedio*. Howard M. Brown's article referred to in note 32 above reports other judgements expressed by Galilei.

[71] See the conclusion to chapter 1.

[72] He must have been a restless soul. In 1559 he was in Schio, in 1560 in Nice. From there he went on to Novara before reaching Florence. Sometime after 1567 he may have been employed by Archduke Ferdinand II of Austria; in 1580 he was organist at the court of Bavaria. In 1583 one of the *intermedi* of *Le due Persilie* (see note 34) was by one Ser Stefano, who may have been our Rossetti. See Allen B. Skei, 'Stefano Rossetti, Madrigalist' in *The Music Review*, 39 (1978), pp. 81–94.

[73] On the use of this term, see the last chapter of this book. Rossetti's book of madrigals à 4, edited by A. B. Skei is now available as vol. 26 of *Recent Researches in the Music of the Renaissance* (Madison, Wisconsin 1977).

[74] From Ceccherelli, *Descrizione*, cc. 6v–8v, it appears that Rossetti was already in the service of Ferdinando dei Medici: 'On the following Sunday, on the fifteenth of the month [February 1567] our Most Illustrious and Most Reverend Cardinal [not yet sixteen years old] held an entertainment in the wide street opposite the Medici house.' The main attraction of the entertainment was a float with a cloud surrounding Juno, fourteen nymphs, and 'two most famous Roman heroes'. Normally Ceccherelli gives first the name of the poet and then that of the composer of the music, but in this case the text is ambiguous: '...the *canzone* composed by Scipione delle Palle a Sienese, and an excellent musician, and the music by Stefano Rossetto concerted à 6, with two trombones, two lutes, a *lira*, a harpsichord, a *cornetto* and a transverse flute'. It is unclear whether Scipione del Palla merely wrote the words of his *canzone* or whether he also composed the music, in which case Rossetti would have been responsible only for 'concerting' it with six instruments.

[75] To my knowledge, Ghisi, from whose *Feste musicali* I have taken the information, did not otherwise draw attention to it. See also H. W. Hitchcock, 'A New Biographical Source for Caccini', in *Journal of the American Musicological Society*, XXVI (1973), pp. 145–7.

the picture of the musical events in Florence before the advent of monody by hinting at some slight, unexpected connection with the Neapolitan *milieu*. We have already met Scipione del Palla as one of the musicians who performed as actors in Neapolitan comedies before the middle of the sixteenth century;[76] in March 1558 he acted in at least one of the *intermedi* performed with *Alessandro* by Alessandro Piccolomini (also from Siena), which the Marquise del Vasto had had performed 'in her beautiful palace at Chiaia' (as well as 'in her theatre that is so ornate') to honour the vice-reine, the Duchess of Alba, on her departure from Naples. A long series of stanzas by Luigi Tansillo survives from that *intermedio*.[77] They were 'recited by the lady Queen Cleopatra' after Act II, while the boat on which she had arrived on stage sailed up 'the river Arno which leads to Pisa' (the setting of the plot of *Alessandro*). As for the performers, we know that

Queen Cleopatra was [enacted by] Fomia, who, when she sings, cannot be compared to any earthly thing, but to the heavenly harmony. Musicians of great excellence and renown impersonated the characters of Mark Antony and others, within and outside the boat: Cornelio was Mark Antony; Scipione delle Palle was Proteus outside the boat; Giovan Leonardo dell'Arpa, unique as a player of that instrument [the harp], was one of Mark Antony's servants. And as the boat came to face those ladies [the duchess and vice-reine, the Marquise del Vasto and others], Cleopatra stood and said some...stanzas *in a style midway between singing and reciting*, with the instruments softly intoning rather than playing [?] after each verse, which resulted in great gracefulness and majesty.[78]

The stanzas sung by Cleopatra were the climax of musical interest in a series of *intermedi* unusual in more ways than one. Three of them were obviously reminiscent of the *intermedi* performed in Florence on the occasion of the nuptials of 1539; they are the three whose verses were written by Tansillo, and were sponsored by Don García di Toledo. Both had been in the 1539 party escorting Eleonora to be bride to Cosimo dei Medici, and had journeyed from Naples by boat, sailing up the Arno at least as far as Pisa.[79] In quoting the

[76] See above, chapter 3.

[77] Published in Luigi Tansillo, *Il canzoniere edito ed inedito*, with an introduction and notes by Erasmo Pèrcopo (Naples 1926), vol. I (the only one published), pp. 257–61. The notes also include excerpts from the pamphlet *Stanze di Luigi Tansillo composte per gli intermedii della comedia* etc. (Mattia Cancer, Naples 1558, 'at the request of Marco Ant. Passaro, bookseller' who Percopo considers to have been the author of the description). Two other *intermedi* (I and IV, but not II) are also recorded and described in the edition of the *Canzoniere*.

[78] Fomia or Fumia was the singer referred to in a madrigal by Antonio Allegretti, published in 1565 in the collection by Dionigi Atanagi, *De le rime di diversi nobili poeti Toscani...libro primo*, and later included by Monteverdi in his *Libro primo* of madrigals (1587). Besides this, Atanagi's collection includes a song, also by Allegretti, which praises 'the masterly and sweet song and playing of madonna Eufemia, a Neapolitan gentlewoman commonly known as Fumia'.

[79] There were four *intermedi*; one before the prologue, two between the acts, and a final one (the comedy, though originally written in five acts, was on that occasion performed divided into three). The first was the 'Dawn' *intermedio* (suggested by the name of the duchess as well as by the Florentine 'Dawn' of 1539). Dawn appeared on a 'white and gilded' float, and recited, but did not sing, her verses; she was preceded by the star Lucifer, accompanied by 'much bird-song', and was succeeded by Apollo and the Muses. For the second *intermedio*, Tansillo wrote no poems; we merely know that it involved Wild Men, centaurs and bears. The third *intermedio* was that of Cleopatra, whose boat appeared 'surrounded by many sea-monsters, and four sirens', and a dolphin, as well as Proteus, already mentioned. The fourth was the float of Night 'black and blue and scattered with stars, and Night with her black and starry cloak, was seated there, and Tranquillity and cupids and the Graces with her'. Night too recited her verses without song. It

Ex. XXXVIII   Scipione del Palla (?). Music for the *stanze* sung by Cleopatra in an *intermedio* by
Luigi Tansillo for A. Piccolomini's *Alessandro*, performed in Naples in 1558. From
Aeri racolti insieme con altri bellissimi aggionti di diversi (G. Cacchio dell'Aquila,
Naples 1577). The only known example lacks the tenor part.

description of the *intermedio* of Cleopatra I have stressed a sentence which
seems to echo some words, previously quoted, by Poliziano,[80] and seems also
to anticipate the style of *recitar cantando* and *cantar recitando* of the new
century. It is especially interesting in that a setting of Tansillo's first two
stanzas is included in a collection printed in 1577 in Naples by one Gioseppe
Cacchio dell'Aquila, the *Aeri racolti insieme con altri bellissimi aggionti di diversi
dove si cantano sonetti, stanze, & terze rime*, edited by Rocco Rodio.[81] This very
short piece (example XXXVIII) consists of two phrases of music, which
correspond to the first two lines of the first stanza and were evidently meant
to be repeated for the following three distichs, and again for the four of the
next stanza. The missing tenor part can be reconstructed fairly precisely, due
to the chordal nature of the accompaniment, in which the bass line faithfully
doubles the rhythm of the singing voice.[82] It is more difficult to imagine the
nature of the instrumental interlude mentioned in the final sentence of the
description given above. It must have been very short, for we are told that
the instruments 'intoned' rather than played; even so, it would have made
the whole series of Tansillo's stanzas exceedingly long if it was repeated after

would thus appear that the use of music (or at least of vocal music) was limited to the third
intermedio, in which after Cleopatra's octaves they all (including Scipione del Palla) sang a
madrigal together.
  [80]   See the conclusion of the first chapter.
  [81]   The frontispiece adds 'Newly reprinted'; no one knows when the first edition appeared.
Cacchio dell'Aquila had printed Rocco Rodio's *Libro di ricercate a quattro voci* in 1575.
  [82]   The bass too (and certainly the missing tenor) has the words set under the notes as though
to indicate that all the parts were performed vocally, while we know for certain that the piece
was intended to have the upper part alone sung, and the other parts played on instruments.

Ex. XXXIX   Scipione del Palla (?). Air on a text by Petrarch (from *Il trionfo d'Amore*). From *Aeri racolti insieme con altri bellissimi aggionti di diversi* (G. Cacchio dell'Aquila, Naples 1577). The only known example lacks the tenor part.

Du _ ra   leg _ ge   d'A _ mor,   ma ben   ch'o _ bli _   qua

Ser _ bar   con _ vien _ si,   pe _ rò   ch'el _ la   giun _ ge

Di   ciel   in   ter _ ra u _ ni _ ver _ sal   an   ti _   qua

each distich. It is more likely, then, that the instruments played only at the end of each stanza, giving the singing voice a short rest and paving the way for the beginning of a new stanza.

Thus we find that a style of setting similar to the one in use at the beginning of the century for the singing of *strambotti* was still being performed in 1558 and being reprinted as late as 1577. The similarity is further increased by the fact that only two parts are added to the upper voice, thus repeating the basic distribution adopted at the beginning of the century to accompany a song on a single instrument, be it a lute, a lyre or a viol.[83] Nor is the similarity restricted to the fragment derived from the *intermedio* in *Alessandro*, for the same recitative manner, found in most of the twenty-eight pieces (twenty-three à 3 and five à 4) of the 1577 *Aeri racolti*, shows that a school of *recitar cantando* existed in Naples soon after the middle of the century. As for the composers,

[83]   See, as examples of early sixteenth-century practice, the two books of *Tenori et contrabassi intabulati* published by Ottaviano Petrucci.

200

Pietro de Ysis and Luigi Dentice[84] are each represented by two pieces, Rocco Rodio, Fabrizio Dentice, Francesco Menta and Tarquinio del Pezzo by one each. Twenty pieces are anonymous, but the only extant copy of the 1577 print has the ascription 'Scipione delle Palle' penned at the head of *La dura legge d'Amor, ma bench'obliqua* (example XXXIX), a setting of a text from Petrarch's *Il trionfo d'Amore* (III, lines 148ff) for three voices. Eleven of the sixteen sonnets in the collection are also by Petrarch. The other pieces include three examples of *ottava rima* (one of them accompanied by the rubric 'To this [*aere*] any other *stanza* can be sung'), two of *terza rima* both by Petrarch (one of them, the beginning of *Il trionfo d'Amore*, accompanied by the rubric 'On this [*aere*] any kind of *capitolo in terza rima* can be sung'), four strophic *canzonette*, and only three pieces setting texts in the free metrical schemes of sixteenth-century madrigals. With the exception of the last and of one sonnet (*Pien d'un vago pensier* with *Ben, s'io non erro, di pietat'un raggio* as its *seconda parte*), all the pieces apply the principle of using the same music for all segments of text with the same metrical structure, and expand such a procedure to the point of re-using the music of the first quatrain of a sonnet not only for its second quatrain, but also for its tercets.[85] All this is in keeping with an idea of music as 'servant of speech', a mere vehicle for the text; at any rate, this is how it strikes us, lacking as it does the warmth imparted to it by, in the words of Caccini, 'the noble manner of singing that I have learned from my teacher, the famous Scipione del Palla'.

I hold Caccini chiefly responsible for the creation of the myth that monody and opera originated in the Florentine *camerata*,[86] for he was the first to propound it. We must beware lest we create a new myth, of a Neapolitan *camerata* centred on Scipione del Palla, from which the Florentine one might have derived. The truth is that the ideas and procedures of both have more distant origins in the musical practice of the fifteenth century. The description of the singing of choruses included in a report on Gabriele Bombasi's *Alidoro*, a tragedy performed on 2 November 1568 in Reggio Emilia in the honour of Barbara of Austria, Duchess of Ferrara, has no connection with either Florence or Naples, nonetheless its language is such that it might seem to be by a member of the Florentine *camerata* (especially as its anonymous author, possibly Bombasi himself, tends to write like a Tuscan), and yet we know that it was written and published well in advance of any musical, or non-musical, gathering in the *camerata*[87] of the Bardi family.

[84]   The printed source merely has 'Dentici'. This cannot have been Fabrizio, whose name appears in full at the head of a setting of the sonnet *Empio cor, cruda voglia e fiera mano*, nor Scipione Dentice, whose activity as a composer only began later.

[85]   The rather inaccurate layout of this edition gives no precise indication as to how the music of the two quatrains was to be adapted to fit the tercets. In most cases people probably continued the custom of giving the quatrains' music the form abbc which became abc for the tercets. Only in the case of one sonnet, the Petrarchan *Pien d'un vago pensier che mi disvia*, is the music given in full.

[86]   In connection with this, see the following chapter, especially pp. 238 and 244.

[87]   In sixteenth-century usage, the term *camerata* indicated a regular habit of meeting similar to what two centuries later was to be called a *conversazione*, and in the nineteenth century a *salon*. Even those texts which gave rise to the belief that the *camerata* was something akin to an academy indicate that in the house of the Count Bardi discussions were held on a range of subjects not exclusively musical. Vincenzo Galilei must have begun to talk increasingly frequently about music not earlier than 1575.

The chorus was one of women of London, one of whom, as usual, spoke in dialogue with the other characters in the tragedy whenever necessary; but then, during the pauses in the action, she sang, or else recited, those *canzoni* that are commonly called choruses. Much thought had been given to these by most excellent musicians, who, having looked deeply into their meaning, wrote the songs for them, imitating the words so felicitously, *that one would sooner call them speeches than songs*. For being of chromatic music, with very few alterations, *they moved at the pace of ordinary speech*, always avoiding any repetition.[88] In the perorations, in the prayers to the gods, in the exclamations, complaints, questions, weeping and sighing [the songs] expressed the affections of the soul as if, far from being fictitious, they came from real feelings of the heart. The songs being composed thus, the bass and middle parts were assigned to a consort of instruments, all soft and subdued, and touched with utmost restraint by skilful players, placed with their consort of instruments somewhere remote and out of sight. Only the treble line which carried the words, was sung by that one lady, who stood with the other women in the forefront of the stage; so that, when it was time to begin and they started together, she with her voice and the consort with the accompaniment, the one near and the other far away, the one in sight and the other hidden, they left the audience in doubt as to whether her singing was joined by any sort of accompaniment, or whether a mere resonance of her voice produced so sweet a sound, or else whether some distant harmony chanced to form such a pleasant concord. Whatever they may have thought of it, this singing of hers was so lovely to listen to and to watch, that I think it will long be remembered and even serve as a model. For this lady had a most delicate voice, combined with a certain natural talent ruled by art and great judgement. And at the right moments whilst she was so displaying her voice, she altered the expression of her face and eyes, and her gestures and movements, to accord with the changes in meaning of the words she sang. So gently did she do this that she charmed everyone, and they feared, hoped, rejoiced or sorrowed as she wished.[89]

These might well be the words of a self-satisfied author, possibly half in love with the singer; what is important, however, is not so much that the music written for *Alidoro* was actually as described, but that in describing it he could formulate intentions and ideas usually ascribed to more recent times. In any case, while we have no way of judging a music that is no longer extant and whose composers are unidentified,[90] we must always bear in mind how

[88]   Quoted from Giovanni Crocioni, *L'Alidoro o dei primordi del melodramma* (Bologna 1938), p. 37 (it goes without saying that the interesting text of *Il successo dell'Alidoro*, the anonymous contemporary description of the performance, has nothing whatsoever to do with the opera yet). The term 'chromatic music' refers to a rhythm notated *a note nere*, brisk and approaching the rhythm of speech. The meaning of 'very few alterations' is less clear. The full text of *Il successo dell'Alidoro* is now reprinted in *Il teatro italiano*, part II, *La tragedia del Cinquecento*, ed. by Marco Ariani (Turin 1977), vol. II, pp. 984–1008.

[89]   *Ibid.* The text indicates in various ways that many of the concepts considered to be characteristically Florentine were in fact older and more widespread: the 'bass and middle parts', the 'concert placed in distant and hidden location', the expressive diction emphasized by appropriate gestures, and even the sense of mystery which could be obtained by a clever distribution of instruments and voices in various locations. It is believed that the author of the tragedy, Gabriele Bombasi, also wrote the description (Crocioni, *L'Alidoro*, pp. 47–9). Particularly interesting is his discussion of the variety of ways in which tragic chorus could be handled in contemporary theatrical practice (*ibid.*, pp. 37–9).

[90]   *Il successo dell'Alidoro* says (*ibid.*, p. 50) that 'besides those of our own city [Reggio], who were many and excellent, from several of the first courts and lands of Italy many famous musicians of our day had here been gathered together for this purpose'; the reference, of course, is not only to composers but to performers also. Crocioni (pp. 55–6) mentions Claudio Merulo, but Striggio too might have been there, for it was precisely in that year that he visited various courts. The music for the tragedy appears to have included an instrumental prelude as well as

relative the concept of expressiveness is; in a climate of prevailingly decorative or descriptive music even a small inflexion, a slightly more pronounced gesture, a hint of rhythmic hesitation or acceleration may have had an emotive effect that we are no longer able to recapture, used as we are to richer fare.

The musical document most directly connected by author and date to the so-called Florentine *camerata* is a piece (example XL) by Piero Strozzi. He was a nobleman and dilettante who also appears, with Giovanni Bardi, as one of the interlocutors who in Vincenzo Galilei's *Dialogo della musica antica e della moderna* (1581) are the mouthpieces for the author's studies in musical history and theory. The piece is a setting of one of two madrigals composed for the *Chariot of Night*, one of the floats, triumphs or masquerades of 1579, which celebrated the wedding of Francesco dei Medici (by now the Grand-duke of Tuscany) with Bianca Capello:

> Fuor dell'umido nido
> uscita colle mie presaghe schiere
> di fantasmi, di sogni, e di chimere,
> la Notte io son(o), che qui nel vostro lido
> di tante liete altere
> pompe e di tanti fregi
> ne vengo a render gratie, o sommi Regi.[91]

From my dank den, with my presaging host of phantoms, dreams, chimaeras, I am Night, who have come to your land, to give you thanks, supreme Majesties, for so many joyful displays, so lofty and ornate.

It was sung, to the accompaniment of a consort of viols, by Night, played by Giulio Caccini, then at the zenith of his career as a singer. (It is thus yet another example of a polyphonic piece performed monodically, even though in its source, the manuscript Magliabechi XIX, 66 of the Biblioteca Nazionale of Florence, it appears in a modernized version for solo voice and continuo.)[92] The piece is not particularly expressive, as Night merely explains who she is and pays homage to the 'supreme Majesties'; at most it may have hinted at her ominous host with the veiled sound of hidden viols within the float. But it flows smoothly, especially the skilfully achieved continuity of the first three

the choruses; I see no justification for Crocioni's guess that other parts of the tragedy were sung. Nevertheless, as a concession to contemporary custom, there were added four 'visible' *intermedi*, though with invisible music, with characters who appeared 'not from those places used by the actors, but rising instead from the ground, appearing in mid-air and descending from the sky'. The orchestration must have been adapted to the theme of the four *intermedi*, which was that of the elements: earth, water, air and fire.

[91] The complete text is given in Leo Schrade, 'Fêtes du mariage de Francesco dei Medici', in *Les fêtes de la Renaissance*, I (Paris 1956), p. 120. A second stanza was sung to the same music.

[92] Ghisi's statement (*Feste musicali*, p. xl, repeated in the introduction to D. P. Walker's, ed., *Musique des intermèdes de 'La pellegrina'*, Paris 1963, p. xiv), that the madrigal was composed for tenor and bass continuo, is not quite correct, as it is known to have been performed accompanied not by one instrument, which could have made use of the guideline supplied by the continuo part, but by an ensemble of viols for whom it was necessary to write out the parts. Besides, it is possible that Caccini, who personified Night, sang in falsetto, transposing the vocal part up an octave. Schrade, 'Fêtes du mariage', p. 121, agrees that the piece was originally polyphonic. *Ibid.*, p. 124, another piece performed in the 1579 entertainments is identified: the madrigal *Qual miracolo, Amore* by Vincenzo Galilei, performed by one voice with a lute accompaniment, and published in that form in Galilei, *Fronimo*. F. Fano, *La camerata fiorentina* (Milan 1934), pp. 21ff., gives a transcription of it.

Ex. XL Piero Strozzi. Night's song, on a text by Palla Rucellai. Performed in 1579 by Giulio Caccini 'on his own and many other viols'. From the version for voice and continuo in the Florence manuscript, Biblioteca Nazionale Centrale, Magliabechiano XIX, 66, fol. 64.

lines, coming to a climax on the emphatic, twice-repeated statement 'I am Night' ('La Notte io son'). It is not at all clear how deliberate was the choice of the fifth mode and a series of modulations involving all the chromatic steps within the octave of F.[93]

A gap of a whole generation divides the *intermedi* of 1539 from the short season of wedding and carnival celebrations sponsored by Francesco dei Medici in 1565–9. And even in Florence, there were no spectacles after 1569 which were important and solemn enough to warrant the printing of a description of them for the purpose of informing allied or rival courts, often one and the same. No comedies with *intermedi* were performed to mark Francesco's second marriage, which gave legal recognition to his long affair with Bianca Capello. Only open-air spectacles were staged.[94] It was not until

[93]   F sharp is required already in the cadence on '*nido*'; G sharp and B natural are needed in the one on '*chimere*', which perhaps also involved the resolution on an A chord with C sharp. E flat is needed for '*alte pompe*', but it could already have been introduced in the chord of C on '*uscita*'.

[94]   The float of Night, already mentioned, formed part of it.

a new generation entered court life that theatrical events of the kind we have been examining again took place. As far as I know, the start of a new phase was first indicated by the performance of *Le due Persilie*, 'a comedy by Giovanni Fedini, painter of Florence. Performed by order of Signor Girolamo and Signor Giulio Rossi, of the Counts of San Secondo. In the presence of the Grand Princesses of Tuscany. On the 16th day of February 1582' (Florentine style, new style 1583).[95] As Mary, who later became Queen of France, was still too young, the Princesses of Tuscany must have been Eleonora, firstborn of Francesco and Giovanna of Austria, who married Vincenzo Gonzaga in the following year, 1584; and Virginia, natural daughter of Cosimo, who in 1586 married Don Cesare d'Este, heir presumptive to the duchy of Ferrara and future brother-in-law of Carlo Gesualdo, Prince of Venosa. Neither comedies nor *intermedi* were performed for the wedding of Eleonora,[96] though in due course she was to preside over such famous spectacles of the Mantuan court as the performances of Guarini's *Il pastor fido* (1598) and Monteverdi's *Orfeo* (1607), *Arianna* and *Il ballo delle ingrate* (both 1609). By contrast, the 1583 performance of *Le due Persilie*, and *L'amico fido*, given for the wedding of Virginia, were performed with *intermedi*.

The music for the 1583 *intermedi* (which do not seem to have been linked by a common thread)[97] was entrusted to six different composers. Three were asked to write only one polyphonic madrigal each, to be sung by various characters; these are individually identified in the description,[98] but must have been less easily recognized by the audience, unless a *scenario* containing a summary of the comedy and its *intermedi* had been distributed.[99] Three other composers had to cope with more complex and much less clear situations. Iacopo Peri 'alias il Zazzerino' wrote the music of the first *intermedio*, which opened with Demogorgon, father of the Gods, and Eternity, singing together 'in music...and in a dialogue', and ended, after a number of scenic surprises,[100] with a song sung by all the characters who had arrived in succession, in which 'Demogorgon started the singing and the others followed him'. The fifth *intermedio*, whose music was written by the 'chapel-master of Their Most Serene Highnesses', Cristofano Malvezzi, unfolded in three distinct episodes: (a) a dialogue between the Muses and Pleasure (who had already appeared in the preceding *intermedio*, 'followed by Youth, Sardanapallus, Wealth, Ignorance and Pride'); (b) a monologue by Sorrow, who started 'singing solo, accompanied by a symphony of various instruments

95 See note 34 above.
96 Instead there were masquerades and jousts. See Ghisi, *Feste musicali*, p. xi.
97 Except between the fourth and fifth *intermedi*: in the latter some of the allegorical characters of the former were again introduced.
98 These were the second *intermedio* (*La casa del Sonno* – the House of Sleep) with Morpheus, young Sleep, Itatone, Panto and two female characters representing true and false Dreams and music by 'Ser Stefano' (Rossetti?); the third *intermedio* (*I campi Elisi* – The Elysian Fields) with Aeneas, the Sybil, Anchises, Mercury, the river Lethe and four souls, with music by Messer Giovanni Legati; and the fourth, in which sang Pleasure, Youth, Sardanapallus, Wealth, Ignorance and Pride, music by the Reverend Messer Gostantino (sic) Arrighi. There is no indication of what instruments accompanied the voices in these or the other *intermedi*.
99 One can already gather from the list of characters given in the last note how difficult it must have been to recognize and distinguish between, for example, real and false Dreams, or Pride and Ignorance.
100 After the dialogue between Demogorgon and Eternity, there followed 'the uproar of Chaos' quoted above, note 34.

from behind the stage', but then 'took in his hands the garment of Pleasure...and fully decked himself with it'; and (c) a conclusion in which Sorrow was 'joined by Sardanapallus and the others [Pleasure's followers], and, being thought to be Pleasure, they all follow him singing: *This is the idol we adore*'. In the sixth *intermedio* 'Love, Hymen, the three Graces, Juno and Venus came on stage...& Love started, singing: *Come, much desired god*'; Alessandro Striggio wrote the music. As a whole, there is no comparison in terms of sheer theatrical display between the 1583 spectacle and those given at court, but it is once more interesting for the variety of ways in which dialogues are used (unfortunately its music too seems to be lost), as well as for the moralizing allegories of its fifth and sixth *intermedi*, which to some extent anticipate those in *La rappresentatione di Anima, et di Corpo* by Emilio dei Cavalieri (1600).

There is little more to be said about the spectacle given for the wedding of 1586, though it should be stressed that, perhaps to compensate for the long pause which had elapsed since the last theatrical event of a similar kind, but more probably to impress the invited guests from the allied and rival court of Ferrara, a great display was then made of theatrical resources, and extreme attention was paid to every detail. The same spirit prompted a wordy, most detailed *Descrizione del magnificentissimo apparato, de' meravigliosi intermedi* by Bastiano de Rossi (Florence, G. Marescotti, 1585, i.e. 1586 new style). It had been decided that 'the comedy...should be recited by the most accomplished actors of whom we know today, and [learned] with the longest, most persevering, most zealous rehearsing ever practised'. Furthermore, once 'so wonderful and novel, so magnificent and splendid an invention for the *intermedi*' had been found, 'a search was made for the most sufficient masters and craftsmen of this town'; and thus 'more than four hundred people [were summoned] for the realization of this work, who have almost continuously practised up to this very day [presumably 16 February 1585/6), when the *Descrizione* was dedicated to Alfonso II d'Este]...All can see, and none can fail to admire greatly, the perfection to which they have brought it.'[101] The comedy was Giovanni Bardi's *L'amico fido*, which, had it been published, would have revealed a new aspect of the many-sided personality of the promoter of the *camerata*,[102] though admittedly one which Bardi himself considered less important than his accomplishments as the inventor and the poet of the *intermedi*, the composer of the music for the last one, and the supreme authority for the staging of the whole spectacle. This is hardly surprising,

[101] The subject of all this activity, which I have reported impersonally, was Giovanni Bardi, Count of Vernio, to whom the grand-duke had entrusted the organization of the spectacle.

[102] Only its title is known, which anticipates that of the better known *Il pastor fido* by Guarini. Bardi was a philologist, interested in Platonic philosophy and consequently in mathematics, astrology, and musical theory, and who wrote as well about the traditional Florentine game of *calcio* (football). As for his literary tastes, he was a Dante scholar and a linguistic purist, so that his comedy must have given him the occasion for a display of Florentine idioms. These qualities led him to be one of the promoters of the Accademia della Crusca. In music, he was not interested solely in theory: we do not know if he actually knew how to play some instrument, but there is certainly evidence of his having more than once acted as a composer. This combination of interests in philology, philosophy and music led him to encourage and finance Vincenzo Galilei's research on ancient music. It is probable that Galilei's ideas, especially his criticism of contemporary contrapuntal polyphony, reflected those of Bardi, who is in fact the main exponent of the theories of musical philology and aesthetics in Galilei's *Dialogo della musica antica e della moderna*. The other interlocutor is, as I have already mentioned, Piero Strozzi,

given that the *intermedi* even took precedence over the comedy in the title of the *Descrizione*. In 1589, three years later, Bardi again decided that it was important for him to concentrate on creating and producing the *intermedi*, which were performed four times with three different comedies. And though he let others write the texts of the *intermedi*, once more he composed the music for one of them.[103] His commitment was all the greater in 1586 because his comedy, *L'amico fido*, was 'the first to be performed in this hall, and the first that the said grand-duke [Francesco I] had ever had performed after his father's death'. 'This hall' was the one 'built by the said Grand-duke Cosimo in that magnificent and most perfect building, known in Florence as the palace of the Officials (de' Magistrati),...which he had started at such expense and brought almost to completion with such magnificence.' It was later called the hall 'of the comedies', and was almost, yet not quite, a theatre.[104] Its size[105] helped, in the *intermedi* even more than in the comedy, to 'make the architect most fertile in his inventions...with a number of machines ascending to, or

[103] It is the last madrigal of the fourth *intermedio*, practically the only known example of his music, recently republished in *Musique des intermèdes de 'La pellegrina'*, critical edition by D. P. Walker, pp. 85–7.

[104] There is no doubt that the hall was constructed in such a way as to be easily adapted to use as a theatre: its size and the raked floor predisposed it to such a use. But in 1585 neither a fixed stage nor a fixed arrangement of seats for the spectators existed – nor do I believe that they ever did so later.

> In this hall, which is ninety-five *braccia* in length and thirty-five in width, and twenty-four high, and whose floor slopes two and one-eighth *braccia* from top to bottom (and it was given this slope that the people in front might not obstruct the view of the spectacles of those behind them) the aforementioned Grand-duke Francesco wished this performance of the comedy to be held...Therefore in the lowest part of the hall *was placed the perspective*, the marvels of which we shall in due course describe, and we shall now speak only of the apparatus. The said hall *was given the appearance of a theatre* by the ingenious artist [Buontalenti] by six steps which surrounded it on all sides as far as the perspective, which took up twenty *braccia* of the length of the hall. In the centre of the great hall, thirty *braccia* in front of the set, was a platform, one *braccio* high above the floor, which had a step in front of it and was twelve *braccia* wide and as many long, gradually losing its vantage [against the rising floor] towards the back...On this platform, all covered with crimson velvet made yet richer by the quantity of gold which surrounded it and with most precious carpets from Alexandria, sat the Princes and Princesses on rich and splendid seats...

The arrangement was not permanent, although it is probable that once dismantled the parts were kept for re-use if necessary. In 1589 Buontalenti rearranged and redecorated the hall; a description of its new appearance is to be found on pp. 7–17 of the pamphlet published then too by Bastiano de Rossi. This time the princes and princesses sat on a dais at the back of the hall. The invention of a new arrangement and decor on each occasion contributed to the novelty of each spectacle: the 1585 description states 'The surrounding crowds having feasted their eyes for some while on these marvels [the apparatus and decorations of the hall, and the lighting]...they fell silent: and the grand-duke gave a signal: and in a moment, before the eyes of the spectators and to their great astonishment, the curtains, which covered the stage, rose, and it appeared that they were transformed into two great rich hangings of red velvet with large and beautiful tassels of gold and silk which hung on either side...' This novel and ingenious system for opening the curtain became a constant feature of the Medicean theatre, but I cannot tell whether it was permanently installed or whether it was set up afresh each time. On the Medicean theatre, see the rather different opinion expressed by Elena Povoledo, pp. 366–8. See also Annamaria Petrioli Tofani, 'Il teatro medìceo', in *Il luogo teatrale a Firenze* (Milan 1975), pp. 105–6, and Ludovico Zorzi, 'Il teatro mediceo degli Uffizi e il teatrino detto della Dogana', in *Il potere e lo spazio. La scena del principe* (Florence 1980), pp. 355–6.

[105] The measurements given in the footnote above correspond to circa 55 m in length, 20 m 30 in width and 14 m in height. The difference in height between one end of the hall and the other was 1m 25.

descending from the sky, flying in the air and rising from underneath the stage, and with frequent changes of scenery'.[106]

The only theme that the 1586 *intermedi* all had in common was that of glorifying the bridal couple.[107] All the themes and characters from previous *intermedi* were called on to help achieve this – of course, with new variations and improvements. The first *intermedio* began with the customary vision of heaven, and through the opening of the sky, which was operated by the Horae, the nuptials of Mercury and Philology were seen. Philology was soon neglected by Mercury, who suddenly felt the urge to start 'to sing solo, to the sound of viols, lutes, harpsichords and wooden organs,...giving orders by his song to a host of Blessings...quickly to descend that very day...bringing the Golden Age back to us [on earth]'. At this point 'the cloud started its descent, and the Blessings, while descending, sang this madrigal, *O fortunati eroi*, with great sweetness, accompanied by lutes, viols, harps and transverse flutes'.[108] In the second *intermedio* 'all the Evils were seen entering the stage...and they formed a semicircle, sitting on some stones, which had appeared as if by a miracle'; from an opening in the ground 'the city of Dis suddenly arose with all its Furies and demons'; and then a boat arrived, 'ploughing the liquid expanse, and on it was Phlegias...who, having landed and moored his boat, started to sing with a harmony well fitting his character, to the sound of trombones and bass viols'. Phlegias prepared to take aboard the Evils, who were driven back to hell by the Medici–Gonzaga wedding; but they, too, had a song to sing before boarding the boat; until, with lesser harmony, 'when the boat had moved off from the shore with great jarring noises and screams, both they and the horrible city were engulfed in a deep chasm; and the demons quickly plunged after them into this cavern; which having swallowed all...as if by magic shut'.[109] Others involved were Flora and Zephyrus, who sang one after the other in the third *intermedio* 'to the sound of one lute and one harp', conjuring up the appearance of Spring with dancing nymphs and

[106] The passage is taken from the description of the 1589 spectacles, but easily fits any contemporary entertainment with *intermedi*.

[107] 'But let us now tell of the marvels and wealth of the *intermedi*...and let us state what was the Poet's intention when, at the start, he set himself to find a plot for the performance of these *intermedi*. It was this: to find one single theme from which all six *intermedi* would spring...But he then decided...to aim at variety above all else. And seeing that it was better that his invention should be many-stranded, he attempted in all ways to make this unity consist of variety and disunity, and in this he succeeded, so that all those good things which befall mortal man, as represented in these *intermedi*, they all appear to occur as a result of this most happy [Medici–Este] wedding' (de Rossi, *Descrizione*, cc. 5v–6).

[108] One is not told whether the gods seen through the opening in the sky were again puppets, or whether the spaciousness of the hall made it possible to use real people. Despite various indications to the contrary, I would be inclined to favour the former hypothesis. The Blessings were Virtue, Honour, Faith, Beauty, Youth, Happiness, Health, Peace, Prosperous success, and Hymen. The descent by cloud is the one discussed above in note 47.

[109] In this *intermedio* too a large part of the action evidently took place without music, though at times with noises of various sorts. After having sung, Phlegias 'began to organize the small ship to take on the Evils waiting there. From within this boat could be heard certain noises of chains and irons'. After the madrigal of the Evils (Ingratitude, Fraud, Envy, Discord, Wrath, Hunger, Plague, War, Fury, Terror – ten in all, as there had been ten Blessings, if one includes Hymen, in the previous *intermedio*), 'Phlegias took hold of the oar...and began to work to bring ashore the boat...When he had finally moored it at the landing, the Evils were made to embark...' All this evidently took place without music.

of 'a garden of trees heavy with fruit', in which birds were heard singing;[110] Thetis, who in the fourth *intermedio* 'started to sing all by herself, most sweetly, to the sound of lutes', until Neptune emerged in his chariot and it was his turn to 'sing all alone, to the sound of lutes, harps, trombones and transverse flutes', ordering the sea to be calm;[111] Juno, who stopped the rain and let a rainbow shine 'to the sound of lutes, harps and harpsichords';[112] and finally two merry groups of Tuscan shepherds and shepherdesses, nineteen of each, who in a chorus asked 'the great sorceress of Fiesole' what caused 'this renewed season', and resumed their singing and dancing and redoubled joy on learning that

> In questo lieto giorno
> congiunto ha insieme il ciel coppia divina.[113]

In this most happy day, heaven has joined a divine pair together.

Bastiano de Rossi quite evidently had no special bent for music; he was possibly more interested in arguing whether *arpe* (his word for harp) was a masculine or feminine term, than in distinguishing its sound from that, let us say, of a *dolzaina*. He mentions many instruments with a peculiar fascination, not uncommon in literary people, for the sound of their names; but seldom bothers to say how many of each kind were used, or to make clear whether they were played on stage, hidden backstage, or disguised behind unusual shapes. Similarly, he reproduces all the words, saying by which character or group they were sung, but giving no technical information on the number of parts in each piece, or the number of singers or players for each part. Beside the names of the composers – Striggio for the first, second and fifth *intermedio*, Cristofano Malvezzi for the third and fourth, and Bardi for the last one – the only specific information concerning music, evidently intended to flatter Bardi, is that the latter 'chiefly wanted the magnificence and refinement of his poem to be allowed to shine; for which purpose he wanted the harmony to be richer, fuller, sweeter, more varied and more

---

[110] At the start of the *intermedio* there was a change of scene ('in an instant there appeared on the stage the view of a marvellous land'), then there were the songs of Flora and Zephyrus, then

> singing, Spring began to appear on stage, accompanied by cupids, breezes, nymphs, satyrs, and the god Pan and Priapus were also there. And while they were appearing thus dancing, the trees were flowering...And when the spectators had seen and heard all this, and while they were still amazed at it...Spring, with all the chorus of nymphs and satyrs, on lutes, harps, mute *cornetti*, trombones, and *dolzaine* began this sound...And when it was finished, the chorus within began to sing to the sound of instruments: and the nymphs, still dancing, resumed the singing.

[111] Thetis was accompanied by fourteen male and four female tritons, and Neptune by twelve nymphs, who sang 'in two rows' after Neptune's solo, and they all finished together. During their song the sea-monsters who had roused the sea submerged, and the sea grew calm. After this, 'the rocks disappeared, leaving a green and flowery meadow', so that Neptune's chariot might better be admired, 'and while these things were being accomplished, the sweet symphony of the instruments could be heard'.

[112] It was an *intermedio* of clouds. Against a dark and stormy sky Juno appeared on a 'clear-coloured cloud'. At her command, the nymphs scattered the tempest, singing 'to the sound of the same instruments, and of trombones, and large flutes', which furnishes us with another example of the use of trombones for something quite other than infernal or nocturnal scenes.

[113] Shepherds and shepherdesses 'came rejoicing and singing to the sound of lutes, harps, *dolzaine*, bag-pipes, bass, tenor and soprano viols, recorders, flutes, transverse flutes, trombones, straight and curved *cornetti*, rebecs and large flutes'. The sorceress replied '(they being silent) to the sound of lutes and harps', and thus the dialogue continued, ending at last with the chorus accompanied by dancing.

artful than any other, and at the same time (which is held to be almost impossible) most clear and the words easily understood; this, too, the connoisseurs will be able to judge when it is published'. The connoisseurs were to be disappointed, as we are ourselves, for, again, the announced publication never took place. Once more, we are deprived of Striggio's music, which from an artistic point of view was certainly the most valuable of all, of the music of Malvezzi, who was a good if not a first-rate musician, and of Giovanni Bardi's greatest musical endeavour, historically especially interesting.

It would be as wrong to classify Bardi as a conservative as to call him a progressive. It would appear that he was open to the ideas of his own time, while being, as is often the case with Florentines, stubbornly attached to certain traditions. Though not as polemical or belligerent as Vincenzo Galilei, he was certainly critical of contemporary polyphony; but this was after all a common trait, shared with many people who wanted to reform sacred polyphony. Bardi's criticism, however, while affected by the moralizing attitudes inspired by the Counter-Reformation,[114] had deeper roots in the complex humanistic tradition of Florentine Platonism: music is not merely the perceptible concord of sounds, but the deep inner relationship by which the poetic word reflects some fragment of the transcendent harmonious world of cosmic truths, and is thus an echo of the universal harmony. Accordingly Bardi's interest was focussed less on instrumental music, or on music in which voices would be handled as instruments (the most flexible and effective of all intruments), than on an ideal of sung poetry in which the singing would echo the poetic contents of the text. Related to this was Bardi's admiration for Dante, enabled by poetic inspiration to penetrate the harmony of the universe. This explains why Vincenzo Galilei, seeking to apply his theories of musical reform, should choose a *canto* (number XXXIII, the episode of Count Ugolino) from Dante's *Inferno* for his secular example, while using the *Lamentations* of Jeremiah for his experiments in sacred music. I rather doubt whether Bardi fully shared Galilei's idea that reviving ancient music was the best possible way to correct the deviations of contemporary music. As a Greek philologist, he certainly felt a desire to know what the music of those remote centuries had been; but most likely he did not think of it as a model to be strictly adhered to, but rather as a more general indication of what should be done. This view must have been confirmed by the disappointing results Galilei achieved in about 1581–2 when he attempted to restore the ancient modes and tuning systems.[115]

Bardi based his musical aesthetics on his belief in the revealing power of

[114]   There is a connection between the moralism of those times and the praise of the virtuous cultural intentions of the *camerata* which met in the Bardi house. This praise was repeated in more than one text commemorating the gatherings.

[115]   Information about it is contained in a letter written by Piero Bardi, Giovanni's son, to Giovanbattista Doni:

> He then had [the audience] hear the lament of Dante's Count Ugolino, clearly sung by a tenor in good voice, against a consort of precisely played viols. Just as it aroused the envy of a large number of professional musicians, so this novelty also pleased those who were real lovers of the art. Galilei followed up this worthy enterprise by composing part of the Lamentations [of Jeremiah] and responses for Holy Week, both sung in the same way in devout company... (in Solerti, *Le origini del melodramma*, pp. 144–5).

The most certain fact is that the voice which sang took the tenor part in a polyphonic instrumental ensemble: 'precisely played' indicates the attention paid, probably, to reproducing the Pythagorean tuning advocated by Galilei. That the whole attempt was a failure is attributed to the envy of the other musicians.

the poetic word, enabled by the gift of inspiration to reach the supreme theoretical truths and harmonies. Accordingly, he mistrusted everything that was aimed at being immediately appealing to the ear, as well as all the practical expedients of musical technique and artistry. In practice, however, such a total denial of musical artistry would have been opposed to the general appreciation of artistry in other fields; hence his attempt to hit on a compromise. We can see this reflected in the peculiar list of superlatives used by Bastiano de Rossi in his 1586 description of Bardi's quest for a harmony that would be 'richer, fuller, sweeter, more varied, and more artful than any other'. His first four requirements define the meaning of the last, and they are all modified by the added condition that the text should be clearly understood ('which is held to be almost impossible'). As a man of the world and a dilettante not completely unaffected by the detested blandishments of polyphony, Bardi may not have been too strict in imposing his terms on his collaborators; as a composer himself, he adopted a kind of chordal polyphony in which the text was usually recited simultaneously by all the voices. Furthermore, he insisted on 'composing by whole lines' (*comporre col verso intero*), that is, considering each line as a rhythmic unit to be preserved in the music. He may have trusted that the proportions of superior harmonies would be reflected within each individual unit as well as in the way they were related to one another.[116]

Bardi was a dilettante: he was not totally committed to or dependent on music but could treat it as just one aspect of his position as a high-ranking nobleman, a courtier, and an arbiter of many a kind of artistic refinement. Such a status had first been officially recognized when he had been put in charge of the spectacles of 1586 and seemed confirmed when in 1588/9 he was asked to organize those planned for the forthcoming celebrations to mark the nuptials of the new grand-duke, Ferdinand I. But his prestige, though not yet his authority, had been greatly impaired when in the autumn of 1588 Emilio dei Cavalieri had been appointed to the newly created post of superintendent responsible for all the artistic activities of the Medici court. He was a Roman, and like Bardi a gentleman of high rank and many artistic talents. He was also a personal friend of the new ruler.[117] Little evidence survives of the tensions between the two rivals, both equally jealous of their prestige and privileges, for social convention limited the amount of overt antagonism they could display, but there is a hint of their mutual hostility in the discrepancies between the official description of the spectacles, by Bastiano de Rossi, and a second one included when the music of the *intermedi* was finally printed. The official description, inspired by Bardi,[118] accurately reflects his intentions,

[116] This preoccupation with 'composing by whole lines' (*col verso intero*) shows that for Bardi the need to interpret the expressive content of the words was at any rate subordinated to respect for its metrical form. It is understandable that he should have criticized an excess of musical expression (cf. note 33 of the next chapter) no less than the lack of it. For a discussion on Bardi's personality see D. P. Walker, 'La musique des intermèdes florentins de 1589 et l'Humanisme', in *Les fêtes de la Renaissance* (Paris 1956).

[117] Despite it being a topic of considerable interest, no one to my knowledge has made a detailed study of the artistic and cultural activities of Cardinal Ferdinando dei Medici in Rome between 1571 and when he was raised to the position of grand-duke.

[118] It is entitled *Descrizione dellaparato e degl'intermedi fatti per la commedia rappresentata in Firenze nelle nozze de' Serenissimi Don Ferdinando Medici e Madama Cristina di Lorena. Gran Duchi di Toscana* (A. Padovani, Florence 1589). On the differences between the first and second editions

but fails to mention the changes introduced in the last stages of the preparations. It is also very inadequate on musical detail, due to the lack of interest of its compiler. It even omits the information, precious for our understanding of the predominant interest in *intermedi*, namely that these, having been created for *La pellegrina* of the Sienese Girolamo Bargagli (which was performed on 2 and 15 May by members of the Sienese Accademia degli Intronati), were then twice repeated with two other comedies performed by the Comici Gelosi (respectively, on 6 and 13 May), *La zingara* and *La pazzia*.[119] The second, later, description, included with the music whose printing the grand-duke commissioned through Cavalieri,[120] more faithfully reflects the changes which the latter had made in the spectacle; quite naturally it is also more precise about the composers of the music, the instruments employed and the performers. Both descriptions show their bias through intentional omissions made at the expense of minor figures of the opposite faction.[121] One wonders what part old Alessandro Striggio would have played in these spiteful skirmishes, had he too been present.[122]

We cannot blame Cavalieri's intrusion for the lack of a single theme connecting all the *intermedi*, for indeed Bardi himself claimed that he was responsible for this, as de Rossi reports:

He [that is, Bardi] did not consider a single plot [for the *intermedi*] to be appropriate, considering that it would be enough for the audience to have to follow that of the comedy. Furthermore, had he chosen a single [continuous] plot, he would always have been committed to following that single thread. There always seem to be good and

see Ulderico Rolandi, 'Emilio de' Cavalieri, il Granduca Ferdinando e l'"Inferigno"', in *Rivista musicale italiana*, XXXVI (1929), pp. 26ff. The differences between the *Descrizione* and the musical edition of the music are largely indicated by A. Solerti, *Gli albori del melodramma* (Milan 1905), II, pp. 15ff.

[119] This is mentioned in the handwritten *Diario* by Settimani in the passages reproduced by Solerti, *Gli albori del melodramma*, II, pp. 17–18. For *La zingara* (and probably also *La pazzia*), it specified that 'it was performed in the Great Hall of the Palazzo Vecchio', which means that the stage machines used on the large stage of the Uffizi hall must have been transported and adapted to a different, and certainly smaller, stage. This detail casts doubt on the entire validity of the information: perhaps the Gelosi comedies were performed in three acts and therefore required fewer *intermedi*, thus simplifying the transfer. From Settimani's *Diario* we also learn that *La pellegrina* was repeated on 15 May 'in the Salone de' Magistrati [i.e. in the Uffizi] at the request of the ambassadors of the Republic of Venice and others who had arrived since the first performance'. Sets and machines for the *intermedi* must have been transferred again, this time in the space of a mere two days.

[120] This is the very rare edition of the *Intermedii et concerti, fatti per la commedia rappresentata in Firenze nelle nozze del Serenissimo Don Ferdinando Medici, e Madama Christiana di Lorena, Gran Duchi di Toscana* (G. Vincenti, Venice 1591) dedicated by Malvezzi to the new grand-duchess. Particularly important is the partbook of the 'Nono' ('ninth voice'), which contains information about the instruments used in addition to the voices.

[121] The most serious omission in the musical edition is of Caccini's aria (fourth *intermedio*), and in the *Descrizione* of Peri's piece (fifth *intermedio*).

[122] The edition of the music records that 'Alessandro Striggio' was employed as a viol player in the first 1589 *intermedio*, and refers to 'the aforementioned Alessandrino' employed in the same capacity in the fourth *intermedio*, causing one to think in terms of the young Alessandro, Monteverdi's future librettist. But our doubts are raised anew when we read that amongst the instruments used for the fifth *intermedio* was 'an *arciviolata lira* played by the masterly hand of the famous Alessandro Striggio'. On the other hand, it would seem strange that Striggio, even if old or ill, should have taken part as a performer without making some contribution, even if less than normal, to the composing of the music. Fenlon, *Music and Patronage in Sixteenth-Century Mantua*, p. 141, seems inclined to think that both Striggios were present. *Ibid.* evidence is given that the older Alessandro died in Mantua in 1592.

bad sides to this: actually, it would have restricted the artist's freedom, without seeming to bring too much novelty to [please] the connoisseurs.[123]

No details are given of the 'single plot' which Bardi may or may not have had in mind; the 'unity' of the six 'fables' he selected is limited to the fact that five of them revive classical myths about music. This 'unity' could almost be extended to include the sixth plot, that of celestial and infernal demons in the fourth *intermedio*, had its unidentified sorceress, who sings 'to summon the demons of the purest region of the air, the one called fire, and to force them to tell how soon the world will be blessed with supreme joy', made it clearer that her magic is accomplished by means of song. The celestial demons immediately appeared on one of the customary clouds and expressed this prophecy:

> Or che le due grand'alme insieme aggiunge
> un saldo amor celeste,
> d'ogni alta gioia il mondo si riveste,
> ogni alma al bene oprar s'accende e punge.
> Volane lunge la cagion del pianto.
> Felice eterno canto
> che più che mai soave in ciel risuona
> di sua felicità speranza dona.

Now, as a bond of celestial love unites two great souls the world is blessed with highest joy; every soul burns and desires to do good. All cause of tears departs. A song of eternal happiness, sounding now in the heavens more sweetly than ever, gives us good hopes of partaking in its bliss.

There was, however, some delay on stage before the 'song of eternal happiness' could be heard. Unexpectedly, and with no further magic command, the setting changed into a Dantesque vision of hell; Furies and infernal demons 'sat subdued in sorrow on those rocks, and started to sing a sad and mournful piece (the work of our poet) to the sound of harps, viols, and citterns, lamenting...the happy events that had been announced by the demons in the cloud'.[124] Bardi, a Dante scholar, paid this *intermedio* set in hell, which comes as a break in the series of musical myths, a special honour by writing the madrigal sung by the Furies and devils at the end of the scene. This was his only contribution as a composer. It is easy to see why he paid a similar honour to the first *intermedio*, for which he wrote the opening words, to be sung by Dorian Harmony. Why he chose to write the words for the choir of sea-nymphs in the fifth *intermedio* is less clear.

Nor can the five *intermedi* illustrating musical myths be seen as expressing, even allegorically, a theory of musical and poetic aesthetics. Had this been Bardi's intention, de Rossi would not have failed to make the point in his description, whereas he merely states that Bardi intended to satisfy the expectations of the audience by providing the usual surprises,[125] possibly

---

[123] *Descrizione*, p. 17.

[124] *Ibid.*, p. 52. The infernal scene is minutely described in the next two pages, with frequent references to Dante: 'one saw old Charon, with his ship, as Dante seems to paint him, with a long white beard', and Lucifer's head 'had three faces: the forward-facing one, as stated by Dante, was red, the one on the right was between yellow and white, and the third was black', and so on, including individual lines and whole passages from Dante.

[125] See the passage quoted above in connection with the 1586 *intermedi* but taken from the 1589 *Descrizione* (cf. note 106).

embellished by philological, astrological and literary subtleties aimed at satisfying himself and delighting the learned. The place where the extensive use of musical myths might seem to be justified is in a surprising statement which anticipates by eleven years some ideas later expressed by Cavalieri in the introduction to the print of his *La rappresentatione di Anima, et di Corpo* (N. Mutii, Rome, 1600). De Rossi writes that 'their maker [of the *intermedi*] has striven to the best of his ability to ensure that all the actions to be accomplished in the plot are performed according to their nature; for instance, if there is to be dancing or singing in the *intermedio*, the plot shall specifically require it'.[126] We do not know whether Bardi and Cavalieri disagreed about who had thought of the idea first, as there is no record on either side of arguments on the matter. However, Bardi's 'natural' dancing in the last *intermedio* was later altered by Cavalieri.

'But let us now narrate the marvels of the *intermedi*', wrote de Rossi after eleven printed pages all devoted to descriptions of the new arrangement of the theatre which Buontalenti had created in the Sala delle Commedie of the Uffizi palace.[127] Their plots are all well known: the Music of the Spheres (I), the Muses defeating the Pierides in a singing contest (II), Apollo's victory over the serpent Python (III), the Apparition of celestial and infernal demons (IV), Arion rescued from the sea by virtue of his singing (V), and finally the Gift of Harmony and Rhythm to mankind (VI), which appeared as the Gift of Dance and Song in the actual performance. Their poetic texts, as well as the essential passages of de Rossi's description, had already been published by Angelo Solerti by the beginning of this century;[128] but it is only in recent years that a full survey of the corresponding music has been made possible by a complete critical edition of the musical print of 1591.[129] This makes immediately apparent how extensive and technically more challenging the sections assigned to professional composers were, compared with the contributions of dilettanti and of singers who themselves wrote the pieces they were called upon to perform. Luca Marenzio composed all the music for the second and third *intermedi* (with one exception which I shall mention later); Cristofano Malvezzi most of the music for the first, fourth, fifth and sixth *intermedi*. Of the others Cavalieri had the largest share, as he composed about half of the final *intermedio*, while the contributions by Bardi, the two Archileis, Giulio Caccini and Iacopo Peri were limited to one piece each. One further distinction

[126]   For Cavalieri's equivalent expressions, see the next chapter, especially note 26.
[127]   The apparatus of the 'great Royal Hall of the palace' is more briefly described in Settimani's *Diario* (see Solerti, *Gli albori del melodramma*, II, p. 17). It was 'all decorated in gold with paintings and statues in relief. All around it were steps one on top of the other, where both the Florentine and the foreign ladies sat comfortably, and in the centre of the hall were the men seated on benches so arranged so that the last could see as much as the first. For the princes and princesses a handsome dais was arranged behind all the others...' This arrangement of the theatre therefore differed from that of 1586, when the princes had sat in the centre of the hall. See *Il luogo teatrale a Firenze*, ed. M. Fabbri, E. Garbero Zorzi, A. M. Petrioli Tofani (Milan, 1975), pp. 105ff.
[128]   Solerti, *Gli albori del melodramma*, II, pp. 15–42. Also Aby Warburg, 'I costumi teatrali per gli intermezzi del 1589', in *La riforma del melodramma* (Florence 1895), reprinted in Aby Warburg, *Gesammelte Schriften* (Leipzig 1932). See also the studies by Federico Ghisi and D. P. Walker which introduce the edition of the music referred to in the next note.
[129]   This is the *Musique des intermèdes de 'La pellegrina'* by D. P. Walker (Paris 1963). It was intended that it should be followed by a second volume to include a new edition of Bastiano de Rossi's *Descrizione* with essays and critical comments.

lies in the fact that Marenzio and Malvezzi were entrusted with the sections demanding greater contrapuntal skills, while the others wrote largely chordal pieces, or ones intended to be performed by a single voice and instruments. There were fewer such pieces than there had been in previous *intermedi*, but this does not seem to have been intentional.[130] The fact that the work was by more than one person in no way reduces its artistic value or its interest. This is partly because the success of all *intermedi* depended chiefly on their variety, and thus they could only benefit from the varied talents of the different contributors. Furthermore even when a large number of people had had a hand in the work, the musical contributions were separated from each other by intervals. The length of these varied, but they were all full of the action and portents which were the essential characteristics of the *intermedi* as spectacles.

It is somewhat ironic that the only reference to the Greek theory of music, the solo sung by the Dorian Harmony at the beginning of the first *intermedio* (example XLI), is, in the description written by a Bardi partisan, attributed to Bardi's main opponent, Cavalieri, a belligerent defender of the excellence of 'our own music'.[131] More plausible is the attribution in the musical print of 1591, where the piece is ascribed to Antonio Archilei, whose wife, the famous Vittoria, sang it from a cloud hovering against a backdrop representing a view of Rome. Even the new attribution, however, does not make too much difference, for the Archileis had been for many years in the service of Cardinal dei Medici and belonged, like Cavalieri, to the group of those who had come from Rome following the new grand-duke. There is no attempt at an antiquarian reconstruction of the ancient *harmony*. With the transparent simplicity of the chords played by a 'visible' lute and two hidden *chitarroni* and with the flexibility and lightness of its vocal coloratura it achieves an *ethos* that is not gravely solemn, but ethereal, serene and crystal-clear, more appropriate to Plato's allegory of a musical cosmos than the answer it receives from the sirens. That the latter's singing is less felicitous cannot be blamed on Malvezzi. He was forced, most probably for practical reasons, to make use of two choruses of low-pitched voices, whose sound we find unsuitable to those mythical beings who in Plato's cosmology presided over the course of the planets.[132] They hint at this task in a light madrigalistic run which they sing more than once in appropriate places:

> Noi che cantando le celesti sfere
> dolcemente *rotar* facciam intorno...

We, who by singing keep the heavenly spheres smoothly *circling* around...

---

[130]   I myself have occasionally referred to a regression of monody in the 1589 *intermedi*. Closer study has however convinced me that no special intention was behind the slight reduction in the number of monodic pieces.

[131]   Above all, it was Peri who asserted this, in the foreword 'To the readers' inserted before the score of *Euridice*: 'Although as far as I know, *our music* was made to be heard on stage with marvellous invention, by Emilio del Cavaliere before any one else...'

[132]   That female choruses often included male voices is a fact which frequently recurs in the music of this period, in which the performers, even if in female attire, were in any case usually men or boys. The 1589 second *intermedio*, entirely female, and the chorus of sea-nymphs in the fifth *intermedio*, both included basses and tenors. The chorus of sirens, Fates and Planets, nevertheless, had a particularly low and heavy *tessitura*; besides it is made up of eight voices

Ex. XLI   Antonio Archilei. Start of the song of Dorian Harmony in the first *intermedio* of *La pellegrina* by Girolamo Bargagli, sung by Vittoria Archilei, 'she playing a *leuto grosso* accompanied by two *chitarroni*'. From *Intermedii et concerti, fatti per la commedia rappresentata in Firenze,* etc. (G. Vincenti, Venice 1591).

in two choruses although there were ten sirens ('two…according to modern opinion, are to be added, i.e. those of the ninth and tenth spheres'). Later on, however, in the triple chorus of fifteen voices, the sirens certainly form two of the three groups.

217

Si _ _ re _ ne a _ mi _ ca scor _ ta,

a _ mi _ ca scor _ _ ta

Son l'Ar _ _ _ mo _ _ _ ni _ _

_ a Ch'a voi ven _ go, mor'ta _ li,

After the cloud with the Dorian Harmony had risen out of sight, and the ones carrying the sirens had descended, the sky opened (by now an established tradition); at which point, 'up there, as well as down on earth, a melody arose, so much sweeter than any that had ever been heard, that it seemed to belong

Ex. XLII Cristofano Malvezzi. Symphony of the first *intermedio* of *La pellegrina* by G. Bargagli (for violas, lutes, four trombones, a *cornetto*, a transverse flute, *chitarrone*, psaltery, cittern and mandola). From *Intermedii et concerti* etc. (G. Vincenti, Venice 1591).

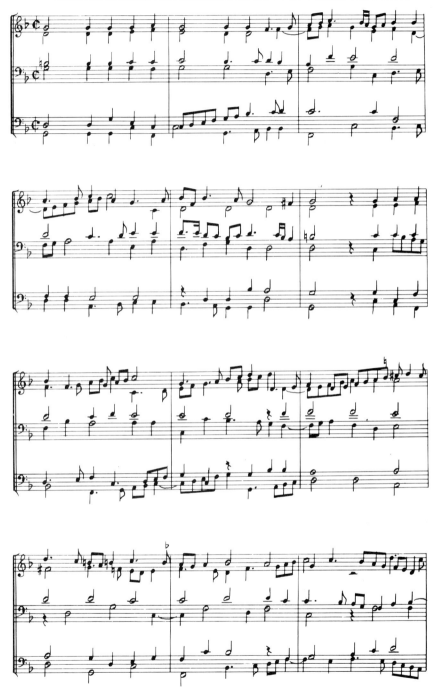

to Paradise'.[133] This was a symphony à 6 by Malvezzi (example XLII), which served as a prelude to the second half of the *intermedio*. Though it is not clearly indicated in the printed score, a dialogue develops in this second half between a new group, made up of Necessity, the three Fates, Astraea, and the seven Planets, who had all been revealed when the sky opened, and the ten sirens in two nearer and lower groups. The Planets were probably responsible for providing the instrumental support. The symphony was played twice, and then 'a lad [endowed] with an excellent voice and charm' (probably meant to represent Astraea) started to sing to the accompaniment of various stringed instruments:

> Dolcissime Sirene,
> tornate al cielo, e in tanto
> facciam cantando a gara un dolce canto.

Sweetest sirens, come back to heaven, but meanwhile let us compete in singing a sweet song.

The group to whom the appeal is made obligingly accepts the invitation and starts to sing a distich à 6 (*Non mai tanto splendore*). The singing then continues with fifteen independent parts grouped in three choruses (an upper one which includes Necessity, Astraea and the three Fates; and two lower choruses formed by the ten sirens on their respective clouds, which are slowly re-ascending. Each chorus is accompanied by its own instrumental forces).[134]

[133] According to the edition of the music 'the following symphony was performed with the aforementioned instruments [two *lire*, two harps, a large lute, a *chitarrone*, a bass and a sub-bass viol which all had accompanied the first double chorus] and in addition [it was played] in the open sky by six lutes, three large and three small, a psaltery, a bass-viol with three tenor viols, four trombones, a *cornetta*, a transverse flute, a zither, a mandola and a *sopranino di viola* played most excellently by Alessandro Striggio'. At the end of the symphony there is a repeat sign, so it is possible that it was played once from the open sky and once on instruments closer to the audience (or vice versa), or else on both occasions by all the instruments. Amongst the instruments which played from the sky are recognizable the complete family of six lutes (which therefore played monodically) and an almost complete family made up of four trombones, the *cornetta*, and the flute. There were only five viols, and I cannot tell which of the other instruments mentioned might have completed the group. In any case there remain two instruments which were not grouped with others of the same sort. It is even more difficult to establish how the eight instruments of the nearer group were arranged to play the six parts of the symphony.

[134] The version of this piece in *Musique des intermèdes*, pp. 18ff, distributes the parts of the dialogue according to Solerti's suggestions. It seems to me more likely that the first chorus was composed of the Fates, Astraea, and Necessity, and the other two choruses of the sirens. The fifteen voices were accompanied by the instruments listed in note 133 above, but the problems of distribution are greater as the more numerous group (the open-sky one) should have been connected only with the first chorus, and the smaller group with the two siren choruses.

Eventually, when the three groups had gathered in the upper part of the stage, they joined forces in the following madrigal à 6, 'sung and played by the same instruments and voices, all parts doubled in the proper proportion to each other; by which [madrigal] the first *intermedio* was brought to its end':[135]

> Coppia gentil d'avventurosi amanti,
> per cui non pure il mondo
> si fa lieto e giocondo,
> ma fiammeggiante d'amoroso zelo
> canta, ridendo e festeggiando, 'l cielo.

O gracious pair of fortunate lovers, to honour whom not only the earth is joyous and happy, but heaven, too, glowing with amorous fire, sings, all smiles and merriment.

Malvezzi is to be congratulated on having succeeded in making such a complex structure joyful and gay by taking advantage of all the resources of contrapuntal writing. These range from massive chordal sonorities to the interplay between blocks of sound whose contrasts were accentuated by their relative positions on stage, and to passages of transparent concertato, in which isolated voices disentangle themselves from the ensemble to introduce florid passages and contrapuntal interplay. Last but not least of the musical factors which contributed to the success of the *intermedio* are the transitions from binary rhythm (often implying a flexible rhythmic variety)[136] to ternary, and the gentleness of the prevailing minor mode.

Marenzio's achievement in the second *intermedio*, which also started with a symphony (à 5, played by 'two harps, two lyres, one bass viol, two lutes, one violin, one *viola bastarda* and one *chitarrone*')[137] and had its climax in a triple chorus with six parts in each group, is by contrast rather disappointing. However, the weakness of the plot must be taken into account; it had very little appeal for the poet, Rinuccini, it was poorly explained to the public, and posed problems for the artist who was to provide a musical interpretation of

[135] Once again the problem of how parts may have been doubled is insoluble, especially as it involves fifteen voices assigned to perform six musical parts.

[136] It is frequently said that the rhythm of Renaissance music was purely quantitative. This is correct only to the extent that an indication of binary measure does not necessarily mean an alternation of accented and unaccented beats. The idea of a kind of music completely unaccented is unrealistic. The accents were perhaps not as strongly stressed as in more recent music, so that the stressing of a syllable in syncopation would have been more readily acceptable, and it must also have been possible for several voices in a polyphonic piece to put stresses on different beats; but accents did exist, and if the music is to be interpreted correctly it is essential to ascertain where the sense of the music, and of the words linked to the music, require that they should fall. These same considerations should also apply in the case of a ternary measure. In practice rhythmic accent and triple metre almost always coincide, though not so completely as not to admit, for instance, the so-called 'hemiola' (two ternary measures accented as if they were three duple bars). The rhythm 'signatures' are in practice indications of tempo (slower or faster) derived from the original proportional significance of the signs. For example, Malvezzi's symphony à 6 should, in my opinion, be interpreted entirely in 3/1 except for bars of 2/1 before the final chord; this 3/1 (notated in the original in duple time) is slower than the 3/1 sections notated in triple time in the successive choral pieces; in the latter, the sections in duple time may actually once more indicate a mixture of duple and triple rhythm. For a wider range of examples see all, or almost all, the musical excerpts quoted in the text.

[137] The instruments are indicated in the edition of the music (the *Descrizione* makes no mention of the symphony) and clearly divide into two groups: five bowed (two *lire*, a bass viol, a violin, a *viola bastarda*) and five plucked (two harps, two lutes, and a *chitarrone*). One may even conclude that the 'perfect' instruments (i.e. those capable of producing complete harmonies), such as especially the lutes, the *chitarrone* and the bastard viol, could be assigned linear parts.

221

it. He would have had either to debase himself by giving the Pierides a weak song, or to make the song of the Muses supremely beautiful in order to justify their victory in the singing contest. In conceiving the plot of the *intermedio* Bardi's sole aim must have been to exploit Buontalenti's 'inventiveness'; more precisely, it was a question of creating an opportunity for him to repeat the sudden metamorphosis of characters on the stage which he had already successfully used in 1569 with Latona's frogs. The change takes place after the musical part of the *intermedio* is over and the Hamadryads, the judges of the singing contest, have themselves finished singing their verdict which favours the Muses. Then, 'as if by a miracle, one could see the losing girls, changed into magpies, go to hide from the others cawing and jumping, while the mound and the grottoes disappeared, and the garden vanished'. The music, mostly chordal, shows a skilled hand and is effectively assigned to the various groups on stage (without the advantage, however, of a more diversified scattering in space), or to even smaller units that the composer creates for greater variety. Its smooth flow even affords some examples of imitation in canon between the choruses, but still basically lacks a poetic afflatus and can only succeed in concealing the emptiness of the plot behind a display of decorative devices. It cannot even alternate soloists and choruses, for the Pierides and the Muses must sing as whole groups, and a choral unanimity is required for the verdict of the Hamadryads. By way of compensation for this, the composer must have asked for and obtained the insertion (not too skilfully managed in the text)[138] of a short initial chorus for three soprano voices, often imitating each other in unison, to which the symphony serves as a prelude (example XLIII). The success of this insertion is proved by the fact that it was often echoed – by Cavalieri in the sixth *intermedio*, and by Peri and Caccini in their first operas.

Marenzio's major reward, though, was that he was asked to write the music for the third *intermedio*, so rich in poetic themes and musical opportunities that it must have been subjected to some pruning to prevent length impairing its effectiveness. After the second act of the comedy, 'the houses [of its stage setting] were concealed by oaks, Turkey oaks, chestnut trees, beeches...and the whole set was changed into a wood. Inside the wood [there was] a dark, huge grotto in ruins; and all the plants around it [appeared to be] scorched and damaged by fire...The wood having appeared (what a new wonder), one could see nine pairs of men and women entering from the left, all dressed as it were in a Greek garb;...and as soon as they came on stage they started to sing to the sound of viols, transverse flutes and trombones.'[139] The text

---

[138] It is not in fact clear that it was the Hamadryads who sang, but it must have been them since they claim to be 'in a harsh and bitter competition...elected to give a fateful verdict'. The song for three voices in which the singers insist on their own beauty ('Nature created us beauteous, perfect in beauty') would normally be thought more suited to the three Graces, but though the *Descrizione* does not say so the Graces must have been attached to the group of the Muses whose song is written for twelve voices in two choruses. The Hamadryads (wood nymphs), however, from having been three become six in the final piece 'O figlie di Piero', in which they form the first chorus of six voices, the other two being those in which Muses and Graces join forces. The introduction of the little chorus in treble voices is not the only sign of hasty and confused modifications, introduced perhaps in the final stage of the lengthy preparations. In this case, the decision may have been at least partly justified by the last-minute inclusion in the cast of 'two girls who serve...the Duke of Mantua' and of 'a child, their brother'.

[139] That is how it appears in the *Descrizione*; in the edition of the music the first madrigal ('*Ebra di sangue*' – 'Drunk on blood') is omitted, and the next one is indeed given as being sung

Ex. XLIII   Luca Marenzio. Sinfonia ('composed of two harps, two lyres, a bass viol, two lutes, a violin, a *viola bastarda* and a *chitarrone*') and start of the first madrigal (accompanied by 'the sound of a harp, and two lyres') of the second *intermedio* of *La pellegrina* by G. Bargagli. From *Intermedii et concerti* etc. (G. Vincenti, Venice 1591).

by two choruses, but with a total of only twelve, not thirty-six, voices. The instruments listed too are different: 'This concert was performed with a harp, two lyres, two bass viols, four lutes, a bass trombone, a *cornetto*, a violin and twelve voices'. The instruments thus were twelve, but it is difficult to establish how they were distributed to support the two choruses, especially when these sang in opposition to each other.

given to this group in de Rossi's description is omitted in the printed score, in which the *intermedio* begins with the musical setting of another text, the one assigned by de Rossi to nine more pairs, who should have arrived after the first ones from the opposite side of the stage; nevertheless, the division into two groups of those present on stage is maintained, and the lament of the people of Delphi (example XLIV) is sung by a double chorus.

Marenzio did not achieve this effect of tragic mourning by means of harmonies charged with pathos, but through the bare emptiness of open fifths and octaves, in two short passages for two soprano parts, which frame a short, tense description of the monster which has plagued Delphi. Once the stage has been set, and the previous events of the drama established, the present anguish is expressed in a series of alarmed questions exchanged by the two choruses. These are almost canonic in form, and yet keep with great restraint within the limits of almost absolute consonance. This emphasizes the expressive dissonances which are reserved for the final question: 'Might Jupiter have heard our desperate crying?' At this point we are confronted with

Ex. XLIV Luca Marenzio. Start of the third *intermedio* of *La pellegrina* by G. Bargagli ('with a harp, two lyres, two bass viols, four lutes, a bass trombone, a *cornetto*, a violin, and twelve voices'). From *Intermedii et concerti* etc. (G. Vincenti, Venice 1591).

an insoluble problem of interpretation. According to de Rossi's description, 'as soon as they had uttered these last words, a serpent, a dragon of incalculable size, meant by the poet to represent the serpent Python, spitting fire and darkening the air all around with smoke, raised its head through the horrid, sombre grotto...Wherefore the unhappy people, catching sight of the wild cruel beast, all together...in a plaintive, sad voice, sang the following words, praying God to rescue them from such fierce, unheard-of evil.' Instead,

226

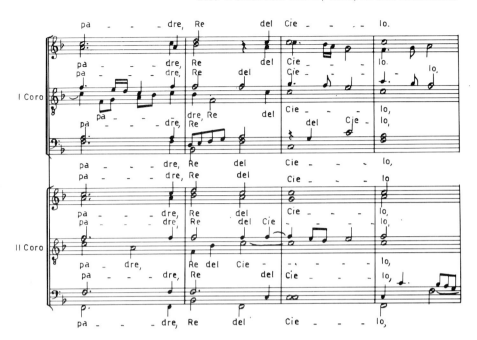

the printed score has here only a short rest, in which we would hate to have to insert the appearance of this huge sixteenth-century Fafner, 'its wings wide open (of a strange colour, between greenish and black, sparkling with mirrors), its horrid huge mouth gaping to show three rows of enormous teeth, its burning tongue darting out with hissing noise and spitting of fire and venom'. If we do not allow this vision to interfere, the singing could resume after the last anguished question, with a splendid transition from a G chord to an F chord, enhancing the trepidation of the following prayer, in which for the first time the two choruses are fully united:[140]

> O padre, o Re del Cielo,
> volgi pietosi gli occhi
> a l'infelice Delo:
> a te dimand'aita, e piang'e plora.
> Muovi lampo e saetta
> a far di lei vendetta
> contro 'l mostro crudel che la divora.

O father, King of heaven, turn thy eyes with compassion to unhappy Delos (sic): she asks thy help, and cries and implores. Hurl lightning, and dart, to take vengeance for her on the cruel monster that is devouring her.

The musical setting manages to combine both madrigalistic and recitative features: it is recitative in a way that is suited to a tragedy, resembling Andrea Gabrieli's choruses for *Edipo tiranno*,[141] in the rhythmic precision and the

---

[140] In this case too the edition of the music omits the first three lines of the prayer (*O sfortunati noi* – Oh how unfortunate we are) so that it begins more effectively with the invocation itself.

[141] Composed for the inauguration of the Teatro Olimpico at Vicenza in 1585 and printed in Venice in 1588, they constituted an immediate precedent of which Marenzio could not have been unaware. On them see Leo Schrade, '"L'Edipo Tiranno" d'Andrea Gabrieli et la Renaissance

almost complete simultaneity with which the text is uttered by all the voices, while it is madrigalistic more in the sober, yet precise, characterization of each sentence than in the expressive dissonance on *piang'e plora* or in the sprightly scales of eighth-notes on *saetta* (a noun made into an exhortative verb by the music).

According to de Rossi's description this is only a preamble: the climax was reached at the moment when

the poet of the *intermedio* had wanted to depict the Pythian battle as represented by Julius Pollux. He tells us that the fight, when it was represented in the music of the ancients, was divided into five parts: in the first Apollo explored the ground, to see whether it was convenient for the battle; in the second he challenged the serpent, and in the third he fought it, in iambic verse...In the fourth that god's victorious slaying of the serpent was represented in spondaic verse; and in the fifth [the god] leapt and danced a joyous dance, signifying his victory. Although the cruel passage of time prevents us from depicting such things with those ancient musical modes, nevertheless, the poet, judging that such a battle, performed on the stage, would give, as it actually gave, great pleasure to the audience, had it represented *with our modern music*, doing the best he could, as a man of great experience in the art, to imitate and revive the ancient one.

There follows a long description of the god appearing from the sky ('to the greatest surprise of all who saw him come, for a beam of light could not have arrived with greater speed, and...nothing could be seen supporting him') and of the five phases of the battle as it was mimed and danced. The corresponding passage of the printed score gives the briefest of information: 'Here a symphony is missing', adding no hint of the attempted imitation of the ancient musical modes. Similarly it does not say whether the missing symphony was by Marenzio (to whom the print assigns all the music of the *intermedio*), or by Bardi (to whom de Rossi's description seems to attribute it). I think it more likely that, following a practice which was soon to become very common, it was provided by an anonymous, possibly very mediocre musician who specialized in dance music. We are ourselves prevented by the 'cruel passage of time' and by the indifference or ill-will of men, from giving an answer to so many questions; we can only stress Bardi's propensity (of which we may also find a confirmation in his *Discorso mandato a Giulio Caccini*)[142] to accept the best that modern music could offer, since 'the modes of ancient music' once more proved to be out of reach.

As for Marenzio, he cannot have found particularly congenial the final part of the *intermedio*, in which all the men and women, 'dancing and singing,...[left] by the same way by which they had entered'. The final double chorus for eight voices unfolds, as befits the plot, in an interplay of the two groups, united at certain times, opposed at others. Their sober chordal

de la tragédie grecque', in *Musique et poésie au XVIe siècle* (Paris 1954), pp. 275ff, and the edition also by Schrade in *La Représentation d'Edipo Tiranno au Teatro Olimpico* (Paris 1960). An earlier edition, almost unavailable, is A. Gabrieli, *Cori dell'Edipo Re di Sofocle*, transcribed and completed by Fernando Liuzzi (Rome 1937) – three partbooks: I do not know if the score too was published. Finally, see Osthoff, *Theatergesang*, I, pp. 326–31, and on the circumstances of the task falling to Gabrieli (it was originally proposed that it should go to Filippo de Monte) and some contemporary comments, A. Gallo, *La prima rappresentazione al Teatro Olimpico* (Milan 1973), pp. li–liv.

142 Handed down in Giovanbattista Doni...*Tomo secondo* (Florence 1973), pp. 233ff.

scansion of the rhythm is enriched by light madrigalistic touches, such as the melismas on the words *fiamma* and *cantiam*; nevertheless, the result is more a march than a dance, the only hint of dancing being a short passage in ternary rhythm on the line *Cantiamo dunque a l'amoroso ballo*. Better suited to the composer's gifts was the prayer of thanks to the winning god, *O valoroso dio*. According to de Rossi's description it should have been sung by 'two pairs of men among those standing along the border of the wood to watch the fight'; but Marenzio made it into another elegant trio of high-pitched voices, chasing each other in imitative entries at the unison; to reach the prescribed number of four voices he just added to them a bass part resembling a vocal continuo. The instrumental accompaniment was light and gentle: a harp and a lyre.

After the novelty of 'the *moresca* representing a fight', the fourth *intermedio* introduced a combination of two traditional themes, namely a magic evocation, which elicited as an answer happy predictions and the eulogy of the bridal couple, and an infernal scene providing the usual sight of Charon's boat, the accompaniment of trombones, and the final precipitous swallowing of the whole, accompanied by 'plaintive crying and screaming'. The sorceress (Caccini's wife, Lucia) entered the stage on a chariot, 'took a lute she had there with her, and to its sound, and to a harmony of large lyres, of basses [?], viols, lutes, one violin, one *arpe doppia*, bass trombones and wooden organs, all playing inside,...began sweetly to sing'. So de Rossi's description informs us, adding also that the song 'and the order of the melody of said instruments was the work of Giulio Caccini, an esteemed musician of our times'. In the printed score Malvezzi claimed for himself the authorship of the symphony, which must have preceded, not followed, the song; the latter is totally omitted. It has been found, however, by Federico Ghisi, once more in the manuscript Magliabechi XIX, 66.[143] It creates an interlude of solo virtuosity (example XLV) inserted between the symphony and the chorus *Or che le due grand'alme*; these, both by Malvezzi and both festive in their G minor key and fluent counterpoint, are related to each other by being both à 6, using the same instruments, and repeating the same ascending scales, which in the choral piece are the musical equivalents of *s'accende* in the text. The aria does not yet represent Caccini at his best, for it lacks a clear formal definition; however, his personal style is already present in the floridity and rhythmic variety of the coloratura and in some hints of harmonic *sprezzatura* (see the recurrent melisma in measures 2, 3 and 4 of the example).

The only musical parallel to the change from a heavenly to an infernal

[143] See F. Ghisi, 'Un aspect inédit des intermèdes de 1589 à la cour Médicéenne', in *Les fêtes de la Renaissance*, I, pp. 145ff, and his contribution to the introduction to *Musique des intermèdes de 'La pellegrina'*, p. xx: the piece appears in an appendix to the same volume. The manuscript, already discussed, is the one in which Ghisi identified two passages of Peri's *La Dafne* and Piero Strozzi's madrigal for the Float of Night, as well as the adaptations for voice and continuo of the choruses of Malvezzi's *Coppia gentil* (appendix to the above, p. 157; compare with the polyphonic version, *ibid.*, pp. 33–35) and *Del vago e bel sereno* (ibid., pp. 112–16), respectively from the first and last *intermedi* of 1589. Caccini's aria would perhaps be considered as the first example of monody with continuo accompaniment were it not for the fact that it too was probably an adaptation of an originally polyphonic piece, though in my opinion this in no way decreases its importance as a step in the direction of monody. The intensification of the sound of the sorceress' lute by means of hidden instruments anticipates the device suggested by Marco da Gagliano for the sound of Apollo's *lira* in his *Dafne*, but the description of the choruses of *Alidoro* have already shown us that the idea was not without precedent.

Ex. XLV   Giulio Caccini. Start of the song of the Sorceress in the fourth *intermedio* of *La pellegrina* by G. Bargagli. From the version for voice and continuo in the Florence manuscript, Biblioteca Nazionale Centrale, Magliabechiano 66.

setting, with the latter's wealth of visual elements, occurs in the already mentioned five-voice madrigal by Bardi, *Miseri abitator del cieco Averno*, which was rather lacking in harmonic variety, possibly because of the stated intention of its author to make it 'melancholy and plaintive'.

In the fifth *intermedio* Amphitrite, sister to Thetis of the fourth *intermedio* of 1586, made an entrance full of royal majesty (see the descending and ascending melody of her final phrase) to pay homage to the nuptial pair:

> ...ad inchinarvi, o regi sposi, vegno
> fin dal profondo del mio vasto regno.

...to bow to you, O kingly pair, I come, from the remotest depths of my vast kingdom.

The same purpose is expressed by her following of Tritons and nymphs, or, at least, by the nymphs:

> ...siamo a 'nchinar a voi, gran regi, uscite.

...to bow to you we have, great kings, come forth.

They all sing, in fact, the four short strophes of an epithalamium, the first sung as a solo by Amphitrite, and the third à 3 by her and two other voices; the answers by the full chorus used the same music for the text of both the second and fourth strophes.[144] As Amphitrite, Vittoria Archilei sang her part, it would seem, without any additional virtuoso embellishments; Antonio, her husband, and their pupil Margherita joined her to sing in the trio.[145] Again we must admire Malvezzi's talent in building a graceful decorative structure on nothing more than a text of emphatic eulogy, mainly exploiting contrasts of sound and rhythm among its short sections.

[144]   The first solo piece was sung by Archilei 'to the sound of a lute, a *chitarrone* and an *arciviolata lira* played by the masterly hand of the famous Alessandro Striggio' – i.e. three 'perfect' instruments to perform the four lower parts of the madrigal à 5. The same instruments, plus a bass and a tenor viol, two lutes, a piccolo (?) and a harp, also accompanied the other sections, perhaps varying the combination in the solo and in the trio. The last choral stanza was repeated twice, and here too the instrumental accompaniment could have varied to include more instruments in the final repeat.

[145]   The edition of the music has: 'loro Alleluia', which I interpret as 'loro Allieua'. This Margherita has often been mistaken for a relative of Caccini.

Besides courtly flattery the presence of Amphitrite with her retinue had no
other purpose than to set the scene for a maritime episode: they vanish from
sight when Arion's ship arrives to the sound of a symphony à 6, also by
Malvezzi.[146] Here de Rossi's description proves once more to be unreliable; its
narrative lacks clarity, it quotes a wrong text, and completely omits the name
of Iacopo Peri as the composer and performer of Arion's song.[147] To Arion's
rescue comes, along with the dolphins, the printed score; it may be as biased
as de Rossi's description, but is at least more precise on things musical.[148] His
song, more Caccinesque than Caccini's for the sorceress, provides remarkable
evidence of the great flexibility of the tenor voices of that time. They were
possibly darker in colour and deeper in range than our modern tenors, but
also more even and smoother in their whole compass, because they tended
to enhance the natural qualities of the voice rather than to develop the
artificial notes of a high register.[149] Arion's vocal part mainly doubles
(although not always strictly) the tenor part of its instrumental accompaniment à 4,[150] embellishing it with garlands of sounds, which we might
find redundant and monotonous, were the song not punctuated by the echoing
answers of two other tenors – another special effect made possible by the
unusual size of the hall. Thus the piece, basically a solo, becomes to some
extent the equivalent of the concertato trios of sopranos already mentioned.
Arion 'sits astern on the galley, dressed as a musician and poet in the ancient
garb, wearing a wreath of laurel, his robe of red cloth woven with gold, fit

[146]   The edition of the music has: 'The following symphony was performed with an *organo
di pivette*...two lutes...a bass viol, a *chitarrone*, a violin...' (I have omitted the names of the
instrumentalists). One gets the impression that the top and bottom parts were given to melodic
instruments (bass viol and violin) while the other instruments played chords. In any case, there
were six instruments, just as there were six parts. The most characteristic touch of instrumental
colour was provided by the *organo di pivette* (possibly an organ with a reed stop) almost certainly
producing a nasal sound. Arion's ship was not the first in the history of *intermedi* (one may
recall, for example, Cleopatra's) and another ship was later to become the central theme of a
1608 *intermedio* – 'The ship of Amerigo Vespucci'.

[147]   According to the *Descrizione* 'one began to hear the song, above a harp...of a single man';
the text of this song, omitted in the edition of the music, incited Arion to enter 'those torbid
and sounding waves'.

[148]   The edition of the music has: 'This Echo was sung by Iacopo Peri known as 'il Zazzerino'
with great artistry *on the chitarrone*, and [listened to] with marvellous attentiveness by the
audience'. The singer might actually have accompanied himself on the *chitarrone*, which was
later to become the instrument most typical of the *basso continuo* (but see what is said below,
note 151). Nevertheless, the harmonies were already written out in full four-part polyphony.
Although the voice part essentially doubles the tenor part ornamenting it with coloratura, it is
nevertheless unlikely that the accompanying instrument omitted that part altogether. Apropos
of this, see note 150, and for the form of the instrumental accompaniment, note 151.

[149]   The range of the tenor part, in the ornamented version (and ignoring for the moment
the differences between ancient and modern diapason) is from bottom C to top F in a tenor clef,
i.e. it covers the range of the stave without having recourse to additional lines.

[150]   As in the solo song of 'Dorian Harmony' in the first *intermedio* and in the one in the sixth,
not clearly assigned to any one character (see page 233 below), the four parts are all given together,
and without words in the pamphlet of the 'Nono' ['ninth part']. In any case, they were performed
by *chitarroni* (combined with a *liuto grosso* in the first *intermedio*) which, by emphasizing the
chordal nature of the accompaniment, eliminates any hesitation we might have about doubling
of the ornamented vocal melody with even the more schematic melody of the accompaniment
(anyway, I doubt that sixteenth-century musicians shared such concern). In the case of Peri's
madrigal there is even less uncertainty, as the main voice doubles both the tenor and the bass
at different times; had the instrumental tenor part been omitted, several chords would have been
left lacking the third, obviously required by the composer.

for a king. In his hands he holds a lyre, built in the shape of our harp',[151] In such royal attire, he seems to rely more on the magic power of his vocal virtuosity than on the emotive power of human pathos, or on the persuasive power of supplication. Alas, he is not as successful as Monteverdi's Orpheus later proved to be with the ornamented version of his aria *Possente spirto*:[152] for 'as the sailors moved towards him with unsheathed knives, he jumped headlong into the sea, dressed as he was; and a great splash of water was seen as he fell, and he then took a while to re-emerge, supported by a dolphin which brought him to the shore'. Quite apart from the great splash of water, this is the most dramatic episode in the whole literature of the courtly *intermedi*; and yet, following Peri's echo piece, no other music is found for it in the printed score, except a final chorus à 7 by Malvezzi, sung by the sailors excitedly rejoicing in the riches they have thus acquired. There is no music for the drama. Nor can we expect even Peri to have placed too much confidence in the moral to be elicited from the *intermedio*: that the gods, if not the humans, favour musicians.

In the sixth *intermedio* we reach maximum disagreement between de Rossi's report and the information given by the printed score, although their discrepancies mostly concern the mode of performance and not the basic ideas of the *intermedio*. In the printed score the text accompanying the customary slow descent of clouds carrying Apollo, Bacchus, the Graces, Muses and cupids, as well as (only mentioned by the score) Hymen and Venus,[153] is altered and shortened. They are descending because Jupiter, 'feeling sorry for the human race, so exhausted and oppressed by worries,...has sent [them] to earth' to bring the gift of Harmony and Rhythm – or else, according to the musical print, of Song and Dance.[154] The text of the answer is, however, unchanged, voiced on earth by 'twenty pairs of men and women', who give no hint of being either exhausted or too worried:

[151] The shape of the instrument is confirmed by Buontalenti's frequently reproduced design for Arion's costume, Peri must have pretended to accompany himself, since the edition of the music states that his song was accompanied by a *chitarrone* (cf. note 148).

[152] See the next chapter.

[153] One gathers that Hymen and Venus were present from the text of the first 'part' of the *Ballo*: 'Behold Hymen and Venus | set foot on earth'.

[154] De Rossi's *Descrizione* certainly corresponds to Bardi's humanist design. 'The poet had these gods appear on stage Apollo, Bacchus, the Graces, the Muses, and cupids who accompany Harmony and Rhythm...as he wanted to represent to us that fact of which Plato writes in the books of his laws' (the relevant passage, from the *Laws*, Bk V, is identified and reproduced in W. Kirkendale, *L'aria di Fiorenza id est il Ballo del Granduca*, Florence 1972, pp. 44–5). The version in the edition of the music sacrifices the humanist element, transforms the abstract gift of Harmony and Rhythm into the more concrete one of Dance and Song, introduces an extended eulogy of the grand-duke and of 'the happy marriage of Lorraine', and replaces the old text of the dance with a new one. Kirkendale's book illustrates the lasting musical repercussions (even in the form of motets and masses) of the 'aria' of the *Ballo*, of which Cavalieri was both composer and choreographer. There is no doubt that it was the second version which was performed after Cavalieri intervened, possibly at the request of the grand-duke himself, who must have found Bardi's Platonism 'too dry'. (The same criticism was later levelled at the first version of Rinuccini's libretto for *Arianna*.) It is of course absurd to think in terms of productions of both versions and alternate performances. The edition of the music, as has already been pointed out, does not name the characters, still less does it indicate which part each had in the dialogue. From the text one gathers that besides Hymen and Venus Flora too was present; Love is not mentioned, but surely must have been there. Besides, the madrigal for seven choruses leads one to think in terms of a (not unusual) opening of the sky and of a stereophonic distribution of all the sources of sound in Heaven, on earth and in mid-air.

> O quale, o qual risplende
> nube nell'aria di sì bei colori?
> Accorrete, pastori,
> e voi, vezzose e liete
> belle Ninfe; accorrete accorte e preste
> al dolce suon dell'armonia celeste.

O what, O what a beautiful cloud is shining in the air with such splendid colours? Come quickly, O shepherds, and you, charming and joyous, you beautiful nymphs; hasten, brisk and wise, to the sweet sound of the celestial harmony.

Both texts were set to music by Malvezzi as two madrigals à 6. The first, initially performed by the instruments alone, was then repeated (to give the cloud more time for its descent) 'with the voices, all doubled'.[155] The second was 'concerted by four lutes, four viols, two basses [viols], four trombones, two *cornetti*, one cittern, one psaltery, one *mandola*, the *arciviolata lira*, one violin, and twenty-four voices.'[156] The trend towards colossal musical dimensions (which we have seen growing throughout the whole history of the courtly *intermedi*) does not stop there; heaven and earth join forces to praise the Medicean couple in a piece for thirty voices, in seven choruses, which was performed by sixty singers and by all the available instruments.[157] But between the two earlier madrigals and this climax of choral and instrumental sonorities a madrigal was slipped in which had not been intended to be part of the original plan, but may have been suggested by the last line of the text quoted above, in which the sweet sound of celestial harmony is mentioned. This is a solo piece, sung to a *chitarrone* by the soprano Onofrio Gualfreducci (impersonating either Amor or Hymen):

> Godi, turba mortal felice e lieta,
> godi di tanto dono,
> e col canto e col suono
> i faticosi tuoi travagli acqueta.

Rejoice, O mortal crowd, in happy merriment; rejoice for such a gift; and with singing and playing soothe your tiring toil.

Had the Dorian Harmony been brought back, a connection would have been created between the first and last *intermedi*; but, since the singer was different, we must also presume he impersonated a different character. The piece must have been inserted on Cavalieri's suggestion; he wrote the music for it, in a style similar to that of the solo madrigal in the first *intermedio*.[158] It also fits

---

[155] 'This madrigal was performed by instruments alone without voices, and they were two *chitarroni*, two *lire*, four lutes, a bass viol, a violin. Then it was repeated with two voices to each part ('con le voci raddoppiate'). So says the edition of the music. Note the presence of the violin and of the bass viol, which emphasized the melodic lines of the top and bottom parts, while the middle ones were performed only by plucked instruments.

[156] De Rossi, *Descrizione*. In this case the four viols plus two bass viols, and the four trombones plus two *cornetti* could be evenly assigned the six parts. It is harder to establish quite how the other instruments were distributed. Evidently the aim was to achieve an effect of sheer choral (four voices per part) and instrumental power, rather than one based on sound colour.

[157] 'The following madrigal for seven choruses was performed with the first above-named instruments and with all the others, and the voices totalled sixty'. The edition of the music proceeds to give the names of some of the more famous of the performers, but gives no information which would enable us to identify the characters.

[158] On grounds of similarity of style one might attribute to Cavalieri the solo sung by Dorian Harmony, but there is no reason to doubt the precise statement in the musical edition that the song was by Antonio Archilei.

well in the broad formal and tonal plan of this first section of the final *intermedio*, which Malvezzi had designed with his usual skill (and with a special airy freshness in the first madrigal, *Dal vago e bel sereno*).

With the seven-chorus madrigal for thirty voices, *O fortunato giorno/Poi che di gioia e speme/Lieta canta la terra e'l ciel insieme*, the mortals have suddenly learned how to sing (as if they had not already sung *O qual, o qual risplende*). The finale, as outlined in de Rossi's description, should have been a dancing lesson, with the gods the teachers and the humans the pupils. At first the gods

> sing on their own up to the end of the second stanza of the song [which has seven such stanzas plus an envoi]; then, to these words, *Movete il piè conforme*, the gods descend to the earth (and, the clouds having vanished [as quickly] as lightning), take those nymphs and shepherds by the hand, and begin to dance with them, still singing and teaching; until, at the end of the line *Muova leggiadramente i passi suoi*, the mortals, dancing with them [i.e. the gods], sing all the remaining part of the *canzone*, supported by a harmony of other instruments and voices coming down from the opening in the sky, so that it seemed that all the angelic hierarchies had assembled there to sing.

Nowhere does the printed score indicate so clearly that the gods teach the mortals how to dance. All the sections for three sopranos must have been assigned to the gods in the final sequence: 'All the trios were sung and danced by Vittoria Archilei and Lucia Caccini and Margherita: Vittoria and Lucia each played a *chitarrina*, the former a Spanish one, the latter a Neapolitan one; Margherita [played] a *cembalino* adorned with little silver bells...'[159] All the sections à 5 must have been assigned to the mortals, except for the last and longest one, in which all the gods must have joined too; but the print does not make any such distinction, mentioning indiscriminately the participation of all the voices and instruments. The three singing ladies were not the only ones to dance; in fact the printed part of the 'Nono' contains detailed instructions for all the steps of the dance, plus two diagrams indicating the positions twenty dancers were to assume at given moments.[160]

The best known fact about this finale is that 'the music of this ballet and the ballet itself were [composed] by Signor Emilio dei Cavalieri, and *the words were written after the air for the dance* by Signora Laura Lucchesini ne' Guidiccioni, a most prominent gentlewoman from the city of Lucca'. The reason for this procedure is easily understood if one considers the musical structure invented by Cavalieri, and its ingenious and most peculiar application of the rule of varied repetition to which dance music was subjected at the time. Only the last of the six 'parts' forming the sequence is not directly derived from the first one, although even this is stylistically related to it;[161] in the other parts the usual procedures of melodic and rhythmic variation make their

---

[159] The purely musical attributes make it difficult to guess which divine characters the three singers represented, but it is quite likely to have been the three Graces. The desire to copy the Ferrarese female trio is obvious (the *Descrizione* of 1589, like that of 1586, was dedicated by Bastiano de Rossi to Alfonso II d'Este).

[160] Choreography and diagrams are reproduced in Walker, ed., *Musique des intermèdes de 'La pellegrina'*, pp. lvi–lviii.

[161] The division into 'parts' can be inferred from the description of the choreography. The first 'part' included the *Ballo* and its *Risposta* (ibid., pp. 140–2); the second runs from 'Che porti o drappel nobile' to 'E i gigli e le viole | si vedranno fiorire' (pp. 142–5); the third from 'O felice stagion' to 'Tessin Ninfe e Pastori | dei più leggiadri fiori' (pp. 145–8); the fourth from 'Ferdinando hor va felic' e altero' to 'Hor te, coppia reale | il ciel rend'immortale (pp. 148–51); the fifth and sixth correspond to the two stanzas quoted later in the text (pp. 152–4).

appearance here and there, but the basic principle is a systematic redistribution of the musical elements first presented in the *Ballo* à 5 and the *Risposta* à 3, which form the first part. The result, an increasingly rapid dialogue between the earthly group (à 5) and the heavenly one (à 3), must have heavily taxed the mediocre gifts of Cavalieri's poetess lady friend. To her relief and ours, men and gods joined forces to sing à 5 the fifth and sixth parts, so that the text, if not actually more inspired, is at least smoother:[162]

> Le querce or mel distillino
> e latte i fiumi corrino;
> d'amor l'alme sfavillino
> e gli empi vizii aborrino;
> e Clio tessa l'istorie
> di così eterne glorie.
>
> Guidin vezzosi balli
> fra queste amene valli;
> portin Ninfe e Pastori
> dell'Arno al ciel gli onori;
> Giove benigno aspiri
> ai nostri alti desiri.
> Cantiam lieti, lodando
> Cristiana e Ferdinando.

May the oaks now secrete honey, and the rivers flow milk; may our souls glow with love, and loathe all impious vices; and Clio trace the histories of such eternal glories.

Nymphs and shepherds together, through these pleasant vales, lead graceful dances, extol the honour of Arno to the sky. May the favour of Jupiter bless our noble desires. Let us sing, happily praising Cristiana and Ferdinando.

The music of the 'Ballo' is mainly chordal, with the single exception of the soprano part entering in imitation, and derives a marked *arioso* quality from being built on a bass line which has a certain affinity, especially initially, with the so-called *romanesca* bass.[163] The music of the *Risposta* begins with a canon at the unison and continues by alternating short contrapuntal passages with others in which the three soprano parts come together to form chords. To achieve the correct effect, the emphasis should be on the continuity of the piece rather than on its apparent fragmentation into short sections which featured the stylized choreographic figures.

Our survey of about sixty years of the history or chronicle of Florentine courtly *intermedi* before the advent of opera began with a study of one work intended to glorify the Medici. It can end on the same note, with the Medicean eulogies of 1589. The custom of performing *intermedi* did not stop then, in

---

[162] If we label the phrases which make up the *Ballo* with the letters AABCDD[1], and those of the *Risposta* aabcdd, the structure of the second part is AAaaBbcDD[1]dd, which is repeated for the third (except that those passages in duple rhythm in the *Ballo* appear in triple rhythm, and those in triple rhythm in the *Risposta* appear in duple rhythm) and for the fourth (entirely in triple rhythm, but with contrasting accentuation for the sections derived from the *Ballo* and those derived from the *Risposta*). The fifth part is a repeat of the *Ballo* with different words, and the sixth, in triple rhythm, is an extension of it, with many repetitions and a strong cadential feeling. For fuller analyses of the *Ballo* see Walker, *La musique des intermèdes florentins de 1589*, pp. 139–41 and Kirkendale, *L'aria di Fiorenza*, pp. 46–9.

[163] On the *romanesca* see the article by John M. Ward in *Die Musik in Geschichte und Gegenwart*, XI, cols. 778–9. Kirkendale, *L'aria di Fiorenza*, p. 20, also notes the affinity.

Florence or elsewhere; in Florence, however, a new more concentrated phase set in, during which opera emerged from the minor spectacles of the Medicean court. The next 'nuptials of the Gods', in 1600, saw the performance not only of Peri's *Euridice*, but also of a new set of *intermedi*, this time woven into the plot of a *favola tutta in musica*, *Il rapimento di Cefalo* by Gabriello Chiabrera, with music written mostly by Giulio Caccini. Later on, for instance in 1608, *intermedi* were once more performed with spoken 'fables' or comedies; and once more we hear stated that they, more than the main action, attracted all the audience's attention. However, they were no longer immune to the influence of opera, and so came to be performed with more music and more solo singing than their original nature required. In at least one case the marvels of solo singing, which had long been restricted to being a subsidiary decorative element, took precedence over the expected miracles of the stage machinery and *ingegni*: the *intermedi* performed in Bologna, possibly as early as 1605, with *Filarmindo* by Rodolfo Campeggi essentially consisted of a short operatic plot, whose acts were *intermedi* to the acts of the spoken pastorale; they were published by the composer of the music, Girolamo Giacobbi, as a separate work with the title *Dramatodia overo...Canti rappresentativi sopra l'Aurora ingannata* (Venice 1608).[164]

The history of the courtly *intermedi* is simply the history of a colossal, as well as multi-faceted, handicraft. We can evaluate its single achievements, but hardly give a comprehensive judgement of their worth. They are a conglomerate of diverse elements held together by some thread of logic (although we have seen how tenuous such logic could be), but hardly susceptible to being turned by this alone into a single work of art. It is pointless to praise or belittle their artistic merit, though from a practical or historical point of view they can be admired for the very large amount of effort put into them. And of course we only know them as faded shadows, occasionally but always imperfectly brought to life by some description or sketch, when these exist.

The same can be said of their music. All too often we have had to lament its absence, or else, in such cases where we are lucky enough to have access to it, to lament the uncertainties about how it was performed. The quality of the music seems to me to have been appreciably better in 1589 than in 1539, for I cannot easily reconcile myself to the contorted rhythms of Corteccia's music. Even in 1589, however, the overall effect consisted of more or less extended patches of instrumental and vocal colour which alternated with long intervals of silence (or even noise); during the latter visual (or even mechanical) elements predominated. We can pay homage to the success of individual pieces, especially to those of Malvezzi, for their consistently high standard, and to those by Marenzio, for their occasional intensity of expression, but not to the results of the whole work. Music did not yet dominate the stage; it was not as active and dynamic a presence as it was later to become in opera.

[164]   A modern edition of part of the first episode and of the complete text has been edited by Giuseppe Vecchi (Bologna 1954).

6 Early opera and aria

Few other genres have their beginnings as precisely determined as opera. Its landmark is the first performance of *Euridice*, with music by Iacopo Peri on a text by Ottavio Rinuccini, which took place on the evening of 6 October 1600, in the Pitti palace in Florence in the apartment of Don Antonio dei Medici,[1] a half brother of the future queen of France, Maria dei Medici. We must dismiss any proposal to consider *Dafne*, music by Iacopo Corsi and Iacopo Peri on a text also by Rinuccini, as the starting point, not because the dates of its various performances are uncertain and a complete score missing, but because both the text and the few surviving fragments of the music[2] make this work seem immature and preliminary compared to the full-fledged vitality of *Euridice*. Also to be dismissed is the challenge coming from *Il rapimento di Cefalo*, text by Gabriello Chiabrera and music for the greatest part by Giulio Caccini, which was performed three days later than *Euridice*, on 9 October, but which was given in the huge Sala delle Commedie of the Uffizi palace as the major spectacle (offered by Grand-duke Ferdinand I himself) in the series of events celebrating the marriage of Maria dei Medici to Henry IV of France and Navarre.[3] *Euridice* had been merely the homage paid to the new queen by a private citizen, Cavaliere Iacopo Corsi; yet *Il rapimento* was practically forgotten soon after its performance,[4] while *Euridice* had the most

[1] The best possible reference for the antecedents and early history of opera is, of course, Donald J. Grout, *A Short History of Opera*, 2nd edn. (New York 1965), chaps. 4–7, and its comprehensive bibliography (particularly sects. 2 and 3). Antonio dei Medici, born in 1576, was recognized by Francesco I dei Medici as his natural son by Bianca Capello, although it would seem that the whole affair of her pregnancy had been a pretence, for she could bear no child. Antonio grew up in the Medici family and escorted Maria dei Medici to Paris after her wedding.

[2] For the dates of *Dafne* and its surviving fragments see now William V. Porter, 'Peri and Corsi's *Dafne*: Some New Discoveries and Observations', in *Journal of the American Musicological Society*, XVII (1965), pp. 170–96. The earliest available text is a libretto printed in 1600; it is reported, however, that every new performance since 1597 (new style 1598) had brought modifications and improvements of both text and music. The former was once more revised for the performance in Mantua in 1608 with completely new music written for the occasion by Marco da Gagliano.

[3] The performance lasted five hours, required more than one thousand men for the handling of the stage machinery, and cost 60,000 scudi; see Angelo Solerti, *Musica, ballo e drammatica alla corte medicea dal 1600 al 1637* (Florence 1905), p. 26. Alois M. Nagler, *Theatre Festivals of the Medici* (New Haven 1964), pp. 96–100, gives a detailed description of the spectacle, and, on p. 95, a much shorter one of *Euridice*. The title of Nagler's fifth chapter, 'Opening of the Uffizi Theatre', is misleading; the Sala delle Commedie was so called because it was occasionally used as a theatre, but was never a permanent one. It was part of the theatrical game of the time to create anew on each occasion the arrangement and decoration of the large hall or courtyard selected for the performance. This probably also applies later to the so-called Barberini theatres in Rome.

[4] Only the final chorus remains, included in *Le nuove musiche di Giulio Caccini detto Romano* (Marescotti, Florence 1602), modern edition ed. H. Wiley Hitchcock (Madison, Wisconsin 1970).

extraordinary success in print among the early operatic scores, rivalled only by Monteverdi's *Orfeo*.[5]

Born under the sign of discord

Even if the printed scores of Peri's *Euridice* were not available to us, a clue to its importance would be provided by the storm of polemical gestures and documents that accompanied and followed its performance. The performance itself was intruded upon by Caccini, who was able to replace part of Peri's music with his own under the pretext that singers who were his pupils could sing only the music written for them by their master. Yet his having disrupted the artistic unity of the work we consider as the first real opera, and having imposed on Peri the same kind of artistic promiscuity (most usual at the time) to which *Il rapimento* was being subjected,[6] was not enough for Caccini, who swiftly proceeded to claim exclusive authorship for his own profit. Shortly after the Florentine nuptials were over, he had already composed and published a complete score of *L'Euridice posta in musica in stile rappresentativo da Giulio Caccini detto Romano* (Marescotti, Florence 1600), which he was able to dedicate to his former patron, Giovanni Bardi, Count of Vernio, on 20 December 1600.[7] Nowhere in the print is Rinuccini named, or the existence and recent performance of Peri's score hinted at, or the fact acknowledged that *favole in musica* had already been composed and staged in Florence since 1591 by Emilio dei Cavalieri. Instead, a reference to certain conversations on musical matters that had been held at a much earlier time in the house of Bardi – in the so-called *camerata* – flatters the dedicatee and lends support to Caccini's contention that he had been writing 'such manner' of music for at least fifteen years, a claim that he was soon to restate at greater length, if not as forcefully, in the foreword of *Le nuove musiche*.[8]

Meanwhile Peri had reacted by having *Le musiche di Jacopo Peri...sopra l'Euridice del signor Ottavio Rinuccini* (Marescotti, Florence 1600; 1601 new style) published.[9] The modesty displayed in this title is an evident rebuke of Caccini's impudence as well as an acknowledgement of Rinuccini's merit. Also stressed – on the title page, in the dedication to the new queen (dated 6 February 1600; 1601 new style), and in the address to the reader – were the facts and occasion of the October performance. Finally, and again in

[5] Peri's opera appeared in two editions – the one of 1600 (1601 new style) mentioned below, and a second one printed in Venice in 1608 – even before the first of the two editions of *L'Orfeo* were published.

[6] Caccini was in charge of all the solo parts – that is, practically the basic play – plus the final chorus; at least three other composers wrote the other choruses, which, combined with spectacular changes of scenery taking place under the very eyes of the audience, formed the *intermedi*, imbedded, so to speak, in the main action.

[7] Caccini had even been Bardi's secretary about 1592; see my 'Caccini', *Enciclopedia dello spettacolo*, vol. II (Rome 1954), col. 1447, and 'Caccini', *Dizionario biografico degli italiani*. A modern edition of the first three episodes of *Euridice* is included in Robert Eitner, ed., *Die Oper von ihren ersten Anfängen bis zur Mitte des 18. Jahrhunderts*, I (Leipzig 1881), 35–76; an English translation of its foreword is given by Oliver Strunk, *Source Readings in Music History* (New York 1950), pp. 370–2.

[8] English translation in Strunk, *Source Readings*, pp. 377–92, and in Hitchcock's edition of *Le nuove musiche*; see below, p. 244.

[9] Facsimile edition ed. Enrico Magni Dufflocq (Rome 1934). An English translation of the foreword is given in Strunk, *Source Readings*, pp. 373–6.

pointed contrast to Caccini's bad manners, Peri makes a graceful bow to both his opponents, Cavalieri and Caccini.

There was indeed a third party to the dispute. Emilio dei Cavalieri was a Roman gentleman whom the grand-duke had brought with him from Rome at the time of his accession to the rule of Florence and had entrusted in 1588 with the supervision of all artistic activities of the Florentine court.[10] Cavalieri had first checked and then superseded the authority of Count Bardi on matters of theatre and music. More recently, however, Cavalieri had found occasion to get away from Florence and to revert to Rome, although his ties with the Florentine court had never been severed, nor his superintendence revoked.[11] Cavalieri's grand manners had prevented him from seeking publicity by having the musical pastorales printed which he had composed for Florence during the nineties. In 1600, however, he was actually the one who started the printing race by permitting, in his aristocratic high-handed way, an obscure editor to give to the printer *La rappresentatione di Anima, et di Corpo novamente posta in musica dal sig. Emilio del Cavaliere per recitar cantando* (Mutii, Rome 1600).[12] The work had been performed in February in the oratory of the Chiesa Nuova in Rome, but the dedication of the print to Cardinal Aldobrandini was dated by Alessandro Guidotti, the appointed editor, on 3 September 1600, the very moment at which the Florentine spectacles for the wedding were being rehearsed.[13] The timing qualifies the print as an unspoken reproach to the grand-duke, who on the occasion of the royal wedding had forsaken Cavalieri's merits as an old friend and faithful servant; among these merits were the plays he had conceived, written the music for, and staged in Florence in 1591 and 1595, insistently mentioned in both the dedication and the address to the reader.

Cavalieri attended the Florentine wedding and possibly helped with the staging of *Euridice*,[14] but left for Rome shortly thereafter. It would have been inconceivable for him to become involved in a public argument with such commoners as Caccini, Peri, or even Rinuccini, but he continued to express his dismay in a series of letters he addressed from Rome to Marcello Accolti,

[10] Biographical information is given in my 'Cavalieri', *Enciclopedia dello spettacolo*, vol. III (Rome 1956), cols. 256–8, in Warren Kirkendale, 'Cavalieri', *Dizionario biografico degli italiani*, and in C. V. Palisca, 'Musical Asides in the Diplomatic Correspondence of Emilio de' Cavalieri', in *Musical Quarterly*, XLIX (1963), 339–5.

[11] Palisca, 'Musical Asides', pp. 343–7.

[12] Facsimile edition, ed. Francesco Mantica (Rome 1912) with preface by Domenico Alaleona; dedication and foreword are reprinted by Angelo Solerti, *Le origini del melodramma* (Turin 1903), pp. 1–12. New facsimile editions have been published in Bologna, 1967 and Farnborough, 1967.

[13] There are no extant letters in Cavalieri's correspondence between Easter and November 1600; so Palisca conjectures ('Musical Asides', p. 344) that 'he must have been busy in Florence with the preparations for the wedding'. It seems to me that the preparation of the printing of *La rappresentatione* must have kept him in Rome; he probably expected to be recalled to Florence to take charge of the nuptial spectacles, but was too proud to make the first move. Hence, his silence and his later complaints that the grand-duke had forgotten his past services in the field of theatre and neglected to take advantage of his experienced advice. Cavalieri was only commissioned to write the music for Giovanbattista Guarini's elegant but perfunctory *Dialogo di Giunone e Minerva*, a laudatory piece involving the descent of the two goddesses on flying machines, performed on 5 October during the official banquet.

[14] Palisca, 'Musical Asides', p. 350. It seems to me that the stage decor and action, and possibly some details of instrumentation, are the matters in which Cavalieri is most likely to have helped; it is strange, however, that Peri, with all his ostentatious good manners, does not mention Cavalieri's contributions in his foreword.

the secretary of the grand-duke. The contents of these letters have recently been made available.[15] His Highness had neglected Cavalieri's proven theatrical experience to avail himself of inexperienced advice – namely that of his half-brother, Don Giovanni dei Medici; as a result, not only had he had his money practically wasted, but also had 'lost that reputation that Florence had always had in such things'.[16] However, a new element of bitterness comes to the foreground, stemming from Rinuccini's dedication of the printed libretto of *Euridice* (Giunti, Florence 1600). Cavalieri complains (10 November 1600) that 'he [Rinuccini] acts...as if he had been the inventor of this way of representing [action] in music'; but 'this was invented by me, and everyone knows this, and I find myself having said so in print [in the foreword of *La rappresentatione*, of which Cavalieri thus acknowledges himself the real author]. Now whoever sees the libretto of Little Frog [Ranocchino, for Rinuccini] will consider me a liar.'[17]

Milder, though equally contemptuous, are Cavalieri's reactions to the printing of Caccini's *Euridice*, which he had already received in Rome on 20 January 1601, when he writes: 'I find nothing in it that annoys me. For my *rappresentatione*, which is printed, having been printed three and a half months earlier, settles all the contentions.'[18] Cavalieri must have realized, however, that Caccini's point was not to claim priority in the writing of *rappresentationi in musica*, but to assert that such *rappresentationi* were in a style that he, Caccini, had invented. In turn, Peri also claimed to have invented and applied to *Euridice* an impassioned style of singing never heard before. To these claims, if my interpretation is correct, Cavalieri gave an oblique answer by encouraging the publication of Luzzasco Luzzaschi's *Madrigali...per cantare, et sonare a uno, doi, e tre soprani* (Verovio, Rome 1601).[19] Luzzaschi's arrival in Rome in the retinue of Cardinal Aldobrandini is reported by Cavalieri on 6 April 1601; and in May, in another letter in which he is critical of Caccini, Cavalieri mentioned having discussed the recent musical events with Claudio Merulo and with Luzzaschi.[20] The latter's belated decision to release some samples of the 'reserved' soloistic repertory of the famous singing ladies of Ferrara seems to me an intimation – cognate to Cavalieri's thinking, and possibly suggested by him – that a refined style of soloistic song had long been in existence, independent of Caccini. In turn, Luzzaschi's publication may have prompted Caccini to restate his claims with the printing of *Le nuove musiche*.

The gist of the whole story seems to be that each contestant was deeply convinced of his own right to the priority he claimed and either failed to see the differences between his accomplishments and those of his rivals or else

---

[15] Palisca, 'Musical Asides'.

[16] *Ibid.*, pp. 351–2. In Palisca's opinion the undated postscript belongs to a letter of 24 November 1600.

[17] Translated by Palisca, *ibid.*, pp. 353–4.

[18] Translated by Palisca, *ibid.*, p. 354.

[19] See the modern edition published by Adriano Cavicchi in *Monumenti di musica italiana*, 2nd series, vol. II (Brescia and Kassel 1966).

[20] Palisca, 'Musical Asides', p. 353 and note 54. Cardinal Aldobrandini, to whom both Cavalieri's *La rappresentatione* and Luzzaschi's *Madrigali...per cantare, et sonare* were dedicated, had taken possession of Ferrara after the death of Duke Alfonso II d'Este and ruled there as a papal legate. It would seem that he had also inherited some of the Este musicians and the critical attitude of the Ferrarese court toward the exploits of its Florentine rival.

was afraid that the slightly different claims made by others might dim his own precious personal glory. Among those not directly involved in the dispute, the general feeling was of a fundamental unity of the Florentine style of singing. This style in turn was considered not too different from the style of soloistic singing practised in other parts of Italy, yet different enough to justify the reluctant admission, about 1628, by an unbiassed Roman observer, that Caccini had been, after all, 'almost the inventor of a new manner of singing'.[21] Whatever differences existed among the opposing claims, and no matter how strongly these differences were felt by the various claimants, they found them difficult to define precisely in words. We may be in a better position from the vantage point of our historical knowledge of later developments; we must be careful, however, not to apply indiscriminately to the music of the early seventeenth century such criteria as are suggested to us by the manifestations of later periods.

Recitar cantando versus *cantar recitando*

'Recitar cantando', generally considered a typical expression of the so-called Florentine *camerata*, stems from Cavalieri, who might well never have attended any of the musical conversations in Bardi's drawing room.[22] Cavalieri himself used the term most casually, as, for instance, in the title of *La rappresentatione* ('*posta in musica...per recitar cantando*'), with no other meaning than that of a play to be acted in singing; and indeed all he claimed was to have been the first to devise and bring to the stage such dramatic actions as could be developed completely in songs and music, contrary to the previous theatrical use of music as an incidental element.[23] It is true that the preface of *La rappresentatione* elaborates on the means by which 'this manner of music, which he [Cavalieri] has restored, may move [listeners] to different emotions, such as pity and joy, tears and laughter';[24] these words, however, were written by Guidotti, or dictated by Cavalieri, under the influence of the news arriving from Florence about the spectacles being prepared there and of much discussion going on in this connection about the emotional power of music. Even so, the blurb puts the accent more on variety and contrast of emotions than on their intensity; nor does Cavalieri claim to have found a special style for expressing them. On the contrary, the mention of one scene

[21]   Vincenzo Giustiniani, 'Discorso sopra la musica de' suoi tempi', in Solerti, *Le origini*, p. 116.
[22]   Bardi left Florence for Rome in 1592, but the years between 1588 and his departure had been a time of veiled but strong animosity between himself and Cavalieri. Anyway, the time of most intense musical activity of his *camerata* had been the late seventies and early eighties, when Galilei was preparing his *Dialogo della musica antica e della moderna* (Marescotti, Florence 1581); Facsimile editions of the *Dialogo* have been published in Bologna, 1967, and Farnborough, 1967.
[23]   All things considered, even the music of the very elaborate *intermedi* of 1589, Bardi's foremost accomplishment, is incidental with respect to the main action of the comedies with which they were performed. They have been published in Walker, ed., *Musique des intermèdes*.
[24]   Volendo rappresentare in palco la presente opera, o vero altre simili,...e far sì, che questa sorte di Musica da lui rinovata commova à diversi affetti, come à pietà, & à giubilo; à pianto, & à riso, & ad altri simili, come s'è con effetto veduto in una scena moderna della Disperatione di Fileno, da lui composta; nella quale recitando la Signora Vittoria Archilei...mosse maravigliosamente à lagrime, in quel mentre, che la persona di Fileno movea à riso: volendola dico rappresentare, par necessario, che ogni cosa debba essere in eccellenza...
(third unnumbered page in the original edition and in the facsimile; p. 5 in Solerti, *Le origini*).

of *La disperatione di Fileno*, in which the singing of Vittoria Archilei 'wonderfully brought on tears, while the *person* of Fileno provoked laughter',[25] hints of mimicry as one of the means of expression. Great emphasis is placed by Guidotti (or Cavalieri) on the 'adornments', particularly dances, that must enliven such '*rappresentationi*' and must not be incidental additions to the plot. For 'there will be more elegance and novelty if they can be made to appear different from normal dances; as would be the case of a *moresca* representing a fight, or a dance originating from sporting games'.[26] As an example of the first, a scene of *La disperatione di Fileno* is mentioned, in which 'three satyrs come to blows, and with this pretext perform their fight singing and dancing to a tune of a *moresca*'; to the second type belongs the central scene of *Il giuoco della cieca*, in which 'four nymphs dance and sing, while they encircle and tease blindfolded Amarilli according to the rules of the game' (the *giuoco della cieca* was similar to blindman's buff).[27]

The latter example is an obvious derivation from Guarini's *Pastor fido*, Act III scenes 2 and 3. Cavalieri and Laura Lucchesini nei Guidiccioni, his dedicated friend who provided texts for the *rappresentationi* of 1591 and 1595, proclaimed themselves followers of the pastoral style of the poets of Ferrara, though the latter were violently opposed by the Florentine Accademia della Crusca of which Bardi was one of the founders.[28] Whether the products of the collaboration between Cavalieri and Guidiccioni had any artistic originality or were merely imitations of famous models is impossible to say because both the texts and music seem to be irreparably lost. They must have been in line, however, with the conception of an artificial, idealized pastoral life, to which conception elegance, ingenuity, and a mild sentimentalism somewhat tinged with sensuousness were more essential than the realistic poignancy of human passions and sorrows. Judging from Cavalieri's sparse written hints and from the score of his late spiritual allegory, which attempts to bring the style up to date with features rather clumsily derived from Peri and Caccini,[29] we can

---

[25] See note 24.

[26] The passage reads as follows in the original:

> Quando si è cantato un poco à solo, è bene far cantar i Chori, & variare spesso i tuoni; e che canti hora Soprano, hora Contralto, hora Tenore: & che l'Arie, e le Musiche non sijno simili, ma variate con molte proportioni,...& adornate di Echi, e d'inventioni più che si può, come in particolare di Balli, che avvivano al possibile queste Rappresentationi, sì come in effetto è stato giudicato da tutti gli spettatori; i quali Balli, overo Moresche se si faranno apparir fuori dell'uso commune havrà piu del vago, e del nuovo: come per essempio, la Moresca per combattimento, & il Ballo in occasione di giuoco, e scherzo: sì come nella Pastorale di Fileno tre Satiri vengono à battaglia, e con questa occasione fanno il combattimento cantando, e ballando sopra un'aria di Moresca. Et nel giuoco della Cieca ballano, e cantano quattro Ninfe, mentre scherzano intorno ad Amarilli bendata, ubidendo al giuoco della Cieca

(see above, note 24). For Cavalieri's skill as a choreographer, see Walker, *Musique des intermèdes*, pp. xxvii–xxix and liv–lviii.

[27] See note 26. We do not know whether Cavalieri used Guarini's text or had a new text adjusted to the new dance steps and new music he had created.

[28] Tasso's visit to Florence in 1590 and the performance there of his *Aminta* in 1590 (1591 new style) are in sharp contrast to the harsh criticism that had been addressed to him in prior years by the members of the Crusca Academy (founded in 1582 for the purpose of 'sifting' good from bad linguistic usage), and particularly by Bastiano de Rossi, the author of the printed description of the spectacles organized by Bardi in 1589.

[29] This is no place for a stylistic analysis and evaluation of Cavalieri's work; what I am concerned with is his contribution to the formulation of the new style, which I consider rather slim. Even the alleged greater sophistication of Cavalieri's continuo figuring (see Frank T. Arnold,

agree with Giovanbattista Doni's opinion of his music: '*Ariette* including many artful devices, repetitions, echo effects, and similar things, that have nothing to do with the good and true theatrical music'.[30] Cavalieri was nevertheless correct in claiming that he had created a new theatrical genre – all in music – and had been the first to make it public with the printing of *La rappresentatione*. His invention, or quasi-invention, expanded the already strong musical component of the literary pastorale, and accentuated its tendency toward a formal organization, while reducing and simplifying this pastorale form to adjust it to the particular exigencies and slower pace of a musical performance. The results, however, though significant when compared with the stiff progress and almost symbolic gestures of the cumbersome 'courtly' *intermedi*,[31] must have been nearer to what we would call a ballet or a pantomime than to an opera.

While Cavalieri's claims centred on genre, Caccini and Peri insisted on the style of singing. This is borne out most clearly by Peri, who, having acknowledged that Cavalieri, 'before any other of whom I know, enabled us with marvellous invention to hear our kind of music upon the stage', immediately adds that 'nonetheless as early as 1594, it pleased the Signori Iacopo Corsi and Ottavio Rinuccini that I should employ it *in another guise*'.[32] It may have been part of Cavalieri's earlier polemics with Bardi to prove that 'our' modern music was as apt as the ancient for the stage; but Corsi and Rinuccini went further to show, with Peri's help, that modern music could be effective on stage even in a genre of dramatic intensity *comparable* to that of ancient tragedy. The evidence of this is grudgingly given by one of Cavalieri's letters reporting the opinion expressed in Rome by Bardi that 'they [the Florentines, including the grand-duke] should not have gone into *tragic* texts and objectionable subjects'.[33] The old rivals were at least temporarily reconciled in their common distaste for the newest trends of music in Florence.

The revival of the ancient tragedy was to be attempted eight years later in Mantua by Rinuccini and Monteverdi.[34] In 1600, nobody knew better than Rinuccini that *Euridice* was no tragedy; yet, in a pastoral frame, the death of Euridice and Orpheus' despair have a poignant directness of tragic pathos, and even the less emotional moments of the action refuse to submit for the sake of music to the cunning engineering and formalistic procedures that seem to have characterized Cavalieri's works. Accordingly, Peri's *recitar cantando* (although he never used the expression) is 'a harmony surpassing

---

The Art of Accompaniment from a Thorough-Bass, London 1931, pp. 35 and 49) is a consequence of the fact that he had in mind a fully realized, multilinear accompaniment, probably conceived on and for a keyboard instrument. (Arnold too, p. 47, mentions his sparse use of stringed instruments for the realization of the continuo.) He, therefore, simulated the external features of continuo writing but missed its 'recitative flexibility and chordal, rather than contrapuntal, meaning' (for which see below, pp. 246ff).

    [30]   From Doni's 'Trattato della musica scenica', chap. 9, in Solerti, *Le origini*, p. 208.
    [31]   For the practice of what I call 'courtly', most elaborate, *intermedi*, see my 'Intermedium', in *Die Musik in Geschichte und Gegenwart*, vol. VI, cols. 310–26, and, of course, chapters 4 and 5 above.
    [32]   Translated by Strunk, *Source Readings*, p. 373 (italics mine).
    [33]   Translated by Palisca in 'Musical Asides', p. 352; to have represented the mythological loves of Aurora and Cefalo was deemed objectionable by Bardi.
    [34]   On the title page of the printed libretto of *Arianna* the word 'Tragedia' is set symptomatically in a larger type than the title and Rinuccini's name.

that of ordinary speech but falling so far below the melody of song as to take an intermediate form',[35] that is, a style of singing normally ruled (we shall later mention the exceptions) by the accent and expression of the text and by the needs of the action rather than by principles of musical organization. Cavalieri's solution had been a stylization and formalization of plots and dialogues to fit the exigencies of dance music and song; Peri's is the opposite and can be described as realistic insofar as it modifies the singing to bring it nearer to speech, either ordinary and unemotional or, preferably, heightened by the urgency of vehement passions.

To my knowledge, neither Bardi's group nor Caccini had ever considered the problem of *recitar cantando* before 1600. But in that year Caccini's words were as swift as his actions; having stated in the very first sentence of the dedication of his *Euridice* that he had composed it 'in music *in stile rappresentativo*', he quickly added that this was 'that style which, as Your Lordship [Bardi] knows, I used on other occasions, many years ago, in the eclogue of Sannazaro's *Iten'all'ombra degli ameni faggi*, and in other madrigals of mine from that time.'[36] The eclogue is missing, but the others are pieces that later became part of Caccini's *Nuove musiche* (1601; 1602 new style), in the foreword of which the sequence is inverted but the sentence the same: 'those fruits of my music studies..., my compositions of airs, composed by me at different times...[are] in that very style which later served me for the fables which were *represented in song* in Florence'.[37] I have italicised the words corresponding to Cavalieri's *recitar cantando*. Caccini contended, however, that his own distinctive achievement was nothing more than the application to the stage of a style he had previously used for pieces that we would classify as chamber music. For the sake of distinction, not to invent a new term, I shall call it here a *cantar recitando*. Caccini's other implication was, of course, that Peri had merely followed his, Caccini's, path.

We may be surprised at the use of the term *stile rappresentativo* for chamber pieces, yet there are other instances of it, independent of Caccini. *Stile rappresentativo* and *stile recitativo*, the former even more common than the latter, soon spread as fashionable and practically synonymous terms, for to 'recite' a play is commonly used in contemporary sources in the sense of 'representing' one.[38] Both terms covered the full range of nuances between the extremes that we now call recitative and aria, as well as, when applied to a theatrical score, choruses, dances, and instrumental pieces. But their actual application to a stage work was a rare occurrence, depending on circumstances of court life over which the composers had little control. Far more frequent was the case of works, conceived for performance in a concert

[35] Translated by Strunk in *Source Readings*, p. 374.
[36] Translated *ibid.*, pp. 370–1.
[37] Translated *ibid.*, pp. 377 and 379. See also H. W. Hitchcock's edition of *Le nuove musiche* (Madison, Wisc. 1970), pp. 43–56, providing a new translation of Caccini's address to his readers.
[38] Indeed most title pages of the time use more cautious expressions, such as, for instance, 'a voce sola per cantare sul chitarrone'. However, Monteverdi's continuo madrigals of 1605 were shortly thereafter styled as *musica rappresentativa* according to Jack A. Westrup, 'Rezitative', in *Die Musik in Geschichte und Gegenwart*, vol. XI, col. 356. Monteverdi himself described his *Lettera amorosa* as being *in genere rappresentativo*. On the other hand, Severo Bonini's *Lamento d'Arianna cavato dalla tragedia del Signor Ottavio Rinuccini* (Magni, Venice 1613) contains considerably more excerpts from Rinuccini's theatrical work than the *lamento* indicated in the title, but terms them *in stile recitativo*.

or 'recital', that projected on an ideal stage either a dramatic scene or the affective reactions of a character to a dramatic situation.[39] This direction was most congenial to Caccini, for there can be no doubt that his *Nuove musiche* of 1602 and 1615 and the pieces in his *Fuggilotio musicale* of 1613(?) were songs – admittedly with a 'recitative' or 'representative' quality – composed by a consummate singer and voice teacher in such way that no audience could ever forget that their performance was the exploit of a singer, that is, *cantar recitando*.[40]

We may, then, oppose Caccini, as a master of *cantar recitando*, to the champions of *recitar cantando*, Cavalieri and Peri. We must keep in mind, however, that from another point of view the eminently singable quality of Caccini's music is nearer to Cavalieri's *ariette* than to the realistic eloquence of Peri's style 'half-way between song and speech'. And finally, a common expressive tendency makes Caccini and Peri into the earliest representatives (if I may use the word) of the new 'representative' or 'recitative' style, from which we must exclude Cavalieri, in spite of his eleventh-hour effort in the score of *La rappresentatione*.

The aesthetic problems of the new style

Stile rappresentativo and *stile recitativo* both point to a mode of performance, be it called a representation or a recitation; and indeed the essential novelty of the new style, whether we consider it from Caccini's or from Peri's point of view, centres on the moment of communication with the audience. Caccini described his own brand of the new style as 'a noble manner of singing', which, he asserted, was intended not only to give pleasure, but also to capture the audience with its 'grace' and 'to move the passion of the mind'.[41] Related to the aim of communication are the two technical features which both he and Peri point out as being most distinctive of their works, *sprezzatura* and continuo accompaniment.

It is impossible to determine which one of the two composers first introduced these two terms, which they both use in more or less the same way. Regardless of who first put them in print, they must have evolved their peculiar meaning during the previous phase of verbal polemic exchanges of which we have no record. *Sprezzatura*, whether or not used first by Caccini for a musical purpose, fits perfectly the Platonistic veneer with which he liked to substantiate his adherence to, and reliance on, the classicistic ideals of Bardi and his group. The word had enjoyed a certain vogue since the first quarter of the sixteenth century, when it had been adopted by Baldassare Castiglione, in his classic and substantially Platonistic treatise on aristocratic manners and accomplishments, to describe the apparently inborn spontaneity and relaxed

[39]   The same idea was already present in many a polyphonic madrigal of the second half of the sixteenth century, although it was contended that polyphony lacked the directness necessary for such a kind of dramatic projection; it was soon to become the basic principle underlying the seventeenth-century cantata.

[40]   My doubts about Caccini's authorship of *Il fuggilotio* are supported by H. W. Hitchcock, 'Depriving Caccini of a Musical Pastime', in *Journal of the American Musicological Society* XXV (1972), pp. 58–78.

[41]   Translated by Strunk in *Source Readings*, p. 383. Stuart Reiner has since pointed out to me that the term *sprezzatura* never occurs in any of Peri's known writings; nevertheless, I am sure Peri knew it and applied the idea in its various aspects.

self-confidence that must characterize the performance of the perfect courtier, no matter how difficult his task.[42] Parallel to Castiglione's meaning, *sprezzatura* had been used during the same century to designate the ease and poise of the consummate dancer.[43] Caccini, too takes the position that complete mastery of the most refined vocal techniques is an essential element of his style, but not the only one. The goal of the singer is to attain whatever spirit there is beyond the letter of music – that is, of Caccini's music – which goal can be reached through the *sprezzatura*, that is, through the intangible elements of rhythmic buoyancy and dynamic flexibility of the performance.

To the same purpose is aimed the reduction of the polyphonic accompaniment to an essential lineal minimum, the continuo, allowing a maximum of flexibility also to the accompanist and insuring expressive predominance and freedom to the singing voice. According to Caccini, the ideal situation would have been that of a singer who could accompany himself and thus exert a unified control on both vocal *sprezzatura* and instrumental accompaniment – he explicitly mentions the practice of 'singing on the theorbo or other stringed instrument'.[44] This could not agree more with the ideas of Peri, who was himself highly praised as an extraordinary self-accompanying singer.[45] Were such a unified performance not possible, it was the task of the skilled accompanist not only to adhere as strictly as possible to the performance of the vocalist, but also to use his good judgement concerning the best way and the precise extent to which the continuo line should be integrated by 'playing the inner voices on an instrument for the expression of some passion, these [inner voices] being of no use for any other purpose'.[46]

The last clause is worth noting not only for its thrust against counterpoint,

[42] The following is Castiglione's text in *The Book of the Courtier*, translated by Charles S. Singleton (New York 1959), p. 43: 'But having thought many times already about how this grace is acquired (leaving aside those who have it from the stars), I have found quite a universal rule...: and that is to avoid affectation in every way possible...; and (to pronounce a new word perhaps) to practice in all things a certain *sprezzatura* [nonchalance], so as to conceal all art and make whatever is done or said appear to be without effort and almost without any thought about it.' Notice the relationship with the 'grace' that some have from the stars. At least one modern dictionary, Policarpo Petrocchi, *Nòvo dizionàrio universale della lingua italiana* (Milan 1887–91), still explains *sprezzatura* as a 'manner full of masterly neglect'.

[43] Transferring the concept of *sprezzatura* to dance and music is made easy by suggestions offered by Castiglione, *Book of the Courtier*, Bk II.

[44] Strunk, *Source Readings*, pp. 381 and 392; the original has *chitarrone*.

[45] Severo Bonini, usually biassed in favour of Caccini, had this to say of Peri:

A much learned singer and composer was Signor Iacopo Peri, who would have moved and brought to tears the hardest heart by singing his works, composed with greatest artfulness, for they were in a tearful style (*concetto*), his own speciality...I shall only say that, in addition to being most gentle in his singing and experienced in the art of composing in the new style, he was elegant and artful in the art of playing keyboard instruments, and absolutely unique in the accompaniment of the singing voice with the middle parts (translated from Solerti, *Le origini*, p. 137).

Bonini's full text is now available in Leila Gallena Luisi, *Discorsi e regole sopra la musica di Severo Bonini* (Cremono 1975). In the *intermedi* of 1598, Peri sang to the *chitarrone*, impersonating no less a person than Arion.

[46] Translated by Strunk, *Source Readings*, p. 378. In the original, 'con le parti di mezzo tocche dall'instrumento per esprimere qualche affetto' has an intimation of levity and restraint that is difficult to incorporate in a translation; I suggest as a freer alternative: 'with the middle parts lightly touched by the instrumentalist to express some passion'. In another passage, Caccini explains that he has tied some notes of the continuo 'in order that, after the [full] chord, only the written note be struck again, it being the one most necessary'. Again, I am suggesting a free interpretation alternative to the translation by John Playford followed by Strunk, *Source Readings*, p. 392; the original has 'perché dopo la consonanza si ripercuota solo la corda segnata, essendo

but also for the implicit admission that the addition of the inner parts was *ad libitum*, justified only by special expressive aims; for the two main lines, voice and continuo, tended to form by themselves a self-sufficient texture. Our musical training and performing habits lead us, when we realize a continuo, to seek for two or three added parts that maintain a smooth linear conduct in spite of their basically harmonic function. This was probably also Cavalieri's approach, stemming from his greater familiarity with keyboard than with plucked string instruments. On the contrary, Caccini and Peri, like all musicians of the time who were used to realizing the continuo on the *chitarrone*, theorbo, or lute, must have thought of a supporting bass line discontinuously coloured by chords, whose size and disposition were conditioned by both the expressive needs of the accompaniment and the fingering of the instrument.

Caccini's *basso continovato* (Florentine for *continuato* or *continuo*) may resemble on paper the *basso seguente* practiced by keyboard players who were in charge of accompanying either sacred or secular polyphonic pieces. It actually owes its name to this resemblance,[47] increased by the fact that the older continuo also may have had figures occasionally added to the bass as a guide to the accompanist wherever more than one harmonization was possible. The two procedures, however, are basically different from the compositional point of view. The old continuo or *seguente* was nothing more than a shorthand notation (replacing a full score or an intabulation) of harmonic successions arrived at as the result of contrapuntal considerations; while the new continuo is a line composed *ad hoc* in view of the rhythmic, harmonic, and expressive needs of the upper part. To put it in the language of the time, the new continuo and its harmonic implications – whether or not indicated by figures, and whether or not fully realized as chords by the accompanist – were entirely subservient to the 'aria' of the vocal part.

We touch here a momentous term, which had been used by musicians at least since the early fourteenth century,[48] but which actually became a key word of the musical language during the sixteenth and seventeenth centuries. Nothing is more puzzling than its ubiquitousness and its oscillation between generic and specialized meanings. It might help in untangling them to realize that in spite of its coincidence in form and sound with the word indicating the atmospheric milieu in which we live, 'aria' has a different basic meaning[49] which we may try to render by drawing a parallel with the English

ella la più necessaria...nella propria posta del chitarrone'. I do not know whether 'posta' refers to the *role* of the *chitarrone* or to some technical feature such as its open strings. The sentence immediately following is one more appeal made by Caccini to the discretion and understanding of the accompanist.

[47] Once more, our distinction between *basso continuo* and *seguente* is based on later practices; however, we should remember that *continuo*, *continuato*, *seguito*, and *seguente* were originally equivalent. An organ player accompanying a polyphonic piece on his instrument could use a score or intabulation, or else a bass line formed with the vocal bass or whatever other part happened to assume temporarily the function of a bass part. This new line was properly said to be *seguente* because it always doubled one or another of the vocal parts; at the same time, it had no rests, even though the vocal parts it followed came occasionally to a halt, and thus was properly said to be 'continuous'. For the older continuo, see Arnold, *The Art of Accompaniment*, pp. 6–9.

[48] See my 'Una arcaica descrizione trecentesca del madrigale', *Festschrift Heinrich Besseler* (Leipzig 1962), pp. 157–8.

[49] It has also a different, though not too clearly determined, origin (*ibid.*, p. 160, note 20).

'countenance'. As 'countenance' can be taken to indicate the features that give a visage its individual physiognomy, thus, 'aria' may be used to indicate the features that characterize a particular melody, and may be, therefore, the equivalent of 'tune'. But 'countenance' also means the behaviour of a person, determined by his intrinsic nature and acquired habits; and similarly 'aria', applied to any musical entity (although preferably to a melodic one), indicates the quality it appears to possess as being, as it were, precisely determined and inflected on an unavoidable course – no matter whether such unavoidability stems from tradition, repetition, and habit or from an inner sense of coherence and finality.

As a rule, there was felt to be a strong contradiction between the nature and qualities of an aria and the melodic qualities of the many lines of a polyphonic composition; for in the latter it was the task of the composer to draw, spin, and weave together at his will a number of melodic lines, each of which could be plausible in itself but usually lacked an aria, that is, a sense of self-possessed determination. In the process, whatever melodic character the individual lines might have had initially – usually more strongly asserted at such climactic points as the entrance or re-entrance of a voice part – soon faded away in the less distinctive function of providing a background or even a contrast to the emergence of other parts. Thus, although the word is seldom mentioned, the concept of aria is deeply imbedded in the foundations of the persistent and manifold sixteenth-century criticism against polyphony.

When every extramusical element is discarded from this criticism, be it the desire for church reform or the dream of reviving a classical art, a constant residuum is the deep dissatisfaction with the fact that polyphony could soothe the ear with soft consonances or smoothly managed dissonances, could elicit admiration for the skill of the singers and the ingenuity of the composer, but lacked the power of captivating and moving its audience. Two explanations were usually given for this state of affairs. According to the first of them, both the structure and the ways of performing polyphonic music hindered the understanding of the texts, with which the aesthetic conceptions of the time identified the emotional message of the composition. Although this criticism was still repeated even by those who, like Caccini, inclined toward the second explanation, matters were not improved by the adoption of such soloistic methods of performance as the one indicated by the phrase *per cantare e sonare*, or any other of those types of performance for which the term 'pseudomonody' has been coined. Thus, the second and more classicistic explanation would seem to have been more to the point, according to which the simultaneous sounding of many melodic lines had the result of neutralizing the expressive message, the ethos that each one of them taken singularly might have conveyed. The latter view is expressed most clearly, to my knowledge, in a letter dated 16 February 1549, by one Bernardino Cirillo, an archpriest of the Santa Casa in Loreto, later the commander of the hospital of Santo Spirito in Saxia in Rome, and also a friend of Cardinal Marcello Cervini (later Pope Marcellus II). Cirillo finally advocated a reform of church music reinstating the practice of monophonic plainchant.[50]

[50] See Paolo Manuzio, ed., *Lettere volgari di diversi nobilissimi huomini...Libro terzo nuovamente mandato in luce* (Venice 1564), cc. 114ff. Another version of the letter, with only slight variants, is given by Pietro De Angelis, *Musica e musicisti nell'Arciospedale di Santo Spirito in Saxia* (Rome 1950), pp. 39ff, from MS 338 of the Biblioteca Lancisiana in Rome. De Angelis also gives another

It was one of the many merits of Girolamo Mei, the real mentor of the so-called *camerata*, to have perceived that no ethos was possible even for each one of the single lines as long as they were determined by the polyphonist's combinatory criteria and not by their inner coherence to a mode.[51] We have only to replace the word 'mode' by 'aria' (and its ethos) to go back to our starting point. For mode in the sixteenth century had long since ceased to be a force that could influence the formulation of a melody, except, to a very limited extent, in the perfunctory observance of intermediate cadences and final goals. Nor could the vanished church modes be replaced by the restoration of the long-forgotten scales and tunings of the ancients, for, in spite of a number of attempted revivals (including Vicentino's and Vincenzo Galilei's), their musical meaning was, then as in our day, elusive. The only available concept was the rather vague one of an aria; certain melodies were felt and said to possess an aria, while it was denied to others (particularly to the lines of a polyphonic composition) on the basis of intuitive criteria whose validity was not diminished by the lack of a verbal definition.

We now begin to discern more in Caccini's *sprezzatura* and continuo than just their most obvious aspects connected with the moment of performance.[52] *Sprezzatura* is not only the self-assurance of the accomplished performer, but also the unrestricted and undiverted naturalness of the melody itself, its 'air' of being entirely self-determined or self-propelled. Once more, Caccini's Platonistic orientation prompts him to use an expression that is no less suggestive for being philosophically amateurish; his music embodies in sounds 'that complete grace which I hear in my mind',[53] stipulating, as it were, for each melody the necessity of a course predetermined by a model in the world of Platonic ideas. From its side, the continuo contributes to the aesthetic aim insofar as it limits its own melodic definition to a minimum that, far from interfering with the free course (the aria) of the vocal part, supports and enhances it. In so doing the continuo exercises a *sprezzatura* of its own. Caccini has already referred to this aspect, in which *sprezzatura* becomes a harmonic quality of the continuo, in the preface of *Euridice*: 'The notes of the bass I have sometimes tied in order that, in the passing of the many dissonances that occur, the note may not be struck again and the ear offended.'[54] Even more definitely he relates *sprezzatura* and harmonic procedures in the blurb of *Le nuove musiche*, where he claims to have used 'a certain noble neglect [*sprezzatura*] of the song, passing now and then through certain dissonances, holding the bass note firm, except when I wished to observe the common practice'.[55]

letter, written some twenty-five years later, in which Cirillo asserts he had discussed such matters with Cardinal Marcello Cervini, evidently before the latter became Pope Marcellus II in 1555.

[51]   C. V. Palisca, ed., *Girolamo Mei: Letters on Ancient and Modern Music to Vincenzo Galilei and Giovanni Bardi* (American Institute of Musicology 1960), pp. 70–5; see also Palisca's 'Girolamo Mei, Mentor to the Florentine Camerata', in *Musical Quarterly*, XL (1954), 1–20.

[52]   See above, pp. 245–7.

[53]   Strunk, *Source Readings*, p. 378. Caccini's insistence on grace – here of inspiration, elsewhere of performance – makes the reference to Castiglione obvious (see above, note 42); he probably considered himself as one of 'those who have it from the stars'.

[54]   Strunk, *Source Readings*, p. 371.

[55]   *Ibid.*, p. 378; but Strunk, following Playford, has 'except when I did not wish to observe the common practice'. The original reads: 'eccetto che quando io me ne volea servire all'uso comune'. The 'common usage' is that of polyphony and counterpoint, of which Caccini intended to avail himself whenever convenient.

Attempts to free melodic invention from the strictures of polyphonic writing had been made long before Caccini and Peri. The custom goes back to the first half of the sixteenth century of trying to fill the modal gap with such substitutes of mode as a Paduan, Bergamask, or Neapolitan aria; the results, however, were, above all, too tinged with local colour and humorous overtones to be able to transcend the level of entertainment and become universal criteria of artistic practice. Particularly instructive in this regard is the history of the *canzone villanesca alla napoletana*, or *aria napoletana*.[56] Initially composed by real Neapolitan composers who set to recapture in its upper line the manners and mannerisms of popular singers, the *napoletana* developed into a widely recognized genre, more and more frequently practised by composers from all over Italy and even by foreigners. In the process, both its peculiar southern flavour and its popular character became gradually attenuated; the name itself acquired a gentler sound as *villanella alla napoletana* and then was often replaced by plain *villanella*, or *canzonetta*. Finally, the genre merged with the generalized vogue of the so-called *musiche ariose*, which came to affect the madrigal itself, whether or not its printed collections were explicitly labelled as *madrigali ariosi*.[57] The constant feature throughout this process is the presence of a straightforward (although by no means dance-like) rhythmic drive, and of simple, well-designed melodic contours of the upper part, minimally affected by contrapuntal upsurges of the lower voices.[58]

Even in the *musiche ariose*, however, the composers' habit of thinking in the traditional terms of contrapuntal procedures (the *prima pratica*) reasserted itself in the observance at all times of precisely determined intervallic relationships between the parts. The resulting thorough harmonization of every single note, eventually with repeated notes to accommodate the text in the lower parts,[59] is strongly objected to by Peri in a passage that parallels Caccini's remarks on harmonic *sprezzatura*. Peri, too, affirms that he has held his bass '*firm through the false and true proportions*'; and this he has done 'in order that the flow of the discourse might not distress the ear (as though stumbling among the repeated notes [brought about] by the greater frequency of chords) and in order that it might not seem in a way to dance to the movement of the bass'.[60]

[56] *Canzoni villanesche* (with or without *alla napoletana*) is used in all collections known to us up to 1565, in which year *villanelle alla napoletana* and *villotte alla napoletana* make their first appearance. Reference to the peasant element is completely eliminated in such titles as *canzoni* (or *canzonette*) *alla napoletana* or just simply *napoletane*, used during the seventies: thereafter, most titles are variations of *villanelle et arie alla napoletana*, or even, particularly in the seventeenth century, *villanelle*. See Werner Scheer, *Die Frühgeschichte der italienischen Villanella* (Nördlingen 1936), pp. 11–13.

[57] The oldest example, to my knowledge, is the *Primo libro delle muse a quattro voci di Ant. Barre et altri diversi autori* (Gardane, Rome and Venice 1555), which had many reprints. Also cf. *Madrigaletti et napolitane a sei voci* in two collections by Giovanni de Macque (Gardano, Venice 1581 and 1582), the first of which had a reprint in Antwerp in 1600.

[58] In 'Tragédie et comédie dans la Camerata Fiorentina', *Musique et poésie au XVIe siècle* (Paris 1954), p. 202, I suggested that the parallel thirds and fifths of the *napoletane* might be the imitation of popular accompaniments on string instruments. One added reason may have been to avoid contrapuntal motions that might interfere with the aria of the upper part.

[59] To a great extent, the madrigal provides the model of the repeated-note monodic recitative – one more instance of revolutionary change depending on tradition. In both, repeated notes served effects of contrast beside being expedient as carriers of the text.

[60] Italics mine; once more, I introduce a few interpretive modifications in the translation offered by Strunk, *Source Readings*, p. 374.

Caccini acknowledged his indebtedness to the previous literature of *musiche ariose* – after all, Scipione del Palla, whom he repeatedly refers to as his famous teacher and alleged model, is known to us as a composer of pieces in that category. Most of Caccini's long-winded discourses, however, refer to a particular development of that genre, in which the lighter texts, dialectal or popular, tended to be discarded, while more and more attention was given to lavish, improvised coloratura.[61] At this point the modern critic is faced with the problem whether or not he should take at face value Caccini's insistence in describing coloratura as an essential expressive element of his music. I am personally inclined to admit the sincerity of his utterances, taking into account on one hand the vividness that could be added to 'those long winding points, simple and double, that is redoubled or intertwined one with the other',[62] by an effective performance, and on the other hand the reactions of an audience conditioned by traditions, habits, and mental associations different from ours. Furthermore, it needs to be seen what Caccini's expressive intents were and precisely what he meant when he spoke of 'moving the mind' of his audience.

Caccini's choice of texts – with the exception of *Euridice*, which he set about to compose for evident polemic reasons – is usually a very moderate one from the point of view of emotional intensity. Even more moderate is his treatment of them. As a rule, he establishes a restrained affective mood with a recitative beginning of the musical phrase (recitative in a modern sense), which is then prolonged and sensuously inflected toward a cadence by large, subsiding waves of coloratura. In spite of his dramatic attempts of 1600, Caccini seems to have been as much opposed as Cavalieri and Bardi to the 'tragic' passional outbursts of Peri's *Euridice*, which he kept slandering for years, describing them as monotonous and, at best, 'funereal'.[63] We may sum up his aesthetic goals as, on one hand, a 'recitative' vividness of performance in the sense described above and, on the other hand, a participation of the audience based on a mild sentimental involvement and, even more essentially, on the *elation of expectations fulfilled by the aria of his music*.

One last point, although a minor one, needs to be made about Caccini. His involvement with vocal coloratura by no means represents the beginning of an era of luxuriant vocal improvisation, which had already been practised for some decades. On the contrary, Caccini is strongly and outspokenly opposed to the whims of singers; he considers his *passaggi* as one of the most important vehicles of musical expression and makes them his own concern, the concern of the composer. It clearly emerges from his writings that, while some freedom was left to the performers in the application of a few vocal ornaments – such as *intonazione*, *trillo*, and *groppo*, which, however, assumed a dynamic, more than melodic, significance in his descriptions[64] – Caccini

---

[61] Pirrotta, 'Tragédie et comédie dans la Camerata Fiorentina', pp. 290–1; the collection which includes the only known piece by Scipione del Palla has the significant title *Aeri raccolti insieme con altri bellissimi aggionti di diversi dove si cantano sonetti, stanze, et terze rime* (Cacchio dall'Aquila, Naples 1577).   [62] Strunk, *Source Readings*, p. 377.

[63] See, for instance, Severo Bonini's text quoted above, note 45. Peri's party retaliated by ridiculing Caccini's abuse of coloratura and comparing him to a certain painter, an expert in painting cypresses, who put them everywhere (see Gagliano, in Solerti, *Le origini*, p. 79).

[64] Concerning *intonazione*, Caccini dismisses the habit of touching first the lower third before coming to the correct pitch; he prefers instead 'to tune the first note in its proper pitch,

required that only such *passaggi* be performed as he, the composer, had provided as an intrinsic part of the aria of the composition. He violently opposed the 'maiming and spoiling' of his music by the singers through ill use of ornamentation.[65] Peri's party, from its side, even criticized Caccini for his insistence on vocal embellishments.[66] It is hard to believe that either criticism could have suddenly halted the habit of *ad libitum* ornamentation by the singers; it was, however, in the nature of the new style to oppose unwelcomed interpolations and to subordinate vocal virtuosity to the expressive requirements of the music as conceived by the composer.[67]

It is difficult to determine to what extent the solutions given by Caccini to the problems of an expressive style of singing were exclusively his own. Peri, although somewhat younger, could match with Caccini much of the same musical background and the experience of a professional singer, to whom, as we are going to see, a soloistic style of *cantar recitando* had no less appeal than to Caccini. As the striking parallelism of both artists' utterances on such matters as *sprezzatura* and continuo is probably the result of competitive interaction, it is conceivable that they affected each other in other matters also during the rapid, but by no means sudden, process of their stylistic evolution.

The differences stem mainly from differences of temperament – Caccini's more lyrical, Peri's more dramatic – and, dependent on this, from the tasks each composer set out to accomplish. As far as we know, Peri, with the exception of an echo-madrigal he had composed and performed for the *intermedi* of 1589,[68] first came to the foreground as a composer with *Dafne*, which is said to have been started in 1594.[69] Accordingly, his problems were from the beginning more strictly representative, centring on the need to give dramatic evidence to a text. He was led to overstress this point, however, in order to distinguish his own from Caccini's accomplishments; as a result, his 'imitation of speech in song', obtained by means of 'a harmony surpassing that of an ordinary speech but falling so far below the melody of songs as to take an intermediate form',[70] has come to be construed as a *dry* recitative, to which the composer himself allegedly pleaded guilty. Actually, even in this

diminishing it [in intensity]' (Strunk, *Source Readings*, p. 382) and thus assimilating it to another of Caccini's favorite idioms, the *esclamazione*; this is half-way between ornamentation and dynamic effects, as are *groppo* (the equivalent of our trill) and *trillo* (a trill on a single repeated note).

[65]   Strunk, *Source Readings*, p. 377.   [66]   See above, note 63.

[67]   I am strongly opposed to any addition of vocal embellishments to the written scores of most seventeenth-century composers, except for some trills (possibly of the repeated-note type) and, later, for some appoggiaturas. The fact is that most composers wrote out ornaments wherever the situation required them.

[68]   Included in Walker, *Musique des intermèdes*, pp. 98–106; the use of coloratura in this piece (often repeated by a 'double echo') is more impressive and refined than Caccini's 'aria' of the fourth *intermedio* (ibid., p. 156). The latter was omitted in the printing of 1591, which had been prepared by Cristoforo Malvezzi following instructions given to him by Cavalieri. The two pieces are commented on in chapter 5, where one lost 1583 *intermedio* by Peri is also mentioned.

[69]   Thus, even if we do not consider the echo piece of 1589, the two composers had at least five years during which they competed with, and influenced, each other.

[70]   Strunk, *Source Readings*, p. 374. The word 'dry' should be avoided because of the precise eighteenth-century technical meaning of *recitativo secco*, indicating a recitative with continuo accompaniment (as opposed to recitatives *con strumenti obbligati* or *recitativi obbligati*), but not necessarily lacking melody.

252

Ex. XLVI   Giulio Caccini, opening of madrigal XI from *Le nuove musiche* (G. Marescotti, Florence 1601–2).

statement from the preface to *Euridice*, the extent to which Peri's music falls 'so far below the melody of an ordinary song' is qualified and restricted by the words that follow that statement; furthermore, we have to remember that an obsession with text was the symptom of the sixteenth-century concern for expression.

Peri's music is quite often even richer than Caccini's in melody, the main difference, which Peri found difficult to put into words, lying in the larger scope and open continuity of his monologues and dialogues, compared with the narrower definition of a set piece that is an end in itself. Caccini from his side was affected as much as Peri by the need for declamatory evidence of the text, which he, too, overemphasized in his prefaces (even in places where other elements are the obvious determining factors),[71] not only because one of the aesthetic axioms of the time was that the text was the carrier of the emotional contents, but also because he usually received inspiration from the text for the initial motion of his melodic phrases. Rhythm and accentuation of the words thus became, too, an intrinsic part of the aria (example XLVI). Like Caccini's, Peri's melody also incorporates the rhythm, accentuation, and dynamics of the text in its aria, but faces different problems of development. The use of coloratura to expand an initial gesture into a melodic phrase is usually precluded to him, as is textual repetition; melodic repetition is also a rare occurrence, needing to be justified by either text or action. At cadences the sense of enhanced finality rounding up the conclusion of set pieces must usually be avoided; on the contrary, new ways must be always found to stress continuity and to inject a new momentum wherever the flow of the dialogue tends to become stagnant. The ways in which Peri copes with these problems

[71]   Strunk, *Source Readings*, pp. 385–91.

Ex. XLVII Iacopo Peri. Fragment of *Le musiche...sopra l'Euridice* G. Marescotti, Florence 1600–1), p. 30.

are manifold. To obtain a faster delivery of often lengthy texts, the supporting harmonies of the continuo tend to become more widely spaced and to extend the harmonic *sprezzatura* not only, as in Caccini's music, to passing notes of coloratura, but to notes accented by syllables (example XLVII). Thus the continuo tends to lose all vestiges of linear conduct, reserving that for the moments of heightened lyrical interest. Its increased harmonic significance tends to avoid cadential successions (although we may feel they are still too frequent); instead, unexpected harmonies, or unexpected shifts of the tonal plane are often used to create diversions and to indicate new moods. Conceding that there are also moments of lesser interest, one nevertheless has to admire Peri's resourcefulness in adhering to his text and yet attaining a definite melodic coherence, resulting in a line endowed with aria (example XLVIII). Finally, the most impressive display of unusual and daring harmonies, often resulting from very unorthodox procedures, is brought about by the 'tragic' moment of most impassioned pathos; and yet this display may lend itself (as in the well-known example of Orpheus' song at the gates of hell) to a formal organization that is not the less remarkable for its obvious derivation from procedures familiar in madrigals.

Caccini contented himself with establishing an affective mood and letting it permeate the short span of his pieces, like a slow, sweet poison flowing through the veins of his coloratura. Peri, more nearly like Gesualdo and Monteverdi, seeks to depict more forceful passions, and feels the urge to plunge into their stream, to follow their meanderings, to explore their depths and shallows. To express not only passion but the dialectics of passion, the mere intelligibility of the text is not enough; a give and take is needed, in which

Ex. XLVIII Iacopo Peri, opening of the first scene of *Le musiche...sopra l'Euridice* (G. Marescotti, Florence 1600–1), pp. 2–3.

music enhances the meaning and accentuation of the words and has its blind forcefulness motivated and guided by them. In this way the rhythmic formulation of the dramatic text and its various degrees of emphasis become the criteria of naturalness and necessity, that is, the aria, of the dramatic melody.

What I have said of Caccini's and Peri's works has been meant to indicate how they stem from, and diverge from, the common ground of musical and aesthetic tendencies of their time, and also to help our further investigation of the dramaturgy of opera. For the sake of completeness, we may add that, in addition to the elements of style listed above, many others were present at the moment of an operatic performance that are not indicated in the scores we possess. They go farther than the 'recitative' *sprezzatura* of the singers with which we have become familiar. These elements include changes of tempi, changes of texture and instrumental colour of the continuo,[72] and possibly also linear interventions of other instruments beyond the basic continuo accompaniment.[73] The fact that these elements were not recorded, and could vary from one performance to the other, does not mean that they were not carefully weighted for a calculated effect. Even the simplest *rappresentatione per musica* was rehearsed for weeks or even months before its official presentation;[74] we delude ourselves, then, when we speak of these elements as being improvised at the moment of performance. Indeed, they were so thoroughly rehearsed and agreed upon that they come near to another characteristic trend of the music of the time, that of *stile concertato*.[75]

The pastoral aura

It may seem paradoxical that aria, if only as an indefinite quality and aesthetic goal, should have been an important factor in the initial formulation of a style which we are accustomed to consider chiefly as recitative. The paradox, however, stems from our habits of thought more than from the factual situation. We still think of the early *stile rappresentativo* too much in terms of the later recitative. (This also, possibly, we think of too exclusively as mere non-aria.) To be sure, there are some barriers that need to be overcome to gain access to a musical idiom whose values were explicitly meant to come

[72] See the instrumental indications given by Monteverdi on pages 36 and 38 of the original score of *Orfeo*; as I have often remarked, such indications were given as a record of what had been done in the original performance and as a guide, but not necessarily a rule, to future performances.

[73] I am referring to the intervention of those instruments that are said by Agostino Agazzari to 'serve for ornament'; see his *Del sonare sopra il basso* (Falcini, Siena 1607), translated by Strunk, *Source Readings*, pp. 424ff.

[74] The Florentine spectacles of October 1600 were being rehearsed every morning as early as 29 August (Solerti, *Musica, ballo e drammatica*, p. 23). Similarly, *Arianna* was already under rehearsal in March of 1608, although the performance took place on 28 May. For the long preparations in Parma, see Irving Lavin, 'Lettres de Parma (1618, 1627–28) et débuts du théâtre baroque', in Jean Jacquot, ed., *Le lieu théâtrale à la Renaissance* (Paris 1964), pp. 105ff; and Stuart Reiner, 'Preparations in Parma – 1618, 1627–28', in *The Music Review*, XXV (1964), pp. 273–301. Elsewhere Reiner, 'La vag'Angioletta (and others)', in *Analecta musicologica*, XIV (1974), pp. 63ff, argues that reasons other than musical delayed the 1608 performances in Mantua; this does not mean, however, that any performance could have taken place without having been carefully rehearsed.

[75] See above, note 70. Too much credit has been given to the etymology of *concerto* and *concertato* from the Latin *concertare*, 'to contend or dispute'; but, also, the etymology from *conserere*, 'to connect or bring together', given as the basic one by Franz Giegling, 'Concerto', and Hans Engel, 'Concerto grosso', both in *Die Musik in Geschichte und Gegenwart*, vol. II, cols. 1600 and 1604, is a half truth. Many elements and words of similar sound concur in the final meaning of *concerto*, but to an Italian of the fourteenth century (Boccaccio), as to those of the sixteenth and twentieth, the main meaning of *concertare* was 'to make sure', 'to reach an agreement'.

alive at the moment of performance. The difficulties are compounded by an unfamiliar notation, in which long notes often demand short values, and the modern reader is given little indication of where expressive and rhythmic stresses need to be placed.[76] Yet by giving indiscriminate credit to all that was written or said in Florence at the turn of the century, and by magnifying it into the myth of a quarter of a century of ineffectual theorizing, we have made it all too easy to fall back on an erroneous condemnation of sterile intellectualism.

The discrepancy between verbal statements and actual deeds is borne out by Caccini himself in the foreword to his *Nuove musiche* of 1601 (1602 new style). Having previously quoted Plato to the effect that music should follow, not precede, speech and rhythm,[77] he finds himself committed to giving embarrassed justifications for the pieces in this collection that he calls *arie* – ten of them, as distinguished from the twelve *madrigali*. For not only do most of these *arie* apply the same music to the various verses of a polystrophic text (thus contradicting the fashionable Platonic slogan), but they even include some light pieces – *ariette*, in a *frottola*-like rhythm – for instance, those numbered as sixth, eighth, and ninth *arie*, which strongly resemble Orpheus' *canzonetta*, *Ecco pur ch'a voi ritorno*, at the beginning of Act II of Monteverdi's *Orfeo*.[78] The fact is that aria in this more specific sense is also present in all Caccini's printed collections, and its purpose, in spite of solemn aesthetic preambles, is to provide entertainment.[79] Nor is the musical quality of the madrigals much different; we may speak of them as unavowed nonstrophic *arie*, having only internal repetitions brought about by repetition of text.

We would be mistaken again if we assumed that Caccini's melic temperament was the reason for an exceptional use of aria.[80] A quick glance at the two *Euridici*, *Orfeo*, or any of the extant early operatic scores will show that, far from being a continuous series of open recitatives, each of them includes a number of self-contained pieces. Limiting ourselves, for the moment, to Peri's opera, we may list in the first place its prologue, with seven strophes

[76] For works in this category, more than for any other style, I am opposed to modern editions that merely strive to reproduce the original notation, adding bars that correspond to the beat but not to the rhythm of music. Such editions avoid not error, but taking responsibility for it and, above all, the process of trial and error through which a deeper knowledge of the music should be gained.

[77] Caccini's declared intent (see the unnumbered folio A2 verso of the facsimile edition) is to observe 'quella maniera contanto lodata da Platone, & altri Filosofi, che affermarono la musica altro non essere che la favella [i.e. speech], e'l rithmo, & il suono per ultimo, e non per lo contrario, à volere che ella possa penetrare nell'altrui intelletto, e far quei mirabili effetti, che ammirano gli Scrittori, e che non potevano farsi per il contrappunto nelle moderne musiche'.

[78] See H. W. Hitchcock's edition of *Le nuove musiche*, pp. 131–7, or the edition by Carlo Perinello (Milan 1919; due to the peculiar format of the edition, page numbers would only be confusing). I do not agree with every detail of Perinello's rhythmic interpretation, yet a comparison with the facsimile, pp. 33–7, will bear out the point made above, note 76. In favour of rhythmic interpretation is a more recent and, I am afraid, not too convincing book by Putnam Aldrich, *Rhythm in Seventeenth-Century Italian Monody* (New York 1966).

[79] 'The thought also came to me that I should compose some *canzonette* in the form of arias, to be used in a consort of several stringed instruments, for the relief of depressed spirits', says Caccini, again in the foreword to *Le nuove musiche* (see the unnumbered folio B1 recto of the facsimile).

[80] Jan Racek, *Stilprobleme der italienischen Monodie* (Prague 1965), places due emphasis on Caccini and the literature of chamber songs deriving from him, but overstresses the importance of Caccini's statements without placing them in their polemic context. Racek's work goes against Caccini's expressed opinion by completely disregarding dramatic monody.

Ex. XLIX Iacopo Peri, Orfeo's madrigal from *Le musiche...sopra l'Euridice* (G. Marescotti,
Florence 1600–1), pp. 8–9.

Ex. L Iacopo Peri, Orfeo's song from *Le musiche...sopra l'Euridice* (G. Marescotti, Florence 1600–1), p. 38.

each followed by a short instrumental *ritornello* (only the bass line is given), and the five choruses, most of them including solo verses, that mark the end of the five episodes.[81] Also strophic, with two verses each, are the songs of Tirsis in the second episode and of Orpheus in the last one, *Nel puro ardor* and *Gioite al canto mio*.[82] *Antri ch'a' miei lamenti* (example XLIX), sung by Orpheus upon his arrival on stage in the second episode, and his rondo-like invocation at the gates of hell, *Funeste piagge*,[83] resemble Caccini's monostrophic madrigals, although both span a wider range of emotions than any of Caccini's pieces. Finally, a number of shorter passages have a distinctive song-like quality. One such passage is Orpheus' triumphal exclamation, *O fortunati miei dolci sospiri* (example L) in the fourth episode.[84]

The fact needs to be stressed at this point that the protagonists, though not the title roles, of both of Rinuccini's operatic libretti are musicians: Apollo, the god of music, and Orpheus, the legendary singer, who, at least in the version of the myth followed by Rinuccini, is the son of Apollo and the Muse Calliope. That their common musical talent was no mere coincidence is indicated by subsequent operas. The title role of Agostino Agazzari's *Eumelio*,

[81] The first episode (rejoicing around Euridice; pp. 2–8 of the facsimile) is concluded by the chorus *Al canto, al ballo*; the second (arrival of Orpheus and friends, announcement of Euridice's death; pp. 8–21) by the responsorial threnody *Cruda morte*; the third (description of Orpheus' grief; pp. 21–8) by *Se de boschi i verdi onori*, a chorus of thanks for the celestial solace descended on Orpheus; the fourth (short dialogue with Venus, followed by Orpheus' singing and pleading until Euridice is given back to him; pp. 28–40) by *Poi che gli eterni imperi*, a chorus of infernal spirits celebrating human daring; the fifth (joyous return of the couple, general singing and dancing; pp. 41–52) by a chorus alternating with an instrumental *ritornello*. A change of stage setting, required by the fourth episode, is indicated on p. 28, and the re-establishment of the original setting on p. 41.   [82] Pp. 11–12 and 46–47 of the facsimile.

[83] *Ibid.*, pp. 8–9 and 29–32.   [84] *Ibid.*, p. 38.

performed in Rome in 1606, is of an allegoric youth who is torn between the enticements of pleasure and vice and the appeals of reason and virtue, but who is also – quite unnecessarily from the point of view of the moral example he is called to give – an accomplished singer.[85] In the following year, 1607, Monteverdi and Alessandro Striggio the younger gave in Mantua another version of the Orpheus myth, which to a great extent parallels the one presented in Florence with Peri's and Caccini's music.[86] Also in Mantua, Apollo was brought back on stage in 1608, when Marco da Gagliano reset to music Rinuccini's *Dafne*. There can be no doubt that all authors deliberately sought to justify singing of songs – *cantar recitando* – by choosing for protagonists such musical figures around whom other singers gather quite naturally.

This way of justifying song is in line with an established tradition of the Italian theatre, according to which the exhibition on stage of one or more characters shown in the act of singing, playing instruments, or dancing was an accepted practice and a gratifying element of variety. We may even add that in no other genre had such a habit been as prominent as in the dramatic pastorale or tragicomedy, in which category, according to the rather rigorous classifications of dramatic genres prevailing during the late Renaissance period, we need not hesitate to place the early operatic libretti.[87] Yet, its obvious intensification in the new-born opera, and the lack of an equally obvious stylistic distinction between the pieces that represent *cantar recitando* and the rest of the score betray the qualms of the creators of the new brand of *recitar cantando* concerning the legitimacy of their creation.

I have previously described Rinuccini's and Peri's approaches to *recitar cantando* as realistic, as opposed to the formalistic approach of Cavalieri. This statement now needs further qualification, for it is evident that no departure from reality could be more conspicuous in a play than the systematic 'imitation of speech in songs'. There is, however, a realism of some sort in Rinuccini's and Peri's concern to provide a justification for their departure from reality, a justification which never before had been felt to be needed by

[85] This score deserves attention not as much for its intrinsic value as for its attempt at musical characterization; each character is given a kind of head-motif, which is repeated with most of his utterances. Like Rinuccini and Peri, Agazzari justified *recitar cantando* as a procedure that had been applied in classic times; he further justified strophic repetition of music by doubting that 'the ancients' had felt obliged to give each strophe new music.

[86] Strong similarities and verbal reminiscences indicate that Striggio had the text of *Euridice* in mind when he wrote his libretto. I even believe that some divergences were suggested by Monteverdi in order to avoid either dramatic situations that had proved their weakness or too obvious repetition of the most successful ones.

[87] The distinction between tragedy and comedy was based on the station of their characters as well as on the tragic or comic nature of the events they described. The tragic fate of highborn persons brought grief to those subject to their rule; the misfortunes of the common people affected only them, with the result that their despair could be laughed at. Concerning the pastorale, its theorist, Guarini, has this to say about its characters (after having 'very well and sufficiently demonstrated' its being 'a mixed story of tragic and comic elements'): 'E, per intenderle meglio, hassi a sapere che gli antichi pastori non furono, in quel primiero secolo che i poeti chiamaron "d'oro", con quella differenza distinti dalle persone di conto, che oggi sono i villani da' cittadini, perciocché tutti erano ben pastori' ('To understand these things better, one has to know that the ancient shepherds of that primal age, called "golden" by the poets, were not as sharply distinct from people of importance as peasants are nowadays divided from citizens, insofar as they were all shepherds'); from 'Il compendio della poesia tragicomica', in G. B. Guarini, *Il pastor fido*, ed. G. Brognoligo (Bari 1914), p. 268.

the organizers of the spectacular symbolic *intermedi*, or by Cavalieri for his dancing and singing figurines. The justification given by both of them in the prefatory remarks to the libretto and the score of *Euridice*, namely, that continuous singing had been used by the ancients in their tragedies, was undoubtedly fashionable, but too simple and also, they probably knew, difficult to maintain.[88] It was evidently intended to forestall the most superficial criticism with an *ipsi fecerunt*. More effective in the long run was the built-in defence which gave *recitar cantando* a motivation by endowing the protagonists of opera with the most exceptional gifts for music and by placing them in the very special climate of the pastorale.

As pastorales the early operatic libretti are rather unusual in their pronounced reliance on mythological legends and characters. Yet a mythological quality had always been present in the pastorale even when no particular myth was referred to, for the world of the pastorale was that of a legendary Golden Age, vaguely located in an imaginary pre-historic Arcadia or Thessaly. In that Utopia-Uchronia – still unspoiled by the artificial needs and rules of social life and still blessed with innocence, naturalness, and freedom – men and women, that is, shepherds and nymphs, were not only happier than in the world we know, but also endowed with a spontaneous feeling for beauty and a natural gift for artistic expression, poetry, and music. The nostalgic dream for a utopia of perfect happiness thus becomes the aesthetic vision of an idealized world, the imitation of which leads not to crude realism but to a more refined, and also more malleable, *vraisemblance*.

Gods and demigods are not too often present in the pastorale; yet they are always around the corner, and whenever they decide to intervene among the humans, their sudden appearance produces awe but no surprise. Nor is any logical fault found in their descending or ascending on wings, flying chariots, or soft puffs of clouds. At other times their invisible presence is made evident either mystically through the cryptic verdicts of oracles or, more poetically, through complacent echo answers – a trick that had already attracted the attention of musicians. Finally, and here is our main point, there is no breach of *vraisemblance* in the fact that the gods are exquisite singers; indeed, to all the characters of the pastoral landscape, the gift is given to express themselves in verse and in a language that has 'a harmony surpassing that of ordinary speech'. This is clearly stated by Guarini in his defence of his pastoral play: 'It is no marvel that the Arcadian shepherds, noblest of all, embellished their speeches with poetic ornaments, being more than any other people in the greatest intimacy with the Muses.' He then goes on to quote Polybius to the effect 'that all the Arcadians were poets; that their principal study, and their

---

[88] A contrasting opinion is expressed by Barbara R. Hanning, 'Apologia pro Ottavio Rinuccini', in *Journal of the American Musicological Society*, XXVI (1973), pp. 240–62. However, I am not convinced by her documents and arguments: Rinuccini, and Peri after him, did not state that 'the ancient Greeks and Romans had whole tragedies sung on stage' as a fact, but only mentioned it to be 'the opinion of many'; furthermore, Rinuccini was fully aware of the difference between a pastoral play (*Euridice*) and a tragedy (*Arianna*). I have never denied the influence of classical ideas on the origin of opera; but such ideas were so widely spread that their influence need not have been exerted only through the social gatherings in the house of Bardi. I have always opposed the idea of the latter as an official institution solely concerned with this problem and wasting twenty-five years in a purely philological and theoretical approach; from it derives the judgement of the first operas as inane attempts weakened by learned considerations.

principal activity was music; that they learned it as children; that their laws required them to do so'; and so on.[89]

Such ideas may have been only vaguely in the minds of Rinuccini and Peri – after all, the combination of drama and music is a recurrent urge in all kinds of historical and geographical situations. Nonetheless, Guarini's ideas were in the air, particularly in Florence, which Guarini had visited first in 1588 and again more than once in 1599–1601, when he was, at least nominally, attached to the Medicean court; his *Compendio della poesia tragicomica*, from which I have quoted, although printed in 1602, was already known in manuscript in Florence in 1599.[90] In my opinion, one result of the strong influence exerted by the theories of pastoral poetry on the early *stile rappresentativo* and opera was a lack of a clear distinction between enhanced speech and song, a lack that once more reaffirms the catholic conception of the style itself, embracing, as it does, the full range of nuances from the most prosaic and matter-of-fact utterances to the most lyrical and even florid outbursts. To be sure, there are songs that are definitely songs – *cantar recitando* – and are usually established as such either by the repetition of the same music for more than one strophe of text (while the 'imitation of speech' obeys the madrigalistic principle that new words require new music) or by some explicit mention of the fact that the characters are indeed singing. There is, however, margin left for doubt. For instance, in Peri's *Euridice* the already mentioned *Funeste piagge* is clearly a song, but it is unclear whether Orpheus' following supplications in dialogue with Pluto and Proserpina are also songs, artfully improvised by the unusual singer, or passionate oratorical arguments.[91] Conversely, in the initial scene, the dialogue of shepherds and nymphs calling each other to share Euridice's happiness and to attend her nuptial preparations is already melodious from its beginning, but it gathers further momentum and culminates in open singing on its final line. The line is repeated three times, with different melodies, by three different characters, and a fourth time by the full chorus; of course, even in the bliss of Thessaly, no shepherd or nymph could ignore the fact that 'Non vede un simil par d'amanti il sole' is a quotation from Petrarch[92] and needs to be put in some sort of quotation marks.

The lack of a clear-cut stylistic distinction was by no means restricted to the earliest operas. Even when the librettists began to separate recitative scenes more sharply from situations suitable for an aria, and began to exercise their ingenuity in providing more numerous occasions for the latter, the distinction was hardly made on the basis of musical style. Monteverdi always remained substantially faithful to the madrigalistic conception of a continuity of musical expression with various nuances. Cavalli's typical arias around and after the middle of the seventeenth century break into what we would consider recitative just at the point where they reach an emotional climax, as in example LI; and vice versa, many of his recitatives suddenly take wing,

[89] G. B. Guarini, *Il compendio della poesia tragicomica*, p. 253.
[90] *Ibid.*, p. 305. See also Vittorio Rossi, *Battista Guarini ed Il pastor fido* (Turin 1886), pp. 123–31.
[91] See the facsimile, pp. 32–7. The same applies to some extent to the songs of Orpheus in Monteverdi's score.
[92] It is line 9 of the sonnet *Due rose fresche e colte in paradiso*; for the music, see the facsimile, p. 4.

Ex. LI Francesco Cavalli, two verses of an aria with *ostinato* bass from *Didone*, Act I scene 4.
From the manuscript Venice, Biblioteca San Marco, Ital., Cl. IV, 355.

even though for only the short flight of one single, more exalted line.[93] Domenico Mazzocchi's printed score of *La catena d'Adone* (Venice 1626; it had been performed in Rome the same year) has two numbers which are labelled *arie recitative* in the index. The same term could be applied to the so-called unornamented version of *Possente spirto* in Act III of Monteverdi's *Orfeo*, as well as, in a somewhat different sense, to many an aria or lament on an *ostinato* bass.

The pastoral aura that made *recitar cantando* plausible was not the only legacy of pastorale to opera. Others, on which I cannot dwell, were the almost unbroken rule of the happy ending, the propensity for the depiction of tender passions, and the participation of comic characters, although on a lower social level than the main roles.[94] Still another deserves to be mentioned because it has some bearing on the use of set pieces. This is the striving of both genres towards a classic balance between, on one side, poetic freedom and emotional intensity and, on the other side, the effectiveness of an impressive formal composure.

It has been said that the pastorale was, after all, the fullest attainment of the Italian Renaissance in its attempt to recreate ancient tragedy. The goal could be reached only by repudiating the tenet that the subjects should be historical – too prosaic and depressing – and by avoiding the insidious shoals of the ethic catharsis – never too clearly understood, and anyway too dangerous in times of intensified control of the arts during the Counter Reformation. Instead, a more tangible catharsis was offered to the audience not only by the pleasurable relief provided by the happy ending,[95] but also by the continuous balance of interest between the contents and the ingenuity of their artistic formulation. On the operatic side, I have deemed it possible, on occasion, to compare Peri's *Euridice* to a frieze of metopes, and Monteverdi's *Orfeo* to the triangular tympanum of a classic temple.[96] Such similes have limited significance, but they try to translate into words the sense of a classic balance, too vividly present in the scores to be viewed as a mere coincidence.[97] Although it was soon to give way to the Baroque conception of a play as a continuous building of tensions, to be released time and again by sudden

[93] Mention needs also to be made of certain recitative units, monologues as well as dialogues, which tend to organize themselves either in terms of an emotional crescendo, or, in more strictly musical terms, by adhering to a fundamental key in spite of dashing modulatory excursions and by exploiting the recurrence of significant phrases in both text and music. Cavalli was particularly fond of such effects.

[94] See my 'Commedia dell'Arte and Opera', in *The Musical Quarterly*, XLI (1955), 305–24. The *commedia dell'arte* exerted a direct influence on opera at a slightly later time than the pastorale; yet pastorale, *commedia*, and opera are only different manifestations of the same general trend.

[95] A similar attitude is explicitly endorsed by Caccini in the passage quoted above, note 79.

[96] In 'Monteverdi e i problemi dell'opera', in *Studi sul teatro veneto fra Rinascimento e Barocco*, ed. M. T. Muraro (Florence 1971), pp. 321–43.

[97] See Grout, *Short History of Opera*, p. 52, for a summary and diagram of the symmetries in *Orfeo*. It seems to me, however, that the overall symmetry has generally been overstressed, for to view Acts I and V as a balance of prelude versus postlude does not take into account that a daring tragic finale was also planned, which challenged Monteverdi more than the mellifluous apotheosis included in the score (cf. note 105 below). I am more impressed by the symmetry in the first act, to be viewed in the general context of text and action rather than as a pure element of musical form. For a similar symmetry in the finale of *La morte d'Orfeo*, see Donald Grout, 'The Chorus in Early Opera' in Anna Amalie Abert and Wilhelm Pfannkuch, eds. *Festschrift Friedrich Blume* (Kassel 1963), pp. 160–1.

changes of mood, the interest in a balanced pattern of organization can still be perceived in some of the Roman operas, for instance, in *La morte d'Orfeo* (1619) and *Sant'Alessio* (1631 and 1634), both by Stefano Landi.

The means available to the composer for achieving this sense of balance were mainly the distribution and interrelation of set pieces, either those belonging to the realistic type – musicians shown in the act of making music – or, even more often, those depending on formal theatrical conventions that had been established and accepted long before the beginning of opera. Such are the prologue and choruses which I have listed above along with the *arie* of *Euridice*. Were we to establish a similar list of set pieces for *Orfeo*, we should add the duets and tercets that are so prominent in its first two acts. Choruses no less than *arie* are self-contained, set pieces; they share with many *arie* a strophic verse-pattern and need even more than *arie* to be reconciled with *vraisemblance*. Yet, despite much Renaissance talk about imitation of nature, and despite the realistic bent of Italian comedy and tragedy, the remarkably unlikely fact that a number of characters could find extempore not only a mutual agreement but also the way of vocalizing it in a harmonious ensemble never seems to have been questioned. In tragedy it was legitimized by classic precedent – indeed, it was one of the most obvious formal features of the model; in comedy it had a less official status, yet it became accepted, usually in the guise of a masquerade, as one possible form of *intermedio*.[98] In a similar way, although playwrights often preferred spoken prologues as the vehicles of their programmatic utterances,[99] sung prologues had also been an admissible choice at least from the beginning of the sixteenth century. The pattern of four-line verses sung by a single allegorical personage or mythological character, which we find applied with such uniform regularity in the early operas, appears to be the continuation of accepted practices in previous theatrical forms.[100]

Prologues and choruses, little more than convenient theatrical properties in the early Renaissance theatre, came to opera with the more exalted status they had acquired in the pastorale with its emphasis on all kinds of artistic devices, and more particularly on those having musical implications. In the same spirit also duets and trios, if not used realistically as the concerted singing of two or three characters, acquired formal importance either as an extension of the Renaissance concept of chorus[101] or as the equivalent of

[98] *Intermedio* usually reminds us of the most spectacular examples, a category apart from the simpler forms which were most currently in use. To the masquerade type belong the *intermedi* of both Machiavelli's *Mandragola* and *Clizia*. Among the other types, I must particularly mention the instrumental interlude; well-known examples are the *sinfonie* of both Cavalieri's *La rappresentatione* and Monteverdi's *Orfeo*. The latter were needed, following the choruses that end each act, to accompany the change of scenery which took place before the eyes of the audience; each *sinfonia* is placed in the score at the end of an act, but actually partakes of the expressive mood of the following act.

[99] Particularly intriguing is the spoken *Proemio* of Cavalieri's *La rappresentatione*, a hybrid between the programmatic prologue and the spoken, humorous *frottole* (no relation, but for the name, with the musical form) of previous religious plays.

[100] The same pattern is also occasionally adopted by heavenly messengers in the course of the plot.

[101] Most usually, a normal operatic chorus was formed when two to six of the individual characters present on stage joined their voices to express a common feeling. See Grout, 'The Chorus in Early Opera', pp. 151–3.

another classic device, the stichomythia.[102] Thus the utopian optimism of the pastoral world, while yielding to the escapist tendencies of the time, nevertheless allowed, through the flexibility of its *vraisemblance*, ingenious formal effects which were the last residuum of the classic ideal.

Recitar cantando and aria in the first decades of operatic history

The history of the first half-century of operatic activity can hardly be described as a straight line. In spite of the initial strong impact of the pastorale, many other influences and occasional or local conditions made their mark on individual works, while, under the persisting habit of humanistic conceptualism, the real motivation was rapidly estranging itself from the essence of classicism. It is not my intention to give here any detailed account of that period, for which I can refer to the basic outline provided by Donald Grout's classic work on opera. I shall limit myself to examining some of the conventions that made *arie* and set pieces possible within the frame of *vraisemblance*, if not realism, which opera had inherited from the rules of the Renaissance theatre.

I have singled out Peri's *Euridice* to mark the beginning of opera as a gentle, lovable, and viable (albeit frail) creature. Its viability as a work of art, however, was not necessarily sufficient to grant viability to its genre against adverse conditions and fierce competition. Opera had to compete against, on one side, the richer articulation of plot and dialogue of the spoken theatre and, on the other, a number of other genres in which music associated with less dramatic but more spectacular action. The competition was especially strong in Florence, where the two sides had long combined their forces in the exhibitionistic tradition of spoken comedies with lavish portentous *intermedi*, while normal court life favoured a number of lesser, more easily staged musical entertainments.[103] As a result, a Florentine phase of the history of opera is practically non-existent, beyond its inception, in 1600, until about the middle of the seventeenth century.[104] The new genre might even not have survived had it not been transplanted and injected with new vigour first in Mantua, then in Rome, and finally in Venice.

In each of these places competition had to be met again and again, and acceptance won, through perseverance, ingenuity, and a certain amount of compromise. In Mantua, for instance, the spectacular apotheosis ending *Orfeo*, as well as the one introduced as an afterthought in the finale of *Arianna* clearly

---

[102] Most duets may be included in the definition of a chorus as given in the preceding note; there are cases, however, in which two characters sing to express individual, even antithetic, feelings. Alternation and reassociation of the two voices are procedures similar to those of stichomythia; in addition, the duets often took advantage of the more typically musical technique of imitation.

[103] The concise but comprehensive survey given by Federico Ghisi, 'Le feste medicee, gli spettacoli teatrali, gli intermedi e la nascita dell'opera', sect. 3 of the article 'Firenze', in *Enciclopedia dello spettacolo*, vol. V (Florence, Rome 1958), cols. 376–81, can be supplemented by M. Fabbri, E. Garbero Zorzi, A. M. Petrioli Tofani, *Il luogo teatrale a Firenze*.

[104] There is no record of new operas performed in Florence between 1600 and 1628 – Francesca Caccini's *La liberazione di Ruggiero* (1625) was a sung ballet introducing a tournament; then, with the exceptions of *Flora* (1628), *Le nozze degli dei* (1637), and *Celio* (1646), one has to wait until a habit of operatic performances was inaugurated by *Tancia* (music by Iacopo Melani) in December 1656.

represented a compromise with the genre of the *intermedio*.[105] In the case of *Arianna*, opera's first conscious attempt to compete with the spoken theatre, the compromise worked also in a different, though related, way. Rinuccini, who had already toyed with the idea of tragedy at the time of *Euridice*, must have been glad when the opportunity arose to produce a regular tragedy, or at least a play with many features of a regular one, having no less a musician than Monteverdi at his side. The experiment, however, more daring than we realize, caused no little concern at the Mantuan court, where the plot was felt to be too dry – too human, that is; for it is a fact that, while the fishermen of Naxos, replacing the shepherds and nymphs of Arcadia in the plot of *Arianna*, can still praise the primeval simplicity of their life, the pastoral aura and the blessed innocence of the Golden Age have completely abandoned Theseus, Arianna, and their retainers. They are but men and women, bound by custom, law and even political considerations, from which arise their troubles, hardly suitable to be put into song unless they reach a paroxysm of despair. The compromise suggested by a committee and realized in the Mantuan performance must have involved not only the already mentioned spectacular and melodious apotheosis, but also a considerable amount of vocal floridity brought about by Venus and Love in the first episode.[106]

The two trends thus inaugurated in Mantua can be viewed as separated in theory, but often intertwined in practice. We can perceive the influence of the *intermedi* in such operas, usually big courtly events, which incorporated danced choruses and grandiose stage effects. These were placed at the ends of acts, evidently to function as *intermedi* – in which category we can place the already mentioned *La catena d'Adone* (Rome 1626), *Flora* by Marco da Gagliano (Florence 1628), and, as late as 1667–8, Cesti's *Il pomo d'oro* (Vienna). To a certain extent one can also recognize the influence of the *intermedi* in the evolution of the prologue, which was first expanded by adding a chorus and spectacular action to the original one-character strophic singing, and later transformed into an extensive dialogue, or dispute, between a number of gods or allegorical characters, requiring a set of its own and, more often than not, ingenious stage machinery.[107] This new type of prologue, however, quite often introduces into the ensuing plot a different level of motivation than that of human actions. This motivation can be expanded by other related scenes (not always placed at the proper place for an *intermedio*) into a counterplot of mythological or allegorical nature, which interferes with

[105] In the case of *Arianna* it is recorded that a committee headed by the Dowager Duchess of Mantua found the plot 'too dry' and suggested modifications (Angelo Solerti, *Gli albori del melodramma*, I, p. 92); it is easy to recognize these modifications in the added dialogue between Venus and Love in the first episode, and the final intervention of the gods, Venus rising from the sea, and Jupiter imparting his blessing from the sky, both of which upset the classic 'regularity' of the play. The original finale must have ended, after the arrival on stage of Bacchus and Arianna, with the triumphal chorus *Spiega ormai, giocondo nume*. For my latest conclusions on the diverging finales of *Orfeo* in the libretto and the score see my 'Teatro, scene e musica nelle opere di Monteverdi', in *Claudio Monteverdi e il suo tempo*, ed. R. Monterosso (Verona 1969), p. 51. New interesting details about preparations in Mantua are given by Stuart Reiner, 'La vag' Angioletta (and others)', in *Analecta musicologica*, XVI (1974), pp. 26–88.

[106] See above, note 105.

[107] The pattern of four-line strophes sung by a single character is still present in some of the earliest Venetian operas. In the *Armida* of Benedetto Ferrari (1639), the prologue is sung by Fortune alone, but the strophic pattern is broken; it is re-established in *Il pastor regio* (1640).

271

the principal plot (although the human characters may or may not be aware of its existence) and often determines the sudden twists of the peripeteia. Well-known instances of this two-level procedure are Cavalli's *Didone* (1640), as well as Monteverdi's *Il ritorno d'Ulisse* (1640) and *Le nozze d'Enea con Lavinia* (1641?).[108] They borrow it from their Virgilian or Homeric models. We also find this procedure applied without any similar justification, however, in most of the early Venetian operas, not to mention those plots which are still completely pastoral or mythological.[109]

One must conclude that, as had been the case for the audience of *Arianna* thirty years before, the Venetian public was not fully prepared for the novelty of *recitar cantando* as the normal means of expression for human beings; accordingly, it was only natural for the librettists to select themes that either still retain the mythological or pastoral aura, or could be developed on a double level, one of which at least would allow the composer a freer hand and compensate for the restraint to which he was obliged when handling human characters.[110] This assumption is confirmed by the fact that even on the lower level librettists and composers multiplied the occasions for *cantar recitando*. In Benedetto Ferrari's *Andromeda* (1637), a group of nymphs concludes a successful boar hunt with singing and dancing; in his *La maga fulminata* (1638), two wandering knights sing a duet while travelling in a boat and are answered by no fewer than three sirens. The convivial singing of Penelope's suitors in *Il ritorno d'Ulisse* is paralleled by a concert offered in *La finta pazza* (1641) to a group of visitors. A festival gives the main characters of *Gli amori di Giasone, e di Issifile* (1642) the opportunity of singing in honour of Venus and Bellona; they are joined by two comic characters, who sing for Bacchus and Priapus, and by three girls, who praise the three Graces. *La Venere gelosa* (1643) has a singing competition which reminds one of *Tannhäuser*. Finally, very few operatic heroines neglect to indicate in a song how free they are, initially, from all concerns of love; many of them are noted for their ability to accompany their singing on the harp or the zither;[111] and one, Aventina of *La finta savia* (1642), gives a full-dress recital when she describes the statues of a garden in a series of songs.

[108] Previous instances are the pastoral counterplot of *Erminia sul Giordano* (Rome 1633) and the assistance given by angels and by the personification of Religion to the protagonist of *Sant'Alessio* (Rome 1631 and 1634) in his fight against the schemes of the Devil. In *Amore trionfante dello Sdegno* by Marazzoli, the personifications of Love and Indignation influence the actions of the human characters, thus also explaining their abrupt psychological changes; in other cases, rivalries among gods also affect the actions of the humans, and their pacification (or discomfiture in the case of an evil power) is a prerequisite for the denouement. Sudden transitions from indifference or hatred to love, and vice versa, are often the effect of Love's arrows.

[109] Mythological pastorales are Cavalli's *Le nozze di Peleo, e di Teti* (Venice 1639), the first opera to be called a *festa teatrale*, and his *Gli amori di Apollo, e di Dafne* (Venice 1640), as well as Manelli's *Delia* (Venice 1639). Benedetto Ferrari's *La ninfa avara* (Venice 1641) has no gods, but is entirely pastoral and is called *favola boschereccia*.

[110] See, for instance, the floridity of the recitative of La Religione in *Sant'Alessio*, Act III scene 5, given by Hugo Goldschmidt, *Studien zur Geschichte der italienischen Oper im 17. Jahrhundert* (Leipzig 1901), I, p. 237. Although Monteverdi did not wait for the pretext of the supernatural to justify his using whatever musical means best suited his intentions, yet in *Il ritorno d'Ulisse* Minerva's, Juno's, and Neptune's vocalizations are the most daring ones and Telemachus is never as melodious as when he travels with Minerva on a flying chariot.

[111] Dafne, in Cavalli's *Gli amori di Apollo, e di Dafne*, asks for her zither and sings; Archimene in *Il Bellerofonte* (Venice 1643) plays the harp. Even later, in Cavalli's *Serse* (Venice 1654), Xerxes falls in love with Romilda by hearing her singing.

The luxuriant growth of the Venetian opera, after its initial phase of adjustment, richly exemplifies the many ways in which composers strove for public acceptance of *recitar cantando*. Yet one has to realize that opera would never have become the kind of spectacle we know without a number of circumstances connected with its previous development in Rome. Strong objections had been raised there by the papal government against the professional *comici dell'arte*, whose performances represented elsewhere a welcome alternative to the more sophisticated, but expensive and infrequent, court spectacles. This gap, only partially filled by amateur performances,[112] gave opera the chance to be more than a tentative competitor of the spoken theatre.

The first operatic performances had been given in Rome by Florentines – as was the case of *Aretusa* by Filippo Vitali, performed in 1621 with the participation of Caccini's son Pompeo as a scenery painter and a singer – or had followed the Florentine pattern musically and dramatically, as for instance Stefano Landi's *La morte d'Orfeo* (1619). A different trend was inaugurated in 1623 with the advent of Maffeo Barberini as Pope Urban VIII and with the emergence of his three nephews as the arbiters of Roman social life; an almost regular habit of operatic performances was soon established. The performances were held every year during the carnival season, or on the occasion of princely visits, in one or the other of the various Barberini palaces, or in the Palazzo della Cancelleria, the official residence of Cardinal Pietro Barberini.[113] Opera thus became the main form of theatrical activity in Rome, and as such it expanded the scope of its plots and the range of its subjects, including, along with the traditional pastoral, mythological, and allegorical topics, plots derived from the most famous poems of Italian epic literature (*La catena d'Adone*, 1626; *Il ritorno di Angelica dalle Indie*, 1628; *Erminia sul Giordano*, 1633; *Il palazzo incantato d'Atlante*, 1642), from hagiography (*Sant'Alessio*, 1631 and 1634; *Santa Teodora*, 1635; *San Bonifatio*, 1638), or even from the *commedia dell'arte* (*Il falcone*, 1637, performed again in 1639 as *Chi soffre speri*).[114] One external indication of change was the gradual

[112] Plays, with or without music, were often performed by the students of various colleges; and, later, performances of comedies were organized by such artists as Lorenzo Bernini and Salvator Rosa.

[113] Although performed in the house of a Baron Hohen Rechberg, *Diana schernita* (1629), with the Barberini lily and golden bees appearing in its finale, can be considered the first Barberini opera. It derives its inspiration from the favourite theme of an old follower of the Barberinis, Francesco Bracciolini, author of *Lo scherno degli dei* (1617); it also makes humorous references to the invention of the telescope by another one-time protégé of Urban VIII, Galileo Galilei. The performances of *Sant'Alessio* seem to have been given first in the older palace in the Via dei Giubbonari, and then in the new one in the region called Quattro Fontane. Concerning the theatre, see above, note 3; Professor Irving Lavin informs me that only in 1639 was some kind of semi-permanent theatrical installation created in the new palace.

[114] The trend of hagiographic plots had already been inaugurated in 1625 with a *Sant'Eustachio*, music by Sigismondo d'India (another *Sant'Eustachio*, libretto by Rospigliosi and music by V. Mazzocchi, was performed in 1643); it lasted at least until 1668, when *La comica del cielo*, text by Rospigliosi (by now Pope Clement IX), music by A. M. Abbatini, was performed. *La catena d'Adone* (1626) and *Il Ciclope* (1630) combined mythology and Christian piety through far-fetched moral allegories. The influence of the *commedia dell'arte*, already felt in the comic parts of *Sant'Alessio* (including a dance of peasants in the costumes of Punchinello, and the comic tricks played on the servants by the Devil), is particularly strong in *Chi soffre speri*. With the expansion of the operatic scope goes the shift from the classic number of five acts to the more practical division into three acts, reducing the number of required *intermedi* from four to two. It was easy, however, to rearrange the number of acts; for Monteverdi's *Ritorno d'Ulisse* we have a three-act score and various five-act libretti.

abandonment of such names as *favola* or *pastorale* in favour of *commedia per musica*, or even simply *commedia*.[115] Under the growing influence exerted on Italian theatrical activity by the Spanish theatre, the term had lost its connotation of a precisely defined comic genre; it meant rather any kind of theatrical action developed mainly through dialogue, and was as neutral as 'opera', a term soon to prevail in the musical theatre.

In itself, the transition to plots derived from epic poems was not too great a departure. The warrior world of Ariosto's and Tasso's tales, the Golden Age of chivalry, was no less unreal and utopian than the Golden Age.[116] However, it offered no specific justification of *recitar cantando*. It would seem then that fewer than two decades of opera had been sufficient to establish continuous singing, initially the privilege of shepherds and gods, as an accepted theatrical convention. Audiences and critics had become accustomed to the novelty and ceased to question its legitimacy; for it is a fact that the willingness of the audience to accept a mode of representation in the theatre, or any other artistic framework, matters more than the author's rationalizations. Once the acceptance is established, usually through mere repetition and habit, the illusion is created no matter how faithful to, or divergent from, reality the representation is.

The desire of the Barberini and their favourite librettist, Monsignor Rospigliosi, to eliminate the often scurrilous performances of the *commedia dell'arte* by equating opera with spoken theatre may have contributed to the rapid establishment of *recitar cantando* as the equivalent of speech on stage. In any case, it is a fact that the enlarged scope of the action, the increased number of characters, the introduction of secondary plots, of peripeteia, of disguise and recognition created large sequences of action in which rapid delivery and communication of the text were more essential than musical setting. The only reason for hesitating to identify this procedure with the later *recitativo secco* is that the latter was chiefly characterized by a mode of accompaniment, not necessarily by a lack of musical interest.[117]

Of course, we are lucky to have in our possession a number of scores from this period. We must realize, however, that they put us only one step ahead of having only the libretti, and in a sense the latter are the most essential clue to works that were basically conceived as plays. As for the music, it was only

---

[115] For instance, in the *Argomento et allegoria della commedia musicale Chi soffre speri* (Rome 1639); for the allegory, see Stuart Reiner, 'Collaboration in Chi soffre speri', in *Music Review*, XXII (1961), pp. 265–82. The habit of referring to operas as comedies, an intriguing and often confusing feature of Roman chroniclers, occasionally spread outside Rome. See Henry Prunières, *L'opéra italien en France avant Lulli* (Paris 1913), which contains many French and Italian letters that refer to operas as comedies. Reiner, 'La vag'Angioletta (and others)', pp. 42–3, note 48, and pp. 85–8, stresses the double meaning of the word *commedia* with early Florentine and Mantuan examples of its use, alternately, for a 'play' or a real 'comedy'. I welcome his additions, which do not disprove my statement about the gradual abandonment of *favola* and *pastorale* in the Roman usage.

[116] Charlemagne and his knights had become the heroes of popular mythology long before Ariosto's whimsical and ironical treatment of them in his epic. As for Tasso, his attempts to reconcile his romantic stories with history were a futile afterthought; his characters derive from Homeric, Virgilian, and Ariostesque models – a literary rather than a popular mythology – to which he merely added his note of pathos. In both Ariosto and Tasso, a host of fantastic or allegorical figures are introduced into the action and the art of magic is often present. However, no character in either Ariosto's or Tasso's works is noted for his musical gifts.

[117] See above, note 70.

1   The Mountain of the Hebrews

2　Fifteenth-century cassone

3   The Triumph of Chastity

4   Float with the Ship of the Merchants and Burghers of Pesaro

5   Orpheus in Hell

6   *Il tempio d'Amore*, comedy by Galeotto del Carretto

7   *La fabula de Caephalo*, by Niccolò da Correggio

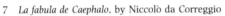

8   The Rotating Mountain with Hades, by Leonardo da Vinci

9   Plan of the rotating stage, and the interior of Hades
with Pluto, by Leonardo da Vinci

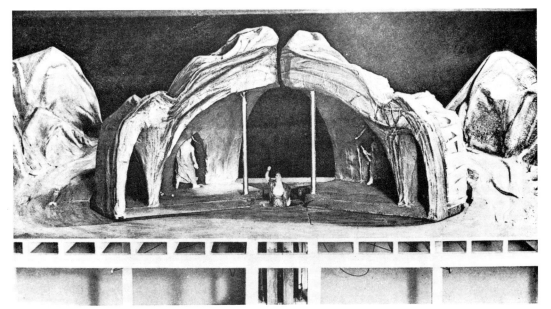

10   Reconstruction of the Rotating Mountain with Hades, from
the drawings of Leonardo da Vinci

11   *La rappresentazione et festa della Annuntiatione
di Nostra Donna*, by Feo Belcari

12 'Paradise', detail of Hubert Cailleau's miniature

13 Devices for Baldassare Taccone's *Danae* performed in Milan in 1496, by
Leonardo da Vinci

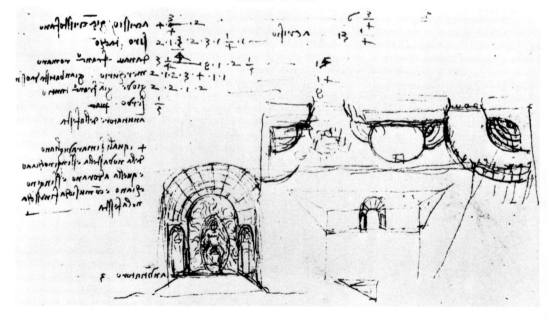

Theatri ex ordine Corinthio, et ex cementitio opere marmoreorum ornamentorum cultu splendido Velitris in foro S. Jacobi saeculo XV exstructi
in quo passionis, et mortis Christi sacer ludus agebatur, quodque anno CIↃIↃCCLXV vastatum, atque in horrea frumentaria conventum fuit
scenographiam, quae forte fortuna superfuit ne insignis operis, veterisque instituti memoria interiret, aere caelandam curavit
Stephanus Borgia a Secretis sacrae Congr. de Propaganda Fide anno CIↃIↃCCLXXX

14   Permanent stage for the *Passion*, built by the Confraternita di San Giovanni, in Piazza
San Giacomo in Velletri.

15   Stage with juxtaposed mansions, for the Valenciennes *Passion*, 1547

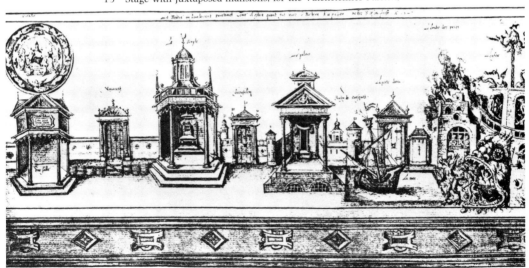

16 Roman tragic scene, possibly inspired by Seneca's
Troades

17 The 'Shield of Aeneas', by Ercole de' Roberti

18 Terence's *Andria*

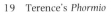

19 Terence's *Phormio*

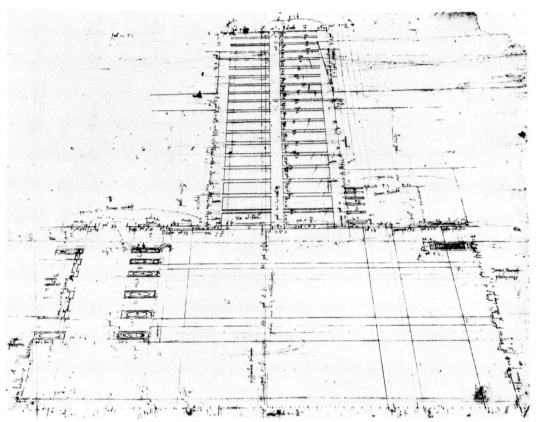

20 Baldassare Peruzzi, plan of the set for the *Bacchides* performed in Rome in 1531

21 Tracing of a sixteenth-century sketch, probably for Ludovico Ariosto's *I suppositi*

22　Comic set by Baldassare Peruzzi

23　Orazio Vecchi, *L'Amfiparnaso*

24   Terence's *Heautontimorumenos*

25   Adriano Banchieri, *Il donativo di quattro asinissimi personaggi*

26　The Teatro Olimpico in Vicenza, 1580–5

27　Seventeenth-century theatre: drawing by Giovanni Francesco Barbieri
known as 'il Guercino'

28 Perspective street: scenographic drawing attributed to Francesco Salviati, sixteenth century

29 *Il granchio*, comedy by Leonardo Salviati

30 Baldassare Lanci, set for Giovanbattista Cini's *La vedova*, performed in Florence in 1569

31 Device to simulate the waves of the sea, eighteenth century

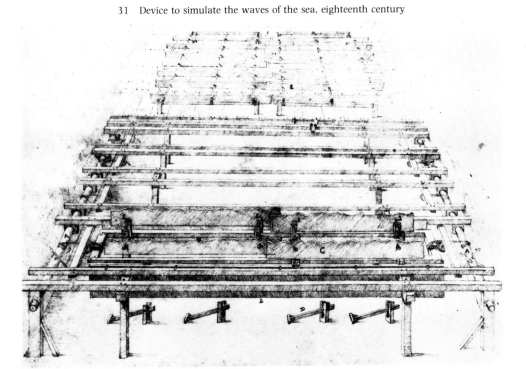

32   Bernardo Buontalenti, set 'for the first *intermedio*', commonly linked to the 1586
Florentine festivals; on that occasion the first *intermedio* was *Giove invia i beni sulla terra*

33   The Medicean Uffizi theatre: engraving by J. Callot from G. Parigi, for the first *intermedio*
of the *Liberazione di Tirreno ed Arnea autori del sangue toscano*, performed in Florence in 1617
(Florentine style 1616)

34 Bernardo Buontalenti, *L'armonia delle sfere*, first *intermedio* to G. Bargagli's *La pellegrina*, performed in Florence, in the Uffizi theatre 1589

35 Bernardo Buontalenti, *La disfida delle Muse e delle Pieridi*, second *intermedio* for the 1589 entertainment

36　Bernardo Buontalenti, *Apollo e Pitone*, third *intermedio* for the 1589 entertainment

37　Bernardo Buontalenti, *Ade*, fourth *intermedio* for the 1589 entertainment

38   Bernardo Buontalenti, *Anfitrite e Arione*, fifth *intermedio* for the 1589 entertainment

39   Bernardo Buontalenti, *L'Armonia e il Ritmo donati agli uomini dagli dei*, sixth *intermedio*
for the 1589 entertainment

40 *Il tempio della Pace*, sixth *intermedio* for *Il giudizio di Paride*, comedy by Michelangelo
Buonarroti il Giovane, performed for the wedding of Cosimo dei Medici and Maria Maddelena
of Austria

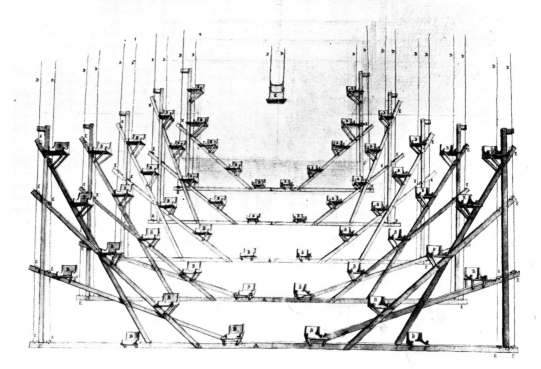

41   Francesco Guitti, 'Device for fifty-four persons', a machine designed for the joust
Mercurio e Marte which was the opening performance at the Teatro Farnese in Parma (1628)

one of the many elements contributing to the projection of that basic outline across the footlights; it was seldom more important than stage design, costumes, acting, the jokes of the comic characters, and, last but not least, what would now be called 'special effects'. The fact that music was only one of the many ingredients in the theatrical recipe explains the great difference of musical interest – one could say of musical dosage – in the various surviving scores. Impassioned recitative is still the centre of attention, alternating for the sake of variety with choruses and dances, in *La catena d'Adone* of 1626; but *Diana schernita* of 1629 (as far as we know, its most immediate successor) develops its satirical and even striptease-like action mainly in a plain parlando style, relieved by only one extensive song of Endymion (Act III) and by a choral finale in which, quite incongruously, Endymion's corpse is changed into the lily and golden bees of the Barberini arms. The parlando style is prominent in varying degrees in the Barberini operas that followed. In *San Bonifatio* (1638), not only is recitative seldom interrupted by arias, but further lack of musical variety is created by the fact – certainly due to the occasion and circumstances of the performance – that all characters, including the devil and a Spanish braggart soldier, are sopranos.[118]

On the whole, the most prominent feature of the Roman opera, and its most typical legacy to the genre, far from being its emphasis on the chorus (often confined to the detachable and interchangeable *intermedi*), lies in its affinity to – actually meant as a refinement of – the mode of performance of comedy. This affinity led, on one hand, to the kind of compelling drive that characterizes the rhythm of comedy and, on the other, since the 'comedy' is after all a musical one, to the creation of points of specific musical interest, functioning in most cases as either preparation or culmination of the 'comic' action – or as a temporary diversion. This does not mean that the 'comic' action was entirely devoid of musical interest; on the contrary, many of the procedures that lend remarkable musical interest to Cavalli's monologues and dialogues had already been attempted in the Roman opera.

The realistic procedure, the song as such, is by far the easiest way to introduce and justify passages of more specifically musical interest, as we have already seen while speaking of the pretexts for song invented by the librettists in Venice. In Venice, however, in the absence of the special conditions that had made Roman opera into a substitute for spoken theatre, the audience had to be gradually introduced to the novelty of operatic conventions. But realistic *cantar recitando* is by no means missing in Rome; we can take as an example scene 4 of Act II in *Chi soffre speri*, where the servants Zanni and Coviello – a Bergamask and a Neapolitan, both familiar characters in the *commedia dell'arte* – entertain a young shepherd and finally succeed in cheating him of his food while singing a *bergamasca* and a warlike song. Act III of the same opera is opened by the same shepherd, who praises his carefree life in a song. This is an obvious reminder of the pastoral tradition; at the same time, however, it is related to the practice of showing a character in the act of singing to himself while performing some usual chore or sport. The selection

---

[118] The Spanish soldier, Capitan Dragon y Vampa Sparaparapiglia, obviously derives from the *commedia dell'arte* and is paradoxically inserted in a classic plot. The 'comedy' was probably performed by young students of a college; a manuscript libretto in the Biblioteca Casanatense in Rome (cod. 1293) includes the *intermedi*, in one of which the difficulties of an all-soprano cast are discussed and a reference is made to the diminutive stature of the performers.

and content of the song, and the activity in which he is involved, as well as additional recitative, are all intended to provide an insight into his personality. Shepherds, young girls picking flowers and adorning themselves, or minor gods stepping on stage to deliver some message, are most likely to be introduced in such a way. The procedure is even more straightforward with comic characters, whose monologue scenes often become a direct address to the audience with satirical or ribald remarks on contemporary life – an even more ludicrous situation when the character is a mythological figure expected to have classic composure.[119]

Serious characters lend themselves less easily to a straightforward singing situation. In their case the monologue takes the shape of a recitative with ups and downs of emotional intensity and occasional changes of mood. Yet Stefano Landi did not hesitate to conclude the monologue introducing Sant'Alessio to the audience (Act I scene 2) with a two-strophe *arietta* summing up the saint's meditation on the vanity of life.[120] In *La catena d'Adone* (Act III scene 1) a philosopher's anguished reflections on Falsirena's rash actions periodically revert to a *mezz'aria* in which he states that 'reason is the loser where sensual passion prevails'.[121] In Monteverdi's *Il ritorno d'Ulisse* (Act I scene 1), the description of things 'returning' in nature assumes aria-like features in Penelope's long self-introductory monologue (the short interruptions of Ericlea do not alter the basic situation); then the thought of Ulysses' continued absence brings the recitative back to a more impassioned (and, therefore, also musically relevant) conclusion.

Penelope's monologue and Alessio's meditation facilitate the transition to lament and prayer, the most impressive set-piece conventions of the early opera, for both of which Monteverdi's example was a decisive contribution. I name the lament first because it had been largely exploited even before the one sung by Arianna in 1608 moved the audience to tears and impressed itself in the mind of every music-loving Italian. After *Arianna* composers became so conscious of the effectiveness of the lament that they abused it to the point of caricature. This is the case in *Aretusa*, which opens with Alfeo declaring to the audience his unrequited love for Aretusa, followed by Aretusa troubled by a menacing dream, by her father fretting over some obscure premonition, by her brother worrying lest something should happen to her while hunting, by a shepherd bringing on stage the sad news of her death and of Alfeo's despair, then by Alfeo himself and a dismal choral finale. A few cases of *cantar recitando* and choruses do not provide sufficient relief from this orgy of musical deploration.

---

[119]   Mercury or one of the Muses is most often cast in such a role.

[120]   Modern edition in Goldschmidt, *Studien...italienischen Oper*, I, pp. 208–9.

[121]   See my 'Falsirena e la più antica delle cavatine', in *Collectanea Historiae Musicae*, II (1957), pp. 355–6, including a partial transcription. We have coined the term *arioso* for this kind of transition from a declamatory pattern to a full, even though short-winded, melody. The seventeenth century used, if any, a number of different expressions. One is *mezz'arie*, mentioned in the index of *La catena d'Adone* as present in the score, but not listed. See Stuart Reiner, 'Vi sono molt'altre mezz'arie...', in *Studies in Music History: Essays for Oliver Strunk* (Princeton 1968), pp. 241–58. Short, not formally organized, melodic passages are sometimes labelled *ariette* or even *arie* in the score of the anonymous *Pio Enea* and of Marazzoli's *Amore trionfante dello Sdegno* (both performed about 1641–2). The inconsistency with which the two terms are used should not be surprising considering that even full-fledged arias were not always so labelled, either out of carelessness in the copying or because of the obviousness of their being arias. Finally, the word *cavata*, which I indicated to be the antecedent of *cavatina*, appears in some later scores, such as the Viennese copy of Sartorio's *Orfeo*.

The lament was initially conceived as a madrigalistic recitative, yet was already formalized to some degree in Peri's *Funeste piagge* and Monteverdi's *Lasciatemi morire*. During the 1620's it borrowed from the rising *cantada* the form of an *ostinato* aria, which I have already qualified as one sort of recitative set piece.[122] Even later, when the contrast between recitative and *ostinato* had lost its impressiveness through repetition, the lament became a plaintive aria, usually prepared by a recitative, and occasionally, but not necessarily, breaking into recitative at its climax.

Even more personal a contribution was the prayer of Act III of Monteverdi's *Orfeo*, where the double version in the score provides us the privilege of catching some glimpse of the growth of a poetic conception. There is no doubt in my mind that the unornamented version of this piece is not a schematic one, to be embellished at will by the performer, but a full realization of the prayer following the oratorical principles of the early *stile rappresentativo*.[123] It is also a prayer in the familiar terms of human misery and of confident hope in a superhuman power. It took a stroke of genius, after having quite effectively conceived the whole series of strophic recitative variations on a repeated bass line,[124] to give the same basic material – the same aria I would call it, and not in a merely formal sense – a completely new and more sophisticated twist, reworking it into an 'orphic' rite, a highly stylized and hieratically formalized incantation, through which a superhuman singer soothes and subdues the forces of darkness crossing his path.

Both as a prayer and as an incantation Orpheus' song left its mark on history. No less than three prayers are included in *Sant'Alessio*: one is the *arietta* mentioned above, an invocation to death to come; a second one is a chorus (Act I scene 5) asking divine protection for Alessio 'wherever he may be'; and the third is again a strophic aria (Act II scene 7), saluting the arrival of death, at last, announced by an angel to Alessio.[125] Another prayer is addressed to Juno by Psyche in *Amore innamorato* (Venice 1642; Act II scene 4), but its music is no longer extant. Aside from these examples, prayers are not too common in the world of opera. We need not to be surprised that the three included in *Sant'Alessio* all follow an aria-like pattern, considering that more than a quarter of a century had lapsed since *Orfeo*. We have more reason for wonder when the magician Falsirena of *La catena d'Adone* evokes Pluto in an '[*aria*] *recitativa per ottave*.'[126] *La catena d'Adone* is probably the last among the Roman operas in which the ideals of the early *stile rappresentativo* are still applied in full vigour. Furthermore, Falsirena's evocation of Pluto is interpreted as a prohibited formula to be uttered in secrecy; the same penumbral concept also applies to Pluto when he reluctantly answers Falsirena's questions, again in a *recitativa per ottave*.

There must have been many other examples of the incantation aria, for

---

[122]   See above, p. 268.

[123]   The full artistic validity of both versions is strongly asserted by the direction at the head of the piece in the 1609 print (p. 52): 'Orpheus sings only one [or 'either one'] of the two parts to the accompaniment of the wooden organ and one *chitarrone*' ('Orfeo al suono del Organo di Legno, & un chitarrone, canta una sola de le due parti').

[124]   The text is a Dantesque *terza rima*, six threè-line verses plus a concluding line. The rhythm of the bass pattern is freely organized, but substantially altered only in the fifth *terzina* and in the final line.   [125]   Goldschmidt. *Studien...italienischen Oper*, I, pp. 217–23 and 230–1.

[126]   Both Falsirena's and Pluto's *arie recitative* are set to a bass pattern repeated for the two halves of the *ottava*.

magicians and enchantresses abound in seventeenth-century opera, as, for that matter, in most of operatic history. Monteverdi's counterpart of Falsirena, the shadowy project of his *Armida*, is to us nothing more than a title;[127] but Armida returns in *Erminia sul Giordano* (Rome 1633), where, with the help of theatrical machinery, she suddenly conjures up the walls of Jerusalem merely because she wants to know how the siege is progressing. She regains the title role in Benedetto Ferrari's *Armida* (Venice 1639) and has a sister in his *La maga fulminata* (Venice 1638). She is the leading female character in *Amore trionfante dello Sdegno* (Ferrara 1641 and 1642), music by Marazzoli to a libretto by Ascanio Pio di Savoia.[128] But plots in which Armida appears are not the only ones to include magic. We need only recall Luigi Rossi's *Il palazzo incantato d'Atlante* (Rome 1642), in which the machinations of magicians form the central theme. Either the scores are lost or composers did not continue to utilize scenes of magic and incantation, for the only other example I can mention from this time is the well-known one of Medea in Cavalli's *Giasone* (Venice 1649).

Monteverdi was also the originator, as far as we know, of the musical description of madness, another operatic feature which enjoyed some success with composers and audiences. Although related to the monologue – it is indeed a monologue even though other characters may be present – the dramatic sequence of musical folly is a comic one, committed not to a crescendo of emotional intensity, but to abrupt shifts from one idea to another, on which the mad character (or the simulator of madness) concentrates time after time with utmost intensity. In Monteverdi's words,

since the imitation of...madness must only consider the situation as it is present, not in its past or future; and since, consequently, the imitation must rest upon each individual concept, not upon the meaning of the whole sentence, then the mention of 'war' shall require imitation of war, 'peace' of peace, 'death' of death, and so forth. Also, since the transitions and imitations shall be enacted in quick succession, she who is entrusted with a role of such primary importance, which moves to laughter and sympathy, such a lady shall of necessity omit any imitation other than the momentary one suggested by the prescribed text.[129]

The role described by Monteverdi is that of 'Licori finta pazza inamorata d'Aminta', to which a larger number of his extant letters refer than to any other of his works. His enthusiasm for this comic pastorale, which he completed in 1627 in a few months of happy work, but which never reached the stage, is made more tantalizing by the fact that both libretto and score are lost.

---

[127]   The earliest mention of this project is in a letter of 1 May 1627 to the younger Alessandro Striggio (see G. F. Malipiero, *Claudio Monteverdi*, Milan 1929, p. 250; C. Monteverdi, *Lettere, dediche e prefazioni*, ed. D. de' Paoli, Rome, 1973, p. 241). The following letters are mostly occupied with discussions of *La finta pazza Licori*; then two letters of 18 and 25 September, also addressed to Striggio, refer to *Armida* (G. F. Malipiero, *Claudio Monteverdi*, pp. 273–4; Monteverdi, *Lettere, dediche e prefazioni*, pp. 284–6. The first one of these letters mistakenly reads *Aminta*) as a work of vast dimensions which would require two months to be finished. *Armida* is mentioned once more in a letter of 18 December of the same year. Translations are provided in *The Letters of Claudio Monteverdi* translated and introduced by Denis Stevens (London 1980).

[128]   Manuscript score without a title in the Vatican Library, Chigi, Q VIII 189.

[129]   Translated from a letter to Striggio in Malipiero, (*Claudio Monteverdi*, p. 252; Monteverdi, *Lettere, dediche e prefazioni*, p. 244). My translation does not agree with those given by Leo Schrade, *Monteverdi: Creator of Modern Music* (New York 1950), pp. 309–10, and Stevens, *The Letters*.

Monteverdi, always faithful to the original comprehensive concept of *stile rappresentativo*, and more extreme in his application than any other musician, must have displayed in the score, and more particularly in the description of Licori's simulated madness, the full riches of musical invention that are present in its tragic counterpart, *Il combattimento di Tancredi e Clorinda* (circa 1626).[130] As it was later revived on the Venetian operatic stage, the 'imitation' of madness, real or simulated, must have relied more heavily on verbal expression, and consequently on a recitative relieved by short insertions of caricatural song. This much transpires, at least, from the only surviving score which contains scenes of folly, Cavalli's *Didone* (Venice 1640). There, furthermore, the sequence of Jarba's madness, although essentially comic, also sounds, if only briefly, a note of his misery. The scores of *La ninfa avara* and *La finta pazza* (both Venice 1641), in both of which madness is a central theme, are lost. To have the music of a similar scene one has to wait until Cesti's *Orontea* (Venice 1649), and then the delirious character is a secondary one and the cause no longer folly but drunkenness.[131]

To express himself in song still seemed incongruous for a serious character,[132] but incongruity, if any was still felt, could only make a comic one more comical. To come on stage singing one or another type of song placed an immediate label on the ribald or the coward, the glutton or the drunkard. In addition to that, comic characters also had a way of expressing their simple wisdom and coarse common sense in aphorisms and proverbs, which needed to be placed in quotation marks by the composer with a shift from *parlando* to an aria-like rhythm and pitch. The Roman *Chi soffre speri* (1637 and 1639) with its multitude of *commedia dell'arte* types provides all kinds of examples of how comic characters can be musically handled. In Venetian operas, following a series of dramatic upsets, a comic character often remains alone to make derogatory comments in an aria, with easy generalizations embodying his practical or cynical wisdom.

The tradition of giving comic characters simple tunes sounding like popular ones goes back to the last pastoral operas. Such are the songs of Pan in both *Flora* (Florence 1628) and *Diana schernita* (Rome 1629); in the former there is also a suggestion of pastoral amoebaean singing, for Pan's couplets expressing his unrequited love alternate with symmetrical, although differently tuned, rebukes of his beloved, also of a rather popular flavour. The popular sound is evident in the two-voice *arietta* of the pages Curtio and Martio in *Sant'Alessio* (Act I scene 3), with its thrice-repeated interlude (three times vocal imitation of instruments, the last time actually an instrumental *ritornello*);[133] this in turn compares with the *strambotti* sung by Zanni, Coviello, nymphs, and shepherds in the first *intermedio* of *Chi soffre speri*. The tradition was to be continued at least up to the time of Melani's *Tancia* (Florence 1657); since Tancia is a peasant girl, she and her rustic lover are

[130]   It is evident from Monteverdi's description that Licori's madness attracted him as an ideal situation for those extreme accents and abrupt shifts of mood that are typical of his *stile concitato*.
[131]   I have given a partial transcription of it following 'Le prime opere di Antonio Cesti' in Pietro Castiglia, ed., *L'orchestra* (Florence 1954), pp. 176–7.
[132]   See Francesco Sbarra: 'I know that such *ariette* as those sung by Alexander and Aristotle will be held to be adverse to the dignity of persons of such stature', translated from the foreword to the printed libretto (1652) of *Alessandro vincitor di sè stesso* (see *ibid.*, p. 164).
[133]   Goldschmidt, *Studien...italienischen Oper*, I, pp. 210–12.

entitled to similar songs.[134] Even without these or similar references to popular singing, however, comic *arie* usually have simple and direct rhythms and an almost syllabic rendering of the text.

To be sure, comic characters could also sing, on occasion, virtuoso or pathetic arias. The first is possible when a character engages in extensive vocalization either because he has pretentions or delusions of grandeur and prowess or simply because he stutters. Concerning the second type, it is a well-known fact that misadventures and despair of an essentially comic character produce a ludicrous affect, which is enhanced the more exaggeratedly pathetic his laments. In both cases, however, the comic effect is doubled by the awareness of the fact that the lowly character is usurping expressive conventions that belong to another class or type.

This leads me to the last of my present considerations, that of situations in which the self-consciousness of operatic conventions lends itself to intentional caricature. This is obviously the case, for instance, in *Chi soffre speri* (Act II scene 11), when the main character decides on, and 'laments', the sacrifice of his favourite falcon to the dinner table and is lamentably echoed by Zanne in his Bergamask dialect idiom, or else in the monologue of Iro in *Il ritorno d'Ulisse*, Act III scene 1.[135] More subtly, but on a larger scale, the parody of operatic conventions is a clue to *Il palazzo incantato d'Atlante* and *Orfeo* by Luigi Rossi (Rome 1642 and 1647) and to a later *Orfeo* (Venice 1672) by Antonio Sartorio.

No momentous conclusions are to be reached through my rambling survey of the conventions which lent opera (as a whole and in its individual aspects) some measure of *vraisemblance*. As it was in the best operatic tradition to end on a compendious choral aphorism, no comment could be here more appropriate than the line ending at once a Chorus of Phantoms and Act I of *Il palazzo incantato d'Atlante*: 'Oh, ch'è lieve ingannar chi tosto crede!' (How easy it is to delude he who wants to believe!).[136]

---

[134]   *Ibid.*, pp. 357–8.
[135]   In this category is also the parody of the incantation scene by Bruscolo in *Tancia*, Act III, *ibid.*, p. 371.
[136]   Originally this chapter had a slightly longer conclusion, in which reference was made to an as yet unrealized project: a discussion of the various uses of the term '*aria*'.

PART II Origins and aspects of Italian scenography (from the end of the fifteenth century to the Florentine *intermedi* of 1589)

ELENA POVOLEDO

1 From Poliziano's *Orfeo* to the *Orphei tragoedia*

These days it is normally assumed that *La fabula d'Orfeo* was presented on a medieval stage, one with sets to represent several places simultaneously, such as those used in Italy for religious plays. However, since a great deal of research[1] has failed to find anything which throws light on the staging of the Mantuan play, all we can do, if we want to get beyond vague generalities, is to refer directly to Poliziano's text. From the stage-directions, and even more from the characters' passing references accompanying and enlarging upon the action, it is in fact possible to find details which link the Mantuan *festa* to contemporary plays, both sacred and secular, and enable us to attempt a reconstruction of the original *mise-en-scène*.

The *Fabula*, which is narrated rather than acted, develops with no break in continuity from Aristaeus' amorous lament to the hideous wrath of the enraged Bacchantes. Despite sudden shifts in place and mood, one single set capable of being adapted to different uses was enough for the entire plot. This set was 'a prettily flowered shady hill', the surface strong enough to be walked on, the interior hollow. It must have been a machine (an *edifizio* rather than an *ingegno*) constructed on a movable waggon or on a stationary *tribunale*.[2] It could have been adapted with few problems to fit the decoration of tapestries and greenery prepared in the courtyard of the Ducal Palace or in one of its upstairs halls. For this was certainly, in Mantua as elsewhere, the typical setting of the sort of festival Cardinal Gonzaga wished to hold. A sizeable area of planking, or more simply just the floor of the room or courtyard, delineated by the tapestries and greenery, constituted the main acting area.

The action begins with a group of characters at the foot of the hill, by a cool spring beneath the shady leaves, where Aristaeus is telling Mopsus, an old man, of the pain his love is causing him. To the sound of Pan-pipes, he chants his beautiful, well-known song:

---

[1]   Cf. Pirrotta in part I, chapter 1 of this volume. On the possible staging of the Mantuan spectacle, see *inter alia* F. Neri, 'Poliziano, "Orfeo" e le Stanze', *Biblioteca Romanica* (1911), pp. 130–1. Without emphasizing the fact, he identified the 'practicable hill' as the only set required in Poliziano's *Fabula*. Although well argued, Ireneo Affò's idea of a pseudo-classical stage, along the lines of the Teatro Olimpico at Vicenza, is absurd: cf. *L'Orfeo tragedia di Messer Angelo Poliziano tratta per la prima volta da due vetusti codici, ed alla sua integrità e perfezione ridotto, ed illustrato dal Reverendo Padre Ireneo Affò* (Venice 1786), notes to the fourth or Necromantic act, also R. Rolland, *Musiciens d'autrefois* (Paris 1908), pp. 21–31.

[2]   In medieval stage terminology, a *tribunale* was a fixed scaffold, while an *edifizio* was a mobile waggon or float, on which could be set either a sculptured religious group or a stage supporting a *tableau vivant*. *Ingegni* were more complex constructions, equipped with mechanical devices to enable the machine to move, and largely used in religious drama. We shall return later to the *ingegni* of F. Brunelleschi and of Cecca, whose work represents the height of perfection achieved by these machines.

> Udite, selve, mie dolci parole,
> Poi che la Ninfa mia udir non vuole.

> Listen, O woods, to my sweet words,
> Since my own Nymph refuses to listen.

It proceeds with the arrival of Tirsis, who 'slides down' from the hill to announce Eurydice's presence nearby. Aristaeus promptly departs, clambering up the hill in search of his beloved nymph. Then Orpheus too descends from the hill, singing Latin verses in honour of the Mantuan cardinal and accompanying himself on his lyre. When a shepherd arrives bringing news of Eurydice's death, Orpheus pretends to leave the scene and wanders round the stage singing of his grief. While he is doing so, the gate of hell, closely guarded by Cerberus and the Furies, is revealed in the side of the hill.

The fact that this vision of the gate of hell had to be hidden from the audience at the start of the play makes the hypothesis that the set was a machine on wheels, and hence more easily turned around, preferable to that of a fixed platform. As we shall see, such a solution would have been neither new nor unusual. If however the mountain was stationary, all that would have been necessary was a closed door, which would have solved the problem according to the acceptable, though old-fashioned, medieval convention of sets with many mansions.

The door opened to reveal Pluto on his throne, flanked by Proserpina and Minos. It is not clear whether Sisyphus, Ixion, Tantalus and the Danaids would also have been visible, enthralled by Orpheus' song. They might have been, but not necessarily: it would have been simpler for Pluto merely to describe their state of trance. From the same door emerged first Eurydice and then the Fury who led her back to Hades. The final episode is set once more at the foot of the hill, where the Bacchantes, having torn Orpheus limb from limb off-stage, sing and dance their humanistic dithyramb.

As far as the staging of *Orfeo* is concerned, it is then obvious that medieval conventions prevailed over the humanistic ideas about the unities of time and place. But it is also true that Poliziano used only those elements of medieval convention which had already passed from sacred to secular drama, and he introduced, in place of allegory and eulogy, a more appealing note of intense pagan, and amorous emotion. Instead of a series of different sets, there was only one, which coped with both settings at once, while the effective evocation of places and images was left to the narrative and descriptive verses.

It is clear that Poliziano had no time to create an entirely novel style of staging in the few days allowed by the Cardinal for the devising and preparation of the play,[3] nor had he intended to. Instead, the *Fabula* reflects his youthful poetic style and whatever theatrical experience he had managed to acquire indirectly as a spectator in his first ten years at the Florentine court, or perhaps quite recently in Emilia or Venice during the 1480 carnival season, the time of his departure from Tuscany and his brief stay in Mantua.[4]

[3] Poliziano, in his dedicatory letter to Messer Carlo Canale, wrote: 'At the request of our Most Reverend Cardinal of Mantua, in the space of two days amid constant tumults, I had composed *La fabula d'Orfeo*, written in the vernacular so as to be better understood by the spectators.' This letter, recorded in the Borromeo, Riccardi, Oliveri and Chigi codices, was also published by I. Affò in the 1786 edition.

[4] I accept the suggestion, made by E. Tedeschi, 'La rappresentazione d'Orfeo' and 'La tragedia d'Orfeo', in *Atti e memorie dell' Accademia Virgiliana di Mantova*, new series XVII–XVIII (Mantua

In the Florence of Lorenzo the Magnificent, most theatrical entertainments were still a mixture of religious and popular festivals. The secularizing effect of the new Medicean culture, with its emphasis on worldly splendour, had not yet begun to change the old institutions or upset the official calendar. Year after year Poliziano had seen the processions in honour of the feast of St John, the *rappresentazioni* of the Annunciation and Pentecost, the festivals of St Batholomew and St Ignatius, and the popular jousts between the rival districts of the town. He would certainly have known the floats used for the sacred 'Triumphs' of St John (plates 2 and 3), the cloud-machines and the *edifizi*, as well as the *ingegni* described by Vasari – Brunelleschi's preserved in the church of San Felice (plate 11), and the one reconstructed by Cecca which belonged to the church of Santa Maria del Carmine. As recently as 1471, to celebrate the visit of Galeazzo Maria Sforza and Bona of Savoy, the main entertainments after the triumphal entrance had been *rappresentazioni* of the Annunciation, the Ascension and Pentecost. In the space of a few days three *ingegni* had been seen in operation in three different churches, and 'their extreme ingenuity caused the Lombards to admire them greatly'.[5] Contemporary accounts do not describe the three *ingegni* in detail, but it is certainly possible that the one still used at San Felice was Brunelleschi's, and not impossible that the one in the Carmine was reconstructed by Cecca for this very occasion. We know nothing of the third *ingegno*, in Santo Spirito, except that it made use of an excessive number of torches: during these same festivities of 1471 'the whole church caught fire because of the many lights lit for such occasions' (Machiavelli).

Cecca's set for the Ascension involved the erection of a hill in the middle of the presbytery of the church: 'Thus Christ was lifted from the top of a hill, most cunningly made of wood, and led to heaven by a cloud filled with angels, leaving the Apostles behind on the hill. It was wonderfully well done.' The 'Paradise', which was inserted beneath the roof directly above a central structure (*tribuna*), consisted of two hemispherical domes one inside the other, painted to resemble a starry sky. In the space between them were 'several large wheels, shaped like wool-winders, and set with large numbers of small candles to represent the stars. These wheels formed ten revolving rings, for the ten heavens, between the centre and the surface of the domes, in a most beautiful and orderly fashion.'[6]

However, *Orfeo* did not require a Paradise set above a hill, but a hill with hell inside it. Poliziano may have seen such hills on the floats used for the feast of St John, like the one admired by Eleanor of Aragon in June 1473, 'with the Resurrection, the descent into Limbo, and the freeing of the Holy

---

1925), pp. 47–74, that the play was staged between 20 March and 21 April 1480, and that it might have been performed in honour of the embassy sent by Ludovico Sforza and led by Giovanni Borromei to renew the 1472 treaties. Pirrotta does not entirely agree with this opinion.

    [5] *Istorie Fiorentine di Scipione Ammirato con l'aggiunta di Scipione Ammirato il giovane* (Florence 1647), vol. XXIII, p. 107. The Sforza visit is also documented in N. Machiavelli, *Storie fiorentine*, vol. VII, p. 28, and in *Ricordi storici di Cino Rinuccini dal 1282 al 1460, con la continuazione di Alamanno e Neri suoi figli fino al 1506 ecc.*, ed. G. Aiazzi (Florence 1840). From Vasari we know that Cecca opened his own workshop in about 1471.

    [6] *Le vite de' più eccellenti pittori scultori ed architettori scritte da Giorgio Vasari pittore aretino, con nuove annotazioni e commenti di Gaetano Milanesi* (Florence 1906); *Vita di Francesco d'Angelo detto il Cecca*, vol. III, pp. 197ff.

Fathers'.[7] Or perhaps he was remembering more pleasing ones used by revellers in a secular context. The idea of a hollow hill, with one side open, belching forth flames and damned souls amidst the clanking infernal wheels and chains, was by no means new in medieval theatrical or pictorial iconography (plate 5). But Poliziano's Hades is a hell at peace:

> Io veggo fissa d'Issïon la rota,
> Sisifo assiso sopra la sua petra,
> e le Belide star con l'urna vota.

I see Ixion's wheel stilled, Sisyphus seated on his rock, and the Danaids standing with empty urns.

This vision of rapture had nothing to do with the horrors of damnation, and this must have made it easier for the poet's imagination to return to the beautifully decorated floats used in the palace entertainments to accompany the encomiastic eclogues or usher in the *entremets*. Even if Poliziano had not seen these in Florence, where the Petrarchan *Trionfi*[8] were perhaps preferred, he would certainly have heard them described by the Medicean ambassadors. And people still remembered the great festivities held in 1475 in Pesaro in honour of the wedding of Costanzo Sforza and Camilla of Aragon. We are familiar with these through a precious manuscript illustrated by Lionardo da Colle, which was written, or at least finished, in 1480.[9]

Thus on Monday 28 May 'a great banquet' was held at court as part of a reception. The hall of the palace was 'festooned with garlands in the classical style, thick with greenery', and decorated with a 'sky', an artifical ceiling of dark-blue cloth with the signs of the zodiac in gold on it, each the size of a man. The stars were made of mirrors, with silver rays, and beside each sign of the zodiac was portrayed the face of its champion: Perseus, Pylades, the Hydra and so on. Gifts were presented before the banquet, and this ceremony was accompanied by mimed and danced *intermedi*, brought into the hall on large allegorical floats. The Hill of the Wild Man, on which the courtiers' gifts were shown, the Queen of Sheba on an elephant carrying

---

[7] Letter by Eleanor of Aragon to her father, dated 24 June 1473, in C. Corvisieri, 'Il trionfo romano di Eleonora d'Aragona nel giugno 1473', *Archivio della Società Romana di Storia Patria*, I (1878), p. 655. Another description of this spectacle has been reprinted in *La commedia del Cinquecento*, vol. II (Series *Il teatro italiano*) ed. G. Davico Bonino (Turin 1977), pp. 398–9.

[8] Triumphs (*trionfi*) were mobile allegorical spectacles commonly used in Italy to celebrate weddings, town festivals and formal entrances into cities. Of literary origin, they were modelled on the Roman triumphs, but later developed into processions of various sorts of differently inspired allegorical floats. Some were celebrations of one individual, such as the triumph of Alfonso of Aragon in Naples in 1443, while others were of basically Roman inspiration, like the one Lorenzo the Magnificent intended to insert into the Florentine procession for the feast of St John. Yet others were scenes derived from descriptions in Francesco Petrarca's *Trionfi*. Cf. on this topic, and on medieval Florentine spectacle in general, C. Molinari, *Spettacoli fiorentini del Quattrocento* (Venice 1961), especially on the *trionfi d'Amore* (triumphs of Love), pp. 16–17.

[9] *Ordine de le noze de lo Illustrissimo Signor Misir Costantio Sfortia de Aragonia: et de la Illustrissima Madona Camilia de Aragonia sua consorte nel anno MCCCCLXXV adi infrascripto*, preserved in the Vatican Museum, Urbinate Codex 899. The description was reprinted several times, though without the miniatures. These however were published by Tammaro De Marinis under the title of *Le nozze di Costanzo Sforza e Camilla d'Aragona celebrate a Pesaro nel 1475* (Rome 1946). The codex, 'written in the hand of Lionardo da Colle servant of the most illustrious master Costantio' is dated 1480, and De Marinis thinks that it was written at the request of Federico da Montefeltro, Duke of Urbino, who had been present at the wedding. The codex is in fact to be found in the Urbinate collection of the Vatican Library.

offerings from the Jews, the Hill of the Israelites, and the 'Company of the Seven Planets on seven small square classical chariots' – all these paraded through the hall. The two mountains were made of wood, 'painted and covered with trees and greenery and various animals, such as hares, goats, deer, bears, rabbits, etc. They were devised with great ingenuity, and easily moved without it being possible to see who was carrying them or who was inside them.' From the first hill emerged the Wild Man and a man disguised as a lion, who fought each other. They were followed by fourteen *morescanti*, who 'came from two sides, almost as if from two grottoes in the hill'. The second hill was surmounted by a 'tower' containing a 'sprite', and on one side had a gate and a drawbridge, out of which came a Jewish elder and twelve *morescanti* (plates 1 and 4).

Federico da Montefeltro and ambassadors from the main Italian cities, certainly including Florence and Mantua, witnessed the festival. In any case, the spectacle at Pesaro, though magnificent, was nothing new. Cardinal Francesco Gonzaga, who spent part of the year living in Rome, knew the entertainments sponsored by the Riario cardinals, and had himself held similar ones at his home near the Campo Marzio. One such entertainment was put on for the New Year of 1476, though no use of floats was made in it. It was described in a letter by the Duke of Milan's representative, Giovanni Marco:

The dinner was splendid, and when it was over there was a fine show of the conflict between the Virtues and the Vices. All the Virtues appeared in female dress and with disguised and painted faces; they were followed by the Vices. A debate was held before the king, as to whether one should lead an Epicurean life or follow the path of Virtue. Then the followers of Vice danced, sword in hand. The Virtues defeated the Vices, and thus the entertainment ended at the sixth hour of night.[10]

The king, probably a 'king of Love', was played by a certain Brugnollo, a young page and one of the cardinal's favourites. 'A handsome youth, beardless and attractive', he presided over the banquet seated at the head of the table, dressed in the robes of a king and decked with jewellery.

The carnival banquet of Cardinal Gonzaga, the parading floats at Pesaro in 1475, and the many other *intramesse* which flourished throughout Italy in the fifteenth century and survived in certain forms into the sixteenth cannot really be considered as true drama. Yet the particular solution adopted by the Mantuan producers of *Orfeo*, half-way between a stage-set and a decoration, was evidently devised in, and justified by, the same context and the same specific conditions of place, action and occasion. In the long run, as Pirrotta rightly maintains,[11] it greatly influenced not only the style of staging, but also the dramatic conception of many of the so-called hybrid dramas.

But whether it was still linked to the formula of convivial diversions and of masquerades, or whether it had already evolved into a recited eclogue, a farce or a fable, the *intermedio* entertainment continued to be seen as an

---

[10]   The letter is quoted by A. D'Ancona in *Le origini*, II, p. 69. That Cardinal Gonzaga, Bishop of Mantua and later of Bologna, also had a house in the Campo Marzio in Rome is borne out by Burckhardt in his Diary: cf. 'Johannis Burckardi Liber Notarum', ed. E. Celani in *Rerum Italicarum Scriptores* (Bologna and Città di Castello 1907–) vol. I, p. 233 note.

[11]   Cf. Pirrotta, part I, chapter 2 above.

integral part of the feast and its ceremonial. In general it remained itinerant, mixing dance and mime, song and recited tribute. Imaginative invention was subordinated to panegyric, and personal allusions or references to recent events were used to up-date each 'fable', so that it appeared to take place in the present. There was no need for a set which would evoke times or places beyond the festival or isolate the illusion in artificial time or space other than those in which the audience lived. All that was required was simply a decorative framework, which would include the festivities themselves, from the palace gate to the dais of the guest of honour. The 'king' of the banquet in Rome, before whom the Vices fought against the Virtues, was involved in the feast. Similarly in Pesaro the bride and groom were involved, through the offerings made to them, while the courtiers themselves danced with the *morescanti* brought in on the great allegorical floats.[12]

Were we assured that we can assimilate the hill of Poliziano's *Orfeo* to those used at Pesaro, then its novelty would have been that the stage machine was divested of its allegorical significance and assumed a primarily scenic function. Seen in this way, not only did the hill represent the woods and Hades, which were the two main settings of the action, but it could also be walked on, so that part of the action could actually take place on it.

Unfortunately, contemporary sources do not support this theory, for they do not so much as mention the names of the set designers, if indeed a set was used, nor that of the director of the festival. It could not possibly have been Poliziano, who was new to such things, and was unlikely to have been Baccio Ugolini, the first Orpheus, for, though he was a poet, musician and lyre-player, there is no evidence that he was skilled in the figurative arts. Alessandro D'Ancona[13] suggests that the man responsible might have been Zafrano, who in 1483, and probably earlier too, was the jester of the Marquis of Mantua. Though jesters were still expected to possess the traditional quality of *jucunditatis lepos* (the amusement of wit/jollity), the nature of their job was actually quite complex by the end of the fifteenth century. There were all sorts

---

[12] Fifteenth-century Italian chronicles are full of descriptions of festivals of this sort. Besides D'Ancona's definitive work, *Le origini*, II, *passim*, one has but to consult more specialized works such as P. Ghinzoni's articles in *Archivio storico lombardo*, 'Nozze e commedie alla corte di Ferrara nel 1491', XI (1884), pp. 752ff, 'Trionfi e rappresentazioni in Milano (secoli XIV–XVI)', XIV (1887), pp. 820–31, and 'Alcune rappresentazioni in Italia nel secolo XV', XX (1893), pp. 958–67; and the works of A. Luzio and R. Renier on the Mantuan court, more particularly, *Delle relazioni di Isabella d'Este Gonzaga con Ludovico e Beatrice Sforza* (Milan 1890); 'Buffoni, schiavi e nani dei Gonzaga', in *Nuova Antologia*, XXVI (August 1891); *Mantova e Urbino* (Turin 1893); 'La coltura e le relazioni letterarie di Isabella d'Este Gonzaga' in *Giornale storico della letteratura italiana*, XXXIII (1899) and XXXV (1900). Also, by A. Luzio alone, *Isabella d'Este e Francesco Gonzaga sposi* (Milan 1908); *Isabella d'Este e i Borgia* (Milan 1915); *L'archivio Gonzaga di Mantova* (Ostiglia 1920/1). Entertainments of this sort survived for quite some time in Venice and were promptly noted down by Marin Sanudo in his *Diarii* (printed in Venice between 1879 and 1902). There exists, in manuscript 1650, fasc. XIV, of the Marciana Library in Venice, a valuable summary of these festivities: 'Articoli estratti dai Diarii di Marino Sanudo concernenti notizie storiche di Commedie, Momarie, Feste e Compagnie della Calza'. Forthcoming are M. T. Muraro, 'La festa a Venezia e le sue manifestazioni rappresentative: La Compagnia della Calza e le Momarie' in a new volume of *Storia della cultura veneta* (N. Pozza, Vicenza), and E. Povoledo, 'Accademie, feste e spettacoli alla corte di Caterina Cornaro' in the proceedings of the meeting on 'La letteratura, la rappresentazione, la musica al tempo e nei luoghi di Giorgione' held in Castelfranco Veneto in 1978. See also the description on pp. 10–11 above.

[13] D'Ancona, *Le origini*, II, p. 361. The real name of Zafrano, or Zafarano, was Ercole Albergati.

of jester, and by then many of them no longer resembled the medieval 'jesting fool', but had become more like professional actors, able to cope with sophisticated spectacles and to organize elegant festivals.

Zafrano was an actor, a poet, a stage-designer and an inventor of mechanical devices. He was in the service of the Gonzagas at least from 1483, and was famous throughout Italy. Alfonso of Aragon, Ludovico Sforza 'Il Moro', and Giovanni Bentivoglio all sought his services. In 1495, to mention just one of the spectacles in which he excelled, he took part in the entertainment organized for the carnival at the Mantuan court. Besides the banquet and the ball, there was a mobile entertainment of the type already mentioned, the main attraction of which was an allegorical farce by Serafino Aquilano. It was followed by an allegory of Zafrano's, 'written by him and composed entirely of his own family, for in Modesty's triumphal cart were four of his children, two boys and two girls, the elder daughter on the summit of the float between two unicorns'. When they reached the guests, the child first recited some verses in Latin, 'with good courage, great modesty and excellent pronunciation', and then some verses in Italian dedicated to the Marquis Francesco Gonzaga.[14]

D'Ancona's theory that Zafrano was involved in the production of 1480 cannot be confirmed, though it is known that subsequently the artist, together with Filippo Lapaccino, was twice charged by the Mantuan court with the preparation of a new performance of *Orfeo*. Both productions were planned to honour Ercole d'Este: the first to be presented at Marmirolo in November 1490, the second at Gonzaga in June 1491. Neither production took place. In 1490 Atalante Migliorotti, who was to have played Orpheus, failed to reach Mantua in time, and in 1491 it proved impossible to complete the necessary preparations in the few days available before the arrival of the Duke of Ferrara. We know little of this stage apparatus, which the two producers considered so important, merely that several enormous 'centaurs' were planned, probably for use in the final Bacchanal,[15] and that the execution of the set design was to be in the hands of two painters, Tondo de Tondi and Luca Leonbeni, at that time busy decorating the villa of Marmirolo.

Atalante Migliorotti, a citharist and accomplished singer, in the service of the Medici court in 1490, was also a close friend of Leonardo da Vinci, who

[14]   The description is to be found in a letter written by Giovanni Gonzaga, brother of the marquis, to his sister-in-law Isabella, then in Milan. This letter is reprinted in *Dalle origini al Quattrocento* vol. II (Series *Il teatro italiano*), ed. E. Faccioli (Turin 1975), p. 700. On Zafrano's activities see D'Ancona, *Le origini*, II, p. 360ff. Serafino Aquilano's farce (published several times including 1877 in Naples where it appeared under the title of *Rappresentazione allegorica data in Mantova nel 1495*) consisted of three allegorical monologues on Pleasure, Virtue and Fame, and the actors made their appearance on floats: see D'Ancona, *Le origini*, II, pp. 365ff.

[15]   Antimaco, charged along with Zafrano and Lapaccino with organizing the spectacle, wrote to the duke on 31 May 1491: 'The centaurs, should they be brought in, need a lot of space: they will leap about as much as they can.' E. Tedeschi, in 'La rappresentazione d'Orfeo', believed that the centaurs were intended for the Hades scene, but surely they are connected more with Dionysiac rites than with the Underworld.

For biographical information on F. Lapaccino, priest, organist, singer and writer of plays, see D'Ancona, *Le origini*, II, p. 358. On Atalante Migliorotti, who, it would appear, at the end of his life served Leo X as architect and supervisor of the papal buildings, see Giorgio Vasari, *Le vite*, ed. G. Milanesi (Florence 1906), vol. IV, p. 53 note 4. On the two painters Tondi and Leonbeni, see S. Davari, *Le ville dei Gonzaga a Marmirolo* (Mantua 1890).

had taught him to play the lyre in his youth, and in 1483 had taken him to the Sforza court in Milan. Because of this friendship, Kate Traumann Steinitz has linked the two performances planned for 1490 and 1491 with two of Leonardo's drawings, now in the Arundel Codex. They depict, in a series of hasty and unfinished sketches, a revolving set of hell, and the machinery to move it. The apparatus could assume two different shapes. The first was a mountainous scene, dominated by a central peak surrounded by a deep valley, perhaps part of the acting area, which was in turn enclosed by a circle of mountains sloping gently away into the distance. The second set was the same as the first, except that the central mountain was opened to reveal the kingdom of Pluto in its hollow interior. Some plans and various technical notes reveal that the central mountain was built on a revolving disk and that the set changed from one form to the other in full view of the audience (plates 8, 9 and 10).[16]

Kate Steinitz has also suggested that the text to be performed in 1490 or 1491 was not Poliziano's original *Fabula*, but the later version known as the *Orphei tragoedia*. Carlo Pedretti, while not abandoning the idea of a new performance of *Orfeo*, suggested 1506–7 as an alternative date for the Leonardo sketches, reckoning that they might have been intended for the court of Charles d'Amboise, the French Governor of Milan, whom Leonardo served between 1506 and 1511. On the basis of the surviving reports, Pedretti's suggestion is the more convincing. Even if Leonardo had drawn the sets simply to please his friend Atalante, and it was impossible for them to be constructed in the eight days available, it seems inconceivable that Atalante would not have conveyed Leonardo's ideas to Mantua, or that Zafrano and, even more, Francesco Gonzaga would then have ignored them and been content to turn to the two painters employed at Marmirolo.

By changing the date, we may even think that they planned to perform a third version – *La favola di Orfeo e Aristeo* – or else another text unconnected with *Orfeo*. But before linking Leonardo's set to one of the versions of *Orfeo*, or to a further unknown work, we must return to a problem merely hinted at above in connection with the 'Mountain–Hades' set of 1480 modelled on the Pesarese floats of 1475. It was not resolved there, because we cannot depend on the analysis of intentions which can only be derived from indirect literary evidence. The problem is to establish how far one can attribute to Poliziano, or to those who adapted his work, the resulting staging technique, which was incapable of rejecting the medieval tradition, but somehow

[16] The Arundel Codex 263 is in the British Museum. Folio 231v shows the plan of the scene with the rotatory apparatus, the cross-section of the cave with Pluto, and other sketches with the plan of the revolving platform, the plan of one side of the hall with an indication 'here they dress', the jars for the playing devils and an upright pole supporting a curtain.

The second folio, 224r, shows the mountainous set, the open mountain, and a device to turn the machine.

F. Malaguzzi Valeri, *La corte di Ludovico il Moro* (Milan 1915) related the scene to *La festa del Paradiso*. K. Traumann Steinitz made a careful study of the two drawings in 'A reconstruction of Leonardo da Vinci's Revolving Stage', *Art Quarterly*, XII (1949), pp. 325–38. She supervised as Roberto Guatelli produced a model which reconstructed Leonardo's *ingegno* and this was shown at the Leonardo da Vinci Exhibition in Los Angeles. A second model was built by J. T. Jones to the specifications of C. Pedretti and K. Traumann Steinitz for the Elmer Belt Library of Vinciana, at the University of California at Los Angeles. On this model, which differs from Guatelli's, see C. Pedretti, 'Dessins d'une scène, exécutés par Léonard de Vinci pour Charles d'Amboise (1506–1507)', *Le lieu théâtral à la Renaissance*, ed. J. Jacquot (Paris, 1964), pp. 25ff.

acknowledged the humanist idea of unity. To what extent were humanist perceptions superimposed on medieval structures, or even absorbed in them?

This is a set of problems which extends beyond *Orfeo*. It originated in the casual mixing of dramatic genres which characterized the end of the fifteenth century. It was helped by the coexistence without attrition of tried and tested stage techniques with the new intellectual curiosity of humanism, which was stimulating but not yet strong enough to bring about completely new forms. The problems involve the whole theatrical production, drama, music and pantomime, between 1480 and 1508, i.e. from the Mantuan festival at which *Orfeo* was performed to the presentation of *La cassaria* at Ferrara, which established the new parameters of Renaissance staging, based on the perspective set. As Pirrotta makes clear, 'hybrid drama' and performances of classical works intermingle in this ill-defined but fertile ground of old and new, so much so that one must consider as 'hybrid' not only texts like *Caephalo*, *Danae* or the two *Timone*,[17] but also the comedies of Terence and Plautus, which become hybrid through the intervention of the translator–adaptor or of the artist responsible for the presentation.

The problems arose, though still in embryonic form, when a new dramaturgic structure involving a plot divided into acts and insisting on the revival at all costs of the three unities of time, place and action, was grafted onto the traditional system.

As *Orfeo* shows, both sacred and secular medieval plays involved continuous action, self-contained to the point of justifying contact between actors and audience. But this continuity was the result of an ambiguous and conventional interpretation of time and space, while the humanist unities were a rational attempt to free the conventions of all ambiguity, and to confer on them a purely scenic and dramatic value. For the academicians of the Renaissance, time, place and action had to be real unities, the action developed as a unified whole, in the length of a solar day, in the unchanging square or street of a city. If this conception was to accept compromise it was in a new way which we shall deal with later. This consisted either in the acceptance of a set linked to a dramatic genre rather than to the requirements of the individual texts, or else in the use of acted *intermedi* to re-establish the continuity which had been broken by the division of the play into acts.

By the recurrent use of multiple and simultaneous mansions,[18] the stage used for medieval sacred plays stressed visually the idea of unlimited time and space, unlimited because these qualities were already implicit in the sacred

---

[17]   Niccolò da Correggio's *La fabula de Caephalo* (ed. in *Opere*, Venice 1513) was performed in Ferrara during the 1486 carnival season. B. Taccone's *Danae* (nuptial edition, Bologna 1888) was performed in Milan in the palace of Giovanni Francesco Sanseverino, Count of Cajazzo, on 31 January 1496. M. M. Boiardo's *Timone* (ed. Scandiano 1500) was written to please Ercole I d'Este, and no one knows if it was performed. Galeotto del Carretto's *La comedia di Timon greco* (ed. Turin 1878) was written in 1498. On the different versions of *Orfeo*, see Pirrotta, pp. 42–46 above. Correggio's *Caephalo*, Boiardo's *Timone* and Poliziano's *La fabula di Orfeo* are all now available in *Dalle origini al Quattrocento*, vol. II.

[18]   The two medieval stage arrangements most common in Europe were the so-called 'set in the French style', with all the mansions side by side in a single line on one stage and viewed from the front, and the so-called 'set in the German style' with mansions on individual stages disposed around an open space such as a square, a courtyard or a market, and viewed in the round. The *ingegni*, of which much has been written in this book, were a typical Italian solution, while the Perran Round theatres were Celtic.

event protrayed, itself eternal and continuously present. Similarly, secular performances, with or without floats, left the imaginary space and time of allegory undefined, but linked them constantly with the present by means of eulogistic passages which turned the allegory into a homage, adapting it to the one spectator it was meant to honour.

Viewed in this way, Poliziano's *Fabula* was still linked in some ways to the medieval conception of uninterrupted time and space, but it was presented without either the mystic support of sacred and therefore eternal significance, or that of a laudatory intention. The Latin ode sung by Orpheus and addressed to Cardinal Gonzaga is a self-contained interpolation which could easily be omitted. I do not believe that Poliziano himself felt an urge towards dramatic innovation; rather, the novelty of his conception determined a new way of depicting these images and expressing them in verse. On the other hand, I find a humanist concern is present in the *Orphei tragoedia*, even though the author did not change the dramatic substance of the text, but confined himself to inserting the episode of the Dryads and dividing the text into five acts, giving them scholarly headings: *Pastoricus, Nymphas habet, Heroicus, Necromanticus,* and *Bacchanalis*. This urge to up-date becomes even more evident in *La favola di Orfeo e Aristeo*, whose plot, as is well known, is enlarged by the addition of three acts. In the first, the *antefatto*, Apollo obtains the lyre for his son from Mercury and Orpheus obtains Eurydice from Diana; in Acts IV and V we witness the purification of Aristaeus through a series of portentous events: the Maenads transformed into trees by Bacchus, the snake turned to stone by Apollo when about to bite the dismembered head of Orpheus. Here too humanist influence is noticeable in the mythological themes culled from Virgil and Ovid, in the division into acts, and in the insertion between the acts of short lyric choruses in octosyllabic lines. But it has not yet reached the point of asserting the classical ideal of the three unities. The action continues to take place, as in the original fable, in unreal time and space.

If I wished to identify common elements in the motives which inspired the three versions of *Orfeo* and Leonardo's set, I would say that the latter is most closely linked to the text of the third version. There is a prevailing element of fantasy in both the final transmutations of the fable and in the surprising movement of the stage mountain which opens and closes.

But, in my view, what makes Leonardo's set important is not so much the possibility of identifying the text which inspired it, but the clue it provides to the dramatic developments at the time. It does not just help us visualize the scene of one or other *Orfeo* text, it is a solution to the problems of late fifteenth-century staging. I should like to call it a 'hybrid' solution, though this involves an arbitrary extension of the term. It is not an altogether unexpected solution, even from Leonardo, as traditional elements remained dominant in the two productions which can safely be attributed to him, *La festa del Paradiso* (1490) and *Danae* (1496), despite their being up-dated by their mythological imagery.

In both sets, the chief element was two *ingegni*, and it is interesting to note how Leonardo's devices take over at least one of the two different types of Florentine 'Paradise'. Much has been written about the form and mechanism of these machines in connection with Brunelleschi and Cecca; Leonardo must certainly have seen them in Florence as a young man.

In *La festa del Paradiso*[19] the text by Bellincioni is of little value in itself, but it shows clearly how traditional elements and classical lore, as well as the stage action and the courtiers' celebration, were already closely intertwined. I think that the text was influenced equally by the desires of Ludovico il Moro, who was responsible for the festivities, and by the dominating presence of Leonardo and his machinery. The plot is thin: Jove, having thanked God for granting supreme beauty to the earth in the person of Isabella, descended from his paradise with the other six planets, to pay homage to the duchess. The constellation having regrouped itself on a hill after the 'flight', Mercury, followed by the other planets, Diana, Venus, Apollo, Mars and Saturn, descended to offer their virtues and powers to Isabella, who was seated in the middle of the hall. Then Jove offered his gift: the three Graces and the seven Virtues, who arrived 'encircled by a cord', guided by Mercury and escorted by seven nymphs bearing large burning torches. Their song ended the play, and Isabella returned to her rooms accompanied by the Graces and Virtues.

In this fragile dramatic fabric, where Jove prays to a Christian god and the planets are identified with pagan divinities, everything is reduced to a common denominator of formal celebration and propitiatory rhetorics. Sacred and profane are mixed, while medieval ideas of astrological divination and nuptial celebration are concealed in myth. Music, song, recitation and pantomime are of equal importance, and even the audience is partly involved in the performance.

The shining machine of Paradise was placed at one end of the disproportionately long hall[20] and dominated the rich decorations from above. The hall was divided about a third of the way along its length by a partition ('a barrier of planks about two *braccia* [58 cm?] high') which seems to have separated the dukes and their retinue who were involved in the performance from the great tiered stand erected for the gentlemen of the court, who were the true spectators and formed the bulk of the audience. Between the ducal dais and the stage was an empty area, surrounded on two sides by benches for the ladies and on the third, at the foot of the stage, by more benches for the masked dancers. It was in this central area that first the dances which preceded the *Festa* and then the parading of the planets, Virtues and Graces took place. Perhaps for acoustical reasons the main group of instrumentalists was located behind the ducal dais, just about where the wooden barrier stood.

The stage was raised above the hall, though still accessible from it. It was itself on two levels. Above stood Paradise, 'shaped like half an egg', with a gilded vault and the signs of the zodiac all around its base. Below, on the stage, was a hill built to be walked on at different levels. The basic plan was the same as the *ingegno* in the church of the Carmine, described by Vasari in his life of Cecca: 'a hill excellently made of wood' at the centre of the presbytery

[19] *La festa del Paradiso*, planned for February 1489 when the marriage between Gian Galeazzo Visconti and Isabella of Aragon was celebrated, was postponed because of the sudden death of Ippolita, the bride's mother. Instead it was performed on 13 January 1490, in the Sala Verde of the Sforza castle. The two main sources of information about the entertainment are Giacomo Trotti's 'Relazione' entitled 'Feste in Milano 1490', which exists in manuscript in the 'Raccolta di varii monumenti istorici e varie narrazioni' in the Biblioteca Estense in Modena and has been published by E. Solmi and re-edited in his *Scritti Vinciani* (Florence 1924), and the text of the performance, in B. Bellincioni, *Sonetti, canzoni, capitoli*, collected by Father G. F. Tanzi and published after the death of the author, in Milan in 1493.

[20] The hall, identified by L. Beltrami, *Il castello di Milano sotto il dominio dei Visconti e degli Sforza 1368–1535* (Milan 1894), measured 62 m × 10 m.

of the church, and a double dome with rotating skies placed above a central *tribuna*.

Jove himself was at the centre of the golden vault, surrounded by the other planets, who were arranged on a mobile support which was disguised so that the figures seemed to be suspended in the void. The amazed Modenese reporter does not furnish us with technical details, but another description, Vasari's, of Brunelleschi's *ingegno* at San Felice,[21] may make good the deficiency. In Brunelleschi's *ingegno* the angelic host which accompanied the flight of the Angel of the Annunciation was supported by a large iron bar ending in an eight-spoked wheel, each spoke in turn ending with a 'flat platform the size of a trencher', on which were seated the children. In the middle of the 'cluster of eight angels' was the mandorla bearing the Archangel. The whole contraption was moved by a double pulley, worked by means of small hand-winches.

In Milan too the mechanism must have consisted of a large stage suspended in the air, supported by strong buttresses, with platforms and an upper chamber capable of holding a second orchestra, the necessary machinery (probably based on the system of counterweights dear to Leonardo's heart), the technicians supervising the machinery, and those charged with the delicate task of looking after the lights. Only the hollow part, gilded and shining, was visible from the hall, while the back of the elevated stage must have been masked by the decorations of 'festive greenery' which covered, and so lowered, the ceiling of the whole hall.

In *Danae*, performed six years later, the mechanical element was even more decisive. Leonardo's contraptions changed the very nature of the play: it lost some of the elements of both the sacred *rappresentazione* and of classical drama, which most critics maintain to be present and mixed together in the text.[22]

The play tells the story of Danae, the beautiful maiden loved by Jove and shut up in an inaccessible tower through the jealous prudence of her father Acrisius. Jove is aided by Mercury, who continually flies between earth and Olympus, but he seeks in vain to convince Danae or corrupt her guardian Sirus. Nevertheless, he reaches the girl in the shape of a shower of gold and fathers Perseus by her. Danae is condemned to death by her father, but is saved by Jove, who transforms her into a star and raises her to the heavens, amidst an explosion of light and sound. At this point there is a coda which takes up the whole of Act V and returns the performance to the spirit and conventions

[21] Descriptions of four *ingegni* survive. One, describing the *ingegni* for the *Annunciation* in the church of the Annunziata and for the *Ascension* in the Carmine seen by Bishop Abraham of Souzdal during his visit to Florence in 1439, is published in D'Ancona, *Le origini*, I, pp. 246, 251. A second, describing Brunelleschi's *ingegno* for the San Felice *Annunciation* (circa 1435), is by Vasari, in Vasari, *Le vite*, ed. Milanesi, vol. II, pp. 375ff. A third also described by Vasari, is of Cecca's *ingegno* for the Carmine *Ascension* (post 1469) and is given in Vasari, *Le vite*, vol. III, pp. 197ff. The reconstructions of Brunelleschi's *ingegni* attempted by V. Marchi (*Mostra di scenografia*, Florence 1933), P. Turchetti, *Enciclopedia dello spettacolo* (Rome and Florence 1954), and Molinari, *Spettacoli fiorentini del Quattrocento*, pp. 39ff, have all been rendered out-of-date by the discovery of a drawing of the machinery of the Annunciation *ingegno* in the *Zibaldone di Buonaccorso Ghiberti* in the Biblioteca Nazionale in Florence (MS BR 229, c. 15v); cf. A. R. Blumenthal 'A Newly-Identified Drawing of Brunelleschi's Stage Machinery', *Marsyas*, XIII (New York 1966–7), pp. 29ff. The Brunelleschi *ingegni* have now been exhaustively discussed by L. Zorzi; *Il teatro e la città* (Turin 1977), pp. 71–6, with bibliography pp. 153–68 and photos of reconstructions in plates 31–42.　　[22] I. Sanesi, *La commedia* (Milan 1954) I, pp. 214ff.

of a fifteenth-century celebratory *intromessa*. A group of singing and dancing nymphs asks Jove for an explanation of the marvel; Hebe descends from the sky to placate Acrisius by revealing to him the divine origins of Danae's lover and of the unborn Perseus; Acrisius regains his youth through joy; and finally Apollo descends from Olympus to sing the praises of Ludovico il Moro, accompanying himself on the lyre.

The fable was therefore classical in content and in its division into acts, but still linked by its dramatic structure to fifteenth-century tradition. It was also unusually animated, with its repeated flights and apotheoses, and the spreading of the action into the intermediate space, suspended between earth and sky. The medieval flights of the Angel of the Annunciation and of the Assumption of the Virgin Mary were originally intended to emphasize the exceptional nature of the mystic event, through the amazement and awe of the watching faithful, but these techniques had now become the main element of the play, and the means, surprise, had become an end in itself.

The scene therefore functioned on the three levels of earth, mid-air and Olympus. It can be reconstructed through the stage-directions in Taccone's text, which are always at pains to mention musical developments and the intervention of mechanical effects. The poet also informs us that the orchestra was invisible: 'the large instruments [were] concealed behind the stage machinery', while the 'fifes, bagpipes, drums and other hidden instruments' were probably concealed behind the upper and lower stages.

However, we do not know what machines Leonardo devised for the flights and apotheoses, how they worked and how they were hidden from the public. Nor do we know the lay-out of the lower stage, where Acrisius' palace, Danae's tower and the prison in which the innocent Sirus ended up, were all set up together. 'Olympus', Taccone wrote, was 'a most splendid heaven', which 'opened all at once' to reveal 'Jove with the other gods, with innumerable lamps resembling stars'. Only a part of this Paradise design is recognizable in a drawing at the Metropolitan Museum (plate 13);[23] it is difficult to make out but is certainly linked to *Danae*.

On the left of the drawing a large niche is depicted, with a divinity enthroned in a flaming mandorla, considered by some to be Danae herself transformed into a star. In his recent interpretation Carlo Pedretti rightly argued that the niche was not placed on the stage proper, but on a mobile

---

[23]   B. Taccone's *Danae* was performed in the Sanseverino palace on 14 January 1496. The drawing, acquired by the Metropolitan Museum in 1917, was exhibited in 1919, its subject being then unknown. It was later identified by Paul Müller-Walde, who authorized Marie Herfeld to publish his findings in 'La rappresentazione della Danae organizzata da Leonardo', *Raccolta vinciana*, XI (1922), pp. 226–8. More interesting is the recent study by K. Traumann Steinitz, which also gives C. Pedretti's interpretation, 'Le dessin de Léonard de Vinci pour la représentation de la Danae de Baldassare Taccone', in *Le lieu théâtral à la Renaissance* (Paris 1964), pp. 35ff.

Besides the 'star' and the cross-section of the scene, the drawing also bears an inscription by Leonardo, which gives the names of those who acted the different parts:

> Acrissio Giàcrisstofaro | siro tachò | danae franco romano | merchurio gianbatista daossmo | Giove Giàfranco tantio | servo piac | anuntiatione dela festa | + i quali si maravigliono della nova stella essinginochiano | e qualla adorano essiangino | chiano e cõmucha finsscha no la festa. | anuntiatore 3

Beloved of Isabella and Beatrice d'Este, Gian Cristoforo Romano was a humanist sculptor, whom Baldassare Castiglione holds up as a model in his *Il cortegiano*. Baldassare Taccone was Ludovico il Moro's chancellor, while Giovan Francesco Tanzi was a humanist priest and a good friend of Bellincioni, whose verses he published.

platform which acted as a lift. The presence of this wide platform does not rule out the use of a hemispherical Paradise as in 1490, but it makes it unlikely. All the above descriptions speak only of 'flights' suspended in mid-air, while the use of a large lift in the gilded vault before the very eyes of the audience would have partly destroyed that element of magic which seems to have been the strength of these spectacles. On the other hand, when not in motion the machine could have been hidden behind the clusters of clouds and lights, which filled the top of the dome. There is not a single element in the drawing which might suggest a dome; on the contrary, the sketch in the lower right-hand corner on which Pedretti bases his interpretation indicates only horizontal planes. By an extension of Pedretti's theory, however, it would be possible to believe that the 'beautiful sky' was placed on a higher platform, either suspended or held up by strong props, as was the case in the less sophisticated *ingegno* seen in Florence in 1439 by the Bishop of Souzdal.[24] The base of the elevated stage must have been fitted with a trapdoor, so that the lifting platform could fit into its opening when raised.

As for the significance of the enthroned figure, the flaming mandorla may indicate Apollo and the words on the left specify a 'herald'. It is then possible that the drawing refers to the opening phase of the spectacle, which might have been envisaged at first as a prologue spoken by Apollo instead of by the author.

This sort of stage lay-out would also help to explain the controversial set

[24]   The *ingegno* was used in the *Ascension* in Santa Maria del Carmine. 'Paradise' was located over the presbytery, which in the fifteenth-century used to be raised. On this raised floor itself stood two mansions, one a castle representing Jerusalem, the other a hill for the Mount of Olives. 'Paradise' was on a wooden platform and was glimpsed through what was described as

> a round aperture, fourteen feet in diameter, covered with a blue cloth on which are painted the sun, the moon and the stars; this represents the first celestial sphere. When the time comes, this curtain is raised, indicating that the gates of Paradise are about to open: and inside sits a man with a crown on his head, representing our heavenly Father...Around him are a number of children.. and a large number of small burning lights. Above this circle, which represents the sky, there is a disc of paper touching the upper circle of another sky on which are painted angels the size of men...From the sky in which sits God there descends on seven ropes a beautiful cloud surrounded by revolving discs: to left and right, angels with golden wings.

The cloud was then to bring Jesus back to Heaven. One can get some idea of the appearance of the 'discs' which rotated around God the Father and around the cloud from the 'Paradise' for the Valenciennes Passion. For the description by the Bishop of Souzdal see *Dalle origini al Quattrocento*, vol. II, pp. 688–92; and see also Zorzi: *Il teatro e la città*, as cited in note 21.

   This technique of Paradise, made up of concentric rings, either never entirely disappeared from stage tradition, or else was revived by the Baroque producers for their special effects. Niccolò Sabbatini da Pesaro is informative about the technical side of the operation: *Pratica di fabricar scene e machine ne' teatri* (Ravenna 1638), vol. II, chapter 54, reads

> At times the need arises in the *intermedi* to represent Paradise. Should this be so, here is how it can be done. A circular opening should be made in the sky, of the same size as Paradise is to be. Then make eight or ten rings out of planks of wood a foot wide. The circles must be of unequal size, i.e. the first larger than the second, the second larger than the third, and so on. Then cover each with clouds; as the circles diminish in size, so the colour of the clouds should fade, until as nearly white as possible. Then fix them one above the other, as it were in the shape of a choir, i.e. with the the largest toward the opening and the others behind, securing them with nails and wooden cross-beams. They must be placed at least one and a half feet apart. Between them put a good many lights, in such a way that the audience cannot see them. The opening in the sky must remain covered by a shutter... then when you want to reveal Paradise, first light those lights, then slide the shutter from over that part of the sky, and the audience will see a most beautiful perspective of clouds, which will truly seem a Paradise.

for Boiardo's *Timone*, where the stage directions repeatedly refer to two 'prosceniums', an upper and a lower, both capable of bearing the weight of several people.[25]

Let us return to the two drawings of Hades in the Arundel manuscript, accurately interpreted by Kate Traumann Steinitz and Carlo Pedretti, who had also supervised the reconstruction of two models based on these drawings. The set must have represented a mountainous area, free-standing and substantial. The central hill was mounted on a revolving platform divided into two parts which, turning in opposite directions, moved towards the back of the stage and showed the hollow interior of the hill to the audience. The two rocky halves of the hill rejoined at the back, and thus formed hell, with niches opening in the walls and Pluto in the centre on his sphere.

There is no point in re-examining the perfect mechanism of the revolving hill, or the system of counterweights identified by Pedretti, which enabled the two halves of the platform to rotate and Pluto to rise from beneath the stage simultaneously. It is more important to emphasize that Leonardo's interest in mechanics and the surprise effect, were in this case subordinated to the pressing, and in my view new, demands of a unified set representing a specific location. One could claim that the device of the hill was derived from a medieval *ingegno*, which had been modernized and perfected by new Renaissance skills, namely by Leonardo's mechanical mastery, and expanded to occupy the whole stage. But in fact the *ingegno* had now passed beyond the medieval convention in which the psychological effect of marvels, like the simultaneity of mansions, could legitimately be detected. In this case the machine served merely as the means of solving a specific problem: how to enable two sets representing different places to be shown successively on stage, by arranging a scene-change in full view of the audience without interrupting the flow of the action.

Even the external appearance was conceived in such a way that, whether the mountain was open or closed, the set would appear as a single unit: now a mountain region, now the cavern of hell against a rocky background. This set could have accommodated not only Poliziano's *Orfeo*, but also the *Orfeo e Aristeo* version. First Apollo and Mercury, then Tirsis, Aristaeus and the lonely Orpheus could all have acted on the slopes of the central mountain, which were strong enough to be walked on. The choruses of nymphs and Bacchantes could have entered via the semicircular valley surrounding the hill, while the sung and danced ensembles (the marriage of Orpheus and Eurydice, the funeral lament, the impious and frenzied Bacchanal) could have moved onto the wide proscenium in front of the hill, which is easily recognizable in one of the sketches of fol. 231v.

In this way machine and appearance became mutually interdependent, and confirmed the basic idea of unity in place and action. One cannot believe that

---

[25] *Timone*, Act I: 'Timon enters from the other end of the proscenium. And first he begins to hoe, then, interrupting his work, he turns his face to the skies and speaks thus...The curtains of heaven open, Jove appears with Mercury, dressed as has already been described, and together they speak as appears below...Mercury leaves Jove seated, and walking about on the upper proscenium, he speaks the following words, his face towards the audience.' In Act II: 'This second act takes place entirely on the upper set. Mercury leads Wealth to Jove...Jove having stood up from his seat walks about so much that he exits, passing through the curtains' (Scandiano 1500). See *Dalle origini al Quattrocento*, vol. II, pp. 516 and 526.

Leonardo derived such a problem, and a coherent solution to it, from one of the three *Orfeo* texts, which could only suggest the pagan setting of the play and the occasions for changing the stage. Perhaps it is not even necessary to look to the rising humanist poetics to find an explanation. Probably, for Leonardo, the new concept of a unified spectacle in a single and identifiable place was a result of his personal experience, and arose spontaneously out of his constant dissatisfaction with his own work. We could even say that if Leonardo had persisted in his theatrical work, he could perhaps have produced a new solution to the problem of handling space in Renaissance dramatic production. It might have been a solution different from the perspective set, just as his mechanical sets were an alternative to the *città ferrarese* ('Ferrarese city') as a means of resolving the tension between the persistent medieval stage-technique and the requirements of a classical style. A third motive force might thus have affected sixteenth-century staging alongside the antiquarian tendencies of the academicians and the perspective solutions of the Renaissance artists. But one cannot even guess at its parameters.

2 The *città ferrarese*

In our examination of the salient features of the fifteenth-century Italian *festa*, we have observed the importance of two main characteristics: the use of hangings, floats and *ingegni* for visual effect, with no constant preference between them, and the employment of the actor–courtier, whose presence was further emphasized by his costume. These festivities cannot be termed true theatre, because for both the audience and the actors the spectacle and the means of its production remained ends in themselves. Music, words and movement all had the same kind of importance, while the set was so designed as to suit sung plot, recited dialogue or danced pantomime equally well.

However, as soon as classical drama, hitherto a monopoly of the literary academies and the humanist schools, began to be incorporated into the varied and flexible conventions of the *festa*, it immediately became necessary to find a different setting for such performances. The first classically inspired set was probably the much discussed *picturata scaena* devised for Cardinal Riario in Rome around 1483, for a comedy put on by the Accademici Pomponiani. Sulpizio da Veroli mentions it in his first edition of Vitruvius, though without enough detail to enable us to reconstruct it visually.[1] The experiment was doubtless followed by others not only in Rome but elsewhere, encouraged by the ever-increasing interest in the performance of classical plays and by the perseverance of scholars in collating, translating and publishing texts by Plautus and Terence. At the same time they were investigating Vitruvius' obscure architectural rules, and checking their interpretations against the surviving ruins of Roman theatres.

Thus by the end of the century a sort of humanist set was developing, of which traces remain in the wood-cuts of the first illustrated editions of Terence, especially in those of the two earliest examples: Trechsel's Lyons edition (1493) and Soardi's Venetian one (1497). Though it is likely that the pictures differed from the original sets, if only because of the engravers' interpretation, some basic elements of the originals must have been preserved, for example, the recurrent design of arches with cloth curtains, arranged in a single forward-facing arcade, only rarely rounded off by two short side pieces. The abbreviated inscriptions across the architrave tell us that each arch corresponded to one 'house' in the comedy.

Without going into the reasons for and against assuming these engravings to be of real theatre settings, it is worth comparing some of them, for example

---

[1] *Lucii Vitruvii Pollionis De Architectura Libri Decem* (Rome 1486), ed. Sulpizio da Veroli, who dedicated the edition to Cardinal Raffaele Riario: 'Tu etiam primus picturatae scaenae faciem quōm Pomponiani comoediam agerent nostro saeculo ostendisti' ('You were the first to show our age the appearance of a painted set, where the Pomponiani could act a comedy').

those for Trechsel's editions of *Andria* (plate 18) or *Phormio* (plate 19) and Soardi's illustrations for *Heautontimorumenos*, with evidence from different sources clearly linked to the theatre. One may cite the clay tablet from Numitorius Hilarus' Columbarium (plate 16) and the marble relief from the Museo delle Terme, both showing a first-century Roman single-story *frons scaenae*, the miniature by Hubert Cailleau showing the stage of the Valenciennes Passion (plate 15), a late and ornate example of a medieval set with multiple juxtaposed mansions, and the Borgia engraving of the Teatro della Passione in Velletri (plate 14), which was a permanent theatre built in a classical style.[2] These different structures, temporary or permanent, are analogous rather than formally related, and the links, which are in any case indirect, are also affected by the stylizing intervention of the engraver. Yet, despite the differences in external appearance, it seems impossible to question the similarity of the structures used in the different stages, the links between stages and sets, and their practicality for acting. In each of these examples, as in other similar ones, we are presented with a wide stage, where the action took place on the whole of the broad, shallow and empty proscenium. The set faced onto the proscenium, and was conceived as a single line, either straight or irregular, formed by a series of pieces of scenery (medieval mansions or arcades with architraves and pediments) next to one another. These were not acting areas but represented specific places pertaining to each character, where the actors could wait in sight of the audience, or through which they could appear.

It therefore seems safe to consider the Terence engravings as iconographically reliable, standing half-way between the pure depiction of reality and artistic license, and to speculate on where the humanist sets they represent stood in relation to medieval tradition on the one hand and the new antiquarian theories of the humanists on the other. This relationship consisted once more in a combination not spontaneously arrived at but intellectual in origin, both cause and result of a long academic debate which lasted the whole of the sixteenth century. Both the Terence sets and the Velletri stage can be interpreted either as medieval stages, with juxtaposed mansions supported by the classical motif of the arcades, or as variants on a reduced scale of the portico, in which the first commentators of Vitruvius saw the image of the Roman *frons scaenae*. But whereas in the Terence engravings the relationship to medieval and classical models is one of mere analogy, the problem is more complex when we consider the stage at Velletri. All the sources agree in calling the building the Teatro della Passione, and no one questions that it was built for the Confraternita di San Giovanni in Plagis, between 1499 and 1530. Yet its external appearance is so close to that of a *frons scaenae* that G. Cressedi (in 1953) rejected the traditional

    [2] See T. E. Lawrenson, 'Les Editions illustrées de Térence dans l'histoire du théâtre', in *Le lieu théâtral à la Renaissance* (Paris 1964). For H. Cailleau's miniatures. J. Jacquot, *La vie théâtrale au temps de la Renaissance* (Paris 1963), exhibition catalogue. For more recent theories suggesting alternative lay-outs for the Valenciennes theatre see E. Konigson, *La Représentation d'un mystère de la Passion à Valenciennes en 1547* (Paris 1969). On the Velletri theatre see A. Gabrielli, *Il teatro della Passione di Velletri* (Velletri 1910); A. Tersenghi, *Roma* (1924), vol. II, pp. 77–80; G. Cressedi, 'Velitrae', in *Italia Romana: municipi e colonie* (Rome 1953), series I, vol. XII, pp. 53–5; E. Povoledo, 'La sala teatrale a Ferrara: da Pellegrino Prisciani a Ludovico Ariosto', in *L'architettura del teatro in Italia dall'età greca al Palladio*, in *Bollettino del Centro di Studi di Architettura Andrea Palladio* (Vincenza 1974); L. Zorzi, *Il teatro e la città* (Turin 1977), pp. 313–18.

interpretation and argued that it was an atypical Roman theatre, with only a stage and without an area for the audience. This hypothesis is unconvincing, above all because it is difficult to accept that late fifteenth-century humanists would have been ignorant of the existence of an intact *frons scaenae*, in annual use and only 30 km from Rome, just when the polemics about Vitruvius and the structure of classical theatres were being revived by the academies. There are two alternatives. Either the theatre was a real *frons scaenae* used by the Confraternity for performances of the Passion, but so ruined by the end of the fifteenth century as to be unrecognizable, so that the repairs made between 1499 and 1530 were virtually a restoration, or else the theatre was built on the ruins of, or near to, an earlier medieval stage like the one at Valenciennes, now adapted to suit new classical ideas. In either case, one must assume the involvement of an architect well versed in archaeology and humanist studies, almost certainly connected with the Accademia Romana.

But we are only interested in classical drama and its production insofar as it provided the context for the development and flowering of the *intermedio apparente* ('visible' *intermedio*), which it did for reasons and within limits discussed above by Pirrotta. For this reason our interest in the 'Terentian set' is restricted, precisely because its nature is debatable and cannot be verified by contemporary accounts. Quite the reverse is true of the type of set developed in the same period at Ferrara, at the court of Ercole I d'Este, which was a lively centre of humanist interests and theatrical invention. There all these controversial problems about sets seem to come into focus and be resolved. The ducal chronicles[3] do not omit a single performance, and there is no shortage of descriptions, though some of them are rather cursory.

Ferrara, like its neighbours Mantua and Milan, to which it was linked by ties of marriage and political interest, was a typical late fifteenth-century court, full of men who were irreverent and yet bigoted. Dukes founded monasteries, yet employed official astrologers; residual superstition found remission in respect for religious observances, and relief in the rediscovery of an idealized pagan mythology.

Ercole had been educated at the Aragonese court in Naples, where he had seen more of jousts and triumphs than literary academies and performances of plays. Above all, he lacked the humanist training which was flourishing in Ferrara, at the school begun by Guarino Veronese in 1429. The school had been founded for Leonello, the celebrated bastard son of the Este family, and he had been its most valuable pupil. When he came to power in 1441 the whole of the court's cultural life was affected by this experience. With Borso d'Este, who knew no Latin, interest in the classics seemed to weaken; plays became once again mere convivial pastimes, while popular festivals and official celebrations increased in number. Even the chapel choir, on which Borso lavished attention and money, performed in the Duomo in public concerts. For Borso the whole population was a potential audience, and his essentially political and propagandist aims were consistent with the trappings

---

[3] See especially the anonymous *Diario ferrarese* (1409–1502) and Bernardino Zambotti's 'Diario ferrarese dall'anno 1476 sino al 1504', both ed. G. Pardi and published in the series *Rerum Italicarum Scriptores* (Bologna 1925–37). See also the 'Diario di Ugo Caleffini' (1471–94), ed. G. Pardi (Ferrrara 1939–40), vols. I–II of the series *Deputazione di Storia Patria* (Ferrara – Monumenti). A selection of the most relevant quotations can be found in *La commedia del Cinquecento*, vol. I: page references are inserted in subsequent notes.

of the old feudal relationship between the lord and his people; protection and loyalty.

The humanist tradition did not die but withdrew into the studio where Battista Guarini, son of Guarino, continued his lessons and where one could still find, as teachers or pupils, Tito Vespasiano Strozzi, Pellegrino Prisciano, Antonio Tebaldeo, and amongst the younger men Niccolò da Correggio and Pandolfo Collenuccio. These were the men who were to be Ercole's cultural advisers after his return from Naples in 1462 and his succession to the ducal title on his brother's death in 1471. And yet, as Adolfo Venturi wrote,[4] Borso's era did not end with his death. For at least a decade, until the war with Venice (1481–3), the whole of Ercole's court was based on the men and institutions inherited from Borso. Then both changed, and 1486 saw the start of the great age of Ferrarese theatre.

A repertory with such a clear classical bias was not limited entirely to Ercole's court: the Roman and Florentine classical traditions were not stillborn. However they carried on with spectacles which must have taken place in a context of student dilettantism, and were thus unlikely to attract much attention. Performances in Ferrara were exceptional because they were integrated into the festival. Though not yet truly public, they were opened to a larger, though still privileged audience, so that they eventually created their own style and tradition.

The first mention of the sort of set which for the sake of simplicity we shall call the *città ferrarese* (Ferrarese city) dates from 1486, and occurs in connection with a performance of Plautus' *Menaechmi*. 'Vidimus effictam celsis cum moenibus urbem/structaque per latas tecta superba vias' ('We saw the town portrayed with lofty walls, its splendid buildings lining broad streets'), wrote Battista Guarini bombastically.[5] The two ducal chroniclers detailed more simply: 'The comedy of I Menechini was recited... on a new stage shaped like a city made out of planks and painted with houses' (Zambotti), five 'houses with battlements, each with its own door and window' (*Diario ferrarese*).

The set was erected in the Cortile Nuovo of the palace, on the side which runs parallel to the Via di Corte Vecchia. The ducal dais was on the opposite side, towards the chapel, while the large audience was between the two. At some point, probably at the start of the first act, a float in the shape of a ship forced its way through the dense crowd: 'Then from the side of the pantry and the kitchen came a flat boat with ten people aboard, with oars and sails like a real one, and there the two brothers met each other' (*Diario ferrarese*).

In the following year's carnival Niccolò da Correggio's *Caephalo* and Plautus' *Amphitrione* were performed. Again the set was erected in the Cortile Nuovo, but along the short side where one now finds the external staircase. The painter Giovanni Bianchi, called Trullo, was involved in the work.[6] The stage

[4] A. Venturi, 'L'arte ferrarese nel periodo di Ercole I d'Este', in *Atti e memorie della R. Deputazione di Storia Patria per le provincie di Romagna*, VI (1887–8), pp. 91ff and VI (1888–9), pp. 368ff.

[5] B. Guarini, 'Elegia', in *Carmina* (Modena 1496), Bk IV. See also Pirrotta p. 40 above.

[6] G. Bianchi, or Bianchini, known as Trullo, was active in Ferrara between approximately 1450 and 1491, the year when he was killed by the painter Bartolomeo Turola (or Belli?). Nothing survives of his work, and the few accounts of it that exist class him amongst those painters who lived in the shadow of Cosmè Tura and Ercole de' Roberti and were employed primarily to do restorative work or such decorations as friezes, ceilings, cornices etc. See Venturi, 'L'arte ferrarese' and L. N. Cittadella, *Notizie relative a Ferrara* (Ferrara 1864), *passim*.

'stretched from wall to wall', and the same set was used for both comedies, 'a *tribunale* of wood and planks painted with houses, in the image of a castle and a city'. In addition to the basic set, *Amphitrione* also had an *ingegno*, a Paradise, probably similar to the one made up of concentric circles at Valenciennes (plate 12). The opening which unveiled the device, obviously intended for Jove's appearance, was also employed along with its lighting effects as an *intermedio* to one act: 'And between the acts more entertainments were performed, especially as a sky had been built high in a corner towards the clock-tower, with lamps burning in the appropriate places behind thin black curtains, and shining like stars; and there were children dressed in white, representing the planets' (Zambotti).

For both the entertainments the appearance of the courtyard was completely transformed by the decorations, but the plan of the temporary theatre was itself simple and not new. It consisted of a raised stage with 'houses' side by side, whose significance will be examined below. Opposite, there was a single forward-facing bank of tiered seats hung with tapestries; on the balconies above there were more places for the ladies. Between the set and the seated spectators a space was left, in which, despite the crowd, a boat-shaped float could be manoeuvred, as in the *intramesse* for banquets in Pesaro or Rome.

In 1489, when Isabella's marriage to Francesco Gonzaga was celebrated, the performance had already moved indoors, to the great hall which occupied the whole of the palace's north wing, in the corner between the Corso and what is now Piazzetta Savonarola.[7] We do not know how this still temporary theatre was organized. In 1491, however, the same hall was used for performances of *Menaechmi*, Terence's *Andria* and the *Amphitrione*, on three consecutive evenings, to celebrate the marriage of Alfonso d'Este and Anna Sforza. It was now organized in a way which seems to be approaching what was to be the typical arrangement of a Renaissance *teatro da sala* (hall theatre). The set, still with four houses and a Paradise in a row, was at one end of the hall, probably the end facing Castel Vecchio. The tiers of seats for the guests were placed round the other sides and must have reached about half-way along the room. The central area and the wide aisle between the stage and the end of the tiers of seats was left free for the dancing which preceded each evening's performance, for the manoeuvring of the ship in *Menaechmi* and perhaps also for the *entrées* of the *intermedi*.

We can only reconstruct the setting of the entertainment by comparing the different surviving accounts of it.[8] The Milanese ambassador wrote to Ludovico Sforza: 'At about the 24th hour we returned to the hall, and sat down in a place near the centre of the hall, which was all tiered and faced four castles, from which the actors were to emerge.' Zambotti makes it clear that the audience was seated on three sides of the hall: 'and there were around

---

[7]   According to information scattered throughout the two *Diarii ferraresi*, the first great hall of the Ducal Palace was in the north wing, and stretched from the entrance hall (which was reached by means of a covered external staircase from the main courtyard) to the side of the palace facing the Castel Vecchio. It was devastated by the fire which in 1532 also destroyed the 'theatre of Ariosto' built there between 1529 and 1530, and again by the great earthquake of 1570. It was rebuilt in another wing of the palace facing what is now Via di Corte Vecchia, as one can see from the plan of Ferrara drawn in 1605 by G. B. Aleotti.

[8]   Besides the two *Diarii ferraresi* already referred to, see also the 'Lettera degli ambasciatori milanesi a Ludovico il Moro (14 February 1491)', in D'Ancona, *Le origini*, II, pp. 130ff. Also T. V. Strozzi, 'Aeolostichon', IV ('Ad Herculem Ferrariae Ducis, de Nuptiis Alphonsi et Annae'), in *Strozzi Poetae Pater et Filius* (Venice 1513), c. 125v.

the hall platforms in the shape of theatres'. Strozzi confirms this: 'Quae populum capiant hinc atque hinc ordine longo/Multiplici surgunt celsa theatra gradu.' ('Lofty theatres rise with many tiers to receive the spectators this way and that in long rows.')

From the *Libri di Munizioni*, which A. Venturi has examined, we also learn that Niccolò Segna 'painted the set and Menechino's [i.e. Menaechmus'] ship for the comedy', while Fino Marsigli 'painted two mountains for the entertainments in the great hall' and 'two snakes for the play of *Amphitrione*', those used in the last *intermedio*.[9]

Except for a break between 1491 and 1498, overshadowed by family mourning and the dangers of the French invasion, plays for the carnival were performed in the great hall almost every year. The chronicles, except those of 1499, add few details of any importance until 1502. Then the accounts of the festivities to celebrate Alfonso's new marriage, with Lucrezia Borgia, give us something conclusive. For the first time a theatrical performance was staged somewhere apart from the normal setting of banquets and balls. These continued to be held in the palazzo, while the theatre was set up in the upper hall of the Palazzo della Ragione, located on the adjacent side of the square. A temporary bridge, leading to the Rigobello tower, joined the two buildings.

Five of Plautus' comedies were performed: *Epidicus*, *Bacchides*, *Miles gloriosus*, *Asinaria* and *Casina*. There was only one set for the five evenings, but at least 110 new and lavish costumes were made for the comedies and their *intermedi*. The first evening, in fact, began with a simultaneous parade of all the costumes in the great hall.

This theatre, the result of fifteen years of experiment, can be regarded as the archetypal sixteenth-century theatre hall, with its mixture of styles. With no awareness of incongruity, the semicircular bank of seating, classical and humanist in derivation, was combined with a stage generated by immediate theatrical needs rather than erudition.

Isabella d'Este wrote to her husband:

...My lord my father...took me to see the hall where the comedies will be acted. It is 146 feet long and 46 wide. On the side adjoining the square and at both ends are built the tiered seats; thirteen tiers with two partitions to divide the women from the men. The women will sit in the middle and the men on either side. The ceiling and the tiers are covered with green, red and white cloth. On the other side, facing the seats, there is a wall of wood, crenellated like a city wall, as high as a man. Above it rise the houses for the comedies, six in number, no different from the usual ones. It is estimated that 5,000 people will be there...[10]

In fact there were 3,000 spectators, according to a later report of Niccolò Cagnolo, a courtier from Piacenza who had come to the wedding celebrations in Ferrara as part of the French ambassador's suite.[11] The bank of seats was greater in width than depth and occupied a good deal of the long narrow room (about 60 m × 19 m). It curved round at the ends, 'with its high and low seats

[9] Niccolò Segna and Fino Marsigli, like Trullo, worked at the court of Ercole I, in the shadow of Ercole de' Roberti. They worked on decorations (state barges, wedding chests, etc) or on the production of stage apparatus, though obviously guided by whoever had ordered the spectacle. See Venturi, 'L'arte ferrarese', *passim*, and Cittadella, *Notizie*, *passim*.

[10] Cf. D'Ancona, *Le origini*, II, pp. 134ff; also *La commedia del Cinquecento*, vol. I, p. 412.

[11] N. Cagnolo's entire letter appears in Zambotti's 'Diario ferrarese', pp. 318–33.

in a circle' (Cagnolo), forming a half-ellipse, bent towards the side of the hall looking onto the square. The ladies and gentlemen were placed here, while the princes and guests of honour sat 'in the middle of the orchestra'. The stage was placed against the other long wall of the hall, probably where the doors were located which led into adjacent rooms. This arrangement was necessary, as between them the play and *intermedi* required many actors, at least five changes of costume (one for each *intermedio*) and the use of floats and spectacular machines. The depth of the entire theatre, which unusually occupied not the length but the width of the hall, cannot have been more than 19 m, and indeed must have been less, owing to the need for a passage-way behind the seats and access stairs for the actors at the back of the stage.

The set was of the same kind as those repeatedly described in Ferrarese accounts from 1486 onwards; we tend to visualize it as a highly specialized variant on the stage with mansions, which was also used for the Ferrarese sacred *rappresentazioni*.[12]

The stage was divided in two. The proscenium, as high as a man and with its plinth painted to resemble city walls, had an acting area 'about 40 *braccia* long and 5 wide', i.e. about 26 m × 3 m (Cagnolo).[13] In the background were the six houses for the comedy, 'no different from the usual ones', that is faithful to the earlier model, with its 'five houses with battlements each with a window and a door' (1486). They were not painted on a wooden screen, but formed a series of small rooms, probably side by side like those in the Terence illustrations. 'And on one side', wrote Cagnolo, was 'the proscenium with several rooms, all crenellated and decorated with turrets, which housed the mimers and the actors who were performing the comedy.' Since the entire proscenium was 26 m long, the façades of the six houses could have been about 4 m wide, and inside they might have measured 4 m by 3. In any case they were large enough to allow floats to be manoeuvred, for we hear of one 'shaped like a unicorn and pulled by a horse', which appeared in the third *intermedio* of *Epidicus*, and another like an enormous sphere which appeared in the second *intermedio* of *Casina* and 'opened in two [halves] in the middle of the proscenium, and inside was a most beautiful music, of lyres and sweet harmonies of voices' (Cagnolo). To summarize: they were still mansions of a special kind, which could be combined with a Paradise–Olympus, as was done when *Amphitrione* was performed in 1491, 'with a sky which opened in a circle on the ceiling of the hall, with planets and music and angelic songs' (Zambotti).

Much has been written on the appearance and arrangement of these houses. Some have interpreted them as a medieval set, some as a series of arches like the one in the illustrations of Terence, and some have gone so far as to suggest that they might have been a perspective view of a city *avant la lettre*, literally painted on a back-board of wooden planks. But since the descriptions clearly specify doors, windows, battlements and turrets, the *città ferrarese* could not

[12] The *Passione*, performed on 20 April 1481 in the Ducal Chapel for Good Friday (Zambotti, 'Diario ferrarese'), and the *Passione*, whose performance in the square between the Ducal Palace and the Duomo was spread over three days, both had this type of stage. For the latter, the set had been erected in front of the palazzo del Podestà (Zambotti, 'Diario ferrarese').

[13] These calculations are based on a unit of measurement equal to 65 cm, since the Ferrarese *braccio* varied according to use: the *braccio* for measuring silk was 68 cm, for wool it was 64 cm, and the architectural *braccio* probably varied still more.

have imitated the classical arcades of the Terentian portico, despite the fact that it appeared to follow the plan of adjacent small rooms. And despite Battista Guarini's description: 'Vidimus effictam celsis cum moenibus urbem/ structaque per latas tecta superba vias', it cannot have been a perspective set; Guarini's description was not published until 1496, and is in any case suspect, given its over-enthusiastic tone.

The novelty of this set could not fail to strike the imagination of the diarists, and later of the rather bored Isabella herself. The diaries all emphasize the limited number of 'houses', the fact that they could be used, and that they sought to convey the impression of a city. This idea of a city, that is of a single and fixed location, is in fact the basis of the Ferrarese set, and involves the rejection of the coexistence of several simultaneous sets, which had been inevitable in the sacred *rappresentazioni*. But in this city of Ferrara there were at most six houses, and the crenellated walls which were intended to limit the view of the city, were painted on the plinth of the proscenium. Bernardino Zambotti's note on Terence's *Eunuco*, which was performed in 1499, is decisive on this point: 'And in front of the stage a wall had been made, with battlements painted like a city, where one could see five houses built with doors and windows, which seemed to be of brick. From these houses the performers made their entries and exits as they were required.'

The only example of a city in a theatrical style to be found in fifteenth-century Ferrarese iconography is the view of the monuments of Rome in the fresco on 'The Month of September' painted by Ercole de' Roberti[14] in Schifanoia (plate 17). The picture is a curious detail, interpreted by iconographers as 'the shield of Aeneas' commissioned by his mother Venus from Vulcan, whose busy workshop can be glimpsed on the left. The city serves as a background to the Capitoline she-wolf feeding the twins. It is set out in three parallel parts, recalling a medieval stage, but with an architectural style which modifies the traditional mansions according to the classical standards enjoined by humanist taste. The city walls are in the foreground, with small turrets at the sides and the Porta Maggiore in the centre, similar to the base of a Ferrarese proscenium, 'made [like] a wall with battlements painted like a city'. Behind there is the piazza, completely empty because the obelisk which should be in the centre has been pushed back. Thirdly, there are the 'houses', a compromise between medieval shops, with their typical doors which also functioned as windows, and classical monuments decorated with architraves, semicircular tympanums and high pediments. There are six buildings altogether, six mansions *sui generis* placed beside one another to form a single irregular façade as in the sets for religious plays: three shops at the back, a fourth building shaped like a crenellated tower reminiscent of the tomb of Caecilia Metella, and a further two buildings just visible at the sides, curving forward to act as wings.

[14] See E. Povoledo, 'La sala teatrale a Ferrara', also note 2 above. For the entire cycle of frescoes in the Sala dei Mesi at Schifanoia, see A. Warburg, 'Italienische Kunst und "internazionale" Astrologie in Palazzo Schifanoia zu Ferrara', in *Atti del X Congresso di Storia dell'arte in Roma* (Rome 1922), pp. 179–93; P. D'Ancona, *I Mesi di Schifanoia in Ferrara* (Milan 1954); R. Longhi, *Officina ferrarese* (Florence 1956, enlarged 3rd edn). Zorzi (in *Il teatro e la città*, pp. 21–5 and the long footnote on pp. 48–54) accepts the shield in this fresco as scenographic evidence, but argues for a quite different iconographic interpretation. His whole semiotic approach to the Schifanoia frescoes is linked to notions of theatrical display.

The shield seems to be inlaid in the body of the fresco, rather than hung, as it should be, from the doorpost of the workshop, and the view of Rome stands out from the rest of the composition as though it were extraneous or a later addition, inserted into the irreverent story of the Triumph of Lust to commemorate some more recent and real event. Perhaps it was painted in celebration of Borso d'Este's triumphal journey to Rome to be invested with the ducal title, and was commissioned by Borso himself in the final months of 1471, or by Ercole some years later in memory of his brother. Perhaps it was a more modest reminder of the journey undertaken by Pellegrino Prisciano, one of the consultant iconographers for the cycle of the months, to search amongst the ancient ruins for the lineaments of the Roman theatre. But whatever the purpose or significance of the small fresco, it cannot be assigned with certainty to a later date or taken as a faithful reproduction of a real theatrical scene. The two cities are not the product of one occasion, but of one culture, a culture characterized by breaks with tradition and by research. They are the product of an outlook common to both the theatre and to painting, a shared way of symbolizing the 'city', the public and official focus of social life, and of portraying it, either on the flat wall of a fresco or in the illusory depth of the stage.

If one cannot go so far as to talk of a perspective set which followed the humanistic principles of the three unities, neither can one speak only of 'mansions', for this would be to ignore a manifestly new element which freed the *città ferrarese* from the traditions of religious drama. It stood between the two currents: the medieval one now in decline and the Renaissance one which was still not clearly formulated. Four or six houses did not constitute a perspective view; they were mansions which had been up-dated in accordance with a new concept of theatre, looking to a classical world but not yet freed from the limitations of hybrid drama. It was therefore a conventional set, planned first in terms of stage practicability, and secondly in terms of scene illustration. However, despite all this it was still intended to resemble a city 'with superb houses and wide streets', in accordance with the ideas of the humanists who filled the palace.

The *città ferrarese* was not a solution to all the problems of staging, it was a highly specific set, and it was entirely derived from the demands of a particular dramatic and recited text. The *intermedi* in fact took place on stage and were interpolated into the comedy between acts, with the intention of filling in the gaps and creating a relaxing digression; but they really had nothing to do with the play, or with the three unities of the humanists. They still reflected the fanciful, grotesque, allusive character of the *intromesse* for banquets, even if the dialogue between actors and spectators which the *entremets* had once instituted by eulogy or personal address no longer existed.

At Ferrara the *intermedi* seem to have taken place mainly on stage from the very first performances. Already in 1487, in the last *intermedio* of *Amphitrione* 'all the labours of Hercules appeared on the stage' (Zambotti). In the 1502 plays this was confirmed quite unambiguously by Cagnolo and the *Diarii* of Marin Sanudo[15] for almost all the comedies: 'on the proscenium, which was in front of these rooms (i.e. the houses with battlements of the set), about 40 *braccia* long and 5 wide, they acted some *moresche* with dancing

[15] See *I Diarii di Marin Sanudo*, vol. IV (Venice 1880), cols. 222ff.

to the sound of drums'. Even the *entrées* of the dancers, 'prepared...within these rooms' came directly from the *città*. But that *città* was not designed for them at all: it was a solution to other problems, those of the play, so that often the *intermedio* added elements of its own, such as a float, a medieval *ingegno* or a pretended rustic arbour.

We have already mentioned the wheeled 'boats' in *Menaechmi* (1486), the unicorn float (*Epidicus* 1502), the 'sphere where four virtues clustered together' (*Casina* 1502) and the 'Paradises' in *Amphitrione* with their 'sky' and shining lights which 'opened in a circle' revealing choirs of children dressed in white 'representing the planets'. But the 'movable rustic arbours' are more significant than these, because they reveal an intention to evoke a scene other than that of the comedy. Sanudo merely hints indirectly at this in his description of the first *intermedio* of *Asinaria* (1502): 'ten Wild Men ran and jumped frighteningly about the stage for a while, then hearing the horn blow, and fearing the dogs and hunters, they fled into the woods...' Then: 'At the third blast of the horn they returned to the woods', from which they re-emerged to capture a lion and a panther, until dancing and 'jumping they gathered at one end of the stage, all ten in a group'.

Recalling the performances of 1491, Tito Vespasiano Strozzi indulged in descriptions of some *intermedi*, including one in which youths adorned with garlands of ivy wove a portico of greenery out of boughs they carried:[16]

> Hic iuvenes ederae tecti viridantis amictu
> pluribus extemplo prosiluere locis,
> atque leveis agili meditantes corpore motus,
> ad numerum coeptos implicuere choros;
> quosque manu tulerant connexis ordine ramis
> texitur, atque nova porticus arte viret,
> moxque resolventes ramorum vincula saltu
> non incomposito corripuere fugam.

Here, all of a sudden, youths adorned with garlands of green ivy leapt forth from many places, and, performing light steps with supple bodies, they began their dancing and wove it to the rhythm. By combining together with good order the branches they had held in their hands an arcade is formed and looks green with novel art. And then, breaking the bonds of the branches with a graceful leap, they took their flight.

But these are exceptional. Like the *intramesse* for banquets, *intermedi* did not require a recognizable setting. They acted on the imagination, by means of costumes rich and varied to the point of exaggeration, so that they were clearly intended to be an unreal disguise, in contrast to the costumes used in the comedies, which resembled everyday clothes of the real world. Of the costumes which were paraded on the ducal stage before the performance of 1499, 133 were for the plays and 144 for the *intermedi*, 'all new'. In 1502 there were 110. The subjects were endless: Moors and Turks, nymphs and soldiers, old-fashioned foot-soldiers and knights on imitation horses, cooks, lunatics, peasants, pagan gods and courts of love, monsters, magicians, wild animals and hunters, old men, young maidens and youths in love. They wore silk clothes 'slashed and embroidered, hose in nine liveries, golden bells and shining ornaments', satin *ziponi* or cloaks of green ivy, veils, furs over nearly

[16] See T. V. Strozzi, *Aeolostichon*, IV ('Ad Herculem Ferrariae Ducis, de Nuptiis Alphonsi et Annae'), in *Strozzi Poetae Pater et Filius*, cc. 125v–31v.

naked bodies. On their faces they wore masks of exotic or deformed faces, on their heads precious head-dresses, wreaths of ivy or 'hair made of tinfoil'.[17]

But who devised this splendour, and in particular who designed the highly unusual *città ferrarese*?

The *Memoriali di spesa* and *Libri delle uscite* of the Este family supply the names of many artists called in to contribute to the work: Niccolò Segna, Giovanni Bianchi called Trullo, Fino and Bernardino Marsigli, Bernardo Brasone. On the other hand, the two great artists who dominated the court and reign of Ercole, Cosmè Tura and Ercole de' Roberti,[18] are never named in connection with spectacles. The former are artists who have become known more for their involvement with the plays than for their paintings, and one always gets the impression from the accounts justifying expenses that they were required to collaborate, in order to give concrete form to someone else's conceptions. A letter written by Beatrice d'Este to her sister in February 1491 implied that the mastermind may largely have been the duke himself:

And I am most certain that these decorations and triumphs are as masterly and elegant as Your Excellency writes to me, for, having been thought up and ordered by our most illustrious father, there is no doubt that all will have been handled with extreme wisdom and perfection, for such is His Excellency's custom.[19]

Certainly Ercole did not act alone, and in the same way as he entrusted Trullo, Segna or the Marsigli brothers with the task of 'painting the stands' and the machinery, so it is probable that to build the latter he made use of Biagio Rossetti, who in the year 1491 designed and directed the construction of the arches for the entry of Anna Sforza. But above all, Ercole must have availed himself of Pellegrino Prisciano, librarian, writer and antiquarian, the duchess' astrological counsellor and the duke's adviser on theatrical architecture.[20] In the Biblioteca Estense of Modena there exists a short

---

[17]   See Pirrotta, part I, chapter 2 above.

[18]   In 1452, Cosmè Tura painted a crest with the device of a unicorn, destined for the winner of the Palio di San Giorgio (Venturi, 'L'arte ferrarese'), and in 1461 he received 166 lire 'for caparisons and cloths to be hung over the armour of the knights' (G. A. Ferrini, *Il torneo delle contrade per il Palio di San Giorgio*, Ferrara 1939). He supplied the designs for the hangings and furnishings of the nuptial chamber at the time of the wedding of Ercole I and Eleanor of Aragon, but there is no evidence of his having been involved in designing stage furnishings. Ercole de' Roberti designed Isabella d'Este's wedding bed when she married Francesco Gonzaga in 1490 as well as the triumphal car on which she made her entry into Mantua (Venturi, 'L'arte ferrarese').

[19]   The letter, dated 23 February 1491, is given by Luzio and Renier, 'Commedie classiche in Ferrara nel 1499', in *Giornale storico della letteratura italiana*, XI (1888), p. 178.

[20]   Pellegrino Prisciano (born after 1435, died 1518) was the son of one of the duke's stewards, and was at court from an early age. Between 1469 and 1470 he was adviser on astrological symbols in the Schifanoia frescoes. By 1475 he was already court archivist. From there he went on to reorganize the large ducal library. He took part in diplomatic activity at the command of the Este family, going several times to Venice and twice to Rome. He was introduced into Italian humanist circles, and lectured on astrology at the Ferrara Studio. His work was varied, and was characterized by intelligence, accuracy, and learning with a touch of pedantry. Besides the slim volume of *Spectacula*, he wrote the *Chronica parva* of Ferrara, both of which are in the Biblioteca Estense of Modena. The exact title of the treatise on architecture is 'Pellegrini Prisciani Spectacula ad Illustrissimum D. Ducem Herculem I' (MS lat. 466). The work would appear to have been written between 1486 and 1501, as in 1485 he wrote to the duke, Ercole, telling him that he had identified the person who was holding the manuscript of Alberti's *De re aedificatoria* which had been missing for some time from the duke's library, and his voyage to

popularizing treatise called *Spectacula*, written by Prisciano between 1486 and 1501. Basing what he had to say on the treatises by Vitruvius and Leon Battista Alberti, the author analysed the setting of classical drama in its individual parts, among other things reconstructing a Roman theatre which he seemed to be holding up to Ercole as the model of an ideal permanent Este theatre. It is likely that in 1502, or even before, the duke and Prisciano had thought of reconstructing a *teatro a l'antiqua* in the court *salone*. However, they only got as far as the banked seating; as for the stage, they preferred to fall back on the usual set with six functional crenellated houses, tried and tested over some thirty years.

Whatever the end result, one can say that Ercole was motivated as much by intellectual pride in an indirectly acquired humanist culture as by direct, and therefore more real, understanding of theatrical practice. These were years of radical change in all the elements of spectacle included in dramatic production on the eve of the Renaissance. The collective and sustained experience of those involved in the Ferrarese theatre (headed by Ercole and Prisciano, but together with Collenuccio, Tebaldeo, Niccolò da Correggio and all those concerned in the Sala Grande theatre) could not fail to hold a position of legitimate authority in this process.

Rome, which he refers to in connection with measuring certain Roman monuments, took place in 1501.

Amongst the more recent studies on Prisciano, see A. Beijer, 'An Early 16th-Century Scenic Design in the National Museum, Stockholm, and its Historical Background', in *Theatre Research*, IV (1962), no. 2, pp. 150ff; and A. Rotondo, 'Pellegrino Prisciani', *Rinascimento*, XI (1960), fasc. 1, pp. 69–110. Substantial extracts from *Spectacula*, including notes and diagrams, are now reproduced in F. Marotti, *Lo spettacolo dall'umanesimo al manierismo: Teoria e tecnica* (Milan 1974), pp. 53–77.

3 Regular comedy and the perspective set

Amongst the other things made by the hand of man which can be viewed with enjoyment of eye and contentment of mind is (in my opinion) the uncovering of a stage apparatus, where within a small space one may see, created by the art of perspective, proud palaces, vast temples, divers houses and near and far spacious squares adorned with various buildings, long straight roads crossed by other roads...[1]

If we wish to identify Italian Renaissance staging with the perspective set defined in 1545 by Sebastiano Serlio, in the scene designs of the *Secondo libro dell'architettura*, we ought to begin in 1508, with the letter Bernardino Prosperi wrote in that year to Isabella d'Este, to inform her of a performance of Ariosto's *La cassaria* which had just taken place. And since, as Serlio goes on to say, 'there are three sorts of stage sets, the comic, the tragic and the satyric', it would be necessary to go even further back, to the first commentators of Vitruvius who unearthed this relatively straightforward message amongst the more obscure passages of his *De architectura*.

The concept of the three classical sets, and hence of a unified scene representing a specific place, easily identifiable from the theatrical genre if not from the text itself, had already been formulated in the humanist circles which had adopted the ideas of Leon Battista Alberti. Even without going back to the *Filodosso* (1425–6), in which, if we follow E. Battisti's interpretation,[2] Alberti's intuitive grasp of the single set seems clear though unpremeditated, it is well known that *De re aedificatoria* had already been finished in 1452 and was circulating throughout Italy in manuscript. Alberti wrote:

And as three sorts of poets operated in the theatres, a machine existed which turned on a pivot and immediately presented to the spectators a side so painted that it seemed now a royal palace for the tragedians, now a scene of ordinary houses for the comedians, and now a wood for the satyrists, according to the requirements of the tale which they wished to perform.[3]

Familiarity with the works of Vitruvius and Alberti, especially after they had been almost simultaneously printed (1485–6), was a requirement for all those who moved in humanist and academic circles. We can see it reflected

[1] *Secondo libro dell'architettura*, in *Tutte le opere d'architettura et prospettiva, di Sebastiano Serlio Bolognese* (Venice 1619), p. 44. The first edition of the *Secondo libro* had appeared in Paris in 1545. The relevant parts, with diagrams, are reproduced in Marotti, *Lo spettacolo*, pp. 190–205. The sentence quoted here appears on p. 196.

[2] E. Battisti, 'La visualizzazione della scena classica nella commedia umanistica', in *Commentari*, VIII (1957), pp. 248–56.

[3] From *L'architettura di Leon Battista Alberti, tradotta in lingua fiorentina da Cosimo Bartoli* (Florence 1550), Bk VIII. Bk VIII chap. 7 of *De re aedificatoria* now appears in latin in Marotti. *Lo spettacolo*, pp. 35–45, with a modern Italian translation pp. 45–52. The sentence quoted is on pp. 40 and 49.

in a wider creative and cultural sphere, in which, as we have seen, noble and courtly drama was not the least important element. The different goals aimed at by the humanist scholars and the court entertainers, in their efforts to put the classical programme into action, soon developed two distinct tendencies and two distinct results. The perspective set of *La cassaria* merely furnishes a more striking example of this. The academicians busied themselves with archaeological research into the surviving remains of Roman theatres or with questions of philology, which led to increasingly accurate editions of the works of classical authors and to illustrated commentaries on Vitruvius. When they made more direct contributions to the development of a classical style of dramatic performance, they occasionally attempted with scholarly integrity to test the validity of reconstructions based on archaeological evidence. More frequently, however, they were forced to work within the framework of court spectacle, over which they rarely had control, so that what they did was subordinated to public expectations and the immediate requirements of staging. On the other hand, the love of the classical felt by those who organized performances was all too often an intellectual pose, at times even a matter of convenience. They were prepared to see something 'eternal and ancient' in any set which displayed a sufficient number of round arches, to equate unity of action with an uninterrupted performance, and to put into action unity of place within the old framework of a set with mansions.

This mixture of elements, which was still operating on the familiar ground of medieval tradition, lasted until the first years of the sixteenth century. As we have already seen, it led to solutions like the stage at Velletri, the Terentian portico and the *città ferrarese*, which resembled one another despite the fact that they were differently inspired.

In *Spectacula*, Prisciano reconstructed the Roman *pulpitum* as a raised stage approximately two metres above the ground, 'completely flat yet divided into three parts'. The outer one, facing the theatre, was to correspond to the orchestra; the middle one, 'in which the plays took place', to the proscenium; the inner area, 'where the houses were depicted', to the stage. Prisciano did not, therefore, identify the Greek orchestra with the Roman *platea* ('square') but considered that it was raised and incorporated into the *pulpitum*.

Before tackling the matter of the three fixed sets, the author described the rear section: making use of what Vitruvius said about the *frons scaenae* and the comic set,[4] he incorporated both in a monumental façade which becomes strangely significant if we read the description of it while keeping an eye on the engraving of the Velletri stage:

And the *pulpitum* was adorned with columns: scaffolds (*solari*): and so that one could go from one to another in imitation of houses with entrances: doors: and with one [door] in the centre royally decorated as a temple ('si como regale per ornamento de templi'): and through which the characters could descend and ascend as the story required.

Prisciano interprets the elements of the *frons scaenae* as 'scaffolds', i.e. as

---

[4] Vitruvius described the construction of theatres in the Greek and Roman styles in chaps. 6 to 9 of Bk V of *De architectura*. Amongst the more recent translations see S. Ferri's *Vitruvio. Architettura (dai libri I al VII)* (Rome 1960), with parallel text. For examples of humanist use of Vitruvius, see C. Molinari, 'Il teatro nella tradizione vitruviana: Da Leon Battista Alberti a Daniele Barbaro', in *Biblioteca teatrale*, 1971, p. 39, and Marotti, *Lo spettacolo*, pp. 95–165.

elevated structures similar to the mansions but intercommunicating and functioning on two levels, ornamented with columns and tympana in a Roman style. The image was not really very different from the *frons scaenae* of Numitorius Hilarus. Yet Prisciano lost his chance of realizing his tripartite stage in Ferrara when, probably at the request of the duke, he left Trullo and Segna to make the *città ferrarese* with its wooden walls, crenellated houses, doors, windows and chimneys.

This atmosphere of second-hand classicism, immune from archaeological influence, is more evident in the temporary theatre which Francesco Gonzaga ordered to be built in Mantua during the 1501 carnival, probably in a hall of the Pusterla, his usual residence. Three classical plays were performed there – *Penulo*, Seneca's *Ippolito* and the *Adelphi* – and one imitative work, *Philonico*.[5] The rectangular room was adorned with an imitation porch (*loggia*) round all four sides (two with eight arches and two with six), which gave it the appearance of a 'building ancient and eternal'. Six of the eight arches along one of the long sides were filled by Mantegna's 'Triumph of Caesar'. An unusual lay-out provided for a corner stage 'where one of the long sides joined a short one', with some tiers of seating arranged at right-angles along the sides facing the stage, distributed between the spectators ('ladies, Germans and others') and the players ('trumpeters and musicians'). The set was almost certainly raised, with a proscenium jutting out towards the audience, and it is reminiscent of some of the Terentian engravings (plate 19), resembling a pavilion with architraves and columns rather than a frontal portico. 'Four tall columns with round bases were to be seen, which supported [the figures of] the four principal winds... Within the scene were golden drapes and some greenery, as required by the plays'.[6] Above the columns, between the four

[5] D'Ancona, *Le origini*, I, p. 381, suggests identifying *Philonico* with Fra Giovanni Armonio's *Stephanium* (ed. Venice 1502). In fact, as happened in the case of Seneca's *Fedra*, which was known as the *Ippolito* after its male protagonist, Cantelmo might have given the *Stephanium* the name of another character, *Philodicus*, changing it to *Philonico*.

[6] The Mantuan theatre of 1501 was described by Sigismondo Cantelmo, a Neapolitan gentleman in the service of Ercole I d'Este, in a letter published by G. Campori, *Lettere artistiche inedite* (Modena 1886), p. 5; D'Ancona, *Le origini*, II, pp. 380ff; and now again in *La commedia del Cinquecento*, I, pp. 421–2. Cantelmo's description is unclear, in spite of its many details, and raises many doubts; the following reconstruction is but a proposal. Cantelmo wrote:

> Its shape was quadrangular, slightly longer than [it was] wide; two opposite sides had eight architraves with columns harmonizing with and proportioned to the height of the said arches. Their bases and capitals, painted most splendidly in the finest colours and decorated with leaves, represented to the mind a building ancient and eternal, full of beauty. The arches with flowers in relief formed a wonderful perspective; each was four *braza* [*braccia*] wide and proportionally high. Within the scene were golden drapes and some greenery as required by the plays. One side was decorated with six panels of the Triumph of Caesar by the inimitable hand of Mantegna. The other two sides opposite each other had similar arches, but fewer in number, each having six of them.

Reckoning 65 cm for the average *braccio*, and taking into account the measurements of Mantegna's panels (2 m 74 × 2 m 74), the surface delimited by the false colonnade must have measured about 24 m × 18 m (the span of the arches being 2 m 74, their total span amounted to 21 m 92 × 16 m 44, to which the size of the columns must be added). Cantelmo spoke first of *architravi*, but then used the shorter word *archi*, thus leaving the nature of the tablature undetermined. As regards the base 'painted most splendidly in the finest colours', it must have been a podium rather than an individual base of each column, that is a false plinth resembling the one which runs all around the Wedding Chamber underneath the figures painted by Mantegna. Such a plinth was needed lest the tiers of seats, correctly assumed by Pirrotta to be placed along two adjacent sides of the wall, should partially conceal the arches. On the longer side opposite to the seats six arches were decorated with Mantegna's Triumph of Caesar, now

winds, 'was a grotto, artificial yet most natural', and above it a sky shining with lights, formed by two concentric wheels. One was contrived with the signs of the zodiac and the other, with Fortune at its centre, was divided into three sections, with 'its tenses: *regno, regnavi, regnabo*'. The base of the proscenium ('frontispiece') was decorated with the 'Triumphs of Petrarch', also by Mantegna.

Despite the impression made on Sigismondo Cantelmo, who wrote to Ercole d'Este about the Mantuan entertainments, this hall did not recall an ancient theatre, nor in my opinion was it intended to. One cannot equate the rows of seats at right angles with a semicircular theatre, while the set combined

---

at Hampton Court in London. The last two arches (or, more likely, the first two on the adjacent shorter side) must have been closed with golden curtains; they served for the players' entrances on stage; the latter was unusually located at one corner. It seems evident that a passage ran between the walls and the false colonnade; it was needed both behind the set and behind the tiers of seats for the audience, which formed a right angle along the two sides opposite the stage. In Cantelmo's words: 'Two sides formed the stage for the jugglers and actors, the other two had tiers of seats assigned to the ladies, to Germans and others, to the trumpeters and musicians. At the corner joining one long and one short side four tall columns with round bases were to be seen, which supported [the figures of] the four principal winds. Between them was a grotto, artificial yet most natural. Above it was a sky shining with many lights like most brilliant stars, and with a mechanical wheel bearing the signs [of the Zodiac], to the motion of which now the sun, now the moon revolved in their proper houses. Within [the grotto] was the wheel of Fortune with its tenses: *regno, regnavi, regnabo*; and the golden goddess herself was seated in the middle with a sceptre and a dolphin. Around the stage, at the foot of the frontispiece, were Petrarch's Triumphs also painted by the hand of the said Mantegna.' The stage, then, was placed at the corner whose four arches were covered by golden drapes; it consisted of the four round columns crowned by the four winds, of the grotto and the wheel of Fortune. If I try to visualize the architectural structure formed by the four columns, I see it more easily in the shape of the 'Terentian porch' – more particularly in its variant with three sides, as in the woodcuts for *Phormio* in the Lyonese edition – less easily in its most common variant as a single frontal porch. If the spaces between columns were screened by curtains as in the Terentian woodcuts, they would have been the main element of the set 'with golden drapes and some greenery' as was required by the plays. Furthermore, if the false colonnade rested, as it is most likely, on a podium, the stage, too, must have been raised and had, as in the Terentian woodcuts, a large platform protruding from the proscenium toward the audience, something like the Elizabethan stage. The grotto must have been placed between the winds on the top of the pavilion formed by the four columns. Its only use must have been that of supporting the wheel of Fortune, itself one more variant of the Valenciennes 'Paradise' with concentric wheels or of the *Ascensione* in the Florentine church Il Carmine. It is possible, of course, that Cantelmo's 'between' referred to the four columns rather than to the four winds; however, the resulting structure would make no sense, being cumbersome and useless for the performances.

Other questions arise about the lost 'Triumphs of Petrarch', of which we have probably a reflection in the 'Triumphs' attributed to the school of Mantegna in the National Gallery in Washington (six tablets measuring about 51 cm × 53.8 cm). In my opinion their being placed, according to Cantelmo, 'dintorno alla scena al frontespizio a basso' must be understood as meaning 'all around the lower part of the proscenium'. The term *frontespizio* was used in the early sixteenth century in the general meaning of 'forefront'; it applied, for instance, to the whole stage in the description of the *Paliliae* (Rome 1513). Here it may be taken as meaning the frontal socle of the proscenium protruding toward the audience. If this had a polygonal shape, like the one shown in the woodcuts for *Phormio*, the six tablets may have been distributed in pairs on each of the front sides in view of the audience.

The decoration of the hall was completed by a profusion of lamps, some of them placed so as to lighten the stage, others hanging under the arches among the standards. The hypothesis previously advanced of a flat tablature finds support in the presence of 'statues, broken or whole, painted with silver, gold and other colours, which stood high above the arches, adding much ornament to the place. Last came the sky, made of dark blue cloth and spangled with stars with such constellations as they revolved that very night in our hemisphere.' See A. Luzio, *La Galleria dei Gonzaga venduta all'Inghilterra* (Milan 1931); A. Luzio and E. Paribeni, *Il Trionfo di Cesare di Andrea Mantegna* (Rome 1940). On the decoration of the hall see also Pirrotta's chapter 2.

the humanist idea of a background of columns hung with gold cloth, and the traditional taste for machines, here represented by the heaven with its concentric wheels. In place of God or Jove at the centre of the wheel there was Fortune, the blind goddess who rules over human events, and in whom the pagan and irreligious idea of chance, and the astrological symbol of a belief by now declining, were fused. If anything, the aim was to recreate the atmosphere of Mantegna's Wedding Chamber, with its few touches of classical revival: the imitation portico which surrounded the room and was raised above the floor on a painted plinth, and the heraldic decoration made of emblems and devices, were committed to posterity in the Wedding Chamber to glorify the house of Gonzaga and were exploited to flatter its great allies, the Emperor of Austria, the King of France and the Venetian Signoria in the 1501 theatre. It would seem that even some of the *intermedi* were to be put to political use in that carnival. The Marquis Francesco wrote to Niccolò da Correggio: 'And then we should like another [*intermedio*] in which Italy, Mantua and ourselves should be introduced, in a comparison or discussion in such a way that the acting of three generous people in discussion is introduced into that *festa* of yours which you have now sent me.'[7]

As far as we know, Mantegna did not supervise the staging of the entertainment. This possibly fell to Zafrano, who is known to have been at Gazzolo in January of that year, along with Fedele of Forlì, working on the hangings for a comedy ordered by Cardinal Ludovico Gonzaga. As we have seen, in the 1491 revival of *Orfeo*, Zafrano was authorized to make use of the court painters, and in those years the whole court was entirely under the influence of Mantegna. Whoever painted the artificial loggia in the hall used for the entertainments either took Mantegna's advice, or else constantly bore in mind the architectural *trompe l'oeil* of the Wedding Chamber in the Ducal Castle, with its broken columns, imitation reliefs and metallic statues, so dear to Mantegna's paintings.

After 1508, the divergence between humanist theory and theatrical practice worked in a different way. The academicians pursued a coherent line of research, trusting primarily to interpretations of passages in Vitruvius and archaeological finds, and drawing some encouragement from occasional rigorous revivals such as the Roman theatre of the *Paliliae*, and perhaps the small Cornaro theatre at Loreo.[8] Theatrical practice freed itself from medieval

[7]   Letter written by Francesco Gonzaga to Niccolò da Correggio, dated 28 January 1501, in D'Ancona, *Le origini*, II, p. 380.

[8]   For the *Paliliae*, celebrated in Rome in honour of the conferring of the Roman patriciate on Giuliano and Lorenzo dei Medici, who were respectively the brother and nephew of the pope, the theatre was erected by Pietro Rosselli in the Campidoglio between Palazzo dei Conservatori and the church of Ara Coeli. It had two 'frontispieces', i.e. two *proscenia*. One led into the quadrangular area where the coronation ceremony took place, while the other, in the background and made up of arches closed by golden curtains, formed a background to the performance of Plautus' *Poenulus*. Amongst the various descriptions, by M. A. Altieri, Notturno Napoletano and Palliolo, the latter's is perhaps the most interesting: *Narratione delli spettacoli celebrati in Campidoglio da Romani nel ricevere lo magnifico Juliano et Laurentio de' Medici per suoi patritii* (Rome 1513). The accounts by Altieri, Palliolo and A. Sereno have been reprinted by F. Cruciani in *Il teatro del Campidoglio et le feste romane 1513* (Milan 1968). The book opens with a long introductory chapter by Cruciani, followed by A. Bruschi's 'Ricostruzione...del teatro capitolino'.

Information on the Loreo theatre is contained in a 'Lettera lunga' by Giacomo Alvise Cornaro,

stage techniques and recognized perspective, which had developed through the figurative arts, as the medium which could most accurately express those elements of realism and unity, already felt to be an incumbent need in the *città ferrarese*.

Perspective thus came to be used rather later in scenography than in painting and drawing. Earlier, despite the information in the work of Vitruvius,[9] the rediscovery of classical theatre had not influenced traditional stage decor to the extent of introducing perspective sets. Perhaps the Latin texts lacked both real immediacy and the power, through the work of the translators, to mirror the society which had rediscovered them. They lacked, in other words, that stimulus to realism which was the *raison d'être* of the perspective set. The perspective set was not so much a realization of the three Vitruvian sets as a response to the needs of Renaissance drama, which was beginning to require an illusion of three-dimensional space, created around the realistic acting of the characters.

If, then, there was a single set, as required by the structure of the comedy, which was in its turn influenced by classical ideas, this was no problem. It made it possible to avoid contradicting Vitruvius' classification of sets and the principle of unity of place, which by now had become a constant element (though not yet the subject of dispute) in the dramatic outlook. Writers of treatises, painters, authors and supervisors were all products of the same cultural environment. Many, like Prisciano, Serlio, and Sangallo, did academic archaeological work as well as being creative artists. Even when this was not the case, they knew and influenced one another. It was men connected with the Renaissance theatre who developed perspective sets, for use in an original repertory, but such an achievement cannot be explained without reference to the previous humanist experiments, of which they were a logical, though independent, development.

As far as we know, the first document in which the term 'perspective' was deliberately used about a set is the letter written in 1508 by Bernardino Prosperi to Isabella d'Este. In it, the writer admiringly drew the attention of his correspondent to the set, its novelty and its creator. It seems to me to be too fortunate to be mere coincidence that this should have happened in Ferrara, in the milieu of Ariosto and Giraldi Cintio, at a time when so-called regular comedy was just coming into being on the stage, and the forms of tragedy and pastoral drama were soon to be renewed. Prosperi wrote:

The best part of all these plays and *feste* has been the scenes against which they were performed, which were by one Maestro Peregrino, a painter employed by the Lord; there is a road and a perspective of a town with houses, churches, belfries and gardens.

written on the death of his uncle Alvise, and published by G. Fiocco in 'Alvise Cornaro e i suoi trattati d'architettura', in *Atti dell' Accademia dei Lincei* (1952), pp. 195–222; 'After the hunt he would have a comedy put on, which was performed in his theatre, which he had made in imitation of the ancient ones, for he had built the stage in lasting stone, and the other part, where the audience sat, he made of planks which could be taken up.' L. Zorzi, in his commentary to *Il teatro del Ruzante* (Turin 1967), pp. 1436ff, questions Fiocco's identification, believing that the description may refer to the Casino Cornaro in Padua or to some other villa belonging to the humanist gentleman. Zorzi reiterates this view in *Il teatro e la città*, p. 317 and footnote.

    [9] The first printed edition was the 1486 Sulpizio one, but the treatise was circulating in manuscript in the first half of the century. L. B. Alberti had already studied it by 1450, and referred to distinguishing sets according to their dramatic genre.

A person cannot tire of looking at it for the divers things there depicted, all cleverly contrived and well-planned, and I think it will not be wasted, but that they will save it to use on other occasions.[10]

Pellegrino da Udine, an artist from the north and educated at the school of Giambellino and the Vivarini, was in Ferrara in March 1508 to serve the dukes as a painter. We know little of his skills in perspective, and it would appear that he was new to stage design. The creative spirit which inspired him was probably Ariosto's; the latter, more than Pellegrino, had felt the stimulating influence of the classical models through the texts of Plautus and Terence, which he had read and seen, and in his youth acted.[11] But he also favoured a new style of drama, more a mirror of life than a nostalgic evocation of ancient fables:

> Nova commedia v'appresento piena
> di vari giochi, che né mai latine
> né greche lingue recitarno in scena.

> I present you with a new comedy, full
> Of various diversions, the like of which
> Neither Greek nor Latin tongue ever recited on stage.

The plot was new, and so was the setting.

Bernardino's vague description becomes a recognizable image if one rereads it in the light of Serlio's account forty years later: 'although this style of perspective, of which I shall speak, differs from earlier rules, for those were depicted on flat walls, and this one is substantial and in relief'. Serlio's perspective set was depicted on a series of successive flats, 'with very long and straight roads crossing others', while previous sets, Pellegrino's included, had been painted on a single backcloth. Thus we can reconstruct the set for *La cassaria*, 'which is a street and a perspective of a town'. There was a street in the foreground, on the proscenium, and the perspective view of a city, Taranto or Metellino, in the background: neither classical nor oriental, but with houses, churches, bell-towers and gardens.

When this lay-out is compared with the text of *La cassaria* and with a sketch preserved in the Biblioteca Ariostea in Ferrara, no contradictions emerge. The drawing is in too poor a condition for an attribution to be suggested, though it has been possible to make a copy of it (plate 21). However, since it depicts the central piazza of Ferrara, it has been considered to be a set for *I suppositi*, and the work of Pellegrino da Udine or of Raphael.[12] The broad and spacious

---

[10] D'Ancona, *Le origini*, II, pp. 394–5; and now in *La commedia del Cinquecento*, I, pp. 413–14. On identifying the city in which the action supposedly takes place, either Taranto or Metellino, see Pirrotta, p. 77, note 6 above.

[11] Pellegrino da Udine (born 1476, died Urbino, 17 (or 23) December 1547), was according to Vasari a pupil of Giambellino, but stylistically he is closer to Alvise Vivarini and the Friuli masters. See A. Venturi, *Storia dell'arte italiana* (Milan 1926), series IX, vol. II, pp. 448–52. L. Ariosto, aged nineteen, followed Ercole d'Este to Milan in August 1493, and, it would appear, acted in the three comedies *Captivi*, *Mercator* and *Poenulus* which the duke had performed at the court of Ludovico il Moro (*Diario ferrarese*).

[12] The drawing attributed to Pellegrino in the Library's old catalogue was shown as the work of Raphael in the exhibition of ancient and modern Italian scenography organized by E. Prampolini in 1950/1, for the Italian Cultural Institutes abroad. Raphael did in fact design the sets for the 1519 Rome performance of *I suppositi*, organized by Cardinal Cybo in Castel Sant'Angelo in honour of Leo X, but the Ariostea drawing cannot be by him. Had it been possible to recognize

square on the backcloth reproduces fairly faithfully the Ducal Palace with the Rigobello tower, and the battlements of the Castel Vecchio in the background on the right. In the foreground there are two large houses, on each side of the proscenium. In conformity with Serlio's instructions, they were probably made of two pairs of flats (one pair sideways to show a perspective view, the other facing forward) fastened to each other. With other buildings painted on the backcloth, the lay-out of the set could also have applied to the one described by Prosperi.

According to the evidence of the text, the action of *La cassaria* takes place in an almost private street between the entrances of two nearby houses, one belonging to Crisobolo a rich merchant, and the other to Lucrano a miserly procurer who keeps two young girls, Corisca and Eulalia for sale as slaves. Though the plot makes use of stock situations of classical comedy, it is enlivened by a humour which is urban and Ferrarese, made up of intelligent cunning coloured with slang and biting allusions.

Erofilo, son of Crisobolo, and Caridoro, son of the Pasha of Metellino, plot, with the aid of the servant Volpino, how to free the two girls without paying for them. Taking advantage of the absence of his older master, Volpino steals a chest full of cloth of gold, which he sends to Lucrano's house as a pledge for the acquisition of Eulalia. Erofilo is to denounce the theft to the Pasha and to accuse Lucrano; then Caridoro is to ask the procurer for the two girls in return for interceding with his father for Lucrano's life. The unexpected intervention of some of Erofilo's servants, who abduct Eulalia to give her to their younger master, and the sudden return of Crisobolo, spoil the plot; as a result Volpino ends up in chains despite his fertile inventiveness. At this point Caridoro's servant Fulcio takes the initiative, and succeeds in extorting the money necessary to pay Lucrano from Crisobolo, to redeem Corisca and Eulalia, and to settle them in the house of the obliging Lena.

The action, which spreads over half a day, all takes place in the short stretch of road between the two doors which alone are identified and necessary to the entrances and exits of the characters. The rest of the scene ('houses, churches, gardens and belfries') is less specific, but the city which one imagines to lie behind the backcloth takes on a life and identity of its own, for there are the houses of Lena and Filandro, Chiroro, Critone and Plutero, the Pasha's palace, the piazza and above all the port which constitutes the other centre of the plot; verbal allusions to them give specific reality to the otherwise undetermined set, while references registering the passing of the

Ferrara in the perspectives which made up the set, Giuseppe Paulucci, the Ferrarese orator who described the performance (D'Ancona, *Le origini*, II, pp. 88ff), would not have failed to emphasize the point. The piazza shown in the drawing appears to have been drawn from life, while it seems that Raphael never actually visited Ferrara.

Even the attribution of the drawing to Pellegrino is hypothetical, merely based on his presence in Ferrara in 1509, though in that case he would have had to destroy the 1508 perspective of 'Metellino' or 'Taranto'. There is nothing to support this idea in Prosperi's letter to Isabella in February 1509. Prosperi wrote: 'for the story took place in Ferrara, as he pretends'. It is therefore not impossible that the sketch is of a later date and belongs to a revival of *I suppositi*, or to the three performances (in 1528, 1530, 1531) of *Lena*, which is also set in Ferrara. Lodovico Zorzi, referring to an article by Donato Zaccarini ('Una scena cinquecentesca con la piazza di Ferrara', in *Bolletino statistico del comune di Ferrara*, for the 2nd quarter of 1925), dates this sketch very much later, after 1550, and denies its relevance to the staging of the first Ariosto plays. See *Il teatro e la città*, pp. 27–30 and footnotes pp. 56–8.

hours and the setting of the sun compress the time-scale of the transition from afternoon to night.[13]

In *I suppositi*, which was performed the following year, also at court, Ariosto moved the action to Ferrara and made it contemporary. Like *La cassaria*, it required only two houses, one belonging to Damone and Polinesta, the other to the false Erostato, yet the rest of the city is alive in the background: the Piazza del Duomo, the palace courtyard, the ducal court of justice, the stalls of the merchants, Porta Leone and Castel Vecchio. One's immediate inclination is to associate the drawing in the Biblioteca Ariostea with this comedy.

Then came the burdensome war between the Este family and Venice, and the long break in theatrical activity. The next chronicle reference is in 1513, in Urbino, where the young Duke Francesco Maria, who had recently become Lord of Pesaro as well, was celebrating a joyful carnival. The theatrical entertainments included Bibbiena's *La calandria*, a comedy (perhaps *Eutichia*) by Nicola Grassi, and a third play by the fourteen-year-old Guidobaldo Ruggeri, with all its parts played by children. Baldassare Castiglione, who was asked to direct the entertainments, wrote in confusion to his friend Lodovico Canossa, describing himself as one 'who had to fight with painters and master carpenters and actors and performers of the *moresca*'. Girolamo Genga, painter and ducal architect, was credited, albeit indirectly, with having made the scenery, by both Serlio, who was in Pesaro in 1513, and Vasari.[14]

The theatre took up the Ferrarese idea of a 'walled city', but extended it to the entire room, involving even the audience, which seemed to look out over the moat of the city contained within two walls. The first wall was depicted on the base of the proscenium, as though it encircled the city, the second stood in the centre of the hall like a barrier, or more likely as a parapet to the lowest tier of seats.[15] The stands for the pipers and trumpeters were

---

[13]   *La cassaria*, Act I scene 2 (the action takes place in daylight). Nebbia, Gianda's servant: 'If Crisobolo returns, what will become of me? Do you not know that as he left this morning he entrusted to me all the keys of the house.'

Act IV scene 2. Crisobolo returns carrying a light: 'I stayed so long at Plutero's house without noticing the time that now night has fallen.'

Act V scene 2. Crisobolo: 'How slow the others are in returning. Imagine what it would be like if I stayed away from home three or four months, if after one half day's absence I find myself so happy.'

[14]   Neither Vasari nor Serlio refers specifically to the set for *La calandria*, but both give one to understand that all the theatrical apparatuses made in Urbino in those years were made by him. Vasari wrote (*Le vite*, vol. VI, p. 317): 'Genga was also retained by the duke in particular to make comedy sets and decorations. As he had an excellent understanding of perspective and sound architectural principles, he made them most beautifully.'

Serlio, who figures as a painter in a 1513 list of participants in a procession in Pesaro, wrote in his *Secondo libro dell'architettura*: 'This is what I saw with my eyes: several sets arranged by the knowledgeable architect Girolamo Genga at the request of his master Francesco Maria, Duke of Urbino. I could appreciate such liberality in the prince, such fine judgement and skill in the architect, and such beauty in what had been done as I had never seen the like of it in any other work made by art.' B. Castiglione's letter is quoted in D'Ancona, *Le origini*, II, pp. 102ff, and in *La commedia del Cinquecento*, vol. I, pp. 445–8, together with another account of the same occasion on pp. 448–52. For a laborious but informative study of the whole festival, see F. Ruffini: 'Analisi contestuale della "Calandria" nella rappresentazione urbinate del 1513: 1. Il luogo teatrale', in *Biblioteca teatrale* 15/16, 1976, pp. 70–139. See, for more information about Genga and the della Rovere. O. Rossi-Pinelli, 'La villa Imperiale di Pesaro come spazio scenico per la corte urbinate', in *L'architettura del teatro in Italia*, pp. 219–34.

[15]   It seems less likely, though not impossible, that the second 'wall' of the moat was at the back of the hall, between the two musicians' stands, as one might be given to understand by the sentence 'the hall became as it were the moat of the city'.

in the two back corners of the hall, and the raised stage was opposite them.

The setting represented an outer road between the city wall and the last houses. Between the stage and the ground was a most natural representation of the city wall with two towers: the pipers stood on one end of the hall and the trumpeters at the other. In the middle was another fine wall: the hall became as it were the moat of the city, traversed by two walls like dams (Castiglione).

The ceiling of the hall was hidden by an awning of greenery, through which passed the rods holding the double row of chandeliers:

Enormous balls of greenery were attached to the ceiling of the hall so that they almost hid the vault, from which also hung wires through holes in the roses. These wires held two rows of candelabra…which shed a great light. The set then depicted a beautiful city, with streets, palaces, churches, towers, real streets and everything in relief, but also aided by excellent painting and properly understood perspective.

Castiglione thus carefully distinguished between 'streets' and 'real streets', having already specified that the set 'depicted an outer road between the city wall and the last houses'. The stage designer had therefore envisaged several streets, represented in different ways. One the 'outer road', which can be equated with the proscenium, was intended to be acted on and was spacious enough to permit the *intermedi* to appear on decorated floats. Other passages, the 'real streets', must have been behind the nearest free-standing houses, and been intended for the entrances of the actors, while finally those simply called 'streets' must have been painted in perspective on the backcloth. At one side, though it is unclear whether of the proscenium or the backcloth, there was a triumphal arch, and in the centre an octagonal temple.

Amongst the other things there was an eight-sided temple in semi-relief, all covered with stucco carvings telling wonderful stories. The alabaster windows were an illusion, as were all the architraves and mouldings of fine gold and ultramarine. In places there was glass looking like real jewels, free-standing figures apparently made of marble, decorated columns: it would take too long to recount everything. This was almost in the centre: at one end there was a triumphal arch…Between the architrave and the vault of the arch the story of the three Horatii was most beautifully portrayed: it looked like marble but was in fact painted. In two little niches…two Victories made of stucco, carrying trophies. On top of the arch was a beautiful equestrian figure…on either side of the horse were two small altars, on top of each of which stood a vessel full of fire, which lasted for the length of the comedy.

These are the only two buildings described by Castiglione and at least one of them, the triumphal arch, was a classical monument, appropriate in that the action was supposed to take place in Rome. Castiglione himself does not insist on the identity of the 'beautiful city', just as Bibbiena does not revert to the idea of Rome after his caustic announcement in the 'Argument':

Do not think that [the characters] *come* from Rome by magic at such speed, for the town you see here *is* Rome. Once she was so great that, in triumph, she easily absorbed many cities and lands and rivers into herself; and now she has become so small that, as you see, she easily fits into your city. Such is the way of the world.

The play's location in Rome is arbitrary; the author is not interested in this to support the mood of the action, nor as a pretext for its development in 'real' time spent off stage. The plot and its subplot are entirely resolved on-stage around Calandro's house, which is the only identified place which the author requests should be added to the road as part of the acting space. Every unforeseen event and every change of mood take place before the eyes of the audience, which is deliberately involved in the characters' way of life, always and only seeking the pleasurable gratification of their senses. The 'enchanted and fantastic realism' written of by Russo,[16] in which love is exalted 'as physical high-spirits, as unrestrainable ardour, as a sort of celebration of body and mind', has nothing in common with the splendid set produced at Urbino. In any case Bibbiena was far off, at the papal court, and the comedy had been written without any thought about what apparatus it would be acted on. Perhaps Castiglione and Girolamo Genga had been ordered not only to entertain the guests, but also to arrange a celebratory show, so that the monumental Rome depicted in stucco and perspective was not so much Calandro's city as the abode of Julius II, the city which recognized Francesco Maria della Rovere as its prefect.[17]

In any case, the commemorative intention of the Urbino entertainments is also confirmed by the politically-inspired nature of the *intermedi*. Four allegorical pantomimes were performed with *La calandria*: the *moresca* of Jason, and the floats of Venus, Neptune and Juno. These alluded, though indirectly and with some distortion, to recent events of the League of Cambrai and the Holy League. Fifth and lastly Cupid sprang from beneath the stage to clarify 'the meaning of the *intromesse* with a few stanzas'. Jason's *moresca* apparently symbolized the war which had taken place 'between those earth-bound brothers, as we now see wars taking place between neighbours and between those who should make peace', while Love who had arrived with Venus' float had 'with holy fire kindled first men and the earth, then the sea and the air, to banish war and discord and unite the world in harmony'.

Thus the perspective city, created by the Ferrarese designers around the gay episodes of Ariosto and intended to be realistic, had already become at Urbino, where the court was maintained by the pope's nephew, a courtly pretext for laudatory display. But even though such tendencies were to recur, with different emphases, in the great entertainments of princes, they always remained exceptional, and linked to exceptional events; comedy was not commonly performed in this way, for comedy was constantly spreading even outside the courts. It was not yet restricted by the conventions of public and professional performance, but was entrusted to the initiative of bands of revellers and of semi-professional companies.

Machiavelli's *La mandragola* is the best example of this aspect of comedy; in the prologue the author himself acknowledges that the setting is a generic one. In the first verses which introduce the comedy (though the rest of the play is in prose) there is no evidence of any intention to depict the Florentine milieu. Psychologically what matters is the presence of the two buildings, Nicia's house and Fra Timoteo's church, in the foreground. The entire action of the play takes place, quite realistically, between them. The author is not

---

[16]   L. Russo, *Commedie fiorentine del Cinquecento* (Florence 1939).
[17]   Francesco Maria della Rovere (1490–1538) had been named Prefect of Rome by his uncle Julius II in 1504. In 1514 he had been created Duke of Pesaro, and the carnival that year was celebrated particularly elaborately.

really concerned with unity of place; what interests him is the 'real time of the action' and thus the 'temporal perspective'[18] which allows the long and amorous night of Lucrezia and Callimaco to pass between Acts IV and V. This is underlined by Fra Timoteo:

They are all snugly at home, and I shall go to the cloister. And you, spectators, do not criticize what we do, for nobody is going to sleep tonight, so that the acts will not be interrupted by time [off]. I shall recite my office; Ligurio and Siro will dine, for they have not eaten all day long, and the doctor will be trotting back and forth from the bedroom to the living room, to make sure the pot keeps on the boil. As for Callimaco and Madonna Lucrezia, they will not sleep, for I know for sure that we would not sleep, were I in his place and you in hers.

This is the only time which really passes off-stage; the rest of the comedy does not require an imaginary off-stage dimension. The city depicted on the backcloth is deliberately vague:

> Vedete l'apparato,
> quale or vi si dimostra:
> questa è Firenze vostra;
> un'altra volta sarà Roma o Pisa:
> cosa da smascellarsi dalle risa.

Behold the setting, as it is shown before you: this is your Florence; another time it will be Rome or Pisa: it's enough to split your sides with laughter.

It is a formula which was to be adopted by many sixteenth-century authors, especially in semi-professional circles. Thus we find in Dolce's prologue to *Il capitano*:[19]

> Questa è Ragusa; un'altra volta Mantova
> sarà o Cremona: e io che forma et habito
> ho di soldato, sarò Prete o Monaco.

This is Ragusa; another time it will be Mantua or Cremona: and I, who have the dress and aspect of a soldier, shall be a priest or a monk.

The occasion of the entertainment and the nature of the audience could thus also influence the intended purpose of the scenery. *La mandragola* was intended for the Compagnia della Cazzuola, an enterprising group made up of artists and rich Florentines, who performed it in 1518 'in the home of Bernardino di Giordano, by Monteloro'. 'The perspective, which was most beautiful, was the work of Andrea del Sarto and Aristotile' (da Sangallo).[20]

[18] See Pirrotta part I, chapter 4 above.

[19] *Il capitano*, a comedy by M. Ludovico Dolce, performed in Mantua before His Excellency the Duke (Venice 1545).

[20] On the date of *La mandragola*, see Ridolfi, *Vita di Niccolò Machiavelli*, pp. 442ff, note 19. On A. Parronchi's suggestion that *La mandragola* was performed in 1518, see Pirrotta, pp. 123–24, note 12 above. There also appear to me to be problems in associating the much discussed panels in Urbino, Baltimore and Berlin with the three comedies referred to by Parronchi, namely *Pisana*, *Falargo* and *La mandragola*. In my opinion the panels are of an earlier date and do not necessarily depict theatrical scenes at all, but idealized views of cities such as were common in marquetry and in the decoration of *cassoni* (cf. P. Schubring, *Cassoni, Truhen und Truhenbilder der italienischen Frührenaissance* (Leipzig 1923). Even assuming that the panels were suggested by real theatrical sets, Lorenzo Strozzi's *Falargo* would have been performed using a set (the Baltimore panel) whose iconography was closer to the tragic than to the comic genre. See also Zorzi, *Il teatro e la città*, pp. 76–8 and 85–7.

Vasari, who provided a report on the performance, did not describe the set, but Machiavelli took care to identify what he considered to be the essential areas on stage:

> Quello uscio che mi è qui in su la man ritta,
> la casa è d'un dottore
> che 'mparò in sul Buezio legge assai.
> Quella via che è colà in quel canto fitta,
> è la Via dello Amore,
> dove chi casca non si rizza mai.
> Conoscer poi potrai
> a l'abito d'un frate,
> qual priore o abate
> abiti el tempio ch'all'incontro è posto,
> se di qui non ti parti troppo tosto.

The entrance which is here at my right-hand is the house of a doctor who learnt a lot of law from Boethius. The road which is shown on that side is Love Alley; whoever collapses there never stands erect again. Later, if you do not leave too soon, you will be able to recognize by his friar's habit what prior or abbot lives in the temple which is placed opposite.

The prologue does not mention Callimaco's house, though the text requires it to be on stage and available for acting (Act II scene 4). The plan of the set envisaged by Machiavelli, if not by Andrea del Sarto and Sangallo, was hardly wider than the 1508 set and can still be construed according to the plan of the 'Ferrarese piazza': a wide proscenium for the main action; at the sides, at the beginning of the raked area, two buildings which the actors can enter (the church on the left and Nicia's house on the right); two symmetrical buildings further upstage (Callimaco's house and an unidentified one) and finally the perspective backcloth. Between the backcloth and the two houses on the right ran Love Alley from which Callimaco, masked and dressed in a beggar's short coat, was to emerge singing.

In any case, most of the comedies written in the first twenty years of the sixteenth century would not require a different stage lay-out. For all its splendid stuccoes and gold reliefs, the size of its trap-doored stage and the array of floats deployed for the *intermedi*, the set used for *La calandria* in Urbino does not seem to have been differently arranged. And yet within a few years scenographic technique, and consequently the ground-plan of the stage, do appear to have changed appreciably. Scenography progressed from the 'picture-perspective'[21] mainly achieved by means of a large backcloth, to a lay-out in depth with successive flats symmetrically arranged within the real space of the stage. The stage itself was lengthened and divided into two areas: the proscenium, which was flat and all available for acting, and the raked area which housed the perspective flats, and which could only be acted on at the level of the first houses. Here Serlio's description is very apt: 'Inasmuch as this style of perspective of which I shall speak differs from earlier rules,

---

[21]   How these 'perspectives as paintings', all depicted on a single plane or else having bas-relief motifs, may have looked can be gathered from the wooden inlays common from the later fifteenth to the early sixteenth century (Federico da Montefeltro's Studiolo in Urbino, the choir of Santa Maria Maggiore in Bergamo, the sacristy of the Charterhouse of St Martin in Naples), as well as from the Lombardesque reliefs in the Scuola Grande di San Marco in Venice.

in that they were conceived on flat walls while this is substantial and free-standing ('materiale e di rilievo'), it is right that we should follow a different road.'

Vasari, who was as vague and imprecise about dates as he was acute and penetrating in artistic judgement,[22] attributed this innovation to Baldassare Peruzzi, a Sienese painter who spent much of his life in Rome, under the protection of Agostino Chigi and the Medici popes:

It is sufficient [to say] that, at the time of Pope Leo X, Baldassare made two sets which were marvellous and paved the way for those who have made them in our own day. Nor can one imagine how he fitted, in such a narrow site, so many roads, palaces and strange temples, loggias and cornices, so well contrived that they seemed not artificial but substantial, the piazza not a small and painted thing, but real and enormous.

One of the two comedies referred to by Vasari was probably Plautus' *Poenulus*, staged in September 1513 by Tommaso Inghirami and Camillo Porzio at the end of the second day of the *Paliliae*, which were held in the Capitol to celebrate the conferring of the Roman patriciate on Giuliano and Lorenzo dei Medici. The second was Bibbiena's *La calandria*, performed in the Vatican in the autumn of 1514, under the direction of its author and in honour of Isabella d'Este.

It is unlikely that the technical innovations alluded to by Vasari applied to *Poenulus*. Even though the writer speaks of a 'perspective so beautiful that one cannot imagine one more so', with 'fine and varied houses, divers loggias and curious doors and windows', it fitted into a much larger and classically-inspired set. Five other painters worked on it, as well as Peruzzi and Pietro Rosselli, the architect of the theatre.[23]

The set for *La calandria*,[24] which was 'beautiful, far more beautiful than the one he had made before', has been identified in turn with each of the various surviving sketches by Peruzzi. However, in my opinion these either date from after 1514 or else cannot be linked with Bibbiena's text. It is therefore difficult to establish when Peruzzi did produce his innovation, and whether it occurred without the cooperation of other artists, as is likely. In any case, it is clear that most of his scenographic drawings display the characteristics of technique and perspective which Sebastiano Serlio later took up and described in their stage form. Serlio met Peruzzi in Rome in the last years of the latter's life, between 1535 and 1537, and became so close a friend that on his death Peruzzi left him a group of drawings, most of which Serlio then used to illustrate his *Trattato dell'architettura*. Three drawings, now

---

[22]   Vasari, *Le vite*, vol. IV, pp. 589ff. Amongst other things Vasari wrote: 'And either before or after *La calandria* was performed, which was one of the first comedies in the vulgar tongue to be seen or heard, it is enough [to say] that at the time of Leo X Baldassare made two marvellous sets, which paved the way for those being made in our own day.' On Peruzzi's theatrical activities, cf. *Enciclopedia dello spettacolo* (Florence and Rome 1961), VIII, cols. 34–7.

[23]   See note 8 above.

[24]   Cardinal Bibbiena's *La calandria*, previously performed in Urbino in 1513, was repeated in Rome in the autumn of 1514 in the Vatican, to honour the presence of Isabella d'Este. Amongst the sketches commonly assumed to be linked to the spectacle is the one which depicts a set and is preserved in the Gabinetto dei Disegni e delle Stampe in the Uffizi (Arch. 291), and the drawing in the Biblioteca Reale in Turin.

in the Uffizi, especially confirm Serlio's debt to the Sienese master. These are a set usually regarded as being for *La calandria*, and the plan and elevation of a set for the *Bacchides*, performed in Rome in 1531 to celebrate a marriage between one of the Cesarini family and a Colonna.

In the words of Francesco Gonzaga, Mantuan ambassador to Rome:

On the first day the bride was conducted to her new house escorted by most of the ambassadors. We danced before and after dinner, through part of the night. On the second day we similarly made merry until dinner, to which almost all the cardinals came. Afterwards there was a performance of Plautus' *Bacchides*, which lasted almost till daybreak. The same happened on the third day, that is dances and a play, which had been composed by a servant of Monsignor Cesarino. The decoration was beautiful, especially the sets of the comedies, considering the smallness of the place, which seemed much greater than it really was by an artful use of perspective.[25]

Even the two Uffizi drawings (plate 20), authenticated in writing on the back by Peruzzi's son Sallustio, show a set which must have covered an area at most 14.20 m wide by 10.55 m deep. The stage was effectively divided into three areas: the proscenium, the nearest section of the raked area and the back-of-stage. The proscenium (at most 1.80 m deep) and the nearest section of the raked area represented a piazza surrounded by the houses of the protagonists, in which most of the action took place. The piazza was 5.10 m deep ('20 *palmi* $\frac{1}{2}$ *dita* the whole piazza' is indicated on the drawing). It was 14.20 m wide at the proscenium and 11.95 m wide at the opposite side, about half-way to the back of the stage. The front of the piazza thus came to form a sort of half-stage perspective, made up of Nicobolo's house ('with shops') on the left, and the house of the Bacchides on the right. Between the two houses opened the *via ad forum*, a foreshortened, not practicable road which filled the back-of-stage, about 5.50 m deep and 2.90 m wide at its entrance. The actors entered and exited not only from the proscenium, but also from two 'streets' ('*via*') about 40 cm wide, situated half-way to the back of the stage, on the far side of the piazza.

It was on this plan, which applies to all the surviving sketches, that Peruzzi built his idealized city, piazza, street or market place, a compromise between realism and the classification of Vitruvius. The first two drawings depict a set for a comedy: an Athenian square, with the houses of Nicobolo, Filosseno and the Bacchides beside the Temple of Apollo with the Via del Foro and the *viridarium* (plate 22). The third drawing, assumed to be the set for *La calandria*, shows a view of Rome in which 'the houses...should belong to noble personages',[26] an ambiguous cross between a comic and a tragic set. The plan differs little from the one we have looked at: beyond the proscenium came the piazza, flanked by four monumental buildings which could be used for acting. In the middle distance there were two more buildings, one on either side, which were possibly acting spaces. One was a domestic house with a shop, the other the church of Santa Maria della Pace, obviously prior to Cortona's

---

[25] Letter by F. Gonzaga published by A. Luzio in *Archivio storico mantovano*, vol. I, p. 23. The two drawings in the Uffizi are marked Arch. 268 and Arch. 269. See F. Cruciani, 'Gli allestimenti scenici di Baldassare Peruzzi' in *L'architettura del teatro in Italia*, pp. 155–72; and, for the performance of 1531, F. Cruciani, 'Prospettive della scena: "Le Bacchidi" del 1531', in *Biblioteca teatrale* 15/16 (1976), pp. 49–69.
[26] Serlio, *Secondo libro dell'architettura*, p. 46r.

restoration. In the background is a view, curiously celebrating the archaeological remains of the city through an arbitrary topography, for it jumbles
together classical monuments and Renaissance buildings: the Colosseum, the
Torre delle Milizie, the bell-tower of San Lorenzo in Miranda, the three pillars
of the Temple of Castor, the obelisk, Trajan's Column, Castel Sant'Angelo, and
in the centre an arch inspired by the Arco degli Argentari in the Foro Boario.

The similarities between Peruzzi's Roman square and the two sets, comic
and tragic, published by Serlio in his treatise are so obvious that they lead
one to wonder whether the former was not the model. The lay-out is the same,
the houses very similar; almost the same classical buildings are reproduced
in the tragic set, behind the central arch. One cannot discount the idea that
the sketch was made for *La calandria*, but there is another attractive
hypothesis: that it belonged to that group of drawings 'of the antiquities of
Rome' collected by Peruzzi, who intended to turn them into a volume not
contradicting but rivalling Vitruvius. On Peruzzi's sudden death, these
drawings may have been left in the hands of Sebastiano Serlio.[27]

So we are back to our original problem: how far can Renaissance
scenography be equated with the three perspective sets illustrated by Serlio
and by subsequent sixteenth-century treatises? How far did the perspective
city of the Renaissance solve all the problems posed by the humanists'
preoccupation with the unity of place, the Vitruvian classification of scenes,
and their subordination to dramatic genre? Is it even necessary to discriminate
in this way, or is not the marvellous geometric perspective, both realistic and
conventional, with its central axis and single focal point the coherent
conclusion and harmonious resolution of these apparently contradictory
elements?

Already in Urbino the classically influenced set of *La calandria* seems to have
been intended as celebratory rather than realistic. Already Peruzzi had fused
the tragic and comic scenes into a single urban view incorporating all the
traditional elements: the piazza with its temples and monuments, the market
with its shops, the inn and the house of the procuress. The satyric scene
preserved its own attributes, except where it came to coincide with natural
decorations, but it was still very rare. Serlio described one such set made by
Girolamo Genga, which he probably saw at Pesaro around 1525:

How magnificent it was to see so many trees and fruits, so much grass and different
flowers, all made of fine silk in various colours. The river banks and abundant rocks
were set with different sea-shells, snails and other small animals, many-coloured pieces

[27] B. Cellini, 'Discorsi sopra l'arte. Dell'architettura', appendix to the *Vita* (Rome 1901), p.
797:

> The said Baldassare had had many talks with the said Bastiano, and had argued with good
> reason that Vitruvius had not given [definite] rules for that most beautiful of the deeds
> of the ancients [i.e. theatre]; thus the said Baldassare had followed his own judgement
> in all the works that he had made in imitation of the ancients. Death however took away
> the poor artist when he had all prepared in good order...But the results of his labours
> had been left with the said Bastiano, who had them printed...There were five of them,
> one of which had been made [by Bastiano while] in the service of King Francis in 1542,
> at which time I [also] served the said King.

Indeed Serlio, too, repeatedly expressed his indebtedness to and admiration of Peruzzi, more
particularly in the proem to his *Quarto libro dell'architettura*. More recent studies are M. Rosci,
'Sebastiano Serlio e il teatro del Cinquecento', in *L'architettura del teatro in Italia*, pp. 235–42;
and F. Mancini, M. T. Muraro, E. Povoledo, *Illusione e pratica teatrale* (Vicenza 1975), pp. 33–40.

of coral, mother-of-pearl and sea-crabs, with so many wonderful things that it would take me too long if I wished to describe them all. I shall say nothing of the satyrs, the nymphs, the sirens, and the different monsters and strange animals, so artfully made that, when they were put on by men and children (according to size) who went about with appropriate movements, they really seemed like live animals.[28]

But the pastoral eclogues, sixteenth-century surrogates for satyric drama, were most often performed in the urban perspective set common to all the entertainments performed for a celebration or carnival. This 'piazza plus road', this monumental market, was in fact the ideal setting for Renaissance entertainments, both the elaborate celebratory court festivals and the less elaborate shows put on by the bands of revellers. When, with the revival of interest in Aristotelian aesthetics in the middle of the century, the arguments about the three unities began again, even the commentators on Vitruvius who had come to reason on the rules of *De architectura* by different routes, adopted the perspective solutions of regular theatre, adapting them to the idea of *versiles* sets and *periaktoi* (to be discussed later).[29]

Between 1520 and 1580, most of our information on the theories and practical experiments of the academicians comes from the Sangallos, Andrea Palladio, and Daniele Barbaro. Already, in a drawing now in the Uffizi and dated between 1515 and 1530, Antonio da Sangallo il Giovane had made use of a tripartite stage bearing no resemblance to the Roman *frons scaenae*, in an attempt to realize Vitruvius' set. 'On the stage was what today we call a set (*apparato*) and it represented a hall, with, on either side, a hospice (*ospitio*) or a room from which the actors emerged. This was provisional, since it could be given three sorts of stage decorations, according to circumstances.' This particular set (*aula regia*) was conceived by Sangallo as an open area, with a few houses merely hinted at, though in perspective. He combined the two elements together, i.e. the *ospitalia* doors and the *versurae*, (the walls at the two ends of the *pulpitum*) and interpreted them as two towers flanking the *aula regia*; this last was understood to be permanent, whereas the *ospitalia* were 'provisional' and could be adapted to the needs of the particular story.

A few years later, and certainly before 1548, Antonio's brother Battista da Sangallo annotated the text of Vitruvius on a printed edition by Sulpizio da Veroli, now in the Corsini Library in Rome. In the margin of the section 'De Tribus Scaenarum Generibus' he drew three perspective drawings in the manner of Peruzzi, labelled *scena comica*, *scena tragica* and *scena satiresca*.

The role of Andrea Palladio was more important and decisive. A member of the Accademia Olimpica founded in Vicenza in 1555, he took an active part in the life and organization of the association. Amongst other things, he was asked in 1561 to build a temporary theatre in the Basilica, for performing Alessandro Piccolomini's *L'amore costante*, and in 1562 the structure was renovated and re-used for the production of *Sofonisba* by Giangiorgio Trissino. Two of the six small frescoes which adorn the Odeon annexed to the Teatro Olimpico give us a picture of the two performances and the classically-influenced theatre, with a semicircular *cavea* and a *frons scaenae*. Although

---

[28] Serlio, *Secondo libro dell'architettura*, p. 47v. See F. Marotti, *Lo spettacolo*, pp. 202–3.
[29] See R. Klein and H. Zerner, 'Vitruve et le théâtre de la Renaissance italienne', in *Le lieu théâtral à la Renaissance* (Paris 1964).

these frescoes were not painted until 1595, and one cannot rule out the possibility that the painter allowed himself to be influenced by the contemporary hall nearby when evoking past performances, nevertheless their trustworthiness is confirmed by the description by the secretary of the Academy.[30] One may legitimately assume that Palladio had already, in 1561, established the architectural solutions to which he gave a definitive form in the last months of his life, when he drew the Teatro Olimpico project, which was faithfully completed after his death by his son Silla.

Both the secretary's description and the two frescoes insist on the coexistence of a *frons scaenae* and a perspective set. The *frons scaenae* had a central arch-shaped entrance and two smaller doors with architraves; the perspective conceived by Palladio and executed by Fasolo and Giovan Battista Zelotti could be glimpsed behind the three entrances. This was an interesting conception, which moved beyond the whole convention of the 'urban view' and included not only the elements of the tragic and comic sets, but also those belonging to the satyric one:

...through the door on the right could be seen houses which resembled those of the main perspective [which could be seen through the central door], and through the one on the left could be seen a landscape with many trees and behind the other doors on both sides (the *versurae*) were other houses. Not everything which showed through the doors was painted, most of it was free-standing, and people entered through these doors, just as they did from the main perspective...

The theatre for which the noble Compagnia degli Accesi of Venice asked Palladio in 1565, for their performance of *Antigone*, a tragedy by Conte di Monte, must have been designed along the same lines. Vasari, while telling us that the artist was helped by Federico Zuccari to make the set, gives us a rather inadequate description of it:

Now Federigo, although entreated to return from Venice, was not able to comply, and so had to stay for the carnival in that city, in the company of the architect Andrea Palladio. Palladio had made for the gentlemen of the Compagnia della Calza a wooden half-theatre in the shape of a colosseum, in which a tragedy was to be recited, and he had Federigo paint twelve great narratives in the set, each seven and a half *piedi* in either direction,[31] with an infinite number of episodes drawn from the deeds of Hyrcanus King of Jerusalem, in accordance with the subject of the tragedy.

While it is justifiable to think of a hall in classical style with a semicircular *cavea*, the arrangement of the set is unclear. Intuitively one would guess that it was a Renaissance panelled decoration. There is nothing either to bear out or to contradict Magagnato's suggestion that the panels were intended to decorate a hypothetical *frons scaenae*.

The Olimpico scene, originally conceived by Palladio, was constructed along different lines by Vincenzo Scamozzi, when he was entrusted with the job in May 1584, after the decision had been taken to open with *Edipo Tiranno*, which was to be produced by Angelo Ingegneri in the translation by Orsato Giustiniani. Lionello Puppi[32] seems to consider this substitution of the

---

[30]   See L. Magagnato, *Teatri italiani del Cinquecento* (Venice 1954), pp. 55ff.

[31]   Approximately 2 m 45 × 2 m 45.

[32]   L. Puppi, 'La rappresentazione inaugurale dell'Olimpico', in *Critica d'arte* (1962), no. 51 pp. 57–64; no. 52, pp. 57–69. See also L. Schrade, *La représentation d'Edipo Tiranno au Teatro*

inaugural text very important. A tragedy by Sophocles was to be performed instead of Fabio Pace's pastorale, as had been intended when Palladio designed his theatre and envisaged behind the three doors of the *frons* a set less important and less visible than Scamozzi's, though still in perspective. But I believe that Palladio's ideas were more conditioned by the restricted space available than by the modest demands of the pastorale. Scamozzi took heed of the advice of Angelo Ingegneri, who required 'a city which resembles as far as possible the place where the story of Oedipus occurred', and proposed to show the walls, palaces, temples and Cadmean gods. But when he came to put these ideas into practice, he decided instead on an 'idealized reconstruction of foreshortened views and perspectives of the streets of Vicenza'.[33] Rather than to the Sophoclean text, Scamozzi conformed to the custom already established from the time when Peruzzi, and following his example the Sangallos, Serlio, Barbaro and the other theoreticians, had used perspective techniques to produce the three Vitruvian scenes.

Palladio had accepted this formula from 1556 when, in illustrating the *De architectura* published by Daniele Barbaro, he imagined three roads in perspective mounted on *periaktoi*, behind the three entrances of the *frons scaenae*. He twice put this into practice in the Basilica theatre: for a comedy, *L'amore costante*, and for a tragedy, *Sofonisba*. Daniele Barbaro, when he published his *Practica di perspectiva* (1568) took the engravings from Serlio's treatise as his model for the three fixed sets. Finally Angelo Ingegneri, when he commemorated the performances of 1585 in Vicenza years afterwards, in *Poesia rappresentativa*, confirmed and defined the convention:

Actually the set is more tragic than comic, and in no way pastoral. Nevertheless with well-chosen changes and additions it could be adapted to all uses...But for tragedy I see in it one very great advantage: that the 'front' [plate 26] (which according to the custom of the ancients represented nothing other than some famous building made as an ornament to whichever city had been chosen as the setting, and from whose arches the actors enter and exit as required) can very conveniently serve as one side of a courtyard or a royal palace, and the proscenium for its piazza.[34]

But if the play being performed was a comedy, the proscenium reverted to being 'understood as a road or other public place of the city'; and not the *frons* but the perspective, worked out on the back with five diverging roads, became the ideal background for the action.

The solution represented by the Teatro Olimpico was unique in its perfection. Scamozzi himself, when he planned the ducal theatre of Sabbioneta in 1588, returned to Serlio's scheme of an urban view with a central axis and a single focal point. This style of set, a product more of comic than of tragic practice,

Olimpico (Paris 1960); G. Nogara, *Cronache degli spettacoli nel Teatro Olimpico di Vicenza dal 1585 al 1970* (Vicenza 1972); A. Gallo, *La prima rappresentazione al Teatro Olimpico* (Milan 1973); D. Gioseffi, 'Palladio e Scamozzi: il recupero dell'illusionismo integrale nel teatro vitruviano', in *L'architettura del teatro in Italia*, pp. 271–86; L. Puppi, 'Le esperienze scenografiche palladiane prima dell'Olimpico', *ibid.*, pp. 287–308; F. Barbieri, 'Il Teatro Olimpico: dalla città esistenziale alla città ideale', *ibid.*, pp. 309–22.

[33] Magagnato, *Teatri italiani*, p. 60.

[34] A. Ingegneri, *Della poesia rappresentativa e del modo di rappresentare le favole sceniche* (Ferrara 1598). See Marotti, *Lo spettacolo*, pp. 299–300.

had by then become indispensable, because of its adaptability. It was at once multiple and single, as the same set remained in place for the whole performance while providing all the necessary locations: the street, the piazza, the church, the house and even the interior, which was suggested by the device of having a character talk from a window. The scene is at once realistic and illusive, for reality was recast so that it was intellectualized rather than historical or illustrative, and while an attempt was made to create the illusion of real space around the actions of the characters, there was no need for this space to correspond to a recognizable milieu. It was a conventional set, since it was conditioned by the dramatic genre and not by the content of the play, but this generic quality could be offset, if the author wished, as soon as the speeches of the characters evoked the atmosphere of the city which was supposed to lie behind the scenes, alive and at times involved in the action.

Aretino's *La cortigiana* is a model example of this. The action is spread over the whole of Rome, starting from the set which represented a street 'in Borghi', not far from St Peter's. Here the characters meet, separate, and find each other again, getting involved in the tangle of a picaresque action without a plot, inconceivable outside the climate of that splendid, sordid, unforgettable papal city. 'A curse be on Rome, on those who live there, and on those who love her and believe in her. And just to spite her, let me say that I believed that the scourge Christ sent, in the hands of the Spaniards, had improved her, but she is now worse than ever.' So ends the first act, with the curse of the Florentine fisherman hoaxed by Rosso. But 'Rome is Rome' and Aretino, though by then a Venetian, still retained a vivid image of it. Flaminio and Valentino go to talk 'in Belvedere'. Rosso, together with 'il Frappa', 'lo Squarcia', 'il Tartaglia' and 'il Targa', comes along the Via della Pace from Campo dei Fiori, and finally the painter and wit Andrea leads the stupid Sienese Maco to visit the city:

A: ...let's go to see Campo Santo, the Guglia, Saint Peter's, La Spina, Banchi, Tor di Nona.
M: Does Torre di Nona ever ring vespers?
A: Yes, by pulling on ropes [i.e. 'tratti di corda' – torture].
M: Amazing.
A: And then we'll go to Ponte Sisto and through all the *chiassi* [narrow streets] of Rome.
M: Is the *chiasso* [turmoil? brothel?] all over Rome?
A: It's all over Italy.
M: What church is this?
A: Saint Peter's, enter to pray.[35]

The portrait of Rome figures in another of Aretino's comedies, *Talanta*: a splendid and tangible Rome, recognizable by its most famous monuments, all visible on stage at the author's express wish.

The performance was exceptional in every way: for the time and place, and for the scenographic procedures which retained the traditional qualities of the perspective city while injecting into it new elements which led it towards solutions of greater moment than can have been realized at the time.

---

[35] *La cortigiana*, Act II scene 3. Written in Rome between 1525 and 1526, the comedy was updated and published in Venice in 1534. The date of its first performance is unknown, but it was certainly performed in Bologna in 1537. For this and other comedies by Aretino, see M. Baratto, *Tre studi sul teatro (Ruzante, Aretino, Goldoni)* (Venice 1964). The 1525 edition has now been edited by G. Innamorati in the Einaudi Collezione di Teatro series (1970).

Written at the request of the Sempiterni, *Talanta* was performed in the 1542 carnival, in an unidentified palace in Cannaregio. The Sempiterni were one of those Compagnie della Calza, once numerous, which had held the field in Venice for more than a century. Noble, wealthy, recognized by the state, they influenced every enterprise promoted by the humanist circles, the jesters, or the first semi-professional extempore actors, favouring a feature of Venetian dramatic activity which so affected its later development, that of depending on multiple initiatives rather than on a single court theatre. Amongst the Compagnia figured the names of some of the best-known young noblemen of Venice, and in the three years for which it survived it put on a display of unprecedented splendour, as if it wished to celebrate an apparently doomed tradition in beauty. The sets for the inaugural ceremonies were entrusted to Titian, a 'famous painter in the pay of the Compagnia for this purpose, and for any machines, *edifici* or similar displays'.[36] However in 1542, wishing to perform a comedy with a completely original set, the Compagnia turned to an artist from outside: Giorgio Vasari, who was among the best-known artists on the mainland and a close friend of the author.

For at least the first half of the century, Venetian theatre, so developed and varied, already bordering on professional organization and able to meet the demands of a public of different social and cultural levels, can be said to have lacked a major school of scenography. Without a court theatre, all the elements were lacking which favoured the development of a coherent tradition by means of a centralized management and a continuity of experience. The Compagnie della Calza had prolonged the life of that kind of set, undefined but elaborately decorated (*scena-addobbo*), which had easily been ousted in the other Italian cities by regular comedy and perspective sets. The semi-professional companies which were establishing themselves and flourishing between 1540 and 1560, following the lead of Burchiella, Calmo and the Armanos, could not or would not go beyond the limits of adaptable repertory scenes along the lines of perspectives imported from the mainland. They may have been assisted by Serlio himself, who was beloved of cultured Venetians of the early Renaissance.[37] These were exceptional companies which recruited their members from amongst the artists and men of culture: merchants, musicians, lawyers and *litterati* who loved to meet in 'virtuous Academies', in palaces or in the shops of Francesco Berettaio or Gaspare Gioielliere, to discuss every discipline, but above all the theatre. At carnival time they formed a company to perform one or two comedies, either as guests of the more wealthy companions in patrician houses, or, acting as their own impresarios, in the halls at San Cassian or Santo Stefano, with admission by ticket. They put on the comedies of Calmo, Giancarli, Dolce and perhaps even of Aretino, preserving them from the imitations of the 'foolish jesters' capable only of 'a farrago of empty words and scurrilous actions'.[38]

[36]   B. Giustiniani, *Historie cronologiche dell'origine degl'ordini militari e di tutte le religioni cavalleresche, infino ad hora instituite nel mondo* (Venice 1697), pp. 105ff.
[37]   See M. T. Muraro, 'Le lieu de spectacles (publics ou privés) à Venise au XVe et au XVIe siècle', in *Le lieu théâtral à la Renaissance*; E. Povoledo, 'Scène et mise en scène à Venise dans la première moitié du XVIe siècle' and 'Scène et mise en scène à Venise de la décadence des Compagnies de la Calza jusqu'à la représentation de l'Andromeda au théâtre de St-Cassian', in *Renaissance, Maniérisme, Baroque, proceedings of the XI Stage International du CESR de Tours*, 1968.
[38]   L. Dolce, *Fabrizia* (Venice 1539). The dedication is to Stefano Rizzo who was one of the actors. Tiberio d'Armano, a semi-professional actor, puts forward a similar view in the dedication

They acted with generic sets, which were identified in the prologue or the text, as in *La cassaria* or the performances of the Cazzuola. In the prologue to Giancarli's *Cingana*, the young Tiberio says:

I would ask you to believe three things which appear a little difficult, for otherwise you will risk missing a large part of the entertainment...The first is that you should believe that these buildings before you are the city of Treviso. And although they do not altogether resemble it, you will deceive yourselves into believing that it was like this at the time when the events which we are about to perform took place.

The street or the piazza remains the focal point of the action, and the text of Giancarli's *La capraria* requires no more than three or four houses for acting in. The same is true of Calmo's *Rodiana* or of Dolce's *Il ragazzo*.

Aretino's early comedies also fit this lay-out. In *Il marescalco*, written and probably performed at the court of Federico Gonzaga, the set represents the piazza at Mantua. All the action takes place here (i.e. on the proscenium and the nearest section of the raked area) in the space of a few hours. The plot hinges on the joke played by the duke on his marshal, compelling him to marry, only to have him discover at his wedding a page dressed as a woman. The characters circle around the marshal in very rapid succession, each adding something to the growing *timor nuptiarum* which grips the protagonist. Although the text implies the presence of three houses, there are only two named locations. One, the house of the marshal, from which there is constant coming and going, is visible to the audience. The other, the palace, is out of sight but dominant, since all those involved in the duke's joke issue from it: Messer Jacopo, Ambrogio, the count, the page and the footman. Giannicco comes from the palace to open the comedy by singing: 'My master takes a bride, my master takes a bride in this town.' He returns to the palace, on an errand for the marshal, towards the end of the second act, slinking away between the count's house and the pedant's house, whilst singing irreverently another malicious song: 'The little widow when she sleeps alone, cannot blame it on me.'

In *La cortigiana*, as we have seen, the scene was set 'in Borghi', but the whole of Rome was present on the backcloth. Similarly in *Talanta* all the archaeological monuments were actually on stage, some painted on the backcloth, some constructed from flats at the side and available for acting, like the six domestic houses explicitly required by the plot. It was a new lay-out, fully developed, and, in 1542, exceptional both in and outside Venice.

Aretino himself had wanted Vasari to come from Florence, and they must have planned the set together. Had the playwright not known the set on which his characters were to act in advance, neither the long promenade made by Vergolo and Ponzio among archaeological remains, nor the unravelling of love affairs around the experienced beauty of Talanta could have been plotted.

No sketches connected with this performance are known, but we can visualize it from the two descriptions left by Vasari,[39] and check our results

of *Didone*, a tragedy by L. Dolce which was performed and printed in 1547: 'whereas on the other hand to see *clowns* appear on stage *with stupid and ridiculous gestures* is usually to the taste of the majority because the connoisseurs are always in a minority' (my italics).

[39] 'Vita di Cristofano Gherardi' in Vasari, *Le vite*, vol. VI, pp. 223ff.; 'Lettera di G. Vasari a Ottaviano de' Medici', *Le vite*, vol. VIII, p. 283ff. Ottaviano dei Medici belonged to a cadet branch

against both Aretino's text and the plans of later sets. Vasari wrote to Ottaviano dei Medici: 'I tell you that the hall where the set was made was enormous, as was the set itself, the perspective of Rome'. In order to gain space, the Sempiterni had actually chosen a building still under construction: 'a large house which was not finished, which had only the main walls and the roof'. It was 40 m long and just over 9 m wide. The stage was a further addition to the 40 m, but it is not clear how deep it was: of necessity the opening of the proscenium was less than 9 m and it was probably raised 2.30 m from the ground, so that it was at the same height as the seated assembly. On both sides of the raked area, along the diagonal axes, were aligned the houses of Talanta, Armileo, the old and wise Venetian Vergolo, Tinca the captain, Orfinio and Blando, and finally Santa Maria della Pace and the Ritonda, i.e. the Pantheon. All the houses had real doors and windows, and 'there were beautiful palaces, houses, churches, and an infinite variety of buildings of Doric, Ionic, Corinthian, Tuscan, Rusticated and Composite architecture'.

The perspective continued on the backcloth, leading to the Arch of Septimius Severus, which was the central focal point of all the intersecting lines of the set and of the lines of vision from the hall. Aretino described them all, one by one, through the mouths of Ponzio and Vergolo: the Ritonda, 'so big and bulky', the 'half-ruined' Colosseum, the dome of St Peter's with its pinnacle 'of strange sharply cut stone', Trajan's column, the Torre delle Milizie, Palazzo Maggiore in the Forum, the Arch of Septimius Severus, 'proud, none prouder', and the statue of Pasquino. In his letter to the Medici, Vasari added Santa Maria Nova, the Temple of Fortune, the Sette Sale, and the Torre dei Conti, while Blando's visit to Santa Maria della Pace to view the Sybils and to the Pantheon to visit Raphael's tomb represent Aretino's homage to the painter he had known in his youth: 'in manner gracious, of noble presence, and witty'.[40]

The set had thus evolved in several ways. It had evolved optically, since Peruzzi's 'piazza plus road' had developed into a single wide and deep road, which emphasized the distance without straining the logical limits of space, even if this eventually developed into the Baroque illusion of recession. The action too had evolved, since more of the raked area was being exploited, and it was usable beyond the fourth house. Finally, a relationship had intentionally been established, by which the set and the decoration of the hall had become complementary, not purely for reasons of ornament.

Actually, by its archaeological illustration of Rome this set recalled the theme of the aulic city, which was now more and more frequent in the great theatrical entertainments, and in which the initial realistic intention of the perspective piazza took on a different meaning. The laudatory theme was echoed in the decoration of the hall by wall panels, which depicted the Venetian provinces in allegorical form, while the great roof panels dedicated to the hours illustrated a dramatic preoccupation new even to Aretino: the unity of time. 'The ceiling of the whole hall was made of wood, divided into

of the family, and had married a sister of Maria Salviati, the mother of the future Cosimo I. For several years he was Cosimo's counsellor. He lived in Via di San Gallo, near the Loggia dei Tessitori.   [40] *Talanta*, Act IV scene 21; Act V scene 21.

four great squares and carved with four large stories: in one was Night, in another Dawn, in another Day, and in the last was Evening...' The four stories were framed by a further twenty-four smaller panels depicting the hours, 'twelve of the night and twelve of the day, which were shown each with a head-dress on its head, made of wings and clock-mechanisms, which varied according to the point in passing time they progressively represented.[41] Time himself was at the head [and end] of the procession of the Hours, the last of whom embraced him, intimating that he had been completely spent'. The passing of the hours was emphasized by the movement of a large luminous sphere placed in the sky above the set: 'a sun which, moved during the performance, gave off a great light, since they had succeeded in making very large balls of glass.'[42]

Even Aretino, whose previous comedies were so antagonistic to the classical tradition, so irreverent, alive and theatrical, with characters raving in the streets of Mantua or of Rome, accepted the three unities in *Talanta*. As Baratto writes: 'the comedy is influenced by the place of its performance, by the prestige of the festival which gave rise to it... The author's mind is less closed to the laws of a cultural world foreign to him, but against which he wishes to measure himself.'[43]

So the set, invented for this comedy, by reflecting its contents, became enriched but also compromised.

[41] This refers to the panel nearest the stage, with Time dividing the hours. There are differences between Vasari's two descriptions of the arrangement of the panels on both ceiling and walls: see J. Schulz, 'Vasari at Venice', in *The Burlington Magazine* (December 1961), pp. 500–11.

[42] The device of obtaining an intense yet indirect light was not new. There is a drawing of such a device by Leonardo, in the Codex F of the Institut de France (fol. 23v) while S. Serlio, *Secondo libro*, p. 48, mentions it at length. The effect was achieved by filling large glass balls with clear or coloured water and placing a light, in another such ball, within them. The Venetian lights of 1542 were evidently exceptional in that the glass-blowers of Murano had been able to provide particularly large balls.

[43] Baratto, *Tre studi sul teatro*, p. 138, and, by the same author, *La commedia del Cinquecento* (Vicenza 1975). A paper as yet unpublished by Christopher Cairns suggested a close relationship between parts of *Talanta* and an identified translation of Terence's *Eunuchus*.

4 'Visible' *intermedi* and movable sets

As soon as the *intermedio* changed from being part of a festivity to being part of a play, and to being acted, like the play, on stage, it began to make its needs felt on that stage. Increasingly, the stage was required to find space for the *intermedio*, if not to adjust visually to it.

In Vicenza, a rich city and most imposing among those of Italy, I made a theatre and a stage of wood, perchance, no, without doubt, the largest made in our time. Where, for the benefit of the marvellous *intermedi* which were performed there, such as floats, elephants and various *moresche*, I wished there to be, in front of the raked floor a level floor, the width of which was 12 *piedi* and the length 60 *piedi*; where I found this very useful and handsome.[1]

So wrote Sebastiano Serlio in 1545. Yet in 1637, in a treatise which popularized an already well-established tradition, Niccolò Sabbatini considered the possibility of a stage all of which could be used, at least by the *morescanti*. It was without a flat proscenium, but had a raked area which stretched from the front of the stage to the backcloth.

Having fixed, as we have said, the placing of the front of the stage, that is the lowest part facing the spectators, it will be necessary to mark its first height on the walls on either side. It should be not less than 4 *piedi*, and made to rise thereafter at the rate of half an *oncia* per *piede* [half an inch per foot?] as far as the back of the stage, will achieve the required ultimate height. This, however, is only when the stage is intended for dancing; if not, it can be raised two-thirds of an *oncia*, which would show off the scene better.[2]

All the experiments from which Baroque scenery derived developed between these two extremes of stage design. From them started its abstract conquest of unlimited spaces, in which the structures lost their specific reference to reality, and the eye and the imagination of the wondering spectator were no longer kept distinct. Peruzzi's 'piazza and street', stretched beyond the dimensions of Vasari's *strada lunga*, became an unlimited receding perspective. As the set acquired an illusory and virtually infinite depth by optical illusion, two conditions fundamental to Renaissance stage design were abandoned: the fixed set and the availability of a large area of the stage for acting. The urban scene fixed for the whole duration of the play gave way

[1] *Secondo libro dell'architettura*, pp. 43–4, in *Tutte le opere d'architettura et prospettiva, di Sebastiano Serlio Bolognese* (Venice 1619). The first edition of the *Secondo libro* came out in Paris in 1545. The dimensions of the proscenium are the equivalent of about 22 m in length, 3 m in width and 1 m 80 in height.

[2] Sabbatini, *Pratica di fabricar scene*, vol. I, chapter 3. All the rules laid down by Sabbatini refer to a stage without a flat proscenium, though not all seventeenth-century theatres were equipped in this fashion.

to an adaptable set, which was seen to change its appearance several times in the course of the same act. The action which had previously taken up at least two-thirds of the stage, now returned to the proscenium and moved nearer to the audience, in order to avoid a direct confrontation between the figure of the actor and the perspective painted on the flats, which would have spoilt the perspective illusion and made the presence of the actor on stage incongruous.

In the view of Sabbatini, which was generally accepted, only the danced *intermedio* was freed from this limitation, as if it were unnecessary for the dances to submit to this logical law, given the absence of real connections of time and place between the set and the *intermedio*. This was so, but only on the surface. The general rule allowed different, at times contradictory, views and solutions which gradually imposed themselves on the rational theories of Renaissance drama, and eventually disrupted them.

When we examined Leonardo da Vinci's designs at the court of Milan, we saw how, in the 'hybrid' plays and in their presentation, the *intermedio* ended up by being confused with the main performance. They shared plot types and scenery, and were both divided between the stage and the hall, involving actors and spectators in a common feeling of celebration and participation. The fact that *Danae*, which was divided into five acts in the classical style, had more 'invisible' musical *intermedi* than 'visible' ones, might be said to provide a sort of negative confirmation of this. As Pirrotta says,[3] such a choice 'was probably dictated by the fact that music was quite often also performed in the course of the acts themselves. The division between them had therefore to be marked more obviously by clearing the stage during the intervals and filling the gap with music coming from hidden sources.'

'Visible' *intermedi* were preferred, at least in Ferrara, for the performance of classical comedies. They displayed an inexhaustible variety of subjects, bearing no relationship to the plot of the main play, and were used in an almost anti-realistic spirit, if we are to judge from the prevalence of grotesque or fantastic elements, the variety of the dances and the sumptuousness of the costumes. They already took place on stage: on the proscenium, occasionally involving some float or piece of machinery.

Regular comedy inherited the *intermedio*, with its meanings and intentions, directly from the classical performances, and as long as it remained the prerogative of court and patrician entertainments, it essentially retained its visual characteristics. The *intermedi* varied in length and importance from occasion to occasion: there was no lack of *intermedi* with music played in the wings, while stage-hands were seen reorganizing the lights and the stage between one act and the next. More often, however, musicians and dancers appeared, carrying their instruments and whatever else they needed for their brief performance. Sometimes there was only one visible *intermedio*. Bernardino Prosperi informs us[4] that in 1508 *La cassaria* 'had the distinction of honourable and good actors, all on stage with beautiful costumes and sweet music in the *intermedi*, and with a *moresca* of drunken cooks who had cooking-pots tied on before them, on which they beat time with wooden rods to the sound of music performed by the cardinal's musicians.' The performance

---

[3]   See pp. 47–8 above.
[4]   See D'Ancona, *Le origini*, II, p. 394. Also *La commedia del Cinquecento*, vol. I, pp. 413–14.

of *I suppositi* ended with a danced pantomime: 'The *intermedi* were all songs and music, and at the end of the comedy Vulcan and the Cyclops hammered out arrows to the sounds of fifes, beating time with hammers and with bells attached to their legs. After finishing this performance of the arrows with working the bellows, they danced a *moresca* with the same hammers.'[5]

At other times *intermedi* came between each act, and occasionally, though infrequently, they were linked by a vague common idea. This could be political or celebratory, as in the Urbino performance of *La calandria* in 1513, or purely visual, as in Zuan Polo's *intermedi* for Plautus' *Miles gloriosus*, when it was put on by the Compagni Immortali in the courtyard of the Ca' Pesaro in San Beneto in Venice (1515).

And between the acts Zuam Polo himself created another new comedy, pretending to be a necromancer who went to hell and found Domenego Tajacalze who was chasing wethers (*cazava castroni*). He came out with the wethers and made a dance with them, then came a music of nymphs, each [beating] an anvil to time and pretending to beat a heart etc. After the main comedy they put the story of Paris and those goddesses and to whom he gave the apple, i.e. to Venus.[6]

It is not clear whether Zuan Polo's grotesque farce took up more than one *intermedio*, as Marin Sanudo's ambiguous 'and between the acts...he created another new comedy' implies, or whether it was limited to only one interval, and then gave way to the chorus of nymphs of love and the story of Paris, with their mythological flavour. None of them had any connection with the Plautine comedy being performed by the Compagni themselves. Many years later, in his poem *Il sogno*,[7] written on the death of Zuan Polo, Alessandro Caravia described the special technique of this farce, which had evidently remained in the great jester's repertory. Zuan tells of the nightmare which had him in hell with his friend Domenego Tajacalze, also a well-known jester, intent on pacifying the wrathful Farfarello:

> Ma pur mi messi un poco a contrafar
> Da Bergamasco, da puttin, da Schiavon
> Facendo certi gesti nel balar;
> E poi me missi a far certe mie berte:
> Tra l'altre mie feci una callesella
> Contrafacendo lingue, hor basse, hor erte...
>
> Da poi mi missi a far da fantolin
> E Domenico a risponderme da vecchio
> Ed io or da Greco, ora da Bergamin
> Per laúto [liuto] sonavo con un secchio
> Cantai molte canzon de Serafin...
>
> A cantar io mi missi a l'improvvisa
> In lode d'ogni diavol de l'Inferno;
> Domenico ancor lui cantò assai versi.
> Di dir all'improvvisa essendo stuffi,
> Per far rider di nuovo ancor i Diavoli

---

[5] D'Ancona, *Le origini*, II, p. 395. Also *La commedia del Cinquecento*, vol. I, pp. 414–15.

[6] *Articoli estratti dai Diarii di Marin Sanudo concernenti notizie storiche di commedie, Mumarie, Feste e compagnie della Calza*, pp. 29–30. *I Diarii di Marin Sanudo*, which run from 1436 to 1533, also exist in a printed edition (Venice 1879–1902). This extract is now cited in *La commedia del Cinquecento*, vol. I, p. 512.   [7] A. Caravia, *Il sogno* (Venice 1542), p. 8.

Si sentassimo in terra ambodoi cuffi
Fingendo di giocar quai putti e piavoli
L'uno con l'altro zaffandosi ne i zuffi
Da cani e gatte ancor facendo sgniavoli

I also tried a few impersonations: as a Bergamask, a child, a *Schiavone* [a Dalmatian sailor, whose main trade was to import wethers], making gestures and dancing. Then I started performing my jests, among them a joke imitating languages and voices, now hoarse, now shrill...Then I started to act as a small child, with Domenico answering me as an old man; as a Greek or as a Bergamask I sang many songs by Serafino [Aquilano], playing on a bucket instead of a lute...I started singing extempore the praise of every devil in hell, and Domenico, too, sang many verses. Then, having tired of improvising, and wishing to get more laughter from the devil, we both sat low on the ground, pretending to play like children and pets, clawing each other's muzzle, as well as making stridulant noises like cats and dogs.

Songs, grotesque dances, acrobatics, assumed dialects and improvised dialogues: the jesting technique contains the essence of all that later became characteristic of the *lazzi* of the *commedia dell' arte*. Nevertheless, however interesting it may be from the point of view of playing styles, the Venetian clowning *intermedio* adds little to our inquiry, if we judge it on the basis of the stage design of the Compagnie della Calza, which had remained faithful to the out-dated scheme of neutral and luxurious decoration throughout the whole of the first three decades of the century. With its rich surroundings of golden curtains and figured tapestries, glittering with lights and framed by friezes and greenery,[8] it perpetuated the characteristics of 'hybrid' staging, as far as it accommodated mummery, classical drama, clowning *intermedi* and dances, without differentiating between them.

The semi-professional companies, and the semi-academic Ridotti who, as we have seen, replaced the Compagnie della Calza as promoters of theatrical activity, preceding and making easier the establishment of the Comici dell' Arte in Venice, either abandoned acted *intermedi* or updated them in accordance with the conventions of music and song used in mainland entertainments. However, in this regard the madrigal *intermedio* did not affect the stage design, even if sung by musicians in costume, like the choruses of nymphs and shepherds in *La mandragola* and in *Clizia*, or the chorus of hermits in Giannotti's *Il vecchio amoroso*. Being usually independent of the plot of the comedy, it had no connection of content or of action with the perspective city standing behind it, even if it made some direct comment on the plot, or accounted for the passing of time as required by the classical rule. We can find a proof of this in Alessandro Piccolomini's *L'amore costante* (1536). In order not to contravene the custom of the Intronati, only musical *intermedi* were used between the acts, while as the finale of an act and therefore within the play itself, fights and *moresche* appeared, justified in theory by the sudden eruption of an armed quarrel and its subsequent settling. Yet the movable set did in part have its origins in the acted *intermedio*, or rather in its special type connected with the great patrician and court entertainments. Scenographically, this coincided with the celebratory 'city', recognized by its main buildings, aligned diagonally on stage.

[8] There are numerous references by Marin Sanudo, *I Diarii*. On the subject of this sort of apparatus see E. Povoledo, 'Scène et mis en scène à Venise dans la première moitié du XVIe siècle', in *Renaissance, Maniérisme, Baroque, proceedings of the XI Stage International du CESR de Tours, 1968*.

Through the complex evolution of set design, the *intermedio* never abandoned those basic features which had made it the ideal interval filler. It tied together the continuous performance which renewed Aristotelian polemic was now calling 'unity of action', it justified the passing of time, it distracted the audience from the operations of the stage hands, and it lessened the inconvenience of the long and enforced stay in the hall.[9] Indeed in some ways these properties were made manifest and highlighted visually by the greater scale which the *intermedio* was assuming in the entertainments. Two issues in particular stand out; not new (in themselves) but resolved in a new way which presaged more substantial innovation. They were the increasingly frequent presence of a tenuous theme which artificially linked the *intermedi* together and prepared the ground for their future independence from the main action, and the visual presentation of the passage of time, emphasized at the beginning or end of an act by the allusions of one of the characters.

We have already referred to this double aspect of the court *intermedio* and to its importance when examining the reasons for the comic set and illustrating two spectacles which, each in its own way, were epoch-making in contemporary Italian life: the Urbino *La calandria* of 1513 and *Talanta* performed by the Venetian Compagnia dei Sempiterni in 1542. It is not by chance that contemporary accounts lead us to Umbrian and Tuscan artists. A theatrical practice which was by then common to the whole country cannot be limited to their schools and to that of Ferrara, but it is impossible to deny that they formed the *avant-garde*, throughout the sixteenth century at least.

The political and commemorative motivation of the Urbino *intermedi* is obvious, as is their lack of connection with the Roman piazza designed for the benefit of the comedy. Castiglione, or Girolamo Genga on his behalf, took care to isolate them within the context of the set, giving to each *intermedio* a recognizable float elegantly decorated. 'The first ['*intramessa*'] was a *moresca* of Jason, who appeared on the stage from one end dancing, armed in ancient style, handsome, with a sword and a very fine shield.' Having yoked the fire-breathing bulls, Jason, still dancing, 'sowed the teeth of the dragon, so that men armed in ancient style gradually emerged from the stage...and these danced a proud *moresca* [showing their intention] to kill Jason, and when they were at the entrance [of Ares' grove] they killed each other one by one...after them Jason went inside, and immediately emerged with the golden fleece on his shoulders, dancing most excellently'. The second *intermedio* was 'a beautiful float with Venus', drawn by doves and accompanied by cupids dancing a *moresca*, 'with lighted torches in their hands with which they set fire to a door, from which emerged nine elegant youths...and they danced another beautiful *moresca*'. The third *intermedio* was 'a float of Neptune drawn by sea-horses, followed by eight monsters dancing a branle'. The fourth was Juno's float, on a cloud, driven by two peacocks and escorted by various dancing birds. At the end of the comedy

a cupid suddenly emerged on stage...who explained in a few stanze the meaning of the *intermedi*...and this was that the first was the battle between those earthborn brothers, as we now see that wars exist between both neighbours and those who

---

[9] The anonymous author of *Il cocchio* complained 'that excessive and stupendous *intermedi* are performed, out of all proportion to the main action', while the ancients did not use them 'except to allow the actors to pause and change their dress, to eat something and, as is said colloquially, *far otta* (to take time)'. Cf. Pirrotta on this in part I, chapter 3 above.

should make peace...Then came Love, who inflamed first mankind and the earth, then the sea and the air with his holy flame, in order to banish war and discord, and to unite the world in harmony.[10]

The allusion to the recent events of the League of Cambrai and the Holy League (1508–12) seems clear, as does the optimistic allegory in the other *intermedio* which took place in the two comedies by Grassi and Ruggeri, performed on the same occasion and using the same set as *La calandria*.

In the said comedy by Nicola [Grassi] there appeared in one of the *intermedi* an Italy all torn by barbarians. Wishing to say some lamenting verses, she twice, as if in extreme pain, stopped her recitation, and thus, as though lost, she left the stage, leaving the spectators to believe that she had forgotten her words. But then in performing Ruggeri's comedy on other days, this same *intermedio* was reinserted, and when she called Francesco Maria to her aid, an armed man appeared with splendid entreaties in a *moresca*, with a naked sword in his hand. When by sword-thrusts and other blows he had driven from Italy all those barbarians who had plundered her, and had returned to her in time to the music of a beautiful *moresca*, he placed a crown back on her head, and she being dressed in a regal cloak of gold, he accompanied her off the stage to the same beat, all of which formed a wonderful spectacle.

The movement of the floats and the vivacity of the dancers who appeared 'on stage from one end dancing', bring us back to the quotation from Serlio, who, precisely for the *intermedi*, wanted 'in front of the raked floor...a flat floor' solidly reinforced. In addition, Genga's set must have had two side ramps as a means of access for the floats, which could not possibly have appeared from the back of the perspective set.[11] The floor of the proscenium also must have had trap-doors for the sudden appearance of the warriors armed in ancient style or of the cupid who recited the epilogue.

Serlio also mentions other stage effects without explaining how they were arranged; however they confirm the presence of ceilings organized in such a way as to allow the appearance and disappearance of machines and the easy manoeuvring of the luminous spheres which represented to the audience the movement of the celestial bodies:

There one sees the horned and shining moon slowly rise, and without the eyes of the spectators having seen it move; in others one sees the rising of the sun and its movement, and at the end of the comedy its setting with such artifice that many spectators are amazed. With artifice, as required, some god will be seen to descend from the sky, or some planet travel through the air...

Serlio's statement confirms a practice which by 1545 had become current and which can easily be documented.[12] Even Vasari, describing the set of *Il commodo* designed by Bastiano da Sangallo in 1539 for the marriage of Cosimo I dei Medici, stopped to speak of the movement of the sun at the back of the stage and of this very simple arrangement which Sangallo repeated and developed several years later in Venice, in Aretino's *Talanta*:

---

[10]   For the two quotations from the *Lettera di B. Castiglione al Vescovo di Canossa*, see D'Ancona, *Le origini*, II, pp. 102ff. Also now in *La commedia del Cinquecento*, vol. I, pp. 445–52.

[11]   Note that in the 1502 entertainments in Ferrara, even the floats like the unicorn one in *Epidicus* and the sphere of *Casina* came from the 'houses' of the set. For the stage lay-out in Urbino see Ruffini, 'Analisi contestuale della "Calandria"', in *Biblioteca teatrale*, 15/16.

[12]   See Pirrotta, part I, chapter 4 above.

Then he arranged with great cleverness a wooden arch (*lanterna*) resembling a chest, behind all the houses; this supported a sun a *braccio* high, made of a ball of crystal full of distilled water, behind which were lit two wax candles, which made it shine in such a way that it really seemed the live and natural sun; and this sun, I say, having around it a decoration of gold rays which covered the curtain, was gradually moved by means of a winch in such a way that at the beginning of the comedy it seemed as if the sun was rising, and that having risen to the zenith of its arch it descended in the same way, so that at the end of the comedy it went below and set.[13]

To supplement Vasari's indications, one can imagine a ribbed track placed at the rear of the stage and hidden by the backcloth. On this track ran the 'wooden arch', which supported the glass sphere crowned by gold rays, perhaps by means of a system of cogged wheels like the one described by Sabbatini.[14] In Florence the sphere was about 58 cm in diameter; in Venice the skill of the Murano glassblowers allowed it to be larger still. In Florence the idea of the unity of time and temporal perspective implicit in the movement of the solar sphere was complemented by the succession of *intermedi*; in Venice, where as far as we know there were no visible *intermedi*, the idea was picked up and commented on visually in the pictures of the ceiling which showed the hours of the day and night, the four quarters of the day (Night, Dawn, Noon, Evening) and 'above the stage...Time, accompanied by Aeolus, the god of the winds, dispatched the hours to their places'.[15]

The comparison between Sangallo's set for *Il commodo*, in the second courtyard of the Medici palace in the Via Larga, and the set erected by Vasari in the house being built in Cannaregio, is interesting in many other ways. Firstly, the unsolved problem of the origin of the so-called *strada lunga vasariana* ('Vasari's long road') which came into its own in Italy towards the middle of the century, but which was certainly anticipated by the set of *Talanta*

---

[13] Vasari, *Le vite*, ed. Milanesi, *Bastiano detto Aristotele da San Gallo*, vol. VI, pp. 441–3.
[14] Sabbatini, *Pratica di fabricar scene*, vol. II, chapter 42. The device described by Sabbatini was intended to create a particular cloud effect, but it could have been used to allow any other sufficiently light object to pass across the sky of the set:

> To create this [cloud effect] you must build eight or ten cylinders made of wooden stakes, at least one foot in diameter and as long as the width of that part of the sky which is to be made cloudy. Then at either end of each place a wheel, which must be cogged and two inches thick and of the same diameter [as the cylinders]...Then lengthwise above the cogged wheels, from the other side, place a wooden groove. Let it be smoothly planed and firmly set in place. It must be a little wider than the thickness of the wheels, and deep enough to take up four inches. Inside it place a piece of wood for each rod, with cogs of the same size as those of the wheels, and positioned above these in such a way that when this piece of wood is moved, the wheels too will turn to the same extent.

The cylinders were manoeuvred by 'four men, above the sky', two on either side of the stage.
In the case of the movement of the sun, all that would have been necessary would have been to substitute for the straight groove a curved guide, it too grooved on its lower side, and to adapt the wheel situated at the base of the cylinders (in this case the lantern supporting the glass sphere of the sun) to a system of small transmission wheels, similar to the one used in a clock mechanism. Extracts from Sabbatini now appear in English in A. M. Nagler, *A Source Book in Theatrical History* (Dover, New York 1959), pp. 86–102.
[15] Vasari, *Le vite*, ed. Milanesi, vol. VI, p. 225. The letter by Vasari to Ottaviano dei Medici complements the later description in the 'Vita di C. Gherardi' (see p. 332, note 39 above). It is nevertheless difficult to specify accurately the position of the fifth panel with Time. For technical reasons it could not have been placed in the sky of the set, closing it. It must therefore have adorned the proscenium arch either on the pediment or, less probably, in the vault of the arch, which was unlikely to have been deep enough to contain it.

and perhaps also by that of *Il commodo*. While in no way belittling Vasari's pre-eminent influence on Italian scenography in the age of mannerism, this possibility would merely confirm Sangallo's originality and the links between him and the painter from Arezzo. The loss of his scenographic sketches is therefore particularly unfortunate. Amongst the most open-minded and restless artists of his time, sensitive to every change in theatrical tastes, Sangallo reacted to the most subtle influences and produced solutions which were only applied more deliberately and more consistently many years later. Vasari recognized their importance and admired him.

At the age of twenty-five, in 1536, Vasari had been one of the painters who executed the set devised by Sangallo for *L'aridosia*, the comedy written and produced by Lorenzino dei Medici, on the occasion of the marriage between Duke Alessandro and Margaret of Austria. The plot was supposed to take place in Florence, and the set

was the most beautiful, not only that Aristotile had made so far, but that had ever been made by anyone, for he had made in it many projections of buildings in relief, and in the middle of the forum a beautiful triumphal arch, which looked as if it were made of marble, all historiated and adorned with statutes, not to mention the roads which receded into the distance and many other things made with beautiful inventions and unbelievable study and diligence.[16]

The mention of several perspective roads, which raises the particular question of their lay-out, also recurs in Vasari's description of the set of *Il commodo*:

In the great courtyard of the Medici palace where the fountain stands, Aristotile made another set which represented Pisa, in which, always improving and varying what he did, he excelled himself. It is impossible ever to put together either a greater variety of doors and windows, or more bizarre and fanciful façades of buildings, or roads or distant landscapes which recede better and act as required by the rules of perspective. Besides this, he reproduced there the leaning bell-tower of the Duomo [of Pisa], the dome and the round church of San Giovanni, with other monuments of the city.[17]

There is no point in checking Vasari's description by comparing the text of *Il commodo* with later sets having an extended lay-out. The fairly unoriginal plot revolves around the amorous misadventures of five young people (two

---

[16] Vasari, *Le vite*, ed. Milanesi, vol. VI, pp. 439–41. *L'aridosia* was performed in the Loggia dei Tessitori in Via San Gallo, though it is not known with which *intermedi*. The expression 'not to mention the roads' is to be understood as 'not to mention the beauty of the roads'. The presence of a second raised stage for the musicians makes this production particularly interesting. For this purpose the back wall of the loggia was knocked down and rebuilt to include within it 'a room like a pit, which was to be quite sizeable, and a platform as high as the stage, to be used for the groups of singers, and above the former he wished to make another platform for harpsichords, organs and other similar instruments, which cannot as easily be moved or changed'.

[17] *Il commodo* 'Commedia di Antonio Landi, recitata nelle nozze del sig. Duca di Firenze e della Duchessa sua consorte l'anno 1539 con gli intermedi di Giovan Battista Strozzi fiorentino' (Florence 1539). The festivities were described by P. F. Giambullari in *Apparato et feste nelle nozze del Illustrissimo Signor Duca di Firenze et della Duchessa sua Consorte, con le sue stanze madriali, comedia et intermedii in quelle recitati* (Florence 1539). Among the more recent studies on the performance of *Il commodo* and on the 1539 festivities, see A. C. Minor and B. Mitchell, *A Renaissance Entertainment* (Columbia, Missouri 1967). For the Florentine festivals see M. Plaisance, 'Espace et politique dans les comédies florentines des années 1539–1551', in *Espace, idéologie et société au XVIe siècle* (Grenoble 1975), as well as his introduction to the critical edition of il Lasca's *La strega* (Abbeville 1976). For Sangallo in general see also Zorzi, *Il teatro e la città*, pp. 92–100.

couples, and an odd-man-out who later discovers himself to be the brother
of the woman he loves), which are complicated by the peevish weakness of
their parents and by the intrigues of a servant and a matchmaker. Only four
usable buildings were required: the house belonging to Leander and
Porphyria, who are brother and sister, one belonging to the doctor, one to
old Lamberto, and the church before which the comedy begins at daybreak,
and where the third act ends at vespers, and which therefore could not have
been the 'round' baptistery. Love, intrigue and matchmaking could have
unfolded just as naturally in Serlio's 'comic set' or in the 'Florentine street'
attributed to Francesco Salviati but held to be post-1565 (plate 28),[18] while
the extended set used for *Il granchio* might appear excessive (plate 29).[19] It
is unclear whether or not the set for *Il commodo* went beyond the intentions
of Peruzzi's 'piazza and street'. If it did, comparing it with the set assumed
to be by Salviati, we could substitute the 'round church' and the leaning tower
for the hexagonal building which in the drawing juts out from the centre of
the backcloth, diverting the sight along two symmetrically diverging lines,
which simultaneously pick up the trajectory of the central receding perspective
and bring it gently to end in the two light arches barely suggested in the
distance.

On the other hand, Vasari does not notice another aspect, itself highly novel
amidst the innovations introduced by Sangallo. As it has to do with the placing
of the *intermedi*, it is of importance to our inquiry:

> The writer of the comedy...was Anton Landi, a Florentine gentleman, and in charge
> of *intermedi* and the music was Giovan Batista Strozzi, who at the time was young
> and greatly talented. But since enough has been written about the other things which
> adorned the comedy, the *intermedi* and the music, I shall say no more...it suffices for
> the moment to know that the other things were in the hands of the said Giovan Batista
> Strozzi, Tribolo, and Aristotile.[20]

[18] Both this and another scenographic drawing attributed to F. Salviati are to be found in
the British Museum. The presence in the foreground of the two loggias which have been
regarded as representing the two wings of the Uffizi Gallery has led Magagnato, *Teatri italiani
del Cinquecento*, p. 46, to maintain that they could not have been by Salviati, who died in 1563.
The two loggias, which also feature in other sets such as the one for *Il granchio*, are not however
an accurate reproduction of the Uffizi architecture and could represent a stylized development
of the traditional Renaissance motif of the porticoed house. The other buildings beyond the two
loggias in the British Museum drawing also repeat themselves symmetrically on both sides of
the road.

[19] *Il granchio*, a comedy by Leonardo Salviati, 'with *intermedi* by Bernardo de Nerli, of the
Florentine Accademia. Brought before the public by the Florentine Accademia in Florence, in
the Sala del Papa in the year 1566, in the consulship of the author', Florence 1566. The Sala
del Papa, in which Martin V and Eugene IV had stayed, was in Via della Scala.

[20] Giambullari, *Apparato*, p. 66, only mentions Strozzi:

> The words and the plot and the costumes of this and of all the other *intermedi* of the
> comedy which will be described in the appropriate places were by our Gio. Battista Strozzi.'
> But Vasari, who knew and admired Tribolo, is more specific in his 'Vita' of the artist:
> 'And this Tribolo made for the costumes of the *intermedi*, which were the work of Giovan
> Battista Strozzi, who was in charge of the whole comedy, the most wonderful and
> beautiful inventions that one can imagine in clothes, footwear, head-dresses and other
> articles of dress (Vasari, *Le vite*, vol. VI, p. 89).

Other details on costume are to be found in part I, chapter 4 above. The catalogues of two
exhibitions are valuable in connection with the iconography of the Florentine festivals: *Mostra
di disegni Vasariani*, ed. A. M. Petrioli Tofani, Florence 1966, and *Feste e apparati medicei da Cosimo
la Cosimo II*, ed. A. M. Petrioli Tofani and G. Gaeta Bertelà (Florence 1969).

Strozzi was perhaps the organizer of the whole spectacle, while Tribolo was in charge of the highly original costumes for the *intermedi*. The first *intermedio*, to cite just one example, was of 'twelve shepherds, each couple differently dressed. The first two were dressed with the long fleeces of red billy-goats and had caps and footwear of the same material', the second couple was dressed in 'bark of trees made in scales surrounded by borders of ivy and other flowers, their boots and headgear of the same bark, decorated with ivy and flowers', the third couple was 'dressed in blue clothes', the fourth in

broom, woven and surrounded by divers olive branches, and with girdles made in the same way. The fifth couple wore white cloth embroidered with ancient birds, but with their feathers tinged with many colours. Their footwear was similar, but their caps with strange novelty were made with a single squab, which with its wings a little lowered and its tail straight down formed a suitably round cap, the neck and head of the squab rising over the forehead of the shepherd. The clothes of the last couple were of plaited straw variously decorated with ears of corn.

Each carried his own instrument, appropriately disguised: some as a branch of ivy, some as a bone or an animal's horn, and so forth.

The author of this description, Pierfrancesco Giambullari, was a more attentive, or perhaps less involved observer than Vasari. While he neglected to describe the perspective 'in order not to mar its beauty by my ill-chosen words', he followed the *intermedi* closely and noticed every unusual aspect of them. There were six of them, including the prologue and epilogue, and the only link between their simple sung action was the passing of time, deliberately proclaimed at the beginning or end of the acts. The spectacle opened with Dawn, who slowly appeared in the East in the sky of the set, and closed with Night, who was also let down from the ceiling to introduce, with her song, the final dance of the satyrs and Bacchantes. The first *intermedio*, of shepherds, supposedly took place in the morning; the second, of nymphs and sirens, at the approach of midday; the third, of Silenus, at the hour of noon; the fourth, of huntress nymphs, towards evening. Throughout, the set was the perspective view of Pisa, but the *intermedi* were performed in three different places: the prologue and epilogue began in the stage sky and finished on the proscenium, the first and fourth *intermedi* took place entirely on that stage, the second and third were off-stage, in the intermediate area between the spectators and the stage which Serlio calls the 'piazza of the theatre'.[21]

Giambullari's description is more admiring than technical: 'Between the spectators and the set, and linked to the stage, was seen a very wide channel, all painted within and without to resemble the Arno. From the seaward side of this, three naked sirens suddenly appeared, each with her two tails minutely worked with silver scales.'[22] The sirens, who had long green hair

[21] Serlio, *Secondo libro*, p. 43v., calls the orchestra 'piazza' and makes a distinction between the *piazza del teatro*, contained within the semi-circle of the steps, and the *piazza della scena*, the wide passage connecting it with the base of the proscenium. In the first half of the century the stage was often called the *teatro*, and the corridor was used by the actors to provide access to the stage, which had neither a backstage nor dressing-rooms.

[22] In the Ferrarese festivities of 1502, and in the Urbino performance of *La calandria* in 1513, the room in which the play took place was decorated so as to represent a city seen from without. The stage represented the city itself, the base of the stage represented the city walls, and the wide passageway between the spectators and the proscenium purported to be the ditch. This traditional idea has been replaced by a different convention, in which the city is separated from the public not by a ditch but by the river Arno. D. Giannotti, in the prologue of *Il vecchio amoroso*, written

with 'head-dresses of shells and snails' were accompanied by three blond nymphs 'dressed in light green muslin' and three sea monsters, 'with branching horns on their heads', dressed in maidenhair fern and lichens. And singing all together they showed that morning had already passed and dinner time was approaching.

In the third *intermedio*, also sung in the Arno, appeared

Silenus, whom Virgil described in his Sixth Eclogue, found at noon by Mnasillus and Chromis and fairest Egle as he rested asleep in a grotto...which showed that in the comedy it was already the hour of noon. And woken by them, and asked to sing, he took between his goat's legs a tortoise shell, in which was a fine *violone da gamba*, and with a bow shaped like a dried snake, he began to play sweetly.

It is possible to reconstruct a plausible, though by no means certain, model of this extremely special scenic device if we look at the so-called 'Salviati set' and at the engraving of *Il granchio*. In both sets the proscenium was joined at each end by two small rostra which, jutting out towards the hall, created a rectangular bay at the foot of the stage. In the *Il granchio* engraving the front of the proscenium (and thus the wall of the bay] was decorated by a female figure representing Florence. In Salviati's set, instead of this figure there was a small flight of stairs linking the stage and the hall. In the 1539 stage the front of the proscenium represented the Arno with Silenus' cave, but it may also have had, in the centre, a small fake or real stairway.

It is Vasari who once more provides us, indirectly, with information about this:

I shall say no more about the stairway which he made in this [set], nor about how greatly they [the spectators] were deceived, in order not to make it appear a repetition of what we have described on other occasions: I shall say clearly that this one, which seemed to rise from the ground onto the floor [of the stage], was octagonal at the centre and square on either side, and had great artistry in its deceptive simplicity ('con artifizio nella sua semplicità grandissima'), for it so graced the perspective above that it is impossible to see a better one of that type.

This excerpt can be variously interpreted. The most obvious explanation is that Vasari, writing many years later, misremembered: the stairway could have been there, and could have been real, to enable the actors and those involved in the *intermedi* to climb onto the stage. It might had had a simple structure, with two small flights of stairs apparently complicated because of the decoration which simulated eight sides. If this were so, Silenus's cave would probably have been located under the octagonal element and framed by the two flights of stairs. Alternatively, seeing that Giambullari does not mention them, we may conclude that the stairs did not exist at all, and Vasari was confusing Sangallo's set with a different one; the actors could have entered from behind the stage, and those involved in the *intermedi* could have reached the Arno directly from the court. This was made possible by the contemporary stage convention which had not yet broken the illusory link between audience and action.

With the *intermedi* of *Il commodo* we have not yet reached the movable

around 1536, suggested a similar solution: the scene represents Pisa, 'And we are acting this comedy for you in the square in front of the church. The street in front of me is the Lungarno. And you, spectators, are watching this feast from within the Arno river. Rest assured, however; you will not get wet.'

set, for only the place of the action changed, not the perspective itself. However, the insistence of the authors (and I think it right to add the name of Giovanbattista Strozzi to that of Sangallo) that the *intermedi* should have an autonomous set is still symptomatic. Developing along natural lines, the *intermedio aulico* later assumed increasingly original characteristics, becoming a dramatic form in its own right. 'Formerly *intermedi* were made which served the comedy', il Lasca protested in the prologue of *La strega*,[23] 'but now they make comedies which serve the *intermedi*.' Growing, and filling more and more of the time allotted to the entertainment, the *intermedio* ultimately came to require a setting different from that of the main performance. By undermining the very principle of the three unities it pushed scenography towards the decisive turning-point of the movable set.

In the light of the experiences of 1539, another piece of information appears plausible. It was supplied in 1583 by Egnazio Danti in his commentary on Vignola's *Le due regole*. Speaking of scene changes accomplished by means of *periaktoi*, the author adds:

And note that while the set is being turned and changed it will be necessary to keep the eyes of the spectators busy with some *intermedio* so that they do not see the walls of the set turn, but only notice that it has changed when the *intermedio* disappears. I have heard that Aristotele da Sangallo had already made a set like this, which changed twice, for Duke Pier Luigi Farnese in Castro.[24]

This historian picked up his information some forty years after the event, and there are no reports contemporary with the performance which confirm it. However Sangallo was actually in Castro in 1543, and it is in any case significant that the idea of a movable set, revolving on *periaktoi*, was traditionally associated with his name rather than with that of his cousin Antonio il Giovane, to whom we have already referred.[25] Bastiano also worked for the theatre in Rome, in the home of Roberto Strozzi, and also in the Palazzo della Cancelleria, where, Vasari writes, Cardinal Farnese had him erect a permanent perspective set, 'in one of the mezzanine halls which give onto the garden, but in such a way that it was fixed there, so that he could use it whenever he wished or needed to do so'.

Sangallo's ideas seem not to have been developed in Florence after he left. Again, Danti gives us to understand how exceptional was the Castro initiative,

[23] *La strega*, by A. F. Grazzini known as il Lasca, written before 1566 and published in 1582, was not performed in the author's lifetime. For il Lasca's opinion on the *intermedi*, see pp. 171–72 above.

[24] See E. Danti's *Commentarij*, on the *Due regole della prospettiva pratica di M. Iacomo Barozzi da Vignola* (Rome 1583); and see note 44 below. Danti's *Commentarij* are now in Marotti, *Lo spettacolo*, pp. 213–18, with the passage quoted on p. 218.

[25] Aristotele da Sangallo was probably in Castro in 1543, as it would appear from a letter written by Claudio Tolomei to Anton Francesco Ranieri (Rome, 27 June 1543).

Maestro Giovan Mangone, the famous and highly-praised architect, has died in these last few days...Now you know Maestro Aristotele, I mean that maestro Aristotele who is so good at perspective and such a skilled contriver of sets, the one I tell you made the stage at Castro and finished it even though he had no time to do so...he wishes to have from the [Apostolic] chamber one of those posts which had been held by maestro Giovan Mangone.

F. Salviati also designed perspectives for the comedy performed in Castro about 1538, when Pier Luigi Farnese took possession of the town. It is possible that, either then or during his stay in Rome, Sangallo met Salviati and his ideas on stage perspective. Antonio da Sangallo is the author of the design (now in the Uffizi) depicting a Roman stage discussed in part II, chapter 3 above.

and immediately goes on to praise another spectacle, which represents the *terminus post quem* in the chronology of the development of movable sets: 'And then I saw a comedy performed in Florence on a similar set, in the ducal palace on the occasion of the visit in 1569 of Archduke Charles of Austria, where the set was made by Baldassare Lanci of Urbino.' But there was inevitably a ferment of ideas in Cosimo I's resplendent city. When the duke had founded the Accademia Fiorentina in 1541 and had housed it in his palace on the Via Larga, he had partly entrusted to it the organization of spectacles, though he himself continued to direct them in his role of member of the Accademia and its main financial backer. They performed at carnival time or on special occasions, in the Sala del Papa in Santa Maria Novella, or in the main hall of the Palazzo Vecchio which in 1540 had become the ducal residence. Generally they put on texts by members of the Accademia themselves, such as *Il furto* (1544) and *I Bernardi* (1547)[26] by Francesco d'Ambra, *Il granchio* by Leonardo Salviati (1566), *I Fabii* by Lotto del Mazza (1567), adorning them 'with sumptuous decorations and full of magnificent pomp, rich attire, and *intermedi* of great appeal'.[27]

As well as the Accademia Fiorentina there were also numerous groups, sponsored by teaching institutions, and bands of entertainers, derived from those of the early Renaissance and made up of artists, noble youths and boys. Pre-eminent amongst these were the Compagnia di San Bastiano de' Fanciulli and the group of the Fantastichi who shared the comedies of Giovanni Maria Cecchi, the Compagnia dell' Arcangelo Raffaello, the Compagnia del Vangelista, and the two groups of schoolboys under Bernardino and Alberto.[28] The omnipresent Medici often attended themselves, and the palace stewards sometimes supplied not only the costumes and fittings but also the services of the court painters. In the years immediately following the 1539 festivities, this task fell to Sangallo: '...and almost each year he made some set and perspective for the comedies performed at carnival time. He had so much experience and aid from nature in that type of painting that he conceived the idea of writing and teaching about it'. Afterwards the artist left the court, disappointed because Cosimo was beginning to prefer Francesco Salviati and Bronzino to him. In the meantime Giorgio Vasari's mannerist talent was gaining ground. Vasari was given a permanent post at court in 1555, and was joined in about 1560 by Baldassare Lanci, as ducal architect, and by Bernardo Buontalenti, as companion to the prince Francesco in his studies. These names stand out today amongst the many which adorned Cosimo's

[26] *Il furto* (ed. Florence 1560) was performed in 1544 'in the so-called Sala del Papa. The *intermedi* were by Ugolino Martelli who later became Bishop of Glandeve in Provence.' *I Bernardi* (ed. Florence 1564) was performed in 1547 'with pomp and elaborate apparatus, in the great hall of the Most Illustrious Duke Cosimo', which was probably the Salone dei Cinquecento in the Palazzo Vecchio.

[27] We will return in a more appropriate place to the *intermedi* of *I Fabii*, which featured a change in full view after Act IV.

[28] The Compagnia di San Bastiano dei Fanciulli performed these plays by G. M. Cecchi: *La moglie* (1545), *Il corredo* (1546), *La stiava* (1546), *I dissimili* (1548), *L'ammalata* (1555), *Il servigiale* (1556). By the same author the Compagnia del Vangelista performed *La morte di Re Acab* (1559), *La coronazione di Re Saul* (1569), *Serpe, ovver Suocera e nuora* (1574), *L'esaltazione della Croce* (1576, for the wedding of the grand-duke), *Acquavino* (1579). The Compagnia dei Fantastichi performed his *Gli incantesimi* (1547), *L'assiuolo* (1549), *Lo spirito* (1549), *Il donzello* (1550), *La maiana* (1551). Bernardino's pupils performed *Il sensale* by F. Mercati (1559), and 'the noble youths of Alberto in their school' put on *La Cangenia* by B. Poggi (1561), while in the Casino of Don Antonio dei Medici they acted *I morti vivi* by J. Pagnini (1602).

court and theatre. They were involved in all the great festivities of 1565, by which the duke, while honouring his German daughter-in-law, wished to amaze the whole of Europe.

The task of planning the festivities, coordinating the entertainments and supplying the inventions fell to Don Vincenzo Borghini, prior of the Ospedale degli Innocenti. Vasari was in charge of translating the inventions into images, planning how to realize them, recruiting the artists, sharing out the jobs and supervising the work. The festivities lasted three months, from 16 December, when Giovanna entered Florence, to 23 March, when there was the great entertainment offered by the Orsini in Piazza San Lorenzo. The spectacles were held on Sundays, at court or in the two great temporary theatres built in the squares in front of Santa Croce and Santa Maria Novella. Amongst all the masquerades, balls, jousts and tournaments, there were only two dramatic productions: Francesco d'Ambra's *La cofanaria*, held in the Great Hall on Christmas Day, and *L'annunciazione*, which revived the lost tradition of *ingegni* in the church of Santo Spirito.

Unfortunately there are no known sketches of the splendid Palazzo Vecchio set for *La cofanaria*, but literary sources more than make up for this. The most valuable of these is the text attributed to il Lasca.[29] Vasari, overburdened with work, concentrated on the plans and left others to put them into practice. The carpentry work was directed by Battista Botticelli, the exterior decoration of the stage was painted by Prospero Fontana, 'the paintings [of the set] were the work of Bernardo Timante, a painter of capricious talent and a favourite of the bridegroom, Prince Don Francesco dei Medici' (Settimani). Also 'the ropes of the sky – and the exits beneath the stage required by M. Gio. Battista [Cini] were the work of Bernardo Timante, known as Bernardo delle Girandole' (il Lasca). It was not Vasari, then, but Cini, the author of the *intermedi*, who was the director of all or part of the spectacle, while Buontalenti, who in his youth had applied himself more to the art of fortifications than to painting, and was loved by Francesco for his 'fanciful mechanical inventions', looked after the system of fly-ropes and the lifts from understage, required for the appearances of musicians and deities.

Even the ten canvasses depicting the main fortresses of the duchy, which temporarily decorated the walls of the Salone dei Cinquecento, five on each side, were designed by Vasari but painted by Alessandro del Barbiere, Giovanni Lombardo (a Venetian), Bastiano Veronese and Turino from the Piedmont. The figures, friezes, garlands and cherubs were the work of Lorenzo Sabbatini of Bologna.[30]

If one compares the measurements and information supplied by il Lasca

[29] On the festivals of 1565–6 and their sources, see Pirrotta, part I, chapter 5 above, especially notes 7 and 10. For the chronology of G. Vasari's theatrical activity and for the names of the other artists who collaborated with him in the 1565 festivals, see E. Povoledo in *Enciclopedia dello spettacolo* (Florence and Rome 1962), vol. IX, cols. 1466–71.

[30] Vasari had already been commissioned to decorate the Salone dei Cinquecento in 1563, but the work was only carried out later, between 1566 and 1571. Battista Botticelli, master carpenter, was in Castro in 1538 with F. Salviati, and he carried out the carpentry involved in the creation of the arches as well as in the rest of the job. Prospero Fontana, a painter from Bologna, was also an Accademico del Disegno in Florence (Vasari, *Le vite*, vol. VII, pp. 82, 410, 621). His works are to be found in Rome and in France. A reconstruction of the Salone dei Cinquecento fitted up as a theatre appears as plate 59 in Zorzi, *Il teatro e la città*, and is extensively discussed on pp. 96–105.

with the dimensions of the still intact Salone of the Palazzo Vecchio, the Medicean theatre appears much more harmoniously proportioned than the Venetian one used by the Compagnia dei Sempiterni, but not vastly different in its general arrangement. The hall is 53 m long, 22 m wide and 18 m high. The north side was filled with seats 'made out of wood for this purpose, which can be fitted together and taken to pieces, and are disbanded and put back in place in eight hours'. The two tiers, obviously intended to be preserved and re-used, were as in Venice parallel to the two long sides of the room, already 2.25 m from the ground at the first tier, and reached from the front, protected by a decorated balustrade, by means of small stairways. Here sat the 60 ladies who had been invited, while the gentlemen arranged themselves in the hall around the ducal stand which was raised on a 'wooden platform with three steps around it for access, covered with fine rugs, on which were placed rich seats variously embroidered in gold' (il Lasca).

The wall paintings, which as in Venice illustrated the provinces belonging to the state, were divided by female cariatids, each of which bore

several large crystal balls a *braccio* [58 cm] high, made with great artifice, full of water of different colours; they reflected those colours by means of a great light which was placed behind that transparent body, and made a dazzling brightness. The cariatids were all worked with silver, to represent the hours of the night, and with other similar balls [placed on the cornices of the stone decoration of the wall of the Udienza side] made up the number of hours spent at the comedy, the meal and the dances which lasted until daybreak. (il Lasca)

The whole of the south side was occupied by the stage, which was also raised 2.25 m above the floor, and had a scenic front which stretched from one wall to the other. The proscenium, which was painted on a collapsible wooden wall, presented a large opening framed by two imitation columns in composite style, 7.55 m high and surmounted by an architrave 2 m high, with frieze and cornices. Thus 11.75 m of the 18 m-high room were accounted for. The remaining 6.25 m were occupied by a pediment decorated with the Medici arms and chiaroscuro figures. On the base of the proscenium were painted three false stairways, one of mixti-linear design in the centre and two, square, shown sideways on each side. Also in the base of the proscenium there were the openings of two passages, one of which led to the apartments of the Prince of Bavaria and the other to the old stairs of the palace.

The set represented Florence, and was now in the shape of a *strada lunga*, unusual in that it did not feature a collection of the most important monuments of the city but reproduced, more or less realistically, the street which crosses the Santa Trínita bridge and links Piazza Santa Trínita and Piazza San Felice:

and the set represented that part of Florence which we call Santa Trínita, in which there was the bridge here depicted in its entirety, as it really was before the flooding of the river Arno in 1557 ruined it, with the road of Via Maggio as far as San Felice in Piazza, which was visible straight ahead of the bridge. And similarly the palaces, and the houses which were around that place [Piazza Santa Trínita] with the addition of a triumphal arch in the middle of it, with the river Arno, and the river Danube at the foot of it, to represent the alliance of Their Highnesses, for whom these so happy wedding festivities were being celebrated. And the set also represented the foremost buildings of the perspective very thoroughly decorated in various ways to make them beautiful; [all of] which with the open lamps together with all the decorations made a magnificent and elegant sight. Giorgio Vasari, creator of these ornaments, had used a barrel-vault ceiling with wooden screens, all covered with cloth, and painted with air full of clouds, which ceiling rotated according to what the whole set was doing. A new invention, this caused the perspective to give a strong impression of depth. (il Lasca)

The engraving of *Il granchio* (plate 29), whilst being very crude, so resembles the scene described by il Lasca that it makes one wonder whether the 1566 perspective was not re-used by the Accademici Fiorentini the following year, in the Sala del Papa. Of course the engraving conveys neither the beauty of Vasari's invention nor Buontalenti's highly original execution of it. Perhaps we should look for both these elements in the symmetrical colonnades which emerge, precious and surreal, from the background of certain paintings in the Studiolo of Francesco I.[31] But it is possible to reconstruct the lay-out of the set: the buildings in the foreground were not so much faithful to real life as varied for the sake of beauty, and shining with lights. Then there were a few of the houses of Piazza Santa Trínita,[32] with four roads, two on each side, 'which were left [open] on the stage for the use of the actors'. The Arno was represented at the back of the stage, between that part of the perspective which was shown on successive pairs of canvasses and its continuation on the backcloth. Even the bridge, which was viewed 'straight ahead', appeared foreshortened towards the back, and if the engraving is to be believed, had the bridgeheads decorated with statues like the present bridge, which was reconstructed by Ammannati between 1566 and 1569. Beyond the bridge, in the centre of the perspective, began the Via di Maggio with medieval houses and Renaissance palaces, amongst which may have appeared the house of the Ridolfi, the Palazzo Corsini or the Palazzo Peruzzi belonging to the Medici. Also in the engraving, about half-way along the street, appears a faint arch cut in half, and even further back crenellated towers and houses which disappear into the distance until they merge with the undulating outline of a hilly landscape.

Pirrotta has analysed the musical and theatrical significance of the *intermedi*, and has shown the nature of the reciprocal interconnections between the acts of *La cofanaria* and its *intermedi*, *La favola di Psiche e Amore*. The *intermedi* were devised and directed by Giovanbattista Cini, set to music by Alessandro Striggio and Francesco Corteccia, and staged by Buontalenti. Again, it is il Lasca who provides us with the details of the action, all of which

[31] Francesco I's Studiolo in the Palazzo Vecchio was created between 1570 and 1579. Vincenzo Borghini conceived the subjects for the cycle of pictures and Vasari directed the task of translating these ideas into painting. The work itself was done by I. Zucchi, M. Cavalori, Maso di San Friano, Poppi, Santi di Tito, G. Stradano, G. B. Naldini, A. Allori, G. Bandini, G. Macchietti, Lorenzo dello Sciorina, G. M. Butteri, J. Coppi, A. Fei, N. Betti, D. Buti, V. Casini and other artists. G. Vasari painted *The Liberation of Andromeda by Perseus*, and Agnolo Bronzino the lunette with the portrait of Eleonora of Toledo.

[32] Commissioned by G. Vasari, G. B. Cini wrote another account which was published by the painter though without the name of the author, entitled *Descrizione dell'apparato fatto in Firenze per le nozze dell'Illustrissimo ed Eccellentissimo Don Francesco de' Medici, Principe di Firenze e di Siena, e delle Serenissima Regina Giovanna d'Austria* (Vasari, *Le vite*, vol. VIII, pp. 517ff). The set for *La cofanaria* is there described: 'in which perspective the vanishing point coinciding most ingeniously with the furthest part of the set along the line of the bridge, and terminating at the end of the street called the Via di Maggio, in the nearer parts was depicted the beautiful quarter of Santa Trínita'.

took place on the stage, with spectacular entrances on machines, and individual entrances at varying distances from the back of the stage.

The performance was opened by Venus, appearing 'most beautiful, all naked and garlanded with myrtle and roses' on her gold chariot encrusted with jewels, pulled by swans and borne by a 'white and excellently counterfeited' cloud. With her were the three Graces, naked and blonde, and the four Horae with 'their wings all painted to resemble butterflies'. The cloud, gently lowered onto the stage, slowly deposited its load of beauties. They were immediately joined by Amor, who 'with no less attractive looks, but seeming to walk about on foot, had been seen to approach from another side', accompanied by Hope, Fear, Joy and Sorrow. Amor was naked, Hope was dressed in green, Fear 'palely dressed', Joy in white and Sorrow all in black. Having instructed her son to pierce the heart of her rival Psyche with his dart, so that she would be given to a mere mortal, the goddess slowly departed on her heavy machine, and with the first act of *La cofanaria* there began an intricate but realistic story of love and misunderstandings.

The second *intermedio*, which mimed the falling in love (suggested off-stage) of Amor and Psyche, with cheerful interventions by the singers, took place at the back of the stage, with successive entries from the sides. 'From one of the four roads, which were left [open] on the stage for the use of the actors, a small cupid' was seen to enter with a *violone* hidden inside a swan. 'But after him, from the four streets of the set just described emerged in the same way and simultaneously from one street amorous Zephyrus..., from another Music...; from the other two one saw Play and Laughter appear, disguised as two little cupids, laughing and joking together.' The choreography ended with the simultaneous entries of four more cupids from the four streets, and the gathering of the entire chorus into a semicircle, in a movement which later became traditional in festive iconography.

In the third *intermedio*, since Amor had abandoned mankind for the beautiful Psyche, the world was seen invaded by fraud and treachery: 'and therefore little by little it seemed as if the floor of the stage rose up and when it had finally turned into seven little hillocks, there were seen to emerge from them, as something evil and harmful, first seven and then seven more Deceptions' dressed in spotted leopard skins, with snake-like legs, and on their heads wigs 'of sly foxes'. And having sung their madrigal, 'they left in good order by means of the roads previously described'.

In the fourth *intermedio* appeared the crimes and brawls provoked by the Deceptions, in the absence of Cupid: 'Instead of the seven hillocks, which had previously been shown on stage, one saw in this scene...seven little holes' from which came, amidst smoke and flames, Discord, Anger, Cruelty, Robbery, Revenge and two Anthropophagi. Each was pushed up by two Furores made hideous by their wounds and their head-dresses of intertwined snakes, from which emerged fire and smoke. They sang together and 'in the guise of warriors danced a new and highly extravagant *moresca*, at the end of which they ran in great disorder about the stage and disappeared, inspiring great fear'.

The whole of the stage floor must therefore have been pierced by trap-doors to permit the simultaneous entry of the singers for the *intermedi*. In addition, there must also have been a wide rail at the back of the stage, cut into the floor parallel to the Arno, to enable Charon's boat to enter at the end of the fifth *intermedio* to pick up the despairing Psyche abandoned by Amor, and to take her, according to Venus' orders, to Hades. This was the last image in a scene which was wholly infernal and obscure in its succession of monstrous visions.

And therefore Psyche was seen coming along one of the roads, clothed in desperation and very melancholy, accompanied by noisome Jealousy, who appeared pale and afflicted like the others who followed. She was identified by her four heads and turquoise dress made up of woven ears and eyes. Psyche was also accompanied by Envy, recognized by the snakes she was devouring, and by Thought or Concern or Worry, whatever one wishes to call her, recognized by the crow on her head and by the vulture tearing at her insides, and by Scorn, or Contempt (*Disprezzagione*) to give her a feminine name, who made herself known by the owl on her head and by her disarranged, torn and shabby dress. These four hit and goaded her until they had nearly reached the middle of the stage when suddenly, with fire and smoke, the earth opened in four places and, as if wishing to split it apart, they took out four most horrid serpents which unexpectedly issued forth.

But the serpents concealed inside themselves four *violoni*, on which the wretched Passions accompanied Psyche's lament.

After this was finished, and each having with a certain gracefulness shouldered her serpent, the spectators were no less terrified to behold another enormous aperture appear in the floor, from which smoke and flames in huge quantities emerged unceasingly. Then suddenly, with fearful barking, infernal Cerberus was seen with his three heads, to whom, obeying the legend, Psyche was seen to throw one of the two flat cakes which she was holding; and after a while Charon accompanied by various monsters appeared in his boat, in which the despairing Psyche took her place in the tiresome and unpleasant company of her four tormentors.

In the sixth *intermedio* the story of Psyche and Amor resolved in joyful images of a happy and peaceful world.

Suddenly a verdant hillock was seen to emerge from the floor of the stage, all covered with laurels and divers flowers, crowned by the winged horse Pegasus. It was soon recognized as Mount Helicon, from which gradually descended that attractive band of cupids already described, and with them Zephyr, and Music and Amor and Psyche hand in hand, all happy and rejoicing because she [Psyche] had returned safe from hell.

And Pan, nine satyrs and Hymen, god of marriage, also descended from the hill, and with a 'new and joyful and very charming dance they brought the entertainment to a graceful end'.

I have described these *intermedi* at length, although they might seem boring to a less than attentive reader, because I feel that it is in them and in the barely glimpsed intentions they reveal, rather than in the acts themselves, that one can discover the most concealed and authentic meaning of this new theatrical world, different and transitional, which to our modern eyes has become identified with the world of Vasari and his collaborators. The two stories ran parallel, contrapuntally. The comedy was realistic and grotesque, made almost surreal by the dramatic conventionality of its intrigues. The story of Psyche was metaphysical rather than a pure fantasy: it pretended to moralize on the main events, 'to give cause to the troubles of the comedy' (Cini), whether its images were sought in the hybrid and platonic yet suspect innocence of a naked and bejewelled Olympus or among the monstrous divinities of a hell forged in the secret ovens of alchemy. While Vasari could not have combined Cini's *intermedi* and Aretino's *Talanta* in 1542, Cini for his part could not have found figures more resembling those of his characters outside Francesco I's Studiolo, painted by Vasari's collaborators between 1570 and 1572.

All the novelties intuitively introduced by Bastiano da Sangallo in the 1539 arrangement were present in the Palazzo Vecchio set, but they had reached the point of breaking with the Renaissance tradition from which they had grown as an answer to precise needs. The basic structures (hall, perspective, machines, costumes) and certain aesthetic attitudes capable of bringing cohesion, such as the ideas of temporal perspective and of abstract celebration, still formed the skeleton of the spectacle, but increasingly they were changing their nature. The original realistic stimulus was not entirely abandoned, but had begun to make way for the figurative ambiguity of mannerism, by which the crisis affecting Counter Reformation man, with his new distrust of the reality which surrounded but no longer sustained him, was translated into indefinable and seductive images.

The hybrid vision of the *intermedi* is the most obvious measure of this change in the invention and formulation of visual shapes. But in a way even the *strada lunga*, an obvious development of Peruzzi's perspective set (and as such possible even to a scenographer like Sangallo), reappears in a different light in the work of the followers of Vasari; we are now in the world of the seascapes of Giorgio Vasari's own *Andromeda*, or in Alessandro Allori's *La pesca delle perle*:[33] a world combining reality and escapism, realism and anti-realism.

The almost faithful portrait of the Via di Maggio was elongated to the point of deformation, and this deformation became 'manner', i.e. an exaggerated expression of individual imagination, defined through form. The lengthening of perspective was here not so much a conquest of infinite space as a disagreement with the idea itself of anything finite. It was left to Baroque scenography, dominated by the dynamic imperative imposed by the new mentality (including the new scientific mentality), to resolve this problem, now only in its infancy, with a different tension and delight.

Whether the actors in *La cofanaria* or the performers of *intermedi* of *La favola di Psiche* emerged from amongst the tall, carefully foreshortened houses of Piazza Santa Trínita made no difference. Venus' cloud descended from the concave sky and Mount Helicon rose from the large below-stage. Musicians and machines stopped in the middle of the set without negating it, but distracted the audience's attention from it by means of surprise. The importance the organizers attached to the element of surprise is confirmed by the presence of the great screen painted by Federico Zuccari, whose splendid sketch for it is still preserved in the Gabinetto degli Uffizi. Whereas in 1539 Bastiano da Sangallo had left the perspective in full view so that it could be admired even before the performance, Vasari covered it jealously:

And the space where there was the perspective for the comedy remained filled for many days, so that it could not be seen, by a cloth 23 *braccia* long and 15 *braccia* high [13.35 × 8.70 m], on which was painted a hunt with a great many figures both

---

[33] What R. Sayce has to say on G. Vasari is most interesting; see his article in *Renaissance, Maniérisme, Baroque, proceedings of the II Stage International du CESR de Tours* (Paris 1972).

mounted and on foot, with dogs and birds, who were hunting in a large and beautiful land. (il Lasca)

The almost physical contact between the play and spectators which Renaissance theatre had quite naturally preserved, had by now broken down. The two sides became isolated, each within its own sphere: illusion and reality – and the new rapport now established among them could only be purely intellectual.[34]

The decorative frame which a designer following Serlio's perspective style had created around the visual picture, in order to bring together the focal points of the set and concentrate the attention of the spectator, had been transformed into a wooden partition which simulated an architectonic structure but which actually separated the set from the hall. The staircase painted capriciously on the plinth of the proscenium was merely a decorative reminder of those steps which until recently had actually linked the proscenium with the body of the theatre and given the actors access to the stage. The new secrecy required by the manoeuvring of the stage machinery had necessitated a rearrangement of the 'set, which was provided inside with platforms, rooms and stairways for both the consort and the actors, so comfortable that while the entertainment lasted, no noise was heard nor disorder seen' (il Lasca).

The seats for the audience surrounded the hall, and the prince's stand in the centre, open to the admiring eyes of the guests, was still a spectacle within a spectacle, but separate. Elsewhere and later on, in the danced balls and open-tournaments, where some parts were played by the princes and courtiers, this free communication between hall and stage reappeared. But within the comedies, the *intermedi*, though they may have carried on a moralizing dialogue with the audience or celebrated the presence of the prince, no longer came to involve them physically in the action.

Finally, let us consider the decoration of the hall. As in Venice, it reinforced not only the established theme of political celebration of the stage, but also the more dramaturgic theme of temporal perspective. However, whereas in the set for *Talanta* the division of the hours depicted on the ceiling and the passing of time marked by the rotating sun at the back of the stage measured the time of the action on stage, in Florence the hours illustrated by the great iridescent balls held by cariatids or fixed to the third wall of the hall (not covered by paintings) did not allude to time within the play but to time spent at the whole entertainment, 'at the comedy, the meal and the dances which lasted until daybreak' (il Lasca).

Some years before the better-known Buontalenti, who was already a favourite of Prince Francesco, another artist emerged from amongst those minor ones who had been involved in the 1565 entertainments. This was Baldassare Lanci.[35] Born in Urbino and a protégé of Girolamo Genga, Lanci reached

[34] On the relationship between stage space, theatrical action and the public in the sixteenth and seventeenth centuries, see the two essays by C. Molinari and P. Bjurström in *Le lieu théâtral à la Renaissance* (Paris 1964). A sketch for the concealing curtain of *La cofanaria* is reproduced as plate 62 in Zorzi, *Il teatro e la città*.

[35] On B. Lanci's theatrical activity see Vasari's biography (Vasari, *Le vite*, vol. VII, p. 641) and in addition E. Povoledo, in *Enciclopedia dello spettacolo* (Rome and Florence 1959), vol. VI, cols. 1192–4.

Florence in 1560 at the age of fifty, having devoted himself primarily to building and military engineering. At the court of Cosimo I he was employed as architect (*architettore*), but he continued to work on fortifications, and it may have been because of his experience of machinery that Vasari put him in charge of the floats used in the last masquerade of Francesco's wedding entertainments on 26 February 1565 (1566 new style), a few days before the start of Lent. The information is supplied by Vasari himself, who mentions it in connection with Lanci's son 'Pompilio, who bore himself excellently in several things in the masquerade called "*della Genealogia degli Dei*" organized by his father, the said Baldassare, particularly in regard to the machines'.[36]

Lanci's work satisfied both his supervisor and the duke, so much so that in the following years, when Vasari was either unwilling or unable to attend to stage decorations because of other more demanding work,[37] the task passed to him. He was responsible at least for the production of the comedies performed to celebrate the two main events which took place before his death in 1571: the baptism of Francesco's first child Eleonora in February 1567 (1568 new style), and the visit of Archduke Charles of Austria, brother of Duchess Giovanna, in May 1569.

In 1568 Lotto del Mazza's *I Fabii* was performed, with *intermedi* set to music by Alessandro Striggio, and in 1569 Giovambattista Cini's *La vedova*, with *intermedi* also by Striggio. Both the comedies were staged in the Salone dei Cinquecento, both had a main perspective representing Florence, with a view of the Palazzo Vecchio, but above all, both presented a startling novelty: the set, mounted on *periaktoi* (rotating triangular wings), changed in full view of the audience at least once in the course of the performance.

While it is almost certain than Lanci did not have to concern himself with arranging the hall itself, as the collapsible tiers of 1566[38] were probably re-used, the same perspective set with the Piazza dei Signori was not employed for both these plays. The two descriptions of the comedies lead on to envisage different backcloths representing the same view seen from different angles, even bearing in mind the fact that sixteenth-century scenography did not insist on a strictly accurate representation of any given place. It is possible that some *periaktoi* painted with civic buildings were re-used, but it is clear that there were different backcloths, both for the two main perspectives and for the two new sets, which changed while the living screen of an *intermedio* protected them (as subsequently advised by Danti in 1583).

A drawing preserved in the Gabinetto degli Uffizi and attributed to Baldassare Lanci (plate 30), does indeed show a scene with a road dominated by the Palazzo dei Signori. It is well drawn and places the artist's scenographic style midway between the Serlian tradition of a market-square and Vasari's *strada lunga*. The right-hand diagonal is devoted to monuments of the city.

36   Vasari, *Le Vite*, vol. VII, p. 641.

37   G. Vasari was involved in decorating the Salone dei Cinquecento and in directing the decoration of the Studiolo of Francesco I in the Palazzo Vecchio.

38   The description of the hall in which *La vedova* was performed is particularly reminiscent of that of *La cofanaria*: 'Seated on the steps around the great hall were ladies who had been invited to the meal that evening. At the south end, was the stage: at a distance from which was a raised platform on which their Highnesses sat down. The rest of this hall was left empty for the spectators and was full of gentlemen and favoured persons who had been permitted to enter freely on that day, a benefit denied to the others', from *Raccolto delle feste* (Florence 1569); and see note 51 below, and the reconstructions (plates 59, 70, 72) in Zorzi, *Il teatro e la città*.

One can see the Uffizi gallery (though it is angled in such a way as to show a foreshortened view of its side where one would expect the front of the colonnade), the Palazzo dei Signori, the fountain 'del Biancone', the Palazzo Uguccioni, and in the distance the dome and bell-tower of the Duomo. The left diagonal is given over to civil buildings: a house with a flowered porch on the top floor, the Loggia dei Lanzi, the expanse of the square, and other houses with shops. The increased depth of the perspective is perceptible in the way the size of the buildings decreases towards the Duomo, but there are none of the branching streets at the back visible in Salviati's set, nor are there hints of more open countryside as in *Il granchio* (plates 28 and 29). It is, then, an elongated road, which could be acted upon perhaps as far as the third entrance, but is contained in a logical space, and with its buildings designed to be in proportion to the size of the actor on stage.

A second drawing, attributed to Baldassare Lanci, thought to be for *La vedova*, and belonging to the Bertini collection in Prato, was exhibited by Licisco Magagnato in the 1974 exhibition at Vicenza.[39] Although the description of the 1569 set supplies few details which may help to identify the sketch, it is probably connected with *La vedova*. In del Mazza's *I Fabii*, the street vanishing into the backdrop of the main perspective must have been the Via della Vaccherreccia, which is not visible in the drawing:

The said scene and perspective was made in this guise: first the ducal palace could be seen near the front (*in testa*) with all its surroundings as far as the end of the Vaccherreccia, then the rest, made up of several structures which represented various palaces and houses of divers kinds, with porches, projecting terraces and other features. At the sides it had façades full of varied and differently counterfeited figures, made as the producers of the comedy had intended them to be. Besides these was at each side a naked figure in relief, admirably foreshortened, made by the hand of the excellent Giovan Bologna [Giambologna], sculptor to the Most Illustrious Prince. These figures, as they were the size of giants, held in one hand a great torch, and in the other a cloth which fell along the wall at the sides of the perspective.[40]

In actual fact the Via della Vaccherreccia joins the side of the square opposite the Palazzo dei Signori, and as one came from the Loggia di Mercato Nuovo the dome of the cathedral could not have been seen in the background. The set changed in the interval between the fourth and fifth acts, and the scene shifted from the Piazza dei Signori to San Giovanni. The Duomo must have been painted on the backdrop, as in the two drawings, while the whole set depicted the Canto della Paglia (between Via de' Cerretani and Borgo San Lorenzo).[41]

The set remained like this until the fourth act. Then, while the *intermedio* was being sung and played (as will be described in due course) it turned so easily and in such an orderly fashion as had never been seen, for all the pieces were so balanced on

[39] For the Uffizi drawing labelled 404P, see *Feste e apparati medicei*, mentioned above in note 20, *passim*. For the drawing in the Collezione Bertini of Prato, see L. Magagnato, *Il teatro italiano del Cinquecento* (Vicenza 1974), an exhibition catalogue, and plate 63 in Zorzi, *Il teatro e la città*.

[40] Alessandro Ceccherelli, *Tutte le feste e mascherate fatte in Firenze per il carnovale questo anno 1567. Et insieme l'ordine del Battesimo della Primogenita dell'Illust. et Eccell. S. Principe di Firenze e Siena, con gl'intermedii della commedia e dell'apparato fatto per detto battesimo* (Florence 1567).

[41] G. B. Cini, in the *Descrizione* of the 1565 entertainments (Vasari, *Le vite*, vol. VIII, p. 551) gives precise information as to the site of the Canto della Paglia, which was also the site of one of the arches devised by G. Vasari: 'in that part, that is, where the road which proceeds from the Archbishopric enters the Borgo di San Lorenzo and forms a perfect cross and cross roads, dividing the afore-mentioned Strada della Paglia'.

certain pieces of iron that even the smallest child could turn them with great ease. This turning made the scene quite different from what it had previously been, for it changed all the houses and their particular features and made the front (*la testa*) to be seen as in reality (*di naturale*), showing the area from the Canto della Paglia towards S. Maria del Fiore just as it really is. All in all, it was a most marvellous artifice.

The printed edition of *I Fabii*[42] returns at the end of the text to this business of the scene-change, supplying some details which are useful because they define the lay-out of the set and confirm that the change took place to assist the comic action.

Be it known to the discreet Reader that besides the rich *intermedi* that were acted with this comedy, there were two perspectives, one of which represented the Piazza del Duca and served for the first, second, third and fourth acts, where one saw the houses of M. Prospero and Ipolito. When the fourth act was finished, the other perspective, richer and more splendid to behold, was turned around, showing the Piazza di San Giovanni. That is the reason why the two afore-mentioned houses do not appear in the fifth act, but only the house of M. Lattantio.

In this way a precedent was established in *I Fabii*, but one which was not followed up, as the *intermedio*, initially used to serve as a machine and a curtain, took over the innovation of scenery and adapted it to its own ends, leaving comedy to continue using a fixed urban perspective for many more years. It is also true that the eventful, but not very new, plot of *I Fabii* could have been performed against any of Serlio's piazzas with two functional houses on either side. Once more, the crux of the plot is the thwarted love of two young couples, the female halves of which never appear on stage. Ippolito loves Livia, the daughter of Prospero, and Tiberio loves Laura, the daughter of Lattanzio. But the two aged fathers, both anxious to have male heirs, have in turn decided to get married again, Prospero to Laura, and Lattanzio to Livia. Also involved is Serafino, an unfortunate marriage-broker, who in his eagerness to satisfy everyone is always just a hair's breadth away from being handed over to the Bargello. Finally, to complicate matters, comes first the intervention of Ormanno, a friend and accomplice of Ippolito, who, in order to give back to Prospero his desired heir, pretends to be Fabio, the son believed by the old man to have been lost at sea. Then, of course, the real Fabio appears. With mistaken identities, misunderstandings and the inexhaustible inventiveness of Ormanno, the final recognition scene is reached: Tiberio is discovered to be the son of Lattantio and the brother of Laura, so the couples have to change round: Ippolito will marry Livia, but Laura will be married to Fabio.

The action of the first four acts centres on the broker's continually upset negotiations and on Ormanno's lies which are constantly being discovered and pieced together again. It takes place between the two houses of Prospero and Ippolito, making use of a frequently repeated theatrical expedient: one group of characters discusses their plans and are overheard by an opposing group 'from around the corner', who prepare to overturn these plans. The other focus, off stage, is the Borgo San Lorenzo, where the young people and

---

[42] *I Fabii*, a 'comedy by Lotto del Mazza, a Florentine cobbler, acted in Florence in the year 1567 in the Ducal Palace after the baptism of the Most Illustrious Leonora, first-born daughter of the Most Illustrious Prince of Florence and of Siena, and of his most worthy consort, Queen Giovanna of Austria', Florence 1567.

Serafino arrange to meet, where Ormanno has his quarters in the Albergo dell'Agnolo and where, as we find out in Act V, the house of Laura and Lattanzio is located. Even though such officers as the Bargello and the Otto[43] are constantly being mentioned, no one ever refers to the buildings depicted in the set (the Palazzo dei Signori, the Loggia dei Lanzi, Vacchereccia) which were evidently chosen more to illustrate Florence and the Ducal Palace than to provide a realistic setting for the comedy. According to Ceccherelli, the authors (del Mazza, and perhaps the anonymous inventor of the *intermedi*) were consulted about the decoration of the 'façades full of varied and differently counterfeited figures', but the only scene to bear out this statement seems to be a later and irrelevant addition: in Act II, Ormanno, having left his horse at the inn, reaches the Piazza dei Signori and looks for Ippolito's house: 'If you please, kind sirs...tell me which is the house of Ippolito Campugliesi.' Ippolito himself, who has not seen his friend for years, replies: 'It is the one which forms the corner, and has those ducal arms above the door.'

So it would seem as if the change of set in the fifth act to the Canto della Paglia, where the action concludes with the attempted abduction of Laura, the recognition scene and the general pardon, and where the only usable house on stage is Lattanzio's, was done purely for effect and was not required to sustain the plot. The final words of the printed edition of *I Fabii* do in fact sound like an attempt at justification: 'That is the reason why the two afore-mentioned houses do not appear in the fifth act, but only the house of M. Lattantio', as if the change had taken place merely at the moment when the comedy was being produced.

The sets, wrote Ceccherelli, changed by revolving on the spot, 'for all the pieces were so balanced on certain pieces of iron that even the smallest child could turn them with great ease'. Sixteen years later, in 1583, Egnazio Danti saw in the system of *periaktoi* (the interpretation of which term had already been a cause of controversy amongst humanist architects) the method used by both Sangallo and Lanci to change their scenes, and explained very simply how they worked:[44]

---

[43] The Council of Justice, which controlled the Bargello, had since 1502 had its seat in the Palazzo del Podestà, not far from the Palazzo dei Signori, on the street leading to the Duomo. The Sala of the Otto di Pratica, on the other hand, was in the Palazzo dei Signori itself. The latter also became known as the Palazzo del Duca in 1540 when Cosimo I went to live there; when, after 1550, Cosimo moved to the Pitti Palace, the Palazzo dei Signori (inhabited by Prince Francesco) was called the Palazzo Vecchio.

[44] E. Danti, *Del modo che si tiene nel disegnare le prospettive delle Scene, acciò il finto della parete accordi con quello che si dipinge nelle case vere, che di rilievo si fanno sopra il palco*, appendix to *Le due regole della prospettiva pratica di M. Iacomo Barozzi da Vignola con i commentarij del R. P. M. Egnatio Danti dell'ordine dei predicatori matematico dello Studio di Bologna* (Rome 1583). There follows a rubric which reads 'the manner of which can be seen from this figure'. The figure itself is accompanied by the following explanations: 'Let the line AB represent the base of the backcloth, and let us assume that one wants to alter this backcloth in the course of the comedy, let us say three times. Three different cloths will be made which will be attached together and which will form a shape similar to a prism or a triangular column with two equilateral triangles at its two ends and whose base, or plantar projection will form the triangle ABC. These three sides will be made of strong wooden stakes with their cross-pieces and will have the cloth nailed in them so that they could be painted. In the centre M of the triangular base a hinge will be fixed and likewise another in the upper end, corresponding to M. These shall be fixed into good wooden beams so that the whole body may turn on them; the latter shall touch the platform only about M and all the rest be free so that it may be easily turned. Likewise, all the tridimential (*in rilievo*) houses will be made triangular in shape; so that, after the first side of the set, LABG, has been

But let us now leave aside the discussion of the difference which exists between tragic, comic and satyric scenes, for others have written enough on this matter, and it is not relevant to our purpose. Here we will merely explain how the scenes are made which suddenly turn, how the painting changes, without the spectator being aware of it, and from the sight of one city section a change is made to another or to a countryside.

The *periaktoi* were nothing more than tall prism-shaped frames, with three or more facets, placed at each side of the stage along the diagonal axes. There were two or more on each side, and they converged towards the backdrop, which was itself made up of a tall prism whose base was much larger than that of the others. Each facet of the *periaktoi* consisted of a reinforced frame, bearing, painted in perspective, some of the elements making up one of the different shifts of scene. In the centre of each prism was a stout wooden beam, the metal tip of which fitted into the floor of the stage. The height of the prism's base was adjusted so that when the construction revolved it did not touch the floor and stick. In *I Fabii*, the *periaktoi* bore only two frames: 'And should we wish to change the scene only twice, we would give it only two sides: and should we wish to turn it four, five or six times, we would give it as many sides' (Danti).

As we have seen, the set for *I Fabii* only changed in the fifth act, whilst in the other four the Piazza dei Signori remained unchanged, with Via della Vacchereccia in the background and the houses of Ippolito and Lattanzio at the sides. But each *intermedio* introduced into the stage a different device, more-or-less conspicuous, which descended from the stage loft or emerged from beneath the stage itself. Together these served to enliven the spectacle and to satisfy the expectations of a public which had become accustomed to associating the courtly *intermedi* with some unexpected novelty.

used for, let us say, Act I, it may be possible to have it suddenly turned around, thus having another landscape come into sight. For side BC will be turned around [and be seen] where AB is. Likewise shall be done also with the houses in relief, turning around to show the sides HA, KI, DE and FG. And for two more *intermedi*, at any point of our choice, we will turn around the other two sides of the backcloth and of the houses in relief. See text in Marotti, *Lo spettacolo*, pp. 217–18.

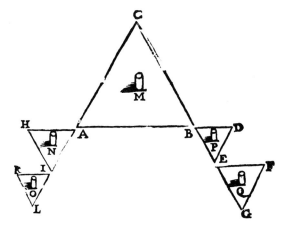

Egnazio Danti's *periaktoi* set, from his edition of Vignola's *Le due regole della prospettiva pratica* (1583)

Inserted between the acts, with a few cautious references to what is happening to the protagonists,[45] the six *intermedi* of *I Fabii* make do without a common theme, but nevertheless remain very tenuously linked together by moralistic allusions, inspired by the recurrent themes of the contrast between passion and conscience, and the precariousness of human fortunes. They were performed in the following order: the tumultuous entrance of the Furies and the Vices; the dispute between Pleasure and Hercules who finally chooses the path of fighting; a chorus of nymphs and shepherds attacked by satyrs; Calumny, according to the scene painted by Apelles; the descent of the Muses and the Graces, later driven off by the Vices; the banquet of the Gods after the birth of Venus.

The first *intermedio* acted as a prologue before the prologue. The start of the spectacle after the opening of the curtain[46] which, unusually, was operated in the Italian fashion rather than falling *ad aulaeum*, was described by Ceccherelli with unusual words: 'And the beginning took place in this guise: when great lights had been lit, the cloth which was stretched over the front of the perspective was suddenly cut and the first *intermedio* emerged.' Namely, 'the head of a snake-like monster with long sharp fangs' was seen before the buildings facing the Piazza dei Signori, 'and when it opened its throat, fire came out of it'. From the throat, 'taken to be the mouth of hell', there emerged 'one by one', first the Furies then Ixion, two Danaids, Tantalus, Tityus, Sisyphus, Salmonaeus and the pick of the depraved heroes of all antiquity.

In the third *intermedio*, the shepherds' entrance with the nymphs was accompanied by the appearance 'in the middle of the scene "of a vaulted (*in botte*) pergola"' which served as a mansion for the first part of the episode. In the Calumny of Apelles, loosely inspired by Botticelli's painting, the stage properties were even simpler: 'a throne, which suddenly emerged from beneath the stage', was intended for the king who was fought over by Truth and Calumny, and was placed, impartially, in the very centre of the semicircle formed by the singers.

The fifth *intermedio*, between Acts IV and V, represents the crux of our research. The action, which took place on two levels at once, was heightened by the virtually simultaneous, startling movement of the cloud machine which descended from the loft and of the scenes which changed by revolving. The manoeuvring of the machines and subsequent choreographic action, which was particularly significant musically because of the alternation of voices and instruments, as Pirrotta has already pointed out, required that the whole of the scenic foreground should be occupied, and thus made use of the *intermedio* as a living curtain. This was as specified by Egnazio Danti: 'And

---

[45] For example in the third *intermedio*, after the arrival of the satyrs who disturb the musical entertainment and after chasing away the shepherds seize the nymphs, Ceccherelli comments: 'which *intermedio* shows that when man thinks himself to be happy and prosperous...some accident occurs which deprives him of all peace of mind, just as one has seen happen with reference to the comedy', *Descrizione*, c. 21 r–v. In addition, see Pirrotta, on the *intermedi* of *I Fabii* in part I, chapter 5 above.

[46] Normally the curtain was used only at the start of the spectacle, and once having been opened did not shut again. Throughout the entire Renaissance the most common form of curtain was the *aulaeum* type, which fell and lay at the bottom of the proscenium, whereas the so-called 'Italian style' curtain in use now, opens from the centre, the two sections of cloth being raised and gathered on either side of the proscenium arch in rich folds.

be warned that while the scenery turns and changes it will be necessary to occupy the eyes of the spectators with some *intermedio*, so that they might not see the walls of the scene change, but only see that it has changed when the *intermedio* disappears'.

In order to hide the workings of the machines and the *periaktoi* Baldassare Lanci further added the proscenium decorated on both sides by the torch-bearing giants painted by Giambologna, which he inserted as a screen between the hall and the set, as Vasari had already done. The decorated proscenium again recalls the sketch attributed to Salviati (plate 28).[47]

The machine used for the Muses and Graces was probably still the one devised by Buontalenti in 1565. Ceccherelli did not describe it, 'as it has often been seen'; but he did not miss the chance of illustrating the device, a scaled-down forerunner of the great 'glories' constructed by the artist twenty years later to honour the marriage of Virginia dei Medici:

The cloud was made in this fashion, of painted cloth, and in the middle was a flat area about one *braccio* wide [58 cms], and long enough for all twelve to have plenty of space there. They were sitting on a small bench and were inside an iron harness which opened and was locked with a clamp as they wished. The said harness was full of cotton wool, so that it had the same appearance as the cloud and could not be seen.

The last *intermedio*, or Epilogue, again took place on two levels, but the upper half of the set, where the Olympian banquet was represented, must have all been faked: 'the said gods were made with painted pasteboard, one by one, making a beautiful show'. The action then concluded on the stage; after 'the sky had been closed, all the gods came [down] on stage, and there were twenty-nine of them, for the stage could have contained no more... After they had formed a crescent from one side of the set to the other, they danced, singing and playing.'

Even in Giovanbattista Cini's *La vedova*, performed in 1569 and referred to by Egnazio Danti[48] as the archetype of the new style of changeable sets, the shift between the second and third acts made up an element of surprise which was an end in itself. In subsequent acts, the new set conditioned the plot of the comedy and the subject of the *intermedi*, rather than being determined by them. When the text of the comedy was published according to its original version, the author, or the editor in his stead, warned the reader with the following note:

[47] Giambologna (Jean Bologne or Boulogne, 1524–80), a Flemish sculptor, 'a truly rare youth' as Vasari described him, did a lot of work for Prince Francesco. In the 1565 entertainments he also collaborated with other artists to produce the temporary decorations for the door of the Duomo.

[48] E. Danti, in the *Commentarij* to Vignola's *Due regole della prospettiva pratica*, claims to have been present at the performance of *La vedova*, but gives an inaccurate description of the scene changes, maintaining that there were in fact three of them: 'And later, on a similar stage, I saw performed in Florence a comedy, in the Ducal Palace on the occasion of the visit of the Archduke Charles of Austria in the year 1569, when the set, made by Baldassare Lanci of Urbino, changed twice. At the start of the comedy it represented the bridge at Santa Trínita and then, as the performers were supposed to have gone to the villa of Arcetri, the second side [of the *periaktoi*] became visible, showing a scene full of gardens and villas such as are in Arcetri, along with vineyards and estates around it. But then the scene changed a second time, and represented the corner of the Alberti home. And while the set was being turned, it was covered and occupied by beautiful *intermedi* devised by M. Gio. Battista Cini...' The set which included the Santa Trínita bridge belonged to the 1565 performance; obviously Danti saw both and, years later, confused the two. See Marotti, *Lo spettacolo*, p. 218.

At the end of this second act, while the *intermedio* was in progress, before everyone's eyes the whole perspective was seen to turn and change most artfully. Having hitherto represented one of the parts of the city, with this change it revealed several of the most magnificent villas and finest gardens of most delightful Arcetri, to which the preceding and subsequent parts of the comedy were very cleverly adjusted. Despite this, it has been felt necessary to let it appear [in print] in the form in which it can be read here.[49]

The plot of the comedy, necessarily restricted between the house of Messer Marino, a Venetian merchant, and the house-cum-inn owned by one Imbroglia, required neither the Piazza dei Signori nor the view of Arcetri. Indeed, one would think that moving the action from Florence to Arcetri immediately after the second act, just when Gostanzo's plot to discover his wife's supposed infidelity is beginning to develop, would have broken the tight and rapid rhythm of the plot, which despite being divided into acts, is nevertheless continuous.

Giovanbattista Cini, who had devised in 1566 courtly *intermedi*, which were overcharged with mannerist and literary images, found instead a new style for the comedy. It was sharp and witty, animated by an entirely new realism, full of *joie-de-vivre*, and at the end brought without hesitation to the most unexpected adventurous conclusion. The action, supposedly sited in Florence, is made up of mostly foreign characters who speak in different dialects (Venetian, Neapolitan, Calabrian and Sicilian), which betrays the growing taste of the public and the author for the increasingly well-established *commedia dell'arte*.[50] The key to the plot is the false news of the death of Federigo, jealous husband of the beautiful Cornelia, who wants to ascertain the truth of certain insinuations concerning his wife's fidelity which he had heard while in Cyprus. Masked, or rather 'transformed, with a habit and a beard, and a patch over his eye' (Act I scene 2), and having changed his name to Gostanzo, Federigo takes a room at Imbroglia's inn. In the house opposite live the Venetian merchant Marino, his daughter Cornelia, Lucilla (a little orphan girl brought up by the merchant), Benetta (an old woman) and the Sicilian Fiaccavento, who pretends to be a bravo, and acts as bodyguard to the women. Amongst the youths who frequent the inn are Galeotto and the Neapolitan Cola Francesco, both of whom are in love with Cornelia and who inform Gostanzo of their apparent good fortune. In fact both have been duped by Benetta, who has kept for herself the gifts sent by Cola to his supposed fiancée, and while pretending to introduce Galeotto into Cornelia's bedchamber has in fact made him sleep with the willing and crafty Lucilla. At the start of Act III Gostanzo begins to weave his ingenious plot, taking advantage of Marino's love for Lisetta, the innkeeper's beautiful wife. First he will find

---

[49] *La vedova* 'a comedy by M. Giovanbattista Cini performed in honour of his Serene Highness the Archduke Charles of Austria on his visit to Florence in the year MDLXIX' (Florence 1569). The *intermedi*, devised by G. B. Cini, were set to music by A. Striggio.

[50] The prologue of the comedy, spoken by Laughter, reads:
> Similarly, [the author thought] that he could use many languages in order to make his fable more cheerful, all of them Italian, however, and easily understood out of a long established practice. Keep your mouths shut, you learned men, and please do not frown...

Then Laughter continues, addressing the ladies: '...But please do not leave: they [the learned] are waiting eagerly to hear these stupid Zanis (as they say) utter some silly jokes.'

an excuse for sending away the innkeeper, then he will introduce the old man into Lisetta's chamber, and will return with his clothes. The servant Burchiello, dressed as Marino, will order Fiaccavento to leave, and Galeotto and Gostanzo will be free to enter the forbidden house. But matters are complicated by the unexpected return of the suspicious Imbroglia, who surprises his wife, while Cornelia and Benetta put the two young men to flight shouting 'Stop! Thief!' Then occurs the improbable *dénouement*. Benetta confesses all, Gostanzo reveals his true identity, and Lucilla reveals her true origins: she admits to being Galeotto's young wife, and Cola Francesco's half-sister, who had been believed dead.

As I have said, nothing in either the action or the dialogue requires the presence of the Piazza dei Signori, which appears to have been introduced purely for show. This hypothesis is borne out by the meticulous care with which the different monuments are illustrated in the Uffizi drawing (plate 30), above all 'a particular place in it: the corner of the Antellesi with the façade of the Ducal Palace, which is shown with the three giants at its base'.[51]

The first two *intermedi* of *La vedova* also take place against the same background. These are dedicated with the aid of Fame, to the celebration of Time Past and Present, and, with the aid of the sorceress Eritone, to the evocation of Time Future. Fame is addressed in the *intermedio* before the prologue by a group of Florentine youths and girls, and Eritone in her *intermedio* by the spirits of great artists of past ages.[52] But as the dialogue proceeds, the author's intentions must have been clearly revealed to the only too well-prepared spectators: the real hero was to be the Ducal Palace, the tangible symbol of past glories, present power and future hope.

Apart from almost unthinkingly establishing a new link between the plot and the stage setting, the *intermedi* to *La vedova* added little, from the point of view of stage technique and visual effects, to the *intermedi* of earlier entertainments. There was an oval gilded carriage for Fame, and for the magical *intermedio* there was a play of spirits, who jumped out from beneath the stage through a trapdoor in the stage-floor. The machine[53] which screened the set while the *periaktoi* were being turned and Florence was being transformed into Arcetri may have been the one usually used for apotheoses (which may also have been used for the final *intermedio*) or another technically not too different one, even if different in appearance. It was made of clouds which moved above the stage, spreading out and coming together again, 'showing those tangles which one is wont to see when they are thick in the sky and collide. And as they met they sang most sweetly.' Obviously the singing was by the male singers, dressed in feminine veils of 'red, yellow, green', tied down to their little chairs and enveloped in the clouds of cotton wool. And 'after their song, the Winds rose up pretending to come from below

---

[51] *Raccolto delle feste fatte in Fiorenza dalli Ill.mi et Ecc.mi Nostri Signori e padroni, il Sig. Duca et il Sig. Principe di Fiorenza et di Siena nella venuta del Serenissimo Arciduca Carlo d'Austria per honorarne la presenza di sua Altezza* (Florence 1569).
Another *relazione* attributed to G. B. Cini also exists: *Descrittione dell'intermedii fatti nel felicissimo palazo del Granduca Cosimo e del suo Illustrissimo figliuolo Principe di Firenze et di Siena: per honorar la Illustriss. Presenza della Sereniss. Altezza dello Eccellentissimo Arciduca d'Austria. Il primo giorno di maggio, l'anno MDLIX* (Florence 1569).
[52] For descriptive details and a study of the *intermedi* from the point of view of their music, see Pirrotta in part I, chapter 5 above.   [53] See note 66 below.

ground, in the same artful manner as the spirits already described, blew them [the Clouds] away and cleared the sky'. Even the blowing of the wind was a musical effect and not one of staging, as the other *Descrittione* shows: 'and they pretended to push the clouds towards the east with their breath, rising and putting to their mouths long silver conch-shells, and they sang...'

The new set required two rural *intermedi* 'with a subject to suit the new perspective'. The first, fourth in the series, was the classical episode of Latona, wandering parched through the Greek countryside with her children in her arms, and insulted by the harvesters who muddied the water she sought to drink. She asked Jove to

reward such villainy appropriately...And suddenly, with masterly art, the whole crowd was seen transformed into frogs, so realistic that even real frogs could look no more true to life. They were seen to leap into the pool, and resuming their *canzone* they were seen to swim about in the water with a thousand most natural gestures, and to sing with gurgling noises, which greatly pleased the spectators.

This is perhaps the first instance of this stage effect, of water and characters in it, which I have come across in the sixteenth-century chronicles. It is the basis for those seascapes full of rocks or surrounded by gentle countryside which were to form a typical motif of piscatorial fables and Baroque scenography. By contrast the Arno required in the *intermedi* of both *Il commodo* (1539) and *Il granchio* (1566) served merely to identify a place, being seen in front of the proscenium plinth in the former, and suggested by the lengthwise view of the bridge of Santa Trínita and by the passing of Charon's boat in the latter.

In Latona's *intermedio*, an additional change took place in the course of the action, for the body of 'clear waters' became a 'marsh full of reeds'. It is unclear whether this was simply a pictorial device or whether the water effects were achieved by the old method of waves cut out of long strips of wood or leather (plate 31), familiar from medieval religious plays,[54] and described in detail by Sabbatini in his *Pratica*.[55] The *Raccolto* does not describe the technical arrangements, but the *Descrittione* supplies the name of the scenographer and explains the simple trick used to transform the peasants into frogs:

On the stage, which, after turning, no longer showed Florence but a place not too far away, beyond the city gates, there was seen first a marsh full of reeds. A number of peasants were seen to approach it, dressed in hats and rustics' smocks, the first gold and the second orange satin. The smock reached to the knees, and a white shirt was draped over it, as is commonly seen.

After Latona's curse, the peasants 'suddenly became frogs, the costume being made in such a way that at the appropriate moment both it and the hat fell off, and there remained the frog costume, which was the work of Bernardo Buontalenti, painter and engineer of our Most Illustrious Prince'.

The fifth *intermedio*, a chorus of Diana's nymphs, did not require any particular stage effects, while the sixth, which concluded the entertainment,

[54] G. Cohen, *Le Livre de conduite du régisseur et le Compte des dépenses pour le Mystère de la Passion joué à Mons en 1501* (Paris 1925), p. 533: 'A Jehan Bracquet, nauvieur, pour son sollaire d'un petit bacquet de bois à mectre sur l'eauwe, avoir esté querir par eauwe Jemapes et l'amener au Rivaige, pour servir à la mer duddit Hourt: VI s'.
[55] Sabbatini, *Pratica di fabricar scene*, vol. II, chapters 27, 28, 29.

took place entirely in the air, with the customary Olympian apotheosis, which despite its exceptional lighting was nonetheless still a static display:

Heaven suddenly opened, and so bright was it because of the lights reflecting on the gold, that one's sight was blinded by a shimmering light which the eye could not bear, so brightly did they shine, spreading shining rays in all directions. Within this heaven, divided into different tiers, one could see a great number of gods artfully arranged, in such a way that it was impossible to discern where they rested, but all appeared suspended and upheld by divine power.

As in the last *intermedio* of *I Fabii*, at least some, if not all, of the gods must have been made of 'individual painted cartoons', but the enthusiastic author of the *Raccolto* makes no mention of this fact.

Much progress had therefore also been made in the art of staging when Bernardo Buontalenti, then at the height of his capricious talent, found himself directing the great entertainments for the wedding of Virginia dei Medici and Don Cesare d'Este in February 1585 (1586 new style). Theatrical performance in the court of Florence had declined after the death of Cosimo I in 1574. The new duke seemed to prefer gay masquerades and shows of chivalric splendour to drama, so Buontalenti's scenic inventions had been devoted to them, their floats and parades. Not even in 1579 when Francesco I's second marriage, to Bianca Capello, was celebrated with public pomp, or in 1584, when Eleonora married Vincenzo Gonzaga, were any theatrical events worthy of note remembered amongst all the jousts.

The performance of *L'amico fido*, with its six famous *intermedi* organized by Bardi, therefore marked a highly sensational resumption, even if the new theatrical event was in fact merely the splendid culmination of many other people's experiments. As far as the stage decor is concerned, one cannot undervalue the influence of the Florentine *festa*; Buontalenti certainly knew these earlier works, and took advantage of them both in laying out the hall and in revolutionizing the stage equipment. However, whatever the fame and qualities of these precedents, none of them had been planned with such clarity and comprehensiveness, or had achieved such consequential results. Only the introductions to the great tourneys 'fought' in Ferrara between 1560 and 1570 had shown anything like this completeness, this harmonious accord between set and theatre, action and theatrical space, intentions and results.[56] In these also, as in the Florentine *intermedi*, the sets (the place assigned to the defending party) changed in full view of the audience, though by different means and for different visual purposes. The fame of the Florentine festivals has undoubtedly been aided not only by the celebrity of their protagonists, but also by the quality of the many documents, both literary and iconographic, which have been preserved in the Medici archives, by the diligence of the Florentine publishers and above all by the readiness with which the grand-ducal press turned many of the sets painted for the Uffizi theatre into magnificent engravings.

[56]   The most important Ferrarese *tornei* were *Il castello di Gorgoferusa* (1561), *Il monte di Feronia* (1561), *Il tempio d'Amore* (1565, for the marriage of Alfonso I and Barbara, the sister of Giovanna of Austria), *L'isola beata* (1569, for the visit of the Archduke Charles of Austria), *Il mago rilucente* (1570). See E. Povoledo, 'Le Théâtre de tournoi et Italie pendant la Renaissance', in *Le Lieu théâtral à la Renaissance*.

The 1586 festivities were in fact performed in a new hall expressly decorated by Bernardo Buontalenti in the part of the palace known as 'of the Conservatori' ('Conservators'), which corresponds today with the Gabinetto dei Disegni and some of the rooms of the Uffizi Gallery. Some printed descriptions of the theatre are still extant, as is a later engraving by Callot,[57] based on a drawing by Giulio Parigi (plate 33), which gives us a fascinating but distorted picture of the room, as the dimensions mentioned by Bastiano de Rossi do not agree with the much larger proportions in the drawing. De Rossi twice described the Uffizi theatre, once on the occasion of Virginia's wedding, and later in 1589, when the new grand-duke Ferdinando I married Christine of Lorraine. There are some discrepancies between the two descriptions and Callot's engraving, especially as regards the decoration, so it is therefore probable that the hall, which was only used for large-scale performances, was on every occasion restored or repainted, especially in the pictorial parts which deteriorated most easily. It is possible that the tiers of seating could be moved when necessary, while the basic stage structure, along with the large machines and the complicated scaffolding of the *tirari* (counterweighted fly-lines) had to remain fixed. This at any rate is the conclusion one reaches from the allusions in the two manuscript diaries by Cesare Tinghi and Francesco Settimani, a conclusion confirmed by Filippo Baldinucci, who wrote a biography of Buontalenti at the end of the seventeenth century and seems to have seen the theatre personally, even if it had been remodelled by then.[58]

It was a typical hall theatre, with tiered seats on three sides, and an acting area in the middle which, if not required by the performance (as in masques, ballets or jousts), was filled with benches arranged around and in front of the prince's dais. The ladies occupied the banks of seating, each of six rows, while the men sat on the benches, though in Callot's engraving they appear to be standing. According to de Rossi, the room measured 95 *braccia* long, 35 wide and 24 high, i.e. approximately 55 m × 40 m, which are roughly the measurements of Vasari's room in the Palazzo Vecchio. The stage, obviously 20 m 30 wide, was only 11 m 60 deep. In order to improve visibility from the hall which was over 43 m deep, the floor was inclined: at the back of the hall

[57] Callot's engraving appears amongst those which illustrate the first *intermedio* of *La liberazione di Tirreno e d'Arnea autori del sangue toscano*, performed in Florence in 1617 (1616), with words by A. Salvadori, music by I. Peri, the dance and combat (*abbattimento*) by A. Ricci, set and machines by Giulio Parigi. The text was published in the *Opere* of A. Salvadori, Rome 1668. The most important descriptions are those by B. de Rossi (see note 61 below). We have taken Vasari's *braccio* to have equalled circa 58 cm in calculating the size of the hall in metres.

Amongst the more recent studies, see P. Rosselli, 'I teatri dei Medici', *Bollettino degli ingegneri* (Florence 1974), no. 7, pp. 3–12. See also *Il luogo teatrale a Firenze* (Florence 1975), exhibition catalogue, pp. 105ff; and Zorzi, *Il teatro e la città*, pp. 109–18 and footnotes. A reconstruction of this theatre appears in plates 69, 70 and 72 of the Zorzi volume.

[58] *Diario di Ferdinando I e Cosimo II gran Duca di Toscana scritto da Cesare Tinghi, suo aiutante de camera da 22 luglio 1600 sino a' 12 settembre 1615*, preserved in manuscript in the Biblioteca Nazionale of Florence and discussed at length by Solerti in *Musica, ballo e drammatica alla corte medicea*.

For the *Diario* by Francesco Settimani, MS in the Archivio Storico Fiorentino, see A. Solerti, *Notizie e documenti intorno la vita di Francesco Settimani fiorentino* (Florence 1875).

F. Baldinucci's life of Buontalenti appears in *Notizie dei professori del disegno, da Cimabue in qua* (Florence 1846), vol. II, pp. 490–532.

Pirrotta does not entirely agree with the view that the Medicean theatre was permanent: cf. p. 208, note 104 above.

it was about 1 m 30 higher than by the stage. About half-way along the room, 17 m 60 from the stage, rose the grand-ducal dais, itself about 7 m × 7 m in size.

In 1586 the decoration of the walls, all painted and in the mannerist style, alternated between architectonic elements and motifs of luxuriant greenery, associating the gods and allegories of classical mythology with images of an opulent and ordered nature. From a balustrade of artificial marble which backed onto the wall on three sides and crowned the tiers of seats, rose a bank of myrtle and fruit trees, about 4 m 60 high, which encircled the hall giving it the appearance of 'one of the most pleasant and graceful gardens'. The high windows were covered by screens depicting the statues of Apollo, Bacchus, Felicity, Joy, Mercury, Hymen, Beauty and Happiness. Between the windows, garlands of leaves and fruit formed ovals containing the images of Jove, Mars, Ceres, Cupid, Juno, Vulcan, Proserpina and Pomona. The system of lighting too was splendid. The hall was lit like day by four sets of equipment distributed between the tiers of seats, the ceiling and the front of the stage: the stage had lights in the loft, the proscenium and on the back of the surfaces of painted scenery. One series of torches was carried by the twenty-four pyramids which divided and decorated the plinth of the first row of seats, their height gradually augmenting in inverse relation to the slope of the hall (from about 1 m 70 to 3 m). Between these pyramids were the steps giving access to the tiers. A second series of candlesticks, set inside baskets of imitation fruit which collected the dripping wax, was supported by the 'markers' which divided the border of greenery into large squares at intervals of about 4 m 50. A third group of candlesticks hung from the proscenium frieze, and the fourth, of twenty-four candlesticks shaped like the bodies of harpies, was suspended from the rosettes which decorated the ceiling of the hall. The centres of these rosettes were slightly raised in order to allow air to enter, while other openings arranged to provide a flow of air were to be found beneath the stage.

The opening of the stage was bounded and its width reduced by two short side walls with artificial niches containing statues of Perspective and Architecture, each carrying in addition to symbolic instruments 'necessary to their work a lighted torch'. The arch of the proscenium was then defined by a draped frieze decorated with gilded cupids and surmounted by an heraldic pediment. The first curtain opened in the Italian style, and was gathered at the side of the stage.

In 1589, the general lay-out remained as it had been in 1586, except for the depth of the stage, which de Rossi indicates had 'the span of 25 *braccia*' i.e. 14 m 50. He also describes a small balcony in the wall facing the stage, 'so that on it could stand the musicians who sang in response to the harmony from the perspective'. There were again six tiers of seats with the artificial balustrade along 'the last row which was rather wider than the others and acted as a railing to enclose the amphitheatre', and 18 torch-bearing pyramids decorating the plinth of the first row. From the 45 ceiling rosettes (gold on an azure field) hung 16 chandeliers of 18 candles each, no longer shaped like harpies but made up of the combined arms of the bridal couple.

On the other hand the decoration of the walls was changed: it was much more like the decoration shown in Callot's engraving. Instead of the espaliers with greenery, eight large Corinthian arches rose from the artificial balustrade, their upper parts decorated with openings showing the sky, and their lower parts with statues in imitation metal. Between the arches were large panels, each 'of imitation Sienese marble with a niche in the centre'. The niches were filled with figures, representing along one wall, starting from the stage, New Comedy and associated with it Instruction, Confidence, Laughter and Hymen. On the other wall was old Comedy, followed by Pastoral, Satyric and Lyrical Poetry. The windows had not been closed, in order to allow smoke to escape, but they were screened by curtains of greenery.

The proscenium was similar to the 1586 one, except for the arms on the pediment, while the lighting had been perfected by the addition of footlights. Above the landing of the imitation staircases which decorated the base of the proscenium was 'a colonnade of balusters, somewhat lower than the stage, and each hid a light, whence issued part of that shining light which illuminated the floor of the stage without inconveniencing anyone'.

On both occasions, therefore, the theatre was equipped with a proscenium which, while not yet architectonic, was already defined in both structure and function. It divided the stage from the hall, while the set, isolated behind the iridescent frame of the proscenium, supported, with all available technical means, the abstract, vaguely philosophical and above all marvellous themes of Giovanni Bardi's *intermedi*. By a curious and progressive inversion of terms, the *intermedi* had by now come to form the main part of the entertainment.

In both the 1586 and the 1589 entertainments, Buontalenti's decorative taste and scenic inventiveness developed along two main lines. Tradition and novelty, equilibrium and dynamic tension seem to alternate in the visual unfolding of the entertainment, based on the two different themes of comic plot and sung action. These form two lines which converge and contradict each other without creating jarring discords; on the contrary, there is in this contrast a useful incentive to comparison. In order better to understand the stylistic duality of Buontalenti and the way the two trends interact, it may be of use to examine these two entertainments at the same time, not only because the plan of the entertainment appears to be repeated, but above all because the 1589 spectacle can be illustrated by consistent iconographic documentation made up of original drawings and contemporary engravings.[59]

[59] Only one drawing preserved in the Gabinetto dei Disegni e delle Stampe of the Uffizi in Florence (classification: 7059F) has been connected with the 1586 entertainments, and specifically to the first *intermedio* of *L'amico fido*, though its subject is by no means clearly identified. Another drawing, also in the Uffizi (5113 arch.), depicting a study for a garden scene with *treillage* motifs can be linked to the second 1589 *intermedio*, *La disfida delle Muse e delle Pieridi*.

A series of original drawings by Buontalenti, connected to the 1589 *intermedi*, are preserved in the Victoria and Albert Museum in London. These depict the first, second, third and sixth *intermedi*, while the fourth *intermedio* 'of Hades' figures in another drawing in the Louvre, Paris. They were studied and published by J. Laver, 'Stage design for the Florentine Intermezzi of 1589', *Burlington Magazine*, LX (1932).

Less convincing is the attribution of a series of theatrical drawings in the collection belonging to the Duke of Devonshire, published by A. Nicoll in *The Development of the Theatre*, 3rd edn (London 1948), pp. 97–101.

The original costume designs, collected in one volume in the Biblioteca Nazionale di Firenze, were studied by A. Warburg in 'I costumi teatrali per gli intermezzi del 1589', in *Commemorazione della riforma melodrammatica, Atti dell'Accademia del R. Istituto Musicale di Firenze* (1895).

In addition to these H. Tintelnot, *Barocktheater und Barocke Kunst* (Berlin 1939), pp. 25ff and *passim*, on Buontalenti and his connection with contemporary culture and art continues to be of fundamental importance. See also *Feste e apparati medicei* (catalogue).

The comedy performed in 1586, *L'amico fido*, had been written for the occasion by Giovanni Bardi, who also wrote the text for the *intermedi*. The six musical acts are linked not so much by a common plot as by a common theme of eulogy: the tribute of the gods who restore to earth its Golden Age in honour of the noble bridal couple. Each *intermedio* represents the gift of one of the gods: 'Jove sends blessings on the earth: hell opens and swallows up all evils; Zephyrus and Flora bring eternal spring; Neptune calms the sea's storms; Juno checks the elements of the air.' The spectacle finishes with a chorus of Tuscan shepherds and shepherdesses who joyfully celebrate the new marriage. The music was written by Alessandro Striggio, Cristofano Malvezzi and Giovanni Bardi.

In 1589 the comedy was Girolamo Bargagli's *La pellegrina*,[60] performed by the Intronati of Siena. Giovanni Bardi had the task of inventing the *intermedi*, which celebrated the Platonic concepts of *musica mundana* and *musica humana* in six allegorical and mythological tableaux (plates 34–9): the Music of the Spheres; the Contest of the Muses and the Pierides; Apollo and Python; the *intermedio* of Hades; Amphitrite and Arion; Mankind being given Harmony and Rhythm by the Gods.

Ottavio Rinuccini, Giovanbattista Strozzi and Laura Lucchesini nei Guidiccioni contributed to the texts. Most of the music was written by Luca Marenzio and Cristofano Malvezzi. Giovanni Bardi, Emilio dei Cavalieri, Giulio Caccini, Iacopo Peri, and Vittoria and Antonio Archilei were also collaborators.

The perspectives remained constant during each of the two comedies, in *L'amico fido* representing Florence, in *La pellegrina* Pisa. Unfortunately there are no surviving pictures of them, except perhaps for a vague hint of the Pisan perspective which can be glimpsed behind the machine of Hades in Epifanio d'Alfiano's engraving of the fourth *intermedio* – but it must be treated very cautiously indeed. However, the descriptions of Bastiano de Rossi, an exaggeratedly enthusiastic admirer of both Buontalenti and Giovanni Bardi, make up for this serious lack of evidence.[61]

The sets of both comedies represented composite views of the two cities, justified more by the sense of occasion than by the requirements of the text. By this very freedom from strict topography they were closer to the depiction of Rome in the set of *La calandria* (1513) or Peruzzi's 'urban scene' (plate 22) than to the perspective sets of *Il granchio* and *La vedova*, which were in their own way realistic.

The lay-out of the sets, with symmetrical side flats, probably on sliding

[60]   *La pellegrina* had been written by G. Bargagli in 1564: he had been commissioned by Ferdinando dei Medici, a cardinal at that time, after A. Piccolomini had declined the task. After Francesco died in 1587 without legitimate male heirs, Ferdinando received a papal dispensation from the cardinalate. By that date Bargagli too was dead. For the censoring of this comedy between its composition and performance see N. Borsellino, *Rozzi e Intronati* (Bulzoni, Rome 1974).

[61]   B. de Rossi, *Descrizione del magnificentiss. apparato e de' maravigliosi intermedij fatti per la commedia rappresentata in Firenze nelle felicissime nozze dell'Illustrissimi ed Eccellentissimi Signori il Signor Don Cesare d'Este, e la Signora Donna Virginia Medici* (Florence 1585; 1586 new style), and see Pirrotta, pp. 207ff above. An extract is printed in *La commedia del Cinquecento*, vol. I, pp. 498–92.

B. de Rossi, *Descrizione dell' apparato e degli intermedi fatti per la commedia rappresentata in Firenze nelle nozze de' Serenissimi don Ferdinando Medici, e Madonna Cristina di Lorena, Gran duchi di Toscana* (Florence 1589), and see Pirrotta, pp. 212ff above.

frames, can be reconstructed from the sets for the *intermedi* of *La pellegrina*, on the grounds that while the iconography could be changed, the basic arrangement of the stage could not. De Rossi's descriptions also suggest the general nature of the perspective of the two cities, which must have been similar to Vasari's *strada lunga*, with a central axis and a single focal point. The buildings, which were in proportion to the height of a man at the front of the stage, decreased in size towards the back, where they changed into one or more open views, which were panoramic but did not strain the limits of logical and definable space, as had happened in Salviati's perspective set (plate 28).

That Buontalenti should have persisted in adhering to the basic traditions of staging comedy is very much in keeping with the age in which he was working. However much *La pellegrina* might stand out because of its vitality from the rest of contemporary dramatic production, it nonetheless contained nothing sufficiently new or stimulating to justify a substantial alteration of the set either by the use of scene changes or, more simply, by changes of imagery. Nor was there any other drama produced towards the end of the century which could have justified such a development. Apart from Tasso's *Aminta*, Giordano Bruno's *Il candelaio* was the one masterpiece of this theatrical genre written after the Council of Trent. So novel are its themes, its style and its language that it alone could have laid claim to space and forms beyond the traditional. So great is the force with which the author projects into the realms of abnormality the brutish image of the corrupt society which surrounded him, that only the most splendid flights of mannerist painting could have done justice to them. But in the sixteenth and seventeenth centuries *Il candelaio* was never performed.

In *L'amico fido*, the text of which is lost, the set dazzlingly depicted Medicean Florence, with the Duomo, Giotto's Campanile, the Palazzo dei Signori, the Loggia dei Lanzi, the Uffizi, Santa Maria Novella, and the Loggia di San Paolo:

There was the more-than-human building of the church of Santa Maria del Fiore, with its dome...and beside it one could see its marble bell-tower...There one could see the new building known as the Magistrates',....His Highness' palace with its miraculous bell-tower, the magnificent porch which we call 'the Pisani's', the corner of the Antellesi and all the other houses. There one could see the venerable church of Santa Maria Novella, with its piazza and the building of Saint Paul which stands opposite it, and the largest and most noble dwellings which that district affords. And these dwellings were so natural and lifelike, that they seemed real to the viewers, being above all perfectly level and most splendid because of the never better illumined opening of far-reaching perspective (*foro*) (since our architect has been the first to discover a way to light it); the background of the said scene was marvellous, and it and the distant view delightfully deceived and dazzled the eyes of the spectators.

According to the description by Bastiano de Rossi, the set for *La pellegrina* was arranged according to a rather more modern lay-out, resembling the one attributed to Salviati. The foreground buildings (obviously those required by the action) were of a natural size, and the idealized view of Pisa, represented by all its monuments, was relegated to the middle ground of the stage and was arranged in three perspectives converging on a single central focus:

One could recognize in it the ancient and noble city of Pisa, since one could see there all that part of the city which the Pisans call *Lungarno*, the bridges, the Duomo with its leaning bell-tower, the church of St John, the noble structure of the Campo Santo [cemetery], the palace of the Knights of St Stephen, with the church which is beside it...and many other churches and houses of great repute. They were so masterfully counterfeited and so resembled the real distinguished buildings of that city, and were so well shown by the splendour of the luminous opening [coming] from heaven to earth which was achieved by concealed lights...And one could wonder not only at this, but also at the way in which the said set was devised. It had three perspective openings, the middle one composed of straight lines, while the other two were composed in all respects of curved lines to counterfeit the said city, the streets of the city being almost all curved.

According to de Rossi this was an entirely new scheme 'in that there is no example I know of curved lines drawn in perspective, or of a set with more than one perspective'. This assertion is partly contradicted by the sketch attributed to Salviati, although this seems nearer to Vasari than to Buontalenti. However, compared with Vasari the set for *La pellegrina* does present some novelties. Instead of two perspectives there were now three, and the side ones did recede in a curvilinear fashion not to be found in any of the *intermedi* sets but which is hinted at, to a certain extent, in some of the 'cloud appearances', particularly those of the fourth and sixth *intermedi*.

The description does not mention the order in which the Pisan monuments were arranged. In the engraving of 'Hades', the Baptistery, and perhaps the palace of St Stephen, appear painted on the backdrop, with the Ponte di Mezzo in front. Other buildings, monuments, domestic houses and perhaps even a church must have filled the wings at the sides. According to the author's intentions (though the comedy had been written many years before and Bargagli had died in 1586) it would have been possible to confine the action to the two buildings in the foreground, which were old Cassandro's house and Violante's inn. Lepida, the wet-nurse Giglietta, Terenzio a false pedant and the servant Targhetta all live in the first house, while, besides Violante, the Pilgrim, Ricciardo her escort, and a German student Federigo with his servant Cavicchia all lodge at the inn. Lucrezio, the other lover, lives elsewhere with his servant Carletto. The whole city of Pisa, with the Studio, the port, the Ponte di Mezzo, the Duomo, the Bargello and even the 'just court of the prince' is understood in the text to be present, but only incidentally. It is not involved in the same way as Rome in Aretino's *La cortigiana* and Caro's *Gli straccioni*, or Venice in the comedies of Andrea Calmo, where the immediacy is deliberate and conditions the play to a much greater extent.

Besides, the whole of the action takes place between the two houses, and is more recounted than acted. Every time a character leaves the stage the audience ceases to think about him. The plot runs smoothly, if somewhat slowly, for the first three acts. One conversation follows another, to inform the audience of events and what has happened before: Lepida, promised by Cassandro to the young and rich Lucrezio, has in fact secretly married Terenzio, who is posing as the tutor of Lepida's younger brother. In order to avoid the planned marriage, Lepida pretends insanity. Lucrezio has only accepted Lepida out of despair, having heard from a friend that Drusilla, whom he had secretly married and left two years ago in Lyons, is dead, and he hopes that Lepida's insanity will prevent their marriage. The Pilgrim is requested by all to heal Lepida, for she is believed to possess miraculous cures.

In reality, she is none other than Drusilla who, believed to be dead in an accident, has come to Pisa to find her forgetful husband. In Act III, the style and tempo of the play alter. The usual Renaissance theme of misunderstandings becomes more intricate, and is coloured by realistic twists and adventurous or pathetic touches. The characters gradually gain individuality, especially the minor characters such as the three servants (one faithful, one stupid and one a knave), the bogus pedant as caricatured by Terenzio, the shrewd nurse acting as Lepida's adviser, and Violante the innkeeper with a generous and elastic conscience. Even with these changes of style the tale does not get entangled: on the contrary, each scene develops a well-thought-out and well-expressed thread, until they combine at the end to clarify the misunderstanding. Lepida, who is expecting a child, is betrayed to her father first by the servant Targhetta and then by the German student who is in love with her and has been watching her closely. Lucrezio, who is at first held responsible, gets most irate; the Pilgrim nearly dies a second death because of it; Terenzio finishes up in the hands of the police. But it is precisely through the agency of the Bargello that the final recognition scene takes place, for all concerned gather there together. Since Terenzio proves to be a German nobleman, and the brother of Federigo, his marriage with Lepida is no longer felt to be undesirable by rich Cassandro, while Lucrezio and Drusilla can be reunited.

The choice of this gay, free-flowing and adventurous comedy was probably made by the duke himself, who was so different in character from his brother; unlike him, he was not over-fond of speculative and inventive recreations. On the other hand the *intermedi* were, as in 1586, entrusted to Giovanni Bardi with his genius for Platonic symbols. Through their music and images, and the mechanical inventions of the restless stage-designer, they expressed the other side of the intellectual and artistic pre-Baroque world, that of an escape into a realm of fantasy transcending reality. This secured its own emancipation by inventing a new balance of forces in tension as opposed to the rational equilibrium of the Renaissance world.

In his recent work on Baroque opera,[62] Cesare Molinari devotes several careful and persuasive pages to the 1586 *intermedi*. After analysing each one in terms of its fundamental dynamism, expressed not so much through the actors as through the successive movements of the stage components which continued to change throughout the play, he locates the significance of their subjects in an almost cosmic scheme which transcended the initial motive of eulogy and moved into more intense and complex realms of contemporary culture. Disregarding the first and last *intermedi* as no more than traditional, Molinari concentrates on the four central ones which 'form an entity whose most important motif was certainly not provided by the intention of flattering the bridal couple, but by that of representing the four elements which according to ancient physics make up the universe'. And further: 'But in reality, for Buontalenti and perhaps even more so for Bardi, the *intermedi* as a whole were meant to represent not so much the elements as the whole

[62] C. Molinari, *Le nozze degli dei* (Rome 1968), pp. 13–34; the quotations used here are from pp. 23–4. An attempt to reconstruct the settings of *La pellegrina* was made by F. Mancini for an exhibition at the Cini Foundation in Venice; see F. Mancini, M. T. Muraro, E. Povoledo, *Illusione e pratica teatrale*, pp. 41–7; the model of the setting for the fifth intermedio, *Anfitrite e Arione*, is still preserved at the Cini Foundation.

universe, divided into its four kingdoms...A sacred play, product of both heaven and earth!' In this ambitious programme of the two artists, Molinari identifies various kinds of response to, and profound analogies with, contemporary culture, above all with the themes of mannerist painting closely associated with Vasari.

The allegorical scheme of the four elements was also repeated with a more obviously philosophical content in the 1589 *intermedi*, and thereafter became customary. Molinari continues: 'Once more the scene represented in turn heaven, earth, sea and hell, and from now on these four elements were to reappear for nearly 75 years in almost all the more elaborate performances of both *intermedi* and operas.' It is probable that for Bardi the four central *intermedi* were, and were intended to be, an allegory of the four elements, while undoubtedly for Buontalenti the four sets of country, sea, hell and heaven represented the natural setting of the *intermedi*, logically supported by the great machines. But the machines and sets which were to be found amongst the properties of any Baroque lyric theatre, including the urban perspective which in the seventeenth century came to be known as the 'city' or 'tragic' set, had by then lost all cosmic or allegorical implications. They were repertory sets and machines, places in which to act, alternative types to the tragic perspective with stereotyped names like *boscareccia* (sylvan), *deliziosa* (a garden with architectural elements), *mare* (marine) and *infernale* (infernal). If we add to these the prison and the throne room, we have the basis of all routine stage sets.

It now remains to consider how far Buontalenti felt and shared the speculative element which fascinated Bardi, or whether something else made him the poet's ideal collaborator: was it rather the fanciful inventiveness of his engineering ability, his taste for mechanical tricks and for surprise effects, in short the urge which led him, a balanced and accomplished architect, to turn the theatre into a fantastic folly.

The surviving scenographic sketches by Buontalenti are inadequate to convey his genius for spectacle; for this we need the help of Bastiano de Rossi's descriptions. The dynamic tension, which constituted the motive force of each *intermedio* was not transferred to the perspective views of the sets, which all appear less developed than the set of *La pellegrina*. Unless the designs represent a first incomplete idea of the staging, and the engravings by Epifanio or Carracci (plates 34–9) a simplification for graphic purposes, not one of the compositions corresponds to that idea of infinitely receding space which, perhaps conditioned by later Baroque iconography, we instinctively associate nowadays with de Rossi's evocations of the cosmos. In all the sets the lateral elements arranged along the diagonals are repeated with identical symmetry: wings of clouds, trellises, leafy trees, infernal rocks and marine rocks. The vanishing point is placed in the distance, and the perspective recedes towards the backdrop, but it does not open into infinity, except perhaps, rather tentatively, in the sky sets of the first and sixth *intermedi*. It is more likely that the perspective either focusses on the apex where the two diagonals join to form a triangle, as in the *intermedio* of 'Apollo and the Python', or else it is intercepted in the distance by some scenic feature, like Mount Parnassus in the *intermedio* of the Muses and Pierides, or the perspective of Pisa which appears behind the infernal rocks of Hades.

Into this optical scheme, which is entirely geometrical and logical, and in proportion, at least in the drawings, to the size of the actors, Buontalenti introduced the second visual element, the machine. With this he introduced and brought to the fore the element of spectacle and motion, the novelty, the real motive force of his great scenic construction. To the prince, dazzled by the light of the torches, the stage, viewed from his dais 17 metres away, appeared like a magic box, on which flickered the changing interplay of images, forms, lights and colours, continually moving and being transformed to the accompaniment of the songs of the *intermedianti*. This total effect was intentional. The authors planned it and obviously achieved it, given the applause received by the two spectacles and the speed with which the new genre caught on even outside Florence. Bastiano de Rossi ends his description with a very suggestive statement: 'For all the parts of the spectacle...taken individually, and indeed the whole spectacle together, can be said to have had a choral effect for size and magnificence, expense and artistry; no such spectacle of this kind has ever been seen since the time of the Romans.'

It has often been discussed whether the sets in Buontalenti's two spectacles, which changed in full view of the audience, revolved on *periaktoi* according to the system described by Egnazio Danti, or instead glided along rails in one of the three ways explained by Sabbatini in his *Pratica*.[63] For want of direct information the argument remains undecided, though given the stage dimensions (20 m 30 × 11 m 60 and 20 m 30 × 14 m 50) it is difficult to believe that there would have been space not only for the technicians' galleries, the hoists for the machines, the mechanics, the orchestra and the actors ready for the stage but also for the cumbersome prisms of the *periaktoi*. The 1589 description makes it clear that the first 'houses' were 20 *braccia* high, i.e. 11 m 60, and that the others diminished in proportion. The hypothesis of sliding wings is confirmed by an observation of de Rossi, still referring to the 1589 spectacle, about the way the wings were lit:

for the wise artist, one who tried to omit nothing which might render his praiseworthy work even more beautiful, artfully arranged that those same lights which lit the perspective, and which were movable and attached to the houses of the perspective, would still provide lighting for the *intermedio* when the set changed (*voltando*), in spite of their being invisible.

Voltando (turning) must here be understood in the not-uncommon sense of 'changing'. In fact, if the lights were fixed to the flats of the perspective set, when the *periaktoi* were turned they would have turned too, whereas if the wings of the perspective remained stationary, the flats for the *intermedi*, sliding in front of the houses, could have made use of the lights already fixed to their supports. On the other hand the flats did not always move along the level of the stage floor: in both spectacles at least two changes were made by lowering machines masked by clouds, and a further two (the marine *intermedio* and the infernal one) were made by structures which rose from beneath the stage.

Bastiano de Rossi's bombastic descriptions probably add a little mystery and confusion to the way the spectacle actually developed, but the *ingegni*, devices and tricks to which Buontalenti resorted were inexhaustible, and if the plan

---

[63] N. Sabbatini, *Pratica di fabricar scene* (1638), vol. II, chapters 4–9, 13–15.

of the spectacle was repeated in the two entertainments, the second appears to me to be in some way a perfecting of the first. If one follows closely the way in which apparitions and mechanical manoeuvres succeeded one another, one is struck by the order in their sequence and by the way in which the different effects, some slow and some violent, alternated and complemented each other. One is also struck by the intelligent way in which music, action, mime and even intentional noises intervened to distract the audience in order to disguise the slowness with which the heavy machines were moved.

The prologue of *L'amico fido* opened with a perspective view of Florence, and at almost the same time as the curtain, the upper part of the set opened to reveal two large clouds, one above the other, both attached to the loft by fly-ropes. The upper cloud, which depicted the Assembly of the Gods, was, with the exception of Jove, probably contrived out of painted images: 'Equally amazing were the foreshortened figures which entirely filled it, and far from the natural world seemed even to transcend into the eighth sphere.' The second cloud was a mobile machine, with seats and hooks, which descended vertically to bring the Blessings to the earth and then ascended with unprecedented perfection: 'for those clouds which were represented by the hand of this artist at the wedding celebrations of the Most Serene Grand-duchess of Tuscany, Giovanna of Austria, of happy memory, and the one which was made by Baldassare Lanci in honour of Archduke Charles, were seen to rise again empty, and the hook was seen'.

One drawing by Buontalenti is traditionally associated with this *intermedio* (plate 32). In it the centre of the scene is dominated by a great eagle, which however is not mentioned in the descriptions. The drawing therefore must either refer to an early idea of the producers (for example for a setting of 'Blessings brought down to earth escorted by Ganymede') or else be connected with some other entertainment.

In the second *intermedio* ('Hell swallows up the Evils') the rhythm of the transformations appears to have been far faster and more lively, undoubtedly aided by the fact that the moving parts rose from understage through trapdoors in the stage floor, and made use of apparatus which was simpler and safer than that which descended from the loft.[64] The transformations followed each other in three sequences. First rose the rocks, on which sat the Evils, forming a 'semicircle, all sad and melancholy, sorrowful, and full of gloom and wrath'. Then the whole of the centre of the stage opened, and from the 'fearful cavern full of cruel fires and dark flames' emerged the enormous machine bearing the city of Dis 'emitting smoke and fire, with all about it its marsh, full of filthy and hideous waters'. On the flaming towers stood the horrible Furies, while around it rushed two bands of shrieking devils, dressed

[64] F. Baldinucci, *Notizie dei professori*, tells the story of the machine constructed in the church of Santo Spirito for the sacred *rappresentazione*. The lowering and opening of this machine caused 'so much fear in the hearts of the musicians, who were representing those heavenly spirits, that suddenly they all lost their wits in such a way that at the height of the singing they all fell dumb for some while, with the exception of the famous singer Giulio Romano, who, continuing the motet and repeating the words "o benedetto giorno", made up to a certain extent for the incident'. Because of this episode Caccini 'was later, as a joke, nicknamed "Benedetto giorno" by the Florentine wits'. Actually Baldinucci is muddling dates and spectacles: the sacred *rappresentazione* in Santo Spirito was held in 1589, while the phrase 'o fortunato giorno' (and not 'benedetto'), begins the great eulogistic madrigal for 30 voices in 7 choirs in the final *intermedio* also performed in 1589. Despite this, the survival of the anecdote is in itself indicative.

in skins, with green and black wigs and enormous bats' wings: 'The sight of the gloomy cavern was most fearful, and so was that of the Furies to be seen on the towers; while the sight of the devils bearing torches lit with a fire which seemed full of pitch and bitumen and sulphur was full of gloom and melancholy and horror.' When the vision reached the height of its tension, there appeared beyond it the boat of Phlegias which bobbed across the stage and stopped to take on board the Evils, and, 'When the boat had moved off from the shore, with great jarring noises and screams both they and the horrible city were engulfed in a deep chasm; and the demons quickly plunged after them into this cavern, which, having swallowed all up, shut as if by magic and there was no sign left to be seen.'

There were more than forty people employed at once (10 Evils, 22 devils, Phlegias, and 2 harpies, and an unspecified number of Furies) and for the ensemble the stage must have appeared overcrowded though not necessarily obstructed. The stage (20 m × 11 m 60) was not much smaller than the average modern stage,[65] but one must take into account the rather cumbersome machinery and the number of mechanics needed to manoeuvre it. There are no known drawings or technical information which refer to Buontalenti's machines, and although the rules set out by Sabbatini in his *Pratica* appear rather elementary compared with Bastiano de Rossi's lengthy descriptions, nevertheless, given the absence of a more sophisticated treatise, we shall have to continue to rely on the *Pratica* all the time.[66]

The third *intermedio*, in which Flora and Zephyrus bring back eternal Spring to earth, took place in a calm and idyllic atmosphere, with two successive transformations, at stage-floor level, by means of gliding flats (or revolving *periaktoi*). The first, at the start of the *intermedio*, suddenly changed the perspective of Florence into 'a wondrous land for its general appearance, in which one saw hills, rivers, skies, torrents, fountains and lakes', but all still 'arid and desolate', as appropriate to a winter landscape. From a 'subterranean cave' emerged Zephyrus and Flora, who with a sweet song invited Spring to come forth. She appeared accompanied by Pan and Priapus, and surrounded by nymphs, breezes, satyrs and cupids. 'And while they appeared thus dancing, the trees were flowering and gradually covering themselves in leaves', the earth was turning green, and water began to flow once more in the lakes and rivers.

In the fourth *intermedio* ('Neptune calms the raging seas'), the action was once more tempestuous, and the machines were operated from below in four

[65] E. Neufert, 'Bauentwurfslehre', fascicles of '*Din-Ausschuss*', Italian edition *Enciclopedia pratica per progettare e costruire* (Milan 1949), pp. 224–5. Neufert establishes the dimensions of a standard stage by calculating them in proportion to the proscenium: width three times that of the proscenium depth twice that of the proscenium, height double that of the proscenium. Since the width varies from 8 m to 14 m and the height from 8 m to 10 m, the standard dimensions of a stage should have ranged between 24 m × 16 m and 42 m × 28 m, and their height between 16 m and 20 m.

[66] N. Sabbatini, *Pratica di fabricar scene* indicates different ways of manoeuvring the machines: using vertical hoists and ropes controlled by winches to move a platform up and down along stout wooden guides made of vertical beams which, attached to the floor of the hall, went through the floor of the stage and reached the loft. For oblique flights, which did not however feature in Buontalenti's arrangements, Sabbatini suggests a machine with a lever action: the platform is attached to a movable support, which is in turn attached by a hinge to the stout vertical beam. The support which acts as a lever is raised and lowered by means of a system of levers acting through conveyor ropes.

sequences: the appearance of the sea with the court of Thetis; the tempest; the appearance of Neptune; calm after the storm. While the flats with the 'harsh sea rocks' were being substituted for the perspective of Florence, the long foamy waves were pushed forward by the mechanics and positioned at correct intervals at the back of the stage (plate 31). Painted on long planks of wood, or on rotating rollers, they reached from one side of the stage to the other, and could be raised, lowered or turned by the men hidden between the wings. They were arranged in such a way as to mask both the rails (or the 'cuts') in the stage floor, along which slid the artificial boats, and the trapdoors through which appeared or disappeared the *intermedianti*, who were either raised by hand or pushed up by a rudimentary system of levers.[67] By alternating 'normal' waves with ones 'all painted black and edged with silver' (Sabbatini) and by raising and lowering them in an irregular fashion, it was possible to create the impression of a stormy sea, and then, by laying them flat on the floor, of the return to calm. Bastiano de Rossi felt that the effect could not be further improved:

And as soon as [Thetis and the sea monsters] had finished their song, the sea appeared all raging and disturbed, and she immediately leapt in with her monsters. The whole scene was surrounded by waves, which by their movement seemed most natural, and within them one could see ships hard driven by the storm as well as savage monsters creating it with swollen human faces which seemed to be blowing.

Once Neptune had appeared on his chariot and had calmed the tempest, and while the nymphs sang in the calm sea, 'the rocks disappeared leaving a green and flowery field' in which the nymphs began to walk, gathering flowers and fish.

Then they returned to the chariot and when they had climbed aboard, rocks began to appear once more, and amongst them Thetis with divers marine monsters, different from the first ones. They played together and bathed, splashing themselves with water...And so much did they play and fish that the chariot was all submerged, and once it had been submerged, neither they nor the rocks were seen any more.

The fifth *intermedio* ('Juno stays the elements of the air') took place entirely above the floor of the stage, in a cloud machine which never descended below the top half of the set, while the most spectacular part of the action, which incorporated brief passages of singing, was played by the lighting effects, by means of which the sky was seen to darken and brighten up again, and flash, being streaked with lightning and rain, and clear with rainbows. The description does not say whether the perspective of Florence remained visible throughout or whether it was in some way screened when the set clouded over:

The sky was seen to dim little by little and to be filled with clouds in such way as to immediately destroy all the brightness of the scene, and it became increasingly darker and more gloomy. And after this it began to thunder and flash lightning with great force; and very soon in the middle of that lightning appeared a cloud of a serene hue in which was a chariot pulled by two large and beautiful peacocks, which as they

[67] N. Sabbatini, *Pratica di fabricar scene*, vol. II: for 'How to represent the sea' see chapters 27–30; for 'How ships are made to appear' see chapters 31–3; for 'How one may imitate a river, which always contains running water' see chapter 35; for 'How to make men emerge speedily on stage' see chapter 20.

moved unfurled their tails like the real ones, and on it [sat] Juno with Iris and her fourteen nymphs...When the cloud had reached the centre of the sky and had stopped there, the thunder and lightning began with all the more force...with stormy rain and large hailstones. When the rain and that ruinous storm had ceased, the rainbow around the beautiful cloud seemed most natural,

and while Juno's song was commanding the nymphs to calm the sky, the latter 'little by little cleared and became limpid and smiling. After the song had ended and the sky cleared, the cloud almost miraculously disappeared'.

It is difficult for us, conditioned as we are by such different experiences of theatre, to gauge quite what effect the progressive darkening of the sky and stage must have had in the context of a sixteenth-century entertainment. One must bear in mind that the hall was smoky but very bright, and that the lights were not extinguished in the course of the performance. The stage, 17 m away from the grand-ducal dais, was lit not only by lights hanging from the proscenium, but also by those scattered throughout its ceiling behind 'sky drops'[68] attached to the flats in the wings and to the frames of the machines. In Juno's *intermedio*, the effect of gradual darkening was largely obtained by sliding cloud-shaped screens in front of the openings in the ceiling by which light entered. It is more difficult to establish whether the proscenium lights were also dimmed, possibly by means of a simple system described by Sabbatini:

Should one wish to darken the stage simultaneously, here is one way of doing it. Have as many cylinders of tin strips as there are lights to be dimmed. These cylinders must be at least half a foot high [approx. 15 cm] and a little less wide, and their upper end should be covered, leaving only a small hole to allow the smoke to escape, and the bottom should be open. This done, each should be positioned above its light, having been opened and arranged as illustrated in the figure below,

that is to say, hung from a wire which runs through a pulley fixed to a stable support (for example the proscenium arch), in such a way that the cylinders remain suspended perfectly vertical, directly above the lights. By loosening the wires, the cylinders will descend 'over the lights, and by this trick they will be obscured. And by returning the wires to their places, the scene will once more be lit'. And by 'attaching as many wires as you can to a single end', the effect of darkness will be rapid and simultaneous.

The cloud-play, which closed and opened and from being dark became bright again, ended with another optical trick, for while the great machine was disappearing into the loft, 'behind the stage one saw a smaller one full of little figures which seemed dressed in the same clothes as those of the larger cloud, so that one could almost believe it to be the large one moving further away on its journey'.

[68] N. Sabbatini, *Pratica di fabricar scene*, vol. II, chapters 37–40, envisages the possibility of an artificial sky with *arie* or *celetti*, i.e. with long strips of wood or fabric painted to resemble the sky and arranged at regular intervals in the depths of the loft. He also describes an artificial sky with a large arched ceiling which, however, is 'broken' both to enable smoke to escape and for manoeuvring different machines such as the canvasses representing clouds or the lights representing the sun.
De Rossi comments on the loft of the Medici theatre when describing the perspective of Pisa used in *La pellegrina*: it was very bright and full of lights 'just as the sky, which because of the fumes was clearly pierced (*sfondato*), and from the holes, although they were not seen, appeared a light so unified that it seemed like that of the noon-time sun...'.

The sixth *intermedio*, in which a band of Tuscan shepherds and shepherd-esses (nineteen couples to be precise) urged on by the sorceress of Fiesole ('Maga Fiesolana') celebrated the joyful event of the ducal wedding in song and dance, required no mechanical wonders but rested on its purely eulogistic content. Only the perspective changed, depicting a flowery field, and behind it 'a wood with various verdant trees, and in it, below a grotto, a large and rich palace surrounded by rocky caves: and around the said grotto, as ornaments for such a dwelling-place, there were fir-trees, cypresses, oak-trees, Turkey oaks, English oaks, chestnuts and so forth...'

As we have said, the *intermedi* for *La pellegrina* repeated the scheme of those of *L'amico fido*, but with variations in the arrangement and a more unified rhythm of the scenic events, making the effect more grandiose but less dramatic and, except in the case of the *intermedio* set in hell, not violent. They dispensed with the scene changes within the *intermedi*, augmented the machines, lengthened the stage and perfected all the apparatus. To begin with, the first curtain opened on a perspective different from the one used in the comedy and certainly unusual, since the front part of the stage reflected the amphitheatre arrangement of the hall at the Uffizi, so anticipating one of those inventions which were to make Bernini famous. Bastiano de Rossi's description, while somewhat confused, leaves no room for doubt on this matter: 'To everyone's eyes, the whole room appeared to be a single perfect amphitheatre (for the perspective, which was opposite to the hall with its Corinthian architecture, was joined to it, and thus completed the amphi-theatre), so realistic and magnificent and of undreamt of beauty...' The author then continues more ambiguously:

The audience believed that the perspective which they saw when the curtain fell, and which they were able to recognize immediately as Rome, was the one where the comedy was to be performed, that there was to be no other perspective, and that the story had taken place in Rome, so excellently had the artist known how to suggest reality and caused the most noble and proudest ancient and modern buildings of the sovereign city to recede from the eye by receding perspective. And below he had depicted the stage on which were to be the actors, so that it not only represented the stage but the perspective too, very realistically.

The stage, then, must have been arranged thus: on the side flats and on a first small backdrop were depicted the large Corinthian arches and the decorations of the amphitheatre which reflected those of the hall, while on the second higher and wider one was painted the view of Rome, simultaneously visible. The amphitheatre was the 'stage on which were to be the actors'.

Agostino Carracci's engraving and the drawing in the Victoria and Albert Museum show the stage already occupied by the cloud-machine and with starry sky effects above (plate 39). In the interests of brevity, instead of de Rossi's description we give here the much more succinct one by Giuseppe Pavoni who was also present.[69] Note that he makes no mention of the

⁶⁹ *Diario descritto da Giuseppe Pavoni delle feste celebrate nelle solennissime nozze delli Serenissimi Sposi, il Signor don Ferdinando Medici e la Signora Donna Cristina di Lorena Gran Duchi di Toscana, nel quale con brevità si esplica il Torneo, la Battaglia Navale, la comedia con gli intermedi, et altre feste occorse di giorno, in giorno per tutto il dí 15 Maggio MDLXXXIX* (Bologna 1589). Pavoni's description is very brief and is slightly different from de Rossi's, but some sentences, identical in the two texts, lead one to think that either Pavoni had before him de Rossi's description, or

perspective of Rome, recalling instead 'certain rocks'. Either he was not present from the start of the performance, or else Bastiano de Rossi inserted into his account an effect which had been contemplated but which never materialized. Pavoni wrote:

In front of the stage were two cloths which covered it. The first was red, and when it had been lowered the set was still covered by another azure cloth, in the centre of which was a woman seated on a cloud. She began to play a large lute and sweetly sing a madrigal, and so playing and singing she was gradually lowered, hiding behind certain rocks, and finishing the madrigal from between them with such a marvellous echo-effect that it seemed as if the king himself was hidden there in very truth. Suddenly the second cloth rose to reveal Paradise with five clouds, i.e. one in the centre and two on either side, which were full of musicians depicted as heavenly sirens and other planets, who with their song made joyful and sweet harmony. And as they were singing in this way, the clouds were rising further towards the sky, and suddenly they disappeared from the sight of the spectators. One part of the sky remained dark so that it seemed like night, and on the other side it remained clear and bright, which caused everyone to marvel at such great artifice. And suddenly the set changed and the perspective of Pisa appeared.

The spectacle therefore began with a cloud scene, and with showy lighting effects, while one gets the impression that the sung part of the action, although influenced by the movement of the machine, was by no means overwhelmed by it. As for the structure of the machine, the illustration shows it arranged on three levels. The first, at the top, was probably contrived out of painted and foreshortened figures of gods in the midst of the splendour of the sun's rays. The other two can be reconstructed on the basis of the 'contrivance for fifty-four persons' invented by Francesco Guitti in 1628 for the Farnese theatre in Parma (plate 41).[70] Just two structures were obviously sufficient to convey the twenty people who flanked the platform, separate from the rest, which was suspended at the centre of the stage. Each structure was formed of a frame, probably rigid, of stout wooden beams, arranged so that besides holding the benches each beam reinforced and fixed the others. The two horizontal and vertical beams on the side were equipped with a series of pulleys (marked with the letter E) through which passed the ropes which extended to the loft, where the winches to be used for manoeuvring them were located. The key to the drawing reads literally:

D – ropes which raise and lower the frames and the seat, all by means of a reel which receives all the said ropes
E – pulleys placed in the frames through which the ropes pass so that the said ropes should not be so strained.

Naturally this is no more than a suggestion or a guide, and it is possible that Buontalenti's *ingegno* was constructed in an entirely different fashion.

In the second *intermedio*, the contest between the Muses and the Pierides, the music seems again to have been the chief element (plate 35). The set changed quietly, with the frames either revolving or sliding at stage level,

that both of them made use of a third common source which may have been Bardi's account. Pavoni's text now appears in *La commedia del Cinquecento*, vol. I, pp. 496–500, along with the description of the same event from Baldinucci's *Notizie dei professori*.
[70]   See E. Povoledo, 'Macchine e ingegni del Teatro Farnese' in *Prospettive*, no. 19 (1959), pp. 49–56.

while the flowery mountain machine emerged from below the stage: 'The perspective changed again, and a new one appeared with mountains, gardens, and fountains amongst which yet another [mountain] came into sight which gradually grew bigger than the others. On its sixteen Hamadryads sat on some bushes. On either side of this mountain appeared two caves. In the one on the right were the nine Muses' and in the other the Pierides. After the Pierides had contended with the Muses and had been judged by the Hamadryads to be inferior to their rivals, 'as punishment for their presumption they were suddenly transformed into magpies, which, jumping and cawing about the stage in the manner of birds, sought to hide themselves from the eyes of men. And in the meantime the hill and the caves suddenly disappeared, and the garden with the magpies vanished, in such a way that the audience hardly noticed it.' While the Hamadryads' hill is recognizable in some pages of the large volume preserved in the Biblioteca Nazionale in Florence, where there is a collection of *intermedi* costumes, the trellis motifs which made up the *deliziosa*, garden with architectural elements, are probably to be identified with those depicted in a preparatory drawing preserved in the Uffizi.[71]

Unlike the others, the third *intermedio* had a wooded perspective (*boscareccia*) which was perfectly triangular in plan (plate 36), and a free flight by Apollo who descended to the woods of Delphi to slay the serpent Python, represented in the guise of a dragon breathing fire and flames. In the fourth *intermedio* we once more find Hades, which recalls the second one in 1586, but it was complicated by the introduction of a machine with the demons of the air which opened the action (plate 37). In Epifanio's engraving, which shows the two successive phases of the *intermedio* simultaneously, the stage seems to be divided into two sections by the great partition of rocks, with holes opening to show other diabolical scenes. In the centre foreground is the monstrous depiction of Lucifer; in the distance, through a curtain of flames, appears the perspective of Pisa which was subsequently covered by the rocks. It is the only one of these *intermedi* which makes use of violent images, and altogether the vision is still that of Dante's *Inferno*. Let us return to Bastiano de Rossi's more effective description: 'In this *intermedio* before the perspective changed, there appeared on a precious chariot of gold and jewels a woman intended as a sorceress by the poet, in disarray and barefoot, her hair loose upon her shoulders and tangled, her appearance proud, her face beautiful.' At her command, the 'demons of the purest region of the air called fire', whose nature, most wise according to Plato, 'was to relate divine things to men, and human matters to the gods', flocked to her on a machine of red clouds. On this occasion, the divine message was the happy annunciation of the grand-ducal marriage. When the sorceress' chariot and the fiery cloud had left the stage, the scene became infernal,

and in an instant was covered in rocks, caves, caverns full of fire and burning flames, and it seemed as if in writhing they sent smoke up to heaven. Once the set had assumed this horror, the stage opened, and revealed a much greater horror: for in opening, it opened hell, from which emerged two bands of terrifying Furies and devils...Hell appeared all fire and flames, and through these flames one could see unnumbered souls, tormented by great bands of devils.

[71]   See note 59 above.

And in the centre of the ice of Cocytus was Lucifer, with his three devouring faces and his enormous bat's wings, surrounded by Charon, Geryon, half man and half serpent, Pluto, Satan and Minos 'dressed in purple but blackened by smoke', the harpies, the centaurs, Cerberus and the Minotaur. The theatre resounded with dreadful cries and laments and horrendous noises until, the cursing having finished in a sad chorus of distress, the gulf reopened and 'hell was swallowed up. The rocks and caves and caverns disappeared: and the scene returned in its former beauty'.

Like the marine *intermedio* of 1586, its equivalent in *La pellegrina*, the fifth, was divided into two sequences, this time independent from each other (plate 38). First came the appearance of the court of Amphitrite, who emerged singing from the waters accompanied by Tritons and nymphs, in a sort of mannerist *tableau vivant* reminiscent of Vasari's *Andromeda* in the Palazzo Vecchio. It was followed by the story of Arion, the citharist, in Plutarch's version. This new marine version lacked the tempest effects, which were replaced by a play of seascapes possibly achieved by the use of a system of card cut-outs. The description is once more by Bastiano de Rossi.

On the fifth occasion the scene appeared full of cliffs, and the stage became a sea of waves surrounded by these rocks which seemed like crumbling mountains, amongst which gushed pure and limpid waters. At the foot of these mountains in the water one could see some small boats amidst the rocks, which the receding perspective of the set so distanced from sight that it was as if one saw a good-sized ship from afar.

In Epifanio's reproduction of the scene, Amphitrite's float and Arion's ship are depicted simultaneously.

The sixth *intermedio* brought the spectacle to a close, as it had opened, with a heavenly apotheosis (plate 39). The scene was veiled by a mysterious effect of lights and moods. The two descriptions by Pavoni and de Rossi provide inadequate explanations of the beautiful engraving which concludes the series. Behind the curtain of large drops (probably painted or projected on a screen)[72] no architectonic elements are visible in the set. The depth of the stage is expressed by the diminishing size of the pastoral characters who are preparing to begin the final joyful dance, and by the semicircular line of the machine with its two levels of clouds on which are seated Apollo, Bacchus, the Muses, the Graces and the other divinities.

Pavoni opens his description with a brief note to the effect that 'the scene appeared all surrounded by golden reeds'. De Rossi makes no mention of this, and perhaps one should imagine the reeds as representing long rays of the sun, reaching from the 'heavenly glory' to mankind. The action opened with the appearance of the Assembly of the Gods, in a roseate dawn sky,

which after opening covered the whole scene with rays of sunshine, whose brightness the eye would not have been able to bear long had it not been shaded by certain vapours...and when the brightness of the rising sun mixed with those vapours rendered the set invisible, seven clouds appeared at the opening of the sky, five of which moved down and came to earth, and two remained up above.

Apollo and Bacchus descended from heaven to bring man the supreme gift

---

[72] B. Buontalenti was known for his 'shadow play', and when barely fifteen he had devised for Prince Francesco a rotating magic lantern. This, according to Baldinucci, *Notizie dei professori*, earned him the nickname 'Bernardo delle Girandole'.

of the gods: Harmony and Rhythm, and beneath these divine auspices the Medici court discovered a new chapter of Baroque scenography. The rational unity of the Renaissance was broken, the logical rules of defined space and unity of action were abandoned. The stage expanded, opening both loft and understage to the heavy machines and to the most bizarre *ingegni*. Whatever route the new Orfeos in Florence or elsewhere were to take toward *recitar cantando*,[73] the visual side of the spectacle was henceforward identified with its freer and more imaginative elements. Imagination prevailed over logic, tension over equilibrium, and movement over unity, and the public echoed the poet's cry

The wondrous show, alas, of the *intermedi*!

[73] All the music for the 1589 *intermedi* is now recorded on EMI Electrola no. C 063-30 114/5, with libretto texts supplied.

Index

by Frederick Smyth

Bold figures indicate the more important references; *italic* figures denote illustrations or their captions. Stage works, other than those which are anonymous or are unattributed in the text (which are indexed alphabetically by title), will be found listed under their authors and composers.

Abbatini, Antonio Maria: *La comica del cielo*, 273*n*
Accademia degli Intronati, Siena, 81, 82, 113*n*, 213, 369
Accademia dei Sereni, Naples, 109
Accademia della Crusca, Florence, 207*n*, 242 and *n*
Accademia Fiorentina, Florence, 158*n*, 174–5 and *nn*, 343*n*, 347, 350
Accademia Olimpica, Vicenza, 327
Accademia Romana, or Pomponiana, 299 and *n*, 301
Accolti, Bernardo, 141*n*; *Virginia*, 37, 77
Accolti, Marcello, 239–40
Affò, Ireneo, 17*n*, 43*n*, 283–4*nn*
Agazzari, Agostino, 257*n*; *Eumelio*, 262–3
Alamanni, Luigi (Lodovico), 77*n*, 127, 139
Alba, Duchess of, 198
Albergati, Ercole, *see* Zafrano
Alberti, Leon Battista, 5 and *n*, 16, 309*n*, 310–11, 316*n*
Alberto, 347 and *n*
Albizo, Francesco d', 29*n*
Aldobrandini, Cardinal Cinzio, 239, 240 and *n*
Aleotti, Giovanni Battista, 303*n*
Alfiano, Epifanio d', 369, 373, 381–2
Allegretti, Antonio, 198*n*
Allori (or Tori), Agnolo (Bronzino), 78*n*, 347, 350*n*
Allori, Alessandro (Bronzino), 353
Alvarotto, Aurelio (Menato), 84
Amadino, Ricciardo, 195
Amboise, Charles d', 290
Ambra, Francesco d': *I Bernardi*, 347; *La cofanaria*, 174, **176–82**, 186*n*, **348–54**, 355*n*; *Il furto*, 158*n*, 347

Ammannati, Bartolomeo, 350
Amore innamorato (1642), music (lost) by Cavalli, 277
Amori di Giasone e di Issifile, Gli (1642), music (lost) by Marco Marazzoli, 272
Ancona, Alessandro d', 81*n*, 86*n*; *Le origini del teatro italiano*, 3, 13–14*nn*, 19 and *n*, 20*n*, 24*n*, 39–53*nn passim*, 73, 82*n*, 94*nn*, 120*n*, 129*n*, 287–340*nn passim*; *La poesia popolare*, 78–9*nn*, 81*n*; ed. *Sacre rappresentazioni*, 12*n*
Angelo Michele, 85
Annunciazione, L' (1565), 348
Antico, Andrea, 32*n*, 75*n*, 92*n*, 122
Antimaco, Marco Antonio, 289*n*
Antonio di Guido, 36*n*
Apuleius, 37
Aquilano, Serafino, *see* Ciminelli, Serafino de
Aragon, Alfonso of, 286*n*, 289
Aragon, Camilla of, 286
Aragon, Ippolita of, 293*n*
Aragon, Isabella of, 293*n*
Aragon, Cardinal Luigi of, 48
Aragon, Maria of, 106*n*
Aragon-Este, Eleonora of, Duchess of Ferrara, 6, 9, 285, 286*n*, 309*n*
Arbeau, Thoinot, *see* Tabourot Jehan
Arcadelt, Jacques, 28*n*, 125*n*, **151**; madrigal, **152–3** (Ex. XXX)
Archilei, Antonio, 215–16, **217–18** (Ex. XLI), 230, 233*n*, 369
Archilei, Vittoria, 215–17, 230 and *n*, 234, 241*n*, 242, 369
Arcimboldi, Giovanni, Bishop of Novara, 8
Aretino, Pietro, 82, 330*n*, 331–3; *La cortigiana*, **330**, 332, 371;

L'ipocrito, 80, 88; *Il marescalco*, **78–80**, 88, **332**; *Talanta*, **330–1**, **332–4**, 339, 340, 341–2, 353
Ariosto, Francesco: *Isis*, 11
Ariosto, Ludovico, 44*n*, 55*n*, 76*n*, 197, 274 and *n*, 316–18 and *nn*, 321; *La cassaria*, 77 and *n*, 291, 311–12, **317–18**, 319 and *n*, 332, 336; *Lena*, 318*n*; *I suppositi*, 48, 77, 317, 318*n*, 319, 337, *Pl. 21*
Aristophanes, 82 and *n*, 128; *The Frogs*, 191, *192*; *Nephelai*, 190
Armano, Tiberio d', 331*n*
Armanos, the, 331
Armonio, Giovanni, 101, 102; *Stephanium*, 313*n*
Arnold, Frank T., 242–3*n*, 247*n*
Arpa, Giovan Leonardo dell' (Giovan Leonardo Salernitano), 107–8*nn*, 188–9*n*
Arrighi, Costantino, 206*n*
Arsocchi, Francesco, 16
Ascanio, Josquin d', *see* Près, Josquin des
Atanagi, Dionigi, 198*n*
Avalos, Alfonso d', 103*n*

Baccio (Bartolomeo) degli Organi, 123*n*
Baldinucci, Filippo, 366, 375*n*, 380*n*, 382*n*
Baldissera, Donato, 103*n*
Banchieri, Adriano (Camillo Scaligeri della Fratta), **118–19**; *Il donativo...*, *Pl. 25*
Bandini, Giovanni, 350*n*
Barbara of Austria, Duchess of Ferrara, 201, 365*n*
Barbara of Brandenburg, Marchioness of Mantua, 55
Barbaro, Daniele, 327, 329
Barbera Salutati, *see* Salutati

Index

Index

Index

Index